D1598153

The Life and Works of
John Knowles Paine

Studies in Musicology, No. 34

George Buelow, Series Editor
Professor of Musicology
Indiana University

Other Titles in This Series

The Life and Works of John Knowles Paine

by
John C. Schmidt

RESEARCH PRESS

Produced and distributed by
UMI Research Press
an imprint of
University Microfilms International
Ann Arbor, Michigan 48106

Library of Congress Cataloging in Publication Data

Schmidt, John C   1941-
   The life and works of John Knowles Paine.

   (Studies in musicology ; no. 34)
   Bibliography: p.
   Includes index.
   1. Paine, John Knowles, 1839-1906.   2. Composers—
United States—Biography.   I. Title. II. Series.
ML410.P138S3   780'.92'4 [B]   80-22511
ISBN 0-8357-1126-9

Illustration 1. (Frontispiece)   Paine as a young man (1857), from a daguerreotype (reproduced in Edwards, *Music and Musicians of Maine*).

Contents

List of Illustrations

Abbreviations

AAJ	*American Art Journal*
BDA	*Boston Daily Advertiser*
BDET	*Boston Daily Evening Transcript*
BET	*Boston Evening Transcript*
BH	*Boston Herald*
BMT	*Boston Musical Times*
BPL	Music Department, Boston Public Library, Boston Mass.
BU	Music Library, Boston University, Boston, Mass.
Dart	Dartmouth College Library, Hanover, N. H.
DJM	*Dwight's Journal of Music*
ESM	Sibley Music Library, Eastman School of Music, Rochester, N. Y.
Fleisher	Edwin A. Fleisher Collection of Orchestral Music, Free Library of Philadelphia (performance materials available)
HMA	Harvard Musical Association, Boston, Mass.
HMus	Isham Memorial Library, Department of Music, Harvard University, Cambridge, Mass.
LC	Music Division, Library of Congress, Washington, D. C.
MC	*Musical Courier*

Mich   Music Library, University of Michigan, Ann Arbor, Mich.

MR   *Musical Record*

NECM   Spaulding Library, New England, Conservatory of Music, Boston, Mass.

NYPL   Music Division, New York Public Library, New York, N. Y.

Phila   Free Library of Philadelphia, Philadelphia, Pa.

PPL   Portland Public Library, Portland, Maine

Smith   Werner Josten Library, The Center for the Performing Arts, Smith College, Northampton, Mass.

Summy   Summy-Birchard Co., Evanston, Ill. (microfilm only; prints are available)

Tufts   Tufts University Library, Medford, Mass.

Wellesley Music Library, Wellesley College, Wellesley, Mass.

Wis   Mills Music Library, University of Wisconsin, Madison, Wis.

Yale   Music Library, Yale University, New Haven, Conn.

Preface

John Knowles Paine holds a unique position in the history of American music. He was the founder of the modern music curriculum at Harvard University, subsequently adopted by colleges throughout the country, that made music and music history part of the liberal arts curriculum. His influence was broad, for he trained a large group of composers, critics, and connoisseurs who until recent decades remained in the forefront of the American music scene. He has been recognized as "the first native composer whose fame has endured as a writer in the larger forms," and in his day was called the "dean of American composers."[1]

For such a significant individual a detailed, accurate biography is definitely needed. No monographs were published during his lifetime, although he received generous attention in contemporary biographical dictionaries and studies of American music.[2] But many facts about his life remained hidden in temporal publication and in unpublished sources. Moreover, a reassessment of Paine's very personality is in order, supplanting the prevailing impression of the dry, pedantic, childlike, impractical professor with the virile, charming, down-to-earth personality that he must have been. This task is the sort that Leon Edel, biographer of Henry James, has called the "search for . . . the figure under the carpet, the evidence in the reverse of the tapestry, the life-myth of a given mask."[3]

The present study will review the life of Paine with special emphasis on little-known facts about his ancestry, his youth and early training, his career as a composer and pedagogue, and his compositions and their performances. This last topic is especially important, for Paine's worth as a composer is the main reason today for a serious study of his career. The second half of the study is devoted to an analytical and descriptive survey of his extant compositions, also including other known works now apparently lost. Along with bibliographical and performance information for each work, descriptive analyses are provided for all published works as well as representative compositions in manuscript. These analyses, accompanied by 437 musical examples, are intended to provide a clear idea of each work and an overall impression of Paine's compositional style.

Many individuals and organizations aided this author in his research for the present study. A complete listing would be difficult, but special appreciation must be shown to the staffs of the many libraries contacted and visited, especially the Portland Public Library, Boston Public Library, Maine Historical Society, New England Historical and Genealogical Society, Music Division of the New York Public Library, Music Division of the Library of Congress, and the libraries of Harvard University and the University of Texas at Austin. Acknowledgment is also owed to Dr. Hugh Payne Greeley, Rev. Dana McLean Greeley, Mrs. Ellen Greeley Bryant, H. Earle Johnson, Laning Humphrey, Richard G. Appel, and Andrew Raeburn, as well as the Unitarian-Universalist Association, Boston Music Company, and Summy-Birchard Company. Special gratitude is due to Professor Victor Yellin, Department of Music, New York University; it was in his course in American music that the author's interest in Paine was initiated.

The following acknowledgments are made for permission to reprint illustrations and musical examples:

Scenes from The Birds of Aristophanes and *O bless the Lord, my soul* reprinted with the permission of the copyright owner, Boston Music Company.

Domine salvum fac Praesidem nostrum, Fantasie über "Ein' feste Burg," and *Concert Variations upon Old Hundred* reprinted with the permission of Harvard University Press.

Quartet, Op. 5, reprinted with permission of the New York Public Library.

Prelude to "Oedipus Tyrannus" reprinted with permission from the score published by Edwin F. Kalmus & Co. Inc.

Illustrations from W. S. B. Mathews, *A Hundred Years of Music in America,* and G. T. Edwards, *Music and Musicians of Maine,* reproduced by permission from the reprinted edition by AMS Press Inc., New York.

Concert Variations on the Austrian Hymn, Concert Variations upon Old Hundred, Concert Variations on the Star-Spangled Banner, Deux Préludes, and *Fantasie über "Ein feste Burg,"* reproduced by permission from *The Complete Organ Works of John Knowles Paine,* published by McAfee Music Corporation, a division of Belwin-Mills Publishing Corporation.

Welcome Home, Valse Caprice, Fantasia and Fugue in E minor, Trio in D minor, Sonata for Piano and Violin, and *Funeral Hymn* reproduced by permission of the Houghton Library, Harvard University.

Soldier's Oath reprinted by permission of the University Archives, Harvard University Library.

Sonata in B Minor for Piano and Violin, third movement, reprinted courtesy of the Board of Trustees of the Boston Public Library.

Paine letter to Hermann Kotzschmar reproduced by permission of the Portland Public Library. *Freedom Our Queen* reproduced by permission from a copy in the Portland Public Library.

Symphony No. 1 reprinted from the score published by Da Capo Press, Inc.

Overture to Shakespeare's "As you like it," Symphonic Poem: Shakespeare's Tempest, Poseidon und Amphitrite: An Ocean Fantasy, A Farewell, Beneath the starry arch, Radway's Ready Relief, Phoebus Arise, The Nativity, Song of Promise, and *Scenes from The Birds of Aristophanes* reproduced by permission from copies in the Isham Memorial Library, Department of Music, Harvard University.

Christmas Gift, Funeral March, Romance, Op. 12, Four Characteristic Pieces, In the Country, Romance, Op. 39, Three piano pieces, Op. 41, Nocturne, Op. 45, Symphony No. 2 "Im Frühling," I wore your roses yesterday, Early Springtime, Moonlight, A bird upon a rosy bough, Hymn for Commencement, Mass in D, St. Peter, Oedipus Tyrannus, The Realm of Fancy, Columbus March and Hymn, Hymn of the West, and *Azara* reproduced by permission from copies in the Music Division, Library of Congress.

I
Life

1

Genealogy, Childhood, and Youth

A biographical study of John Knowles Paine frustrates the historian because of the paucity of original material, such as letters, diaries, and other memorabilia, which were destroyed according to his widow's will after her death. Her motivation is unknown. Certainly the facts of Paine's life and career that have come to light give no clue to the reasons for her wish. For if any nineteenth-century American artist may be said to have lived the pure life free of the hint of personal scandal or misbehavior, it was Paine.

To fill the vacuum of personal items, therefore, one must turn to published works of individuals who knew Paine personally or who include material contributed by such persons. The most important of these works is George Thornton Edwards' *Music and Musicians of Maine*,[1] which includes a 20-page section on Paine, including many responses solicited from former students; many details of early Portland history supplied here would be otherwise unavailable or difficult to find. Two students of Paine, Richard Aldrich (A.B. 1885)[2] and Mark Antony DeWolfe Howe (A.B. 1887),[3] have written important biographical essays, with much original material included. A third, Walter R. Spalding (A.B. 1887, A.M. 1888),[4] Paine's successor as Harvard music chairman, provided two studies of the music department at Harvard, including additional insights into Paine's life and teaching career. Further original and invaluable material is found in an unpublished thesis by Kenneth Creighton Roberts, Jr.,[5] who had the foresight to consult a number of other students and acquaintances, as well as several relatives of Mrs. Paine, while they were still alive. Many details of the Paine family life may be seen in the letters of the historian and Harvard colleague, John Fiske,[6] who was one of Paine's closest friends. Aside from these sources, biographical information had to be gleaned by a meticulous search of newspapers and periodicals. Many one-sentence items from gossip columns, as well as passing references in longer articles, have filled in a number of biographical gaps. Among the unpublished sources may be mentioned a few letters that have been preserved, as well as records of the Harvard faculty, Boston West Church, and several performing organizations.

The Paine family branch of which John Knowles Paine was a member traces its American lineage to "Thomas Paine of Eastham," born in Cranford, England, around 1612, who immigrated to Cape Cod and died 16 August 1706; records show him in turn to be a descendant of the fourteenth-century Sir Thomas Paine of Market Bosworth, England.[7] Traditionally, the Paines have considered Thomas of Eastham to be the son of one "Thomas Payne, of Yarmouth," obviously a man of prominence, mentioned often in the Plymouth Colony records between 1639 and 1650. Regrettably, no further records mention Thomas of Yarmouth, and there are no direct ties between him and Thomas of Eastham. The astronomer Robert Treat Paine possessed a summary of the tradition, quoted by a descendant[8] in a discussion of the problem:

> The following is the Genealogical Acc^t given by Barnabas Payen Esqr of Hartford Thomas Paine [Payne] emigrated from Great Britain to America AD 1622 & brought his only son Thomas who was abt 10 yrs old & had lost one eye by an arrow before he came to America. . . .

Thomas Paine, the son, settled in the part of Eastham now called Orleans, and attained prosperity as a cooper and a builder of several gristmills in the locality. Around 1650 he married Mary Snow of Eastham, whose mother, Constance, and grandfather, Stephen Hopkins, the Pilgrim, had come over on the *Mayflower* in 1620,[9] and whose father, Nicholas Snow, immigrated on the *Anne* in 1623.[10] Thomas and Mary Paine had ten children, two of whom were direct ancestors of John Knowles Paine. Joseph (ca. 1667–1712), the youngest son, continued the Paine family name directly to the composer. In 1691 he married Patience Sparrow (1675–1745), great-granddaughter of *Mayflower* immigrant Elder William Brewster, whose daughter Patience (d. 1634; imm. *Anne*, 1623) married Thomas Prence [Prince] (ca. 1600/01–1673; imm. *The Fortune*, 1621), a governor of Plymouth Colony. Hannah Prence (d. ca. 1698), daughter of Thomas and Patience Prence, married Captain Jonathan Sparrow of Eastham, whose father, Richard Sparrow, was in Plymouth by 1635; both Hannah and Jonathan had been widowed prior to their marriage, and Patience Sparrow was their second child.[11] Joseph and Patience Paine settled in Harwich, in the section now called Brewster.[12] Eleven children were born to the marriage; the third son, Richard (1699–1775), was the composer's great-great-grandfather. In 1726 Richard Paine married Phebe Myrick, daughter of Joseph and Elizabeth (Howes) Myrick; Phebe's grandfather, William Merrick [Myrick] (1603–1688/9) had immigrated on the *James* in

1636, and a maternal great-grandfather was the Rev. John Mayo,[13] called as minister to the Eastham congregation in 1655, whose members included Nicholas Snow, Thomas Prence, Edward Bangs, John Doane, Richard Knowles, and William Merrick [Myrick] (all ancesters of John Knowles Paine). Richard Paine worked as a blacksmith, and he and his wife first lived in Truro, later moving to Eastham,[14] where their 10 children were born. Joseph Paine (1741–1827), their seventh child and second son, and the composer's great-grandfather, left Eastham for Maine around 1780.

A second line of descent from Thomas and Mary (Snow) Paine culminated in Joseph Paine's wife, Phebe Rich (1746/7–1828), whom he married in 1767. Phebe's great-grandfather was an older son of Thomas and Mary Paine, Thomas (1657–1721), who in 1678 married Hannah Shaw (ca. 1662–1713), a daughter of Jonathan and Phebe (Watson) Shaw.[15] One of their children was Phebe Paine (1699/1700–1748), who became the wife of Paul Knowles of Truro on 28 February 1722/3; a daughter of this marriage, Ann, was Phebe (Rich) Paine's mother. Paul Knowles was a great-grandson of immigrant Richard Knowles (d. 1670–75), first mentioned in Plymouth records in January 1637/8.[16] Richard's son, John Knowles (killed by Indians in 1675) of Eastham, married Apphia Bangs (1651–ca. 1707) in 1670. Apphia was the daughter of Edward Bangs (1591–ca. 1678), an influential freeman in Plymouth and later Eastham, who had immigrated with his wife Lydia aboard the *Anne* in 1623; Lydia's father, Robert Hickes [Hicks], had come to Plymouth two years earlier on the *Fortune*.[17] Col. John Knowles (1673–1757), second son of John and Apphia Knowles, married Mary Sears (1672–1745), granddaughter of immigrants Richard Sares [Sears] (d. 1767; in Plymouth in 1633) and George Willard (first lived at Scituate);[18] Paul Knowles was the fourth of eight children born to John and Mary (Sears) Knowles. Ann Knowles (1723–85), Paul and Phebe Knowles' firstborn, became the wife of Uriah Rich (1723–1801) of Truro in 1743/4; of their 11 children, Phebe Rich was the second oldest. Uriah, like his wife, was a descendant of immigrants Edward and Lydia (Hicks) Bangs. Another daughter of these immigrants, Hannah Bangs (b. ca. 1644, d. after 1677), married John Doane (d. 1707), son of Pilgrim immigrant Deacon John Doane;[19] their son, Isaac Doane (1670–1754), numbered among his children Hannah Doane (b. 1702/3, d. after 1754), who married Richard Rich (1698/9–ca. 1742) and became the mother of Uriah Rich. The Rich ancestry began with immigrant Richard Rich (ca. 1642–1692) of Dover Point, New Hampshire; his son Richard (1674–1743) of Eastham and Truro; and grandson Richard (1698/9–ca. 1742), also of Eastham and Truro.[20]

To this point the various family lines had stemmed, in the main,

Illustration 2.   **The Ancestry of John Knowles Paine.**

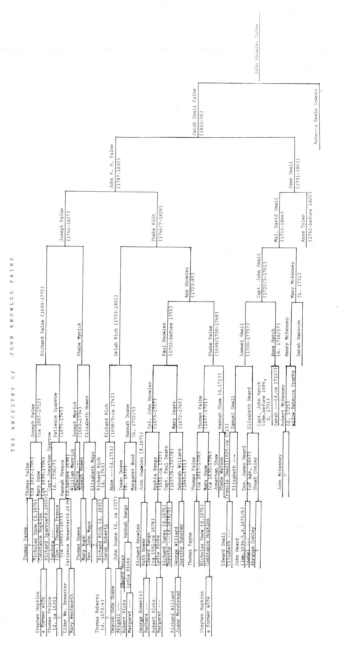

from immigrants to Plymouth Colony and the vicinity of Cape Cod. Several of the immigrants had traveled together—Stephen and Constance Hopkins and Elder William Brewster on the *Mayflower*, Thomas Prence and Robert Hicks on the *Fortune*, Nicholas Snow, Richard Sparrow, Edward Bangs, Lydia Hicks, and Patience Brewster on the *Anne*—and descendants of all immigrants named thus far eventually came to live in Truro or in Eastham, on the tip of Cape Cod. However, when Joseph and Phebe (Rich) Paine moved to Standish, Maine (15 miles northwest of Portland) in 1780, lineages were introduced from those who had settled elsewhere in New England. Joseph and Phebe's youngest son, John K. H. Paine (1787–1835), took as his wife Jane Small (1791–1863), of Limington, Maine, a sixth-generation descendant of immigrant Edward Small of Bideford, County Devon, England.[21] Edward's son Francis (1625–ca. 1713), who settled in Kittery, Maine, obtained in 1668 a large tract of land, 20 miles square, between the Great and Little Ossipee rivers, extending from the Nechewanick River to the Saco River. Limington, Jane's birthplace, was part of this territory, and the Small male descendants in her lineage, as well as most of the families into which they married, lived in Kittery, Scarborough, or Limington.

Efforts to trace the remainder of John Knowles Paine's genealogy have been fruitless to date. John and Jane Paine's son, Jacob Small Paine, father of the composer, married Rebecca Beebe Downes (1808–60) in 1833. Rebecca, like Jacob, was a native of Maine, but records of her birth seem not to have survived, and her parents' names are unknown. However, immigrants named Downes or Beebe had settled in areas of Massachusetts and Connecticut by the mid-eighteenth century, and it may be assumed that Rebecca Beebe Downes was of the same long-established Yankee stock as was her husband.

As noted above, the first Paine ancestor of the composer to live in Maine was his great-grandfather, Joseph Paine (1741–1827), a native of Eastham, Massachusetts. After his marriage to Phebe Rich (1746/7–1828) in 1767, the couple continued to live in Eastham, where seven children were born to them—Myrick, Joseph, Richard, Phebe, Uriah, Thomas, and Huldah. Sometime after the birth of the youngest, Huldah, on 15 February 1780, the family moved to Standish (then called "Pearsontown" or "Pearson and Hobbstown")[22] in the Maine district of Massachusetts, where three more children were born—Freeman (b. 8 August 1782), Joshua (b. 25 April 1785), and the composer's grandfather, John Knowles—usually given as John K. H. Paine[23]—(b. 20 March 1787).[24]

John K. H. Paine and his brothers were all "yeomen," or farmers, of Standish. John, however, was also a cooper, according to reports cited in Spalding's *Music at Harvard*, and in 1811 built a gristmill. Of far more musical interest was his activity during the War of 1812, when he made fifes, drums, flutes, and bassoons for military use, and was a fife-major for a company of soldiers. Later in life he was known chiefly as an organ builder, a vocation that must have evolved from this earlier experience. According to Edwards,[25] one of his earliest instruments may have been a small organ for the Second Parish (Congregational) Church in Portland, which was replaced by "a new and more powerful organ" in 1820; however, the fact that the original Second Parish organ was installed in 1798[26] would make doubtful such an assumption, unless Paine were the builder of an interim or additional instrument.

As a result of the vocations that John K. H. Paine pursued, he achieved enough financial success to purchase, on 8 January 1819,

> . . . a certain one hundred acre lot of land numbered twelve in the third division of lots in the Town of Standish lying at the outlet of Watchick Pond so called.[27]

Paine paid Portland merchant Enoch Preble $141 for title to this property. Either the value of the land increased rapidly or Paine possessed a shrewd business sense, for on 18 November of the same year he sold to four of his brothers—Myrick, Joseph, Jr., Richard, and Joshua—for $100 each, shares in a small, though important, portion of the lot:

> . . . Four fifths of five and a half acres of the hundred acre Lot in the third division of Lots in Standish and which lot is numbered Twelve. . . . To contain five and ½ acres together with four fifths of a Grist Mill, standing thereon; which piece of Land and Mill are not to be subject to division. . . .[28]

Possibly this was the same mill that Paine had built in 1811, according to Spalding. One may suppose that the other four brothers also owned or rented farmland—they were all designated "yeomen" in the deed, although John was now described as a "Miller"—and would find part interest in the mill a definite advantage.

At the age of 23, on 22 February 1810,[29] John K. H. Paine was married to Jane Small of nearby Limington; intentions were declared in Standish on 28 December 1809[30] and later in Limington on 4 January 1810.[31] Later in the year their first child was born—Jacob Small Paine, who was the composer's father. Other sons born to the marriage were David, who became an organist and music teacher, Samuel, and William, a trombonist, and composer of the hymntune "Wells"; William took over the Paine Music Store in Portland after Jacob's death in 1856.[32]

The Paine family moved 15 miles southeast to Portland sometime around 1830 (they were not listed among residents of Portland in the 1830

U. S. Census), but professional musical relationships were begun earlier. One of John K. H. Paine's first organs was built at his shop in Standish in 1828, according to M. A. DeWolfe Howe, and it possessed sufficient lung power to enable its sound to be heard at a distance of two miles.[33] Later it was installed in the Temple Street Baptist Church in Portland, and was lost when the church was destroyed in the great fire of 1866.[34] Paine entered into a partnership with Thomas J. Sparrow (possibly a relative). According to Edwards,[35] the firm in 1831 operated from Market Row in Middle Street; newspaper advertisements during 1833 gave the address of the Paine & Sparrow "Organ Manufactory" as "Nos. 7 & 8 Union Street."[36] The business relationship ended two years later—on 28 August 1835—when Paine died.

In addition to his pioneer activity as a manufacturer of musical instruments, John K. H. Paine played an early part in the history of American band music, for soon after Maine became a state in 1820, he organized a band in Portland. According to Edwards, the original group was very small, consisting of a fife, a tenor drum, a bass drum, a bugle, and a clarinet.

> . . . At first the critics were not inclined to take this "band" very seriously and disparagingly alluded to it as the "Saccarap Band," but band-leader Paine persevered and with the assistance of his son, Jacob S. Paine, a marching musical organization that commanded the respect of his fellow citizens was given to the town.[37]

Jacob soon became leader of the band, and organized it in 1827 as the Portland Band. He continued in this role until 1843, when he was succeeded by Daniel Hiram Chandler (1818–?).

Soon after arriving in Portland, Jacob Paine opened a store, establishing a trade as an "umbrella and musical instrument maker."[38] The association of these two products was not as unlikely as it might seem, since a woodworking skill and the use of ivory was common to both; and presumably the sale of umbrellas would have provided an economic hedge against the rainy weather so discouraging to the outdoor use of band instruments. A description of Paine's umbrellas may be read in an October 1833 advertisement:

> UMBRELLAS.
> At J. S. Paine's Manufactory
> Corner of Middle and Court - Sts.
> Will be constantly found a large assortment of Silk, Gingham, Cotton, and Oil Cloth *UMBRELLAS*, (of his own make) which he will warrant to be of the first rate article, for sale at the Factory prices for cash.
> ALSO—French Silk de. a light article for summer use, those from the country who buy to sell again, will find it to their advantage to call as above.
> ☞ Old Umbrellas covered and rapaired [*sic*] at short notice.[39]

In addition to the instrument and umbrella trade, the business soon included sheet music, publishing, and the sale and lease of pianos—Jacob Paine was the distributor for Chickering pianos for most of his professional career in Portland. For some years during the 1840s he was in a partnership, Winship & Paine, located at 111 Middle Street, dealing in "hats and musical instruments."[40] But by 1850 he was at his own store at 113 Middle Street, and enjoyed a gradual increase in the sale of Chickerings. An 1851 advertisement shows that he had prepared for the growing volume,

> . . . (having made an addition and improvement in my ware room, to meet the increasing demand for the above instruments) . . .[41]

After establishing himself in a successful business, Jacob Paine made a decision to start a family. On the evening of 7 November 1833 he was married to Miss Rebecca Beebe Downes by the Rev. George C. Beckwith, minister of the High Street Congregational Church in Portland.[42] The couple at first lived "at Mrs. N. Kimball's," on Free Street.[43] Later their place of residence was at 201 Cumberland, presumably a rented house, as Jacob Paine owned no property.[44] Five children were born to the marriage, Helen Maria (1834–91), who gained local prominence as a contralto soloist, John Knowles (b. 9 January 1839),[45] Ann Rebecca (b. 1840, d. before June 1850), Alma G. (1842–49), and Adelaide (1848–56).

Portland, the birthplace of John Knowles Paine, is located on the Maine coast, about 110 miles northeast of Boston and 45 miles northeast of Portsmouth, New Hampshire. The original town is situated on a peninsula three miles long and a mile wide, bounded by the Fore River (or Casco River), Casco Bay, and Back Cove. Its deepwater port is the nearest to Europe of any in the United States. Portland at first was called Falmouth Neck and was part of the town of Falmouth, organized in 1719. In 1786 Falmouth Neck was incorporated as the town of Portland, and from 1820 to 1832 served as the first capital of the State of Maine. Its population in 1800 was about 3,700;[46] later census figures indicate a steady growth:[47]

> 1830—12,598
> 1840—15,218
> 1850—20,815
> 1860—26,341

Portland was an important commercial center in the early nineteenth century. It was an important port of entry, and its shipyards supported many related businesses—ship building, sail weaving, etc. Lumber and paper products were an important industry, as were iron foundries, textiles, publishing, and printing. There were numerous carpenters, painters, furniture makers, cordwainers, and even manufacturers of musical instruments, including Jacob Paine, the composer's father, and Charles P. Carlton, first secretary of the Haydn Association (1857), a piano maker.[48] Constant improvement in transportation facilites enabled Portland businesses to claim effectively all of Maine and part of New Hampshire as their territory.[49] The first cheap transportation was the steamboat—the "Patent" began runs between Portland and Boston in 1824,[50] and in 1830 there were two weekly overnight trips available.[51] By 1850 the weekly trips had increased to three, with an equal number to Bangor, and other service to Eastport, Maine, and the British maritime provinces.[52] And in 1860 there were twice weekly trips to New York, while the number of Boston voyages increased to five a week, with new service added to Bath, Augusta, and surrounding towns.[53] The first railroad to serve Portland— the Portland, Saco, and Portsmouth Railroad—began operation in 1842.[54] In 1850 it offered three daily trips to Boston.[55] By the same year the Atlantic and St. Lawrence division of the Grand Trunk Railroad of Canada already provided service to South Paris, Maine; in 1853 Portland became the southern terminus for overnight trains to Montreal that connected with weekly steamers to Liverpool.[56] In the 1850s and '60s several additional lines supplied transportation to such Maine towns as Bath, Waterville, Saco, Bangor, Auburn, and Lewiston; as well as Island Pond, Vermont; Portsmouth, New Hampshire; and Boston and Lowell, Massachusetts. Connecting stage lines to many other communities completed the transportation network,[57] and enabled Portland to become the business center of northeastern New England.

The Paine music store was an important factor in the musical life of Portland in the 1830s, '40s, and '50s, and its proprietor was highly influential among the musicians and music lovers of the city and its surrounding area. Music instructors would obtain students through inquiries left at the store, concert tickets could be purchased there, and local composers could arrange to have their works published. During this period there were never more than two music stores in existence at any one time, according to listings in the *Portland Directory* issues,[58] giving Paine a near monopoly in the field. Jacob Paine was a Trustee (1840)[59] of the Portland Sacred Music Society (the first choral society in Maine to present a complete oratorio, in existence from 1835 to 1841), and also served as a Councillor. His brother David was its organist from 1837 to 1841, and was responsible for an 1839 publication entitled:

> The Portland Sacred Music Society's Collection of Church Music consisting of Psalm and Hymn tunes, anthems and chants, composed and compiled under the special patronage of the Portland Sacred Music Society and adapted to the use of the choruses, choirs and the social circle arranged with small notes for the organ or pianoforte compiled by David Paine, organist of the Portland Sacred Music Society and the Park Street Church. . . .[60]

Helen, Jacob's daughter, was one of the Society's altos and a frequent soloist. Her performance, at the age of 16, in the 8 October 1850 presentation of Rossini's *Stabat Mater*, for example,

> . . . displayed a compass and quality of voice, and power of enunciation which delighted the audience, and gave great promise of future excellence. She was loudly encored. . . .[61]

One example of Jacob Paine's influence, which incidentally may have contributed to the decline of the Sacred Music Society, was the aid he gave to the English conductor, bass soloist, and composer (operas and songs, including "Kathleen Mavourneen") Frederick Nicholls Crouch (1808–96), who had come to America in 1849 to sing with the Max Maretzek Italian Opera Company. One may assume that "Jacques Paine" in the following excerpt from Crouch's autobiographical sketch was really Jacob Paine ("Jack"? "Jake"?):

> . . . The results [of the opera performance] failed to recompense the outlay in New York, as well as in Boston, where the opera died of starvation, leaving me with a sick wife in a city where I did not know a living soul.
>
> I finally met Jacques Paine, a music dealer of Portland, Me. By his advice I lectured on the oratorio "Messiah" before the Boston Handel and Haydn Society, the members singing the choruses. Finally I was engaged as conductor and translated for them Rossini's "Stabat Mater." . . .[62]

Perhaps Paine also interested Crouch in coming to Portland, for the singer gave a concert in the old City Hall, singing his "Kathleen Mavourneen" as well as bass solos from *Messiah, Creation*, and other oratorios. He was received with enthusiasm, and soon thereafter the Sacred Music Society—at the time without a conductor—voted at its 20 May 1850 meeting "that we recommend to the Society to engage Mr. Crouch to lead the Society."[63] Crouch agreed to serve for an annual salary of $300. However, he seems to have been quite an eccentric, controversial figure,[64] arousing the disfavor of many, for on 29 May the Society reconsidered its vote and decided not to hire him after all. Resulting from this action were charges and counter-charges, threats of legal action, and rifts that nearly tore the

Society apart. Jacob Paine, because of his close personal contact with Crouch, in all probability was in the center of the dispute. He may have been the man responsible for Crouch coming to Portland in the first place; perhaps he also was among those who advocated his employment by the Society. Without question Paine thought highly enough of the singer's professional skills to secure him as a voice teacher for Helen,[65] and Paine's Music Store directed inquiries from students on Crouch's behalf, according to a September 1850 advertisement.[66] Helen also appeared on several concerts with Crouch, including a 3 May 1852 program at City Hall.[67] Whatever the connection, Jacob Paine seems thereafter to have decreased his involvement with the Sacred Music Society. At the 21 May 1851 annual meeting he was elected to the Board of Trustees, but declined to serve.[68] He did serve on an arrangements committee for a June 1851 concert of the *Stabat Mater*,[69] but a year and a half later, at a quarterly meeting on 18 December 1852, his membership was terminated:

> . . . On motion the names of the members of the Society were read, and the names of those to whom objections were made were marked. On motion of Mr. Shaw the names of those marked were taken up in order, and the following members were discharged from their membership viz Richard Pennell Chas C Tolman F W. Staples John Chickering W^m E Smith. James N Davis. Dr. S H. Tewksburg. D H Chandler. P Willey Geo W. Willard & J S Paine. *Voted* That the Sec^y notify the members of their discharge. Voted that the Sec^y be instructed to call upon the members marked and request payment of dues. . . .[70]

It would be interesting to know if there were any further reason why these members were dismissed, and if non-payment of dues had been the only justification, what was the cause of these members' dissatisfaction. These were not unimportant citizens: several were leading musicians, including Pennell, organist of the Third Parish Church; Willey, long time member of the Portland Band; Chandler, the celebrated conductor of the band; and Paine himself. There obviously was bitterness felt in the Paine household, for at the next "election of ladies" in May 1853, Helen was no longer listed as a member.[71] However, she continued to perform in regular concerts, such as those of the new Orchestral Society, and sang at a 28 February 1854 chamber concert at "Paine's Piano Forte Room," which also featured Hermann Kotzschmar, Henri Jungnickel, Crouch, and a Madame Zimmerman.[72]

Helen Paine continued her musical training with two other Portland teachers. With Madame Sophia Ostinelli, at one time the organist for the Boston Handel and Haydn Society, she studied voice and piano. And she became an accomplished pianist under Hermann Kotzschmar[73]—the most influential musician in Portland—who was the first to help shape the musical career of her younger brother, John Knowles Paine.

As a Portland boy, John Knowles Paine benefited by three major influences on his musical development—the European tradition, brought over by trained professionals visiting or settling in the city; native culture, such as sacred music, ballads, and instrumental music, which were nurtured by Yankee musicians in the region; and the active musical climate of the Paine family itself, with at least three generations of leadership in the musical life of Portland and the vicinity. European musicians—competent conservatory-trained professionals—came to America in increasing numbers during the mid-nineteenth century, many to establish permanent residency in the young nation. These individuals presented the latest European styles and tastes in music to their American listeners (sometimes condemning, unfortunately, the works of self-taught native composers as crude and unworthy, unfashionable and deserving oblivion). Most were very active as teachers, their efforts resulting in greatly improved performance standards and more cosmopolitan tastes among their pupils and admirers. Portland, being a port city and a center of commerce, was visited by a number of European musicians. Of those who chose to remain, one of the first was Paul Louis Ostinelli, who came to Portland in 1823 with his wife, the former Sophia Hewitt, daughter of the composer and publisher, James Hewitt.[74] Ostinelli, who had achieved the Grand Premium at the Royal Conservatory of Paris, made his Boston debut in 1818[75] and soon became concertmaster of the Philharmonic Society;[76] it was stated that he, "as an orchestra leader and violinist . . . was without a peer in America at that time. . . ."[77] In 1822 he married Sophia,[78] who was well known locally as a teacher, organist, and concert pianist. The Ostinellis did not remain in Portland long, for they were back in Boston by 1828.[79] But Mrs. Ostinelli returned to Portland about 1837 and taught piano and voice[80] until her death in 1846;[81] Helen Paine was one of her students.

Of the immigrant musicians, the most important and influential was Hermann Kotzschmar, who, during a career of 59 years, was a major force in the musical growth of Portland and the entire region.

Hermann Kotzschmar, born on 4 July 1829 in the small town of Finsterwalde, Brandenburg, was a member of a very active musical family. Both his father, Gottfried Kotzschmar, and his grandfather had been *Stadtmusiker* for the town.[82] When still a young boy, Hermann began to study with his father—piano, organ, and orchestral instruments, including violin, clarinet, flute, and horn. At the age of nine the young musician went to Dresden, where he studied piano and organ under Hayne and composition with Julius Otto for five years.[83] By the age of 12 Kotzschmar was sufficiently advanced to be included in the second violin section of an orchestra in Dresden. Two years later he joined another performing group, this time to play first violin, viola, and alto trombone.

At age 19, in the summer of 1848, Kotzschmar and a friend organized a 22-piece band, called the Saxonia Orchestra, and made ambitious plans for an American tour.[84] In November, after a tedious two-month voyage aboard a sailing vessel, the small group of musicians arrived in New York.[85] Within a short time Kotzschmar was able to secure an engagement for the orchestra, playing for the winter season of Fry's Italian Opera.[86] The company played three weeks in New York, five weeks in Philadelphia, and closed in Boston. With no future engagements in sight, the Saxonia Orchestra disbanded, and its members scattered.[87] Kotzschmar, however, remained in Boston during the spring months, playing trumpet (or cornet) and violin whenever the opportunity allowed.

As summer approached, one Gurefeldt, a musician who was to direct the "Jibbenainosay" band at the Union Street theater in Portland, accepted an offer to join the faculty of a young women's school, and offered Kotzschmar the chance to take his place.

> After some hesitation [Kotzschmar] replied that he must sleep over it before deciding but so great was Mr. Gurefeldt's anxiety to learn his decision that he went to Mr. Kotzschmar's room at four o'clock in the morning with the query "Have you decided to go?" and the little affirmative "Yes" proved the decisive turning point in Mr. Kotzschmar's life. That day he left for Portland, Maine. . . .[88]

In July 1849 Kotzschmar began as leader of the tiny orchestra at the "Portland Museum" on Union Street, a theater run by a Joseph Proctor. There were only four in the group, but they were all German musicians with thorough training.[89] Kotzschmar played piano, and fellow Saxonia member Henri Jungnickel was cellist. The violinist, one Reinecke, later returned to Germany and became a "great musical director in Berlin."[90] Little is known of the fourth musician, Faulwasser—including his instrument—except that he later died in Boston. Reportedly, the orchestra was a greater attraction than the theatrical fare itself. Business seems to have suffered, for in 1850 Proctor sold out and the group of musicians disbanded. Kotzschmar, who had already taken some private pupils, began to make teaching his primary occupation.[91] Perhaps the close of the theater orchestra was in some ways a relief for Kotzschmar, for theater audiences expected lightweight, often banal music, and this was a period of the "driest of hack work" for him.[92]

Kotzschmar's talents as a pianist were quickly noticed in Portland. On 4 December 1850 the Sacred Music Society voted him pianist (organist) at an annual salary of $50;[93] Henry S. Edwards, organist since 1841, had conveniently resigned.[94] Kotzschmar appeared as a soloist with the society on 16 March 1851, and was the recipient of benefit concerts in 1850 and 1853.[95] He continued as organist until the society ceased to be active in 1854, and was instrumental in organizing its successor, the Haydn Association, in 1857.[96] In 1851 Kotzschmar began duties as organist for the First Parish Church, a position he held until 1898. The church at first had only a small organ, installed in 1821, but a new, larger instrument was purchased in 1853. His organ training had been only rudimentary, but his fine musicianship enabled him to excel in his post.[97] He was an outstanding improviser as well,[98] a talent that certainly must have won him greater esteem.

Within a short time after arriving in Portland, Kotzschmar most likely became close friends with Jacob S. Paine, whose music store was the "musical head-quarters of Portland."[99] Paine published a number of Kotzschmar's compositions and arrangements. The first to appear was announced in a 6 July 1850 newspaper item:

> NEW MUSIC. We have just received from J. S. Paine, the publisher, the "Juliana Polka, as performed by the Saxonia Band. Composed by Swoboda, and arranged for the Piano Forte by Herman[n] Kotzschmar." It is a very pretty thing. Paine has constantly on hand an excellent assortment of new Music.[100]

Within a month[101] a second pianoforte arrangement was published: *Thine Is My Heart, Galopp, as performed by the Saxonia Band, Composed by Liehmann*. A third Kotzschmar arrangement published by Paine, undated but doubtless from this same time, was *Sommer's Saloon Polka, As played by the Saxonia Band, composed by Gungl*. . . .

Soon the first of Kotzschmar's original compositions was ready for the public, according to an October announcement:

> NEW MUSIC. We have received the "Commercial Street Polka," being the first of six popular pieces for the piano forte, consisting of Polkas, Waltzes, and Quick Steps, composed and respectfully dedicated to the ladies of Portland, by Hermann Kotzschmar. The lovers of good music are greatly indebted to Kotzschmar for this fine composition. It is published by J. S. Paine, 113 Middle street, where all the new music may be found.[102]

In December the second of this series, the *Diamond Cove Waltz* was issued.[103] The third—and seemingly last—number in the projected series of six was *Dandelion Polka*, op. 10, which was announced in April 1852.[104] Other compositions published by Jacob Paine included *Distaffina Polka*, op. 14 (1852),[105] *Vilikins Valse* (1855),[106] and *Tremolo on Balfe's celebrated song, We May Be Happy Yet* (1855). Four Kotzschmar songs "published by the author" in New York in 1852—and sold in Portland at Paine's—were *Immortality of Love, A Ballad*, op. 4, *When will ye think of me my friends*, *dedicated to the members of the Saxonia Band*, op. 5, *The First Prayer*, op. 6, and *Our Yankee Girls*, op. 8.[107]

Kotzschmar continued to compose throughout his life, and a significant amount reached publication. Probably his most popular work was the *Te Deum in F*, first published in 1866 by G. Schirmer. His sphere of influence was increased substantially in 1869 when the Haydn Association, upon reorganizing following the Civil War hiatus, elected him as its conductor. He continued in this capacity until the society disbanded in 1898, and built it into a strong performing group that set a high standard for choral music in the state. At various times, Kotzschmar also was conductor of the Weber Club (a men's chorus), the Philharmonic Orchestra, the Orchestral Union of Portland, and choral societies in Gardiner, Lewiston, and Brunswick. He died in Portland on 15 April 1908. Four years later his memory was honored by the installation of the Kotzschmar Memorial Organ, a 177-stop Austin pipe organ, in the auditorium of the Portland City Hall. Its donor, Cyrus Hermann Kotzschmar Curtis, president of the Curtis Publishing Company, was the son of Cyrus Libby Curtis, originally a trombonist in the Portland Band[108] and a longtime close friend of Kotzschmar. Edwards states that the elder Curtis used his influence to obtain the initial Union Street Theater employment for Kotzschmar,[109] an assertion in apparent contradiction to the earlier newspaper reports cited above. The son, namesake of the musician, as a boy ". . . learned to play piano and organ from watching and listening" to Kotzschmar at the First Parish Church.[110] Curtis, in presenting the organ to the city, stated that Kotzschmar was

> . . . preeminent in this city as an organist, composer and teacher, a man who was loved by all classes for his kindly spirit, his high ideals, and his devotion to music.
> He cared little or nothing for material things or for fame—he never sought them, but here is his monument—a monument to one who DID SOMETHING to make us better men and women and to appreciate that indefinable something that is an expression of the soul.[111]

John Knowles Paine was ten years old when Hermann Kotzschmar first arrived in Portland. It is not known when the youth started his music studies, but conceivably the instruction began soon thereafter. The professional relationship between Kotzschmar and Jacob Paine was initiated by the first few months of 1850, and presumably a bond of friendship and respect would have developed between the two men. Jacob certainly was well aware of his son's musical talent and would have wished for him to learn from such a skilled and well trained musician. Kotzschmar, in turn, would certainly have heard the boy play while visiting the Paine family, and would have recommended that formal study be started. In these teenage years the youth obtained a thorough grounding in piano and organ that would serve him well in his advanced study in Berlin. He also studied theory and composition with Kotzschmar, and produced a string quartet (op. 5) at the age of 16.[112] What other works the young composer may have completed can only be speculated, as none seems to be extant. It is possible, however, that one or more of these early compositions may have survived in another version dating from the Berlin or later Boston years.

Young Paine received his general education in the Portland public schools. Official records from this period were lost when the Portland City Hall was destroyed in the great fire of 1866. However, from roll books and published grade sheets in the collection of the Maine Historical Society, we do learn that he attended the Portland High School for boys for six terms from 1851 to 1853 (age 12 to 14). He enrolled in March 1851, and was listed as a student for the terms ending 2 August 1851, 26 February, 30 July, and 20 September 1852, and 4 March and 5 August 1853; lists for earlier and later terms do not include his name.[113] No listing of graduates has survived, but we may assume, in view of his remarkable academic record (to be discussed below) and the absence of any apparent complications that would have forced him to discontinue, that John Knowles completed the requirements and received his diploma. The published reports include course grades, attendance, and deportment, and show him to have been an excellent student. His lowest grades were given in his first term: in a 4-point system, he received 3.5 in Grammar and 3.6 in both Arithmetic and Geography.[114] A year later Arithmetic and Grammar had improved to 3.9 and 3.8.[115] His highest grades were in 1853—4.0 in Geography, Philosophy , and Meteorology, and 3.8 in Latin.[116] Paine missed 16 half-days, including 12 due to sickness, during his first term, but his attendance improved, and he achieved a perfect record in the July 1852 and March 1853 reports. Even his attitude and conduct seem to have become better as he continued his studies, for a mark of ''2'' in Deportment on the August 1851 and February 1852 reports was replaced by ''1,'' the best possible mark, on the subsequent reports.

It is reasonable to assume that, after finishing high school, Paine divided his time between his studies with Kotzschmar and his assistance in the family store. A general picture of the scope of Jacob Paine's music firm may be gleaned from his 1852 *Portland Directory* advertisement:

Piano Fortes

J. S. Paine

No. 113 Middle Street, Portland

Dealer in Piano Fortes, manufactured and warranted by J. Chickering, Boston. A full assortment of 6, 6 1/2, 6 3/4 and 7 octaves will be constantly found on hand at the manufacturer's lowest prices. Piano Fortes to let.

> Also, constantly on hand a large assortment of Sheet Music. Instruction and Music Books of every description. Bertini's and Hunton's Piano Forte Schools constantly on hand, together with a general assortment of Musical Merchandise.[117]

Being a leading merchant in his field, Paine provided a display of Chickering seven-octave and grand pianos for an 1854 Mechanics' Fair in Portland.[118]

In addition to his piano and sheet music sales, Paine was active in music publishing, as was mentioned above in the discussion of Kotzschmar. He also added works of other Portland composers to his catalog, including D. L. Downing (*Florence Polka*, 1854), E. K. Eaton (*Martha Redowa Polka*, 1856), Melville C. Milliken (*Casco Polka*, 1855), Signor Serafino Rebbechini ("The Vow," 1855, from *Album of Italian Songs*), and H. A. Whitney (*Little Annie*, 1856).[119]

In the midst of much business success and—we may assume—family happiness, three tragedies befell the Paine family, all during the summer and autumn of 1856. On 24 June the Paine store was ruined by a "disastrous conflagration":

> The most destructive fire that has devastated our city for many years, occurred on Tuesday morning last, and consumed, in the business center of the city, about a dozen stores, two hotels, a church, two large livery stables, several dwelling houses, workshops, and smaller buildings. It broke out about 3 o'clock in a shed attached to the Codman house, on Temple St., and soon swept away the stable, the Casco House, Codman House, Temple St. church, and crossing Temple St. completely gutted Muzzey's row of eight three and four story brick stores. Several dwelling houses on Temple St. were also destroyed, also Fernald's tailor shop in the rear of Barbour Block, and a number of buildings in the rear of Exchange St. Most of the property on Temple St. was owned by Samuel J. Anderson; John Mussey owned the stores on Middle St., and Elias Thomas the Casco House, which was uninsured. The storekeepers burnt out, are—P. & L. Merrill; Miss Trow & Drinkwater; Miss Chadbourne; H. P. Storer & Co.; J. R. Corey & Co.; L. D. Hanson & Co.; N. I. Mitchell; Merrill & Quinby; J. S. Paine; Edmund Winship; C. Dyer and F. E. Pray, tailors. . . . Most of the goods in the stores were saved. . . .[120]

In the midst of the confusion resulting from this disaster, the Portland City Council found the state of ruin an appropriate time to widen Temple Street, a north-south street, by widening its eastern side 10 feet. In addition,

> . . . the Winship and Paine stores, at the corner of Middle Street, on the westerly side of Temple street are also to be cut off, thus avoiding the sharp angle that now exists at that entrance. . . .[121]

Consequently, it was necessary for Jacob Paine to move his salvaged merchandise and relocate his business. In August he reopened in a building one block further west on Middle Street:

. . . Our friend, J. S. Paine, the music dealer, who was somewhat suddenly turned out of his old stand by the fire, a few weeks since, has taken up position again at No. 162 [= 152] Middle St., corner of Cross St., up stairs, where he is ready to stand and deliver, as of old. That he is as musical as ever, we have evidence in two "Gems of the Minstrelsy" just published by him, and now lying on our table, entitled "*Rosa May*" and "*When I saw sweet Nellie Home*. . . ."[122]

The Paine family, certainly strained and tired from this trying ordeal, was soon to be saddened by the death of the youngest child, Addie, aged 8 years, 3 months, on 8 August.[123] But still greater grief and shock was felt on the death of Jacob Paine himself on 26 September, at the age of only 46.[124] The admiration he had inspired among Portland citizens was reflected in the *Transcript* eulogy:

. . . Mr. J. S. Paine, whose musical establishment has long been well known in this city, died last week, and was buried on Sunday—his funeral attended by the Musical Associations, Choirs, Portland Band and a crowd of citizens. The band played a beautiful dirge over the dead body of their friend. . . .[125]

Upon his father's death, John Knowles had to assume the responsibility of head of the household. Important decisions were made quickly, and only three days after Jacob's funeral, on 8 October, the following advertisement appeared in the Portland *Eastern Argus*:[126]

John K. Paine,
Teacher of the Piano Forte,
152 Middle Street.
References:—Hermann Kotzschmar,
D. H.Chandler,
Dr. Thomas,
Geo. A.Churchill.

The notice was repeated daily until mid-April 1857, and also appeared in the weekly *Transcript*, beginning 11 October. John's references were leading musicians in the community. Kotzschmar by this time was well on his way to becoming the most influential teacher in the state. Chandler, who succeeded Jacob Paine as conductor of the Portland Band in 1843, improved the organization so that it was considered "The band" of western Maine in the years prior to the Civil War.[127] Dr. Charles W. Thomas was a bass soloist active in Portland music circles, and had been prominent in the First Parish choir during the early 1840s.[128] Churchill, a commission merchant active as a tenor soloist, had conducted the Portland Orchestral Society for a time during the 1850s, and in February 1857 would be elected First Vocal Conductor of the new Haydn Association.[129] It is not known to what degree John was successful as a teacher during the next two years, but Edwards, in *Music and Musicians of Maine*,[130] identifies one student as George W. Marston (1840–1901) who, like Kotzschmar, built a career as a composer, teacher, and performer active in the musical life of Portland and the state of Maine.

John's headquarters for teaching remained at the family store, which now was managed by his uncles, William and David. The upstairs quarters Jacob had occupied after the June fire proved inadequate, and in December the store relocated at No. 2 Free Street. An advertisement first appearing on 22 December 1856 shows the business to be little changed from former years:[131]

Paine's Music Store
Has been removed from Chambers, 152 Middle st.
—to the—
Corner of Cross and Free Sts., and junction of Free, Cross and Middle streets; where we continue to receive
New and Popular Music of Every Variety!
Music not on hand will be ordered with promptness.
Chickering & Son's Piano-Fortes,
—and—
Prince & Co.'s Celebrated Melodeons,
to be found at this store only, as we have the Agency for this City.
The above instruments will be sold at Manufacturer's Prices, with their warrant.

Pianos to Let!
Orders for tuning promptly
attended to at short
notice!
☞ The public are informed that we are now ready to
Repair Umbrellas and Parasols,
. . . at . . .
Paine's Music Store, Corner of Cross and Free Sts.

A later advertisement boasted William Paine's establishment as having "the largest stock of Sheet Music in the state," as well as continuing as an "Umbrella and Parasol Manufactory."[132] The brothers continued to publish new music, and Portlanders so honored in 1857 included Eaton (*Paddy Carey Cotillion*, *Waltz and Polka*)[133] and Whitney (*Memories of Parting*, *Fading Away*, and *Nellie Hood*);[134] also issued were third editions of Downing's *Florence Polka* and Kotzschmar's arrangement of *Thine is my Heart*.

Young Paine had studied with Kotzschmar for some years and had advertised as a teacher for seven months before he received his first public exposure as a performer. This was as an assisting artist on an instrumental and vocal concert given by violinist Carl Gartner on 1 June 1857 at Lancaster Hall; others participating were tenor Samuel Thurston, bass John

L. Shaw, and the Portland Orchestral Society,[135] presumably conducted by G. A. Churchill. Apparently Paine's participation was not considered much of a drawing card, for a newspaper promotional article did not mention him:

> . . . The programme promises the *best* miscellaneous concert that has been offered to the public this season. In addition to four choice pieces to be performed by Mr. Gartner, which alone will be worth ten times the price of a ticket, it contains among the vocal selections, the beautiful terzetto from *Belesario*, a duetto—favorite song of Grizi and Mario—from Il Trovatore; and a spirited martial song, composed by Dr. Callcott, with orchestral accompaniments; and for the Orchestral Society some of their favorites, and also a beautiful Romanza arranged by Mr. Gartner. . . .[136]

No review appeared of the concert, and no further information is available about Paine's place on the program. Within the month, according to Edwards, on 25 June 1857, he made his first public appearance as an organist, "acquitting himself with great credit."[137] Again, notice in the press seems to be lacking.

However, Paine was soon to achieve recognition before the public, for in its meeting on 6 August 1857, the Haydn Association,

> . . . On motion of S. Thurston, Voted that Mr. John K. Paine be the Organist of the Association.[138]

The new choral society had just been organized on 9 February 1857, with George A. Churchill and Samuel Thurston as its first and second vocal conductors;[139] and had presented one oratorio, Haydn's *Creation*, accompanied by the Portland Orchestral Society, on 4 May, repeated on 5 and 27 May.[140] Just after Paine's election, the Association began work on Handel's *Messiah*:

> Haydn Association.—This Association, we learn, will rehearse the Oratorio of the Messiah on Monday evening, Aug. 10. Shall we not have the pleasure of listening to this sublime production at some early day?[141]

After months of rehearsing, the Haydn Association announced a performance of *Messiah* to be given 25 December 1857 at the Chestnut Street Methodist Church, whose large new sanctuary—numbering 190 pews[142]—and new pipe organ had just been completed in June.[143] Paine was to play the full accompaniment on the organ, without help from any orchestral instruments; he was the only person named in the newspaper advertisement:

The Messiah!
The Haydn Association
will give a
Grand Concert
at the
M. E. Church, Chestnut Street, on
Christmas Night, Dec. 25th.
When will be performed Handel's
Oratorio of the Messiah!
John K. Paine will preside at the Organ.
Tickets 25 cents each, to be had at Paine's
Music Store, Breed & Tukey's, H. Packard's,
E. Shaw & Co's., E. C. Andrews' and at the Door.
Concert to commence at 7 1-2 o'clock precisely.
Chas. P. Carlton, Sec'y[144]

A large crowd attended this concert, according to the Association records:

The Oratorio of the Messiah was performed in very good style to a large and attentive audience. The Chorus numbered upwards of 100. Receipts were $109.96.[145]

The performance drew many compliments, especially Paine's accompaniment:

The performance of the Oratorio on Christmas evening at the Methodist Episcopal Church on Chestnut street, was a very fine affair. Much credit is due to the solo performers, and the choruses were rendered in a better manner than we have before heard them. Paine's performance on the organ elicited commendation from every one. The church was filled in every part. . . .[146]

On 1 January 1858 the concert was repeated, with net receipts given to the Chestnut Street church. Again the performance was praised:

Quite a large audience was in attendance at the Chestnut Street Methodist Church, on New Year's evening, to enjoy the repetition of the Oratorio of "The Messiah," by the Haydn Society. The performance was highly satisfactory, and the playing of the Organ by John K. Paine, won much approbation. The "Pastoral Symphony" carried us, as by magic, from January into the green fields in July. It was a gem. . . .[147]

Net proceeds paid to the Chestnut Street church were $100, and the Association announced intentions of giving two more concerts during the season.[148]

By this time Paine and his teacher had recognized the need for him to begin music studies in Europe. An organist sufficiently accomplished to execute satisfactorily such a difficult accompaniment as that to the *Messiah* would need more specialized training than what was available in Portland; naturally a European education would be far more prestigious, as well as thorough, than one gained in Boston or New York. Kotzschmar's training in organ had been minimal, and he was the first to realize that Paine needed a change in teachers and to recommend his going abroad. Such a venture would involve considerable expense, and the Paines did not have the financial resources to take care of it. To raise the funds, John decided to give a series of three concerts early in 1858; the first announcement appeared on 21 December 1857:[149]

SUBSCRIPTION CONCERTS!
JOHN K. PAINE

RESPECTFULLY announces to his friends and the public, that he intends to give

THREE SUBSCRIPTION CONCERTS,
to enable him to
Complete his Musical Education in Germany.

☞ The Concerts to take place in the months of January, February and March.
☞ He will be assisted by talented Artists at home and from abroad.

☞ Subscription List now open at PAINE'S MUSIC STORE. Subscription Tickets for sale at the usual places.

Among the first assisting talent to be enlisted was the Haydn Association. At a Government meeting on Saturday evening, 2 January,

. . . On motion of J. L. Shaw Voted the Association be recomended [sic] to rehearse for John K. Paine's Concert, to be given the last of this month. . . .[150]

Two evenings later the society approved these plans:

. . . Voted to assist John K. Paine at his concerts, as recomended [sic] by the Government. . . .[151]

Later in the month the Association also granted him the use of their hall on Thursday evenings for orchestra rehearsals.[152] Participants in the first concert on 28 January are named in the following advertisement:[153]

John K. Paine's
First Concert
will take place
at Deering Hall,
on Thursday Evening, Jan. 28th,
Assisted by the following talent;
Mr. Carl Gartner, Solo Violinist
Mr. Henry M. [Jungnickel],
Solo Violoncellist
The Orchestral Union,
Mr. H. Kotzschmar, Conductor

. . . and the . . .
Haydn Association,
Mr. George A. Churchill, Conductor
Single Tickets, 50 cts—- two Tickets, 75 cts—three Tickets, $1,00. [*sic*]

Press notice of the concert was quite favorable, but failed to reveal further details:

> The concert at Deering Hall, on Thursday evening last, being the first of a series for the benefit of John K. Paine, was, so far as numbers were concerned, a perfect success. That capacious Hall was filled to repletion, with a fashionable and good-natured audience. The performances were received with much gratification throughout the evening, and it gives us much pleasure to record the success of so worthy and talented a young man as Master Paine. We trust he will be entirely successful in putting a European finish to his presently highly respectable musical education.[154]

The second concert, originally planned for February, took place on Friday, 12 March, and required a last-minute change of program. Assisting artists were to be Jenny Twitchell, alto, of Gardiner, and John L. Shaw, bass, with the Orchestral Union under Kotzschmar.[155] But a schedule conflict arose:

> Owing to some mistake in regard to dates, Mr. Paine is unable to procure the services of Miss Twichell [*sic*] for his concert on Friday evening, but has secured instead Mrs. Harwood the fine soprano of Boston. Miss Twichell understood the concert to be on Friday week and was under engagement for Friday of this week. Mrs. Harwood is said to be an equally choice singer, and therefore this contretemps, which had well nigh brought a failure, will in no wise mar the success of the concert.[156]

Concern among the performers for success must have been high, for Twitchell was considered "the popular vocalist,"[157] while Harwood was an unknown in the city. On the morning of the concert, an article appeared in the *Eastern Argus* praising Mrs. Harwood and quoting extensively a very favorable *Boston Journal* review of a recent concert on which she appeared. An additional program detail also was highlighted:

> . . . Among the attractions offered we notice a grand duett upon two piano's [*sic*] by Messrs. Kotschmar [*sic*] and Paine—the *Leviathan March*—which received such a hearty encore at the last concert. To hear this piece, alone, is worth the price of admission. . . .[158]

The *Leviathan March*, "composed by our townsman Professor Hermann Kotzschmar and by him dedicated to the Boston Germania Serenade Band,"[159] depicted a monster steamship of that name that was regularly in the news. William Paine had published a version for piano in February, and included as its cover "a colored lithograph of the big steamship, as she appears with all sail set on her six masts, and smoke issuing from her fire smoke pipes."[160]

The 12 March concert "drew a full house,"[161] and the sympathetic audience was pleased with the entertainment:

> . . . The old favorites of Portland, Messrs. Kotzschmar, Shaw, the Orchestral Band, &c., as well as the beneficiary of the evening,—were most cordially received.—Mrs. Harwood, of Boston, the female vocalist, made a good impression, and the audience cheered her during the evening with hearty good will. . . .

Harwood's singing removed any misgivings about her being a second choice:

> . . . She has a sympathetic voice, that finds its way at once to the heart of the hearer. It shew [sic] itself in the first song, "Auld Robin Gray," and drew out a round of applause at the close of the second stanza, and an encore at the close, which would take no refusal. She made her mark in all the pieces she sang. . . .

The *Leviathan March* was performed by the orchestra; perhaps the piano duet announced earlier had been the version performed on the January concert.

> . . . The Orchestral Union, under the lead of Mr. Kotzschmar, played the "Leviathan March" and "Champagne Gallop" admirably. . . .[162]

Of course Paine was warmly greeted:

> . . . Master Paine's performance on the piano forte brought an *encore*. This young gentleman gives evidence of much musical talent, which we trust the proceeds of these concerts will enable him fully to improve. . . .[163]

Proceeds from the large sale of tickets added a welcome increase to Paine's educational fund:

> . . . The concert must have been successful pecuniarily, and we are glad of it, for the beneficiary is a young man with excellent musical talents, and is a close student— the means will help him to gratify his aspirations for a finished education in his favorite department.[164]

Less than three weeks later, on Wednesday, 31 March, Paine gave his last concert. Assisting were Jenny Twitchell, trumpet soloist Heinrich Kehrhahn, clarinetist Carl Krebs, Chandler's Portland Band, and Kotzschmar's Orchestral Society.[165] Attendance was good, but the two newspaper reports were at variance. According to the *Eastern Argus*, Deering Hall ". . . was crowded to excess, every available seat being occupied. . . ."[166] But the *Transcript* stated: "The hall was well filled, but such a programme should have packed the house. . . ."[167] This latter review provided a detailed account of the concert:

> . . . The audience expressed their delight with the performances by frequent and long continued applause.
>
> Master Paine opened the concert with a well executed piano solo. His touch was very skillful, combining brilliancy with precision. The clarionet solo, by Krebs, was a rare treat. He produced some surprising effects on that difficult instrument, and was very prepossessing in his manner. Mr. Kehrhahn gave a superb cornet solo. He plays with great ease and freedom; the notes he produced were very spirit stirring, and won the loud applause of the audience. But the most charming performance was the singing of Miss Jenny Twitchell. She rendered "I am the Boyedere," and the Scotch songs, with bewitching effect. Her vocalization is marked by sweetness, both of voice and expression. . . .
>
> The Portland Band rendered the difficult passages from "Il Trovatore" with admirable harmony and precision. We never heard our favorite band do better. Last, but not least, the Orchestral Union gave us the "Champaigne Gallop" in spirited style.—Under the efficient lead of Mr. Kotzschmar this company is a great credit to the musical ability of our city. . . .

Public response to these three concerts was certainly satisfying to Paine, for they showed the fondness that people of Portland felt for him. Moreover, news of such unusual talent and ambition in so young a musician had spread to Boston, where John Sullivan Dwight, arbiter of musical taste, had made note of Paine in his prestigious *Journal* following the third concert:

> Master Paine, a young pianist, has been gratifying the musical people of Portland, Me. with a series of concerts (to the end, we infer, of bridging the way to a higher Musical education in Europe.)[168]

Financially, the results of the series, though helpful, proved inadequate to sustain his three years of study in Berlin. His sister Helen, who had begun a teaching career, provided the remainder of his support.[169]

Paine was soon to leave Portland, but he first participated in several more musical events. Just before his last concert, on 28 March, he was one of 77 "General Managers" for a "Grand Ball! and Musical Soiree! complimentary to The Portland Band . . . ,'' along with Kotzschmar, William Paine, Churchill, and Shaw.[170] In April the Haydn Association presented a pair of concerts at the Chestnut Street Methodist Church, Neukomm's *David* on 21 April and Haydn's *Creation* on the following evening. Paine was organist for both performances, although a full orchestra—led by Kotzschmar and augmented by several guest Bostonians—was on hand to accompany the singers. Soloists were Miss A. V. Atwood, soprano, Samuel Thurston and W. F. Twitchell, tenors, John L.

Shaw, bass, and Boston baritone Myron W. Whitney; G. A. Churchill directed the combined forces.[171]

The last mention of Paine in the Portland press was in connection with a Kotzschmar concert in Deering Hall on Thursday, 6 May; the young musician assisted in the program, along with Mrs. Harwood of Boston, clarinetist Krebs, and the Orchestral Union.[172] Attendance was sparse because of inclement weather, and the performers repeated the program on the following evening.[173] On 26 May the Haydn Association ended its season with a miscellaneous concert, consisting of six choruses (mainly from oratorios the society had performed previously) and a group of solos.[174] No indication is given in newspaper reports concerning the accompanying forces used, but it is probable that Paine, still the Association organist, was at the keyboard. However, it is possible that he could have already left the city, preparing to embark from New York to Germany, in which case Kotzschmar or someone else could have played.

On 1 June 1858 the Haydn Association held its Annual Meeting, and

. . . the usual vote of thanks, were [*sic*] tendered . . . to Mr. J. K. Paine. . . .[175]

It was not noted whether Paine was there to accept this recognition in person. If he did attend, this would have left a bit more than a month for him to resign from the Haydn Association, prepare for his trip, and travel to New York City, from which port he sailed for Europe on 7 July. Meanwhile, the Haydn Association needed to replace him, and on 17 July selected as pianist Henry S. Edwards,[176] who had been Kotzschmar's predecessor in the same capacity for the old Sacred Music Society.

On leaving Portland, the young musician brought to a close the first important period in his musical development. He had been reared in an environment stimulating to musical growth, for his father and uncles were active professionals. They in turn had been inspired by their father, a pioneer in American organ building. It would be reasonable to assume, moreover, that John K. H. Paine began his musical growth as a youth, in the midst of an already existing—albeit informal and amateur—family musical tradition. No record has survived, but one may imagine earlier generations of the Paines, Riches, Knowles, Myricks, and others participating in the singing schools so common to New England communities, singing the Psalms at church, and perhaps playing a fiddle or flute at home. Paine's ancestry stems from the very first English immigrants to New England. These Pilgrims were cultured people, many with developed skills in music. Certainly the love of music—as well as the innate talent—

would have passed from parent to child, setting the background for the outstanding careers of these last three generations.

Probably much of the music John Knowles Paine was exposed to during his childhood was homespun American music—fuging tunes, Psalms, band music (marches, quicksteps, quadrilles, etc.), dance music, minstrel songs, parlor ballads, and salon music for piano; many of his father's publications were in these categories. But John also had many opportunities to hear European concert music, including the Sacred Music Society concerts and recitals of local and visiting artists. When the young musician began his training with Hermann Kotzschmar, his studies of the European masters would have intensified. Kotzschmar's compositions that were published during these years were rather lightweight, owing to commercial dictates, but his skill and knowledge were thorough and his taste presumably was high. The grounding thus established blossomed during the three years in Berlin, and enabled John eventually to attain at least a small degree of international stature. Paine insisted on being considered a *universal* composer, who just happened to be a native resident of the United States. Conscious attempts to write "American" music by injecting folk elements, etc., to him only produced cheap, undignified results; of course, many younger colleagues disagreed. But Paine's convictions were important, for he strove for a universal standard by which music of American composers would be judged on an equal basis, rather than as quaint novelties from an exotic frontier land. Only thus, Paine felt, could the American composer rid himself of the handicap of public bias—whether negative or positive—and attain his full potential.

2

Years of Preparation: 1858–1864

With the conclusion of his three subscription concerts, the 19-year-old Paine had shown himself to be an accomplished professional in the local musical sphere. Under the tutelage of Kotzschmar he had developed a "very skillful" touch at the piano, "combining brilliancy with precision."[1] For the past year he was organist for the Haydn Association, gaining valuable experience; his first-rate accompaniments for the two *Messiah* performances attracted wide notice. Paine also had achieved a great degree of maturity as the only male in the immediate family since his father's death in 1856. Surely he must have spent many hours working in the music store, as well as supplementing the family income by giving piano lessons. Local leaders of Portland's musical life who held him in high esteem included his teacher Herman Kotzschmar, George A. Churchill, conductor of the Haydn Association, Samuel Thurston, voice teacher and assistant conductor of the Haydn Association, and Daniel H. Chandler, conductor of the Portland Band; these men had guided his early career, and they were among the participating musicians in the subscription concerts. Paine had obtained all the training possible in Portland, and for a young man of such obvious talent, a period of study in Europe, preferably Germany, was mandatory, both for growth as a musician and for stature in the profession. Moreover, the musical experiences available in the small city of Portland were extremely limited when compared to those in Boston and New York; opportunities in Berlin, in turn, greatly overshadowed what Boston and New York had to offer. And Paine certainly had the self-confidence and ambition that would motivate him to work toward the very highest goal—professional training in Europe.

News of the young Paine's accomplishments and ambitions spread beyond Portland during these years. Such musical information was considered more newsworthy by journalists of those days than ours. Besides, the professional musicians of Portland must have mentioned Paine's brilliance to their colleagues in other cities; certainly Kotzschmar, whose reputation as a teacher and a composer of vocal and light instrumental music was well established regionally, would have voiced great pride in his pupil. By whatever means the knowledge spread, the young organist attracted the interest of Boston musicians, and a report of his three sub-scription concerts appeared in the 10 April 1858 issue of *Dwight's Journal of Music*. Paine apparently visited Boston at about this time, for he gained the acquaintance of the celebrated Beethoven scholar, Alexander Whee-lock Thayer (1817–97), who had spent the past two years in Boston and New York cataloging the extensive library of Lowell Mason.[2] Thayer had begun his Beethoven research in Europe in 1849, returning to the United States in 1852 to join the staff of the *New-York Daily Tribune*. Handi-capped by ill health, he resigned this position in 1854,[3] returning to Ger-many to examine Beethoven material in the Royal Library in Berlin.[4] But his condition and lack of funds forced him to return again to the United States. With substantial help from Mrs. Mehetabel Adams, of Cambridge, and from Mason,[5] he now planned to return to Berlin and travel thence to Vienna, where he would complete his Beethoven biography.[6] Because of the broad knowledge of the Berlin musical life gained during his resi-dence there, it was probably Thayer who presuaded Paine to pursue his studies in that city (Kotzschmar was trained in Dresden, and perhaps would have retained partiality for his own teachers). Thayer must have been attracted by the young musician's drive, maturity, and talent, while recognizing his unpreparedness for life in Europe, for he offered to ac-company Paine during the ocean voyage, and later to occupy neighboring rooms in a house in Berlin. The many references to " 'John,' a Portland boy,"[7] in Thayer's "Diarist Abroad" column in *Dwight's Journal* provide fascinating glimpses of the first months of their adventure.

On what date John Paine left Portland to begin his trip is not clear. At the annual meeting of the Haydn Association on 1 June 1858, ". . . the usual vote of thanks, were [*sic*] tendered . . . to Mr. J. K. Paine . . .";[8] whether he was there to accept their appreciation in person was not noted in the records. If he did attend the meeting, he would have to have left Portland within a matter of days, traveling probably by rail to Boston to meet Thayer; together they would continue the trip to New York, where Thayer renewed contacts with many friends, especially his former col-leagues on the *Tribune* (most likely including the composer William Henry Fry, an editorial writer and music editor). Being in New York must have been quite an exciting, perhaps disquieting, experience for the small-town boy. New York's music season had not yet ended for the summer; the season of Italian opera continued until 26 June, with works such as *La Traviata*, *Il Trovatore*, Auber's *Masaniello*, and Pacini's *Saffo*. A Grand Musical Festival took place at the Academy of Music on 27 June, advertising "over 300 performers" and "all the professional musicians of the City of New-York and neighborhood"; W. H. Fry was the orator.[9] Another musical attraction was the Mendelssohn Union Concert on 24 June, offering Beethoven's *Ruins of Athens* and Mendelssohn's *Athalie*.[10] At about this time the new Cooper Institute, built by Peter Cooper at a cost of over $600,000, began its project of offering free lectures and instruction; a new State Arsenal was built; and the cornerstone for St. Patrick's Cathedral would be laid in August.[11] City life was quieter at that time than during the previous year, when bank failings and the resulting panic caused frequent riots, robberies, and murders. But crime remained a problem augmented by the squalid, impoverished, corrupt, and unpoliced conditions of many areas of the city. Growing numbers of recent immigrants added to the element that was difficult to control.[12] Typical was the "disgraceful fight" on 23 June at a lager beer saloon

> . . . between a party of musicians who had assembled there. In the course of the row knives, tumblers, decanters, bottles, and other weapons were used in the freest manner. Several persons were severely cut and bruised, but none received any dangerous wounds. . . .[13]

Of course, Paine, in the company of Thayer's friends and colleagues, doubtless was not directly exposed to this class of musicians, but mere knowledge of such events must have been quite alarming to the young man from Maine. One musician whom Paine probably did meet was Charles C. Converse (1832–1918),[14] the young American composer, who soon would return to Germany to be a fellow student of Karl Haupt in Berlin.

Plans were made to depart on the sailing vessel *Athena*, a Boston-built, German-owned ship, which left New York on 7 July.[15] Thayer was reluctant to leave, feeling that his two-year stay in America was far too short; he did not relish taking

> . . . such French leave of so many friends, and should now feel more fully the length of my visit home. But the ship was ready, my companion was anxious to be off, a delay of a day might cost us a month—and so, on the 7th of July, at sundown, we were already beginning to feel the Atlantic swell down by Sandy Hook. . . .[16]

On 3 August the *Athena* reached the Isle of Wight and on the 5th the vessel was towed up the Thames, to be anchored at the Victoria dock. During the stay in London, the passengers decided to spend nights on the ship to avoid delays with customs officials.[17]

Thayer's report describes the changes in London since his last visit and the many buildings—the National Gallery, St. Paul's, Westminster

Abbey—that he and Paine visited. At Westminster Abbey they attended
a service and considered the anthems well sung:

> . . . seldom have we—myself and "John," a young organist—more thoroughly en-
> joyed pieces of sacred music than those thus heard.[18]

On Sunday, 15 August, a performance of Mozart's *Requiem* at St.
George's Catholic Cathedral, Southward, had a profound effect on the
two companions. The music was performed as a part of the funeral service, and the mood was very different from that of a concert hall
performance.

> It was useless to resist it. "John" soon had his face hid, and so was mine before half
> a dozen stanzas of the *Dies Irae* were finished. Neither could laugh at the other for
> his red eyes.

Leaving London, the ship docked at Bremerhaven on Monday, 23
August, and the travelers continued on a small steamer, reaching Bremen
after dark. Paine and Thayer spent the night in the Stadt Frankfurt hotel,
and were awakened the next morning by band music from the square
outside. There, a wind band of oboes, flutes, clarinets, and bassoons gave
a concert, beginning with a German chorale, and played a variety of
pieces, concluding with the Mendelssohn Wedding March in honor of a
local official's wedding anniversary. Thayer described the beauty and precision of their playing as far superior to that of American "blowers of
bastard *brass* instruments," and added that almost any of its members
could appear in Boston as a soloist. This was Paine's first encounter with
a European band; ". . . upon [him] it worked like magic."[19]

   Berlin, the destination of the two travelers, by this time had achieved
a position of great political, economic, and cultural influence. As capital
of the powerful Prussian state, it was becoming the most important city
in Germany. Following a period of unrest in the late 1840s, political
oppression had assured greater stability, which aided the economy and
allowed the government to institute an extensive program of social welfare. Berlin was experiencing a great commercial growth as a major railroad center and distribution point for iron, grain, and wool; a population
boom gave impetus to the construction of huge apartment complexes.[20]
Most important among the centers of Berlin's intellectual life was Berlin
University, with its assemblage of outstanding scholars in all fields, including music; Adolf Bernhard Marx (1795–1866), the theorist, was a
member of its music faculty as well as a co-founder of the *Stern'sches
Konservatorium*. Leaders in Berlin's concert life included Wilhelm Taub-

ert (1811–91), musical director of the Royal Opera and court *Kapell-meister*, Julius Stern (1820–83), *Königlicher Musikdirector*, founder of the *Stern'sches Konservatorium*, and director of the *Stern'scher Gesangver-ein*; Giacomo Meyerbeer (1791–1864), *Generalmusikdirector*, who still conducted productions of his operas; and Hans von Bülow (1830–94), *Hofpianist* and principal master of pianoforte playing at the *Stern'sches Konservatorium*. Other active musicians included Eduard Grell (1800–86), director of the famous *Singakademie*; Robert Radecke (1830–1911), or-ganist and pianist recently arrived from Leipzig, who had begun an im-portant series of choral, orchestral, and chamber music concerts; and Theodor Kullak (1818–82), pianist and pedagogue, who had helped found the *Stern'sches Konservatorium*, then left it to start his own *Neue Aka-demie der Tonkunst*. Singers on the Berlin opera stage included soprano Johanna Wagner (1826–91), the adopted daughter of Richard Wagner's brother Albert; soprano Louise Köster, tenor Theodor Formes (1826–74); and bass August Ludwig Fricke (dates for Köster and Fricke were not available).

The two Americans reached Berlin about 27 August and quickly began taking in its musical life, although the city was still in the summer off-season period and concerts were relatively few. Performances at the Royal Opera House numbered only about three a week, including Mey-erbeer's *Robert the Devil* and *Huguenots*, Mozart's *Don Juan*, Spohr's *Jessonda*, Auber's *Lac des Fées*, Cherubini's *Wasserträger*, works by Donizetti, and one or two ballets. Kroll's theater scheduled a similar number of performances, including works such as Auber's *Le Domino Noir*. About three good symphony concerts were to be heard weekly, "a great falling off." The Stern singing society also suffered from vacation absences, with "but about 100 voices present" at weekly rehearsals; Thayer and his companion enjoyed their "rather good concert" on 14 September, hearing part of Mendelssohn's *Lobgesang*, Mozart's *Ave Verum Corpus*, and other short pieces, They heard the Lutheran *Domchor* each Sunday, and Paine felt that the choir "sings, and that on the whole there is some music to be heard here."[21] A 29 September performance of *The Magic Flute* was a first-time experience for Paine, "whose emotions were written in his face."[22]

Paine was indeed fortunate to have Thayer's help in getting settled in Berlin. Native landladies were known to charge English-speaking stu-dents 12 thalers a month for a room that a German student could rent for 8 thalers; the non-German student was a "goose to be plucked," and also caused more trouble and expense for the landlady.[23] But Thayer's familiarity with the language and customs solved such problems.

> John and I are particularly favored. We are in a two-story house, in a *woodyard*, right upon the great Friedrich St., within six or eight minutes of the opera house, on the lower floor. He has the large room, and I the two smaller.[24]

Paine's chief teacher in Berlin was Karl August Haupt (1810–91), with whom he studied organ, counterpoint, and composition.[25] Haupt was an outstanding organ virtuoso, "the greatest player in Germany . . .—and probably—nay, doubtless in the world."[26] He was an enthusiastic disciple of Bach—in whose style he improvised variations on the organ[27]—and he instilled this enthusiasm in his students. It was said of him that his kindness and patience, extended to visiting artists and students, was as well known as his virtuosity.[28] Haupt played Bach in the so-called German style, that is, with a minimum of shading. According to contemporary explanations, pipe organs of that day were incapable of nuance or effective crescendos. Organists seem not to have practiced terraced dynamics; instead, in performing fugues, they normally used the full organ or an *organo pleno* throughout.[29] Haupt is said to have played "streng gleichmässig *ff*."[30] Paine was also reported to have been "not a showy player . . ."[31] and to have "played Bach and Beethoven in the German academic way of his time. . . ."[32] Haupt's teaching was evident in Paine's use of dynamics in Bach, according to one reviewer's complaint regarding an 1863 Boston recital:

> The strain upon the organ suggests a vast deal of unnecessary labor on the part of the seven perspiring wind-raisers in the ante-room.[33]

In his teaching, Haupt pioneered a more efficient method of pedaling,

> . . . preferring the use of heel and toe in scale passages, never crossing the feet, except in cases of absolute necessity. . . .[34]

Paine helped to introduce this technique to American organists. The score of his *Concert Variations on the Star Spangled Banner*, published in 1865, included "signs for the application of the feet to the pedals"—now in common use—which the composer stated were "invented by Haupt of Berlin. . . ."[35]

Haupt's contrapuntal ability was evident from writers who would often link the two skills: "[Paine,] ein Schüler unseres bedeutendsten Orgelvirtuosen und ausgezeichneten Contrapunctisten A. Haupt . . . ,"[36] as well as from the fact that his counterpoint text, written after he became director of the *Königliches Institut für Kirchenmusik* in 1869, was so popular that it appeared in an English translation.[37]

Most students of Haupt held him in high esteem.

> . . . I cannot tell you how Haupt's pupils respect that man for his learning, and love him for his goodness. . . .[38]

He in turn was pleased with Paine's talent and drive, and must have rated him high among his students. Within a few months of the young organist's arrival, Haupt remarked that he "will make a *great* organist."[39] After a recital Paine gave at the *Parochialkirche* (Haupt's church), a correspondent for the London *Musical World* noted that Haupt,

> . . . generally speaking a stranger to "wreathed smiles," could not restrain the satisfaction, mingled we feel certain with a touch of pride, which he inwardly felt, manifesting itself upon the mirror of his soul.[40]

This pride did not diminish through the years, for Boston critic Philip Hale, who studied with the great teacher in 1883–84, later recalled:

> [Haupt] was never weary of extolling the rare industry of a pupil that was very dear to him—Professor John K. Paine of Harvard University.[41]

Paine's two other teachers in Berlin are said to have been Gustav Wilhelm Teschner (1800–83) in singing and *Königlicher-Musikdirector* Friedrich Wilhelm Wieprecht (1802–72) in instrumentation.[42] Teschner seems not to have been mentioned as Paine's teacher until the appearance of biographical articles from about 1880 onward; however, if Paine himself provided the information for such articles, their factual basis would be assured. His studying with Wieprecht is first mentioned in 1861.[43] A close friendship with Wieprecht can be inferred from Paine's 1866 statement:

> . . . Old Wieprecht is the same good old soul. He is very kind to me and takes great interest in my affairs. . . .[44]

An 1863 advertisement, after Paine had returned to Boston, describes him as "Instructor of the Organ, Piano, Musical Composition, and the various departments of Military Music . . . ,"[45] the latter skill doubtless learned from the royal bandmaster. Such ability was certainly timely enough during the height of Civil War activity!

Paine's academic affiliation during his years in Berlin remains obscure. His main studies were with Haupt, the organ instructor at Theodor Kullak's *Neue Akademie der Tonkunst*. Later, in 1860, Haupt joined the staff of the *Königliches Institut für Kirchenmusik*, and became its director in 1869. Any institutional affiliations of Wieprecht and Teschner do not appear to be revealed in contemporary sources, although an 1858 review mentions a performance by the Kullak institute's instrumental class, led by Wieprecht.[46] Biographers who have mentioned institutions with respect to Paine have reported that he attended either the *Königliches Institut*, the Kullak *Akademie*, or the *Hochschule für Musik*.[47] Thayer considered Kullak's academy and its rival, Julius Stern's conservatory, as the two best music schools in Berlin, and that Kullak's organ department under Haupt was superior.[48] This would suggest that Thayer might have advised Paine to enroll in Kullak's school; the three years Paine spent in Berlin would conform to the normal three-year course prevalent in the conservatories.[49] Moreover, Paine's arrival date in Berlin would have given him just enough time to find his footing and become accustomed to the new sounds of German before the 1 October enrollment date. However, a report from Thayer about American students in Berlin listed Converse and Paine as students of Haupt, one Pattison as a student of Haupt and von Bülow (then a member of the Stern Conservatory staff), and one Pease, of Cleveland, "studying in Kullak's school,"[50] this last phrase perhaps implying that the other three students were not enrolled in a school.[51]

According to "Bostonian," who may well have been Thayer himself, Paine was a warm, friendly person, "portly," with an "open and cordial smile. . . ."[52] His dedication to his studies is seen in an account relating the long hours of practicing spent in his room—"Bach's fugues, Haydn's 'Military' Symphony, 4 hands, another American aiding," and the Kreutzer Sonata.[53] Pleasurable temptations often had to be withstood:

> [John] good-naturedly rises from his pedal-piano, through which, a moment ago, he was driving J. S. Bach on all fours (*his* "fours," not Bach's). "Well, John, will you go to the Concert?" "Thank you, no; I must have my organ lesson for to-morrow learned." "What's the Symphony this afternoon?" "Seventh, I am sorry to say"— and a look of ineffable longing crossed his expressive face,—but behind it is that unmistakeable background of resolution, which belongs to genius, and which can always say: "Get thee behind me, Satan," when the true divinity beckons forward. So I leave John and go out of the gate to the sound of Fugue.

A similar anecdote was told by John Towers, a fellow student and roommate of Paine's:[54]

> . . . It was my good fortune to have for a room mate in Berlin, a veritable pattern of diligence and an excellent fellow to boot. He was an excellent example to follow, both as to diligence, integrity and honor. If I failed to realize the importance of the fleeting moments, he certainly made up in his own person for all my defects in this direction. Work was his motto, and he was as faithful to it as any man—not excepting Mendelssohn himself—I ever met. His chief study was the king of instruments, the organ, and close upon this, musical composition. He seemed to never tire of dividing his time between them, and it was difficult for me to induce him to take outside

exercise. I particularly remember one burning hot summer's day, when I felt so prostrate, or lazy, if it be preferred, and I sauntered into my companion's room faintly hoping we might together take a breather on the river or elsewhere. I found him in the most ariel costume imaginable "pegging away" at a passage for the pedals—he had a set adapted to his piano—and I watched and watched him go over the same passage at least twenty times, the perspiration dripping freely from him on all sides, until I could stand it no longer, and I passionately implored him to wind up, and come out into the cooler open. "Not," he replied, "until I have played it a hundred times," and he was as good as his word. It might naturally be supposed that such effort and such determination would result in producing a master hand on the organ and in the world of composition, and in this case the expectation has been fully realized. The young gentleman who set me and others this good example is now Prof. John K. Paine, A. M., musical director of Harvard University, a master musician of whom America may very justly be proud. His modesty is so great that he would be angry with me for thus unearthing the past, but I think no apology is needed, where the object is to show the oncoming generation that there is only one road to Parnassus, which is rugged and steep and beset with difficulties, which only can be overcome by determination, perseverence and high, and may I not say, holy aspirations.

Such drive and self-discipline we have seen to have been characteristic of Paine since he was quite young; his excellent high school marks, his early compositions, and his accomplishments as an organist under Kotzschmar are clear examples. His self-reliance was developed, in addition, as a result of his father's death and his need to assume the role of the head of the household. Regrettably, Paine was required to grow even more as an individual during these Berlin years, for his mother died on 21 October 1860,[55] during his last year of study. There is no record that he returned; such a trip would have been futile, for he could not have reached Portland until weeks after the funeral. One must imagine his emotion upon first hearing the news. We cannot know the amount of affection Paine felt for his mother, but however close they had been, the word of her death must have been shattering indeed to the student so far from home. But this tragic event must not have broken Paine's determination, for in his remaining months in Berlin he was to perform brilliantly, both as an organist and as a composer.

Contemporary periodicals preserve record of three organ recitals Paine played in Berlin during his student years. Some writers report concerts in "several German cities."[56] as well as a London recital in 1861 "that won for him commendation"[57] but further details are elusive. The first Berlin recital—probably in December 1859 or early January 1860— was reviewed in the 21 January 1860 issue of the London *Musical World*. The writer proclaimed that Paine's playing was "perfection," although "the resonance . . . marred the effect greatly"[58]—the building was not specified.

A second recital—in the *Parochialkirche*—was again reviewed in

Musical World; the correspondent complimented Paine's "classic taste, his sterling abilities, and his indomitable perseverance. . . ." Notables in the audience included the American Ambassador, Joseph Albert Wright (1810–67), former governor of Indiana (1849–57) and U. S. Minister to Prussia (1857–61; 1865–67); Hermann Grimm (1828–1901), art critic, teacher, and novelist, and son of Wilhelm, one of the two brothers Grimm of *Grimm's Fairy Tales*; *Kapellmeister* Wilhelm Taubert; "and several of the most renowned *maestri* of Berlin."[59] Taubert especially was delighted by the program and offered Paine "a few kind words of encouragement"—a welcome development, as

> . . . the musical critics of the place, for some reasons best known to themselves and heaven, are pleased to ignore his performances.

The following note—from "The Diarist" of 12 January 1860—makes mention of a familiar musical celebrity:

> Paine is the topic of talk in all the musical circles. Clara Schumann has heard of him, and I took him down to her a day or two since. He is to go again and play some of his music—a sonata, and fugues.[60]

Another writer recalls the "unusual success attending his performances before the Royal Family of Prussia."[61]

In addition to pieces by Bach, Mendelssohn, and Louis Thiele (1816–48; Haupt's predecessor at the *Parochialkirche*), Paine played compositions of his own on each of three Berlin programs. These included the following:

> Prelude and Fugue in G minor
> Fantasy and Fugue in E minor [op. 2[1]]
> Concert Variations on the Austrian Hymn [op. 3]
> Concert Variations upon "Old Hundred"

Paine's fugues showed himself to be "a thorough comprehender of the king of fugues."[62] While the first two pieces especially reflect the influence on him of the Bach revival, the other compositions, in general, were typical of the repertory popular at that time among German organists.[63] His Austrian Hymn variations were described by a London reviewer as "extremely original, and . . . natural, and—music."[64]

Paine's third concert was played on 19 April 1861, also at the *Parochialkirche*, just before he left Berlin for London. Again there was an invited audience. Included on the program were pieces by Bach (including the Trio Sonata in G and the Fugue in G), Thiele, and Mendelssohn, as well as his two variations listed above.[65] Critics were enthusiastic about

Paine's "most amazing technique" and pedal dexterity,[66] his clarity of style, and his "perfect mastery over the mechanism of the instrument."[67] His Bach interpretations were especially praised.

Reviewers of the concert disagreed over Paine's accomplishments as a composer, at least to a degree. The writer for the *Voss'sche-Zeitung* termed Paine a composer in the best sense of the word, and described his variations as "happily laid out" in a formal sense, with a good use of counterpoint. Only the opening variations of "Old Hundred" showed Paine "had not yet fully emancipated himself" from textbook rules. The *Neue Zeitschrift* columnist found the composer inferior to the virtuoso. His Austrian Hymn variations, while showing talent, did not have the musical maturity of a composer "standing on his own feet."

By 27 April 1861 when Paine arrived in London, the *Musical World* looked forward to his "appearing before a London audience, both as an executant and as a composer."[68] During his short stay "he won the applause of the most educated critics of the city."[69]

In these three years Paine had received intensive training in and constant exposure to German musical culture—an invaluable experience that formed the basis of his entire career. His virtuosity as an organist had already attracted the many German critics and musical cognoscenti, and it was to place him in the forefront among organists upon his return home. Paine's love for the music of Bach was cultivated during this period, and he was one of the first organists to perform this repertory in the United States. Three years of study with Haupt had also provided a thorough grounding in counterpoint and composition that was to produce a conservative, classical discipline in the 21-year-old American and which became an important part of his individual compositional style. Perhaps the most important result of Paine's sojourn in Berlin as far as his career was concerned was prestige, for Americans regarded European musical training as vastly superior to anything domestic. With the German stamp of approval, opportunities would open up to Paine with an ease that even in his most vivid imagination he could not have dreamed. By 1875 the boy from down East would be appointed full Professor of Music at Harvard.

When Paine returned to the United States in late spring of 1861 (he arrived in Portland on 18 June 1861 aboard the *Jura*, from Liverpool via Quebec[70]), both his personal life and the country had been changed by extraordinary events. With his mother's death the previous October, there were only two remaining members of the immediate family to come home to—his sister Helen, married to lawyer William Allen, and his grandmother, Jane Paine, still living at the house at 9 Portland Street. The music store remained under the management of his uncle, and was now known as "William Paine's Music Store."[71] Besides these events of purely personal import, the returning native was faced by the fact that musical organizations for the most part, including the Haydn Association, had suspended activities for the duration of the Civil War. It is not clear why or under what circumstances Paine avoided the draft. He was, after all, 22 years old and, as far as is known, in good health. Besides, from what we know of his financial resources, it is doubtful that he could have gathered together the money, then close to a year's ordinary salary ($400), necessary to provided a substitute.

After the young musician arrived in Portland, we may suppose that he spent many hours discussing his European experiences with his old teacher, Hermann Kotzschmar, who more than anyone else was responsible for Paine's sojourn. We know that he composed a "remarkably fine" *Agnus Dei* "in the strict church style" for Kotzschmar's choir at the First Parish Church,[72] and practiced faithfully on the church's organ. For about the end of July, Paine played a recital in which he included his Concert Variations on the Star Spangled Banner.[73] Also about this time[74] he met the editor of the *Boston Musical Times*, who reported:

> . . . Mr. Paine very kindly permitted us to enjoy an hour's unalloyed pleasure in listening to his rare interpretation of the music of the great master of that grandest of instruments, the organ.
> Mr. Paine plays with remarkable clearness and vigor, and his pedal playing is most admirable. Bach's fugues were given with a rare power we have not heard excelled, and a trio sonate of the same composer, in which two manuals and the pedals are simultaneously employed, was played with a clearness and individuality of parts, and at the same time so elegantly interwoven and shaped into a perfect whole, as to at once indicate the talent of the performer, as well as the lofty genius of the composer. . . .
> [Paine] is a devoted worshiper of . . . Johann Sebastian Bach. He revels in the wealth of the life-long labor of the illustrious master. He would have the world love Bach as he loves him, and he sincerely believes that the world has only to know him as he knows him to love him equally as well. He is a missionary of Bach, and Bach has no more enthusiastic a worshiper, nor so admirable an interpreter in the United or Disunited States of America. . . .
> . . . We shall be happy to welcome him in Boston. . . .

The young organist gave a farewell concert at the First Parish Church in September. He was assisted by the church choir, which sang his *Agnus Dei* and *Benedictus*.[75] In October he made the final break with his youth and embarked on the next phase of his career. The move to Boston was inevitable from the time in the late 1850s when he decided to further his musical education by going to Germany, because his native town did not possess the cultural resources he needed. However, Paine was well-known and admired in Portland, where he had spent his entire youth, and it must have taken much courage and self-confidence to abandon the security of his home community to face the more sophisticated audiences and compete with his musical peers in Boston. Such a move is but another example of Paine's never-ending ambition that was to culminate in his Harvard professorship and ultimate recognition as a leading force in American music.

Paine did not have to wait long to find out how wise his decision to move had been. On 1 November he was introduced to the Boston musical community at an afternoon recital in Tremont Temple to an invited audience "of two or three hundred personal and musical friends."[76] Dwight, writing in his *Journal*, thoroughly approved of the program—all was of "the solid school of proper organ music"[77] he had long promoted. The description of the Austrian Hymn variations reflects the critic's enthusiasm and philosophy:

> The variations . . . were exceedingly ingenious and interesting, with no clap-trap about them, showing the labor of a composer and not of a show organist, the effects being those of the composition not of the combination of stops or the ear tickling effects of the imitation of instrumental tones.

As gratifying to the ego as his initial reception, symbolized by Dwight's comments, may have been, even more significant, in a practical way, was an offer two weeks later of a position as organist for historic and prestigious West Church, indicated in the church records for 16 November 1861:

> Mr. Loring from the Committee on Music reported that . . . in the opinion of the Committee it was deemed desirable to change the organist and submitted the following motion which was unanimously adopted
> *Voted*: That the Committee on Music be authorized to employ Mr. Paine as Organist at a salary of Four hundred dollars per annum.[78]

Besides this prospect of security, Paine must have been delighted by the fact that he would be master of a new organ built by the Hook Brothers, the leading organ builders in Boston, which the church earlier that year had raised a subscription to purchase.[79]

Dr. Cyrus August Bartol, minister of West Church, had been a member of the staff since 1837 and had recently been raised to senior pastor after the death of his predecessor, Dr. Charles Lowell (father of the poet James Russell Lowell). Bartol, a leading Unitarian clergyman in Boston, was a graduate of Harvard divinity school and maintained close ties with the college. Referred to as "the last of the Transcendentalists," he identified with many progressive causes, and was an active member of the Radical Club during the 1860s and '70s.[80] It was through friendships with

Bartol and others in his circle that Paine soon received the opportunity to begin as the Harvard organist.

Paine accepted the West Church position and began his duties on Sunday, 24 November 1861,[81] replacing Joseph Sharland, who had been there since 1853.[82] According to the *Boston Musical Times*, Paine

> has stepped at once into the most refined of our musical society. He will teach the organ and piano, and the theory of music. He will also give particular attention to the proper construction of Military Bands, a department of music in which he is particularly well versed, having studied under Wieprecht, the most distinguished Band instructor of Europe.[83]

He must have made an extraordinarily favorable impression upon the West Church congregation, for, although he was organist and choir director for less than three years, an 1893 newspaper story on the church listed only Paine as "the organist"—ignoring his four successors—and commented that the music was "famous" and "the quartette choir was unrivalled in Boston."[84] A former parishioner reminisced after the congregation disbanded in 1892:

> There were no automobiles or Sunday concerts then. After a sufficient sum was raised to purchase a new organ, Mr. John K. Paine became the organist, and I can remember how we lingered at the end of the morning service, to hear those magnificent toccatas and fugues, by Bach.[85]

Given the close ties between West Church and Harvard, along with Paine's almost instant success, it was probably not too surprising that the young musician soon was offered the position of Teacher of Sacred Music as well as director of music and organist at the college. But this was a mixed blessing, since the Harvard organist's duties normally included playing for Sunday morning services. The West Church post was too rewarding financially for him to resign (his salary was raised to $500 for 1863[86]), and Harvard was at a loss as to how to otherwise fill its vacancy. A compromise was made whereby he was to direct the rehearsals and select the music,[87]

> . . . presiding at the organ in our [Harvard's] daily morning service, and furnishing a substitute on Sundays.[88]

Nevertheless, Paine resigned the position at West Church effective 1 April 1864,[89] the explanation given by *Dwight's Journal*:

> The West Church will sadly feel the loss of [Paine]; but Harvard University . . . has long been eager to secure more of his services, especially as organist and choir director on Sundays, and Alma Mater's arguments have been persuasive.[90]

He had begun his music lectures the previous June and certainly would have wished to spend more of his time at the university. Also, West Church was in a financial bind at that time, and was considering the possibility of changing

> . . . from the present system of a hired choir of four voices to that of a larger volunteer choir from the Congregation, to be trained by a teacher employed for that purpose at the expense of the Society. . . .[91]

Such an arrangement would probably have required a great deal more of the organist's time.

So, at the age of 25, Paine's career took a dramatic turn forward, less than three years after his return from Europe. Fortunate for him that he was not required to serve in the bloody war that was taking place not too far away. He began his music lectures the previous June to classes noticeably lacking the many men of Harvard who had left to fight for Lincoln and the Union.

3

Early Years at Harvard: 1862–1866

At the time Paine arrived in Boston, music played only a small role in the academic life of Harvard University. Although there were such extra-curricular activities as the Pierian Sodality orchestra (1808) and outside private instrument lessons, music was recognized officially only as part of the compulsory daily chapel service.[1] In 1855 Levi Parsons Homer was appointed Musical Instructor and Organist of the college,[2] and the following paragraph from the 1856–57 catalogue gives his duties:

VOCAL MUSIC
Instruction in Music, with special reference to the devotional services in the Chapel, is open to all Undergraduates.
The course will extend to the higher branches of part-singing.
Separate classes for graduates will be formed if desired.[3]

This description was repeated without change until the catalogue of 1861–62.[4]

Homer died on 10 March 1862 at the age of 39,[5] and the following week—on 17 March—the college faculty voted to engage Paine for the duration of the term,[6] his references coming from such distinguished men as John A. Lowell, temporary Chairman of the Corporation—who first suggested that he be hired[7]—from West Church pastor C. A. Bartol, and from Francis B. Crowninshield (A.B. 1829), Fellow of the Corporation.[8] On 18 March Acting President Peabody[9] wrote to the young musician, engaging his services as "teacher of Sacred Music" at $500 a year on a temporary basis, "to terminate on the 11th of July." If the engagement were mutually satisfactory, the contract would be renewed as a permanent appointment.[10] Paine immediately took over the classes in vocal music.

Soon afterward—on 25 March—the new instructor was also employed as director of music and organist, at an additional $350 annually, his total salary thereby equaling that paid to Homer.[11] To save money,

Peabody tried to get through the semester by having these functions performed by amateurs, but, this proving unsatisfactory, worked out instead
the compromise discussed earlier in which Paine would serve as daily
organist, train the choir, and provide a substitute for Sunday morning
services.[12]

The young musician from Maine immediately made his presence
known on campus. "The students already perceive a new touch upon the
keys . . . ," remarked the *Boston Daily Advertiser*.[13] A former professor
Henry Wadsworth Longfellow, after hearing Paine play on the chapel
organ, declared him "a fine organist, young and full of promise."[14] But
all was not well because of his lack of academic status. Peabody surprisingly confided some misgivings to another applicant for the post which
Paine now held:

> 1st, he is not a man of college education or college experience, and though in every
> way pleasing in manners and character, I regard his success with classes of collegians
> as problematical. And 2dly, he has an organ in Boston which he is unwilling to resign,
> and, should his success be all that we can hope, it still remains possible that he will
> find no acceptable substitute as Sunday organist here. . . .[15]

To be sure, the phrase—"The [undergraduate music instruction]
course will be extended to the higher branches of part-singing"—was
omitted from the *Vocal Music* paragraph in the 1862–63 catalogue,[16] perhaps reflecting the administration's concern regarding Paine's lack of an
Ivy League experience. But his popularity among the undergraduates was
so great that a committee of law students presented a resolution on
30 September 1862 to the law faculty, requesting their help in persuading
the new teacher to organize a class in Vocal Music for the law students.[17]

Incidentally, this class was the cause of an early clash between Paine
and the administration. Since instruction of law students was not part of
his contract, in January he requested the Steward's office to bill them
individually, and was subsequently described as seeming "very much
aggrieved" when required to obtain permission for this procedure from
the newly appointed President Thomas Hill. W. G. Stearns, the Steward,
felt in no uncertain terms that Paine should collect his own money.

> There is, at present, a strong feeling in form of crowding every thing into the term
> bills; but when the term bills are presented, a good deal of feeling is manifested,
> sometimes, at finding what are considered extraordinary charges; and all the scold-
> ing,—to say nothing of occasional swearing, comes on the back of the Steward.[18]

One may assume, after this negative reaction, that Paine made his own
collections.

Another incident from the beginning of Paine's Harvard career also deserves mention. Though it may not have contributed to his ultimate success, it does illustrate a central feature of Paine's personality, namely, a willingness to chance administrative displeasure when he felt he was in the right. Paine discovered that the chapel roof was in urgent need of weather-proofing, for otherwise the next severe storm would seriously damage the organ.[19] In fact, there was water in the organ already, rendering parts of the instrument unusable, and immediate repair was necessary. Finding a competent repairman may have been perhaps a reason for the administration's delay in remedying the situation, for the builders, Simmons & Wilcox, had dissolved their partnership.[20] However, the young college organist found it necessary to complain quite strongly before the Harvard officers would free the requisite funds from their war-tightened budget, and in a long since time-honored way he may have let the press know his feelings. For shortly thereafter the following observation appeared in the Boston *Daily Advertiser*:

> It is a pity that Harvard has not an organ good enough for such a player, but Mr. Paine's skill must make up for the defects of the very unsatisfactory instrument which the college owns.[21]

At least some of the Harvard Corporation thought Paine was the source of this negative publicity, while he, on his part, had to allay their suspicions and also discount another speculation that rivalry between former partners of the Simmons & Wilcox firm was responsible. Finally Acting President Peabody, convinced of Paine's innocence, came to the conclusion that the article was written by

> a neighbor, and under the influence, of the Hooks [rival organ builders], who left no means unemployed to obtain the contract for building the College organ, (and it would have been to our advantage had they succeeded). . . .[22]

Apparently there was quite an enthusiastic rivalry between the different camps of the Boston organ world,

> . . . a set of musical friends who are as bitter and unscrupulous in assailing the work of other organ-builders, as political partizans are in blackening the good deeds of their opponents.

Paine, although refraining from criticizing the college instrument in public, tacitly proclaimed its unsuitability by playing all his recitals on other organs—chiefly at Tremont Temple and especially at West Church on the new Hook—"a fine organ of many registers and accordant voicing."[23] Included among his West Church recitals were two, on 25 October and 1 November 1862, for the benefit of the Sanitary Commission,[24] a Civil War counterpart of the Red Cross.

On 6 October 1862 Thomas Hill (1818–91), grandfather of the American composer Edward Burlingame Hill (1872–1960), was named President of Harvard University by the Board of Overseers. Plans were begun for the ceremonies, to take place on 4 March 1863 at the First Parish Church (Unitarian), Harvard Square—"Rev. Dr. Newell's Church."[25] Paine, who by this time had created quite an impression as a man not to be overlooked in matters musical, took steps to insure his participation in the festivities. Hardly had he been welcomed as a new member of the Harvard Musical Association on 19 January 1863 when he began to organize members of this musical establishment "to form the nucleus of a choir to sing some classical chorus by Mendelssohn, & c., at the approaching inauguration. . . ."[26]

Accordingly, at the inauguration, music by the "Germania Band"[27] was followed by the singing of the hymn, "A Mighty Fortress Is Our God," by the college choir and the H. M. A. glee club, led by the Harvard organist. After Hill delivered his inaugural address and received the college keys, charter, and seal, he "took his seat in the president's chair amidst the applause of the audience, and the choir sang 'Domine, fac salvum Presidem . . . ,' "[28] which Paine had composed for the occasion. At the close, the choir sang a chorus from Mendelssohn's *Antigone*, a significant choice by Paine in light of his subsequent composition of music and choruses for *Oedipus Tyrannus* almost 20 years later.

Within two weeks of the inauguration, President Hill initiated an "extended course of lectures" at Harvard—open to all present and former members of the Harvard community (except undergraduates) at no charge and to other interested persons for a five-dollar fee.[29] Included on the list of instructors was the college music teacher, who gave four lectures on Musical Form during the month of June.[30] As a result of President Hill's broad vision, Paine for the first time had the opportunity to teach material of academic substance. This humble beginning would eventually culminate in academic recognition and credit for music at Harvard.

The University Lectures were continued the next fall with eight lecturers, and Paine offered "Instruction in Counterpoint and Fugue" every Saturday, beginning 15 October 1863.[31] Commented his successor, Professor Walter R. Spalding:

> To some unknown administrative genius music owes the pious deception by which instruction in counterpoint and fugue was smuggled into the scheme of University Lectures.[32]

Within a few weeks of President Hill's inauguration, the Harvard musician again appeared before the public, leading the same choir of about 30 male voices and the Germania Orchestra in a concert on 28 March at Chickering Hall. Proceeds from the concert raised funds to distribute copies of Francis J. Child's song book, *War Songs for Freeman*, to the members of the Union Army.[33] Included on the program were the "Bacchus" chorus from Mendelssohn's *Antigone* and Paine's *Domine, salvum fac Paesidem nostrum* (with suitably altered words: "Domine, salvum fac Patriam nostram"), both numbers fresh from the inauguration, and a dozen war songs. In addition, Paine led the orchestra in the Mozart G-minor symphony, and four soloists performed the third and fourth movements of his own string quartet, written when he was but 16. "For so youthful an effort it showed much artistic skill and genial conception," said John Sullivan Dwight in a review.[34] Tickets for the program sold well, although a snowstorm prevented anything but "a comfortable crowd" from showing up.

One of the most significant musical events that occurred during Paine's early Boston years was the installation of the large pipe organ in Music Hall in 1863. Work on the organ was begun in 1857,[35] but the Civil War delayed its installation. The instrument was built by the E. F. Walcker firm of Ludwigsburg, Württemberg;[36] reportedly, Paine had some influence in its design and building during his student days in Berlin.[37] Bostonians recognized the need for an organist to match such an outstanding instrument, and the following view was expressed in August 1861, soon after Paine's return to America, in the *Boston Musical Times*:

> We . . . would suggest to the parties having the charge of the new organ for the Music Hall, the securing, if possible [Paine's] permanent residence in this city. . . . We surely ought to exert ourselves to obtain his presidency over our long arriving instrument.[38]

In March 1863 the organ finally arrived at Boston by way of the brig *Presto* from Rotterdam. Friedrich Walcker, son of the builder, was on hand to supervise the workmen.[39] Estimates of from four to six months were given for the time required to erect the instrument and provide necessary renovations to the hall.[40]

Excitement mounted, of course, as the installation neared completion. Boston music lovers—at least a privileged few—must have enjoyed observing the fascinating process. A record of one visit by Paine has been preserved by the poet Annie Fields, wife of the author and publisher James T. Fields:

> *September* 1st.—A cold storm by the sea-shore, but there was great pleasure in town in the afternoon. [Henry Wadsworth] Longfellow, Paine, Dwight, and Fields went

to hear Walcker play the new organ in the Music Hall for the first time since its erection. Afterwards they all dined together. . . .[41]

A first hearing of the new organ—the "private test"—occurred on 31 October 1863 before an audience of about a thousand, made up of subscribers and stockholders of the Music Hall Association, city officials, and other invited guests. At first, the entire organ case was hidden by a huge green curtain, and those arriving wondered if they would be able to see the organ at all. For at least 15 minutes improvised organ music sounded from behind the curtain—"invisible, impersonal, as befits organ music," ". . . in sweet and careless voluntary. . . ."[42] The audience listened, as well as noticing the many improvements made in the hall during the preceding months,

> . . . when suddenly the gaslights flashed forth, and the curtain began slowly and majestically to descend, revealing first the full length of the cherubs with their gilded instruments surmounting the domes of the two central towers; then the chaste beauty of the ribbed and rounded domes; the the triple columns of huge silvery pipes, with St. Cecilia throned in beauty on the summit of the arch between; and so little by little the whole breadth and grandeur of the superb *façade*. . . . The silence of the rapt audience gave way to a murmur of delight; then round on round of applause swelled in a long crescendo with each new phase of the disclosure, all rising to their feet unconsciously. . . . The old world has many a great Organ built away into the architectural wildernesses of its great cathedrals; but was there ever an Organ cheered and clapped before in the assembly of the people?

Present at this event were five of the organists who would be giving the inaugural concert two nights later; each gave a brief performance on the new instrument. First to appear was G. W. Morgan, who played his own transcription of the *William Tell* overture, one of the most popular works in his repertory throughout his career. After an address by Dr. J. B. Upham, President of the Music Hall Association and Chairman of the Organ Committee, B. J. Lang was the next to perform, playing

> a sweet Andante of Mendelssohn, and a part of [Rinck's] flute concerto, tickling the ear of the curious.

Dwight, in his report of the occasion, expressed dissatisfaction with some of the executants' taste in the performance of music not composed specifically for the organ, but was pleased by Paine's choice of music:

> . . . One deeply musical soon wearies of all the pretty fluting and mixing of tone-colors, merely to try effects, of all the sentimental solo-singing upon this stop and that stop, making a *Vox humana* of each one of them, and ear and soul begin to crave the grand, rich volume of the full organ, infinite and satisfying as the ocean, rolling out of the great thoughts of God, and swallowing in oblivion all the little wearying

personalities of the smaller music. It was a comfort, therefore, when Mr. Paine unstopped the full organ, and in strong and lusty tones, with grand unfathomable basses, (such as those colossal pipes there promise), poured out the roaring, foaming, lifesome tide of Bach's *Toccata* in D minor. Many at first may find the continued sound of the full organ confusing and monotonous; but, depend upon it, the ear learns to love and crave such glorious great sonority; it cannot be too great, provided it be musical, its tones all pure, well blended and proportioned, as they here are.

Following such a musical climax—at least a climax according to Dwight's thinking—Eugene Thayer played his own *Marche Triumphale*, and John Willcox closed the informal concert with a group of pieces, some improvised, and all planned to show his skill in registration.

At last the 2 November 1863 date arrived for the inauguration of the organ. Tickets for all 2,654 seats in the house were sold out in advance at the very high price of $3 each (commented Dwight: "it might safely have been *five*")—and orders had been placed by people from as far away as Chicago.[43] When the audience entered the building that night, again the large organ was covered by the green curtain, and again soft music oozed from behind the veil. Following is the program of the concert:

Part I.
1. Ode, recited by Miss Charlotte Cushman.
2. Opening of the Organ, by Herr Friedrich Walcker, son of the eminent Organ-builder, E. F. Walcker, of Ludwigsburg, (Kingdom of Wurtemberg.)
3. (a.) Grand Toccata in F .... Bach
   (b.) Trio Sonata in E flat; for two Manuals and Pedal:
      1. Allegro moderato. 2. Adagio 3. Allegro .... Bach
            By John K. Paine, Organist at the West Church, Boston, and Musical Instructor at Harvard University.
4. Grand Fugue in G minor .... Bach
      By W. Eugene Thayer, of Worcester.

Part II.
1. Grand Double Chorus: "He led them through the deep," and Chorus: "But the waters overwhelmed their enemies," from "Israel in Egypt." .... Handel
      By George W. Morgan
      Organist at Grace Church, New York.
2. Grand Sonata in A, No. 3: Con moto maestoso—Andante tranquillo—fugue—maestoso .... Mendelssohn
            By B. J. Lang, Organist of the Old South Church and of the Handel and Haydn Society.
3. (a.) "Lamentation in Parasceve ....⎫
      "Kyrie" and "Sanctus," from a Mass ....⎬ Palestrina
   (b.) Movement from the Anthem, "O give thanks," .... Purcell
            By Dr. S. P. Tuckerman,
            Organist at St. Paul's Church.

4. Offertorium in G .... Lefebure Wely
     By John H. Willcox, Organist
     at the Church of the Immaculate Conception.
5. Hallelujah Chorus .... Handel
     By G. W. Morgan.[44]

After Miss Cushman read the ode, which was written for the occasion by Mrs. Fields,[45] Walcker played a few chords to display the
"power and resources of the instrument."[46] As he took his seat, the
curtain was lowered to the floor. *Harper's* described the impressive sight:

> The case itself is so floridly ornate that the impression is bewildering. There is a
> consciousness of pipes, medallions, busts, flags, instruments, scrolls, caryatides,
> carved lattices, arms—a mighty mass of elaborate workmanship rather confusedly
> mingled, of which the dark huge caryatides and solid paneling of the base are much
> the most agreeable. Yet the whole is so vast that any fantastic fancy of decoration
> seems not too daring. . . .[47]

To enhance the effect of such a rare event, the "dim, religious" light shed
by the conventional gas fixtures was supplemented by a specially constructed electric lamp suspended from the upper balcony. Dwight found
the timing of this display most unfortunate:

> The effect was startling, brilliant, but disturbing to the more important portion of
> the musical exercises which then came in order. . . . Now all was flutter and excite-
> ment, all were wondering and exclaiming at the glorious *sight* so suddenly revealed,
> pointing out its beauties one to another, and so forth. . . . This dazzling, unquiet,
> tremulous light was a new and an irresistible distraction, and it lasted long enough
> to render the larger part of the audience insensible to more than the mere sound of
> the whole first part of the music, which was all by Bach, the master of masters in
> the true organ music. . . . Not until that nervous jack-o'-lantern got its quietus, did
> the mass of the audience really begin to listen and appreciate. . . .[48]

The organists had been asked to choose their share of the concert
in such a way that all schools of composition were represented;[49] unfortunately, the program was too heavy for much of the audience. Only
Morgan's Handel and Willcox's Lefébure-Wély were encored.[50]

> . . . Notwithstanding that it was distinctly agreed upon that the program should not
> be lengthened by even a single repetition, . . . Morgan was recalled seven times amid
> the most deafening applause! Seven times, and performed three additional pieces,
> namely, "God Save the Queen," "The Star-Spangled Banner," and an impromptu.[51]

Paine's Bach did not fare nearly as well. People who hoped for spectacular entertainment did not find this music approachable, especially in severe interpretations by Haupt's pupil:

> The fugues of Bach, difficult though they be—with winding roulards and chromatic passages—with questions and answers—are not relished when played with a full, unvarying organ from beginning to end. Tempest and sunshine is the order of Nature—not continued roarings and thunderings.[52]

Little planning seems to have been made for displaying individual ranks, combinations, and solo voices, so desirable in a dedication program; apparently there was a lack of contrast both in volume and timbre. (Dwight, however, in his review,[53] felt that Paine's registration of the Bach trio sonata, "on soft stops, with alternation and contrast of voices," offered significant contrast to the toccata's "inexhaustible suggestion as of the ocean rolling in upon the beach.") But the performers "acquitted themselves with great credit, and the whole affair proved a triumphant success."[54] After the concert ended, a large number of the audience remained to inspect the organ case, which was again illuminated by the electric lamp.

Nationwide interest in the large Music Hall organ and in its first concert elicited wide coverage in the press, including this bit of humor from the *Washington Star*:[55]

> "The Monster Organ"
> ... It requires six able-bodied organists to manipulate this immense musical machine. ... They were selected with reference to avoirdupois as well as musical qualifications, their weight ranging as follows:

	Lbs.
Paine,	180
Thayer,	200
Lang,	175
Tuckerman,	213
Willcox,	192
Morgan,	245
Total	1,225

> When in the grand crescendo passages these six organists rose simultaneously from their seats, and receded a couple of paces, rushed forward in line, throwing their collective weight of over twelve hundred pounds upon the pedals, the musical explosion—for by no other name can it be designated—was terribly grand. . . .

Additional exhibitions were given during the following weeks; crowds for these were not as large as for the opening program, but the enthusiasm continued high. Paine played on 5 and 22 November, as well as in December. On these programs his repertory again included Bach, as well as Mendelssohn, Thiele, and a number of his own compositions. Critical comment again ranged from grumbling criticism of his Bach interpretations and his colorless registration[56] to the praise of his delicate rendering of Mendelssohn and his Bach, played with a "clearness and nicety that we have never heard equaled in America."[57]

The Harvard organist performed on the Great Organ regularly through mid-1866, both in solo recitals and as a soloist with the Orchestral Union. His reputation spread to other cities, and in early 1864 he played two concerts at St. George's Church in New York, where he was "warmly welcomed by the more serious musicians and amateurs."[58] On the second of these recitals (9 February) the young gentleman played three of his compositions as well as the usual Bach and Mendelssohn; soloists and the Trinity Choir assisted. The program "was very ably discussed."[59]

Paine's high level of concert and academic activity established after his return from Europe not only was maintained but even increased. During 1864 he presented six solo concerts, appeared in a joint recital with Tuckerman and Willcox (on 3 January), was the soloist for two Orchestral Union programs, and performed with other artists in concerts for the Unitarian Festival (24 May) and for the benefit of the National Sailors' Fair (12 November). All of these programs took place in Music Hall. The following list includes all the works the organist played on the aforementioned occasions; as usual, his own compositions and those of Bach were most numerous.

J. S. Bach
    Prelude in E Flat, S. 552
    Prelude and Fugue in G [probably S. 541]
    Prelude in C
    Toccata and Fugue in D Minor, S. 565
    Toccata in F, S. 540
    Passacaglia in C Minor, S. 582
    Pastorale, S. 590
    Trio Sonata in C Minor, S. 526
    Canzona in D Minor S. 588
    Chorale Preludes: Schmücke dich, S. 654
          Aus tiefer Not, S. 686
          O Mensch, bewein' dein' Sünde gross, S. 622
          An Wasserflüssen Babylon, S. 653
          Christ, unser Herr, zum Jordan kam, S. 684
Paine
    Fantasy and Fugue in E Minor, Op. 2[1]
    Concert Variations on the Austrian Hymn, Op. 3[1]
    Concert Variations on the Star-Spangled Banner, Op. 3[2]
    Concert Variations upon Old Hundred
    Fantasia Sonata in D Minor [probably Op.17]

Offertories Nos. 1 and 2 (B Minor)
Caprice
Fantasia on the "Portuguese Hymn" (*Adeste fideles*)
Reverie suggested by Longfellow's "Song of the Silent Land"
Thiele
    Toccata in E Flat Minor
    Grand Concert Piece in C Minor
Mendelssohn
    Sonata No. 4 in B Flat
    Sonata No. 5 in D
August Gottfried Ritter (1811–85)
    Sonata in A
Transcriptions of works by Handel, Mozart, and Gluck

In his solo recital on 17 January 1864 an assisting quartet sang his *Benedictus*, a composition already performed in the summer of 1861 at Portland.

Much of the young musician's time continued to be devoted to his duties at Harvard, where he taught three classes: Freshman "lessons in elementary music and vocalization," Sophomore "part singing, reading at sight and vocalization," and the Chapel Choir "practice in sacred music, with reference to the services in the Chapel."[60] His standards must have been quite high, probably more strict than his predecessor, judging from his academic reports:

> The instructor has found some difficulty, in imparting thorough musical knowledge to many of his pupils; for the want of regular attendance, on their part:—especially, in the Choir: and he respectfully recommends the adoption of strict rules, relating to the attendance and membership, in the music classes.

Membership in the Choir, which had numbered 26 and 23 during the two semesters of the 1862–63 year, dropped to 9 in the fall of 1862. Such a reduced number was definitely a threat to Paine's continued employment in the position. Besides the obvious impact of the Civil War, one may suggest many other possible reasons for the drastic reduction in numbers. Paine's strict enforcement of attendance rules would have altered any comfortable, informal air that may have existed formerly. Doubtless his choice of music was more difficult and less popular in style than the student singers cared to learn and perform. Those Seniors who left the choir through graduation in 1863 were the last students to have been recruited by Paine's predecessor; some may have already dropped out because of loyalty to Homer. The more businesslike approach and the reduction of fraternal conviviality during rehearsals certainly dampened the choir's attractiveness to new recruits. But regardless of these factors, Paine needed desperately to build membership in the Choir in order to show his success as its director. An avenue he may have chosen is suggested by the membership description of the Choir, which for 1862–63 was "composed of Juniors and Seniors," but the next fall was "composed *principally* of Seniors and Juniors" (emphasis added). Quite possibly he was augmenting the number with lower classmen, graduates, or even outsiders. This apparent change in membership policy must have been successful, for enrollment increased to 17 the following spring.[61] However, the administration did not wish to give Paine too free a hand in remedying weaknesses of the Choir program, for on 12 September 1864 the faculty

> Voted, That Mr. Paine be requested to furnish immediately a list of members of the College Choir, and that in future no person be allowed to leave or to join the choir except by a special vote of this Board.[62]

During the 1864–65 academic year the Chapel Choir was divided into a Sunday Choir and a Morning Choir; Paine did not specify membership requirements in his report to the overseers. He was able to direct both choirs,[63] having resigned his Sunday duties at West Church the previous April. Perhaps Paine had felt he was spreading his talents too far in holding both positions. As long as he continued at West Church, he certainly lacked complete control over the musical standards for the Harvard Sunday services. Dwight's comment that ". . . Alma Mater's arguments have been persuasive . . ."[64] may have referred to an ultimatum to Paine: he must make a final choice between the two institutions. Whatever pressure the administration may have applied, the young instructor doubtless decided that it would be more profitable to concentrate his efforts in a single direction. If he could succeed in broadening the scope of music at Harvard, it would enable him to exert a strong influence on a large number of future musicians, and, not incidentally, assure him a rewarding, prestigious career.

Such a desire to improve the academic standing of music is seen in this request following the spring 1863 semester:

> The instructor respectfully recommends the formation of a class in elementary musical theory; a knowledge of Harmony being highly important to those who wish to cultivate thoroughly their taste in music. And as the study of Counterpoint and Fugue has been introduced already in the course of University Lectures, it is quite proper that the foundation of this more advanced and developed branch of musical theory now open to all Graduates—should be laid in the Undergraduate department.

The University Lecture course in Counterpoint and Fugue was "given to a few students regularly once a week" during the fall 1863 semester. A course in Harmony and Counterpoint was first taught in 1864–65, apparently replacing the Freshman and Sophomore vocalization classes. This class was quite small, enlisting six members in the fall and only one in the spring; total music enrollments for 1864–65 were 31 for fall and 23 for spring, reflecting the drop in attendance throughout the college no doubt caused by the war.

Details of Paine's private life during this time are exceedingly scarce. Possibly he had already become acquainted with his future wife, Mary Elizabeth Greeley, who lived in Boston with her family at their Summer Street residence (next door to the estate of Daniel Webster).[65] A clue to Paine's place of residence is found in the 1862–63 Harvard catalogue, which listed him as living at a "Mrs. S. Humphrey's."[66] Few of his later friendships would have developed at this time, although he doubtless was acquainted with John Fiske and George Osgood, who were undergraduates at the time. Other documented acquaintances were men far his senior, such as Dwight and Longfellow. It is not known whether he kept in touch with his sister, the only other surviving member of his immediate family. But on 17 March 1863 his grandmother, Jane Paine, died in Portland,[67] and he may have attended the funeral, inasmuch as he and his sister, Helen Allen, were heirs. In any case, the other heirs and the Paine siblings sold Grandmother Paine's house and property to David Paine of Natick, Massachusetts, for $75. The transaction took place in Portland on 26 September 1863, but the young musician attached his signature in Boston and was described as a resident of that city (rather than Cambridge).[68] With the death of his grandmother and the sale of her property, another tie with his youth in Portland had been severed.

By far one of the most important friendships that began during Paine's first years at the college was with John Fiske (1842–1901), the philosopher and historian, who had spent his undergraduate years at Harvard, and who included Paine in planning his 6 September 1864 wedding to Abby Morgan Brooks at Appleton Chapel, Harvard.[69]

> . . . We are going to have Uncle Edmund Willson marry us, assisted by Dr. A. P. Peabody. And John K. Paine will play the organ. Our wedding will be the *first* in Appleton Chapel.[70]

Fiske was a neighbor to the talented organist for the rest of his life, and their association was a close one. Paine stimulated his interest in music and guided his occasional efforts as a composer. In turn, Fiske publicized Paine's music in numerous writings, and introduced him to many friends and acquaintances, including leaders in fields such as publishing, biology, history, and government. Through his friendship Fiske played an important role in making Paine totally acceptable among such people, teaching him the social graces expected of those with good breeding. With this

acceptance, and aided by Fiske's strong—albeit sometimes overly par-
tial—literary support, Paine became quite a celebrity.

The stature and influence of the new music instructor in his lowly position
at Harvard grew slowly during his first years there. His university lectures, deprived of real academic recognition, eventually were discontinued but formed a precedent to be resumed successfully after President
Eliot's inauguration in 1869. Paine had already introduced some academic
meat into the noncredit music instruction assigned to him, a significant
improvement over the job done by his predecessor, Homer. These noncredit courses were to become the first of the music electives later granted
academic recognition under Eliot's administration. In the meantime, he
strove to win greater respect and recognition for music in the University
community. An important example was the Harvard "Commemoration
Day" ceremonies following the close of the Civil War in 1865. Dwight,
a frequent supporter of the Harvard musician, wrote favorably and quite
enthusiastically about the music in his *Journal* of 5 August 1865.[71] He
prefaced his comments with a statement giving historical perspective:

> . . . Our academic festivals hitherto have had little to boast of in this particular. A
> band to march by, and to bray brass music in the church between the "parts," has
> been the only participation of the Divine Art therein. A teacher of singing has for
> some time been employed in the University,—a step very tardily and hesitatingly
> taken. In the hands of Mr. J. K. Paine, a thorough musician and most earnest artist,
> this office has acquired somewhat more importance, and the "Musical Director" of
> the College is making himself, his art and function more and more respected. Through
> him, Music as Art, and in a worthy academic sense, for the first time figured in one
> of Alma Mater's public solemnities, at the inauguration of President Hill. . . . On
> "Commemoration Day," wider scope and more unstinted means were given to Mr.
> Paine, for music worthy of the occasion. . . .

For the morning church services Paine had assembled a 60-voice mixed
chorus, made up of Harvard students and graduates, members of the
Harvard Musical Association, and others from Cambridge and Boston.
These singers, accompanied by an orchestra of 26, performed part of
Bach's cantata *Ein' feste Burg*, the opening chorus and the "Sanctus"
from the Cherubini *Requiem*, a re-harmonized *Old Hundred* with orches-
tral accompaniment, and "a rich and stirring *Gloria* from a Mass which
Mr. Paine has recently composed."

> The performance was on the whole very effective, and it made a deep impression.
> And yet it was done under all sorts of discouragement; it was almost impossible, at
> this season, to gather the same singers together at any two successive rehearsals; it
> was hard to collect the materials of an orchestra; there was but one single chance of
> full rehearsal *with* the orchestra; and finally the organ-loft into which all these ninety

musicians had to be packed was close and uncomfortable, and the place discouraging and deadening to all music. Yet earnest effort, as the event proved was not thrown away; the spirit of the day carried it against all obstacles. . . .

A dinner, under a huge tent, was interspersed by many speeches and poems and greetings from numerous generals and admirals. Music included "luscious strains" by the band of Patrick Gilmore (1829–92), later to gain notoriety with his Peace Jubilees. Three partsongs were performed by a 30-voice male chorus. Paine had composed one of these songs for the occasion, *The Soldier's Oath*, with words by Rev. C. T. Brooks; others were Flemming's *Integer vitae*, and Oliver Wendell Holmes' "Union and Liberty," sung to the *Russian Hymn*. Dwight concluded his report of the event by asking his fellow Harvard alumni the following:

> . . . Will they after that experience, longer ignore the claims of Music among the other "Humanities" which they are ever so ready to endow within the halls of Alma Mater? And shall the College go a-begging even for the means of putting the Chapel organ in repair, so that it may be fit to second the efforts of such a man as Mr. Paine to place high Music on its proper footing in a University of such renown?

However, in spite of Dwight's eloquence, music was not to gain a place among the other humanities of Harvard for another four or five years. Until President Eliot's administration, proposals for the inclusion of music courses in the academic curriculum continued to encounter stiff resistance in the Harvard Corporation. An example of this hostility is evident in historian Francis Parkman's (1823–93) Cato-like remarks at faculty meetings: "Musica delenda est."[72] In this climate, the support of such a respected music critic as Dwight surely helped to develop a more favorable attitude toward music in the academic community.

Dwight's second question of the alumni reflected a chronic problem existing at least since the time the Harvard organist was hired—the poor mechanical condition of the chapel organ. Paine's complaints to Acting President Peabody in 1862 have already been mentioned. Apparently, any resulting repairs must have been unsatisfactory, for the organ was still quite unreliable. Some work was begun on the organ during the 1865–66 academic year, underwritten by private contributions. Three subscription concerts were held in Appleton Chapel during June 1866

> . . . to raise funds to reimburse Mr. Paine and others who had at their own expense had important repairs and additions made to the college organ. . . .[73]

Because of the approaching end of the semester, these concerts had to be given before repairs were completely finished, and certain "accidents" occurred which were annoying and frustrating to the musicians.

> For instance, the great lungs repeatedly gave out before [Paine] was able to go uninterruptedly and grandly through with the famous Bach *Toccata in F*; one or two pieces had to be omitted altogether and others substituted, while others were disturbed by the rattling of the mechanism in certain stops, especially in accompaniment. . . .

Despite these shortcomings, the programs were well received by a large crowd "of the most refined character." Financial proceeds were liberal, but not sufficient to cover the repair expense. Paine was assisted in the three concerts by an amateur mixed chorus of about 16 voices "who have been practising good things during the past season under his direction; . . . their performance was uncommonly good in point of precision as well as expression."[74] Two soloists from Boston, a Mrs. Gilbert and a G. H. Powers, also took part.

The first concert took place on Saturday, 9 June, 1866, at 4:00 o'clock; the following program was announced (spelling and punctuation as in original advertisement):

1. Organ Solo—Prelude and Fugue in A minor .... J. S. Bach
2. Selections from the Requiem .... Mozart
    a. Chorus—Lacrymosa. b. Chorus—Sanctus and
    Hosanna. c. Quartette—Benedictus.
3. Andante and Allegretto from Organ Sonata in B flat .... Mendelssohn
4. Chorus—Salve Regina .... Hauptman
5. Organ Sonata in E minor .... Ritter
6. Selections from Lauda Sion .... Mendelssohn
    a. Soprano Solo and Chorus—Sit laus plena.
    b. Quartette—In hac mensa. c. Chorus—Decti
    sacris. d. Soprano Solo—Caro cibus.
    e. Quartette and Chorus—Ecce panis
7. Organ Solo—Toccata in F .... J. S. Bach[75]

The closing *Toccata in F* received the flawed performance described above; which other pieces were omitted and what numbers were substituted did not receive mention in the reports. A second concert, at first announced for 16 June, was held on the eighteenth; the following was planned (punctuation as in original advertisement):

1. Organ Solo, Toccata in D minor .... Bach
2. Chorus Ave verum .... Mozart
3. Bass Solo from St. Paul, O God, have mercy .... Mendelssohn
4. Organ Solo, Choral Vorspiel.................................... Bach
5. Chorus from Samson, Awake the trumpet's lofty sound .... Handel
6. Organ Solo .... J. K. Paine

      a. Andante con variazioni b. Caprice
7. Soprano Solo, Ave Maria .... Franz
8. Selections from Christus .... Mendelssohn
      a. Trio for Tenor and bass voices b. Chorus.
      Daughters of Zion. c. Choral
9. Organ Solo, Fantasia and Fugue in E. Minor .... J. K. Paine[76]

Dwight's review[77] called the Mozart "perfect, only too short," the *Christus* selections "very impressive," and the *Samson* chorus

> . . . as effective as it well could be with so few voices (the room, however, gave them great sonority).

The same reviewer found Paine's *Andante with variations* to be "musician-like, of rather a tamely respectable old cut, . . ." and the *Caprice* "something like a song without words, captivating by its grace and freedom, and somewhat original," but was more favorably impressed by the *Fantasia and Fugue*,

> . . . in which Mr. Paine seems to us to have most successfully studied and wrought, though of course at a distance, in the spirit of his great master, the master of all true organists.

Excerpts from three major choral works comprised the bulk of the third program on 20 June, which was filled out by two Bach organ works—the Prelude in E Flat and the Fugue in G Minor—and some excerpts from Mendelssohn organ sonatas; a Mozart Andante was omitted because of a malfunction of the organ. Two arias and the final chorus from the Bach *St. Matthew Passion* were "the great novelty" of the program for Dwight, who praised this exposure to the choral music of Bach, flawed though it was by the singers' uneasiness with the Bach idiom and the inadequacy of the chapel organ to produce an effective accompaniment. Other unfamiliar music included the Introit, Gradual, and Sanctus of the Cherubini *Requiem* and three movements from Paine's new *Mass*. The *Confiteor* chorus of the *Mass* favorably impressed Dwight as being

> . . . learned, ingenious in treatment, both of voice parts and accompaniment, and full of strong religious confidence in tone,—free from what is commonplace, or dry, or feebly sentimental,—churchlike and not operatic. . . .

A tenor solo, *Quoniam*, so charmed the audience that it had to be repeated. The singer, unnamed by the reviewers, doubtless was George L. Osgood (1844–1922), a member of the Harvard graduating class and a close friend of the college organist, soon to depart with him for Germany to further his music training. The *Dona Nobis*, according to the *Boston Musical Times* critic, "charmed all hearers with the spirit of peace which the music breathes." Dwight took greatest notice of this movement's "power and beauty," asserting that it had been

> . . . treated gravely, and not in that light, almost playful operatic style in which so many Masses, those of Haydn and Mozart included, have indulged. . . .

These three excerpts, which according to the *Boston Musical Times* were "greatly enjoyed by the audience," and the performance of the *Gloria* on Commemoration Day the previous summer were the first introductions of Paine's *Mass* to the music public. The first complete performance, with orchestra, would take place the following year in Berlin, adding to his stature as an established composer and musician. His high standards of musicianship and taste are shown in his choice of music for these three concerts, for aside from his own compositions, most of the selections were by composers familiar to audiences today, and many are still performed. These choices show his ability to distinguish great music from merely fashionable.

A month after the last concert the successful organist and composer sailed for Europe, thereby ending the first stage of his Harvard career. In the four years of his employment on the campus, he had earned great respect for music in the college community, though it remained a non-credit discipline. Academic content of the music classes had increased steadily, and the choir's singing and general morale had apparently improved under his direction. Topics related to music began appearing among Harvard commencement speeches, including *Musical Form* and *Felix Mendelssohn* in 1864 and another on Bach in 1866, prepared by George L. Osgood.[78] Paine's University Lectures, though discontinued, provided a basis for future lectures and courses, and the quality of music provided for university ceremonies noticeably improved. He continued his activity as an organ recitalist, and was still "generally acknowledged to be the first organist in the country." In the first months of 1866 he gave 10 solo concerts at Boston Music Hall on the great organ, the last being on 11 July, just a week before his departure. In March he was asked by the Mason & Hamlin Company to endorse their Cabinet Organs in advertisements,[79] further proof of his growing celebrity. His standing as a composer had increased with the publication of several works: *A Christmas Gift* for piano, published by G. D. Russell of Boston in 1864; a *Funeral March in memory of President Abraham Lincoln*, also for piano, published in 1865 by Beer and Schirmer of New York; his *Star Spangled*

Banner Varied for Organ, released by Ditson in November 1865; and the "beautifully engraved" score of his *Mass*, released by Beer and Schirmer in time for a notice in the 7 July 1866 *Boston Musical Times*. With these accomplishments and the international recognition to be gained during his forthcoming European visit, Paine attained the reputation vital to his campaign for academic recognition of music at Harvard.

4

Triumph in Berlin and a Transition Period: 1866–1869

Paine's second journey to Europe was in marked contrast to his first eight years earlier. He was now a recognized professional composer and academic teacher with great prospects. This time it was he who played the part of experienced traveler to one of his Harvard students, George L. Osgood, who accompanied him on his quest. The two left before the semester had officially ended, for commencement exercises took place on 18 July, the same morning that their ship, the steamer *Cuba*, departed Boston.[1] As noted earlier, Osgood had prepared one of the commencement speeches, entitled "Thesis: Conditions of the Appreciation of the Music of Sebastian Bach," a topic showing his teacher's obvious influence. This paper could not be delivered by its author, but whether it was read by another was not reported. Osgood earlier had been praised by Dwight, albeit anonymously, for his performances in the three Harvard concerts given earlier in the spring.

> . . . We know not where else in the country to look for a tenor of such pure, refined, expressive quality, of good power and compass, controlled by true, chaste musical feeling, as that which lent such charm to the quartet, and which belongs to a young gentlemen of the present graduating class. Properly nursed and developed, it would be invaluable in oratorio and other higher uses. . . .[2]

Evidently the young singer took Dwight's suggestions seriously, for according to a contemporary report the young tenor now planned to study the "Italian method of singing" with a European teacher. Later, after he returned home to Boston to establish a successful career as a recitalist, teacher, conductor, and editor, he became along with his erstwhile instructor an important member of the Boston musical establishment. While in Europe, he studied for three years with Ferdinand Sieber, Haupt, and Robert Franz, and for another three years with Francesco Lamperti; after a successful series of concert appearances in Germany, he toured the United States in 1872 as tenor soloist with the Theodore Thomas orchestra. The singer participated in performances of many of Paine's vocal works; most notable was his singing the leading role in the incidental music to the Harvard production in Greek of Sophocles' *Oedipus Tyrannus* in 1881. He led the first performance of Paine's cantata, *Realm of Fancy*, in an 1882 concert of the Boylston Club, an organization which he conducted from 1875 to 1893 and transformed from a male choir to a mixed chorus of over 200 voices. His *Guide in the Art of Singing* (1874) reached its eighth edition within 20 years. Osgood lived "in the beautiful suburb of Brookline," and his name frequently was mentioned in the social columns of the Boston newspapers; he was "a member of many of the best clubs of Boston. . . ."[3]

Paine may have had many motives for travel abroad at this time. He had been teaching for four and a half years, and had been working around the clock to establish himself in Boston-Cambridge cultural and intellectual circles. But the most important motive was, now that he had achieved recognition at home, to test his mettle as a composer in Europe. He had indeed asked for and been granted a leave as early as January 1864.[4] We do not know precisely why he waited until two years later to take advantage of this permission, but no doubt he had received some encouragement concerning performance of his most ambitious work to date: the *Mass in D* for soloists, chorus, and orchestra. His reason for traveling at this time was to superintend the performance of his *Mass* before a European audience, thereby gaining the prestige of European critical recognition. According to the *Boston Musical Times*, he had planned to produce the work in London, giving a few organ recitals "of a purely classical character" as well.[5] This may have been so during the dark days of the war for Prussian supremacy over Austria. But in a victorious Berlin and because of the high position Germany held in music, Paine felt a successful audition of his mass would be more significant there internationally.

The *Cuba* docked at Liverpool on 26 July 1866,[6] and the two musicians traveled to London. Paine later wrote to Dwight:

> . . . On route for the continent I stayed a week in London. Davison was very kind and hospitable to me. I was with him every day. He is the same kind hearted Englishman, but like all his country men, sets Mendelssohn up, pulls Bach and Schumann down and won't hear a word of Wagner. We often spoke of you and Boston. . . .[7]

James William Davison (1813–85) was quite a powerful friend for the young American to have in England, as he was editor of the *Musical World* and music critic of the London *Times*. He had given him substantial journalistic coverage during the years of study in Berlin, and would continue to do so.

The war that had raged throughout the German-speaking portion of Europe had caused much alarm in the rest of the western world. The conflict had been started by Prussia, which dissolved the German Confederation, desiring instead a union of the north German states with itself as the dominant influence. A second union was formed of German states south of the Main river. Prussia's chief rival, the now defeated Austria, was excluded from either union, stripped of territory, and fined $10 million (75 million francs) in war expenses. Prussia had begun the fighting over her "concern" for Schleswig-Holstein; she later annexed the Elbe duchies except for Danish Schleswig. This tumultuous political situation had a disastrous effect on music in Germany, as the correspondent for the *Evening Transcript* reported:

> The war has dispersed nearly all the vocal and instrumental solo artists in Germany. Pianists and vocalists have taken flight by dozens, and are thronging into London and Paris. Several of the opera houses are closed, others are closing, and at Carlsruhe the performances came to a sudden end, for the reason that the principal male singers were drafted into the army.[8]

Dwight had expressed his worries in regard to the two musicians' trip:

> May the war not interfere with the musical tour which they have promised themselves.[9]

Fortunately, the fighting largely had ended by the time Paine left England, and he apparently encountered little inconvenience on a "never-to-be-forgotten tour in Switzerland and on the Rhine, . . ."[10] including a stay at the Lake of the Four Cantons in Switzerland.[11] He arrived in Berlin about 20 September and soon realized that the prospects for having his mass accepted for performance were quite discouraging. Flodoard Geyer, whom Paine deemed "the best musical theorist and critic in Berlin,"[12] described with sympathy the situation in the *Berlinische Nachrichten*:

> [Paine] undertook this long journey in order to bring out his work first here in Berlin, as it were the cradle of his culture. This surely is as much a recognition of German Art, as it is a testimonial to the way in which the *musica sacra* is cherished and appreciated here; and indeed a flattering compliment to the critical judgment of the public and the press. Coming back over the sea with warm, full heart and with a certain home feeling as it were, Mr. Paine might have expected that one of our institutions, capable of performing a Mass, would undertake his or assist in bringing it out. But no; insurmountable obstacles and difficulties presented themselves, such as occur only in the art of music and oppose themselves to any speedy development of an artist. . . .[13]

Neither of the two leading singing societies—the *Singakademie* and the *Stern'scher Gesangverein*—could be interested in performing the *Mass*. According to Osgood, several weeks were lost "in waiting for [their] assistance . . . which, through the jealousy of several musicians, was continually deferred. . . ."[14] Geyer reported that he was the first to advise Paine himself to prepare and direct the performance. Others who agreed included *Musikdirektor* Wieprecht and Prof. Sieber, Osgood's voice teacher. With this advice, according to Osgood,

> . . . Mr. Paine resolutely set about forming an independent chorus of his own. Although a stranger, he succeeded in organizing a chorus of more than two hundred voices who took so much interest in the work as to attend the rehearsals three and often four times a week, in all sorts of weather. . . .

Alexis Hollaender, writing in the *Neue Zeitschrift für Musik*,[15] also remarked on the difficulties that the young composer encountered, especially the problems of conducting rehearsals with his limited knowledge of German. However, Hollaender felt that Paine and his singers had a good rapport, and the difficult work was thoroughly rehearsed. Several of the critics were also impressed with the work in progress, including Geyer, who stated in the *Spenische Zeitung*:

> A genuine German musical spirit breathes through the work, which, built up in the school of Bach and Handel, yet reveals throughout the writer's own creative power. Especially is the *Crucifixus* of worth; it reaches some of the best models[16]

Much of the American musician's time now had to be devoted to the preparation of the forthcoming performance.

> I shall have to give up the idea of spending much time in London if I wish to bring out my Mass here, for it will take several months to do it.[17]

When not involved with rehearsals, he renewed old friendships, including those with Grimm, Wieprecht, and Governor Wright. In a letter to Dwight he recounted attending the first Royal Orchestra soirée of the season.

> It was refreshing to hear a grand orchestra again, and I enjoyed it exceedingly. . . .

Occasional side trips were not excluded.

> In a few weeks I shall take a vacation for ten days to go to Leipzig. I want to hear the Gewandhaus concerts and become acquainted with [Robert] Franz and other notabilities. . . .

Although far away from America, the young traveler kept in touch with current happenings during the turbulent political era that followed Lincoln's assassination and the inauguration of Andrew Johnson.

> I hope you don't impeach the President. He deserves it no doubt, but I think it is a dangerous weapon. It is partly the fault of the people, for we ought to be more careful whom we select for our public servants.

The above comment appears to be the only surviving indication of Paine's opinions regarding American politics. We do know that he highly admired President Lincoln, and composed two works in his memory—the *Funeral March* . . . (1865) and the tone poem, *Lincoln*, left unfinished at his death.

Osgood proceeded to study voice with Prof. Sieber, whom Paine described as "educated in the best Italian school, being a pupil of Mitsch." Ferdinand Sieber (1822–95) had spent six years in Italy, composed songs, published vocalises and vocal methods, and was well trained.

> He takes a great interest in Osgood and I notice already a great improvement in the delivery of his voice. If he had gone to an Italian teacher I doubt whether he would have found any more skill in the treatment of the voice, or many of the other accomplishments which Sieber possesses.

After sufficient financial backing was assured and the *Mass* began to take shape in rehearsal, a performance date was set—16 Feburary 1867 in the *Singakademie* hall. Karl Liebig's orchestra of fifty players was enlisted,[18] along with four soloists—soprano Strahl, alto Würst, tenor Geyer of the *Domchor*, and bass Zschiesche.[19]

The February evening of the performance was certainly one of the most memorable of the young composer's life. Critic Geyer described those present:

> A particularly musical audience, including nearly all the distinguished musicians of our city, attended the performance, which took two full hours.

Osgood noted that the hall was "full to repletion," and added:

> . . . The interest in the occasion was heightened by the presence of the Royal personages, the Crown Princess [Victoria], Princess Royal of England [eldest daughter of Queen Victoria of England, and wife of future Kaiser Friedrich III], who accepted Mr. Paine's personal invitation to be present; Prince Alexander and Prince George—the latter a fine musical connoisseur; and others of the Court, who joined in the repeated bursts of applause which greeted the composer at the end of the performance. . . .

Reviewers unanimously praised the performers on their thorough preparedness, their enthusiasm, and their musicianship. Paine's American companion gives a most dramatic description of the performance and its effect upon the audience:

> Both singers and players seemed to vie with each other in their efforts to carry the separate movements through with precision and expression. The fugues were sung with fire and with feeling, and in the more difficult passages, the chorus lost not a single note, nor varied a hair's breadth from the pitch. Especially noticeable was the last movement of all. The two hundred voices came as it were from one mouth, so precise and in exact time. This number, the "Dona Nobis Pacem" begins piano, in a beautiful flowing measure, original and unique in style, and after a fine climax in crescendo gradually dies away to the faintest pianissimo. The audience through the entire house sat perfectly hushed; and after the last sound of the voices had died away not a person stirred till the few closing measures of the orchestra in the lightest piano and finally pianissimo had been given, and the players themselves had relaxed their efforts. There was breathless silence at the last moment. Then succeeded a perfect storm of applause, and the composer was immediately surrounded by his friends, by musicians from the audience and by his own chorus, offering their congratulations. . . .

German reviewers felt, in the main, that this new composition was a success musically. The Berlin correspondent for the *Leipziger Allgemeine Musikalische Zeitung*[20] recognized the rich fruit of German musical study in the composer's taste and technique; the *Mass* was "the delightful sign of beginning artistic development across the ocean." The Berlin *National Zeitung*[21] cited his "faithful conscientiousness and insight" in his studies, his "clear methodical spirit," and his "integrity of purpose and calm intensity of application. . . ." "Nowhere does he show us the traces of unskilful workmanship, whether in the fugal movements or in the freer, more homophonic parts." Hollaender, in the *Neue Zeitschrift*, praised the musical material from which the different sections were developed, and singled out the fugal sections, "which sometimes reach the strength of their models, particularly Handel." Geyer judged the work as satisfying overall, continuing:

> The Mass is the work of a musician, who is justified by earnest study in writing a score like this, peculiarly calculated for the co-operation of the organ. Most of the movements are well planned and well managed. The text is treated according to the traditions of the masters, and we may say with a devout feeling, often a presentiment of the highest. As to finding wholly new ways, to be sure, as to seeking out still stronger contrasts in invention than the greatest masters, especially Bach and Mozart, could do—to this perhaps only a later period of life might lead the artist. . . .

To be sure, the *Mass* was only the first large-scale composition the young American had written. It was to be expected that there would be aspects to be criticized. Hollaender found the work lacking in unity and in textual characterization, with the different sections being just so many pieces of music. He excepted from this comment the *Dona nobis pacem*, which he called "a music piece of great noble expression, in which the author shows himself for the first time to be inwardly moved and speaks on behalf of this. . . ." The Leipzig writer found fault with the "quite remarkably difficult" melodic writing in several of the solo sections. He also felt that the contrapuntal writing was unconvincing: "a few *Schul-fugen* do not amount to a polyphonic work." Geyer called the *Benedictus* "far fetched and not very singable," remarking that it "imposes a hard task upon the singers, even in the entrances, without being beautiful." In his opinion, also "the *Kyrie* seems to set in too frequently, and the contrast of the *Gloria* and *Pax hominibus* is not sharp enough." But Geyer found many more features to compliment, and chided some of his fellows:

> . . . At any rate all those who went away too early, some of our colleagues among them, missed many of the best things, which the Mass conceals toward the end.

It did not matter, however, that some of those in attendance were not sufficiently interested or attracted to remain for the entire presentation. Nor did the reservations expressed by the Berlin critics lessen the significance of this event in Paine's career. His *Mass*, moreover, did deserve the criticism concerning a too-strict reliance on textbook rules and a general lack of boldness. The most noteworthy aspect of the entire project is his successful challenge of the disinterest, lack of cooperation, and outright hostility in the Berlin musical community—successful to such a degree that he, a foreigner and only 28 years old, could draw together a fiercely loyal, hard-working chorus of 200 voices to prepare a program, amply backed financially, that would attract a large, sophisticated, and eventually highly appreciative audience. This combination of courage, intense drive, optimism, and charisma was to serve him well in his coming fight for an academic music department at Harvard. In the meantime, his prestige had risen immensely, for he was now recognized internationally as an important, if not yet major, composer, and one who was to help place America "on the map" musically. His place in the eyes of his contemporaries was exceedingly important at this point; Osgood gives a representative view:

> [The ovation following the concert] was an interesting sight. To know that the young composer standing there was an American, made the hearts of his countrymen present—and there were many—swell with pride. We were proud to know that at last we had our representative in this most beautiful of arts; and to see the phlegmatic German at length heartily acknowledging that in America we not only have time and ability to make money, but that we can send forth artists, and those too who bid fair to stand in the very front rank.

Paine returned to Boston on 14 March 1867[22] in triumph, but not so speedily that he did not have an opportunity of enjoying his victory in Berlin for a fortnight after the performance of the *Mass*. Doubtless he wished to gather all the local reviews; the various Berlin criticisms reprinted by Boston periodicals following his return most likely were made available by him. Osgood's 27 February letter to the *Transcript*, cited above, in all probability was delivered by the returning musician. Another reason for lingering, according to the *Boston Musical Times*,[23] was his intention to give a few organ recitals, although it is not known whether such concerts did take place.

Back in Cambridge, Paine immediately resumed his duties at Harvard, where the spring term was already in session. Had he overstayed his leave? Dwight had reported him to be on leave "until March,"[24] and a 26 February letter from Paine's substitute organist F. A. Carpenter to President Hill complained:

> Mr. Paine engaged me to play for him only last term, and no arrangement was made with reference to his being absent any part of the coming term. . . . If I am to play at Cambridge next Sunday & if I am to provide for prayers, it is necessary that I should know it at once, that I may get some one to supply at my own church next Sunday. . . .[25]

How the problems for both the college chapel and Carpenter, caused by Paine's delayed return, were solved is not known, for the regular organist was not on his bench until Sunday 17 March.

The next most notable event was Paine's participation in the Inauguration Concert of the New England Conservatory of Music on 30 March 1867. The conservatory had just opened at Music Hall on 20 February 1867 with a faculty of 13.[26] At the concert, four singers, three organists, and a pianist shared the program with an orchestra led by Carl Zerrahn.[27] Paine played his *Fantasia and Fugue in E minor*, which was encored.[28] He soon thereafter joined the faculty, and in the February 1868 catalogue was listed among the Piano, Organ, Church Music, and Harmony and Counterpoint instructors.[29] Other professional activity during the remainder of 1867 included 10 solo recitals on the Music Hall organ, the first of which Paine presented on 22 May.[30] Additional public performances included one on 14 October, a demonstration at the Boston factory, along with organists S. P. Tuckerman and J. H. Willcox, of a new and highly praised Hook organ built for the Westminster Presbyterian Church of Elizabeth, New Jersey.[31]

He also played for the memorial service on 26 November for Governor John Albion Andrew (1818–67), the popular Massachusetts politician who achieved fame through Fugitive Slave Law cases and who, foreseeing the Civil War, organized the militia to be ready within a week's notice. Organ pieces for the service were Paine's transcription of "Wir setzen uns mit Tränen nieder"—the final chorus from the *St. Matthew Passion*—and a Bach chorale.[32] Dwight was in charge of the music, which also included selections by an orchestra and by the Handel and Haydn Society.[33]

In addition to his institutional affiliations at Harvard and the New England Conservatory, the ambitious young instructor solicited private students in a *Transcript* card that appeared throughout the fall of 1867, offering instruction in "Musical Composition, Piano and Organ Playing."[34]

Paine's prestige as a composer and success as an instructor was given an additional boost, beginning in 1867, by his gradual acceptance as a member of Boston-Cambridge society. During the summer he was a frequent visitor at the John Fiskes, who had bought a house on Oxford Street where he doubtless met Fiske's Harvard friends, including the psychologist William James (1842–1910), Harvard history professor E. W. Gurney (1829–86), Harvard mathematics professor J. M. Peirce (1834–1906), and mathematician and evolutionist Chauncey Wright (1830–75). Nearby neighbors of Fiske included Henry Wadsworth Longfellow, William Dean Howells (1837–1920), Charles Eliot Norton (1827–1908), James Russell Lowell (1819–91), Francis James Child, and Asa Gray (1810–88), all of whom would call in the Fiske home and issue return invitations.[35] Certainly the Harvard musician, being such a good friend of Fiske, must have been included in many of these social activities, an assumption documented by subsequent events.

Acquaintances and friendships with such important persons in so many diverse fields doubtless played an important role in Paine's cultural development, providing much knowledge and insight denied him by his lack of a university education. These associations also began to benefit the composer professionally, for such men came to respect him as a gifted musician, an intelligent, witty companion, and eventually a social equal, offering him encouragement and support. One early example of the extraordinary faith and admiration such men held for him is seen in the following *Transcript* notice published late in October 1867:[36]

> Mr. John K. Paine: Dear Sir—We have heard with much pleasure of the approbation with which your Mass was received last winter by the severely critical audience of the Berlin Sing-Akademie. In the hope that your efforts and your success in a noble and difficult region of art may be recognized and appreciated by your countrymen, we would suggest that you take measures for the production of your composition in Boston the coming season. Assuring you of our hearty coöperation in any way in which we can be helpful,

We are sincerely your friends,

Benjamin Peirce,	J. R. Lowell,
Thomas Hill,	H. W. Longfellow,
R. E. Apthorp,	F. J. Child,
B. A. Gould,	John S. Dwight,
J. P. Putnam,	B. F. Dwight,
H. W. Pickering,	H. Ware,
J. Baxter Upham,	Sam'l Jennison,
Theron J. Dale,	B. J. Lang,
C. A. Bartol,	Wolcott Gibbs.

One might assume from this advertisement in Boston's most prestigious journal that these individuals were prepared to underwrite the substantial financial risk such a production entailed, tangible proof of their "hearty coöperation." Paine's Berlin triumph had received generous coverage in the Boston press, and the resulting excitement and anticipation would certainly help make this local hearing a success. However, when the response to this appeal was not as immediate or as great as had been anticipated, a repetition of the item in January 1868 was followed by this accompanying statement:[37]

> Mr. Paine having signified that it would give him much pleasure to accept this invitation, his friends think it advisable to ask subscriptions in order to secure the cost of the undertaking. If the required number of tickets are taken, the Concert will be given on Easter Sunday Evening [12 April 1868], at the Boston Music Hall, with a full chorus from the Handel and Haydn Society, the Orchestra of the Harvard Musical Association, and the best solo talent. Subscription tickets will be one dollar each, with secured seats.

Such a statement corrects the possible inference from the original letter that the named gentlemen were prepared to pay all the bills if the concert were a failure financially. Instead, it was now understood that the performance would not take place unless enough tickets were sold. Soon after the ticket sale had begun, on 1 February, Dwight wrote optimistically that "it is now pretty certain" that the concert would take place, ". . . subscriptions having come in liberally and eagerly. . . ."[38] The *Boston Musical Times* of the same date numbered the chorus at "about two hundred selected voices," and felt, regarding solo voices, "that if the Mass is given, Mr. Paine will do all in his power to have the best."[39] On 29 February the *Mass* was "now in vigorous rehearsal," according to Dwight.[40] But this was the last published mention of the planned performance. Apparently the subscription drive failed and plans for the concert were abandoned quietly. Though one can imagine the disappointment of the singers, who were already in active rehearsal, how much more intense must have been the sense of defeat felt by Paine in his native land, especially after all the acclaim the work received in Berlin. Such a failure is but one example of the frustrations of the American composer. No explanation for the cancellation was given in the press; in fact, because no mention was made, some modern writers have assumed that the *Mass* was actually performed as scheduled.[41] But surely if the performance had taken place *Dwight's Journal*, at least, would have provided publicity and a review; the periodical is silent! And, in a fall report of the Handel and Haydn Society, the following wording implies that the Easter program did not take place:

> . . . There is some thought of giving, later, . . . Mr. Paine's Mass, which surely is entitled to a hearing after the praises that it won in Berlin. . . .[42]

These plans were not developed further, and apparently the *Mass* never enjoyed a complete performance in the United States during the composer's lifetime.[43] However, this was the only major work of his that was not performed in its entirety for the Boston-Cambridge musical community, except, of course, for his opera *Azara*, which was never staged and which was performed only in concert version with cuts.

Throughout 1868 the active musician's time seems to have been well filled by his duties at Harvard and at the New England Conservatory. Activities at Harvard remained similar to those of previous years, including playing for chapel services, training and directing the choirs, and teaching the noncredit classes in music. At the New England Conservatory of Music, he taught piano and organ, as well as classes in church music and in harmony and counterpoint. This teaching assignment, potentially more demanding than that at Harvard, would certainly have required a large segment of his schedule. His solo recital appearances on the Music Hall organ seem to have been limited to two, both around the time of the cancelled *Mass* performance—an 8 April 1868 concert, which closed with his *Star-Spangled Banner* variations,[44] and another a week later, on 15 April.[45] He also was a participant in the concert life of the New England Conservatory. Biweekly Classical Chamber Concerts, "at which the choicest works of the great masters have been performed by the teachers and others," were presented "for the purpose of forming a refined and elevated musical taste in the pupils."[46] At a concert at Chickering Hall on 13 May 1868, Paine was joined by fellow instructors Henry Suck, violin, August Suck, cello, and Miss J. E. Houston, soprano. The three instrumentalists performed the Beethoven Trio in D, op. 70, Miss Houston sang songs of Schubert and Schumann, and Paine played three of his own piano compositions—*Sonata in A Minor*, op. 1, *Marcia Funèbre*, and

Impromptu, Welcome Home.[47] The last two pieces may be identified more specifically as *Funeral March in Memory of President Abraham Lincoln*, op. 9, published by Beer & Schirmer in 1865, and the unpublished *Welcome Home to my Darling Lizzie! from John. March 31, 1868, Cambridge*. "Lizzie," of course, was Mary Elizabeth Greeley, who became his wife 16 months later.

On a 14 December 1868 concert, also one of the New England Conservatory series, Paine accompanied Henry Suck in the Beethoven G-major violin sonata. He also performed as piano soloist the Chopin C-minor *Etude* (from op. 10), his own *Fantasie Stück* [*sic*], op. 12 (published in 1869 as *Romance*), and his *Four Piano Pieces*, op. 11 (published in 1872 as *Vier Character-Stücke für Piano-forte*). Paine and Suck were assisted by J. F. Rudolphsen, who sang a Meyerbeer aria and Schubert's *Ungeduld*.[48] As may be inferred from the above-named compositions, Paine was active as a composer in the smaller forms during these years. The first four of his piano works to be published date from this period. He also produced at least three songs—*Early Springtime* (1866), with text by President Hill, *Mondnacht* (1867), setting a poem of Joseph Eichendorff, and *Spring* (1869).

Meanwhile, at Harvard several events had occurred which were eventually to end in the recognition of music as a regular part of the academic curriculum. During 1868 President Hill resigned, and on 29 May 1869 Charles William Eliot (1834–1926) was elected as the new president. Eliot was to apply his educational theories, many considered radical, in the coming years. Among these were the reorganization of the various university departments, the requirement of entrance examinations, and the liberalization of the curriculum through a wide use of the elective system. Music was one of the first to benefit from this last policy, probably to a large degree because of Eliot's encouragement. Eliot's father, Samuel A. Eliot, had played a similar role in forwarding music; during his term as Boston mayor (1837–39) music was authorized as a branch of instruction in the public schools, and Lowell Mason was hired as Superintendent of Music. Walter Spalding, successor to Paine as chairman of the Harvard Music Department, described Eliot's attitude toward music:

> . . . President Eliot has often stated to the writer his conviction that music is one of the most desirable of educational subjects, for the student therein is being trained in his mental powers, his ability to draw fine distinctions, in his ear, his eye, his imagination, his emotions; and on the executive side, in his hands and feet; that is, in a comprehensive coördination of his whole make-up, mental, spiritual, and physical. All the greater credit redounds to Eliot for this attitude, because by temperament he

did not respond profoundly to music. He loved music, however; heard it often in his home thanks to Mrs. Eliot, who had a remarkably pure soprano voice; and through his children and grandchildren he felt its liberalizing and tonic force. . . .[49]

Eliot was inaugurated on 19 October 1869, to the sounds of Paine's *Domine salvum fac Praesidem nostrum*. By this date the year's work was already under way at the college, and the academic innovations were not yet instituted. But changes were rapidly made.

One of the first steps towards legitimizing music and its leading exponent at Harvard was decided upon at the 29 May 1869 meeting of the Harvard Corporation that elected Eliot president:

Voted, that the Degree of Master of Arts, be conferred on . . . John Knowles Paine.[50]

With this act, the Harvard music instructor was given the credentials required in order to hold professorial rank at Harvard, namely, a Harvard degree.

Paine reached another milestone, in his personal life, on 7 September 1869, with his marriage to Mary Elizabeth Greeley (1836–1920) of Cambridge, daughter of William E. and Myra A. (Smith) Greeley. The Rev. Peabody—the Harvard chaplain—performed the ceremony. Miss Greeley was also a native of Portland,[51] where her father had been a commission merchant. Business interests had brought the family first to Salem, where they lived on Chestnut Street,and later to Boston.[52] Edwards, in *Music and Musicians of Maine*,[53] quotes the following description of Mrs. Paine from a 1927 letter written by her nephew, Dr. Hugh Payne Greeley:

. . . She treasured the 75¢ ring that [Paine] gave her more highly than any other possession. They had about Seventy-five Dollars when married. Young Paine went to Eliot, President of the University and urged that music should be taught in American Colleges. Eliot finally said, "If you will teach without pay, you may do so." Paine took it up with his bride and she wisely counseled him to do so, even if they had to live on the edge of starvation. At the end of two years Yale offered the pioneer Music teacher of America a salary and Eliot quickly matched it . . .

[Paine's] wife cared for him as for a child. She stood between him and the world. He was a guileless trusting man, living in his own world of music and of friendship, wholly unaware of the schemes and selfishness that surrounded him. She managed the household. She kept him from interruption when he was composing. She husbanded his small salary and made it answer all needs. She entertained his friends, and widened the circle constantly. She fought his battles for him, dictated the terms of his contracts, defended him before the President and faculty of the college, and saw that the furnace was attended to, and the house painted at the proper time. . . .

During a 2 July 1970 telephone interview, Dr. Greeley told the present author of an incident between Mrs. Paine and the Harvard president:

> Paine was a very simple man. He couldn't have gotten very far without a strong-minded wife. Once President Eliot, who enjoyed riding his bicycle, rode into the front yard and knocked on the window, wanting to talk to Mrs. Paine. She said, "If you want to talk to me, you'll have to come into the house."

Another nephew, William Roger Greeley, gave a similar description of the Paines:

> [Paine] was emotionally a boy, charming, entertaining, but immature. He was not interested in practical affairs. We often spoke of him in fun, asking each other if he even knew where the furnace was, whether the bills were ever paid, etc. Lizzie took care of all these things. She was as responsible as he was carefree. She fought his battles with President Eliot while he stayed home and read detective stories. She even persuaded that august arbiter of the affairs of Harvard to change his mind after he had announced that he was sending Henry L. Higginson to represent Harvard at the great musical festival in Germany [International Wagner Festival, Berlin, 1903], and to make a second announcement that John Knowles Paine would be Harvard's representative. She was more like his mother than like a wife.[54]

Mrs. Paine's strong-willed, independent nature was an asset in dealing with his absent-mindedness, as seen in the following anecdote told by Spalding:

> Once on a shopping tour to Boston [Paine] completely forgot Mrs. Paine, left her in a store, and rushed home to compose. He came to a realization of mundane affairs only late in the afternoon when that noble lady appeared before him with the words, "Oh, John, haven't you missed me all this time?"[55]

And her strong support would also manifest itself in a far more gentle fashion. Composer John Alden Carpenter (1876–1951), in his Harvard student days, would occasionally have tea with the Paines,

> . . . during which J. K. produced some of his favorite puns and pretended to be unaware of the sweet and peaceful presence of Mrs. J. K. whom we all, and he, adored.[56]

Even with the survival of memorabilia, letters, and diaries, it is difficult to reconstruct accurately a man's life. So when faced with the destruction of such material, carried out according to Elizabeth Paine's last will and testament,[57] the problem becomes even more onerous, and the act of destruction itself must be weighed in the balance for its own significance. Since it is not possible, given these handicaps, to present a single story, one way or the other, about Paine's personality, it becomes necessary to paint two possible pictures of the composer as a man and a husband. In one, Paine is an aggressive, confident, self-disciplined, shrewd, and sometimes brash young man who sails to far-off Europe on little more than a shoestring to develop his talent, who lands a prestigious Boston church position, and then secures an even more coveted appointment at Harvard, who several times stands his ground against the Harvard administration, and who—undaunted by the discouragement of a German superior attitude toward American composers—succeeds in producing and conducting his *Mass* in Berlin before a more distinguished and appreciative audience. On the other hand, there is the portrait—painted especially by the Greeley descendents—of the absent-minded, passive, naive, innocent individual who lives solely in his own world of music unconcerned with mundane affairs, and who allows his wife to run the house, make all the financial decisions, fight his battles, plan his social life, and care for him more like a mother than a wife.

Nevertheless, there are two ways in which these views may be reconciled. First, it is possible that John and Elizabeth had known each other since early childhood in Portland, that their friendship grew strong, despite years of separation, and that his aggressiveness and confidence were but the result of her encouragement and push, through a correspondence now destroyed. Accordingly, after the marriage, made possible (or practical) by his success, she assumes the initiative directly; she exerts her strong will and he withdraws into his world of music and composition. However, the facts of the matter make this hypothesis somewhat uncertain. The Greeleys left Portland while Elizabeth was still a child, and her girlhood was divided between Salem and Boston.[58] If such were the case, a friendship dating from the Portland days is unlikely. But even if they actually had known each other during the time before Paine's departure in 1858, it is improbable that this relationship could have been serious, especially in view of the difference of three years in age. It is more probable that the friendship began after Paine settled in Boston. Possibly Elizabeth, a Unitarian, visited West Church, where Paine was organist—although this congregation may not have been the most convenient to the Greeleys' Summer Street house—simply because she knew he was a Portlander. She certainly may have attended Paine's organ concerts there and at other churches such as Tremont Temple, where the former boy from Portland performed, for this would have been one of the few forms of public entertainment proper for an unescorted young woman. Also, according to an obituary, ". . . upon her marriage to Prof. Paine she was brought into another circle of intellectual people, . . ." which perhaps suggests that she had not known Paine long enough or well enough before the wedding already to have gotten to know his Harvard friends.

A second profile—perhaps more acceptable—might portray Paine as indeed the young, virile, confident composer. He retains these traits after marriage, and it is only toward the end of his life, when his position at Harvard is secure, but when his health is deteriorating, that Mrs. Paine assumes the dominant role witnessed by the Greeley nephews. After all, they could only have remembered the last 10 years or so of Paine's life. The man they knew was a different man—deformed by the psychological and physiological impact of diabetes, arteriosclerosis, and possibly minor strokes. A gradual change of this kind, especially if caused by poor health, was far more likely the case than any abrupt change of personality. And doubtless Mrs. Paine, in her affection and concern for her husband, recognized them by assuming a far more responsible and dominant role.

Whatever the relationship between John and Elizabeth Paine may have been, she aided him in his growing maturity as a composer, and strengthened his intense desire to better the educational opportunities available in the field of music. With Eliot's accession to the Harvard presidency, conditions had finally ripened for the growth of a solid, respectable academic music department for the first time in the history of American colleges.

5

Public Recognition and Harvard
Professorship: 1869–1875

Within eight years of his move to Boston from Portland, Paine had reached a high plateau of professional security that would continue throughout the rest of his life. The success of his *Mass* in Europe enhanced his position as a composer, even though efforts to perform the work in the United States had failed. This professional acceptance was proved by Eben Tourjée's invitation to join the faculty of a new music school, the New England Conservatory. And his future had brightened considerably. Friendship with Fiske had provided many social contacts with Harvard faculty members and other intellectuals. After Charles William Eliot's appointment as president of the college in 1869, the elective system was inaugurated, promising an increase in the number of music offerings in the Harvard curriculum. And Paine, having received the A. M. degree *honoris causa* in the same year, could look forward to an eventual permanent faculty appointment. Finally, in his new bride, Mary Elizabeth, he had gained a faithful companion, a person to encourage and support him, and, on occasion, fight his battles.

At this point in his career, Paine began again to expound his knowledge and theories before a public audience. He was stimulated in this pursuit by his wife and by President Eliot, as well as by other colleagues and admirers. An early instance was a 23 September 1869 National Musical Convention speech at Music Hall, *The Musical Profession: A Plea for thorough musical culture*,[1] the title of which belied its strong challenge to the musical establishment, which was dominated by performers. In it he stressed the need for a far more intensive grounding in harmony and thoroughbass, counterpoint, fugue, composition, and analysis. Additionally, he called for more serious attention to consistent practice, rather than mere reliance upon inborn aptitudes.

> All this is important, if we consider it merely as educational, without the sole aim of making composers, but simply musicians. There is a notion that all depends upon

the natural gift of talent or genius, whereas full as much depends upon its constant and proper exercise.

Such a wide and thorough indoctrination in musical knowledge in America would directly result in a much more favorable attitude toward the American composer and an encouragement of his efforts.

> It may be asked, why trouble ourselves about musical composition at home, when we have the repertory of all European composers to draw from? The enthusiastic will answer that the utmost possible in music has not been accomplished; that we must look for new and undiscovered effects and attainments. Surely the devoted artist with lofty ideal and untiring zeal will be rewarded with new revelations; and we Americans have a right if not a duty to compete in this trial. . . .

Paine voiced the need to raise the status of the musician in America, stressing the necessity for instrumental or vocal competence as well as for overall cultural development. Americans of that era, in the main, looked down on serious music as a career, approving only such commercially successful areas as balladry, minstrelsy, popular religious songs, band music, and virtuosity. Paine had to face this form of opposition all through his career—most notably in his attempts to develop the music department at Harvard—and he devoted much effort to gain wider acceptance for serious music in America. Here he expressed his feelings strongly:

> When American musicians are conscious of having studied liberally with the high aim of becoming *masters* in every sense, they will have more self respect; then all narrow and ignorant prejudices against their profession—sometimes held by quasi-cultivated men of other walks of life—will vanish, and all true lovers of art and science will recognize this worth. Musicians should seek every way of self-improvement. Mental training, intercourse with cultivated people, systematic reading, etc., should be precious to the artist, who, next to the preacher of religion, will look upon his as a sacred calling and strive to make himself worthy of it, serving God and man.

He ended this surprisingly direct and forceful manifesto by addressing himself to those who had it within their power to effect change. Paine called upon the wealthy to support the arts, thereby giving the same advantage to be found in European countries, where the court and nobility and "the upper class of society give their constant sympathy and support to men of talent." Such backing in America would help "an original, national school of composers" to grow and flourish.

Ideals such as these had been his since the beginning of his career, and it was these attitudes toward the value and dignity of the music profession that he fostered in his Harvard teaching and his public lectures. True to self-imposed standards of art and ethics, Paine called upon the musical establishment to reform its own house by eschewing the quest for the dollar. With the prevalent lack of musical knowledge or critical judgment, many musicians with minimal training, ability, or taste were able to achieve fame and success among the unsophisticated American public. This low standard was supported by "the constant issuing by music publishers of trashy compositions." These individuals catered to current fads and exploited the public's enjoyment of spectacular effects. Without doubt, professionals such as these resented and felt threatened by the Harvard composer's attacks. It is likely also that they did not subscribe to the code of ethics and standards of professional dignity upheld by Europeans. A published letter, prompted by some reportedly unethical manuevering of one such individual, shows Paine's opinions of this kind of activity:[2]

> *Editor Orpheonist and Philharmonic Journal:*
>   My Dear Sir,—I am informed by President Eliot that no consultation whatever has been held with Dr. Peck (or Peek) in regard to the establishment of a school of music in Harvard College. It is a false statement, but, though I read it sometime since in a New York paper, I did not think it worth while to contradict it. It is hard to believe that the musical profession has so many unprincipled men in its ranks. I hear every day of this and that one who has committed some bad act or other. The name of *musician* instead of being associated with all that is pure, noble and dignified, is of doubtful sound, in this country.
>
>   Yours, with my best regards,
>   John K. Paine.
> Cambridge, November 12, 1869.

Unfortunately, no other references to this episode seem to have survived. However, one may imagine Paine's alarm, for after having spent seven years patiently laying the groundwork for the gradual introduction of music courses as a legitimate part of the curriculum, he now hears rumors about an undistinguished trade school for singers and fiddle players being planned for Harvard University! Members of the Corporation who already were skeptical of music's academic value, finding herein new justification for their misgivings, could easily have ended the venture forthwith. This "Dr. Peck (or Peek)," in announcing plans to invade Paine's territory, seems a threat to the very future of the college musician. Paine's letter, while deploring ethical standards of some American musicians, doubtless was actually intended to ensure his continued role at Harvard.

During the academic years 1869–70 and 1870–71 Paine's teaching duties at Harvard remained the same as in previous years. A corporation vote on 18 June 1870 excused him from playing for Sunday services "on condition that he provide a competent organist for that duty"[3]—a decision that probably did not change his situation to any real degree. He directed the music for the cornerstone laying for Alumni Hall on 6 October 1870.[4] As a composer he was active, being "hard at work" on the oratorio *St. Peter* at the time of a September 1870 report;[5] the work was completed by Spring 1872, for portions were performed at an April 1872 New England Conservatory concert and during the World's Peace Jubilee two months later. He participated in the musical life of Boston, sharing organist duties with George E. Whiting at the 7 June 1870 choral festival of the National Musical Congress at Music Hall. An outgrowth from the 1869 Peace Jubilee, the event featured a chorus numbering over a thousand voices, conducted by Patrick Sarsfield Gilmore, Carl Zerrahn, and Eugene Thayer.[6] The next year the Harvard musician was listed as one of the directors of the Congress following the June 1871 convention.[7] In the fall of 1870 he became organist of the Music Hall Society, replacing J. B. Sharland,[8] who also had been his predecessor as organist of West Church.

One of President Eliot's first actions affecting the college music instructor significantly was the revival of the University Lecture series for the 1870–71 academic year. Paine was included in this first offering, and presented 18 lectures on "The History of Music" at Wesleyan Association Hall, Boston, on Saturdays at noon, beginning 3 December.[9] Each lecture received extensive newspaper coverage, and by way of reprints in *Dwight's Journal of Music* we may gain insights into the emphases he was to make in his forthcoming music history course at Harvard, especially his views regarding contemporary music. Topics of the lectures ranged from "Music of the ancient nations; music in the early centuries of the Christian era; and Ambrosian and Gregorian song" to "The New German Music." But though his intentions were noble, he was limited to a considerable degree himself by the basic attitudes and misconceptions of the day concerning medieval and Renaissance music. Thus, he strongly demythologized Guido,[10] and revealed to his audience that Renaissance composers commonly included "vulgar and offensive words"[11] in their church compositions. In discussing eighteenth-century music, however, he was on more secure ground and showed his deep admiration for the music of Bach, at the same time revealing his disdain for those Americans who did not share his views. Bach was

> . . . the greatest sacred composer and the most intellectual composer who ever lived. Those who find his music cold and passionless are ignorant of his style.[12]

Perhaps most important are Paine's views of contemporary music, for they show the attitudes fostered in him by his German training and which he in turn transmitted to his students. These statements in the main show him to be of conservative persuasion, unsympathetic to newer, more radical developments. He felt that Italian opera ". . . reached its climax in the achievements of Rossini, and since the close of his active career, it has gradually declined, . . ." with Bellini, Donizetti, and Verdi regarded merely as "imitators and successors."[13] Beethoven was called "the representative musician" and "the artist and poet of the nineteenth century"—music had not progressed significantly since his death.

> . . . The lamented deaths of Mendelssohn and Schumann arrested at its full career the onward course of the traditional art of music. Had these leaders of the musical world lived to the present hour in the active practice of their art, the relative prominence of later musicians, like Wagner and Liszt, would doubtless have been modified by their living influence and example.[14]

Paine attacked Wagner's political, social, and religious views, dismissing them as "the vagary of a wild dreamer." He denounced Wagner's desire to unite the arts, explaining, ". . . A concession robs each art of its highest prerogative." He also disliked the abandonment of the traditional aria and chorus:

> To banish the air from the opera is unjustifiable, because its aesthetic influence is too great. On the same grounds the chorus and concerted movements are fully justifiable, even if they arrest for a moment the further action of the drama.

Also unacceptable to the lecturer was the choice of mythology as the "genuine source of the ideal drama"—such an emphasis would "not stand the test of criticism." Paine spoke to a sympathetic audience, for few Bostonians had had opportunity to hear more than a few brief excerpts of Wagner's music, and students were actively discouraged from studying his works (see p. 89–90). Moreover, well-publicized details of Wagner's personal life and his views on religion and politics would have been highly offensive to the average New Englander. In a gesture towards fairness, however, Paine concluded his discussion with a slight concession to Wagner:

> No one will doubt that Wagner is a man of remarkable character and a genius, but neither his head nor his heart have been altogether right. He has been led astray by vagaries. His pernicious theories have marred all his later music, yet here and there wonderful beauties come to light in his scores. His best music has an element of popularity in it.

The speaker brought his series of 18 talks to an end with an overture for musical growth in America:

> Who knows . . . but that another and younger people may yet rejuvenate the life of music? As patriotic and art-loving Americans, . . . let us hope that this will be the

mission of our own land. May it lift the veil that now shrouds the future of this
beautiful art.

These lectures attracted an appreciative, often large, audience.
Among those attending the first one were

> . . . ex-President Hill of Harvard University, Rev. Mr. Alger, Mr. John S. Dwight,
> Mr. Carl Zerrahn, and many of the musical artists and teachers of the city.[15]

But perhaps the most significant and charming aspect of the lectures were
the musical examples played by Paine at the piano; he also assisted in
some of the less demanding vocal demonstrations. Five professional soloists sang regularly during the series, and a chorus ranging from 12 to 20
voices performed examples of Renaissance music, including motets of
Josquin and Lassus, a Palestrina *Gloria Patri*, a Giovanni Gabrieli work
"which seemed decidedly modern in style,"[16] and madrigals of Dowland
and Morley. The University Lectures were repeated during 1871–72, and
Paine again delivered his series on "The History of Music." His lectures
began earlier in the season—on 19 October—and the number of sessions
was increased to 20.[17]

Paine's strong views on the music of Wagner and Liszt were also
aired publicly in his *Inaugural Lecture of the Department of Musical Composition, History, and Aesthetics, in the College of Music of Boston University . . .*, delivered before the student body on 28 October 1872;[18] he
held a professorship in this department until 1877.[19] After stating that the
Handel oratorios, Mozart operas, and Beethoven symphonies are the
"grandest conceptions" in their representative genres, he again gave his
view of later developments:

> In vocal music, if we compare the scores of Liszt and Wagner with those of Mozart
> and Handel, we witness how far the "music of the future" has departed from a vocal
> method, from the harmony and symmetry of design, clearness and directness of
> expression,—moderation and simplicity, which are two important elements in all art.
> The technics of music, with Wagner, Liszt, and their adherents, have become so
> extremely involved and complicated, both in composition and performance, that there
> must soon be a healthy reaction. The only hope for the present and future is the
> adherence to the historical forms, as developed by Bach, Handel, Mozart, and Bee-
> thoven, in church music, the oratorio, opera and instrumental music. [Schubert,
> Mendelssohn, and Schumann] . . . were able to stamp their works with their own
> peculiar individuality and originality without contradicting the past. They, like all
> true artists, recognized the historical sequence and progress of all natural develop-
> ment in art. Such must be the course of the composers of the present and future.

The most extensive discussion of Paine's attitudes towards Wagner,
Liszt, and Berlioz appeared in an article, "The New German School of

Music," included in the April 1873 *North American Review*[20] and prompted by the publication of Wagner's *Gesammelte Schriften* the previous year. This essay is a revision and expansion of the lecture on the same topic given as part of the Harvard University Lecture series. Again he criticized Wagner's political, religious, and social theories, his literary style, his ability to portray character, and his standing as a dramatic poet. Wagner's "infinite melody" is labeled as a "falsity," and his use of leading motives—a "mannerism"—as a mere "substitute for real delineation of character" which may easily become "pedantic and tiresome." The unity of the arts Paine dismissed as unoriginal and superficial. But he commended Wagner on his theatrical prowess:

> One grand effect succeeds another in logical and natural sequence; yet nothing, apparently, is introduced for the sake of mere effect.

Moreover, he credited Wagner with being true to the dramatic action of the play, and uniting action, scenic display, words, and music for best effect. Despite the absence of tunefulness, Wagner's music is described as

> . . . declamatory in a powerful degree; it is true to the metrical accents of the verse, and expresses vividly the meaning of the words. In this respect he stands out prominently as a progressive master, and will exercise a decided influence on the dramatic music of the future.

He praised Wagner's skill in orchestration to heighten dramatic action and to create atmosphere. He found some themes "noble, characteristic, and pleasing," although most are "somewhat coarse and formal," and the works in "free thematic form" have a "want of refined beauty" when compared with similar works of Schumann or Mendelssohn. Wagner's innovative instrumental effects are labeled superficial, and "do not impress us as the spontaneous and sincere utterance of a profound musical nature." The writer's rather biased summary includes the following:

> . . . The unprejudiced critic must acknowledge that Wagner is a man of wonderful energy and talent,—at the same time one whose head and heart are not entirely right. His erroneous theory has marred all his recent music. He has tried to institute a reform or revolution through the intellect rather than by the spontaneous and gradual growth of concrete musical thoughts, the offspring of real musical genius.

According to critic Henry T. Finck, then a Harvard student of the class of 1876, Paine and Fiske had

> . . . put their heads together and concocted . . . [this] article in which my idol [Wagner] was completely demolished, pulverized, annihilated.[21]

The Harvard instructor had objected strongly to Finck's playing through Wagner scores on the University Hall piano:

> . . . he was greatly distressed and warned me solemnly that I would corrupt my musical taste.

It is remarkable what a substantial change Paine was to experience in his attitude toward Wagner's music. Beginning with emphatic, dogmatic statements about the evils of Wagner, Paine gradually began evolving a new approach to composition, reevaluating the immense value of Wagner as a composer. Finck already noticed such a change in the music to *Oedipus Tyrannus*; in a *Nation* review following the January 1882 performance at Booth's Theatre in New York he observed Paine's debt to Wagner:

> . . . in these choruses . . . he unconsciously reveals his admiration for a composer whose theories he condemns. . . .[22]

Perhaps in response to this comment, Paine wrote to Finck on 31 January 1882:

> I want to take this opportunity to say that my opinions regarding Wagner and his theories have been modified since you were in College. I consider him a great genius who has had a wonderful influence on the present day. I will reserve my ideas on this subject until we meet.[23]

Much later, on 25 March 1900, he told Finck of his opera *Azara*:

> You will find that I have entered upon a new path in all respects—in form, thematic treatment, instrumentation, etc. All dramatic composers must learn from Wagner, yet I have not consciously imitated him in style, etc.

Later, on 27 May 1900, he added:

> I have followed throughout the connected orchestral rhythmic flow, and truth of dramatic expression characteristic of Wagner.

Throughout his career Paine increased his use of "Wagnerisms" and professed his admiration for the composer, and by 1903 he represented Harvard University at the unveiling of the Wagner Memorial in Berlin.[24] Such a change shows him to have had an open mind, and definitely sets him apart from others of the traditional German school, who continued their neoclassicism throughout their careers.

Whatever effect his views may have had regarding such controversies as the genius or heresy of Wagner, or the musical value of such non-German composers as Chopin, Berlioz, or Liszt, perhaps Paine's strongest influence was seen in his students. They did not always agree with his convictions in all respects, but came to admire and respect him as a teacher and advisor, and developed under his leadership as musicians and composers. Composer Arthur Foote (1853–1937), a Harvard student in the early 1870s, gave a typical report:

> . . . I owe [Paine] a great deal. . . . He was not one of the born teachers, but certainly he could give generously. Looking back at some of the fugues, etc., of which I have preserved the manuscripts, I am surprised to find how good the result of our work was. His influence was always for what was strong and good in music. . . .[25]

Organist Henry M. Dunham (1853–1929), who studied at the New England Conservatory during Paine's first years there, described an event in one of his classes, which, incidentally, affords us one of the few glimpses of Paine in a not-uncommon pedagogical situation:

> One day, being rather late in preparing my lesson in fugue, to save time I borrowed my subject from some samples of subjects in Cherubini's Treatise on Counterpoint and Fugue. After the Professor had pretty thoroughly mangled it as a bad subject I had to confess its source. The Professor was sometimes a little profane and he indulged himself a little now, claiming that it was a bad subject anyway.[26]

Dunham reported finding much inspiration from Paine's classes. He also related the following example of Paine's deep personal interest in his students:

> I had not yet . . . acquired much faith in myself. One day Professor Paine stopped me on the stairs and said, "Dunham, why don't you do more work?" "Why?" I asked. "Because you have talent." As that advice is vividly recalled even to-day, the advice probably did sink in some.

Dartmouth music professor Charles Henry Morse (1853–1927) also studied with Paine during the 1870s, both at the New England Conservatory and at Boston University—organ, counterpoint, free composition, orchestration, and music history. Morse regarded Paine as

> . . . America's greatest composer by far and [I] am proud of the fact that I found him not only an inspiring teacher but a very warm personal friend. He was a most sincere and honorable man, incapable of anything petty or narrow. He wrote his first Symphony when I was studying with him and brought his first drafts with penciled sketches of the instrumentation to our classes in orchestration, a most helpful object lesson.[27]

Incidentally, Paine's professorship at Boston University was an achievement that must have impressed many. The position was attained through his association with the New England Conservatory; the two schools were associated, sharing faculty and facilities, and the Boston University department functioned as a graduate branch of the Conservatory. Eben Tourjée, director of the Conservatory, was also dean of the College of Music in Boston University,

> the only university in this country where music has its professorships on the same basis as other intellectual and aesthetic studies.[28]

Course offerings and facilities at Harvard were meager at this time when compared to those at the New England Conservatory. Finck wrote of his student days:

> When I studied harmony and the history of music with Paine the class gathered in a large room in the basement of University Hall. A piano was provided. Occasionally, by way of diversion, Paine and I played a Beethoven sonata for piano and violoncello.[29]

Paine's associations with his more gifted students often led to their inclusion at social occasions. Finck continued:

> I also frequently played with him at his residence, where I had the privilege of meeting some persons noted then and, more so, later on; among them John Fiske, Rose Hawthorne (daughter of the great novelist), and Amy Fay, just back from her studies with Liszt. . . .

Until the introduction of the Harvard elective system under President Eliot in 1870–71, the only academic instruction in music available to Harvard students was noncredit, by individual private lessons from Paine, doubtless with remuneration also handled privately. But in the 1871–72 catalogue there appears for the first time, under Elective Studies, a course in music:[30]

> Theory of Music.—(Harmony.—Counterpoint and Choral [*sic*] Figuration.—Free Composition.—Song, march, dance, and rondo forms).

Such a printed description seems to be quite ambitious for a one-year course meeting three times weekly, and some of the instruction must have been superficial. The class attracted the modest number of 11 students— 2 seniors, 2 juniors, and 7 sophomores[31]—and academic music instruction had begun at Harvard. It seems puzzling at first consideration that Paine would have begun his course offerings with such a dry subject as theory, rather than the potentially more interesting topic of Music History or Music Literature that had proved so successful in his University Lecture series. It was not until the fourth course, introduced during the 1874–75 academic year, that students were given the opportunity to study music history;[32] previous courses were all in theory. Perhaps it was easier to

justify the intellectual discipline required in the learning of music theory
as belonging to the university concept; studying the esthetics or philosophy of music would have been more questionable. Prevalent attitudes
are seen in the report to the Board of Overseers for 1872–73;[33]

> . . . The very idea of a University is incomplete if it do [*sic*] not include Music in its
> full circle of the elements of culture, and count it one of the "humanities." For Music
> is a *science*, and Music is a *language*; and on these grounds at least it claims a place
> among the branches of literature and science, even if it be still a question whether
> the University idea shall cover the idea of *Art* as such. . . .

Initial standards were high—the courses were not to be of the popular
variety in which "all might learn a little, none would learn very much."

> . . . What a University is bound to furnish is: a systematic scientific course of in-
> struction to just those students, even if there be barely three such in a hundred, who
> are disposed to enter somewhat deeply into the theory and practice of Music, and
> pursue it as far as their best zeal and opportunity will warrant. . . . Here is a handful
> of young men who have some sort of an ideal of a musical life before them; they
> want to get a musical education; they would devote themselves to this specialty; but
> at the same time they would do it in that large sense of general culture which con-
> stitutes the very atmosphere of a University; they would cultivate themselves as *men*,
> as gentlemen, at the same time that they pursue a special training. . . .

In 1872–73 the course offering was expanded to two—*Harmony.—Counterpoint and Choral Figuration.—Simple forms of Free Composition.—
Song, March, Dance, Prelude, etc.,* meeting for two hour-long sessions
each week, composed of 3 sophomores and 3 juniors, and *Imitative Counterpoint.—Canon.—Free Composition (Thematic Treatment),* meeting three
times weekly, comprised of 3 juniors.[34] The Overseers' committee found
Paine and his students "in earnest in their work," with "intelligent devotion" to their subject. A passage from the report outlines the subject
matter and emphases of Paine's two courses:

> . . . The text book for the first course has been Richter's Manual of Harmony, pre-
> pared for the Conservatorium at Leipzig; and the half dozen young men seem to have
> mastered the principles and the examples there laid down, and to be well at home in
> all the important chords, the rules of modulation and progression, the conditions of
> suspension, the analysis of melodies into phrases, motives, periods; the laws of the-
> matic treatment, &c.; and even to have acquired some practical facility in the simple
> harmonic accompaniment of given melodies, and the strict contrapuntal handling of
> a subject.
>   Having fulfilled the first year's course of what may be called musical *Grammar*,
> we find the pupil in the second year employed on the more interesting, and (if he
> chance to have some inventive gift) inspiring topics of the *Syntax* of the art. He now
> learns something about *imitative counterpoint* and the melodic progression of parts

in polyphonic harmony; he tries his hand at composing a figurative counterpoint to a given Choral. He is taught the laws of Canon. And then he is initiated into the structure and the use of various musical *forms*,—the architecture (so to speak) of music; such as the Song form, the several Rondo forms; the Minuet and Scherzo forms; and, richest and most complete of all, the so-called *Sonata* form, peculiar to the opening Allegro movement of a Sonata, a Symphony, a classical Quartet, &c. We have seen movements from Sonatas, &c., by Haydn, Mozart, Beethoven, submitted to the student for analysis as illustrations of these forms, and he has not failed quickly to identify the distinctive formal character in each. If it were a Rondo, for instance, he would tell which form of Rondo. And what is more, in their own essays at the composition of simple little Rondos, none of the pupils have seemed helpless, while one or two have given signs of something like spontaneous faculty or talent, which possibly, if cultivated, may make composers of them. . . .

Students in this second class used as a textbook Wohlfahrt's *Guide to Musical Composition*, with works of Cherubini and Marx utilized as secondary resources.

Based on the success of these first two years of electives in music, Paine's academic stature grew within the academic community and was, at last, recognized officially in a 2 June 1873 vote of the President and Fellows of Harvard that appointed Paine Assistant Professor of Music.[35] The action was confirmed by the Board of Overseers on 12 June,[36] and he became the first to hold such a position in an American university.

A third course was added in 1873–74; *Fugue (in two, three, and four voices; Double Fugue, &c.).—Instrumentation.*[37] Enrollment consisted of two students, both seniors, who had completed the earlier two courses "with distinction, and who appear to have exceptional aptitude for such studies." (Doubtless one of these students was Arthur Foote, who graduated in 1874 and remained another year to earn the first A. M. ever awarded in music.) Dwight mentions the high quality of the two- and three-part fugues and the four-part Pedal Fugues completed in this class, as well as the skills shown in orchestration. However, the lack of facilities for performing student orchestrations was so frustrating that Paine decided to eliminate instrumentation from the course in future offerings.

The second course, *Imitative Counterpoint.—Canon.—Choral Figuration.—Simple Forms of Free Composition: Song, March, Dance, Prelude, &c.—Thematic Treatment*, attracted three pupils in 1873–74, all of whom had completed the first course. Much time was spent in analysis of Mozart and Beethoven sonatas. Original composition included rondos and other forms as well as two-part inventions in the style of Bach, with which Dwight was "well impressed." The beginning class of five students—*Harmony.—Chorals in four-part Harmony*—gained some understanding of "the principles of harmony, modulation, suspension, organ-point, &c., &c., and more or less readiness in filling out the harmony of figured basses, and in harmonizing chorals. . . ." Dwight felt, however, that further grounding in fundamentals of theory was necessary, and suggested that the study of harmony be increased to two years.

In its 1874 report, the committee for examining the music department voiced similar criticisms, as summarized by Dwight:[38]

> . . . The examiners . . . suggested . . . whether perhaps Mr. Paine was not trying to cover too much ground, considering the limited time the students have for it amid so many other studies, and whether it would not be wiser to give more time to making them more thoroughly grounded in the earlier stages of Harmony, plain Counterpoint, the harmonization of Chorals, &c., rather than attempt to carry them into Instrumentation, when no orchestra or opportunity of trial of their exercises existed in the college. And also whether the teacher's influence need be limited to the inducting of a very few students into the dry theory of Counterpoint; whether he could not do something also toward interesting the mass of undergraduates in music as a matter of taste and refined social culture, accustoming them to the hearing of the best works of the masters. . . .

As a result of these suggestions, for 1874 the topics harmony, chorale harmonization, and "plain counterpoint" were covered in the first two courses, rather than in only the first.[39] The third course was devoted to "special instruction in the higher branches of Imitation, Fugue, &c.," with one senior enrolled; instrumentation was eliminated. A fourth course was introduced, *History of Music*. Twenty had agreed to enroll by August 1874,[40] a greater number than any other music course had attracted, although only six actually took the class. Such a course would appeal to a larger number of students, especially if it included ". . . such practical illustrations as [Paine] may be able to command. . . ." What kind of performances did take place in the class is unknown, but the previous quotation brings to mind the difficulties inherent in teaching a non-technical course in the history of music without chorus, orchestra, or recordings, relying mainly upon the piano for musical examples. Judging from Dwight's description, Paine's lecture was rather unattractive by modern standards:

> . . . The Professor lectures on some period of the history in a familiar conversational way, while the students take notes. The next time, having consulted authorities meanwhile as recommended by the teacher, they are questioned on the points of the last lecture, and take notes on a new instalment of the history. . . .[41]

Some idea of the depth of material covered in Paine's courses may be gained by studying the examination questions submitted to the classes in June 1875.[42] Each test was lengthy, and assumed mastery of extensive skills or subject matter on the students' part. For Harmony, 20 questions required writing at least 15 musical examples (including irregular resolutions of dominant sevenths and four 4-part harmonizations) plus providing rules for 13 problems in harmonic progression or voice leading (such as the correct use of suspensions, appoggiaturas, organ point, and passing notes, the ways of modulating, and the restrictions in use of the $\frac{6}{4}$ chord and of covered fifths and octaves). Counterpoint students were requested to produce six examples, three of them in double counterpoint, as well as giving rules for each species. Students in Imitative Counterpoint and Fugue composed a four-part imitative prelude on *Vom Himmel hoch* and a two-voice fugue, besides answering other questions on the fugue. Students in the History of Music course were required to provide five detailed composer profiles and to write lengthy essays on six historical topics.

Probably most beneficial to the music department's popularity during 1874–75 was the weekly series of "social musical performances" on Thursday evenings, featuring Paine as well as student instrumentalists and singers. Concerts were held throughout the year in the music classroom—

> . . . a small and very uninviting place for it, to be sure, and the poor square piano being not eminently sympathetic or responsive to the best artistic intentions. . . .[43]

Attendance was large and closely attentive, the audience being

> . . . evidently . . . bent on knowing something about the several composers, and the forms and style in which they wrote. . . .

One program at which Dwight was present began with a Handel fugue, a Bach sarabande, and a Mozart "gigue," all played by Paine, who gave historical and critical notes before each piece. The concert continued with the tenor aria, "Dalla sua pace," from Mozart's *Don Giovanni*, sung by Ernest Szemelényi, a student; some Mendelssohn *Songs without words*; piano works and songs of Schubert and Schumann; and a Beethoven sonata. Such a change in department offerings had an immediate effect on student interest, for tentative enrollment in music electives for 1875–76 was double the amount registered in 1874–75. (Enrollment figures were included in each annual catalog.)

The cumulative reward of Paine's talent and industry, notwithstanding the seemingly overwhelming odds against him and his chosen discipline as a legitimate part of America's most prestigious academy, was the proposal during the summer of 1875 by the President and Fellows to establish a Professorship of Music; this action was approved by the Board of Overseers on 14 July.[44] Accordingly, on 30 August 1875 the President and Fellows of Harvard College

> Voted to proceed to the election of a Professor of Music
> Whereupon ballots being given in it appeared that John Knowles Paine, A.M. was elected.[45]

But still, such an election did not satisfy the doubts of all observers; a *Harper's* skeptic stated:

> The attempt to establish a chair of music in connection with Harvard University is not yet *un fait accompli*; there is no fund, no endowment.[46]

When the result of the August meeting was communicated to the Board of Overseers, it referred the question to a committee on 4 October and finally approved the election on 13 October.[47]

With his new rank, Professor Paine held a mandate to broaden the Harvard educational experience in music as far as resources would allow. As Dwight observed,

> . . . this musical professorship will be what he will make it; he has to create it as the sculptor moulds the clay; indeed he has been creating it these fourteen years, by humble means and processes, which it is to be hoped will now blossom to the light and bear good fruit.[48]

The 36-year-old musician from Maine had finally arrived.

6

Compositions: 1873–1880

During the years in which Paine established the music elective system at Harvard and attained the rank of full professor, at the same time serving on the faculties of the New England Conservatory of Music and Boston University, he also managed to continue his efforts at composition, and completed a number of works. The first major work was the oratorio *St. Peter*. By September 1870 he was already "hard at work,"[1] and apparently had completed it before February 1872, when he informed *Folio's* editor that he "has not published his oratorio of 'St. Peter,' but hopes to do so, soon." *Folio* added then that the work "is highly spoken of"[2]— suggesting that it may already have circulated among Boston musicians, at least to some extent. *St. Peter* received its first performance—in excerpt—at a New England Conservatory concert in Wesleyan Hall on 2 April 1872. Paine accompanied Mrs. C. A. Barry in the Recitative, "And lo! Judas came," and Air, "The Lord is Faithful and Righteous."[3] An unnamed reviewer praised the performance and the work:

> . . . But the most interesting number to the crowded audience was the selection from Mr. Paine's unpublished Oratorio. Of course an orchestra was needed for the full effect; but the composer himself, presiding at the piano, could indicate quite well his own intentions; and the Recitative, telling how Christ was seized, was of a noble thrilling character, with a stormy and appropriate accompaniment. The Air which followed, with violoncello obligato *[sic]*, was ever beautiful and tender, chaste in style and neither common nor affected.[4]

A far more public exposure of *St. Peter* occurred at the mammoth World's Peace Jubilee organized by Patrick Gilmore and held in Boston in June–July 1872. The monster chorus of 20,000 voices, combined with half as many instrumentalists, was part of an event unique in history. Johann Strauss, one of the celebrities imported to give the event an international flavor, communicated his impressions to an associate in Vienna:

> . . . The giant Coliseum, elegantly constructed and perfect in acoustic arrangements, has an auditorium capable of seating over 50,000 persons. Besides this, the

musicians number some 1500 instrumentalists and nearly 20,000 singers. A monster organ, blown by steam-power, noble in tone and overwhelming in its effect, is reared at the back of the grand platform. When the European idea of the standard of music in America is considered, the realization of so successful an undertaking is simply wonderful. It was only made possible by perfect organization and the willingness of everybody to make personal sacrifices, and labor unceasingly for the general good. Thus it is that the reputed fable has become a present truth.

When I consider the grand effects of the fresh voices of the chorus, the splendid orchestra, and the mighty organ, I am forced to confess that the Jubilee is a superbly impressive enterprise. And this noble impressiveness results not only from the large masses of performers, but also from the talent and admirable precision with which all the music is executed.

From all portions of America the people flock to join in the festivities, and every day witnesses assemblages of upwards of 50,000 persons. . . .[5]

Such a situation provided a poor setting for the public introduction of *St. Peter*, however. The singers doubtless must have been familiar with the music, for Ditson had published a collection of the numbers to be sung at the festival in advance of the event. Included were two works by Paine, a Choral *[sic]*, "How lovely shines the Morning Star," and a Chorus, "This is the witness of God," both "From the Oratorio of 'St. Peter,' soon to be published."[6] Both were performed on the opening day, 17 June 1872, and Paine conducted the chorus, organ, and orchestra.[7] Unfortunately for Paine, his rather cerebral music followed immediately after Verdi's *Anvil Chorus*, in which "100 anvils [were] played upon by 100 selected members of the Boston Fire Department."[8] Few works would have had a chance of being heard effectively after such a spectacular ". . . inauguration of the golden age of universal peace by the anvil chorus . . . ," and Paine's music suffered. A Boston *Post* reviewer wrote that the chorus,

> . . . although . . . not a badly constructed work, is entirely unfitted for an occasion of this kind, and fell flat on the audience. . . .

Dwight, who had been vocally hostile toward the entire festival concept, cried that Paine's chorus, "a scholarly and clever work," was "sacrificed. . . ." He complained in general that

> . . . it was but a left-handed hospitality that was extended to the classical selections; they went through with the form of introduction and were soon quietly bowed out. . . .

St. Peter was to wait until June 1873 to be performed in an appropriate setting, when it received its premiere in Portland. Paine had worked carefully, and had modeled it after the Bach passions and Mendelssohn oratorios. The text was chosen from scripture, and was divided into two parts, of two scenes each:

> *Part I.* The Divine Call. The Denial and Repentance.
> *Part II.* The Ascension. Pentecost.

Following Bach's example, Paine included several traditional German chorales, but supplied an explanation of this practice to ward off accusations of plagiarism.

> The melodies of the three Chorals contained in "St. Peter," have been selected from the Lutheran Choral Book, and arranged with original harmony and orchestration by the composer of the present work. This is in accordance with the custom among foreign composers of introducing into their sacred compositions the old, popular choral melodies, which are the peculiar offspring of a religious age. (For example, the melody of "Sleepers awake," in "St. Paul," was composed by Praetorious, 1604, being simply arranged and harmonized by Mendelssohn. This custom is further exemplified in "St. Paul," and in the Passions Music and Cantatas of Sebastian Bach.) It is deemed necessary to make this statement, in order to prevent any misapprehension that otherwise might arise as to the origin of these three melodies.[9]

In composing the solo arias, Paine had apparently learned a lesson from the criticisms of his *Mass* regarding undue difficulty and impracticality in the vocal lines.[10] Now, reportedly, he frequently consulted a prominent voice teacher, John O'Neill of the New England Conservatory faculty, as questions would arise about vocal passages.[11] Paine, whose relationship with John Fiske by now had matured into a permanent bond, of course had shared his creation all along with his friend. Fiske wrote after the Portland performance:

> . . . I shall always be glad to reflect upon the fact that I have been present at the very birth of the thing; hearing Paine explain it on the piano for two years past, going to the rehearsal, helping him correct the ill-written orchestral parts, and seeing the first presentation of it in his native town on June 3d. . . .[12]

The vocal score of *St. Peter* was released by Oliver Ditson early in 1873. An announcement of new Ditson publications in the 8 February issue of *Dwight's Journal of Music* included both commendation and qualification:

> We may well be proud of a full-grown Oratorio, the work of an American, and having a good promise of taking its place among works of "the masters." Do not undertake it with the idea that it is an easy Cantata. The composer did not mean easy music. He meant classical and good music, which will cause and repay study.[13]

Music critics gave *St. Peter* wide notice, for it was immediately viewed as a milestone in American music. A writer for the *New York World* published in a 31 March article a lengthy description of the work, and, though reserving final judgment until after hearing it, made the following observations:[14]

> . . . It will appear that, so far as mingled lyric and dramatic treatment of the subject is concerned, the oratorio of "St. Peter" is constructed upon sound principles of art. . . . We are safe in saying . . . that if the composer wields the resources of modern instrumentation as readily, or nearly as readily, as he handles the other tools of his art, a brilliant future may be predicted for this work. The melodies . . . flow along with an easy spontaneity; they are of the kind that are pleasant in the singing and that haunt the memory afterward. Of the intricacies of counterpoint Mr. Paine has acquired a mastery that one would gladly see more often emulated by modern composers. . . .

Other criticisms also appeared during the months preceding the Portland performance, taking on the character of a first-rate artistic controversy between Boston and non-Boston critics, which seems to testify to Paine's national importance. W. S. B. Mathews, without having heard the work in actual performance, excited controversy with his 13 February 1873 *Nation* article.[15] The author must not have been impressed with Paine's wordsetting, mastery of counterpoint, or, for that matter, with the fact that Paine was in the avant-garde of the back to Bach movement in the United States. His remark that ". . . one must be very much in love with Bach, and very little influenced by the modern taste for lyric forms, not to find a certain dryness in 'St. Peter . . .' "[16] demonstrates Mathews' problem in understanding what Paine was up to. The critic's pleas for more melodic interest in oratorios also misses the essential point of Paine's conscious attempt to model his work upon Baroque religious music drama:

> . . . The lyric moment in an oratorio is at once the moment of greatest passion to the singer and most complete repose to the listener . . . because . . . the conviction that the singer has at last quit "fooling around" in recitative and settled down to a steady pull at singing, is especially reassuring to the average listener.

Mathews judged Paine's libretto to be "the real false step in the book." He stressed the need in a text for dramatic interest and sentiment, and moments of great passion. Use of the chorus should be justified by a heightened emotional state, according to the reviewer; it should not express a text that would be equally effective when sung by a soloist. Mathews also stressed need for contrast between tender or poetic (aria) and dramatic (recitative), soft and loud, conflict (solos) and unity (chorus). In all these areas he found the libretto to be wanting. He lamented that the text did not supply ". . . at least one genuine musical chorus in each part." Mathews also did not find ". . . enough attention to the tender and simply *musical* for the best impression upon the public." In general, he felt it likely that the work

> . . . would not be entirely available for public performance. But with judicious omissions we see no reason why it may not prove of permanent value.

This criticism in New York's *Nation* prompted an acerbic rebuttal in Boston's *Atlantic Monthly*, doubtless by music editor William Foster Apthorp (1848–1913), who had studied with Paine at Harvard in 1863–67. Apthorp deplored the situation that

> . . . so much of very doubtful value has been written about [St. Peter] by musicians and would-be musicians, who, although differing somewhat from one another in their expressions of opinion, all agree in claiming to know all about the oratorio itself, and to have, by some means or other, succeeded in dropping salt on the tails of all its musical and dramatic subtleties.[17]

He attacked Mathews' criticism of the dramatic worth of Paine's libretto, and quoted numerous texts from *St. Peter* that were indeed rich in dramatic or emotional possibilities. Apthorp also focused on a statement of Mathews—"The old oratorio [e.g., of Bach or Handel] was too devotional, too monotonous in its emotional range, to serve as an amusement"—and exclaimed,

> But who ever thought of an oratorio in the light of an *amusement*? Let it be said to Mr. Paine's honor, that, at all events, he has not tried to be amusing in his work, to make his oratorio something to be listened to *entre le cafe et le cigare*!

Apthorp criticized Mendelssohn for the "purely sensuous development of a sensuously beautiful melody" in such movements as "He watching over Israel," "Blessed are the men that fear Him," and the close of the Whirlwind Chorus in *Elijah*; these numbers supposedly contain nothing of the "distinctly *religious* element." Mendelssohn's "*Lied ohne Worte* element," "nothing but charming" in his lighter works, "has only served to weaken and impoverish his great religious works." Moreover, "the sensuous character of [Mendelssohn's] melodies," according to Apthorp, "seems rather of the indolent, sentimental, day-dreamer sort than the result of an over-passionate nature."

> We can only congratulate Mr. Paine upon having made a manly stand against this tendency to purely sensuous melody, which is one of the greatest blemishes in the prevailing religious school of music of our day. . . . Throughout the whole of Mr. Paine's St. Peter the music is persistently of a religious character, never inclining to sentimentality. . . .

And Apthorp demolishes Mathews' philistine suggestion that the serious composer should cater to the taste of the average listener:

> An artist does not work for years, putting his whole heart, soul, and being into his work, merely to furnish people with an aesthetico-intellectual anodyne,—to give them music which they can passively enjoy without the exertion of thinking.

Plans to perform *St. Peter* were under way more than a year before the Portland concert took place. At a 4 March 1872 rehearsal, the Haydn Association in Portland

> Voted, To subscribe for One Hundred and Fifty copies of John K. Paine's "Oratorio of St. Peter."[18]

Two weeks later, at an 18 March rehearsal,

> A letter was rec'd and read from John K. Paine, in relation to his new Oratorio, "St. Peter."

Advance subscriptions were a common factor in the publication of new large-scale works, for the financial risk to the publisher was otherwise too great. Perhaps a subscription notice elicited the references to *St. Peter* in the February 1872 *Folio* referred to above. Copies of the newly published vocal scores appear to have been delivered to the Portland society early in December 1872, for at its 13 December rehearsal the Association

> Voted. To examine editions of Paine's "St. Peter."[19]

Weekly rehearsals on the new work began on Monday, 6 January 1873. The secretary elaborated:

> [These rehearsals] were spent on rehearsing a new Oratorio, "St Peter," by J. K. Paine, formerly a "Portland boy," and it seems but just, that Portland should be the first to give it a public performance.[20]

Hermann Kotzschmar, Paine's former mentor, was the director of the society, and carried out

> the long, arduous and patient work of drilling and inspiring the Chorus—a work which required pluck as well as ability.[21]

On 24 March, the members voted unanimously to perform *St. Peter* in public, and the Government of the society voted to engage the Germania Orchestra of Boston for the occasion.[22] On 31 March the Government scheduled the date of the performance and set ticket prices—50 and 75 cents. Paine's influence was soon felt, first by letters read on 4 April, and later in person as he conducted rehearsals on 12, 19, and 26 May.[23] The performance took place on 3 June; a description may be read in Fiske's 5 June letter to his mother.

> I went down to Portland by Monday's steamer "Forest City." Listened all day Tuesday to the rehearsal of John K. Paine's Oratorio "St. Peter", and was present at the grand performance Tuesday evening under Paine's baton. The orchestra—our Boston orchestra—was not quite familiar enough with the work. There was no organ. And the Portland chorus of 150 voices was not powerful enough to give full weight to the grand choruses, which need a choir of 400 voices at least. But the chorus-singing was finer than that of the Handel and Haydn. All things considered, it was a grand success. The oratorio is certainly a very great work—probably the greatest work in vocal music since the Elijah; and it was pleasant to see Paine crowned with glory in his native town, where everybody calls him John. Portland is swelling to the bursting point with excitement over this affair. There were nearly 3000 people present—rather a big audience for a small town.[24]

Fiske wrote a lengthy review of the performance for the August 1873 *Atlantic Monthly*.[25] Again he complimented the chorus on its artistry and discipline, but lamented the fact that the small group of singers could not hold its own in the massive climaxes, resulting in severe imbalances with the orchestra. Although Paine's instrumentation was judged "excellent," these instrumental parts were

> . . . rather clumsily rendered by the orchestra, whose doings constituted the least enjoyable part of the performance. There was too much blare of brass, whine of hautboy, and scraping of strings. . . .

The ages-old problems, inadequate rehearsal time and inaccurately copied orchestral parts, were the chief culprits here.

> For a moment, at the beginning of the orchestral lament, there was risk of disaster, the wind instruments failing to come in at the right time, when Mr. Paine, with fortunate presence of mind, stopped the players, and the movement was begun over again,—the whole occurring so quickly and quietly as hardly to attract attention.

Soprano soloist for the concert was a Portlander, a Mrs. H. N. Weatherbee. The other three soloists were active in Boston—Adelaide Phillipps, alto, George Osgood, tenor (both artists of national stature), and J. F. Rudolphsen, bass, who sang the role of Peter. Mrs. Weatherbee apparently was not as seasoned a professional as were the Bostonians:

> [She] showed thorough culture and true artistic feeling; but, urged by too generous an enthusiasm, and trusting in a very powerful and flexible voice, she too frequently took part in the chorus, so that, toward the last, she showed signs of overexertion.

For the most part, the solo parts were "admirably done." The audience was especially pleased with Rudolphsen's "fine bass voice."[26]

Paine himself was well satisfied with the performance, as he related to Kotzschmar in a 7 June 1873 letter:[27]

> . . . I was delighted with the way the Choruses were sung; there was not one that was not well rendered. The orchestra and soloists required more acquaintance with the composition to do it full justice. These parts will come out better and make a more brilliant effect under more favorable circumstances. As a whole, however, the concert was a noble success and reflects great honor upon Portland. . . .

He also wrote of future plans for the work, and entered into a comparison of Kotzschmar's group with those in Boston:

> . . . The newspapers all give favorable notices of the event and there seems to be a universal wish to hear the oratorio in Boston. Zerrahn says he shall use his influence to have the H[andel] & H[aydn] Soc. bring it out at their festival next spring. The only advantage the music could have under their treatment would be the massive effect of choruses like "Awake thou that sleepest," "The 3rd day he rose again," and "Great & Marvellous." So far as musical expression, clearness of articulation, promptness, etc. are concerned the Portland Chorus stand far above other American choruses. I heard that Zerrahn and others think that I make use of too many dynamic marks in the choruses (such as pp<>mf>etc.) I am of the opinion that there is no reason why any choral music should be exempt from the law of expression. If a chorus can be taught to sing with expression then the composer should aim to make his music expressive, and one has only to examine "Awake thou that sleepest" and "Great and Marvellous" to see how grand and effective the changes from soft to loud are made. This criticism I hold to be a real compliment, proving that in this respect the oratorio marks a progress in chorus music. For my part I am tired of the long continued shouting which marks the performance of oratorios in Boston. Music without expression degenerates into mere noise. . . .

Common to most written reports of the Portland performance of *St. Peter* was the hope that the oratorio would soon receive a Boston performance. The Handel and Haydn Society was the best qualified, of course, and plans were soon under way to prepare such a performance. At its summer 1873 meetings the Society's board of government made plans for the May 1874 Triennial Festival. Theodore Thomas' orchestra would be engaged, and works to be prepared and presented would include, among others, the *St. Matthew Passion* of Bach, Mendelssohn's cantata *The Sons of Art*, Dudley Buck's *Forty-sixth Psalm*, and Paine's *St. Peter*.[28] At its first rehearsal on 5 October 1873 the Society began work on *St. Peter*,[29] which reportedly required nearly as much rehearsal time as the entire remainder of the festival. According to Dwight,

> . . . it was close, serious, laborious study; not a little up-hill work in it,—more work than recreation. Indeed it was a common complaint among the singers that, in many of the choruses, the music did not help them, did not inspire them, take them up and carry them along with it, by that sort of charm which made the difficulties of Bach, for instance, or of Mendelssohn or Handel, or even the Ninth Symphony, melt away

before them to their own surprise; here they had but to delve away still wondering whether it was grateful soil that they were turning up. . . .[30]

Dwight himself found much to question in the new oratorio:

> . . . We could not feel a unity or positive individuality of style. We seemed now among traditions of Bach and Handel, now with Mendelssohn, and quite as often felt the chill of "new school" and "the future. . . ." We could not feel at home in its strange, restless and elaborate accompaniment . . .; nor in such frequent, sometimes abrupt changes of the key; nor in so many figures; nor, generally, in a certain nervous restlessness that seemed to pervade the work. We missed that beautiful repose which is characteristic of great art. . . .

These judgments he had made prior to the concert, based primarily on his study of the vocal score and attendance at rehearsals of the society. Many of his doubts were dispelled by the full performance, and he gave it a cautious endorsement. However, Dwight continued to worry that Paine had been influenced by the extravagances of Wagner, Berlioz, Liszt, and the "new music:"

> . . . We have still our doubts about the chief instrumental pieces, namely: the gloomy Introduction, with its strange modulation from B flat minor into the C major of the opening chorus: "The time is fulfilled," and the "Lament" of Peter after the Denial, both of which still seemed to us overstrained and vague, as if they had caught the new disease, the restlessness that leadeth nowhere, of the music of our day; and so too, in a great part of the accompaniment, even when the voice sings peace, an almost feverish excitement is still kept up in the orchestra. . . .

According to Fiske's August 1873 report in *Atlantic*, Paine had striven, in composing *St. Peter*, to avoid repeating clichés that he viewed as overused in commonplace religious music. The traditional authentic cadence preceded by a six-four tonic triad,

> . . . now become so hackneyed from its perpetual and wearisome repetition in pop-ular church music, seems to be especially disliked by Mr. Paine, as it occurs but once or twice in the course of the work.

Paine obscured the "ordinary effect" of the six-four in "He that over-cometh" with unconventional partwriting in the divided sopranos. More typical of his authentic cadences was the use of a tonic pedal or of a dominant pedal culminating in a major ninth. Several choruses, instead, evaded the situation by use of plagal or phrygian cadences. Fiske observed that these cadential devices ". . . as preferred by Mr. Paine have a certain sort of superiority by reason of the very incompleteness with which they express finality. . . ." Of "great value" expecially in sacred music is the phrygian cadence, which ". . . leaves the mind occupied with the feeling

Illustration 3 and 4. John Knowles Paine letter to Hermann Kotzschmar, Cambridge, 7 June 1873 (in Portland Public Library).

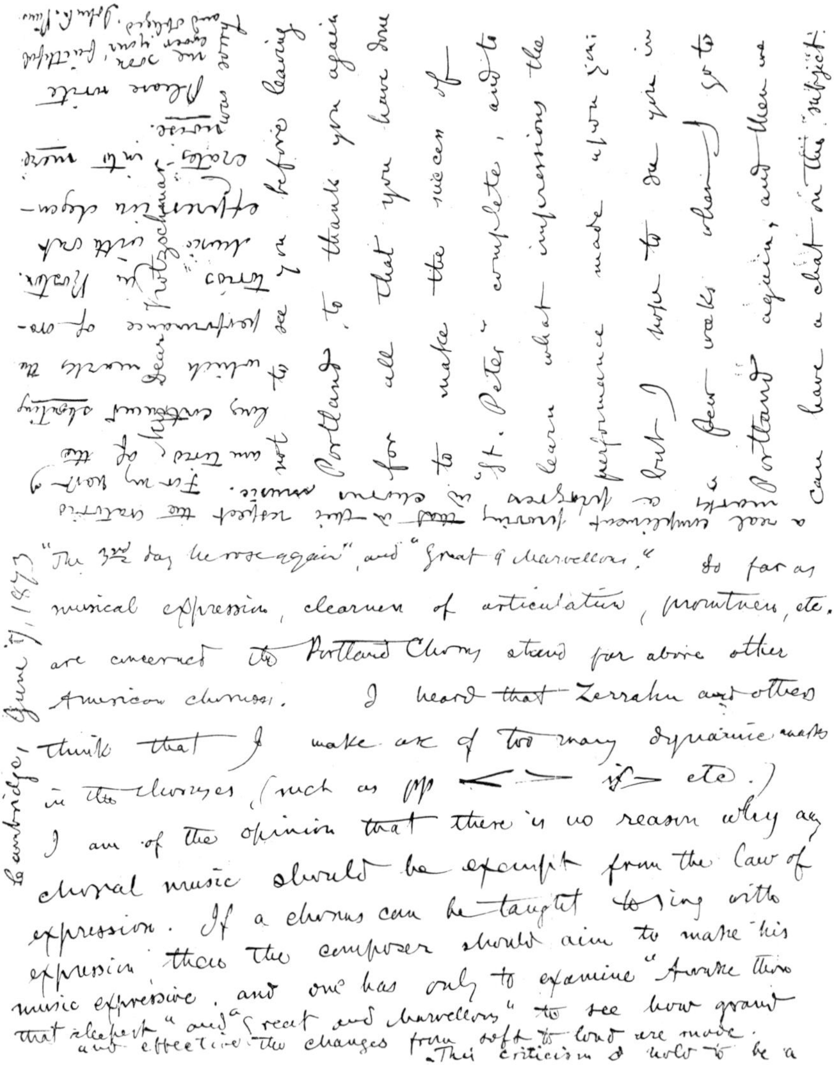

"The 3rd day he rose again", and "Great & Marvellous." So far as musical expression, clearness of articulation, promptness, etc. are concerned the Portland Chorus stand far above other American choruses. I heard that Zerrahn and others think that I make use of too many dynamic marks in the choruses (such as pp $<$ $>$ sf etc.) I am of the opinion that there is no reason why any choral music should be exempt from the law of expression. If a chorus can be taught to sing with expression then the composer should aim to make his music expressive, and one has only to examine "Awake thou that sleepest" and "Great and Marvellous" to see how grand and effective the changes from soft to loud are made. This criticism I hold to be a

Illustration 4.

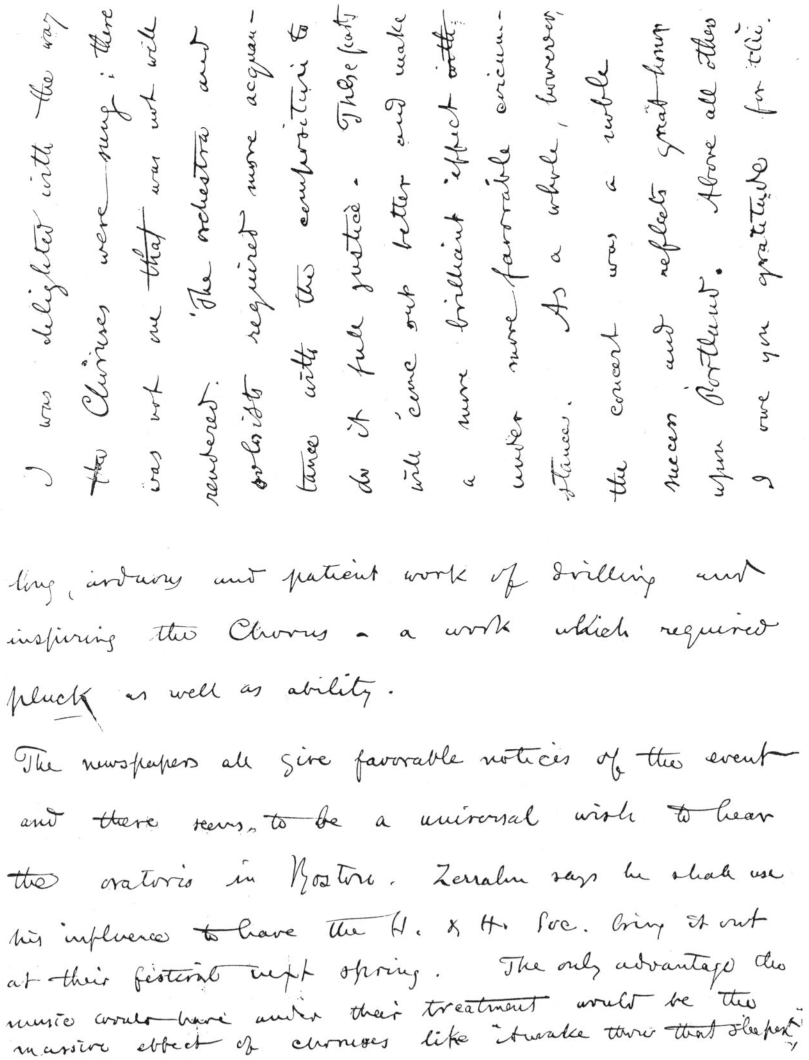

I was delighted with the way the Chorus were sung; there was not one that was not well rendered. The orchestra and soloists required more acquaintance with the composition to do it full justice. The [facts] will come out better and make a more brilliant effect with a more favorable circumstances. As a whole, however, the concert was a notable success and reflects great honor upon Portland. Above all others I owe you gratitude for the

long, arduous and patient work of drilling and inspiring the Chorus — a work which required pluck as well as ability.

The newspapers all give favorable notices of the event and there seems to be a universal wish to hear the oratorio in Boston. Zerrahn says he shall use his influence to have the H. & H. Soc. bring it out at their festival next spring. The only advantage the music would have under their treatment would be the massive effect of choruses like "Awake thou that sleepest,"

of a boundless region beyond, into which one would fain pene-
trate. . . .'' Fiske reported that these subtleties were unconvincing to
some hearers; for them, ''. . . Mr. Paine's cadences have seemed unsatisfactory, their ears have missed the positive categorical assertion of finality which the $^6_4$ cadence alone can give.'' A *Globe* writer concurred
with this basic observation, commenting that *St. Peter* ''has not the marks
of what may perhaps be termed popularity in it . . . ,'' and ''has not the
elements in it which make it a thing for the heart to feel.''[31]

The Third Triennial Festival, at which *St. Peter* was performed,
lasted for six days, 5–10 May 1874. Major choral concerts were presented
each evening, with additional concerts and recitals programmed for the
afternoons. A repeat of *Elijah* the evening of 11 May extended the festival
an extra day, and the culminating effect was an oversaturation of musical
events resulting in waning enthusiasm and uneven attendance on the part
of the public, as well as a loss of $4,000 in ticket sales.[32] Paine's oratorio,
as a new, unknown work, suffered from this over-programming, for it was
presented near the end of the festival, on Saturday evening, 9 May. Moreover, it was given the evening after the *St. Matthew Passion* and the night
before the *Messiah*, and was certainly the one that an average concert
goer would have chosen to miss instead of these two familiar masterpieces. As a consequence, according to Dwight, ''. . . the audience was
not so large as we had hoped to see. . . .'' Even Paine's Harvard community let him down, according to a *Saturday Evening Gazette* story.[33]
A large group of students, after planning to turn out ''in full force to do
honor'' to Paine's work, decided at the last minute to go instead to see
the ''Peerless Queen of Burlesque,'' Lydia Thompson, who was appearing at the Howard Athenaeum with her ''Mammoth Burlesque Company.''

A much larger, longer-trained chorus, a more accomplished orchestra, and the large organ at Music Hall combined to give *St. Peter* a far
more adequate performance than it had received in Portland. The chorus
singing was ''excellent,'' according to Dwight, and the *Globe* stated that
the work was ''more than fairly given.'' Again, however, the performance
suffered from inadequate rehearsal with the orchestra; solo passages for
soprano and alto especially were marred by this defect. Soloists for the
concert were Mrs. Julia Houston West, soprano, Adelaide Phillipps, alto,
Nelson Varley, tenor, and J. F. Rudolphsen, bass; Phillipps and Rudolphsen had also sung at the Portland premiere. The performance in the
main seems to have been fairly well received. Dwight reported that

> the chorus singers and the audience, when they sang in it and heard it as a whole,
> liked it a good deal better than they ever thought they should. . . .

Apthorp, reviewing the festival for *Atlantic*,[34] found the Society's performances to be a "positive triumph." He judged Paine to be "most at home when he is most original . . . ," and observed:

> One cannot look through [Paine's] compositions that are spread over the last five or six years, without being struck by the ever increasing, at times really startling, originality of his aesthetic conceptions.

Apthorp was qualified to make such a general evaluation, for he doubtless had gained acquaintance with many of Paine's works during his studies with the composer at Harvard. Minor works of Paine did not escape the writer's notice. For the October 1872 *Atlantic*[35] Apthorp wrote a review of Paine's *Vier Character-Stücke für Piano-Forte*, op. 11, performed by the composer in an 1868 New England Conservatory faculty recital and recently published by Forbert of Leipzig, and gave them "almost unqualified praise." The reviewer found the four pieces "most free in form and full of genuine, unforced, at times almost startling originality." Although they did not "lie quite so easily under the fingers as might be desired, . . . where there is so much genuine merit, such a consideration becomes of secondary importance."

And Apthorp continued to give favorable notice to Paine's works, at first in *Atlantic*, later in the *Transcript*. Fiske, too, who was a far closer personal friend of Paine, continued to champion his compositions. The earlier *St. Peter* review that he wrote following the Portland performance was the first of many such occasions. Besides understandably feeling grateful for Fiske's public gestures of praise, Paine sincerely found in him and his family sympathy and congeniality. Often the childless composer would accompany the proud father as he wheeled the children, Maud and Harold, through the streets of North Cambridge and Arlington in their specially designed double perambulator.[36] Musical evenings were frequent in the Fiske home, and Paine and Osgood were constant participants. At times these evenings were broadened into public occasions. In a letter, Fiske described "the sixth and last Parlour Concert" on 18 December 1874 as including an audience of 100 people. Paine's Piano Trio, op. 22, dedicated to Fiske, was

> "brought out" being here played for the first time. Altogether I call it a MAGNIFICENT evening, long to be remembered.[37]

But, apart from these informal concerts, Paine's public appearances as a performer became fairly rare. He seems to have abandoned an active organ recital schedule; a 25 May 1870 recital, a 17 May 1871 concert, and another on 9 March 1872—all at Music Hall and sponsored by the New

England Conservatory[38]—would appear to have been his only solo appearances. Occasionally he would perform during orchestral programs, such as playing the organ part for Liszt's *Die Hunnenschlacht* at a December 1872 Theodore Thomas orchestra concert,[39] or performing the Bach *Prelude and Fugue in A Minor* for a 19 March 1874 Harvard Symphony Concert.[40] And apparently, according to reviews, he had not lost his performing skill. This latter Bach performance was praised, along with the wry observation that ". . . few would have been aware, had it not been announced beforehand, that the organ was not in tune."[41] Occasionally there were other programs in which Paine took part; for example, he performed in Beethoven's piano trio, op. 70, no. 1, during a soirée featuring violinist Christian Suckow on 15 March 1872.[42] Duties at Harvard also included occasional public appearances as performer or conductor. Perhaps among the more notable occasions was the 23 June 1874 dedication of Memorial Hall (consisting of Alumni Hall and Sanders Theatre[43]), a building commemorating Harvard students killed in the Civil War. Paine was in charge of music for the exercises, and led "a select chorus from the Handel and Haydn Society"[44] in Beethoven's "Hallelujah" from *Mount of Olives*, "Happy and blest are they" from Mendelssohn's *St. Paul*, and "The Heavens are telling" from the Haydn *Creation*.[45]

Several writers, in reviewing Paine's first successful major work, *St. Peter*, lamented that he had not written a symphony; instead, he had chosen a genre in which he would be strictly bound by the requirement of setting a libretto, thereby limiting his compositional freedom. Paine obviously was encouraged and guided by these observations, for the subsequent five major works from his pen were all for the orchestral medium. These were the *Symphony in C Minor*, op. 23, and the *Overture to "As You Like It,"* both receiving their premieres in 1876, the *Symphonic Poem: "The Tempest,"* op. 31, first performed in 1877, the *Duo Concertante in A for Violin, Violoncello, and Orchestra*, op. 33, introduced in 1878, and the *Symphony No. 2 in A "Im Frühling,"* op. 34, completed in 1879. The first of these, the C-minor symphony, was probably begun—at least in initial sketches—soon after the completion of *St. Peter* early in 1872, and served as a valuable pedagogical example for Paine's orchestration classes at the New England Conservatory. Its exact completion date remains obscure, but Paine must have finished work on the manuscript by early 1875 in order for it to have been considered for inclusion in the Boston and New York 1875–76 concert season. The latest possible date for completion may perhaps be calculated more accurately after noting an observation in a review of the New York premiere on 5 February 1876. Theodore Thomas, who chose the work and introduced it both in Boston and New York, is the subject of the following comment:

> . . . Charged with obstinately refusing to accept any compositions from American writers, he replies by producing one that he had accepted eight months before the charge was made. Having presented to him a work which he finds, on careful examination, to be worthy of a place in his repertoire, he gives the public a chance of judging and enjoying at the earliest convenient moment. . . .[46]

If one assumes that the public had not been informed of Thomas' plans to prepare and conduct Paine's symphony until the advertisements of the concerts appeared in January 1876—thereby allowing that the above-mentioned charges could still have been made in January—the latest that Paine could have finished the score and had it accepted by Thomas would have been May 1875. Doubtless this transaction took place at a still earlier date. Quotation of the interval "eight months" in the above excerpt suggests that the information was supplied to the reviewer from Thomas himself, thereby enhancing its reliability.

Paine's symphony received its premiere at the fourth Theodore Thomas symphony concert of the season at Music Hall, Boston, on 26 January 1876. Ten days later—on 5 February—the Thomas orchestra performed it in New York at a Saturday matinée at Steinway Hall. On 19 February the symphony was repeated "by request" in Boston at a Thomas Saturday matinée concert at Music Hall. And a year later, on 27 February 1877, the work was included on a Thomas orchestra program at Sanders Theatre, Cambridge. Interest in Paine's work was exceptionally high, and the first three performances produced a large number of reviews, published in a variety of newspapers and journals. Public reception of the performed symphony was favorable, and often very enthusiastic. Dwight described the excitement of the "entire vast audience" at the first Boston performance:

> . . . each several movement being followed by applause lasting several minutes, and most spontaneous and sincere, culminating at the end of the work in a storm of *bravos* and a general call for "Paine," who was led upon the stage by Mr. Thomas, and modestly, with evident gratification, bowed his thanks to the still applauding multitude of friends.[47]

The concert, which began with Paine's symphony, continued with two more Boston premieres, the Rubinstein fifth Piano Concerto and a "very long" duet from Wagner's *Flying Dutchman*. Two hours had passed before the concluding work, the entire Beethoven *Symphony No. 2*, was even begun. Both Boston performances of the Paine were "good," according to the May 1876 *Atlantic Monthly*, and the February matinée performance was "even masterly."[48] Fiske wrote of the concert in a letter to his mother, mentioning that the symphony was introduced "amid the wildest applause that I ever witnessed at a concert."[49] He supplied more detail in a June 1876 review for *Atlantic*:[50]

> . . . Whatever anxiety or lack of entire faith any one may have felt beforehand must have been removed by the very first phrase, which with its rushing bass and powerful stroke of chords (as if with some resistless hammer of Thor) proclaims at once the technical skill and boldness of design that belong only to masters of symphonic writing. The feelings of the listeners, taken captive at the outset by this vigorous attack, grew more and more excited. . . . The pauses between the movements were made unduly long by the applause in which this excitement sought to vent itself; and at the end there burst forth such a storm of delighted approval as, during many years of concert-going, we had never before witnessed. . . .

A *Boston Daily Advertiser* writer observed:

> The impression produced upon the audience by the work was unmistakably one of pleasure and satisfaction, and the manifestations of delight were so spontaneous and hearty as to prove the feeling to be no mere outgrowth of friendly prejudice.[51]

Demonstrations of audience approval were more reticent at the New York performance. Concert-goers had had to choose between attending the Thomas orchestra program and hearing the famed soprano Theresa Tietjens (1831–77) in *Norma* at the Academy of Music. As a result, "it was by no means a full house, but there was at least a fair array of listeners, who bestowed upon the performance a close and intelligent attention. . . ."[52] ". . . An annoying noise from the heaters in the hall" detracted from the effectiveness of the third movement. This was not Paine's home territory, and his not being in attendance prevented any personal feeling for him or any magnetism on his part from favorably affecting the listeners' judgments. And doubtless the New Yorkers were mildly skeptical of Boston's overwhelming acclaim for the work, for "there seemed to be a good deal of hesitation on the part of the audience in pronouncing an opinion." The "resistless hammer of Thor" which opens the work apparently was not effective, for the first movement was "rather coldly received." Perhaps the performance of this movement was inferior to that in Boston. During the second movement the listeners became more receptive, and "at its conclusion the applause of the audience was warm enough to show that Mr. Thomas had not made a mistake in producing the work." Praise was also bestowed upon the two concluding movements. "Certainly the audienced liked [the third movement] very much, and the orchestra seemed to like it greatly," wrote the *World* reviewer.

Approval was not unanimous, however. After hearing the work, a *New York Times* reviewer did not feel that Paine

> is possessed of particular originality in thought or method; and the impression of the whole effort, yesterday, was that the musician had occupied fifty minutes where half that time would have been sufficient to have had his say.

But for this exception, however, published criticisms were highly complimentary. The May *Atlantic* observed that Paine "has made a long stride in handling the orchestra since he wrote his *St. Peter*." According to the Boston *Saturday Evening Gazette*,

> it was a genuine surprise, even to Mr. Paine's warmest friends, in the fluency of idea, the freedom from dryness, the apparent spontaneous flow of thought, and the graceful flexibility of style, that distinguish it from beginning to end.

Dwight, for one, listened to the work "with pleasure and surprise," observing after the Boston premiere that the composer had used "much greater freedom" than when he wrote *St. Peter*. "Faultless construction" and "noble contrapuntal harmony" were recognized Paine trademarks, according to the *Tribune* writer, who was delightfully surprised by "the easy flow of melody and the poetical taste in the instrumentation, especially in the employment of the wind instruments. . . ." Individual movements singled out as exceptional included the first, *Allegro con brio*, and the third, *Adagio*. For the *Boston Daily Advertiser* reporter, ". . . the close of the first movement is . . . the strongest, as it is certainly the boldest and most dramatic part of the symphony. . . ." Most writers considered the *Adagio* to be the high point, calling it "the gem of the symphony" *[World]*, the "most attractive" *[Gazette]*, or "the best of the whole work . . . , this alone would stamp [Paine] a master of the orchestra" *[Tribune]*. Osgood, Paine's nearby neighbor and good friend, who supplied a technical analysis to the *Boston Transcript*[53] after studying the score, also considered the third movement the "most attractive:"

> It is perfect in its form, and beautifully scored. There is a certain pose about it that satisfies. Its architectural design and detail harmonize. It is a love poem running over with happiness, tender, sweet and of exquisite refinement. The instrumentation of the whole work is masterly, and one is impressed with the wonderful command of the infinite details of composition which Mr. Paine possesses.

Osgood revealed the fact that this movement, "both in composition and scoring, was a feat of astonishing rapidity and in inspiration uninterrupted in its flow from beginning to end." The *Saturday Evening Gazette* described the "lovely theme" of the *Adagio*:

> It flows calmly and sweetly after the manner of those continuous melodies with which Wagner has made us so familiar, and it has much of the rich sensuousness that marks that composer in his more placid moods.

Such a comparison with Wagner is denied by the *Nation* reviewer, who argued against the abandonment of sonata form, and continued:

> Such a work as Mr. Paine's symphony is in itself a protest against the inferences which might be too hastily drawn from the recent prevalence of compositions in the various styles of Raff, Rubinstein, and Liszt. Indirectly, it is a protest against unreserved acquiescence in the methods of composition of which Wagner is the great representative; although, with his close adherence to the classical form, Mr. Paine has drawn upon modern sensuous resources of instrumentation to no less extent than Wagner. . . . Both in melodic development and in orchestration the significance of Mr. Paine's work lies in its attempt to attain originality of musical expression without deserting classical form. . . .[54]

Paine's symphony was one of three works performed at a Theodore Thomas orchestra concert of American music on 26 July 1876 in Philadelphia during the Centennial Exposition. The concert opened with William H. Fry's symphony, *A Day in the Country*, and concluded with Alfred H. Pease's *Piano Concerto No. 1 in E flat*. Reviewer "C.H."[55] approved of selecting Fry and Paine as American composers representative of

> the two eras of American Music—the one when it whistled as it went for "want of thought," the other after the culture of half a generation had set up the American art intellect on something like a level with that of other nations.[56]

"C.H." named Paine "the most scholarly of all American composers." His symphony "is unquestionably the best large orchestral work yet produced by any native composer . . . ," showing ". . . the brain and handiwork of a master." This writer and another *Dwight's Journal* correspondent, "L.B.B.,"[57] strongly urged that Paine be commissioned to write a fitting work for the closing of the Exposition, or, this being impossible, that the symphony be played at the ceremony. This enthusiastic recommendation was engendered—at least partially—by the scandal felt by conservative American musicians over the commissioning of Wagner to write a march for the opening ceremonies on 10 May. Dwight voiced the indignation of many when he complained of the overblown commission fee: "$5000. *[sic]* for one noisy March,—more probably than

Beethoven got for all the Nine Symphonies!" He speculated further:

> . . . there are several musicians in any of our cities, even Americans, who could have
> composed all that was needed in the shape of March for that day.[58]

Two Americans did receive the honor, along with Wagner, to be
commissioned to compose works for the opening ceremony—Paine, who
set a *Centennial Hymn* by John Greenleaf Whittier, and Dudley Buck
(1839–1909), then assistant conductor of the Thomas orchestra in New
York, who wrote a cantata, *The Centennial Meditation of Columbia*, with
words by Sidney Lanier. Texts by American poets were supplied to the
two composers ". . . in order that their works should have a still more
distinctively national character. . . ."[59] Paine's hymn was a far more modest contribution than Buck's cantata, but was called a "success" by a
New York Tribune correspondent who reported the event:

> There was only one thing that the *Centennial Hymn* could be, and that was a simple
> choral melody. Mr. Paine has made a beautiful piece of work, and put into it true
> religious feeling and great elevation and dignity. As it poured forth from the throats
> of the 800 ladies and gentlemen of the chorus, with that superb orchestral accom-
> paniment, I think the whole audience—at least all of it which got near enough to the
> stage to be within the influence of the music at all—felt a stirring of the heart.
> Certainly when it was over the character rather than the amount of the applause,
> accompanied as it was with a little indescribable movement in the crowd, showed
> that the music had hit its mark.[60]

Thomas' orchestra formed the nucleus of the instrumental band, which
numbered about 150. An H. L. Roosevelt pipe organ had been installed
in a transept of the building and spoke through a window just over the
singers' heads. It played along with the orchestra, and was "effectively
used" in Paine's hymn.

All of the music composed for the Exposition was immediately published. Paine's, issued by H. O. Houghton of Boston, was reviewed in
the July 1876 issue of *Atlantic Monthly*[61] as showing

> . . . plainly the master's hand in its calm, reposeful beauty. It is a very perfect piece
> of plain choral writing, and we should place it in the foremost rank among the many
> modern attempts at *original* composition in this style.

The entire hymn, with piano accompaniment, was published in the June
Atlantic.[62] Its attractiveness and timeliness helped place it on a number
of programs. Bostonians first heard the work at a June Boylston Club
concert conducted by Osgood; Paine had provided the arrangement for
male voices.[63] Local Independence Day festivals included the singing of
Paine's hymn in cities such as Groton[64] and Portland.[65] The Worcester

County Musical Association included it at the annual Festival in October.[66] Theodore Thomas conducted all of the centennial music at a Boston concert on 15 November 1876.[67] Perhaps a truer sign of the *Centennial Hymn*'s popularity was its inclusion in a 27 August 1876 popular concert on Boston Common by T. M. Carter's band.[68] This same organization also performed the hymn during several summer concerts in 1880.

Three other works of Paine also received their first performances during 1876. A *Sonata for Piano and Violin in B minor*, op. 24, was played for the first time at George Osgood's 11 May concert at Mechanics Hall. Ernst Perabo, pianist, and J. C. Mullaly, violinist, performed the work, after which

> . . . the delight of the audience culminated in such enthusiasm and repeated plaudits that the composer had to rise in his seat and bow his acknowledgments.[69]

Reviewers seemed favorably impressed. Dwight called it

> . . . a spirited and genial work, and seemed written *con amore*, as well as with much skill and learning and no lack of fresh invention.

The *Advertiser* described the composition as "a very fresh, interesting and agreeable work . . . ," finding the last movement

> . . . exceedingly brilliant throughout, at times excitingly so by reason chiefly of a certain fierce dramatic quality which also characterized [Paine's] symphony. . . .[70]

Perabo repeated the work at his first chamber concert of the season on 27 October at Wesleyan Hall, again assisted by Mullaly. According to Dwight, the critics again praised the work, saying that it improved with a second hearing.[71] At his second concert, on 3 November, Perabo performed a new Paine work, a *Romanza and Scherzo* for piano and cello, op. 30, along with Adolphe Hartdegen, cellist. It was received with "interest" and "delight" by the audience, though judged "less in itself and its pretensions" than the piano-violin sonata.[72] Perabo continued to support Paine at the third concert, on 10 November, where he played the *Four character pieces*, op. 25. The *Advertiser* found them "less interesting on the whole" than the other Paine works included in the concert series.[73]

Paine's second major work to receive its premiere in 1876, his *Overture to Shakespeare's "As You Like It,"* op. 28, in F, was first performed on 21 November by the Theodore Thomas orchestra at the first subscription concert to be held at the new Sanders Theatre at Harvard University. The audience was "both large and critical."[74] As the *Advertiser* reviewer pointed out, Paine wrote primarily a work of absolute music, and was not influenced by "ultra-programmists" such as Berlioz. Instead, the composer "has treated his fine theme suggestively, with real dramatic discrimination, but without any attempt at coarse realism." Dwight was pleased by the work in his review, calling it "rich, varied, musical, consistent and symmetrical, with a more genial flow than anything we have yet had from its accomplished author."[75] Concerning its reception, he added:

> The orchestra . . . played it *con amore*, and the audience received it *con furore*, the composer being compelled to rise in his seat and bow acknowledgment.

Bostonians had their first opportunity to hear *As You Like It* at the first of two concerts for the Old South Church Preservation Fund, given by the Thomas orchestra on 20 February 1877. An announcement in the *Advertiser* assured the reader: "Mr. Paine's overture alone will repay one for going."[76]

Two more Sanders Theatre subscription concerts in the first season included works by Paine. At the third concert on 17 January 1877, Perabo and Hartdegen again performed the *Romanza and Scherzo*, which "improved upon a second hearing"[77] and "deepened the great impression which it had already made."[78] In the same program, Clara Doria (1844–1931), accompanied by Otto Dresel, sang the *Matin Song*, which attracted praise for its "pure simplicity and elevation of sentiment." On 27 February, at the sixth concert, the Thomas orchestra performed the *Symphony in C minor*. The *Romanza and Scherzo* was heard once more at a 24 June 1878 concert at Wellesley College, again performed by Perabo and Hartdegen.[79]

Although Paine seems to have ceased entirely giving public organ recitals by the mid 1870s, he continued to serve as organist for occasional orchestral concerts. For the Bach *Magnificat*, with orchestral score "completed" by Robert Franz,[80] performed on a Thomas program of 1 March 1876, he played the organ part "in the masterly manner which might have been expected of him. . . ."[81] He also assisted at an April Handel and Haydn Society performance of Mendelssohn's *Hymn of Praise* and Rossini's *Stabat Mater* at which Mlle. Tietjens, in her last Boston appearance, was featured as the soprano soloist.[82] Paine's importance in the general musical community may be learned from the report of an 11 March reception for Tietjens, for he gave one of the seven speeches at this elegant occasion sponsored by the Papyrus Club. Following the dinner at the Revere House, the great diva favored the 80 in attendance by singing "Home, Sweet Home."[83]

Teaching duties at Harvard and the New England Conservatory continued to require much of Paine's time, and his reputation continued to grow. He sought to widen his scope of influence, and on 22 March 1876 again he began his series of lectures on the history of music.[84] He also was listed among the lecturers for the New England Normal Musical Institute that summer at East Greenwich, Rhode Island,[85] an outgrowth of the New England Conservatory.

During the summer of 1876 Paine's friendship with John Fiske resulted in a meeting with another person of historical significance. The Fiske family spent much of August in the village of Petersham in north-central Massachusetts. Paine and his wife must have shared this vacation, for Fiske wrote to his mother of 12 August, detailing a recent delightful day with "much music in evening by John K. Paine."[86] About a week later—on 21–23 August—Fiske was graced with a visit from Professor and Mrs. Thomas Huxley, recently arrived from England;[87] Paine was much in evidence in Fiske's report:

> On Monday the 21st I went to Athol to meet [the Huxleys]: we had a jolly drive over to Petersham; they were enchanted at the view and the fragrant pine woods. After dinner music and then yarns in [James Brooks'] office before a cheery open fire of hickory logs. . . . Tuesday morning grand walk with the Huxleys and Paines taking along some of the children, to Tom Howe's farm, returning by Ansel Stowell road and Picnic Grove. . . . In the evening there was much music by Paine, George Osgood—who had just arrived—J[ohn] F[iske] and chorus. . . .[88]

During both evenings there was "free social intercourse" between the guests, the Fiske and Brooks families, and a few invited guests, "including the Paines, Longfellow's daughter Edith, a daughter of Hawthorne, and poet Christopher Cranch."[89] Cranch was a longtime acquaintance of Paine's, and is referred to as "our old friend" in an 1892 letter to Dwight, written when the poet was on his deathbed.[90]

Testimony of yet another of Paine's friendships is found in a December 1877 Fiske letter:

> We have been to a delightful grouse and potato salad supper party at Bro. Paine's. In the evening when the music was going on full tilt, William James called with his dog, and said dog howled and bellowed at the music and had to be banished to a distant room, amid peals of laughter.[91]

If the noted psychologist-philosopher felt free to call with his dog, he must have been a frequent visitor in the Paine house, and he and Paine must also have shared many thoughts and attitudes. Paine's esteem in the eyes of his friends John Fiske and William Dean Howells (editor of *Atlantic*) must have been an important factor in the publication of his *Matin*

Song in the January 1877 issue of *Atlantic Monthly*. An October 1876 announcement predicted in the coming year

> . . . contributions to each number of original music by such composers as J. K. Paine, George L. Osgood, Dudley Buck and Francis Boott, with words by some of the most distinguished Atlantic poets.[92]

The venture apparently was not carried through as first planned, for in an April 1877 note to Howells, in which Paine acknowledged receiving a check and the returned manuscript, he added:

> I regret that your original plan could not be carried out, but fully appreciate the reasons why it was abandoned.[93]

Most important of the performances of Paine works during 1877 was the premiere of his *Symphonic Fantasy—Shakespeare's Tempest, in D minor*, op. 31, "composed expressly" for a 29 March Harvard symphony concert.[94] However, plans had to be changed, as a last-minute item announced:

> It has not been found possible to prepare the orchestral parts for Mr. J. K. Paine's "Tempest" Symphony, but his overture to "As You Like It" will be given. . . .[95]

According to the reviewers, the audience enjoyed this repeated performance of the earlier work, despite roughness, woodwind pitch problems, and evidence of insufficient rehearsal on the part of the Harvard Musical Association.[96] As a result of this delay, the first performance of *The Tempest* took place on 2 November, not in the Boston area, but in New York, at a Theodore Thomas orchestra concert at Steinway Hall.[97] The *Tribune* reported that the composition created a "very favorable" impression, and commented on the "somewhat meagre" scoring, "done, as a rule, excellently, and with careful discrimination."[98]

On 13 November 1877 the Thomas orchestra again performed *The Tempest*—this time on the first subscription concert of the season at Sanders Theatre in Cambridge. A reviewer for the *Courier* was most enthusiastic, ranking it as "the finest thing [Paine] has done yet," with "absolutely masterly" use of the orchestra. In this work the writer found Paine taking a "decisive stand on the side of the most modern symphonic school"—the anti-Wagner school—representing Schumann, Brahms, Raff, Rubinstein, and Saint-Saëns.[99] Another writer, reporting for the *Advertiser*, also complimented the composer on the new work, although qualifying his praise with the following:

> . . . We must say that Mr. Paine has attempted a very great deal, in a very short space, in the work and that he does not, and cannot, yet realize with his music all

> the ideals which Shakespeare's wondrous play creates in verse. In his "As You Like
> It" overture, where less was attempted, the result was, we think, more satisfac-
> tory. . . .[100]

Dwight also felt that Paine's *Tempest* was "by no means so clear and satisfactory" as *As You Like It*, although he "found much in it to admire." The enthusiastic reception the work was awarded by many newspaper critics seems to have surprised Dwight, who was amused by their conflicting identifications of dramatic events supposedly portrayed in the music. He disapproved of their overuse of superlatives in describing the work—especially in the *Courier* article—and admitted, ". . . so far we cannot feel that this music is 'Shakespearian.' " Dwight concluded,

> We cannot help thinking that the composer would have done better to have kept to
> his original design of making an Overture, instead of a Symphonic Fantasie or Poem
> *à la* Liszt or Saint-Saëns. That might have been equally suggestive and Shakespear-
> ian, and more satisfactory as music.[101]

Dwight described *The Tempest* as being "in the form, if form at all it has, of the modern *Symphonische Dichtung*," feeling probably that Paine had betrayed the cause of classicism by employing such an anti-classical, Lisztian genre. This criticism undoubtedly disturbed Paine; certainly it inspired Fiske to write a rebuttal in the form of a lengthy letter to the editor of the *Advertiser*, dated 4 December.[102] Fiske used numerous superlatives in describing *The Tempest*, and declared that it and the earlier *Symphony in C minor*

> . . . can hold their own in a comparison with almost anything that has been achieved
> by old or recent masters.

He defended Paine's choice of genre, and found its merits to consist "as much in the freedom and originality of its general form as in the intrinsic beauty of the musical ideas . . . ," adding that its

> . . . originality is obtained without the slightest disregard of that orderly thematic
> treatment which is the indispensable basis of all good music. . . .

Fiske devoted the rest of his letter to a discussion of forms appropriate to the subject matter, and concluded that the work may be divided into four fairly orthodox movements, organized respectively in prelude form, song form, rondo, and sonata form. In a later response, Dwight protested that he had not criticized Paine's use of form, only that the suggestion that listeners should watch for extramusical suggestions detracted seriously from appreciation of the form. He smiled at Fiske's comparison to works "by old or recent masters," for "these are the pardonable and no

doubt sincere superlatives of friendship. . . ." Dwight likened these ex-
aggerations to a more familiar comparison of works:

> In the same way we hear just now the "Brahms fanatics" placing the new C minor
> Symphony upon a level with Beethoven's and christening it "the tenth Symphony,"
> forgetting what Schubert, Mendelssohn, and Schumann have created in this form.[103]

The Boston music public heard another performance of *The Tempest* at
Music Hall on 8 December 1877, during the fourth Theodore Thomas
concert of the season. Attendance was poor—the hall was "far from
being full." Dwight found "more beauties" in Paine's composition, and
enjoyed it more than at the earlier hearing in Cambridge.

Another of Paine's contributions to the chamber music repertory
received its first performance in 1877—the *Larghetto and Scherzo* for
piano, violin, and cello, op. 30 [doubtless = op. 32]—at a 9 February Perabo Chamber Concert in Wesleyan Hall. A reviewer found the work to
have "remarkable force, vividness, and grace," all characteristic of its
author, and commented in particular on the "great melodic beauty and
a strong rhythmic sweep" of the scherzo.[104] Opus 32 was heard on
11 December 1877 at a subscription concert at Sanders Theatre, performed by Perabo (piano), B. Listemann (violin), and Hartdegen (cello).[105]
Dwight found it "the finest" of Paine's works in this form, and also
singled out the scherzo as "quite original and piquant."[106]

Certain Paine compositions received hearings during 1877 on programs by pianists of note. According to a newspaper announcement, Amy
Fay performed an unnamed "morceau" on a 7 May recital at Lyceum
Hall, Old Cambridge.[107] The following evening she played Paine's *In the
Country*, 10 sketches for the piano, op. 26, "a charming series of delicate
idyls . . ."[108]; the 10 had been published the previous year by George D.
Russell & Co.[109] Miss Fay performed five pieces from the set at a
16 October recital at Union Hall. Dwight judged them "charming" and
"happily contrasted," being played "*con amore*" and "with grace."[110]
Perabo, at a 22 June program at Wellesley College, played two of the
Four Character Pieces, op. 25.[111]

But surely the most impressive event to include performance of any
Paine works for piano was a concert of American compositions given by
pianist Annette Essipoff (1851–1914), a student of Leschetizky, during
her American tour in the spring of 1877. According to H. T. Finck,

> It is related that when Mme. Essipoff wanted to make up a program of American
> compositions, she experienced difficulty in finding the requisite number of pieces
> coming up to the required standard.[112]

Essipoff played her American concert at Steinway Hall, New York, on 5 May 1877, the last of eight concerts,[113] and concluded a series of six at Boston's Union Hall with a similar program on 12 May.[114] Paine was represented by his early *Marcia Funèbre* and by three sketches from *In the Country*. Other American composers included on Essipoff's recitals were New Yorkers S. B. Mills, William Mason, F. Brandeis, R. Hoffman, H. Carter, E. Parsons, and H. Maylath, Bostonians Perabo, Sherwood, and Foote, as well as Gottschalk.[115] At her Boston concert, Essipoff "was in a happy mood, and played with the utmost brilliance and verve, using her most poetic style" upon Paine's sketches and the pieces by Perabo and Mason.[116]

Paine's keyboard compositions were honored by their inclusion in the new five-year curriculum at Wellesley College for 1877–78. His were listed among "Concert pieces by modern writers" for the fourth year of piano study, and he was one of the composers of "Grand Studies, Preludes, Fugues, Toccatas, Fantasias, and Variations" studied by fourth year organists.[117]

Boston singers did not neglect Paine's compositions, and the *Matin Song* was a special favorite. One of its early performances was by Fanny Kellogg, a prominent Boston artist, at a 26 November 1877 program at the Essex Institute in Salem, Massachusetts.[118] Earlier that year Miss Kellogg was the beneficiary of a complimentary concert at the Hotel Preston in Swampscott. Paine, also a guest at the house, was one of those performing.[119]

Harvard duties for Paine during 1876–77 remained much the same as in previous years. He continued to teach the four courses described earlier, *Harmony*, with twelve enrolled, *Counterpoint*, numbering six, *Canon and Fugue.—Free Thematic Music*, which attracted nine.[120] According to the Visitation Committee report, Paine's *Harmony* and *Counterpoint* courses achieved results "more encouraging than ever," although the Richter textbooks were judged "sometimes rather far-fetched and abstruse. . . ." Members of the committee also complained about what they felt as a "too large" emphasis on "matters of antiquarian research rather than of present interest" in the *History of Music* course.

> At least half of the hours given to what was done before Bach and Handel would have been, in their judgment, better spent upon what has been done since.[121]

Paine directed the series of vocal and instrumental concerts given in Sanders Theatre. He also began a series of recitals in Boylston Hall on 26 April 1877;[122] these, according to the committee report, were

> . . . continued with interest and profit, which would have been still greater if a better instrument and a larger hall could have been provided for them.

It is unclear whether these were his own solo recitals or, rather, programs which he planned and oversaw and in which he was perhaps an occasional performer. Paine still continued to provide music for chapel services, in addition to his other college duties. An October 1877 newspaper item announced happily,

> . . . Professor Paine has secured a triple quartette for the chapel, and the present college choir is the best known here for years.[123]

Composing was not neglected in Paine's routine. At the beginning of the year, it was announced:

> Professor John K. Paine is at work upon a new musical composition, to be called the "Spring Symphony."[124]

Work on this new symphony must have progressed rapidly, for an October report outlining the 1877–78 Sanders Theatre series mentioned the probability of bringing it out "at the last concert in April."[125] This predicted performance did not occur, probably due to a delay in Paine's finishing the score; a first performance did not take place until 1880. Another announced Paine premiere that did not materialize was planned for the 1877 triennial May Festival of the Handel and Haydn Society. The opening concert on 16 May was to begin with "a festival overture and chorus, written for the occasion by Mr. John K. Paine. . . ."[126] Perhaps Paine's other duties prevented him from completing the work in time for its preparation by the Society. Contemporary writers are silent on these details.

A major work of Paine's, the *Duo Concertante for Violin and Violoncello, with Orchestra, in A Major*, op. 33, received a hearing at a 23 April 1878 Thomas Orchestra subscription concert at Sanders Theatre. At this program, the sixth and last of the second season, the *Spring Symphony* was originally scheduled to be played; however, it doubtless was not completed in time, and the *Duo Concertante*, an earlier work, was substituted. Dwight called it "elaborate, brilliant, richly scored, and abounding in bravura passages for the two instruments in the foreground." The soloists, identified as "Messrs. Brandt and Hemmann," played "very skillfully," although their parts were often obscured by the over-bright orchestration, and the cello "often struggled at disadvantage to keep up with all the rapid movements of its lighter and freer leader." Dwight mentioned that the middle movement, *Adagio molto e cantabile*, was "particularly beautiful," and added, "the work was warmly applauded. . . ."[127]

In earlier years Paine would spend his summer vacations at various locations—Boston area sea resorts, inland villages, Europe, and doubtless some years remaining in Cambridge. But in 1878 he and his wife visited the Isles of Shoals, off the Atlantic coast near the Maine-New Hampshire border, beginning a practice they continued throughout his life. The family of poet Celia Thaxter (1835–94) owned a resort hotel, Appledore House, on Appledore Island, and the first notice of Paine's visit appeared in July 1878.[128] Fiske wrote an account of the first days:

> Just back from a visit to Appledore. Went Saturday [6 July] with the Paines, taking Maud [Fiske's daughter], arriving there at noon. After dinner we all went over to Star Island in "Tea-Kettle" alias "Fire-Fly," and explored the island. Robert and Alice Jones came in evening steamer. The night was cold; made hot Jamaica toddy in my bedroom.
> Sunday morning Paine and I rowed Sister Paine, Miss Alice Jones and Maud around Appledore Island. Afternoon called at Celia Thaxter's and played some Chopin to her, by urgent request. The piano had a beautiful tone. . . .
> Monday evening . . . called at Mrs. Thaxter's and had a real concert by Bro. Paine: he played "Moonlight Sonata" most beautifully. Delicious milk-punch in "crypt."[129]

Celia Thaxter was delighted to meet Paine, and was greatly cheered by his presence at the Shoals.

> When I came down here, I never in my life had been so low in my mind. I missed my mother so I knew not which way to turn. But Heaven sent down here a musician, who played Beethoven to me morning, noon, and night the livelong summer, and cured my sick soul as a splendid tonic cures a sick body. Mr. and Mrs. Paine, from Cambridge,—Professor Paine, you know, of Harvard,—happened to come here,— came for a week and stayed six and more; and though he did not intend to play, and I never asked him, he found out how much it was to me, and played to me hours every day. I cannot tell you what it was to me. . . .[130]

Appledore House, since its opening in 1848, had become a small summertime intellectual and artistic gathering place, attracting literary notables such as James Russell Lowell (1819–91), Henry David Thoreau (1817–62), and John Greenleaf Whittier (1807–92), and artists such as William Morris Hunt (1824–79) and Childe Hassam (1859–1935).[131] Many of the Harvard faculty spent their summers there. This strong representation from the Cambridge campus no doubt encouraged a 25 July performance of an "Arion Quartette of Harvard Students" at Appledore House.[132] Paine was not the only musician to enjoy Shoals. William Mason, the famed pianist, had been visiting Appledore regularly since 1863. In his autobiography he mentions Paine's first discovery of the resort, and adds that he

> . . . came year after year without intermission. After a year or two he had a piano sent down from Boston for the summer and placed in the reception-room in Celia

Thaxter's cottage. I had the pleasure of Mrs. Thaxter's acquaintance, but up to that time simply in a formal way, and beyond a call on my arrival and one upon taking leave, I had little association with her; Professor Paine, however, quickly formed a habit of playing Beethoven's sonatas to her, and she very shortly showed a delight in music, and especially in Beethoven's sonatas, with which she became quite familiar.[133]

Mason interested Julius Eichberg in coming to the Shoals in 1864, and the noted violinist also began to spend his vacations there.

He brought his violin with him, and with Mr. Paine frequently played compositions of Bach for piano and violin.

The decade of the 1870s was a vital period in Paine's career as a composer, for during these years he grew from a young unknown to the "dean" of American composers. Recalling the list of works introduced during this decade suggests his relentless drive in attempting to place his music before the public. After failing to have his *Mass* performed in America, the maturing musician gained his first triumph in the widely publicized Portland premiere of *St. Peter*, hailed as a milestone in American music. Triumph was sweetened when the work was subsequently performed by the prestigious Handel and Haydn Society in Boston. Doubtless through his tireless efforts and those of his friends, the merit of his works became known to influential musicians such as Theodore Thomas, Carl Zerrahn, and Ernst Perabo. Thomas, especially, played an immensely important role in agreeing to introduce the orchestral works in his subscription concerts, and exposed Paine to acclaim in New York through performances of the *Symphony* and *The Tempest*. And it was certainly Thomas who secured the *Centennial Hymn* commission, enabling the composer to earn great national distinction. During the 1870s and early 1880s Paine was at his most prolific as a composer. Because of the fortunate circumstances surrounding the performances of and acclaim for his works, these years held for him his greatest popularity as the leading composer in America.

7

Spring Symphony and Oedipus Tyrannus: 1879–1881

Public acclaim for Paine as a composer grew steadily during the 1870s. His numerous works premiered during this decade were welcomed with increasing enthusiasm by the audiences and critics of Boston and New York. He had received a high honor among American composers in his commission for the Centennial Exposition ceremony. Evident in all these events and accomplishments during the decade are Paine's unfailing drive, self-confidence, and willingness to battle the *status quo* in order to right a wrong or to improve artistic or professional standards. This devotion was needed to sustain him in what must have been a very exacting schedule, including full-time teaching duties at two institutions, maintaining his performing skills, providing music for daily chapel services, and producing a significant compositional output—worthwhile occupations that could have been sufficiently rewarding to him. But Paine's self-imposed standards and ambition must have prevented him from being fully satisfied with these achievements. After all, America was merely an insignificant province in the music world, and acclaim in his native country only was of limited value in giving an American composer stature. What would satisfy him was a European success, a taste of which the still young composer had had with the performance of his *Mass* in Berlin. Now, after he had matured, having two symphonies and other orchestral works to his credit, and hopefully no longer writing *Schulfugen*, he was ready again to confront a European audience. Evidently he made contact with some of his Berlin friends early in 1879, informing them of his ambition and asking for their help, for he received an encouraging response, reported in the *Advertiser*:

> Professor J. K. Paine of Harvard University has been invited to produce one of his symphonies at the leading orchestral concerts in Berlin, and will probably send his second symphony, op. 32, recently completed, for its first production this summer.[1]

Here was the opportunity to repeat the triumph he had enjoyed 12 years previously with the performance of his *Mass* in the imperial city. It is indicative of his self-confidence that he chose to submit his new *Spring* symphony, rather than one of his earlier orchestral works that had already received critical approval at home. Paine undoubtedly spent a lot of time polishing the work, which showed a noticeable growth in musical expression. The *Spring* symphony was also one of his last works for orchestra alone, and reportedly it remained the favorite among his compositions in this medium. But Paine's endeavors to obtain a European hearing for his new work were frustrated, for little more than a month later a second newspaper item announced:

> Professor J. K. Paine will go over to Berlin this summer to superintend the performance of his first symphony in that city.[2]

This substitution was certainly disappointing to him. The C-minor symphony, an earlier work, could not display his current compositional skill and ideals. However, to balance out his bad fortune, Paine's chances for having the new composition performed at home were quite good. The Harvard Musical Association was soon to announce its plans to perform the symphony for the coming season,[3] and the Boston Philharmonic Orchestra had similar intentions. In addition, Arthur P. Schmidt of Boston was to publish the score in 1880 as the result of a successful subscription, making it the first American orchestral work ever to appear in print. Engraving of the plates was done in Germany,[4] and Paine was probably able to consult with the printers during his visit.

The Paines left for Europe immediately following the 25 June commencement formalities at Harvard. First on their itinerary was a short stay in London and a visit with Fiske, who had recently resigned his Assistant Librarian post at Harvard and begun a career as lecturer and historical writer.[5] They were to surprise him with the news that at the recent commencement he had been elected to the Board of Overseers of the college. The friends arrived at Fiske's Great Russell Street residence on 8 July, as he described in a letter to his wife:

> This morning I heard a cab stopping in front of the house, and, going to the window, much to my delight, I beheld brother and sister Paine in said cab, rapped to them on the window-pane, whereat they looked up and smiled. It was noon when they came and Paine was very hungry. I took them to Kettner's and they agreed with me that it was a very toothsome place for a lunch. . . .[6]

During the next few days Fiske spent much of his time with the Paines, as they enjoyed the sights of London:

> Wednesday, July 9. Met the Paines in the morning in the nave of Westminster Abbey and took them out to Richmond, most delightful spot on earth. . . . Lunched at the

Star and Garter, and had a beautiful row on the Thames. The Paines were *astonished* at the beauty of the scenery and thought it a day in fairyland. Getting back to London we three dined together at *Simpson's Divan*. Sister Paine was tired out and went back to the hotel.

Fiske's circle of friends in London included many prominent people, and Paine accompanied him at several social events:

In the evening [9 July] Paine went with me out to Macmillan's at Upper Tooting, where Mrs. Macmillan was having a great "reception" with gigantic spread. I gorry, *[sic]*, what a champagne punch!! I gorry, didn't it fizz and sparkle, and wasn't it cool and nice! A great tent was erected on the lawn, communicating by covered-way with the great window of the drawing-room. The tent was brilliantly illuminated, and as you looked into it from the drawing-room the effect was simply magical. There was a superb band of music, and dancing went on in the center of the tent. Both the dining-room and the library had huge tables set, groaning with multitudinous grub, decked with countless bottles and decanters, while the punch-bowl was as big as the iron kettles they used to boil martyrs in. It was an entrancing scene. . . . Mrs. Macmillan looked queenly and sweet. The Simes were there, and George Grove, Ralston, Henry Holt, Thomas Hardy the novelist, and Miss Otté, who pleased me as much as she did years ago at Trübner's. The Simes, Holt, Paine, Miss Otté and I returned to town in the same railway carriage, in high glee telling funny stories and Paine making the most perfectly diabolical puns, driving Miss Otté nearly into convulsions. . . .[7]

Fiske being their guide, the Paines were able the next day to renew acquaintance with Mrs. Thomas Huxley, who had visited with them during an American visit three years previously, as well as to enjoy the marvels of London's subway system:

Thursday, July 10. . . . Took the underground at 1 and reached the Paine's hotel at 1.17—distance about the same as from the Battery in New York to Central Park! Lunched at the *Café Royal* with the Paines, and took them via the underground to Huxley's. The underground and its arrangements have something impressive about them, and duly impressed sister Paine, who, on emerging into broad daylight after a long railroad ride, during which we had once changed cars on to a different line, couldn't get it out of her head that we had got into a different city, and several times spoke of *going back to London!* When I told her that we had been under streets and solid blocks of houses all the way, the fact seemed to be hard for her to take in. . . . And nobody was at home but Mrs. Huxley. She received the Paines with great cordiality and we had a very pleasant call.[8]

Probably the most exciting event of Paine's visit in London was his inclusion in Fiske's 14 July "Social Punch Party" from 8 to 12 at the Great Russell Street rooms. Fiske had wished to make a "social rejoinder" for the many courtesies he had received, and planned the event with the aid of his friend Nikolaus Trübner. Eighteen guests were invited, including ten Englishmen—Lord Arthur Russell, M. P., Thomas Hughes, M. P., Huxley, James Bryce, Herbert Spencer, W. R. S. Ralston, James Sime, Trübner, Frederick Macmillan, and W. Fraser Rae—and eight Americans—Paine, Henry Adams, J. W. White, Moncure D. Conway, Henry James, Henry Holt, Haven Putnam, and Willard Brown. All planned to come except for Bryce, Macmillan, White, and James; Russell and Hughes could not attend because of an urgent meeting of Parliament, and Spencer forgot the engagement.[9] The following day Fiske described the affair in a letter to his wife:

> "Terremenjuous" spree last evening! The punch (which Hezzy [i.e., Fiske] carefully concocted out of lemons, oranges, pineapples, strawberries, rum, brandy, claret, and apollinaris water) was unanimously pronounced an unparalleled work of art, and they all drank it just as though they liked it. The connoisseur Trübner was here before any one else, as I had dined with him; and he saw me put in the finishing touches; and when he tasted it, he said he had never tasted a more delicious punch. I had a mountain of ice in a big bowl and it was cooling unto the palate. Bro. Paine, who staid with me all night, says he doesn't feel the slightest trace of headache this morning, though he drank freely; and if he's all right, I 'spect they all are. I know I am.
>
> We had a truly *glorious* time, and kept it up till one o'clock. Thanks to Trübner, I had some very good cigars to offer 'em which I don't know how to buy in London myself. All sympathized with Hezzy's scheme for next year's lectures. Huxley was the great wit of the evening.
>
> Bro. Paine and I are now waiting for breakfast.[10]

The descriptions of these few days in London offer strong evidence once again of the great benefits Paine received from his close friendship with Fiske. By now he had certainly achieved the polish and grace that put him at ease among people important in social, literary, philosophical, and government circles. He was no longer the diffident provincial, but instead was able to delight and entertain sophisticates such as those he encountered during this visit, an ability that had been and would continue to be absolutely necessary to the furtherance of his career.

Further details of Paine's London visit are lacking. It is probable, however, that he called upon his old friend, music critic James William Davison, for the following notice appeared in the 19 July 1879 issue of Davison's journal *Musical World*:

> Professor John K. Paine, of Harvard University (U.S.), one of the most distinguished of contemporary American musicians, is paying a short visit to this country on his way to the Continent. It is a pity that he should have arrived so late in the season. One of his orchestral works (symphonies especially) would have been right welcome amid the deluge of pretentious rubbish with which we have been for some time

overwhelmed. It would, at all events, have acted as an antidote, Professor Paine being a musician of the health-restoring kind.[11]

The Paines doubtless remained in London until the end of July. Their departure was noted in the 9 August *Musical World*:

> Professor John K. Payne [sic], the eminent American organist and composer, has left London for the Continent, intending to visit the chief musical towns of France, Italy, and Germany. His stay among us has been very short, but we are glad to hear that he intends returning to England in the course of October, when, let us hope, we may hear some of his compositions publicly performed.[12]

No mention is made in either item of Paine's plans to have a work performed during his visit in Berlin. German periodicals seem not to have mentioned his visit at all. Certainly the projected performance of the C-minor symphony must not have taken place, possibly as a result of the same apathy toward American works that Paine had encountered 13 years earlier with his Mass. The length of his stay in Berlin is unknown, and it is left for one to speculate how long Paine struggled before resigning himself to the failure of his mission. Quite possibly he and his wife returned to London early in October, as suggested in the news item above. Apparently none of his works was heard there, either, for Davison would have certainly reported any such performance in *Musical World*. Paine's return visit is not mentioned in Davison's journal, if indeed he did return to London before sailing for America.

Paine's leave from Harvard seems to have been somewhat open ended. At a 25 September 1879 meeting the Harvard Board of Overseers confirmed the appointment of

> . . . William S. Fenollosa, A. B., instructor in music during the absence of Professor Paine during 1879–'80.[13]

Fenollosa, an 1875 Harvard graduate, had earned an A. M. degree in 1876 after studying music theory with Paine.[14] A pianist, he also was a faculty member of the New England Conservatory and was developing a career as a concert artist; he and Paine were both directors of the new Euterpe music society formed earlier that year. Surely the interim appointment was made on Paine's recommendation, for neither were the high academic standards of previous years in danger of being compromised, nor was Paine's position. Fenollosa taught for "a few weeks"[15] during the professor's absence. Paine no doubt was back in Cambridge before the end of October, as an 8 November 1879 notice in *Dwight's Journal* indicated:

> There is to be a series of five classical concerts in Sanders Theatre, (Cambridge), this season, under the direction of Professor J. K. Paine. The entire number will be

given by the Boston Philharmonic Club, with Mr. Listemann conductor, and a symphony will be produced at each concert. . . .[16]

Certainly for him to have the responsibility of planning the programs and directing the crucial subscription drive, Paine must have been back and hard at work. Success in this campaign was especially important, for a series of five concerts planned for the previous season featuring the Brooklyn Philharmonic—probably conducted by Paine—had to be canceled after only 260 of a required 700 persons subscribed.[17] The following excerpt from a review of the 18 December 1879 concert of the new series suggests Paine's first-hand participation:

> These concerts are given under the management of Prof. John K. Paine, and the select character of the program attested his good judgment and taste.[18]

Paine probably resumed teaching his six courses[19] sometime before the middle of the fall semester. Certainly the momentum was high by the time the spring half-year began on 9 February 1880; soon afterward, the following announcement appeared in *Dwight's Journal*:

> Prof. J. K. Paine, of Harvard College, contemplates a series of chamber concerts in Boylston Hall, on the college grounds, before the close of the present season. The students are becoming more and more interested in good music, and the Professor's classes in harmony, counterpoint, musical history, etc., are much fuller than they have ever been before.[20]

But Paine needed to be back in Cambridge for a much more compelling musical reason—two local orchestras were each planning to produce his "Spring" symphony. At least one of these performances—that of the Harvard Musical Association—had been planned before Paine left for Europe, for this intention was announced in an H. M. A. Concert Committee report printed in the 5 July 1879 issue of *Dwight's Journal of Music*:

> . . . Among the orchestral compositions which it is the intention to present, may be named the following:—
>   SYMPHONIES: *New*: Posthumous Symphony in F, by Goetz; "Symphonie Fantastique," by Berlioz; Second ("Spring") Symphony, by J. K. Paine. . . .[21]

The exact performance date of 11 March 1880, however, was apparently not settled upon until after the first H. M. A. concert in December, when it was announced in *Dwight's Journal*:

> The new feature of the seventh concert [11 March 1880] will be Professor Paine's "Spring" Symphony,—its first public performance. . . .[22]

Contrary to this statement, the first public performance actually took place a day earlier—on 10 March 1880—at the first concert by the Boston Philharmonic at Sanders Threatre. The "success of the proposed course" of five concerts mentioned earlier had been "substantially secured" by early December, and Bernhard Listemann's orchestra, "increased to 40 instruments," planned to perform at each program.[23]

The concerts were quite representative of late 19th-century programming in their length, repertory, and the mixing of genres. Also noteworthy, besides the double premiere of Paine's second symphony, was the duplication of the participants as indicated by Sherwood's, Listemann's, and no doubt other musicians' presence on the stage for both concerts.

The Boston Philharmonic Orchestra concert, given in Sanders Theatre at 8:00 P. M. on 10 March 1880, included the following program:

Overture: "Fingal's Cave," .... Mendelssohn.
Soprano Aria: "Ach nur einmal noch im Leben,"
    from "Titus." .... Mozart.
      Miss May Bryant.
"Spring" Symphony in A major, No. 2 (first time) .... J. K. Paine.
    Introduction: Adagio Sostenuto (A minor), Allegro
    ma non troppo (A major); Scherzo,—Allegro (D minor);
    Adagio un poco moto (F major); Allegro giojoso [sic]
    (A major).

Concerto for Piano, in E. flat, Op. 73 ["Emperor"] .... Beethoven.
    (Two movements), Adagio un poco moto.—Rondo Allegro.
      Mr. William H. Sherwood.
Siegfried's Death and Funeral March from
    "Götterdämmerung" .... Wagner.
Songs with Piano-forte.
    a. Rastlose Liebe (Restless Love) .... Schubert.
    b. "Ein Stündlein wohl vor Tag" .... Franz.
    c. Romanze .... Brahms.
      Miss May Bryant.
Overture to "Der Freischütz" .... Von Weber.[24]

Paine's new symphony also appeared on the Harvard Musical Association concert the following afternoon at 3:00 P.M. at Music Hall, Boston, as a part of the following program:

Overture to Collin's "Coriolan," Op. 62 .... Beethoven.
Fourth Piano-forte Concerto, in G, Op. 58 .... Beethoven.
    Allegro moderato (G).—Andante con moto, (E minor),
    Rondo vivace (G).
      William H. Sherwood.
"Spring" Symphony .... J. K. Paine.

Piano-forte solo: Middle movement of Fantasia in C.
    Op. 17 . . . . Schumann.
        Moderato, sempre energico.
        William H. Sherwood.
    Overture: "Becalmed at Sea, and Prosperous Voyage."
    Op. 27 . . . . Mendelssohn.

According to Dwight's review in his *Journal*, both performances were competent, although the earlier concert was handicapped by an inadequate number of players.

> At Cambridge, [the symphony] . . . was played quite well, all things considered, for the first time, by the Philharmonic Orchestra, somewhat enlarged, under Mr. Listemann. The Orchestra was larger, and the interpretation yet more satisfactory in the Harvard Symphony Concert, when Mr. Zerrahn conducted, with Mr. Listemann at the head of the violins. . . .[25]

Zerrahn's "large and well-trained Orchestra"[26] provided a superior hearing of the work; the Listemann orchestra, even "somewhat enlarged" from the 40 musicians announced the previous December, was too small to do justice to Paine's rich scoring. Dwight was not the only writer to remark on this deficiency, for a *Gazette* reporter commented similarly in a review of the same performance:

> . . . The orchestra did it but scant justice on this occasion, though there was no lack of conscientious zeal on the part of the performers to acquit themselves with credit. . . .[27]

Most reviewers were strong in their praise, but nearly all except Dwight did find fault with the work for its extreme length. *Courier* writer "A. A. B." noted after the first performance that ". . . the symphony is, . . . if anything, a little long." The same paper, following the H. M. A. concert, complained much more strongly that the symphony was

> . . . of needless length, or, if not that, that the want of contrast and the general modesty of color produced the impression of length. . . .

Dexter Smith in the *Musical Record* concurred:

> It is quite lengthy; possibly too long.[28]

The *Advertiser*, whose enthusiasm was unqualified after the first concert, also made a similar criticism after the second program:

> . . . the work impresses us as too long, and that it would really gain in strength if submitted to some curtailment.[29]

And the *Gazette* reviewer, after hearing Paine's new composition for the second time, also felt that the first movement especially would "benefit by pruning." But Dwight rose to defend this new creation of his friend:

> . . . If you found this [first] movement "long," hear it until you know it, and you will forget all about the length, just as you never think of age when a soul that has kept its youth converses with you. The fact is, it is just long enough,—that is to say, complete.

Other criticisms included a lack of "well-defined melody" noted by the *Musical Record* reviewer, as well as a certain dissatisfaction felt by the *Courier* writer:

> . . . If we were asked to name the chief characteristics of the work, we should say, a want of repose. We are constantly tantalized by bits of melody of the most exquisite form which comes to the surface like the crests on foam tipped billows, then disappear before we are hardly aware of their presence. . . .

On the whole, the *Courier* reviewer judged the work as

> . . . a decided advance upon the author's first symphony in point of treatment, if not in matter. . . .

and added charitably, but not without further criticism:

> It will doubtless improve upon [repeated] hearing, and much that seemed cloudy will become clear.

This reviewer was alone in his cool reception of Paine's new symphony; other writers were quite enthusiastic. A report of the 10 March premiere in the *Gazette* is typical:

> . . . [The symphony] is a great advance upon anything [Paine] has previously given to the world in flexibility, easy and prolific flow of idea, profound, yet graceful scholarship thoroughly under control, poetic fancy, refined imagination, and that effect of spontaneity in thought which is credited to inspiration. The symphony is delightfully clear from beginning to end. Its learning, which is great, is unobtrusive, and properly falls into its place as a means and not an end. Taken altogether, it is by far the finest work hitherto written on American soil by an American composer. . . .

Apparently most auditors did not share the *Courier* reporter's impression that much was "cloudy" in the work. According to the *Gazette*,

> . . . it was enthusiastically received by a very critical audience, which was none the less delighted because the symphony was wholly comprehensible at a first hearing. . . .

The *Advertiser* enlarged upon this observation:

> [The symphony] will doubtless gain much upon other hearings, but even upon its first audit it entirely charmed and held the great company of critical hearers. We do not believe that this quick appreciation on the part of the listeners is any indication of shallowness or thinness in the work. Indeed, we assert the very contrary. In none of Mr. Paine's other compositions has his learning been more deeply drawn on than in this. But the inspiration and enthusiasm which attended the production of this work are evident enough. The symphony seems to have been conceived at a white heat, and its author's scholarship appears in the fulness of his thoughts and the freedom with which they find utterance. In truth, the symphony shows more than this; it is marked everywhere by a strong shaping imagination, and is constantly touched by a fine poetic fancy and grace. . . . Every part of the work is full of interest and will reward close study, we are sure. . . .[30]

Audience response to the premiere was hearty and enthusiastic, and the composer was called upon to receive their applause. A reviewer for the *Transcript* predicted confidently:

> . . . The ovation showered upon the modest composer last evening was but the first fruits of a new fame to be won for him by this masterpiece, classic and solid in form and matter, and yet enriched with the modern style and vitalized with the modern spirit of musical art. As it marks a new departure in his own career, it also marks an epoch in the development of art in America, and sets the standard of excellence on the very highest plane.

But the most colorful account of the audience reaction, cited by Richard Aldrich in the *Dictionary of American Biography*,[31] related that

> ladies waved handkerchiefs, men shouted in approbation, and the highly respected John S. Dwight, arbiter in Boston of criticism, if not of manners, stood in his seat, frantically opening and shutting his umbrella as an expression of uncontrollable enthusiasm.

Response to the symphony at the second concert was perhaps even more favorable, according to the *Advertiser*:

> It was received with much warmth, the applause gaining in force with each part of the symphony, and, at the close, the composer was called to acknowledge the favorable reception of his work amid much enthusiasm. . . .

Echoed the *Transcript*:

> Mr. Paine had another most enthusiastic greeting from his Boston audience yesterday, being cheered with loud "bravos" on appearing upon the platform, and again applauded as he returned to his seat.

Although most reviewers reported on audience reaction to both concerts, none gives a definite indication of the size for the first program. Little more is supplied for the H. M. A. concert the following day, except that

> . . . Despite the snow storm and general cheerlessness of the day, a good audience assembled. . . .[32]

Several of the newspaper reviews of the premiere concert were quite lengthy and detailed, suggesting that they may have been prepared at least partly in advance. Most noteworthy was the *Advertiser*, which contained an intricate movement-by-movement description that must have been supplied by someone well acquainted with the work—perhaps the composer. A number of writers singled out individual movements for special praise. Most appealing to them was the second movement, the *Scherzo*, or "May night fantasy." Even the *Courier* reviewer enjoyed this section, calling it "peculiarly attractive" and judging it to be "the most original number of the work." The *Musical Record* also considered the *Scherzo* to be the "best portion of the composition," and declared that it was the only part of the symphony that did not lack "well-defined melody." Paine's scoring in the first movement was complimented in the *Gazette*:

> . . . The instrumentation is exquisitely rich, and is fruitful in almost numberless delicious combinations.

Additional favorable comment referred to the last movement, which the *Musical Record* praised highly:

> . . . The breadth and strength of the *finale* evinces the work of a master. The treatment of the brass is in the Wagnerian method. . . .

This movement provided material for the *Courier* writer to compliment as well:

> . . . It is only in the *finale* that Mr. Paine avails himself of the full and most sonorous resources of the orchestra. Here we have a broad choral melody for the brass which reminds one somewhat of a like movement in the introduction to the *Meistersingers*; this movement is well conceived and produced a noble effect. . . .

These two highly successful and widely noticed presentations of Paine's *Spring Symphony* added greatly to his reputation as one of the leading composers in America. Bostonians were to have a number of further opportunities to hear the work within the next two decades, the first being a 3 February 1881 Harvard Musical Association concert at Music Hall.

This performance was originally planned for the 16 December 1880 concert, but was postponed,

> owing to the non-arrival of the score and parts, which are being printed in Germany.[33]

This complication was overcome by the following month; a 29 January issue of *Dwight's Journal* announced regarding the *Spring Symphony*:

> It has been published—score, parts, and four-hand arrangement—in Germany, and may be had at Schmidt's music store.[34]

Availability of the published score added to the listeners' enjoyment of the H. M. A. performance:

> . . . The symphony was heard with the closest attention, copies of the score, which has been recently published, being in the hands and closely followed by the eyes of many auditors. . . .[35]

The work was well received, perhaps even more so than at its first performance. According to *Dwight's Journal*, Paine's symphony was the *"pièce de resistance"* of the concert, and

> . . . more than confirmed the fine impression it made last year.[36]

The *Musical Record* reviewer concurred that the symphony "improves much upon a second hearing," and admitted its attraction for Boston concertgoers:

> Probably the fact that Prof. John K. Paine's "Spring Symphony" was to be again performed had the effect of augmenting the size of the audience . . . , for there were many more present than at the previous concerts of this series. . . .[37]

Probably the delay in receiving the score and parts from Germany contributed toward a slightly less than perfect performance, for *Dwight's Journal* remarked:

> . . . The orchestra took to it warmly and gave a clear and conscientious rendering on the whole, although a few more rehearsals might have improved the light and shade and certain points of phrasing. . . .

A similar delay may have been the reason for omitting the planned performance of the *Scherzo* from the 7 January 1881 concert of the Boston Philharmonic.[38]

Performances of the Spring Symphony continued. It was in the repertory of the new Boston Symphony Orchestra. Theodore Thomas also accepted the work, and it appeared as well in concerts of the Brooklyn Philharmonic and the Chicago Orchestra during the years when he was conducting these organizations, the first being a 2 August 1882 summer concert in Chicago. An organ arrangement of the *Adagio* was included in Henry M. Dunham's *Select Arrangements for the Organ* (A. P. Schmidt, 1888).[39] Five other performances of the *Spring Symphony* give testimony to Paine's prestige. On 5 July 1887, the *Scherzo* of the symphony was performed during the Music Teachers National Association convention in Indianapolis. On 15 November of the same year, Frank van der Stucken included the entire work on an American concert at Chickering Hall in New York City. Both of these performances demonstrate Paine's continued stature as a leading composer and this symphony as a representative work. In 1892 three performances, all conducted by the American, Franz Xavier Arens (1856–1932), again showed these qualities, but this time before European audiences: on 30 January the Berlin *Signale für die Musikalische Welt* reported that the *Spring Symphony* was played at an "Amerikanischer Componistenabend" in Berlin; a similar program took place during the spring at Weimar;[40] and on 5 July, in Vienna, the "Internationalen Musik- und Theater-Ausstellung" presented a "Symphonie-Concert der Componisten und Gastdirigenten Aufführung von Werken Amerikanischer Componisten," in which the first two movements of Paine's work were included.[41] Unfortunately, these European performances did little to further American reputations on the continent. Typical was the *Signale's* review following the Berlin concert:

> . . . The public showed only slight interest in the enterprise, and from an artistic standpoint the results were not worthy of note.[42]

Such a review must have been severely disappointing and certainly not surprising to the composers, for Americans of Paine's stamp must have already gotten accustomed to the generally held European attitude that, while the rich republic could produce excellent steel and tobacco, it was too soon for it to make gentlemen or artists. Of course, none of the compositions played on these concerts measured up to the works of the greatest European masters, but at least Paine's *Spring Symphony* was definitely the equal of major works by his European contemporaries of the second and third rank. This bias was not only to be the misfortune of the nineteenth-century American composer, but also would, to a large extent, continue to plague his twentieth-century successors. Thus, Paine had to be satisfied with mere hearings of his works, albeit received courteously, probably patronizingly, and without enthusiasm. The only real acclaim he would find was to be at home.

Indicative of his local prestige was the regular inclusion of Paine's compositions on programs presented by his compatriots. For example,

two of his former pupils played organ works of his on solo concerts during
1879: C. H. Morse ended a June organ recital at Wellesley College with
Paine's *Star Spangled Banner*;[43] and H. M. Dunham paid similar homage
at a 28 May Music Hall recital.[44] Much earlier, on 6 November 1874,
Dunham had included the same work on another Music Hall recital, part
of the New England Conservatory series.[45] Paine's organ music was occasionally to be heard in cities other than Boston, as for example at a June
1881 recital in Chicago by H. Clarence Eddy.[46] The vocalist most faithful
to Paine continued to be his old friend George Osgood. Typically, at a
7 February 1881 program by violinist Timotheus Adamowski, Osgood, an
assisting artist, included Paine's *I wore your roses yesterday* among his
selections.[47] Local pianists also continued their admiration of the Harvard
composer: on a 24 January 1879 recital at "his rooms," William H. Sherwood included "Farewell" and "Welcome Home" from Paine's set, *In
the Country*, Op. 26;[48] and "Romance," from *Four Characteristic Pieces*,
Op. 25, formed a portion of the program played by John Orth at Mechanics' Hall on 12 April 1880,[49] and repeated on a New England Conservatory recital at Wesleyan Hall five days later.[50] Ernst Perabo played
the "Dance" and "Romance" from the Op. 25 set at his 12 April 1881
matinée at the Meionaon; the *Advertiser* found them "graceful and charming. . . ."[51] Paine's chamber music was not ignored. His "Larghetto"
from the *Trio*, Op. 32, appeared on a 23 August 1879 New England Conservatory program, performed by Turner, Suck, and Rietzel, all faculty of
the New England Normal Institute.[52] Paine, of course, was in Europe at
this time and would have been unable to hear the concert; regardless, the
performers must have thought highly enough of this work to include it in
their repertory on its own merit, not just to flatter the composer. His B-
minor Violin Sonata, Op. 24, was heard once more at the concert formally
opening the new Wellesley College of Music on 30 May 1881. William H.
Sherwood was the pianist, with Charles M. Allen of the Beethoven Club
as the violin soloist.[53] Paine's earlier orchestral music also continued to
appear on programs in the Boston area, including the *Overture to "As
You Like It"* on a 5 May 1881 "Request Programme" of the Boston Philharmonic Society, and the *Symphony No. 1* on a 16 March 1882 concert
of the same organization.[54] Paine himself was still active occasionally on
the concert stage. For example, he accompanied Osgood in songs of
Franz, Schubert, and Handel at a 13 March 1879 New York Philharmonic
Club concert at Boylston Hall.[55] He further influenced Boston's concert
life as a member of the program committee of the Euterpe music society[56]
and through his control of all the musical programs at Harvard. After the
failure of the Boston Philharmonic in January 1881, Paine became president of the Board of Directors of a reorganized Philharmonic Society of

Boston on 9 February 1881; he served in this capacity until the end of
the following concert season, resigning in May 1882.[57] In addition, his
teaching duties were still the same as those of previous years, with one
exception. In 1879 the Harvard Annex (later called Radcliffe College)
came into being, enabling women to receive private college-level instruction from Harvard faculty; remuneration was $3 per hour for individual
teaching and $1 each per hour for classes. A newspaper report named
Paine among the faculty who had consented to be available for instruction,[58] and in 1879–80 he had his first pupil under this new arrangement.[59]

In the fall of 1880, a student-initiated project provided the inspiration
for Paine's next major composition, one that many writers have considered his finest—the incidental music for Sophocles' play, *Oedipus Tyrannus*. A *New York Tribune* report, quoted in *Dwight's Journal*, gives an
early mention of the plans:

> The Harvard students having decided to rival the success of the Oxford students in
> producing a Greek play, looked about for some one who would undertake the leading
> part and finally found an excellent man in Mr. [George] Riddle [Harvard instructor
> in elocution], who has undertaken to learn seven hundred lines of Sophocles's "Oed-
> ipus Tyrannus" before next May. The remaining characters will be taken by students.
> Though the work has but just started, it has received more than the necessary impetus
> by the intense interest already felt by professors and students. Professors [J. W.]
> White and [W. W.] Goodwin are to drill the actors in pronunciation; Professor Charles
> Eliot Norton will plan the costumes, with reference, of course, to strict historical
> accuracy; the one scene is to be designed and superintended by a prominent architect,
> and George Osgood will lead the chorus. Sanders Theatre is admirably adapted to
> a Greek play, and, if the plans are brought as near historical and dramatic perfection
> as they already promise, the production of "Oedipus Tyrannus" will be an epoch in
> the history of classics at Harvard.[60]

Dwight's Journal added that since Mendelssohn composed no music to this
play of Sophocles, "Prof. Paine has been invited to try his hand at it."
Great progress was made in the ensuing month, and on 20 November
Dwight's Journal reported:

> Prof. J. K. Paine, at Harvard, is said to be getting on very successfully in the com-
> position of music for the chorus in the proposed performance of the *Aedipus [sic]
> Tyrannus* of Sophocles. The members of the chorus, who have already rehearsed the
> numbers so far finished, speak of them with admiration, as being music altogether fit
> and noble.[61]

Poet Celia Thaxter, spending her first winter in Boston, visited the
Paines and heard the music as it was being written:

> I am in the midst of the awful and thrilling music of the Oedipus Tyrannus, and it
> curdles my blood; we are all steeped in it, for J. K. P. goes on and on composing it

all the time, and the tremendous chords thrill the very timbers of the house. It is most interesting![62]

Norton, professor of the history of art at Harvard, described his involvement with the play's preparation and gave his reaction to Paine's music in a 31 January 1881 letter to poet George Edward Woodberry:

> . . . I began on Saturday evening by receiving the men of the Greek play for a rehearsal in my study. It was a most interesting exhibition, and a new experience in College life. Professor White is the head of the undertaking, and the actors and the chorus have taken up the work with the same spirit with which our men have devoted themselves to the work of the crew or the nine. Their zeal and their industry are rewarded by a surprising success. Riddle has the part of Oedipus, Opdycke of last year that of Jocasta, Howe of '81 is Creon, Guild of '81 Teiresias, Manning of '81 is the priest. They already have the larger portion or the whole of their parts to perfection. They rehearsed about half the play the other night. Riddle's voice and his pronunciation and delivery of the Greek are admirable, and the other men are all excellent. The tragic quality of the drama is forced home upon the spectator with an effect one would not have anticipated. The music for the choruses is striking, too modern in quality to accord perfectly with the character of the play. But we cannot give the play as the Greeks represented it: we must be content with what will be a very striking modernized reproduction. It is a great gain for culture that this interest in a classic work should be so strong. . . .[63]

Within a short time Paine completed the music, and rehearsals continued in earnest. In a 17 March 1881 newspaper advertisement the Committee of Arrangements—Professors Goodwin, White, and Paine—announced 17, 19, and 20 May as the scheduled performance dates. Regular ticket sales were to begin on 4 April. The committee also provided information regarding musical forces:

> . . . The music for the choruses has been composed for this performance by Professor J. K. Paine; and the choral odes will be sung by a dramatic chorus of fifteen students, assisted by a supplementary chorus composed chiefly of graduates, with orchestral accompaniment.[64]

Publication of a vocal score, with Greek and English words and piano accompaniment, was announced in the same advertisement for 30 March, to be available by mail from the Arthur P. Schmidt firm, its publisher, for a price of $1.25.

Soon afterward, feature articles appeared in many periodicals and newspapers. A passage from the *Advertiser*, providing information about plans for the musical performance, is especially significant because it appeared in a mass circulation newspaper, indicating the interest in artistic projects among the general public.

> . . . A few feet in front of the orchestra circle and parallel to it a screen will be placed, and behind this will be concealed a supplementary chorus of fifty voices and an orchestra of thirty-two pieces led by Listemann, which will be made up of the best instrumental performers in Boston. The supplementary chorus will be chiefly composed of Harvard graduates residing in Boston and vicinity, and will contain many who are prominent in the musical circles of the city. The music is arranged so that the altar chorus sings the strophes and the full chorus joins in on the antistrophe. This is a departure from the old Greek custom, which only allowed a chorus of fifteen to sing, but Professor Paine, in composing the music, decided that it would be best to sacrifice the letter of the custom for the sake of the grand effects to be produced by a larger number of voices. The managers of the play have been so fortunate as to secure the services of Mr. George L. Osgood, who will sing a tenor solo in the fifth chorus. Professor Paine has devoted much time and labor to drilling the several choruses, and will personally direct the music when the play is presented. . . .[65]

The producers decided against including choral dance, "so prominent a feature in the Greek drama," for fear it would "prove a failure." Instead, "a simple rhythmic movement" would be incorporated into the chorus actions, "so slight as to preclude the possibility of its seeming absurd. . . ."

Public excitement about *Oedipus Tyrannus* continued to rise, and on 5 April, the first day of ticket sales, the response was overwhelming. Speculators were in great abundance: the first two persons in line purchased between 400 and 500 tickets, and after the first six had reached the window, reportedly all the best seats in the house were taken. Most of the opportunists were Harvard undergraduates![66]

Newspaper articles devoted to the forthcoming production appeared in the *Advertiser*,[67] where it occupied two columns and was reprinted in *Dwight's Journal*.[68] Its author was a Harvard student, George Albert Burdett (1856–1943),[69] who was to graduate that spring with highest honors in music.[70] Possibly this study was done as a degree requirement; probably it was completed with Paine's close guidance. Burdett opened his analysis with a discussion of the composer's attitude toward Greek music:

> . . . Professor Paine, at the very first, abandoned all thought of attempting to reproduce or to imitate Greek music, believing that any such attempt would inevitably result in failure, or be incongruous to such a degree of irritation as to do serious detriment to the impressiveness of the play. We can, at best, only theorize regarding the true character of the music of the ancient Greeks. . . . Music is the latest and perhaps the most marvellous growth in the realm of fine art, and that its unexampled development into its present efficiency as an art of expression is wholly the work of the last two centuries. In the light of this consideration Professor Paine saw that it

would be possible to stimulate the imagination to such a degree that a livelier sympathy with the story would be excited in the audience than otherwise be attained. He has, accordingly, written his music for male chorus and full orchestra. . . .

The writer's ensuing description of the performing forces discloses additional details to those included in an earlier *Advertiser* article:

. . . The chorus will consist of about seventy-five voices, of which fifteen—members of the Glee club with a very few exceptions, and all students—will constitute the acting chorus. These will enter singing the first chorus, and will group themselves on either side of the *thymele* where they will remain to the end of the performance. This *thymele* or altar will be situated on the "floor" of the auditorium, which will serve the purpose of an addition to the stage and which will be used by those engaged in the performance of the music. The remaining sixty voices—for the most part from the Apollo and Boylston clubs—will constitute a supplementary chorus, which will sit with the orchestra in a semicircle between the audience and the acting chorus; from the latter they will be distinguished by a screen three feet in height, separating the two choruses. The orchestra of thirty-five players will be composed as follows: Six first violins, four second violins, three violas, three violoncellos, three double basses, two flutes, two oboes, two clarinets, two horns, two trumpets, two bassoons, three trombones, and a pair of kettledrums. Professor Paine believes this to be the smallest orchestra adequate for the purpose, and even in this the string band can hardly produce the body that is to be desired.

Burdett continued with a lengthy analysis of the prelude and six choruses, beginning with a discussion of the opening instrumental movement:

. . . In the prelude the attempt is made to epitomize the play, to show the spirit and essential life of the whole tragedy in utmost concentration; to make a reflection in miniature of the whole work. . . . The prelude . . . foreshadows that powerful contrast which is the very marrow of the tragedy—that between the fair appearance and the horrid reality in the condition of Oedipus. . . .

Following this was Burdett's description of the six choruses. The conclusion he reached in his article must certainly have been a reflection of his teacher's concepts and philosophies:

In general it may be said that the music is meant to be strongly expressive of the spirit of classic tragedy. Although polyphonic writing prevails in the choruses, affording, as it does, incomparably greater opportunity for dramatic expression,—still the unisonous arrangement of voices is freely used, which, with the elevated character of the themes and the larger scope of their development, gives a distinctive temper to the music, and one in harmony, we are disposed to think, with the immortal dignity of this masterdrama. The predominance of the minor modes, together with the nature of the harmony and the majesty of most of the cadences, may be expected to raise the music to the elevation of religious awe.

On 14 May a public dress rehearsal was observed by "a choice audience, which occupied every seat" of Sanders Theatre.[71] The two hour and 55 minute play "passed off with a smoothness which testified to the immense labor, learning and ability of the men who conceived and executed the plan." Principal actors were "remarkably good," and Paine's music was found to be "an actual revelation of creative power and beauty."

> The delight of the exacting company of spectators was shown in many ways, applause being abundant and enthusiastic, and the chief actors being once recalled in the middle of the tragedy. It is certainly to be hoped that no recalls will be made or answered in any such fashion at any of the regular performances, however much the audience may be pleased; such an interruption of such a tragedy is most absurd and malapropos. . . .

The first performance of *Oedipus Tyrannus* on 17 May 1881 was doubtless the outstanding cultural and social event of the season. Included in the audience were such distinguished persons as Henry Wadsworth Longfellow, Oliver Wendell Holmes, Ralph Waldo Emerson, George William Curtis, Julia Ward Howe, Governor John Davis Long, Charles Eliot Norton, William Dean Howells, Alexander Agassiz, and Professor A. P. Peabody, the university chaplain.[72] John Sullivan Dwight was both justifiably proud as well as accurate in describing the performance as

> the most complete and thoroughly artistic presentation of a work of pure, high Art, that this part of the world has ever yet achieved out of its own resources.[73]

Professor Norton disclosed his pleasure in a 22 May 1881 letter to Woodberry:

> The play has been more than a success;—it has been the most interesting event in College life and studies for years, and it will have great effect in quickening the interest in classical studies. The most powerful impression it has made is that of the excellence of the Greek drama,—especially in form. The unities have asserted and justified themselves. The old play, produced under conditions so different from those under which it was originally brought upon the stage that its whole external character was changed, has proved of such intrinsic power as to have hardly less effect upon a modern and foreign audience than upon its first hearers. The dramatic quality of the play was marvellously brought out in the acting. The acting was all as good as perfection in knowledge of the parts, and general intelligence, could make it. But it was all too sentimental and realistic; and full of incongruities to one who measured it by Greek modes of expression. The young fellows have really done themselves high credit, and Mr. Goodwin and Mr. White are greatly satisfied and pleased. . . .[74]

The distinguished audience seems to have agreed with Dwight and Norton, according to the *Advertiser* reviewer:

> There can be no doubt that the performance was remarkably successful, and afforded very great and peculiar pleasure to a critical audience. That many of the spectators

had moments of weariness, as most of us have them in listening to modern plays, we do not doubt: but the general experience of the evening—as the faces of the spectators fully demonstrated at its close—was one of excitement and satisfaction. The generally anticipated difficulty of following the book of the play vanished upon trial; nearly every one present seemed to have made some preparation for the event, and those who had not so prepared themselves could not have been more troubled than on witnessing a French or German piece. The action, indeed, was generally so expressive that any quick-witted spectator familiar with the general purpose of the scene could follow the performers without serious interruption. . . . The acting as a whole was remarkably and surprisingly good. . . .

Perhaps the weariness of the audience may be further explained by the fact that not only was the performance entirely in Greek but also the printed programs. In reference to Paine's music for the play, the *Advertiser* writer remarked:

> . . . We must now say, with emphasis, that it marks—to our apprehension—the highest point which his genius as a composer has reached. It is learnedly and effectively scored for the instruments, and the vocal effects produced are almost of the highest order. It is Greek in its spirit, and expresses the tragic pathos peculiar to the situation of *Oedipus* with wonderful imaginative vividness and grasp. The melody is always pleasing and in at least three of the six numbers is very beautiful.

Paine's old friend, Dwight, felt none of the general audience's ennui, and revealed his gusto and enthusiasm for the music:

> . . . Adding lift and inspiration to the whole, making the three hours seem short, [was] the beautiful, strong, fitting, manly music composed by Professor Paine, and finely sung by seventy-five sweet, manly voices, with full orchestra accompanying symphonically, the vigorous, rich strains, which seemed to spring instinctively, by "pre-established harmony," out of the large and ever-changing rhythm of the Sophoclean verses. . . .

A *Boston Saturday Evening Gazette* reviewer was equally complimentary to the music, and paid

> . . . a warm tribute of praise to Mr. Paine for the judicious way in which he has treated the voices throughout. Of his use of the orchestra it is scarcely necessary to speak. It will be taken for granted that there is no flaw in it. It leans towards the methods of Wagner, but is nowhere sensational or in questionable taste. The music of *Oedipus* is, we think, in advance of anything Mr. Paine has hitherto done. It shows expansion and maturity in every direction, and upon it he may safely found a claim to lasting reputation.[75]

The anonymous critic, for the time being, was perhaps more perceptive than either Paine's chief journalistic patron, Dwight, or he himself may have known. Though he may have been referring only to the transformation of themes and orchestration in the prelude, he was foretelling the future of Paine's ultimate shift towards "the methods of Wagner" in the yet to be conceived music drama, *Azara*, of the 1890s. Previously, more sensitive Bostonians had noticed certain traces of *Meistersinger* in the *Spring Symphony*.

The *Gazette* writer found Paine's third chorus, in which Oedipus, Creon, and Jocasta converse with the chorus, as "most dramatic:"

> Taken altogether, this number impressed us as the most thoughtful and the finest piece of work we have yet had from Mr. Paine.

But the fourth chorus was the "least interesting," according to the same reviewer, "labored in effect" and lacking "continuity of idea and feeling. . . ." The *Advertiser* also faulted this number, as lacking "invention."

Performance of the music at this first presentation was "very good on the whole," according to the *Advertiser*, "correctness and spirit being the rule." Most of the singing was "strikingly and exceptionally good," and the musicians seemed to have been "inspired by the music and the occasion." The music surpassed the standards attained at the formal rehearsal in all details except for Osgood's solo in the fifth chorus:

> [he] sustained the solo last night with his usual taste and artistic fire and feeling, but his voice was not in good condition, and the number failed of its full effect and indeed of the effect easily reached on Saturday night.

Costumes were "beautiful in their colors and fabrics," often "graceful and pleasing." "Particularly superb in tint and texture" was Riddle's "kingly robe."

The following two performances of *Oedipus Tyrannus* were equally successful, and on 24 May a fourth representation was announced for Friday evening, 27 May, "for the benefit of Mr. George Riddle, who has so ably sustained the leading part."[76] Competition to gain admission to this performance was fully as keen as with the earlier three. A Thursday newspaper item revealed:

> As early as four o'clock yesterday afternoon about thirty persons were in line at the University bookstore in Cambridge, waiting for tickets to the final performance of "Oedipus Tyrannus" in Sanders Theatre tomorrow evening. The line was lengthened considerably during the evening, and there will probably be a very large number of purchasers present when the sale opens, at nine o'clock this morning.[77]

This additional performance was "in all respects as successful as the preceding ones."[78] The audience was enthusiastic, and apparently more demonstrative in its approval than at the earlier presentations. The first entrance of George Riddle, beneficiary of the performance,

> . . . gave the signal for the beginning of the enthusiasm which did not abate until the
> last note of the postlude was sounded. *Oedipus* was three times called out, and
> *Jocasta* once. Mr. Paine was also compelled to recognize the applause. . . .

A fifth performance, projected perhaps because of the favorable reception
accorded the production, had been planned for the following week but
was canceled, no doubt because of final examinations and the preparations for commencement. As a consolation, the players were allowed to
keep their costumes as souvenirs.

But this was not to be the end of *Oedipus Tyrannus*. During the
summer enthusiasts suggested presenting performances at Boston and
New York theaters. An August 1881 report in the *New York Tribune* dis-
cusses plans:

> There is a possibility that the "Oedipus Tyrannus" may be given in New York the
> coming season provided the authorities at Harvard are assured that the performance
> or performances would be well attended. The play is to be repeated at Cambridge
> some time in the winter; and it is stated on good authority that if the New York
> Harvard club will guarantee its success, one or possibly more representations will be
> given in this city. Here then is a capital chance for the Harvard club to perform a
> real service to the more cultured class of the community. For the production of the
> immortal tragedy of Sophocles would be a positive pleasure to many of those who
> were unable to go to Cambridge last spring, and who have feared that with the close
> of the college year the opportunity of hearing the Greek play with the accompanying
> music of Professor Paine was lost. . . .[79]

Within a few months these plans were completed, according to a *Transcript* announcement early in October:

> Mr. George Riddle is to "travel" with the Greek Play, playing his part in Greek to
> the others speaking in English. Miss Georgia Cayvan, whose piquant vivacity in
> "Pinafore" is well remembered, is to be the *Jocasta*. A large and well-trained singing
> chorus will form part of the troupe, and the fine orchestral music of Professor Paine
> will be given as at the original production. . . .[80]

Doubtless the Greek-English macaronic presentation was a concession to
the public. This compromise aroused the indignation of a number of critics, one of whom, a certain "A. A. H.," New York correspondent for
the *Advertiser*, complained following the later New York performance
without even attending the show:

> The Greek play, or rather the Graeco-English play, has been given at Booth's. I did
> not go thither to see it. . . . For Mr. Riddle's use of the Greek, while the rest of the
> company availed themselves of the vernacular, no excuse would seem possible. The
> "hash drama" is hardly endurable when a necessity. . . .[81]

But the general public did not allow such misgivings to dampen its enthusiasm, for before the Boston opening at the Globe Theatre,

> The advance sale of seats shows that there is a very lively interest in the enterprise.[82]

Performance dates were announced for Monday through Saturday, 23-28 January 1882, "every evening and Saturday matinee."

Opening night was a success. "The audience was large, and, on the whole, though cool and critical, was exceptionally interested."[83] Scenery and costumes were similar to those at the Sanders Theatre presentations, and part of the parquet floor was used for instrumentalists and vocalists, similar to the Harvard production. The combined chorus was made up of singers from Boston and New York, and between 35 and 40 musicians—also from both cities—comprised the orchestra conducted by George W. Chadwick. The *Advertiser* commented favorably:

> For a first public performance the music was . . . well done, and the manner of its doing reflected much credit upon Mr. Chadwick. There was some roughness in the orchestral work, and some feebleness and hesitation in the choral, but there were no serious disasters, and we prophesy that after one more repetition all will go most satisfactorily. The gentleman who took the solo part in the famous No. 5. of the music sang sweetly and truly, if somewhat timidly. The music itself grows more and more wonderful upon each new hearing. The introduction seems to us the noblest piece of instrumental music ever composed by an American; and the second chorus takes, in our judgment, the same rank among the vocal compositions of this country. . . .

Most of the audience must have shared the *Advertiser* reviewer's fascination for Paine's music, but not to so great a degree:

> . . . Some of the customary impatience and bad manners was shown at the close of the evening, when a majority of the company found it impossible to yield to the request of the programme, and wait for the end of the orchestral postlude; but during nearly all the performance a quiet and fixed attention was paid both to the music and the acting. . . .

The *Oedipus* company opened a similar production at Booth's Theatre in New York on the following Monday evening. Critical response was mixed—both the *Tribune* and the *Times* found details of the production unsatisfactory, although the *World* "speaks approvingly of the costuming and the setting of the play."[84] But all writers seemed unanimous in their praise of the music, which the *Times* called "beautiful and masterly"[85] and the *World* "a wonderful creation and a successful attempt to produce something harmonious in effect with the Greek drama. . . ." In a more lengthy commentary, no doubt written by Finck, the *Nation* was equally complimentary:

> . . . None of [Paine's earlier concert works], in our opinion, equals in originality of conception and scholarly treatment his music to Sophocles' tragedy, which to our taste is the most finished specimen of musical workmanship produced in this country. Professor Paine's devotion to Bach and Beethoven is well known, and the legitimate influence of these masters is revealed in most of his works, especially in its polyphonic structure and clearness of form. But in these choruses he also unconsciously reveals his admiration for a composer whose theories he condemns. The vigorous and melodious treatment of the bass in the "Oedipus" music, the chromatic progressions and modulations, the avoidance of stale cadences, the use of the brass in moments of passion, and the brilliant, full, and rich instrumentation in general, as well as the earnest endeavor to reproduce musically the emotional contents of the language, are all so many tributes to the genius of Wagner, from whose influence no modern composer has yet succeeded in emancipating himself. By this we do not intend to imply any plagiarism, but merely to mark the author's place in the musical world. Professor Paine's music is his own. It has individuality of style, and his themes impress themselves on the memory at once, and gain in beauty by repeated hearing. . . .[86]

The above comparison of the music of Paine and Wagner, already hinted at previously, is noteworthy, for it shows how strong an impression Paine had made in voicing anti-Wagner views in public lectures and publications earlier in his career. But by this time Paine's views had mellowed considerably, as we have seen in his letter to Finck. His assimilation of additional Wagnerisms into his musical procedures would be a logical result of such a change of attitude.

Although the New York performances at Booth's Theatre were the last times that Paine's music was heard in the context of the Sophocles play, it did not cease to be heard; rather, the prelude, choruses, and postlude, immediately began to appear in concert programs, and have continued to be heard even in recent years. The first concert performance of any of Paine's incidental music took place just before the Booth's Theatre presentations—at a 28 January 1882 New York Chorus Society concert, conducted by Theodore Thomas, at which the second and fifth choruses were sung. These "aroused the greatest curiosity on the part of the audience,"[87] for the work had not been heard in the New York area. These two movements were repeated, coupled with the orchestral prelude and postlude, at the 17–18 March regular rehearsal and concert of the Brooklyn Philharmonic Society and Philharmonic Chorus at the Brooklyn Academy of Music.[88] At the concert, the Academy was "crowded in every part," and the performance "strengthened the favorable impression created at its first hearing at the rehearsal. . . ."[89] Tenor soloist Theodore J. Toedt and the male chorus "performed Prof. Paine's music in admirable style," according to the *New York Times*,[90] but the *Nation* found more favor with the orchestra:

> ... The instrumental parts, including the prelude and postlude, have never been played before with such passionate energy and such a "stereoscopic" display of all the lines and colors of this interesting composition; and if the vocal part was not equal to the instrumental in smoothness, some allowance must be made for the uncommon difficulty of the work. . . .[91]

Doubtless this superior performance resulted both from the full-sized orchestra—as opposed to the thirty or so in the threater orchestra—and from Thomas, the experienced conductor—in contrast to Paine's or Chadwick's more limited abilities in this role. The March concert was originally planned for a 17 December 1881 date;[92] possibly the performance of Paine's work was postponed because of a lack of rehearsal time, or perhaps to coincide with the Booth's Theatre presentations. For whatever reason, this date proved convenient for Paine to attend:

> ... Interest was heightened in the case of the performers and a few other persons by the knowledge that the composer was himself listening to it from one of the front seats in the balcony. He heard a spirited and correct performance. . . . He expressed his admiration for the work of Mr. Thomas in observing how faithfully and intelligently his music had been studied. Professor Paine was the guest of a committee of gentlemen headed by George William Curtis, and after the concert was entertained at the house of B. F. Frothingham, where he had occasion to learn that New-York is not behind Boston in appreciation of his learning and creative talent.[93]

A first concert performance of the *Oedipus* music in Boston occurred during an Apollo Club concert at Music Hall on 15 February 1882, repeated five days later. The club confined its presentation to Choruses 2, 5, and 6; Mr. C. Chenery sang the tenor solo. Accompaniment was provided by an orchestra—"large, made up of excellent material, and in fine order, doing good work under Mr. [B. J.] Lang's direction. . . ."[94] The *Advertiser* reviewer welcomed the opportunity to hear this music

> under circumstances more favorable to steadiness of nerve than have attended their theatrical performances in Cambridge and Boston.

The writer called the work a "masterpiece," and judged that its illustration of Sophocles' tragedy was equally successful as Mendelssohn's music for *A Midsummernight's Dream*. The Apollo Club also performed *Oedipus* selections in two later seasons—in 1884 the 4th chorus was included in a 30 April and 5 May pair of concerts,[95] and the following year it was repeated, along with the orchestral prelude, on 29 April and 4 May.[96]

Also, the first chorus appeared on a 29 November 1887 Apollo concert.[97] Another local society, the Arlington Club, performed a chorus from the work on a 9 January 1883 concert; Chadwick was its conductor.[98] The Arlington Club also included the first chorus on its 28 May 1884 program; this time Arthur W. Thayer conducted the group, for Chadwick had just resigned.[99] In later years portions of the work were heard in more distant cities. In 1888 the Arion Music Club of Milwaukee performed Choruses 2, 3, 5, and 6 at a 28 February concert, and the Apollo Club of Chicago combined these same choruses with the orchestral prelude and postlude two days later.[100] The Loring Club of San Francisco programmed *Oedipus* in their 1885 season,[101] and later performed the second chorus on 5 February 1890,[102] repeating it with the orchestral prelude the following year at a 29 April program.[103] The club again sang portions of *Oedipus Tyrannus* at an April 1903 concert.[104] In 1892, listings of works to be performed by massed groups for the Chicago World's Fair included the *Oedipus Tyrannus* music;[105] whether it was actually performed seems not to have been reported. A last complete performance of the *Oedipus* music in Paine's lifetime was heard at a 26 November 1895 concert of the Apollo Club at Boston Music Hall, with George Riddle, reader, and William H. Rieger, tenor; Paine conducted the prelude. The concert was repeated at Sanders Theatre.[106] No further performance of the choral movements of Paine's incidental music seem to have taken place, except for a 50th anniversary concert in 1921 by the Harvard Alumni Chorus and Sinfonia Glee Club, with Chadwick as the conductor.[107]

That portion of the *Oedipus* music to establish the most firm position in the concert repertory was the orchestral prelude. Its first performance as a separate entity was on a Boston Symphony Orchestra concert on 11 March 1882, with Paine as conductor. Interest was exceedingly high in this last concert of the season, which was given

> to an audience crowding every portion of the sitting and standing room. There were many unable to gain admission. It is stated that at the public rehearsal of this concert—which occurred on Friday afternoon—there were over two thousand people turned away![108]

The presence and participation of the composer greatly increased audience enjoyment:

> . . . The entrance of Prof. Paine to conduct the "Oedipus" music was the signal for a general welcome from the audience, and, upon the conclusion . . . , the composer was again and again recalled to acknowledge the appreciation of the merits of the music and the playing of it by the audience. . . .[109]

This was the opening piece on the program, and its effect must have been impressive. According to the *Globe*,

> . . . The music has hardly had so fair an opportunity to be judged on its merits before, and Mr. Paine is to be congratulated on the success of the experiment. . . .

Although Paine was most qualified to interpret the work, he did "not shine by any outward graces as a conductor," according to the *Transcript*. As a result, according to the *Journal*, "the players seemed at times not fully *en rapport*," and the *Courier* observed:

> The musicians had evidently not become entirely used to his beat, but no serious breaks occurred, and the noble sequences and the effective string passages in the bass were finely done. . . .

Louis C. Elson, writing for New York's *Music*, assured the reader that "there were no mishaps . . . ," and spoke of his "hearty admiration" for the work.

The close association of the *Oedipus Tyrannus* production with Harvard was in evidence at the 250th anniversary of the University on 7 November 1886: included on the program was the *Oedipus* prelude, played by the Boston Symphony Orchestra.[110] The same orchestra also performed the prelude during four subsequent seasons—in April 1894, under Emil Paur, at Boston and Cambridge; in April 1899, under Gericke, also at Boston and Cambridge; in April 1907 in Boston under Muck; and in both cities in December 1923 under Monteux.[111] Other Boston performances included a 2 July 1886 Music Teachers' National Association concert, at which Chadwick conducted,[112] a 31 December 1891 Boston Philharmonic Orchestra program, led by Listemann,[113] and a 22 May 1908 100th anniversary concert of the Pierian Sodality Orchestra at Sanders Theatre,[114] conducted by Philip Greeley Clapp.[115] Domestic performances also included a "novelty concert" in New York during 1885,[116] an American concert at the National Conservatory of Music in Washington, D. C., with Frank van der Stucken, on 26 March 1890,[117] a program by the Buffalo Symphony Orchestra, under John Lund, at the New York State Music Convention in Buffalo on 27 June 1894,[118] a 23 June 1899 concert by the Cincinnati Symphony Orchestra, led by van der Stucken, for the Music Teachers' National Association convention in Cincinnati,[119] and, quite recently, a December 1953 pair of concerts by the Cleveland Orchestra.[120] The Prelude appeared on two European programs: Frank van der Stucken included the work on a 12 July 1889 American concert at the Trocadéro Palace during the Exposition Universelle in Paris;[121] and in 1903 Paine represented Harvard at the Wagner Festival in Berlin, where he received a gold medal and heard his prelude performed in a 3½ hour international concert on 4 October.[122]

These two compositions—the *Spring Symphony* and the music to *Oedipus Tyrannus*—separated by only a year in their first performances, were the most respected and well-known of Paine's entire *oeuvre*. A typical appraisal appeared in an article of appreciation, written soon after the composer's death by Philip H. Goepp, a Harvard undergraduate from the early 1880s.[123] The symphony he judged as

> probably the best of all Paine's compositions, regarded as a single work of largest dimensions.

And Goepp felt in 1906 that it had not become dated; instead, it

> . . . to-day holds the freshness and continuity of interest, the expressive beauty of its melodic themes, the warmth and delicacy of the harmonies,—especially the nobility and power of the climax.

But the *Oedipus* music was the "high point" of Paine's Harvard career. The significance of the inclusion of its prelude in the 1908 Pierian Sodality anniversary concert, mentioned earlier, is discussed in a review by Edward Burlingame Hill:

> It was peculiarly fitting that the programme should begin with the Prelude by Paine as a tribute to his pioneer efforts in behalf of collegiate education in music. From an unpretentious beginning has sprung a department which has produced many musicians, composers and critics of undeniable standing, who have had a distinct share in the making of American musical history. This prelude, conceived in a serious, classical spirit, is instinct with nobility of sentiment. . . .[124]

Goepp, who attended the original *Oedipus* production, felt that

> . . . the music . . . was the best of the feast. As often happens, the incidental becomes the essential. What saved the great impression of the tragedy, made it more than an antique revival, was the rich, melodious, noble setting of choruses and prelude. . . . Everything conspired to make a rare success; the devoted absorption of Mr. Paine, who was at the height of his power, the grandeur and novelty of the subject, the splendid seriousness of the audience for whom he was writing.
>
> From the purely musical standpoint, . . . Paine's setting of the *Oedipus* choruses have to-day, after twenty-five years, the same potent charm as on their production. In view of the rapid changes which the art of music has undergone in this interval, such a test is proof of a high degree of beauty. It may be said with confidence that a renewed general hearing will result in a far higher estimate of the work than has hitherto prevailed. . . . The *Oedipus* choruses will prove one of the greatest works of modern music. . . .

8

The Mature Composer: 1882–1906

With the success and popularity of his *Spring Symphony* and his "Oedipus Tyrannus" behind him, and although performance of his music began to diminish, Paine was acknowledged as America's leading composer and became a model for younger American musicians. Louis C. Elson, expressing an opinion held by many contemporaries in the musical intelligentsia, stated in June 1882 that Paine was

> . . . by far the best and greatest composer that America has ever possessed.[1]

John Fiske, in an article written for *Appleton's Cyclopaedia of American Biography* in 1888, echoes the generally held esteem of Paine abroad:

> By eminent critics in Germany, Prof. Paine is ranked among the foremost living composers, . . .[2]

a characterization copied by the *Musical Record* in reviewing Paine's *Island Fantasy*, calling him "this foremost composer."[3] Elson maintained his opinion of Paine. After hearing a performance of the *Oedipus* prelude 12 years later, he wrote:

> . . . In spite of the rapidly increasing number of American composers Prof. Paine is still *Primus inter Pares*. It is the writer's opinion that in "Oedipus Tyrannus" American music reached its high-water mark for the present, that no native composition may be ranked with it in dignity or sustained power. . . .[4]

Nor were judgments of Paine's merit limited to contemporary opinions. Writing almost two decades later, Henry T. Finck, the music critic of the *New York Evening Post* and a Paine student, described his former teacher as

> the first American composer whose works evince a musical scholarship worthy of the great Germans, while being at the same time imbued with creative fancy. . . .[5]

H. E. Krehbiel, an important American cultural journalist and writer on music history, considered Paine to be one of the

> . . . most notable composers of America [who] have in a manner kept pace with the changing ideals of Germany, . . .[6]

and styled him

> . . . the dean of the faculty by virtue of the length and dignity of his career, and the opportunities for influence which his position as Professor of Music in Harvard University has brought him. . . .

A. J. Goodrich, in *Complete Musical Analysis* (1889), used the Spring Symphony as a model for young American composers.

Notwithstanding such critical acclaim, the composer was being denied performance commensurate with his reputation, according to the press. The *Boston Sunday Herald*, in its Christmas 1887 issue, lamented that Wilhelm Gericke, Boston Symphony Orchestra conductor, had not given Paine's orchestral works more frequent hearings, and opined that the professor "is the most eminent composer in this country and the peer of any living musician."[7] And the *Boston Home Journal*, in 1891, complained about the neglect of "America's Greatest Composer:"

> The name of Prof. John K. Paine has not been seen for a long time upon the concert programs of this city. . . . And yet there is no doubt that today Professor Paine stands easily at the head of American composers. There are many young composers of talent in this country, there is one at least in this city, who has positive marks of musical genius, but no one in the United States has as yet attained the self-control, the discriminating taste, the purity of thought and logic of development shown in the ripe works of this highly endowed man. The neglect and indifference of those high in authority, and the carelessness of concertgoers, as regards the compositions of Professor Paine, are a commentary upon the real condition of music in this city, and it seems as though its cultivation is fictitious, a thing of fashion, an ever changing mode.[8]

Despite these first suggestions of a developing trend that would eventually result in genteel neglect, Paine continued actively to compose. During the last decades of the nineteenth century a number of performances may be noted annually, and most years saw a first performance or a publication of another Paine work.

The first pieces the composer completed after *Oedipus Tyrannus* were both for chorus—*The Realm of Fancy*, op. 36, and *Summons to Love* (or *Phoebus, Arise*, op. 37); both received their premieres during the spring concert season, 1882. Within the year they were published by Schmidt. First to be performed was *The Realm of Fancy*, a setting of the

John Keats poem, by the Boylston Club at Music Hall on 2 March 1882.
George Osgood conducted the mixed chorus and orchestra; soloists were
Annie Abbott, soprano, Mrs. Jennie M. Noyes, alto, Charles R. Adams,
tenor, and G. R. Clarke, bass. A reviewer from the *Advertiser* praised
Paine's setting of the poem:

> . . . That it aptly and beautifully illustrates that poem is a simple but strong statement
> of the new and remarkable proof which it affords of the versatility of its author's
> genius. . . . A little concentration and simplification it certainly needs, to reach the
> popular ear; but we do not know what we have not a right to expect of a composer
> who can put such words as
>
> > All the buds and bells of May
> > From dewy sward or thorny spray
>
> and
>
> > Every leaf and every flower,
> > Pearled with the self-same shower,
>
> into music, which comes to the ear like a bunch of apple-blossoms to the eye and
> nostril. . . .[9]

Comparison with Paine's recent Greek triumph was inevitable:

> . . . The hand of the composer of the "Oedipus" music may be recognized two or
> three times in phrases which seem for a moment directly taken from that work, but
> is steadily recognized in the nervous vigor and freedom and fulness of the style. The
> instrumental introduction in which the horns are set to play a strain worthy of those
> of Elfland strikes the keynote of the composition at once. It is almost too rich, too
> bounteous in its dainty forms and lovely turns and phrases; it is instinct with quick
> and delicate fancy throughout; and its best passages are as truly and gracefully poetic
> as Keats's finest lines. . . .

The second cantata, *Summons to Love*,[10] setting the poem by the sev-
enteenth-century minor Scottish poet William Drummond of Hawthorn-
den, was first performed less than two months later at an Apollo Club
concert at Boston Music Hall on 26 April. It was written for the club,
and called for a tenor soloist (W. J. Winch), male chorus, and orchestra;
B. J. Lang was the conductor. The program attracted the largest crowd
of the club's season, and the new work again invited comparison with its
composer's previous efforts:

> . . . Prof. J. K. Paine's "Summons to Love" is a beautiful work, the characteristics
> of the composer of the "Oedipus" music being strongly noticeable. . . .[11]

The *Advertiser* reviewer seemed almost to be overwhelmed by this "remarkable work":

> . . . It is written in a style of magnificent fulness, which crowds the mind and the heart of the listener, and portions of the composition—especially the first strophe—may be open to the criticism of being too grandiose for the words. After the entrance of the solo, however, the sense of the auditor becomes accustomed to the "high key" of the composer's color,—if we may use a bit of the aesthetic slang of the period. The first solo passage is of a thrilling beauty and does not permit an anti-climax of emotion even after the strenuous movement of the choral introduction, the change in the theme from the realm of fancy to that of feeling being vividly shown. . . .[12]

Throughout the remainder of the composition, continues the reviewer, are heard numerous "musical phrases richly colored to fit the picturesque text, but, as before, always full and fervid. . . ." At the conclusion,

> . . . the poet's direct word concerning "her who all should grace" is uttered through the same solo voice in a salient sky-piercing phrase of wonderful originality and significance. . . .

Unfortunately, the chorus apparently lacked polish, perhaps because of insufficient preparation:

> . . . It is certain that at a second concert they can make a great advance on this performance in that they retain all their present intensity and vivacity of delivery, and supplement the same by increased smoothness and finish.

Both works received at least one more performance during Paine's lifetime. On 25 March 1897, Geroge A. Burdett, organist of the Central Congregational Church in Boston, led his Newton Centre "Singers" in a performance of *The Realm of Fancy*. In its second year of existence, the chorus numbered about 80, and was assisted in this concert by Caroline Gardner Clarke, soprano, and Almon J. Fairbanks, piano. According to the *Herald*,

> . . . it is claimed that the difficulties of this work have proved stumbling blocks to its production by older and more experienced societies, but as the "Singers" rendered it quite as well as they did anything else during the concert, they may feel very proud of themselves and their success. . . .[13]

Phoebus, Arise (as *Summons to Love* was later called) was performed twice in 1902. The Orpheus Club of Cincinnati, Ohio, included it on their closing concert on 27 April 1902, and planned to repeat the concert on a later tour.[14] In Boston, the Apollo Club, conducted by Emil Mollenhauer (1855–1927) and accompanied by piano, sang the cantata in a Chickering Hall concert on 13 November 1902. Again resulted a comparison with *Oedipus Tyrannus:*

> . . . As Prof. Paine put into his "Oedipus" music quality which was conformable to the spirit of Greek tragedy as we moderns understand it, so he gave a sterling old English ring to the Drummond stanzas and stirred an enthusiasm in the listeners which would not be satisfied until he rose and bowed. . . .[15]

The *Herald* social editor called the cantata "the piece de resistance of the evening. . . ."[16]

Paine's next composition—*The Nativity*, op. 38[17]—was still another cantata, composed for the sixth triennial festival of the Handel and Haydn Society in May 1883. For its text he selected 11 of the 27 stanzas in the hymn from John Milton's ode, *On the Morning of Christ's Nativity* (1629). Such a commendable choice did not go unnoticed by classically educated Bostonians. John Sullivan Dwight concluded a lengthy description of the cantata with the following:

> Surely every one will wonder that no great composer ever thought before of finding a sublime subject for his art in this wonderful ode which Milton wrote when he was only twenty-one years old. What a theme for Handel, whose genius had such affinity with that of Milton![18]

The *Advertiser* reviewer also praised the composer's choice:

> . . . Mr. Paine's selection of such words is a new illustration of the careful judgment and critical taste that he has for a long time shown in the choice of texts for his vocal compositions, the chief of which has been taken from the Scriptures, from Sophocles, Keats and John Milton. . . .[19]

Dates of composition are obscure for *The Nativity*, but the composer certainly must have completed the score—and most likely the publisher Arthur P. Schmidt had issued the vocal score—prior to the earliest announcement of the forthcoming concert on 2 February 1883:

> All students and amateurs of music, as well as the general public, will be interested to know that Professor John K. Paine has written for performance at the next triennial festival of the Handel and Haydn Society a cantata, called "The Nativity," for solo voices, chorus and orchestra, to the words of Milton's immortal "Ode" upon the same theme.[20]

Performance of this new work was scheduled for the second concert of the festival, on 2 May 1883, to be followed by the Cherubini *Missa Solemnis* in D minor. At the opening concert the previous evening a small audience heard Rubinstein's *Tower of Babel*. The crowd was "small, but enthusiastic" at this second program, according to Dwight. Soloists were

Emma Thursby, soprano; Mathilde Phillipps, alto; George W. Want, tenor; and Myron W. Whitney, bass; all who sang "very smoothly," according to the *Advertiser*. The Society, however, did not provide as satisfactory a contribution:

> . . . The choral work was fairly well done, but no better than that there was no fiasco, and nothing approaching a fiasco, but not a little of the singing in the more difficult choral numbers produced a "mussy" effect. . . .[21]

A reviewer for the *Transcript* offered an explanation for the weakness in performance:

> . . . [It] was far better than one had a right to expect in the circumstances. There had been by no means enough rehearsal, but what will you? The composer had agreed to have his work ready by a certain time; the work was not ready, since music cannot be ground out like meal from a mill, and every composer worthy the name is at the mercy of his genius. It is, after all, better as it was; for who would not prefer having an imperfect performance to having an imperfect work? . . .[22]

At the podium was the composer, who

> . . . was warmly greeted by chorus and audience upon his appearance. The cantata undoubtedly produced a good impression, and it will add substantially to the reputation of the man who is now recognized as, beyond all rivalry, the first composer of America. . . .

A lack of popular appeal was a serious defect of this cantata, according to the *Advertiser*:

> . . . It is true that the work as a whole is not likely to achieve much popularity with common audiences, or, as a whole, to excite the enthusiasm even of companies of well-cultivated listeners until they have become entirely familiar with it. The difficulty is owing to the character of the music written for the first half—or, say, the first five stanzas—of the poem. The composition here has many beauties, it is true; it is refined, scholarly, agreeable writing, by no means barren in its ideas or uningenious in its forms. Some of its beauties are rare and unique. . . . But . . . this portion of the cantata is somewhat heavy and produces the effect of monotony. The great submerging wave of vocal tone, always sweet and sonorous though it be, lacks strong, original, and varied effects, and too much reliance is placed for coloring upon the orchestration, which, with all its cleverness, is not equal to the burden put upon it. . . .

More acceptable to the writer was the following passage for soprano solo and chorus; Part II, "The shepherds on the lawn," for the solo quartet and chorus, was

> . . . an absolutely exquisite bit of idyllic poetry in music, . . . and worked up with an eloquent and appropriate elaboration not unworthy of Handel himself. . . .

However, as if to make up for the frankly negative feelings about the beginning of the cantata, the writer can find only the highest words of praise for Part III, the final chorus, a setting of stanzas 13–15 of the Milton hymn, which

> . . . will rank, we think, as the greatest achievement of Mr. Paine's career thus far. . . .

Since these words are so unequivocal, it might be in order here to describe what motivated the *Advertiser's* music critic. Paine's setting of the text is indeed effective and brilliant. And perhaps more interesting to the student of this composer is the word-painting—unusual for Paine—found with these lines:

> And let the bass of heaven's deep organ blow;
> And with your nine-fold harmony
> Make up full concert to the angelic symphony.

At the first appearance of the word "blow" the organ reinforces the orchestra with a *fortississimo* low C, held as a pedal point for four bars. Two bars later the composer sets the syllable "nine-" to an A-minor chord voiced in nine parts: SSAATTTBB—a spectacular division which is not continued. Within three bars the normal four-part choral texture is resumed. Such obvious text setting possibly considered by the composer as a concession to public taste could not have been a more fortuitous creative decision, for it seems to have rescued this otherwise worthy but dull piece. Dwight's analysis considered this finale to be the "strongest chorus" of the work, and found especially remarkable its conclusion, where the chorus sustains its final notes beyond the close of the last orchestral chord:

> [The chorus] is jubilant and more exciting to the close, where the voices hold out the last chord as long as they have breath. . . .

In complete agreement was the critic from the *Advertiser*, who also noted the effect on the crowd:

> . . . The whole of this chorus is magnificent and imposing, and in its final phrases it fairly reaches the point of sublimity, as the united voices cling in an ecstasy of joy through measure after measure to the single work which epitomizes the fruition of their hopes of Heaven and the hereafter. This was recognized at once as a true triumph of genius, and more than justified the great burst of enthusiastic applause with which Mr. Paine was rewarded and by which he was recalled to the stage. . . .

The success of this premiere encouraged the Handel and Haydn

Society to perform the work a second time six years later, at a 29 January 1888 concert at Music Hall; the soprano soloist was Gertrude Franklin. The cantata was followed by the Berlioz *Te Deum*, and Dwight complained that the orchestra—enlarged for the Berlioz—tended to obscure the chorus[23] in the Paine work. Louis C. Elson, in reviewing the concert, compared the two works and found *The Nativity* far more significant than the *Te Deum* that followed:

> . . . The greatest pleasure of the evening was derived from the opening work. Not as grand as "Oedipus Tyrannus," which we regard as the high-water mark of American music, "The Nativity" is yet a great work in the native repertoire, or, for the matter of that, in any repertoire whatsoever. Sufficiently contrapuntal to belong to cantata classics, its loftiness of treatment does not debar most melodious effects appearing, and its Pastorale alone outweighs in merit the greater part of the Berlioz work. It is thoroughly singable, and the chorus and soloists seemed to enter with zest into its performance. . . .[24]

But Elson found the orchestral support unsatisfactory, "being rigid and inelastic in the extreme." The "large audience" again found the work's conclusion especially enjoyable:

> . . . The final choruses went superbly and aroused the chief enthusiasm of the evening.

The Nativity was also presented—fully or in part—in two other cities within the decade. During the 1886–87 season in New York, Part II of the cantata, "The Shepherds on the lawn," formed part of a Chickering Hall Symphonic Concert, with Frank van der Stucken, conductor.[25] And the Handel and Haydn Society of Pittsburgh included the entire work in their 1887–88 schedule.[26]

Bostonians had one more opportunity to hear *The Nativity*, at the sixth annual concert of the People's Choral Union on 22 March 1903. This was an amateur organization, described as follows in an announcement of the concert:

> . . . The work of the union is both philanthropic and educational, and it is interesting to know that the gratuitous labor of the instructors of the union is heartily appreciated by those who have come to gain a knowledge of sight reading and singing through their efforts. . . .[27]

Samuel W. Cole conducted the concert, for which preparations were begun the previous October.[28] At this time Paine's *Nativity* and a Weber cantata, *In Constant Order (In seiner Ordnung schafft der Herr*, op. 36), were announced as the "main numbers of the schedule"; compositions by Mozart and Edgar Stillman Kelley completed the program. Soloists were Mrs. Evta [*sic*] Kileski-Bradbury, soprano; Alice Mabel Stanaway, alto; Clarence B. Shirley, tenor; and Leverett B. Merrill, bass; assisting were the Boston Festival Orchestra[29] and organist Jennie Weller.[30] *Transcript* reviewer "R.R.G." commented very favorably on the work and on Paine's standing as a composer:

> . . . This work of Mr. Paine's was interesting to hear once more. It has much in it that is beautiful. . . . Mr. Paine has still to be removed from his place as the first of American composers, a place he holds firmly. . . .[31]

The *Herald* writer also praised

> . . . Prof. Paine's noble and beautiful cantata, founded on Milton's grand, yet tender hymn—a composition that inclines toward the best form and spirit of English sacred music, but has its touches of later fancy and modern grace, in no wise detracting from its religious nature. . . .

Paine's creative talent benefited Harvard when he set a Latin text by Professor James Bradstreet Greenough[32] as a *Harvard Commencement Hymn* or *Commemoration Hymn*, composed in 1862; a sextodecimo copy of Paine's *Hymn for Commencement*, with words by Greenough, dated 1862, is. in the Library of Congress music collection. W R. Spalding recalls the Glee Club singing "Professor Paine's Commencement Hymn" on 11 December 1882.[33] The *Hymn* was first published commercially by A. P. Schmidt in 1883, and doubtless immediately came into regular use. The *Commemoration Hymn* was sung at the 250th anniversary of Harvard University on 7 November 1886[34] and the score was included in an appropriate collection published by Schmidt.[35] Paine's tune subsequently appeared in several Protestant church hymnals, set to different texts.

Older works of the composer also continued to appear regularly on concert programs; these new cantatas and the *Oedipus* music did not lessen the public interest in earlier Paine compositions. One such work was the *Piano Trio in D minor*, op. 22, which had been performed privately much earlier—at an 18 December 1874 Fiske "parlour concert" where it was "brought out," or played for the first time. Its first public performance was at a 16 February 1882 concert at Wesleyan Hall, played by pianist Carlyle Petersilea, violinist Leandro Campanari, and cellist Wulf Fries.[36] A year later the Mueller-Campanari Quartet played a much earlier work—the youthful *String Quartet*—on a 26 February 1883 concert.

The *Sonata for Violin and Piano in B minor*, op. 24 (1875), enjoyed four performances during the 1880s involving two Boston pianists. William H. Sherwood and violinist Alfred de Sève played the work during the 1884–85 concert season, billed inaccurately as the "first performance in Boston."[37] Sherwood included the sonata on a Boston program of

American compositions, 8 November 1887, with Leopold Lichtenberg, violin.[38] He repeated the work two weeks later at a 22 November concert in Frank van der Stucken's Festival of American Composers at Chickering Hall, New York; Gustav Dannreuther was the violinist.[39] Carlyle Petersilea and violinist Charles N. Allen also included the sonata on a Union Hall chamber concert in Boston, 1 May 1886. A Carl Baermann concert at Union Hall, Boston, on 20 March 1891, provided another hearing of the *Larghetto and Scherzo*, op. 32 (1877), heralded as a "new work." Louis C. Elson, in reviewing the concert, remarked that Paine

> . . . in these later days is writing in a more romantic and earnest manner than ever before. In the "St. Peter" days, he was controlled by rules, but now he is their master, and the earnest depth of the larghetto and scherzo for piano, violin and cello and the freedom of the form, reminded of Schumann in his best period.
>
> The larghetto had a climax absolutely grand, and the scherzo was rather of the dramatic Chopin type than in the playful Mendelssohn vein. The hearty enthusiasm which followed its performance may have been a protest against the prosiness of some of the American music we have recently had, as well as a tribute to the composer (who was compelled to bow from his seat among the audience), and to the fine performance. . . .[40]

On 29 December 1898 the *Larghetto and Scherzo* appeared on an Adamowski String Quartet concert at Association Hall, Brooklyn;[41] the same composition also was included on one of the ten Harvard chamber concerts given during the 1898–99 season.[42] A *Trio for piano, violin and 'cello*—"first time"—was played at a 4 December 1899 Kneisel Quartet concert at Association Hall, Boston; performers were Mrs. Maas-Tapper, piano, Max Zach, and H. Heberlein.[43] There are no extant works in this medium that were still unplayed at that time; possibly the work was the *Trio*, op. 22, which had not had a public performance since 1882.

Another early work, the amusing *Radway's Ready Relief* for unaccompanied male chorus and bass solo, apparently received its first public performance at an Apollo Club concert on 25 April 1883. The club published the music privately, copyright 1883 by Davenport Bros.; later printings were issued by Oliver Ditson. Information about the date and circumstances of its composition is scarce, and the year has been placed variously as 1863 or 1864. The Ditson printings state "Composed in 1863" on the title page, and this date is also mentioned in the *Advertiser* review of the 1883 Apollo concert. However, a note from Paine to the *Musical Record*,[44] in response to a reader's question, gives the later year:

> *To the Editor of the Musical Record*:
> "Radway's Ready Relief" was composed in 1864, a youthful jest on my part,

suggested by an advertisement I saw in the newspaper, and written for some friends of mine in Portland, Me.,—my birthplace.

Yours, very truly,
John K. Paine.

Cambridge, March 11, 1884.

Whichever is more accurate, certainly the composer was more than "barely past twenty-one" when he wrote the song, as M. A. DeWolfe Howe states in his *Musical Quarterly* article on the composer.

The advertisement mentioned in the above note extolled the miraculous virtues of a popular quack patent medicine. Its greatly exaggerated claims were set playfully in an overblown, pompous dramatic-overture style, including a florid recitative for the soloist and some rather difficult passages for the chorus. At the climactic words,

> . . . And for sale everywhere, by all apothecaries in the land, including Chelsea Beach. Ask for Radway's Ready Relief. . . .

the bantering composer concluded with a parody of the F-major finale of Beethoven's *Egmont Overture*, including the piccolo part in the last five bars (originally "To be whistled."). Paine's ready wit and his love of punning are seen on the title page of the Apollo Club publication: ". . . Composed by Dr. Dolore." The setting "proved rather trying to the club" at its 1883 concert, according to the *Advertiser*,[45] and the *Transcript* critic noted that "at one time the chorus came almost to pieces. . . ."[46] But the latter enthusiastically praised the humor in the work:

> . . . Mr. Paine's "Radway's Ready Relief" is one of the most heartily humorous musical jokes that we know of. . . . The music cleverly takes off both the Handelian contrapuntal and the modern picturesque styles, the burlesque solemnity of the writing being infinitely comic, the whole ending with a side-splitting parody on the Finale to the "Egmont" overture. . . . The very excellence of the writing and the purity of the musical form add another element of ludicrousness to what is, in conception and execution, one of the most overwhelming bits of humor we know of in all music. . . .

The *Advertiser* reviewer also had enjoyed the piece:

> . . . It is a trifle in one sense of the word, but is exceedingly ingenious and one of the most genuinely humorous bits of music that we have heard for a long time. It is serio-comic, of course, and nearly all the chief forms of the most sedate composers are used in turn with droll effect. In the solo—which was smoothly sung by Mr. Babcock—the series of roulades is very comical, but even that is not so funny as the steady melodic sweetness and dynamic softness that characterize the music which directly follows, and is fitted to the words, "The continued use of Radway's Ready Relief cured him." The closing phrases are very involved and intricate, abounding in runs and roulades, and written sometimes in the mode of a fugue, sometimes in that

of the canon, but all have a very humorous effect, which reaches its height with the help of some unexpected notes from the piccolo. . . .

The Apollo Club repeated *Radway's Ready Relief* the next year at their pair of concerts on 20 and 25 February 1884.[47] In the following years performances were heard in other cities as well, including Cincinnati's Apollo Club, B. W. Foley, conductor, which sang the work on 12 April 1888;[48] Albany's Schubert Club, which included *Radway* on a 26 February 1891 concert;[49] and New York's Mendelssohn Glee Club, conducted by Joseph Mosenthal (1834–96), which included the work on the opening concert of their eighteenth season.[50] A strongly negative comment about *Radway* resulted from this last concert, in the opinion of reviewer "H.H.," who saw no humor at all:

> . . . It is . . . a matter of regret, and was evidently so regarded by some of the truest friends of the [Mendelssohn] club, that it should have blotted one of its fair programmes with the words of Mr. J. K. Paine's song, with which the concert was concluded, and have given its attention to such trash. The title of this delectable composition is "Radway's Ready Relief," and the words set forth *in extenso* the value of that compound. Since the position of the Mendelssohn Glee Club makes it impossible to believe that its programmes would be used for the purpose of advertising a patent medicine, one is forced to the conclusion that the words of this song are intended to be facetious. As a matter of fact it would be difficult to imagine anything more haft [sic] witted and silly. Their perusal is calculated to produce an emotion of profound melancholy. If "Radway's Ready Relief" possesses the medical value which Mr. J. K. Paine claims for it, it would be a good thing for him to saturate himself freely with it before he writes another song. But for the Mendelssohn Glee Club the kindest advice is to avoid "Radway's Ready Relief," and thereby get rid of pain. . . .

In comparison to the appreciation—or lack of it—resulting from concert hearings of *Radway's Ready Relief* during the 1880s and 90s, probably a much greater enjoyment accompanied numerous private, informal performances among family and friends. A letter of John Fiske describes musical activities at the Isles of Shoals during 18–20 August 1890, with a concluding performance of *Radway* at the Thaxter cottage:

> Monday went to Appledore, Isles of Shoals, taking Abby and Maud. . . . It was devilish hot in Boston, cool at Appledore. Had a deluge of music all through the visit. Monday evening orgy of Beethoven and Chopin by Paine, and beautiful songs by Clara Doria Rogers. . . . Tuesday morning . . . ramble on rocks with the Paines. . . . Wednesday went to the Pavilion with Abby. In afternoon songs in big hall with Maud's accompaniment, also songs by Maud. . . . In evening had fine audience to hear "Las Casas", also given in big hall. From there to Celia's parlour for another hour of music. Piano by Miss Henrietta Dana, more songs by Clara Rogers and songs by me. Miss Dana and Miss Benedict accompanists. And we had "Radway's Ready Relief" by Paine, which brought forth peals of laughter. . . .[51]

Much of Paine's compositional effort must have been directed toward small forms during the early years of the 1880s. A song, *The clover blossoms kiss her feet*, carries the date 1 October 1882; it was never published. It set a poem of Oscar Laighton, a brother of Celia Thaxter and one of the managers of the Appledore House, Isles of Shoals. In 1884 Arthur P. Schmidt published a set of four songs, op. 40: *A bird upon a rosy bough* (Celia Thaxter), *A farewell* (Charles Kingsley), *Beneath the starry arch* (Harriet Martineau), and *Music when soft voices die* (Shelley). Only one performance of any of these is known—an Arthur Foote concert (according to his *Scrap-book*) at Chickering Hall, Boston, on 15 March 1887, on which George J. Parker sang *A farewell*;[52] in reviewing the concert, the *Post* found this "among the best" of the songs, while the *Advertiser* approved of its "good commonplace style."[53] Three other programs, also in the Foote scrapbook, list performances of Paine's most popular song, *Matin Song*—a 15 December 1884 recital by a Mrs. Otis Rockwood, soprano, at Temple Grove Seminary, a recital of American Songs on 15 March 1886 by Lillian E. Stoddard at the Northwestern Conservatory of Music,[54] and an American Music Society concert in Boston, 25 May 1893, with Mrs. Anne Kennard-Martin.[55] Singer Emil Tiferro, a good friend of Paine, included his songs on recitals, such as the one on 16 March 1895 at Steinert Hall; as often happened, the specific titles were not supplied in the press, but *Matin Song* quite possibly was among those performed.[56] Later performances of *Matin Song*, listed in the *Musical Courier*, include a program for the Woman's Club of Evanston, Illinois, on 8 January 1901, including both *Matin Song* and *I wore your roses yesterday*, along with the *Nocturne*, op. 45, for piano;[57] a November 1903 recital by Paul Savage at Hyde Park, Massachusetts;[58] a May 1905 program at the American Institute of Applied Music, New York;[59] and a 16 November 1905 recital by Harrison Bennett, bass, at Steinert Hall, Boston.[60]

Several published piano works also added to Professor Paine's esteem as a composer in the smaller forms. A *Romance*, op. 39, dedicated to Prof. J. B. Greenough (author of the text to the *Harvard Hymn*), was the first to appear, published by Ditson late in 1883;[61] a "New Music" item in the *Advertiser* included it among "several things of more than commonplace character" from Ditson's latest publications.[62] In 1884 the earlier *Romance*, op. 12—originally published in 1869 by Koppitz, Prüfer, & Co.—was reissued by Schmidt; the *Advertiser* found it "of . . . length and solidity. . . ."[63] At about the same time Schmidt also issued "three bright little things"—*A Spring Idyl*, *Birthday Impromptu*, and *Fuga Giocosa*—comprising op. 41, copyright 1884. *A Spring Idyl* was dedicated to

Miss Sarah D. Hoppin, and *Birthday Impromptu* was inscribed to Harvard Professor W. G. Farlow by way of a musical pun, "Fa low:"

A MON AMI

This composition was first published separately in 1882 in a private edition. A contemporary review of *Birthday Impromptu* announced approval:

> The hand of the skilled musician is apparent in every bar of this exquisite little trifle. There is also a freshness and originality pervading it, that is exceedingly fascinating, and slight as it is, (being the merest sketch), it contains a wealth of idea, that one fails to find in many compositions of far more pretension.[64]

Fuga giocosa used as its subject the tune, "Over the fence is out, boys." "It has . . . been pronounced by musicians a real inspiration," according to Edwards,[65] and was cited as a contemporary ideal in Goodrich's *Analysis* and Spalding's illustrations for *Music, an Art and a Language*.[66] In 1889 A. P. Schmidt published the *Nocturne*, op. 45, the last of the composer's piano works to be put into print. According to W. S. B. Mathews, this was not a recent composition:

> . . . This nocturne, . . . after remaining unwritten for years and frequently played by the author at the request of his friends, was then written down, in which form it remained unpublished for quite a long time. . . .[67]

Mathews continues with a rather quaint description of the piece:

> . . . It is an excellent melody and effectively written. The mood of the nocturne is properly that of a quiet sadness, or confidence, such as is engendered by the darkness and the serious reflections which naturally spring up in the mind when the incitation of the sense of sight is temporarily shut off.

Records of performances of piano works are scarce. Some that are known include *Spring Idyl* on a 3 July 1884 concert at Case Hall, Cleveland;[68] the same work on an all-American program by Calixa Lavallée in Boston[69] in May 1885;[70] and the *Fuga giocosa* at an Emil Liebling recital in Chicago during May 1886.[71] Mrs. H. H. A. Beach played the *Nocturne* at a Tremont Temple recital on 27 February 1891; Paine "was in the right balcony to hear it. . . ."[72] Amy Fay continued to include Paine works regularly in her "piano conversations," although there is no indication that she played any from op. 39, 41, or 45. Three of her programs from about the turn of the century were a Chickering Hall concert in New York on 18 October 1898 (the *Musical Courier* announcement failed to mention the Paine work);[73] a January 1900 Conversation at the Wanamaker piano store in New York, on which she played the first five pieces from *In the Country*, op. 26;[74] and a third in Peekskill, N. Y., on 17 January 1901, when she again performed *In the Country*.[75]

Two further long-unpublished works, issued in 1892 by Arthur P. Schmidt, were given French titles: *Deux Préludes pour l'orgue composés par John K. Paine*, op. 19. Prelude No. 1, in D flat, is marked "Larghetto," the second, in B minor, "con moto." Both compositions probably may be dated from the composer's first years in Boston, given the low opus number, but owing to a conflict in titles it is difficult to ascertain when they were composed or played. An *Offertoire* is listed among the pieces that Paine played during the 1863–64 season at Music Hall.[76] Then, on a 30 July 1864 Music Hall recital, he played an *Offertoire in B minor, No. 2*, that Dwight called "a new one."[77] Among the composer's works that he played during the 1865–66 season were an *Offertoire in B-flat*, the *Offertoire in B minor*, and an *Organ Piece in D-flat* (twice).[78] It is possible that the *Offertoires* are the same as the *Préludes*, thereby explaining the French title in a publication intended for an American and German market; French influence had become much more fashionable, for many young American organists were choosing to study in France.[79] One may easily assume that the *Offertoire in B minor, No. 2* is the same as the *Prelude No. 2, in B minor. The Organ Piece in D-flat* may have been the *Prelude No. 1*, with the *Offertoire in B-flat* being a separate composition no longer extant. However, it is quite possible that *B* flat was substituted for *D* flat as a printer's error, either on the part of Dwight or, more likely, originating with the printed program from which he compiled his list; if so, the *Offertoire* and *Organ Piece* may have been the same composition.

Few performances of the *Preludes* are mentioned in contemporary periodicals, reflecting the relative decline of the organist's prestige from earlier decades when Dwight and his colleagues were influential. Three performances of the *Prelude in D flat* are known, however. On 7 April 1900 William C. Carl (1865–1936) played it at a meeting of the Gamut Club at Old First Presbyterian Church, New York,[80] and, in Boston, Arthur Foote included the work at his Old First Church recitals on 4 February 1904 and 9 February 1905.[81] More popular were the two sets of variations on national anthems. William C. Carl included the *Variations on the Austrian Hymn* on two New York recitals—a February 1890 organ concert of American compositions at the Church of the Incarnation,[82] and an American composers' song recital at which he assisted, at the Mendelssohn Glee Club hall on 23 April 1897.[83] Carl played a Paine composition

(unnamed in the report) at a 3 November 1895 recital at Old First Presbyterian Church, New York, where he had served as organist since 1892,[84]
and had included organ works of the composer on other programs at the
church.[85] Organist Everett E. Truette, at a Tremont Temple recital on
5 January 1887, performed a Paine composition puzzlingly titled *Variations on the Russian National Hymn*.[86] Perhaps the Austrian hymn variations were actually played. There is nothing to suggest that Paine wrote
a composition using the familiar melody by Alexis Lvov. However, for a
time Russia used for its anthem the tune common to "God Save the
Queen" or "Heil dir im Siegeskranz," on which Paine based a fugue;
Truette could have played this, though he would have needed to play from
manuscript, for it was never published. The most-often played set of
Paine's variations during the last decades of his life was the *Concert
Variations on the Star-Spangled Banner*, doubtless because of its popular
patriotic appeal. Organ concerts held in conjunction with the World's
Fairs of 1892 (Chicago) and 1904 (St. Louis) provided opportunities for
this work to be heard. Harrison M. Wild, organist at Chicago's Unity
Church, included the *Variations* on a recital series given October 1892–
March 1893.[87] The work appeared on a student recital at Boston's Sleeper
Hall in March 1892.[88] J. Warren Andrews, organist at the Church of the
Divine Paternity in New York, ended a 19 July 1904 concert at the St.
Louis World's Fair with the *Star-Spangled Banner* variations,[89] and closed
a 22 December 1904 recital at his church in New York with the same
composition.[90] And Organist James W. Hill ended a 17 January 1906 re-
cital at the First Universalist Church, Haverhill, Massachusetts, with the
Fugue on Star-Spangled Banner.[91]

During the 1880s and '90s Paine's major orchestral works continued
to be played by the leading orchestras of America. The *Spring Symphony*
was performed at least eight more times—wholly or in part—during the
dozen years following its first performances in Boston and Cambridge.
One of the most important was at the Brooklyn Philharmonic rehearsal
and concert on 30–31 March 1883, when the composer conducted the
first hearing of the work in the New York area. The Friday afternoon
rehearsal drew an enthusiastic capacity crowd, despite a snow storm.
The *Times* called the symphony "ambitious," praised its scoring, and
found it inspired:

> The symphony is not merely a technically correct piece of musical joinership, but
> contains themes which are skillfully treated and managed with boldness and origi-
> nality. In the second part of the first movement, there are reminiscences of a passage
> in the Pastoral Symphony so marked as to excite instant attention, and at other points
> there are indications of a study of Beethoven's methods. The third movement is very
> graceful and will be likely to be the favorite portion of the work, though the fourth

movement is the most impressive and contains a strong, stately theme which is admirably treated. . . .[92]

After the Saturday concert, a writer for the Brooklyn *Eagle* assessed the symphony as "the finest composition that has as yet emanated from the pen of [an] American composer," noted its "profound scholarship," originality, and richness of instrumentation, and opined:

> Mr. Paine has been happily successful in shaping a safe course between the new school and the old; and while the tendencies of the symphony are perhaps more in the direction of the former than the latter, there are yet unmistakable evidences that the author is strongly imbued with the influences of the older masters, particularly Beethoven. . . .[93]

A *Tribune* review[94] following the Saturday concert spoke of Paine as being "easily foremost of American composers" and called the symphony "a serious, important and totally beautiful work." That it was "scholarly and learned" was affirmed by the reviewer, who preferred, however, to stress "the quality of [Paine's] thought, and that seemed to us fresh, delightful, and abundant." Most typical of the composer appeared to be the interior movements:

> The second and third movements we judge show more clearly than either of the others Professor Paine's affinities and the influences which most move him. They remind us of three masters, Beethoven, Wagner, Berlioz. This implies formative influence upon the composer merely, not slavish imitation in his work. . . .

Programmatic elements in the first movement were effective, according to the *Tribune* writer, who also found the "chorale-like paean" in the finale to be "simply thrilling." A reviewer for *The Nation*[95] declared that the last movement ". . . marks the climax not only of the *Spring Symphony*, but of its author's creative power." Praise was given for the "brilliant, clear, and effective instrumentation:"

> . . . Professor Paine has the true orchestral instinct, and is in this respect immensely superior to Herr Max Bruch, for instance, who has just left Liverpool to pay this country a professional visit. . . .

The *Nation* judged that "excellent workmanship" was "combined with originality of invention," and found fault with only the "extreme length:"

> In this respect a good lesson is taught by Beethoven's Eighth Symphony, which was played at the same concert and only consumed about half as much time—twenty-three minutes. . . .

A year later Paine again conducted the *Spring Symphony*, this time

at a Boston Symphony Orchestra rehearsal and concert on 28 February
and 1 March 1884. The *Advertiser* reviewer remarked that the composition "gains in interest" with repeated hearings:

> . . . The writing is learned, and the harmonic treatment often requires close attention;
> but on better acquaintance many fine things came out which at first observation did
> not catch, and the vein of melody proves to be richer and more varied than a single
> hearing would imply. The symphony was received with evident pleasure, and Mr.
> Paine was presented with a handsome bouquet, from which depended an exuberance
> of broad blue ribbon. . . .[96]

The *Andante* (third movement) was included on a 17 June 1885 Music Hall Popular Concert, conducted by Adolf Neuendorff. The program
was devoted exclusively to works by Boston composers; "local pride and
patriotism were duly considered"[97] in this observance of Bunker Hill Day,
a local holiday. Frank van der Stucken included the *Spring Symphony* on
the first of his American concerts at New York's Chickering Hall on
15 November 1887.[98]

The last two known performances of the *Spring Symphony* occurred
simultaneously in Boston and Chicago on 8–9 April 1892. The Boston
Symphony Orchestra concert was given in Music Hall, led by Arthur
Nikisch. Reviewer Louis C. Elson, who considered the symphony "as
yet the best work in this form which America has produced,"[99] was
greatly dissatisfied with the performance:

> The Spring Symphony has been much better played in this city than it was on this
> occasion; . . . the nobility of the finale was thoroughly eliminated. In this finale there
> is a broad and massive theme like a hymn of thanksgiving, in splendid contrast with
> the bubbling joy of the other themes; the composer marked this "Meno mosso, e
> Maestoso"; three times does this occur, and three times was it *dis*regarded. What
> should have been majesty became mere bluster, and even the Allegro Giojoso became
> a wild Allegro Furioso. Possibly the conductor, but newly accustomed to our climate,
> endeavored to adapt the Spring Symphony to New England conditions, but I cannot
> believe that Prof. Paine had a Boston spring in mind when he evolved this tone
> picture, and in any case his marks of Tempo should have been respected without
> regard to the local thermometers.

On the same two days the Chicago Symphony Orchestra, conducted by
Theodore Thomas, began the eighteenth concert of its first season with
the *Spring Symphony*. Also on the program was the aria, "Oh God, My
God, Forsake Me Not," from *St. Peter*; George E. Holmes was the soloist.[100] Paine was present at this concert, as may be seen from his 6 April
letter to Mrs. Anna Lyman Gray:

> I regret that I shall be unable to accept your very kind invitation for Saturday
> evening, but I am going to Chicago this afternoon to be absent from home a week,

so that I shall lose the pleasure of seeing you and hearing my symphony at the Music Hall: two things to regret, especially the former. . . .

I am invited to Chicago by Theodore Thomas, who is to give my Spring Symphony with his orchestra while I am there. I am also going to lecture on Beethoven & Schubert—with illustrations by a Quartet Club—before the Twentieth Century Club. . . .[101]

A final appearance of the symphony on a concert program was also in Chicago, but for a far less ambitious medium: the Amateur Club included a piano duet performance of the *Scherzo* in its March 1899 program of springtime music.[102]

Paine's major attempt to combine program music with symphonic form, his *Symphonic Poem: Shakespeare's Tempest* (1877), no longer aroused the controversy of its first performance; rather, it became one of his most popular orchestral compositions, enjoying eight performances during the 1880s in Boston, Chicago, Philadelphia, and New York. Paine conducted the work on a 10 March 1883 Boston Symphony Orchestra concert; the performance was repeated at Sanders Theatre, Cambridge, on 22 March, the composer again conducting.[103] The audience that heard the Boston concert was "one of the smallest of the season," owing both to the inclement weather and to the fact that many musical Bostonians were elsewhere enjoying Adelina Patti at the opera.[104] But those in attendance were receptive and demonstrative, according to the *Musical Record*:

... Mr. Paine was warmly received as he stepped upon the stage to conduct his work, which was enthusiastically applauded. . . .[105]

The *Advertiser* added:

... On his retirement from the conductor's stand [he] was recalled with great enthusiasm. . . .

The reviewer for the *Advertiser*, apparently agreeing with John Fiske's description of the work on the occasion of its first performance in 1877, complimented the work highly for not abandoning traditional formal procedures, despite its Shakespearian program:

... From such a title and such full detail of explanation of the work given to the listener in advance, one might well be excused for jumping to the conclusion that it would be found to be of the sensational character so common in modern "programme" music, in which form and purely musical sentiment are made subordinate to mere vividness of material suggestion; but the alchemy of genius turns even the basest elements to pure gold, and so Professor Paine, so far from being hampered by the conditions under which he placed himself in undertaking this work, has cunningly made these conditions to serve as suggestions and sources of inspiration in building up a structure of noble beauty and symmetry, whose chief value is purely musical, and its descriptive features merely embellishments. . . . The work . . . , like everything else that has as yet come from Professor Paine's pen, is musical in the best sense of the word. It reflects not only great learning, but fine intuition, . . . and the composer's consummate command over the resources of the orchestra has enabled him to put his thought into such tangible shape as to enforce his thought with great clearness. . . .

Paine had revised the score of *The Tempest* prior to the Boston concert, and the *Transcript* remarked about its "somewhat remodelled and improved shape;"[106] other reviewers, however, seemed unaware that the work was not new and had indeed been performed some six years earlier. The revised version was next performed at a Brooklyn Philharmonic concert on 28–29 November 1884, under Theodore Thomas. The nature of the revisions is described in a *Nation* review:

> [The Tempest] is one of [Paine's] best works, and Mr. Thomas and his orchestra gave it an interpretation which insured it a warm reception by the large audience. The composition is not new, having been written about eight or nine years ago and produced heretofore in Cambridge, Boston, New York, and elsewhere. Some improvements, however, have been recently made in the instrumentation; the second movement has been enlarged, and the coda rewritten. As it now stands it not only gives evidence of the scholarship to be expected of a Harvard professor, but of originality of invention and rare felicity in modulation and instrumentation, especially in the second movement, which, with its broad, flowing melody and really exquisite orchestral coloring, is a thing that any contemporary European composer might be proud of. . . .[107]

But not all the New York critics were as generous as the *Nation*. The Brooklyn *Eagle* felt that the work created ". . . only a mildly favorable impression, . . ."[108] and the *Tribune*, while noting that the composer's

> . . . reverence for the old masters appears in this music which charms one by its simplicity and directness and its melodic character, and shows the training of its author in its strict adherence to the well-established rules of the ante-Wagner-Liszt school. . . .[109]

nevertheless considered *The Tempest's* opening storm scene weak in contrast with the one in Wagner's *Flying Dutchman* overture, which—perhaps unfortunately—followed it on the program. The *Times* felt the work

> . . . can scarcely be described as happily suggestive of the ethereal quality of the Shakespearean poem. . . . Mr. Paine's music bears the same relation to the play that the performance of the most skilled of scenic artists who attempts to realize by means of paint and canvas the fairy pictures of "A Midsummer Night's Dream" bears to the scenes conjured up in the dullest of imaginations by a perusal of Shakespeare's text. . . .[110]

Despite this negative comment, the *Times* reviewer found "great excellences" in the work, for Paine "has not succumbed to the Wagnerian influence." He praised the "well defined and symmetrical" themes, and even found many to have a "distinct sensuous beauty." Significant because it seems to have been universally noted was Paine's "full, muscular, and richly colored" orchestration:

> . . . though it is always sonorous and powerful, the composer never resorts to eccentric combinations or to the familiar modern methods of concealing poverty of thought by means of scientific din. . . .

A Boston audience heard *The Tempest* again at a 6–7 November 1885 rehearsal and concert of the Boston Symphony orchestra, when the *Advertiser*, who called Paine's work "noble, poetic and richly varied," complained incidentally about conductor Wilhelm Gericke's tendency to program many German works and too few by contemporary American composers, as well as about sloppy performances. Especially vexing to the reviewer was the lack of uniform bowings:

> . . . This irregularity was noticeable . . . especially in the adagio of Mr. Paine's symphony *[Tempest]*, where the various bowing of the first violins was extraordinary. . . .[111]

Theodore Thomas included *The Tempest* in his Summer Garden Concerts in Chicago on 6 August 1885 and 28 July 1887,[112] and in the fall of 1887 presented it at a Thomas Symphony Concert in New York on 21–22 November.[113] Among the other performances of the work was one given at a Friday afternoon public rehearsal of the Brooklyn Philharmonic on 17 February 1888, with Thomas conducting; this "rehearsal" was actually a concert in its own right, for the program on the following Saturday evening was devoted to Mendelssohn's *Elijah*.[114] Thomas also conducted *The Tempest* in Philadelphia at a 7 April 1888 concert of the Philadelphia Orchestra,[115] and much later led the Chicago Orchestra in a performance during the fall of 1898.[116]

Paine's overture to *As You Like It* (1876), which seems to have gone unperformed since a March 1877 Harvard Musical Association concert, was revived for Theodore Thomas' Summer Garden Concerts in Chicago during July and August, 1889.[117] On 3 December 1896 it opened a concert of the Manuscript Society of New York at Chickering Hall; Silas G. Pratt conducted a 55-piece orchestra.[118] Bostonians had an opportunity to hear the work at the opening of a 26 November 1899 Music Hall popular concert, one of a series given under the auspices of Mayor Quincy and the city's music committee; Emil Mollenhauer was the conductor.[119] "The house was crowded to its utmost capacity, . . ." for the featured soloist of the evening was the pianist Vladimir de Pachmann.[120] A Municipal Concert on 29 January 1901 devoted entirely to music of American composers began with *As You Like It*. A 50-piece orchestra was again conducted by Mollenhauer; the concert, given in Tremont Temple, was sponsored by the Music Commission of Boston. Other composers represented on the program were Henry K. Hadley, Horatio Parker, E. A. MacDowell, George E. Whiting, John A. O'Shea, Arthur Foote, and George W. Chadwick.[121] The *Symphony No. 1*, which also dates from 1876, appeared on a 10 April 1891 concert of American orchestral music, conducted by Walter Damrosch, at the Metropolitan Opera House, honoring the 50th anniversary of the founding of the *New York Tribune;* only the *Adagio* movement was played.[122]

Paine's last work for orchestra—the *Island Fantasy*—was completed in April 1888,[123] and received its first performance by the Boston Symphony Orchestra under Wilhelm Gericke, conductor, at a 19–20 April 1889 rehearsal and concert. While most of Paine's orchestral pieces are programmatic, this fantasy and *The Tempest* are unique because of the presence of explicit extramusical associations. The composer supplied a description to Louis C. Elson, who included the following "authorized synopsis" in announcing the Boston premiere:

> The subject of the "Island Fantasy" was suggested by two beautiful paintings of Summer Island scenes by Mr. J. Appleton Brown, to whom the work is inscribed. The title "Fantasy" should be taken in its literary rather than its musical sense; for the character of the composition is not at all that of the fantasie of which the Bruch concerto, played this year by Mr. Loeffler, is a specimen. Indeed the principal section of the work is in one of the simpler "rondo" forms, containing two varied statements of the principal theme, two elaborate episodes and a coda. To this is prefixed an introduction in which fragments of the themes, elaborated later on, are used as the foundation of music which depicts in a masterly manner the summer sunshine and calm and the summer storm, which are the contrasted subjects of Mr. Brown's paintings.[124]

One may assume that these two paintings were in the Paines' possession at the time, for according to the will of Mary E. Paine, "two Pastels by John Appleton Brown, 'The Inn at Appledore' and 'Moonlight' . . . ,'' were bequeathed to the President and Fellows of Harvard University, "to be placed in the Fogg Art Museum."[125] Doubtless the composer had the Isles of Shoals in mind, as well as these paintings, while he composed the symphonic poem during the mid–1880s. But the tie with Brown's paintings was not mentioned in a descriptive paragraph for a 2 July 1890 performance under Theodore Thomas at the Music Teachers National Association convention in Detroit.[126] This note was similar to the following description which accompanied the 6 July 1893 performance at the Chicago World's Fair, also with Thomas as conductor:

> This work was suggested by the memory of summer days passed at the seashore, midst the varied scenes of ocean life, calm and sunshine, murmuring breezes and rippling waves alternating with surge and storm.[127]

The same paragraph, with minor changes in wording, appears at the beginning of the score published in 1907 by Breitkopf & Härtel as *Poseidon und Amphitrite. Eine Meer-Phantasie. Symphonische Dichtung.—An Ocean Fantasy. Symphonic Poem*. No mention is made of Brown's pastels, and the dedication to the painter is omitted. The change of emphasis to the Poseidon legend is curious; perhaps Paine preferred its universality to the limited local interest of Brown and the Isles of Shoals.

Reviewers and the public received the work with fairly consistent good favor. Elson, in covering the Boston premiere, typically referred to the composer as a father figure in American music, and found considerable evidence of continued growth and development:

> . . . A work by Professor Paine is always a great event in American musical annals. Hector is still Hector, and he forces many other American composers into the lesser role of Astyanax. The work is in strong contrast with the works of his earlier period. In that epoch he allowed his skill to predominate, and emotion was obliged to remain in the background. At present he brings romance, melody and poetry to the foreground, although his skill underlies it all. The fantasy is not as fantastic as most of the compositions with this title, but is in proper Rondo form, with a good amount of development and extension thrown in. The themes are altogether beautiful, and the orchestration is worthy of any existing composer. The use of the harp and flute in contrast with the powerful brass passages is very striking; the horn has some phrases of most romantic order, and the delicate tremolo of the violins is as suggestive of summer calm as anything could be.
>
> The work won a very decided success, and at its close, when the composer was called for, his appearance on the stage elicited a grand burst of enthusiasm.[128]

In the following season *An Island Fantasy* received a New York hearing during a 10–11 January 1890 rehearsal and concert of the Philharmonic-Society of New York. Theodore Thomas was the conductor, and this was the sole performance of any Paine work by the Philharmonic.[129] Reception of the work was favorable, despite an unfortunate circumstance that prevented a "striking" effect from the harp part:

> . . . Criticisms of Professor Paine on the score of the use of a pianoforte are, of course, based on a misapprehension. Illness of the society's harpist compelled the substitution of the pianoforte for the harp—a sorry makeshift.[130]

A writer for the *Times* complained as usual that the piece was

> . . . a composition so thoroughly sentimental in spirit and so rich in instrumentation that it sounded heavily and languorously sweet between the clear sculptured roundness of the Mozart work [Symphony No. 39 in E flat] and the intense, concentrated joyousness of the Beethoven opus.[131]

However, the *Tribune* reviewer found the fantasy "worthy" and "masterly:"

> . . . It is always a pleasure to hear Professor Paine's music, for even when he fails to impart to it that warmth of feeling which compels sympathy, he is sure to interest by the nobility of his musical thought and his freedom from the vulgar and the common place. . . . The dignity of the Philharmonic Society's repertory suffered nothing from the admission of "An Island Fantasy," but a potent hand was extended to the cause of American music—a cause which every sincere lover of the art and every true patriot has at heart. . . .

Theodore Thomas conducted two other performances of *An Island Fantasy* during 1890—the 2 July program at the MTNA convention in Detroit mentioned above, and at one of the Chicago Summer Night Concerts.[132] The work also was represented at a 25 September 1890 concert at the Worcester, Massachusetts, Music Festival; Paine was the conductor. Two fellow American composers also participated—J.C.D. Parker (1828–1916), who led his *Redemption Hymn*, and Victor Herbert, who directed his *Serenade* for string orchestra.[133] At the Chicago Exposition in 1893, Thomas conducted the fantasy at least once, at a 6 July "Concert of American Music in Recognition of the Music Teachers' National Association." Americans represented besides Paine were van der Stucken, Chadwick, Foote, Nevin, Helen Hood, and MacDowell.[134] The composition may have been played a second time at the Exposition, for the Bureau of Music, Chicago, in a 20 October 1893 letter to the *American Art Journal*, reported that it had been performed twice.[135] The work was last heard during the 1894–95 season, when it was played by the Boston Symphony Orchestra under Emil Paur at its 1–2 March 1895 rehearsal and concert; it was repeated on 25 April at Sanders Theatre, Cambridge. The *Herald* spoke of "genuine pleasure" in again hearing the work at its Boston performance. The writer praised the "poetry, grace of sentiment and depth of feeling;" the audience agreed:

> . . . It was heartily and appreciatively applauded, and it continued until Mr. Paine made his appearance on the stage. . . .[136]

In a four-year period Paine accepted commissions for three new compositions, all for large festivals. The first was written for the Cincin-

Illustration 5.   Portrait of Paine (from Mathews, *A Hundred Years of Music in America,* 1889).

nati "Centennial" May Festival of 1888, the latter two for the Columbian Exposition in Chicago during 1892–93. Music director for both of these events was Theodore Thomas, who was also responsible for commissioning a Paine work for the 1876 Centennial Exposition in Philadelphia. For the Cincinnati May Festival Paine wrote the *Song of Promise*, a cantata for solo soprano, chorus, organ, and orchestra, setting a poem by George Edward Woodberry (1855–1930),[137] and published by the John Church Co. of Cincinnati. Lilli Lehmann was the soprano soloist for the performance, held on 22 May. The Festival Chorus consisted of about 600 singers. Thomas conducted his New York orchestra of 108 players, with Arthur Mees (1850–1923) as organist.[138] The *Song of Promise* was the "great feature" of the festival, "according to the most eminent critics who were present."[139] Paine himself was there. Rose Fay, who married Thomas two years later, related a conversation with the composer during a rehearsal of Beethoven's Sixth Symphony:

> While it was going on, J. K. Paine, the composer, had slid quietly into the hall and sat down beside me. He had just arrived from Cambridge, having come on to hear the peformance of his new Cantata, "Song of Promise," which was to be given at the Festival.
>
> "What fire Thomas puts into that orchestra, and what wonderfully sensuous colors he gets out of those instruments!" he exclaimed.
>
> "Yes," said I, "but he has some very remarkable artists in the orchestra, you must remember."
>
> "That is true," said Paine, "but he does it all the same with any musicians he conducts. Why, I am sure he would make even *me* do it if I went up on the stage and blew one of those horns, this minute—though it might happen that I would squawk occasionally," he added prudently.[140]

Despite the success of the *Song of Promise*, it appears never again to have been performed in its entirety. Only the soprano aria received another hearing, in a quite poor rendition by Alice Wentworth at a 14 January 1892 concert of the Boston Philharmonic Orchestra. According to Warren Davenport,

> . . . This composition, written for the artistic and vocal capacity of Lille Lehmann, overweighted the abilities of Miss Wentworth, who has a light and not well grounded voice, which, with a not well rendered accompaniment by the orchestra, placed the composition in a bad light. . . .[141]

Other reviewers found Wentworth to be "especially over-weighted and embarrassed by the somewhat transcendental character" of Paine's aria, which "made demands on her powers which she was scarcely able to fulfill."

For the World's Columbian Exposition in Chicago Paine composed the *Columbus March and Hymn* and the Columbian song, *Freedom, Our Queen*. The commissioned work that aroused the most interest and attained the greatest popularity was the former, written for the ceremonies on 21 October 1892 dedicating the buildings of the exposition. First public notice that Paine would contribute to the musical portion of the exposition was made in a late December 1891 announcement that he would compose "an important orchestral work" and Arthur Foote a vocal work, "both to form a part of the programmes to be given during the progress of the fair."[142] At about the same time the composers were announced for the opening ceremonies:

> . . . Prof. J. K. Paine, of Harvard University, and E. A. McDowell [*sic*], of Boston, have been selected to compose the music for the opening of the World's Fair in Chicago. Mr. Paine will write an orchestral selection and Mr. McDowell compose the music for the ode.[143]

Perhaps the promise of an intensive musical concert situation in Chicago, led by Paine's friend Theodore Thomas, and the recognition given in the commission, gave rise to a rumor circulating in April 1892:

> There is talk about Professor J. K. Paine's removal to Chicago. It is undeniable that sluggish Boston does not always appreciate the prophet at her gate; but it is to be hoped our composer will not leave the land where he is steadily rising in popular estimation. The West may be quicker, but is not the East more steadfast?[144]

Unfortunately, no further hints of this possibility exist in the press or in available private papers. The source of this rumor would be a fascinating discovery.

Paine completed his *March and Hymn* by midsummer, for John Fiske mentioned in a 12 August 1892 letter:

> Brother Paine dropped in at dusk and played his new World's Fair Columbian March.[145]

Words to the hymn were original, and were widely reprinted:

> All hail and welcome, nations of the earth!
> Columbia's greeting comes from every State[.]
> Proclaim to all mankind the world's new birth
> Of freedom, age on age shall consecrate.
> Let war and enmity forever cease,
> Let glorious art and commerce banish wrong,
> The universal brotherhood of peace
> Shall be Columbia's high, inspiring song.[146]

An octavo edition of the Hymn was soon published by the Oliver Ditson Company, Boston—the Library of Congress copyright copy is dated

24 September 1892. Descriptions of the work began to appear in the press. One of the earlier offered the following praise:

> . . . To state that the composition is wholly worthy of the fame of the foremost composer of America, is but to give it the commendation it so richly merits. Those who attend the dedicatory exercises of the Exposition will greatly enjoy the interpretation of this grand "Columbus March and Hymn."[147]

An interview between the Boston correspondent of the *American Art Journal* and the "genial professor" yielded the first authoritative description of the work:

> . . . He was not to be found in his beautiful home on Hawthorn street, near Brattle, but was accessible in his instruction room, in the old Law School Building, at the angle of Harvard Square.
>
> Though busy with a class of young gentlemen, he presently found time to exchange greetings with his visitor, and for a short walk and longer conversation a few moments later, when the class was dismissed. It was in the first brief chat, however, that the professor communicated the general facts in regard to his Columbus March and Hymn, as he entitles it. . . .
>
> The Professor said that this was really the first time he had given out even such a brief synopsis, and that in a day or so it must be sent to Chicago, for public and press use. . . .[148]

The statement supplied to the *Journal* was brief and somewhat informal. Paine greatly revised and expanded his description before sending it to the press and to Chicago. Resulting was this piece, which appeared in the December *Musical Record*:

> "The Columbus March" is in symphonic form, with two leading themes in strong rhythmical contrast with each other; subordinate melodies are also employed. An extended introduction prepares for the leading theme. The work opens with a fanfare of trumpets, with full, short chords of the whole orchestra, followed by a unison of all the wind instruments (a monologue in recitative form). Then comes the first hint of the leading theme, and a gradual crescendo to *ff* of the whole orchestra; a pedal point on the dominant and a long chord is held, then, after a pause, the theme enters.
>
> The March is not made up of repeated divisions like the usual form with cadences and pauses, but is more continuous and connective, like the movement of a symphony. In the coda there is a reminiscence of the introduction with the trumpet fanfare and pedal point, which forms the climax of the instrumental part, and leads, through a long trill of the soprano instruments, sustained by the full harmony of the orchestra, to the hymn, which opens in unison of all the voices *ff*. The Hymn is in 3-2 time, *maestoso*, and stands in marked contrast to the 4-4 time of the March.
>
> The orchestration of the Hymn is so written that it may be played in connection with the March as an orchestral piece without the vocal chorus. The March is in D-major, but the tonality of key changes often. Many rhythmical effects appear

scored for the following-named instruments: one piccolo, two flutes, two oboes, one English horn, three clarionets, three bassoons, four horns, three trumpets (or more), three trombones, one tuba, three tympani, large and small drums, triangle and cymbals, string quintet, organ. The March and Hymn are about fifteen minutes long.[149]

Thousands of musicians were on hand to perform at the opening festivities. George P. Upton later described the occasion:

> The inaugural ceremonies took place October 21, in the stately Manufacturers' and Liberal Arts Building. The dedication music, which was performed under [Theodore] Thomas's direction, included "Columbus March and Hymn," written for the occasion by Prof. John K. Paine; dedicatory ode, music by G. W. Chadwick; Mendelssohn's cantata, "To the Sons of Art," accompanying the award of medals to the master artists of the Exposition; Haydn's chorus, "The Heavens are telling"; Handel's "Hallelujah" chorus; the "Star Spangled Banner" and "Hail Columbia," with full chorus and orchestral accompaniment; and Beethoven's chorus, "In Praise of God." The musical forces for the occasion were composed of the following musicians of Chicago: Apollo Club and auxiliary, 700; the World's Fair Children's Chorus, 1,500; surpliced choirs, 500; members of quartette choirs, 200; German societies, 800; Scandinavian societies, 200; Welsh societies, 200; orchestra and bandsmen, 300, besides 100 drummers for a few phrases in the Chadwick music, and six additional harps.[150]

Some fascinating details of the performance are supplied by the conductor's wife, who provided a more generous estimate of the number of singers:

> . . . As everything was on such a vast scale, Mr. Thomas had 5,500 voices in his chorus, two hundred players in the orchestra, two large military bands, and two drum corps, of fifty each. The latter were stationed in a balcony above, on either side of the stage. As he could not speak to this great body of performers, by reason of the distance, and they could not see his baton distinctly, he did not use one, but instead held a handkerchief in his hand, gathering in the ends so that they could not flutter, but leaving enough of it visible to catch the eye of even the remotest singer on the top row. As the time for each of the musical numbers drew near, he gave a signal to the two drum corps, who immediately began a long double roll, which started softly, swelled louder and louder, fell and rose again in obedience to the hand which held the handkerchief, until every performer had found his place, every instrument was in position, every eye fixed on the conductor, and every listener spellbound in attention, and then, CRASH! the sound was like the last trump, and the attack of these thousands was as sharp and steady as in an ordinary concert. . . .
>
> The musical numbers were all received with enthusiasm, and the works of the American composers, Chadwick and Paine, brought out hearty applause. . . .[151]

Excitement was widespread in the huge audience. The correspondent for the *Advertiser*, perhaps forgetting for the moment the monster Boston Peace Jubilees of 1869 and 1872, showed a typical response:

> . . . Mind cannot conceive nor pencil describe the scene that was presented when the last of those that had participated in the parade were seated. On the platform were representatives of every country in the civilized globe. Before them the largest audience that has ever assembled since the day upon which the creator said, "Let there be light." Little time was occupied in preliminaries. Without waiting for a signal, the orchestra broke forth with the opening strains of the Columbia march, arousing the audience to a high pitch of enthusiasm. . . .[152]

But not all were as favorably impressed by such numbers or hoopla. A correspondent for the *American Art Journal*, echoing John Sullivan Dwight's exceptions to such productions, said in reviewing a later performance of the work in July 1893:

> . . . Paine's march and hymn is the same work which was performed in such a farcical manner at the inauguration last fall. It is very well scored and produces a good effect.[153]

Dwight, of course, had voiced loud criticism of Patrick S. Gilmore's National Peace Jubilee in 1869, with over 10,000 singers and a thousand instrumentalists, and his 1872 World's Peace Jubilee, using almost twice as many performers. Two excerpts from Paine's oratorio *St. Peter*, included in the 1872 program, "fell flat on the audience. . . ."

Although the exposition buildings were inaugurated on the appropriate day of the Columbian quadricentennial, the actual exposition itself did not open until the following May. Formal opening ceremonies were held on 1 May 1893. Musical works included the *Columbus March and Hymn*, Beethoven's *In Praise of God*, and Handel's *Hallelujah Chorus*; participating were a chorus of 1,500, orchestra, and military bands. Several works by women composers, including a commissioned *Jubilate* by Mrs. H. H. A. Beach, were performed at the opening of the Woman's Building.[154]

Theodore Thomas, Musical Director of the Bureau of Music, planned a very ambitious series of concerts to take place during the six months of the exposition. A long list of works to be performed was released, including Bach's *St. Matthew Passion*, Handel's *Messiah*, and Beethoven's *Ninth Symphony*. American composers were to be well represented by Paine, Chadwick, Foote, Bristow, Bird, Shelley, MacDowell, Templeton Strong, and van der Stucken. Among the proposed works of Paine were the incidental music to *Oedipus Tyrannus*, *The Tempest*, *An Island Fantasy*, and the *Spring Symphony*.[155] Unfortunately, Thomas' wishes were not fulfilled. Budgets were cut when attendance failed to meet expectations of the commissioners of the Exposition, who were understandably more concerned with balancing their books than with costly programs of music. However, not all of Thomas' problems with the administration were fiscal. A typical clash of ideals occurred over the forthcoming appearance of pianist Ignace Paderewski in May 1893. Paderewski intended to play his own Steinway, but since the Steinway Company had refused to exhibit in the exposition, the commissioners forbade its use. Thomas threatened to resign, and, the commissioners relenting temporarily, Paderewski was allowed to use his Steinway. Nevertheless, friction between Thomas and the commissioners continued because of conflicts of interest between his artistic standards and their commercial imperatives. Many professional musicians, alarmed at these conflicts and at the possible failure of Thomas' concert plans and even the prospect of his dismissal or resignation, banded together in support of the leading American conductor. Paine was among the first to respond, and sent the following telegram to the president of the Columbian Exposition Commission:

Boston, Mass., May 19.

H. N. Higinbotham:
    I feel bound to telegraph you unsolicited, urging you to stand immovable by Thomas, and not to sacrifice the highest musical interests of the Exposition because of any friction or difficulties in the management. In the eyes of the musical world it would be an outrage on justice and a fatal blunder to dismiss one who stands for the right and has done most for musical art in America, and whose place as director cannot possibly be filled.

John K. Paine
Professor of Music, Harvard University.[156]

Apparently some of the disagreements were resolved for the time being, for Thomas continued his duties into the summer. His symphony concerts were poorly attended, partly because of the cost of tickets. Eventually the music budget was severely cut, and on 4 August Thomas resigned as musical director, suggesting that

. . . for the remainder of the Fair music shall not figure as an art at all, but be treated merely on the basis of an amusement. . . .[157]

Some of Thomas' plans were carried out before his resignation, however. Of the scheduled Paine works, *An Island Fantasy* did receive two hearings, as noted earlier. The most popular *Columbus March and Hymn*, already performed at the 21 October and 1 May opening festivities, appeared on later concert programs as well. Two that were reported were a 4 July 1893 concert in Festival Hall, which it opened,[158] and an 11 August free concert, attracting an "immense audience," where again it was first on the program.[159] Additional performances apparently were not reported, for the Bureau of Music later declared that the *Columbus March and Hymn* had been heard, "without chorus, three times. . . ."[160] And a correspondent, reviewing the 11 August concert, remarked

> I have heard the Columbus march and hymn by Paine at least six times at these concerts, and it is very effective.[161]

Freedom, Our Queen, with words by Oliver Wendell Holmes, was written for the Exposition Children's Chorus, directed by William L. Tomlins, and received three performances.[162] The first concert of the "chorus of 1,200 piping youthful voices" closed with Paine's song; Thomas directed the orchestral accompaniment.[163] Another performance that was reported occurred at the eleventh concert of the Children's Chorus on 26 June, where again it was the concluding work; the 114-piece Exposition Orchestra again was conducted by Theodore Thomas.[164]

Performances of the *Columbus March and Hymn* away from the Exposition seem to have taken place only while the Fair was still in operation; apparently public interest waned rapidly thereafter. The Chicago Orchestra, under Theodore Thomas, played the work on a 20–21 January 1893 matinée and popular concert at the Chicago Auditorium.[165] Two weeks later, on 3–4 February, the Boston Symphony Orchestra, under Arthur Nikisch, ended its concert, augmented by the Boston Symphony Chorus, with the same composition—it "was not well performed."[166] On the other hand, *Freedom, Our Queen* gained a renewed popularity when it was published in a four-part arrangement by Novello, Ewer, & Co., in 1902. One later performance was at a children's chorus concert at the Saengerfest des Norwestens [*sic*] in Milwaukee on 30 July 1904. Considering this choice of music, it is not surprising to learn that Theodore Thomas was musical director and conductor of the 100-piece orchestra.[167]

The last commission that Paine received—which resulted in his *Hymn of the West*—was also for performance at a world's fair, the Louisiana Purchase Exposition of 1904 in St. Louis. American poet and critic Edmund Clarence Stedman (1833–1908) wrote the words, which amounted to five stanzas. When these arrangements had been made was undisclosed, but a 12 March 1904 notice from St. Louis announced the forthcoming musical features of the fair, including:

The official hymn, by Prof. J. K. Paine, of Harvard University. The official march, by F. Van der Stucken, of Cincinnati.[168]

These compositions received their first hearing at the opening ceremonies of the fair on 30 April. Performing forces were far more modest than those of the Chicago fair in 1892:

... The new "Invocation Hymn," by J. Knowles Paine, was rendered by a chorus of 450 voices, under Alfred Ernst's directorship.[169]

To fulfill his commission Paine wrote a 25-bar hymn, in D major alla breve—conservative and similar to others of his works in this genre. The hymn is preceded by a 41-bar orchestral introduction, based on the first phrase of the hymn; it is typical of the composer's style, but the remarkable frequency of chromatic modulations shows the great appreciation Paine had developed for Wagner's music by this time.[170]

Two further performances of the *Hymn of the West* received notice in the press. On 19 February 1905 it was the first choral work in a program by the Handel and Haydn Society, Emil Mollenhauer, conductor, in Symphony Hall, Boston. According to the *Herald* social editor, ". . . every seat was occupied in Symphony Hall . . . and a number of people were standing . . . ,"[171] for Lillian Nordica was the featured attraction. The music editor of the same newspaper showed his approval of the Paine *Hymn*:

... It is a sturdy setting of Mr. Stedman's poem. It is straightforward, broad, manly music, worthy of the occasion, and effective when performed without reference to the source of inspiration. The composer bowed from the stage his acknowledgment of the loud applause. . . .[172]

On 25 April 1905 the *Hymn* opened the third concert of the Syracuse Music Festival. Mollenauer again conducted, leading the Boston Festival Orchestra; assisting was the Syracuse Music Festival Chorus.[173]

The height of Paine's popularity as a composer was reached about the time of the Harvard Greek play, *Oedipus Tyrannus*, and even the less musical among the Harvard community and alumni recognized him as responsible for its appealing music. Twenty years after the play's overwhelming success, students at Harvard presented another, Aristophanes' *The Birds*. Performances were produced by the Classical Club of the university, and again Paine supplied the incidental music. In sharp contrast to the earlier production, *The Birds* received almost no advance publicity, and seems to have been received as a successful but typical student presentation, not the historic event of 20 years earlier. The public performance was given on 10 May 1901, with a public dress rehearsal and a private performance occurring earlier on 6 and 8 May.

How much preparation preceded these performances were not divulged in the published reports, but it would be a reasonable assumption that, as with *Oedipus*, the first plans were made in the previous summer, and rehearsals would have been held through most of the academic year. Paine had completed his music before the end of December 1900, as may be seen from a 30 December 1900 letter of John Fiske:

> . . . Yesterday Fiske Warren brought Lopez and Patterson out here for a call in my library. Miss Alice Longfellow dropped in and joined us in a cup of tea. As Mary was carrying out the tray the front door bell rang and in came Brother Paine. Played his "Birds of Aristophanes". Finding him in a bland mood I "made hay while the sun shone" and got him to give us Chopin's G-minor Ballade.[174]

Performances were held in the Fogg Art Museum, and the production was supervised by Professors Goodwin, White, Wright, Moore, Gulick, and Winter of the Greek department. Warren A. Locke, organist and conductor of Appleton Chapel, directed the 20-voice chorus, which was composed of the Harvard Glee Club and "several of the best singers of Boston;" they had been "practising for some time. . . ."[175] A supplementary chorus, largely graduates, was seated in the orchestra; only a piano was used for accompaniment.

According to the reviews, *The Birds* was staged "with brilliant success."[176]

> Very effective music was written especially for the play by Prof. John Knowles Paine, Mus. D., head of the musical department at Harvard, who officiated at the piano as accompanist, while Warren A. Locke, whose thorough and skilful training is to be credited with a large part of the success of the presentation, conducted the singing.

The 8 May private performance was "very well attended and the audience showed enthusiasm."[177]

In the following year Paine's music to *The Birds* received another complete performance, although not in context of the play, at a 7 March 1902 concert of the Apollo Club, Emil Mollenhauer conductor, at Chickering Hall. The program was limited to works by American composers, and Paine's received the following comment in a newspaper announcement:

> . . . A special feature will be Prof. John K. Paine's scenes from the "Birds of Aristophanes," with the pianoforte accompaniment played by the composer. This

is an unusual concession of Prof. Paine's for he rarely allows himself to appear in public. . . .[178]

The concert was a success, and the scenes from *The Birds* impressed the audience very favorably, judging from the *Herald* review:

> Of all these [works on the program], Mr. Paine's composition was the most important. In a sense it is a kind of cousin-german to his "Oedipus" music, being solid, compact, and sufficiently different from the music of the day to be easily accepted as classic and Grecian. Being attached to a satirical comedy instead of a tragedy, it is, as compared with the "Oedipus," lighter and more generous in [melody], more varied in rhythm, and never so sombre and abstruse in harmony. There is a short orchestral prelude (condensed for the pianoforte) which is apparently intended to suggest the "wild region between earth and heaven, the home of the birds." The first choruses have rather the movement of a march, but soon this is changed for a gayer, more elastic and undulating rhythm, and later there is more grace and joy, together with a certain dignity, in the final epithalamium. As the composer was a participant in the performance, it may be assumed to have been in accordance with his wishes, but to us the effect seemed too steadily loud and heavy, and to have needed qualification and relief when the easier movements entered. . . . The singing was animated and strong, and all went well. . . .[179]

Dramatic continuity was provided by a short portion of text being read between each chorus. Presumably, the club sang from newly published copies of the vocal score, which was copyrighted in 1902 by Gustave Schirmer, Jr., and published by his firm, the Boston Music Company.

Paine composed *The Birds* for male chorus and orchestra—the manuscript score and parts were available from the publisher—but both complete performances used only a piano; the orchestration was never performed in its entirety. However, the prelude later was extracted and received four orchestral performances. The first was at a 27–28 February 1903 matinée and concert of Theodore Thomas' Chicago Orchestra. According to the *Musical Courier* correspondent, the prelude was "fairly well received," and was described typically as "an exceedingly well constructed work, thoughtful in character and refined in workmanship. . . ."[180] More enthusiasm is seen in the Chicago *Musical Leader* report:

> . . . The mastery of the instruments, as shown by the composer, is colossal, and the sensibility to grace of expression and dramatic instinct are evidenced in the various episodes depicted. On the whole the work was received with great favor and proved to be one of the most interesting orchestral works of the American writers today.[181]

Bostonians first heard an orchestral performance of the Prelude to *The Birds* of Aristophanes at the third Chickering "Production" Concert at

Chickering Hall on 9 March 1904. The composer conducted his work, which opened the program. Chickering Hall was "not as well filled as it should have been," but Paine was "warmly applauded."[182] Apparently the performance suffered in the small hall, according to the *Herald* reviewer:

> . . . Prof. Paine's overture would sound better in Symphony Hall. It is an eminently festal piece, and there is more than once the suggestion of the sweep of the Aristophanic chorus. We should like to hear it in a hall where it would have more elbow room. . . .[183]

Such a performance occured the following year, when the Boston Symphony Orchestra included the Prelude at its 17–18 November 1905 rehearsal and concert at Symphony Hall. Large audiences "completely filled" the auditorium at both occasions.[184] *Transcript* reviewer Henry Taylor Parker extolled the universal, non-American qualities he found in the music, comparing it with a Tchaikovsky work also on the program:

> . . . There is not a hint, again, in the prelude to "The Birds" that Professor Paine is a born New Englander who has lived there all his life, and who was the best of teachers those many years at Cambridge. Was it of Aristophanes who had taken him out of New England, out of himself, and set him to writing, like that volatile Slav thousands of miles away in Russia, for the pure sport of the thing? By every sign he had as much fun in the making and scoring of that prelude as we listeners had in hearing it. The dry-as-dusts will discover whether there are "worthy" musical ideas in it, properly academic ideas for an academic function. For our part, we neither know nor care. We do know, and it seems much more to the point, that much of it sounds and swings and clicks like a chorus in Aristophanes' own verse with an orchestra, instead of Greek choristers, to sing it. There is the joy of living in the prelude. For the moment, though it is hard to imagine, the good professor turned pure pagan.[185]

On 28 December 1905 the Boston Symphony performed the Prelude to *The Birds* again, at a Sanders Theatre concert in Cambridge. Gericke and the orchestra members took this occasion to express publicly—for the last time, as it turned out—their affection and admiration for the retired Harvard music professor:

> [Paine] was obliged to leave his seat in the audience and bow acknowledgements from the stage at the conclusion of the number. Conductor Wilhelm Gericke beckoned Prof. Paine to do this, and the audience showed its approval by vigorous applause, which was augmented by the members of the Boston Symphony Orchestra and also by Mr. Gericke. . . .[186]

The Symphony may also have performed the Prelude on one of its five concerts given in Washington, D. C., during the 1905–06 season, for Paine was among the composers whose "novelties" were announced for the series,[187] and *The Birds* was the only Paine work in the orchestra's repertory during that season. However, the records of the Boston Symphony Orchestra do not list such a performance, and the series seems not to have received detailed coverage in national periodicals.

From the foregoing performance history of Paine's larger works during the last decades of the nineteenth century, one may discern a growing lack of interest in his music on the part of the musical public—or, perhaps, performing organizations themselves. During the 1880s, within any given year one may find that several of his works were performed, and by different orchestras and in different cities. But in the succeeding decade performances were fewer, often only one in a year, with apparently no orchestral performances at all in 1897. Paine had devoted all his compositional attention to *Azara* and had produced no new orchestral works to reawaken public interest. This, in addition to the conservative nature of his compositions and, of course, the ever present anti-American artistic bias, may help to explain the decline in performances.

It is unfortunate that the public had begun to lose sight of Paine, for he had undergone a noticeable switch in compositional style. No longer bound by the classicism of the Beethoven-Schumann-Mendelssohn tradition, he had explored more and more the possibilities of the tone poem and exhibited the influence of its major exponents. Moreover, he had belatedly joined the Wagner camp, adapting its rich chromaticism and colorful orchestration, and studying the innovations of the music drama. Significantly, a major portion of Paine's creative effort during this latter half of his career as a composer was devoted to the opera *Azara*. This was the supreme effort of his life, and caused him the greatest disappointment in its failure to reach production. Paine apparently had begun work by the spring of 1883, for a June item announced simply, "Prof. John K. Paine is composing an opera."[188] Further details were slow to come; a December 1885 notice read:

> Mr. John K. Paine is said to be composing the score as well as the libretto of a grand opera on a Spanish subject.[189]

This report was accurate, although the setting was Provençal, not Spanish. In writing his own libretto, Paine was following the example of Wagner, whose music he had come to admire and assimilate into his own style. However, Paine's literary skill may not have been as great as Wagner's, as Professor Spalding later observed:

> Azara would have been more likely to succeed had some able dramatic poet prepared the libretto. Several such offers, in fact, were made by leading literary men, e.g., W. D. Howells and T. B. Aldrich.[190]

But, as Hugh Payne Greeley remarked:

> Prof. Paine took the liveliest satisfaction in the writing of the libretto of his opera "Azara." His mind for months was full of this composition, and he would recite portions of it gleefully to callers at the house.[191]

Out-of-town friends also heard about the composer's literary project. In 1886 he wrote of his progress to his former student, Henry T. Finck, music editor of the *New York Evening Post*. Finck later quoted a portion of the letter:

> "I have got a splendid subject for a romantic opera in three acts. Scene laid in Provence in 11th century. I am writing my own book—have got about 200 lines done. I will show them to you if you do not object. Please keep it private till I have seen you."
>
> He did come to New York and we talked over the matter minutely over a bottle of Chianti. . . .[192]

A great incentive to proceed with the opera occurred when Theodore Thomas promised to bring it out with a new institution for opera in English, the American Opera Company, organized in 1885, for which he was Musical Director.[193] Regrettably, the company disbanded in 1888 in financial ruin. This is one example of the many obstacles that faced the American opera composer wishing to secure performance of his works. The usual problems of audience prejudices against American music were compounded by the great expense involved in producing opera. Financial backing was difficult to obtain and often unreliable. Performance standards of traveling companies were low, and local productions on the star system were uneven and unjustifiably expensive. The only repertory house in the country was New York's Metropolitan Opera House, and at that time its future remained uncertain. Paine obviously gave much thought to the problem of opera production in America while composing *Azara*, and in 1892 published the article, "Shall We Have Endowed Opera?"[194] in which he proposed that all leading cities establish permanent resident opera companies, with opera houses, in the European manner, but with required endowments provided by "private endowment by one or more of our millionaires," rather than by the government. Such would be a great incentive to music in America:

> If such an opera were established on the plan that I have indicated, a native school of music would in course of time grow up, and we should have American opera given chiefly by American artists. I do not mean by this that foreign talent should be excluded; on the contrary, the *personnel* should be truly cosmopolitan. The repertory should embrace the operas of all schools. A protective policy pursued in the arts would be folly. But the fundamental characteristics of the institution should be American, and we should feel that it was a part of our national life. Certainly for the future of American composers this is the only way by which they can ever expect to accomplish much in this branch of music. . . .
>   . . . If each of our larger cities had such an institution, our people would become interested in the opera, would form the habit of patronizing it, and would fall into that state of mind with regard to it in which the French and Germans are, and thus make it a permanent institution. . . . Our composers, singers, and musicians of all classes would have an incentive to put forth their best energies, and the result would be that we should develop an American opera which would in time take rank with the finest achievements in music. . . .

During the summer of 1886 Paine continued to write, and on 9 October it was announced:

> Mr. John K. Paine has finished the libretto of his opera. The scene is laid in the Alhambra at the time of the Moors in Spain.[195]

The reference to the Alhambra in Spain would appear to be a misstatement, for Paine's libretto was based on the 13th-century *chante-fable*, *Aucassin et Nicolette*, with the dramatic action occurring in Provence. In any case, Paine began the long task of composing the opera, and a November 1886 item duly noted: "John K. Paine's opera progresses."[196] This seems to have been the last mention of the project in the music press for a period of 10 years.

Incidentally, there is a small possibility that Paine may have changed his conception of the opera while working on it, or perhaps that he had begun work on an earlier opera that he either abandoned or reworked into *Azara*. A biographical article in Champlin's *Cyclopedia of Music and Musicians*, dated 1890 and giving a detailed list of the composer's compositions, includes among them "Mirabel, romantic opera in 4 acts (MS., not yet finished)."[197] Unless this entry is assumed to be an error, it would imply a great amount of revision or changes in planning, for the three-act *Azara* would have required an extensive libretto reorganization over a four-act *Mirabel*. Unfortunately, no other references to *Mirabel* seem to exist, and surviving manuscripts provide no insight. Another unfinished opera was attributed to Paine by W. S. B. Mathews in a 1900 article:

> . . . Later Professor Paine has devoted himself to opera. For a long time he was at work upon a "Falstaf" [*sic*] which has never been performed. . . .[198]

This certainly is an oversight on Mathews' part, for on the very next page Walter R. Spalding provided a detailed description of the newly completed *Azara*.

As the knowledge became more widespread that Paine was writing an opera, speculation arose over whether he, the leading American composer, was or should be composing a truly *American* opera. The desire for serious music to be recognizably American grew quickly in some circles during the final decades of the century, fostered to a great extent by the popularity of musical nationalism in Europe, where non-German composers strived to assert their ethnic identities by using idioms characteristic of folk music from their native countries. The nationalistic composer who exerted the greatest influence upon Americans was Antonín Dvořák, who was artistic director of the National Conservatory of Music in New York in 1892–95. Dvořák showed a deep interest in American music, and prior to his coming to New York he expressed his thoughts on American opera during an interview:

> "Do you think . . . it is possible to build up a native opera in the United States? . . . An opera distinctly national in its tone, dealing with American events—with Indians, for instance—written by Americans and sung and played by Americans."
> Dvorjak [*sic*] smiled grimly, "So far as you have gone, I say yes, it can be done after many years, but as to music, ah! that is another thing. America can have native music, but national music never. The libretto may be American and the performers also American; but no such thing as American music any more than German or French music. America will have to reflect the influence of the great German composers just as all countries do. . . ."[199]

But after coming to America, once he had actually immersed himself in the great diversity of the American cultural scene, Dvořák reversed his opinions and now found the music of the blacks and the American Indians extremely attractive. His *New World* symphony reportedly strived to capture the exoticism of this repertory. For Americans, though, Dvořák's newly discovered vein of melody seemed particularly inappropriate to its new symphonic address. Critic Philip Hale, after hearing a Boston Symphony Orchestra performance of what he called the "Congo Symphony," observed:

> . . . More and more am I convinced that Dvořák [*sic*] wrote the slow movement after seeing "Uncle Tom's Cabin" or Milt G. Barlow "in his great impersonation of the aged contraband." Mr. Paur and the orchestra should use burnt cork at the next performance of this pleasing work.[200]

Understandably, many including Paine echoed Hale's attitudes, not only to Dvořák's music but to his words. To the suggestion that American composers utilize Negro melodies in their style, Paine voiced his disagreement, though in more reasoned language:

> . . . Prof. John K. Paine thinks that if Dr. Dvořák has been correctly reported he "greatly over-estimates the influence that national melodies and folk-songs have exercised on the higher forms of musical art. In the case of Haydn, Mozart, Beethoven, Schubert, and other German masters, the old folk-songs have been used to a limited extent as motives; but movements founded on such themes are exceptional in comparison with the immense amount of entirely original thematic material that constitutes the bulk of their music." Prof. Paine thinks the ideas attributed to Dr. Dvořák may have been mere pleasantry on his part. . . .[201]

Paine spoke further on this subject, rejecting the ideology of parochialism in art and especially in opera; he gave his feelings about American opera during an 1896 interview with a writer for *Music*:

> . . . Speaking of composing American opera, I differ with [*Music* editor W. S. B. Mathews] very widely on a point there—in regard to localization and patriotism in music. No one but Dvorak and Grieg has ever, to my mind, succeeded in that sort of thing, and Dvorak distinctly missed Americanism when he attempted to base his work on negro melodies. No. Not even in the great masters of Germany or Italy do you find such localization. They are great because they are individual, not because they are local or patriotic. There is, to be sure, a certain definite manner we term the German school, and another Italian, and so on. It is barely possible that we may at some time have a representative American school. But I doubt it very much. The time for such a thing is past. We have now not national, but international music, and it makes no difference whether I compose here or in St. Petersburg, so long as I express myself in my own way. For instance, [Mathews] often says we should choose subjects from American history for American grand opera. Not at all. If I should ever choose to write an opera, I should be as likely to lay the scene in Provence as in America. Such nationalism is beneath music.[202]

Of course, as can be seen in his last reference, he was defending a position taken 13 years previously, in 1886, when he decided to "lay the scene [of *Azara*] in Provence." Paine was not about to scrap his opera project because of Dvořák's or Mathews' admonitions. Soon after, his libretto appeared in print,[203] and by March 1897 there was talk of a performance:

> Prof. J. K. Paine has advanced so far with the score of his romantic opera, *Azara*, that it is expected that the Boston Symphony Orchestra will perform selections from it this spring.[204]

In 1898 the opera was completed; a July article disclosed the news:

> . . . It is gratifying to be able to close this article, by the courtesy of the composer, with the announcement that Paine's long awaited three-act grand opera, "Azara," is at last finished. He showed me the manuscript—an imposing pile. The scoring is for fullest orchestra, the book is by the composer, in rhymed verse of various metres, the scene is laid in Provence, and the subject is romantic, developing tragic elements, but with a happy conclusion. It is being translated into German; but Heaven forbid that this work, which may well prove to be the first great American grand opera, should have its first performance in a foreign land.[205]

Such enthusiasm in the press so far had had little effect on performance prospects of the work, but the momentum continued. An October announcement added:

> Prof. J. K. Paine has put the final touches to the orchestral score of his grand opera. It is entitled "Azara," and deals with a romantic Moorish subject. He has been his own librettist.[206]

Not only was the musical press caught up in the excitement of this period of gestation, but also Paine's students were witnesses of the composer's enthusiasm for his chef-d'oeuvre. John Alden Carpenter, a former pupil, later reminisced:

> . . . I was fortunate to be under his guidance when he was in the throes of *delivering* the last pages of his opera, and there were magnificent moments watching those stubby fingers and marvelling at that "composer's voice" struggling with "Azara" and her companions from

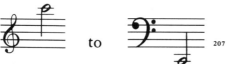

to   [207]

Another unidentified student gives us, incidentally, a picture of Paine quite unlike the pinched puritan of most accounts. In referring to *Azara*, Paine said that one scene required four trumpets in the orchestra and four strumpets on the stage.[208] Frederick S. Converse recalled the composer's satisfaction with his work:

> . . . He did not mind pointing out the superiority of certain features in his opera, "Azara" over certain features in "Tannhäuser. . . ."

Paine shared his delight in the newly completed opera with Finck in two letters. On 25 March 1900 he wrote:

> I wish I could play you the whole opera. You will find that I have entered upon a new path in all respects—in form, thematic treatment, instrumentation, etc. All dramatic composers must learn from Wagner, yet I have not consciously imitated him in style, etc.[209]

Later, on 27 May 1900, he added:

> I have followed throughout the connected orchestral rhythmic flow, and truth of dramatic expression characteristic of Wagner.

Louis C. Elson remarked on this Wagnerian element in *Azara*:

> Time has mellowed [Paine's] views of Wagner as it has eliminated the pedantic element from his later music. Any one listening to the forest music in "Azara" will readily see that the composer believes in the best points of the Wagnerian methods.[210]

Walter R. Spalding, the composer's associate on the Harvard music faculty, doubtless had opportunity to become quite familiar with the opera as it neared completion. He furnished a glowing description of the finished work—one of the first—which was published in 1900:

> Professor Paine has written his own libretto as well as the music, and both words and music show genius of the highest order; the words in their dramatic power and poetic beauty, and the music in that it is free and original in spirit while preserving symmetrical form and proportion. . . . The opera is romantic in spirit, with a thrilling plot of many tragic situations and a happy denouement. The action centers around the invasion of Provence by the Saracens, and the music is strikingly characteristic in its use of oriental color, while the dramatic portions are of great vigor and intensity. The style may be said to be Professor Paine's own, for it is neither like that of the modern French opera with its somewhat lighter mixture of the serious and the comic, nor like that of Wagner with its long monologues and extreme use of leading motives. The subject of the opera is not mythical, but one of human interest, and it makes an instant appeal to the enthusiasm and emotion of the hearer.
>
> All musicians who have made a study of "Azara" are convinced of its great originality, its striking harmonies and melodies, masterly orchestration, dramatic power and picturesque scenic features. "Azara" makes a new epoch in American music, and it will be a shame if this opera is not first brought out on the stage in the land that produced it.[211]

Despite Paine's enthusiastic, total commitment to the performance of his new opera and the sincere encouragements and persuasive arguments of many in the press, *Azara* was not to be "first brought out on the stage in the land that produced it"—in fact, it was never staged at all, an unhappy example of the prejudices then current in the opera world. The closest *Azara* came in its brief performance history was in an abridged concert version, given by the Cecilia Society a year after Paine died.

The first portion of *Azara* to be performed publicly was its ballet music, the "Three Moorish Dances," which formed part of a 9–10 March 1900 concert of the Boston Symphony Orchestra. Other compositions on the program were Smetana's overture to *The Bartered Bride*, Lalo's *Symphonie espagnole*, and Beethoven's 7th symphony; the Smetana was substituted for the announced Goldmark overture, *Sappho*, although there was "no truth in the report that [the latter] was ordered off the program by the city authorities"[212] because of its immoral connotations. Paine's music impressed *Musical Courier* correspondent Emilie Frances Bauer quite favorably:

> . . . Every line of [the "Moorish Dances"] reveals the mastery with which Paine wields his pen. Even as a ballet suite they are not light in any sense, but are musical, melodious and rich in color.

And the *Herald* reporter, undoubtedly Philip Hale, offered generous praise:

> Prof. Paine's Moorish dances from his manuscript opera were the novelty of the occasion. Of course, they lose something in being heard apart from the stage incidents which they were intended to supplement, especially as they are not in the light, tripping style of conventional ballet; but they are, nevertheless, pleasurable in the hearing by reason of their flowing themes, their free, rhythmic swing, their rich and picturesque orchestration and their strong suggestion of appropriate local color.
>
> The treatment of the melodies is ingenious, and at times exceedingly elaborate, but invariably clear and striking in its vigorously marked individuality. It is easy to imagine, interesting as they are detached from their place in the opera, that they would gain greatly in effectiveness with their proper essentials of dancers, action and scenery and in the stage situations that called them forth.
>
> What now seems a little serious for ballet music would then undoubtedly disappear, and the true meaning of the whole would be more strongly emphasized, and the comparative sobriety of the music better understood. However, it was gratifying to hear these pieces even under the disadvantages named, for they showed the composer in the maturity of his powers, and in a style of composition which he had not before essayed.[213]

The performance, led by Gericke, was "of a quality that must surely have delighted the composer." The audience applauded "with vigorous enthusiasm," and Paine "left his place in the auditorium to bow his acknowledgments from the stage. . . ." The performance was repeated in Cambridge a week later at a 15 March Boston Symphony concert at Sanders Theatre.[214] And during the next fall Theodore Thomas led the Chicago

Orchestra in the work at its 26–27 October concert. According to reviewer Florence French:

> . . . The most popular and tuneful number was Paine's "Moorish Dances," which, with their Oriental coloring and rhythm, found many admirers. . . .[215]

When the Moorish dances were repeated by the Boston Symphony on 18–19 December 1903, Boston reviewers indulged themselves in praise for the exotic novelty of this ballet music. Wrote "R.R.G." in the *Transcript*:

> . . . Three charming Moorish dances, very modern, fascinatingly melodious, with a wide variety of piquant rhythms, the whole clothed in orchestral dress now delicate, now resplendent in color. The dances are not Moorish in name only; they seem steeped in the very atmosphere of Andalusia. . . .[216]

And the *Herald* observed:

> . . . Prof. MacDowell of Columbia honors his university by writing Celtic sonatas and New England idyls for the piano; Prof. Parker of Yale is addicted to the oratorio habit; but Prof. Paine writes an opera with a ballet of Moorish dancers, and thus bears witness to the fact that Harvard University encourages the cultivation of the more humanizing arts. The dances gave much pleasure. All of the themes are melodious and some are characteristic; the orchestration is now piquant, now sumptuous. The music is decorative and picturesque, as well as for the steps of dancing girls. It suggests the opera house with its peculiar atmosphere, the set scene, the entrance and the evolutions of the ballet. The dances were heartily applauded, and Prof. Paine rose from his seat on the floor and bowed his acknowledgements to audience and conductor and orchestra. . . .[217]

Two weeks later members of the Harvard community received another opportunity to hear the Moorish dances, when the Boston symphony included them on a 7 January 1904 Sanders Theatre concert.[218] And on 16 January Gericke led still another performance of this music on a Boston Symphony concert in New York's Carnegie Hall.[219] Perhaps a most convincing indication of the popular appeal of the Moorish Dances was their transcribed appearance on two concerts by the Sousa Band. The first, on 11 May 1902 in New York's Metropolitan Opera House, attracted an audience that "completely filled the building." Paine's dances were among the "most effective" of the novelties on the program; they "brought out to advantage the band's full resources," and "aroused much enthusiasm. . . ."[220] Six years later the band again played the Moorish Dances at a 9 October 1908 concert featuring Boston composers at the Boston Food Fair.[221]

As gratifying as was this acceptance of the ballet music, Paine nat-

urally was far more concerned about staging the entire opera, and explored every possible source of encouragement. One of his earliest contacts was Ernst von Schuch (1846–1914), conductor of the Dresden Opera, who directed three orchestral concerts in New York during the spring
of 1900.

> Prof. Paine, of Harvard University, had a conference with Herr von Schuch, before
> the latter's departure for Europe, as to the advisability of producing his opera "Azara,"
> in Germany. He played selections from the score to the Dresden conductor, who was
> greatly pleased with its dramatic as well as musical merits, and declared that every-
> thing now would depend on the libretto, which is also from Prof. Paine's pen. It
> would be gratifying to Prof. Paine's friends to hear that the American composer is
> to be rewarded for his ten years' labor.[222]

Apparently von Schuch was only one of a number of influential German
musicians who possessed an interest in seeing *Azara* performed, for within
the year arrangements were made for the vocal score to be published, on
a subscription basis,[223] by Breitkopf & Härtel of Leipzig. The German
translation had been completed by Karl Pflueger, and Paine had written
a piano arrangement of the score. Early in the summer of 1901 Paine
reportedly traveled to Europe,[224] doubtless to collect the proofs from the
publisher, and in July the composer was correcting them while on vacation, as seen in a letter to his former Radcliffe student, Mabel Daniels
(1878–1971):

> . . . I have received and corrected the proof of Azara up to Page 258, and hope to
> get the rest in a week or two. I find it exacting work; one has to be so careful, what
> with the notes and the words in two languages. I went over it four times, and dis-
> covered something to correct up to the last. . . .[225]

In October 1901 the newly published scores were released.[226] Soon thereafter writers talked of an expected European performance:

> . . . Probably Europe will hear it first, and that may be pretty soon; for the Leipsig
> [*sic*] publishers, Breitkopf & Hartel [*sic*], who also issue the handsome subscription
> issue in this country, believe in the opera and are taking energetic steps to bring it to
> the favorable consideration of the principal German opera houses.[227]

The publication of *Azara* attracted much notice in the press. Most extensive was the *Herald* review,[228] whose proportions compare with those of
Burdett's review of *Oedipus* 20 years earlier. The writer began with a
lengthy synopsis of the plot, outlining its dramatic complexities. Following was a discussion of Paine's treatment of the story; first, the libretto:

> In presenting this tale, which is primarily tragic, and incidentally one of romantic
> love, Prof. Paine has been . . . both poet and composer. His libretto is interesting and
> good—not lackadaisical in its sentiment or turgid and melodramatic elsewhere.

The rhyme comes easily and often daintily, and the rhythms are frequently and markedly varied, as suits with the swiftly shifting situations. . . .

After further textual analysis, the writer continued with a discussion of the musical setting, at first recalling the composer's earlier music for the Greek classic tragedy, *Oedipus Tyrannus*:

In his 40 years at Harvard, Prof. Paine has not lived only with the "grand old masters" of fugue, counterpoint and classic lore. There has been room in his taste for the modern and the slight; he has exercised in many departments of composition, from classic symphonies and overtures to the exuberant current humor of "Radway's Ready Relief." In this score he has written elastically and with diversified treatment; but his science is not more difficult to find by those who know how to look than are his melodies, which lie all along the surface of his work.

He has adhered to modern custom, in that every act is continuous in its progression; but he has recognized the still indestructible feeling for form, by bringing each air or scene to its own perfect conclusion and then building a little bridge—perhaps of only a few bars—over which one passes by easy and scarce noticed steps to the next matter.

He has no long tirades, the most extended declamation being broken up into terse, pithy portions, each of which has its own rhythm, color and accent, according to his belief that it is not natural for a person to deliver several consecutive sentences in just the same way, but rather to give each its own value.

Leading motives are used sparingly and to clear purpose. . . . Various themes are transferred, . . . but as sentimental suggestions, chiefly. . . .

No attempt has been [made] to give anywhere a distinctly oriental or troubadour quality to the music, and the only introduction of anything peculiar is the adoption for some of Malek's airs of the Moorish scale with its one odd interval and the embellishment of them with the frequent rough roulades to which such peoples—possibly often by mere accidents of a furious expression—break up and confuse the headlong course of their wild cries.

The scheme of harmony is modest, and the modulations unforced; yet powerful and exciting effects are constantly obtained, as when, just as the last finale comes, there is a series of strikingly brilliant enharmonic progressions around the prolonged shouts of the chorus. . . .

Such a lengthy description illustrates the enthusiasm the reviewer felt for this new opera. This reaction was far from unique; words of praise came from as far away as Berlin and the *Musik- und Theater-Welt-Zeitung*, which declared:

The enterprising music publishers, Breitkopf & Hartel [*sic*] of Leipsig, deserve great credit for making it possible for the public to become acquainted with an extremely interesting foreign opera, "Azara," by John Knowles Paine. . . . [He] is a composer of refined and pure feeling, whose music is rich in melody, perfect polyphony, charming form and strongly marked characteristics. As one of the "moderns," he has conceived the orchestral part with brilliant effects of color, yet he never burdens the voice parts with heavy orchestration. He does not strive for striking originality, but attains this by virtue of his power and gift of invention, creating in his own manner remarkable effects and captivating tone pictures. . . .[229]

W. S. B. Mathews, editor of *Music*, also praised *Azara*, but predicted its disappointing future:

> For a number of years Professor Paine, of Harvard, has been working at a grand romantic opera upon a Saracen object. The work having been some time completed is here issued in vocal score. It makes a portly and elegant volume of 374 pages. The subject is one which admits of and invites scenic splendor, and no doubt the orchestration and general musical handling have been created with the same possibility in view. It is an important work, and it is a pity that there is very little chance of its being heard upon the stage in the lifetime of its author—not that the death of the author would tend to simplify the production of such a work, but simply that the conditions are such that "No American need apply"—at any stage or orchestral door, saving only with a comic opera, in which line American works are now supreme. . . .[230]

As soon as the vocal scores were available, plans were made for public presentations of excerpts from *Azara*. The first was a soprano aria from Act II, Scene 3, included on a 4 February 1902 concert of the Cecilia Society, B. J. Lang, conductor. The society lost no time in hearing the music privately, as noted in the 3 November 1901 *Sunday Herald*:

> Mr. Lang had a special treat for the Cecilia at last week's rehearsal, a reward for all the extra drilling over the Bach mass. It is quite in keeping, too, that the Cecilia should have the first taste of Mr. Paine's new opera, "Azara." The long soprano aria was sung by Mrs. [Alice Bates] Rice, whose voice seemed the very echo of the nightingale she apostrophized.[231]

The rehearsal performance is also mentioned in a *Musical Courier* item, but an allusion to an earlier Cambridge performance remains puzzling— further details are wanting:

> . . . It will be remembered that Mrs. Rice sang the principal role of John K. Paine's "Azara" when it was given at Cambridge; the other evening she sang a portion of the music at the St. Cecilia rehearsal, everyone being most enthusiastic. Mrs. Rice holds one of the most important church choir positions in the city, being the soprano soloist at King's Chapel, where B. J. Lang is organist.[232]

The February concert included, besides the *Azara* excerpt, works by other Boston composers—Loeffler, Parker, Foote, and Margaret Ruthven Lang—as well as by Tchaikovsky, S. J. Taneyev, Franck, Cornelius, and Hahn. Soprano Alice Bates Rice, accompanied on the piano by Lang, "aroused much enthusiasm"[233] in her performance:

> [Mrs. Rice]—who had taken the not common pains of committing it to heart—sang

smoothly, gracefully and simply the long soprano scene, "Softly the Balmy Zephyr Sighs," from Prof. Paine's "Azara," giving pure, distinct and easily carrying tones to the many high passages. The scene pleased, but necessarily lost value by its isolation from its contrast and from the causes which give it rise and reason in true opera. . . .[234]

Critic Warren Davenport praised the work highly, but found Mrs. Rice's performance inadequate:

The aria from Professor Paine's recently composed opera "Azara," sung by Mrs. Rice, is from the beginning of the third scene of the second act, where Azara sits upon the bank and listens to the murmur of the forest and the sea, a situation in the delineation of which this most eminent of American composers, in the orchestral scoring, has wrought with rare beauty and skill in its poetic charm.

It was given with piano accompaniment, played by Mr. Lang delightfully and appreciatively.

One could but imagine its effect, however, under these conditions.

Mrs. Rice exerted herself to meet the requirements of its strains, but it demands the capacity of a Nordica, or Gadski, at her best, to encompass the nobility of its melodic flow and the breadth of its masterly conception.

What a wonderful libretto is the book of this opera, the inspired effort of the composer himself. In both lyric and dramatic value it is of surpassing excellence. . . .[235]

Perhaps Mrs. Rice's difficulty with the part may be excused when one learns that the composer initially intended the role for a singer of international reputation, Maine soprano Emma Eames (1865–1952); according to a 1905 newspaper editorial comment:

. . . We remember that when Mme. Eames was with Marchesi in Paris Prof. Paine was then thinking of her as the heroine of his opera, then not completed. What an opportunity the singer now has to repay the learned professor's kindness. Her friends in New York insisted that Mr. Conried [manager of the Metropolitan Opera] should hire her this season, although the aesthetic manager in his heart of heart is bitterly opposed to the star system. Why does she not insist on a production of "Azara" with herself as heroine? Johanna Gadski learned English in Walter Damrosch's "Scarlet Letter." Mme. Gadski thus paid tribute to America. But Mr. Damrosch was born in Breslau, not even in Hoboken, N. J. Prof. Paine is a New Englander. He was born at Portland, Me., and reared there. . . . Mme. Eames happened to be born at Shanghai, but she is of Maine stock, and she has the true New England accent even in French opera. She should not rest, she should not allow Mr. Conried to rest until Prof. Paine's opera sees the footlights.[236]

The "kindness" referred to above dated from the 1884–85 season, when Eames, then a young voice student in Boston, helped with the musical illustrations for a course of lectures Paine delivered in Chickering Hall.[237] Eames described the experience:

> During the Boston period it was my good fortune to attract the attention of Professor Paine, of Harvard University, a composer and teacher of undisputed merit. He engaged me, with three others, to illustrate his lectures on the history of music, beginning with the Gregorian chants, which we sang from the quaint square notes, and continuing with the Italian school, the French troubadour songs, the early English, the French and German folksongs, and concluding with the last work in 1884 modern music. These lectures were given both in Boston and at Harvard. Mamma and I went frequently to Cambridge for supper, as the evening meal was called, with Mr. and Mrs. Paine to "make music." He often had some particularly interesting pupil as another guest, and it was there I met Henry Finck. . . . There also I met Celia Thaxter. . . .[238]

Eames mentioned her gratitude to Paine during a conversation with Elson following one of her 1889 performances in *Faust* at the Paris Opéra:

> Miss Eames spoke of Professor Paine with much regard and admiration. "You don't know how much good he has done me," said she, "for he kept me at work on old, old music, ancient masses and all that, until I could not help acquiring a correct taste. . . ."[239]

Later Elson

> . . . asked Professor Paine what music he had given to Miss Eames in her student days. "Dufay, Des Pres, Di Lasso, and the old Flemish school," he replied. . . .[240]

With the success of the Cecilia Society concert and the publicity it provided for *Azara*, other performances of excerpts from the opera soon followed. One of the first was a 6 March 1902 organ recital by Ralph L. Baldwin at the First Church of Christ, Northampton, Massachusetts. Presumably the "Song of Triumph (from opera Azara, Act I.)"[241] was played in an adaptation by the performer. On 15 April 1902 baritone Stephen Townsend presented "two airs" from *Azara* on a Steinert Hall recital in Boston. Unfortunately,

> . . . those songs were least agreeable and least commendable in which he seemed to be taking most pains and making the most continuous exertion. Thus, the vocal and nervous tension evident in the two baritone airs from Prof. Paine's "Azara" made his tone hard and his phrasing stiff. But there was a handicap against him there, because such strong and dramatic things lose effect and fail to give a singer support when taken out of their stage context, while their high range and general exactingness render them too severe for the beginning of a song recital, just as Verdi's "Celeste Aida," [*sic*] put at the opening of his opera, is an overweight for almost any tenor. . . .[242]

Piano accompanist Alfred de Voto was "not in good touch with the 'Azara' songs." Doubtless more satisfaction was found in another performance of "Softly the Balmy Zephyr Sighs" by soprano Alice Bates Rice, this time in a solo song recital at Steinert Hall on 18 March 1903; Jessie Downer-Eaton was the piano accompanist.[243]

All of these were merely short excerpts from the opera, and there had been no opportunity for listeners to gain any impression of the general scope and content of *Azara*. The first attempt to fill this gap occurred on 7 May 1903 at Chickering Hall, a concert performance of scenes from the opera under the direction of Ephraim Cutter, Jr. No orchestra was available; Cutter accompanied the performance at the piano. According to a newspaper announcement, he and Paine planned to produce those portions that would make the story clear, and would

> . . . present the airs and scenes upon which the composer lays most stress, as portraying the passions and bearing the beauty of the opera. The whole first half of the first act will be given, and scenes 1, 2, 4 and 5 from the second; the final scene, with the great troubadour's song will be given as the selection from the third act. . . .[244]

A chorus of 30 voices assisted in the performance, and the soloists— none of them leading singers—included Grace Lowell Bradbury, Rebecca W. Cutter, Mrs. Vernon A. Lyman, Mrs. Albert Thorndike, Ernest R. Leeman, David A. Tobey, Ralph E. Brown, and George A. Tyler. The concert was well received; a "large and distinguished audience" listened with "fixed attention, unfeigned interest and warm, quick applause. . . ."[245] The musicians, though relatively inexperienced, gave a good performance:

> All had fresh, clear, strong young voices, knew their music thoroughly and sang enthusiastically and well, no small amount of the music having been learned by heart. Mr. E. Cutter, Jr., was at the pianoforte, and had so well trained his singers that they really needed no conducting or direction, but went on confidently and correctly.

The composer himself played his piano reduction of the orchestral scene opening the second act, and at the close of the concert "was greeted with enthusiasm and received a huge laurel wreath."[246]

With this first performance of a major portion of the opera, musicians were able at last to form initial judgments of the work. The *Herald* writer found the work successful as an opera, and opined that it held greater affinity to the later Italian school than to the works of Wagner:

> "Azara" is frankly an opera of these days. . . . The opera would associate itself rather with the later work of Verdi than with that of the German school derived from

Wagner. The vocal flow is continuous, but it shapes its phrases more often into the melodic form than into that of the recitative, . . . while the orchestral accompaniment, also disposed to be melodious and not encumbered by philosophical connections of thought, is picturesquely illustrative of the primary idea.[247]

William F. Apthorp, who reviewed the concert for the *Transcript*, left the concert troubled that the effectiveness of the opera as a dramatic work had not been proven, for the performance was too fragmented:

> . . . The question which first presents itself is: Do the selections sung last evening give an adequate idea of the prevailing style of the whole work? I am forced to think that they hardly do; it seems to me that they represent only the more lyrical moments in the opera, and that the more dramatic passages—that is, the more purely dramatic—were left out. For the style of what I heard last night seemed too purely musical to be conceivable throughout a modern work for the stage. Not that the music is not essentially dramatic, for it is; Professor Paine seems to have found himself quite at home in the dramatic musical atmosphere. But that it does not strike me as always effectively scenic; that is, I cannot imagine a great deal of dramatic action going on while it is sung. . . . This music often [seems] more to furnish a striking commentary upon the action than to be itself the medium for dramatic expression. In other words, it seems to me that I have heard only the culminating points of the action of "Azara," musically expressed, but not the dramatic scenes that connect these culminating points. It is like hearing, say, Handel's "Samson" with all the recitatives left out.
> . . . What differentiates the merely generally dramatic composer from the specific opera-writer is that keen sense for the optics of the stage, for making the music intrinsically scenic, which we find in all the truly great opera composers, from Gluck and Mozart to Wagner.[248]

Aside from these misgivings, however, Apthorp was very pleased with the composition he heard:

> Looking at the music for and by itself, simply as music, it bears the composer's earmarks from beginning to end. It is surely up to the best he has done. The writing is, perhaps, more facile and flowing than in some of his previous things; it is frankly melodious, in the modern sense of the term, and often singularly effective. One wishes more than ever that one could hear the whole work, given as it should be, on the actual stage.

Two years later Cutter directed another concert performance of *Azara*, this time at his own home, on 14 March 1905. Some 125 "society people" attended.[249]

Efforts to obtain a staged performance for *Azara* resulted in disappointment and failure. For a few years there was hope, however. Especially encouraging was the rumor in 1903 that Heinrich Conried, manager of the Metropolitan Opera, was open at last to the possibility of producing an opera in English:

> They begin to talk again in New York, reports the *Sun*, about the probabilities of Mr. Conried taking up Mr. Walter Damrosch's "Cyrano de Bergerac," and there is pressure being brought to bear on behalf of Prof. John K. Paine's "Azara." Either would seal Mr. Conried's disposition to give opera in English.[250]

And even more promising:

> Boston must make a push for "Azara," now that Mr. Conried has virtually determined to do one opera in English at the Metropolitan.[251]

However, the 1903–04 opera season continued to exclude American opera. The *Herald* music reporter described the discouraging state following the December Boston Symphony Orchestra performance of the "Moorish Dances:"

> . . . There are two operatic companies in the United States that could produce "Azara": Mr. Conried's and Mr. [Henry W.] Savage's. The former manager has gone to the trouble and the expense of preparing an English version of an opera by Smetana, a Czech; and he purposes to revive certain operas that have had only a short-lived popularity in the United States. Mr. Savage does not hesitate to produce with his company "Othello" and "Tosca" and he will bring out an English version of Puccini's "Mme. Butterfly." Neither manager is considering the production of "Azara," so far as we are informed, and Prof. Paine is looking forward to a production in Germany, for which a German text is already provided. It seems a pity that a serious opera by an American composer of established reputation should not first see the footlights in the land of his birth. Mr. Walter Damrosch was luckier with his "Scarlet Letter;" he had his own opera company; but it is not every composer that can afford this luxury. . . .[252]

Two years later, in 1905, prospects again were bright:

> There is a possibility that "Azara," an opera by Prof. J. K. Paine, an American composer, will be produced at the Metropolitan Opera House next season. ... .[253]

But the news was disappointing when Conried announced plans for the 1905–06 season that fall; a writer described Conried's interview with the press:

> . . . And again he says that he will produce Prof. Paine's "Azara"—"if he can get the company to study it"; in other words, if they will condescend to busy themselves with an American composition.[254]

The above reporter was criticizing Conried for alleged submissiveness in dealing with the artists at the Metropolitan. Many continued to apply pressure, including Finck:

> I did all I could to help Paine. I made personal appeals to Emma Eames and Geraldine Farrar to interest themselves in the rôle of Azara, and they were not deaf to my appeals; but nothing came of it. A guarantee fund of $10,000 was discussed. We got up a petition to Conried signed by Carl Schurz and many other eminent men, and that manager seemed favorably inclined, but nothing was done.[255]

Efforts to obtain a staged performance continued after the composer's death in 1906, but once more they resulted in failure:

> An interesting, if not gratifying, condition in regard to foreign domination in American opera came to light when in 1907 there was a proposition to stage "Azara" under Conried's management. Persistent attempts failed to discover, in either Boston or New York, an operatic contralto or bass who could sing in English well enough to be entrusted with the parts. Neither could the chorus, an important factor in this work, sing other than Italian.[256]

Although the hopes of gaining a staged performance eventually were abandoned, *Azara* at last received a concert performance with orchestral accompaniment at a 9 April 1907 concert of the Cecilia Society at Symphony Hall, B. J. Lang, conductor. The performance was substantially complete, but there were omissions.[257] Alice Bates Rice, who had performed the first vocal excerpt from the opera at a 1902 Cecilia concert, sang the title role. Other soloists were H. F. Merrill, Rainulf; George Deane, Gontran; Mrs. Bertha Cushing Child, Odo; Earl Cartwright, Aymar; Stephen Townsend, Malek; Mrs. Rebecca Howe, Garsie; Adelaide Griggs, Colas; and James M. Rattigan, a Huntsman. Critic Delbert L. Loomis commented about the music and the performance:

> Regarding the music to which Mr. Paine set the words of his life work, it may be said that it is characteristic in the minutest particular of the writings of this able musician. There are several remarkably brilliant orchestral effects, one of particular note being the introduction to the second act. As a whole the opera is certainly a work of great merit and at no time does it fall to the level of the mediocre.
> The soloists sang their parts intelligently and were accorded generous applause. The excellently trained chorus gave the concerted numbers in admirable style.
> The opera is in three acts. . . . Each act contains several scenes and at points the work is dramatic in the extreme. . . .[258]

In a major review for the *Transcript*,[259] Henry Taylor Parker complained indignantly about the cuts that were made:

> If a deed of pious respect is to be done at all it ought to be worth doing completely. To honor the memory and the work of the late Professor John Knowles Paine of Harvard the Cecilia performed last night in Symphony Hall his opera, "Azara," that

occupied his leisure from teaching for ten years and that he cherished above all the rest of his music. The Cecilia could not set it upon the stage with singing actors and all the resources and trappings of an opera house. It had inevitably to give it a concert performance, with "soloists" in conventional evening dress, holding their music books in their hands, with a chorus in a surrounding semi-circle and with singers and an orchestra little accustomed to the large or the sharp theatrical accent that opera demands. In all these respects the Cecilia was not to blame, and its audience readily accepted these limitations. But if "Azara" was to be performed at all and for the first time on any stage, why was it not performed in its entirety? With the cuts that were made, the performance last night continued for two hours and a half nearly, but with no more than the usual signs of restlessness amongst a few in the audience. The omissions would have filled barely another hour. . . . Those who wished to hear the opera for its own sake—and they were considerable—wished to hear it in the form and proportions with which it left Professor Paine's hand. Their interest and their curiosity would have made three hours or even three hours and a half in the concert-room tolerable. It is by no means unlikely that "Azara" may never again be sung anywhere. Yet here it was deliberately shorn at a concert reiteratedly in honor of the composer. . . .

Parker disclosed that the omissions, all lengthy passages for orchestra alone, left unplayed some of Paine's most beautiful music and severely affected the formal proportions of the work.

. . . Why did Professor Paine, well aware of the dramatic and pictorial capabilities of the modern orchestra, write so little for it apart from the voices, listeners might have asked—and did ask last night? In fact he wrote much for it. He wrote preludes for each of his three acts, and they were reduced to a few measures of unmeaningful introduction. In the dark of the glade between the forest and the sea, in the first scene of the second act, the fleeing Azara and Aymar escaped from the king's pursuit, sleep the sleep of the weary and the hunted. Clouds huddle and pass, till the moon is clear. The mists of the dawn gather and rise; the sounds of the wood and the waves stir; come the light and the freshness of the morning. Faint fall the steps of the watching wood nymphs. There is nothing in the whole opera to compare with this episode in poetic imagination and in ethereal and iridescent quality. Professor Paine has given it to the orchestra. He used to call it his "orchestral scene." Nowhere, so far as the printed page may indicate, has he written more beautiful music. Yet it was ruthlessly omitted last night. . . .

Another omission was the ballet music, the "Three Moorish Dances." These of course had already been heard by the Boston public, for the Symphony had included them on concerts in 1900 and 1903, but their potential effectiveness in context was denied.

. . . Professor Paine intended that they should stand in their due place in the opera, and they are as vivid music as it contains. Again, by common agreement of those that know the score, the music that falls to the choruses of Saracens and to Malek, their chief, is the most interesting in itself and the most telling dramatically of all the opera. Upon it Professor Paine lavished long study of Moorish intervals and of the general manner of Moorish song. Then he gave it characterizing, dramatic or lyric significance. It provided the element of contrast and incisiveness that "Azara" abridged seemed to need much. Yet, last night, the omission of the prelude to the first act cut away some of this Saracenic music and the reduction of Malek to a musical and dramatic shadow in the closing scene of the same act cut away more. Of this Moorish music, too, were the omitted dances. It is not merely the intrinsic interest or worth of the omitted passages that condemns these excisions. It is the fact that they altered and even distorted the proportions of the opera and deprived the music of pictorial, dramatic and contrasting elements that it lacks far less than it seemed. It is an old story that Mr. Lang is not a very expert orchestral conductor, and of course audiences are restless under lengths; but as the occasion was, his first, his only duty was to Professor Paine's score as it stood. . . .

Parker criticized Paine's libretto, as did other critics, calling its narrative "detailed and devious," and finding in it "the germ of the peril of monotony. . . ." But he felt that Paine often overcame this drawback, relying on "the expressiveness of his music" for dramatic appeal, and compared him both with Wagner and the modern masters Puccini and Strauss.

> . . . In form [Azara] is neither of the old nor of the new. Professor Paine weaves no Wagnerian symphonic web with the singers as so many added voices to the dramatic tone-poem. He does not cultivate characterizing and endlessly developed and intertwined motives, but he uses sparingly recurring significant phrases for his personages and their dominant passions. Now and then, too, an orchestral cadence or an instrumental detail is curiously Wagnerian. He knew not in the nineties the elastic parlando that Puccini and his Italians have brought to such expressive power or the dramatic significance they have given to harmonies, rhythms and instrumental timbres. Yet he writes, as they at bottom do, in melodious musical dialogue that broadens with the dramatic situation into sustained song, concerted voices, or piled climax. Unmistakably there are good set tunes in "Azara," but the dramatic moment and not the composer's will summons them. The voice is almost always Professor Paine's chosen and most significant instrument. He never, indeed, reduces the orchestra to a mere accompaniment; yet he never makes it the most dramatic and communicative element in the opera, and he has little notion, beside Wagner, or Puccini, or Strauss, of its theatrical possibilities. Again he takes the middle way. In a measure, he shuns the modern passion for musical characterization; yet he does characterize Malek and his Saracens vividly, and in their music he attains the dramatic significance, the theatrical incisiveness, that he often misses elsewhere. . . . Professor Paine excels, as in some of his choral pieces, in the upbuilding of the large climax, in the marshalling of the long and dramatic crescendo. Naturally, with such powers, he has not spared his ensembles and his choruses, but again as a true musical dramatist he makes them spring naturally out of the course of the action, and return naturally to it again. . . .

Despite many moments of expressiveness and beauty, Parker found that the first two acts, as they were performed in the concert situation, were dramatically unsuccessful.

> . . . The whole effect . . . was of a lacking dramatic accent and pungency. The music had seldom the strange magic or the strange power of opera at its fullest. It neither transported nor gripped.
>
> With the third act, and rather curiously, came this missing enchantment, accent and pungency. The few measures of the prelude, Gontran's air to the spring, music that had the moist freshness of May sunshine, the chorus of the trooping knights and ladies to the fete—all brought atmosphere. The music began to transport. The ranked choristers and all the rest upon the prosaic platform of Symphony Hall vanished. There stood the castle court. Beyond were the sea, the sky, the hills and the drenching sunshine. Out of the arched gateway came the many-hued train of Gontran's court. And to them flocked the Moors, bright and tawny at once as was the characterizing music, who were to make their sport. The music was graphic, as of an animated tone-picture. In memory at least the vivid dances followed. Then Azara, escaped from her Moorish prison, but still disguised. Then the pursuing Malek, disguised too and of dark purpose that was in his musical speech. Now, at last, the whole musical fabric, the whole dramatic situation, has gained an intensity that it had never had before. It held it through Azara's rhapsodic narrative of her exile and wanderings—music that for the first time gave her body and character in her tones. In the midst was the true dramatic stroke and suspense of Malek's interruption; and then the quick advance to the delicately rapturous climax of her song. For quick foil—and here again was another dramatic and theatrical stroke—came the Saracen's attempt to kill, and then his own self-murder. And the musical contrast in the return, in his dying words, and of the strange, remote, penetrating note of Saracenic song with half-chivalrous, half-exotic flourishes, was still more potent. Only with the conventional ensemble of a conventionally happy ending did the illusion flag. For one act of "Azara," at least, Professor Paine had written, as it seemed, unmistakable and compelling music-drama. And what American composer of opera—for "The Pipe of Desire" is only one act long—has yet done more?

The closing reference to Frederick Shepherd Converse's work—the first American opera to be performed at the Metropolitan Opera—may suggest what might have been in store for *Azara*, had Paine lived and been able to promote a full production. With *The Pipe of Desire* (1910), the Metropolitan Opera had at last recognized American opera, following it a year later with Victor Herbert's *Natoma* (produced by the Philadelphia-Chicago Opera Company), Horatio Parker's *Mona* in 1912, Walter Damrosch's *Cyrano de Bergerac* in 1913, and Herbert's *Madeleine* in 1914. But George W. Chadwick's 1912 opera, *The Padrone*, was refused by the Metropolitan Opera Company and never performed;[260] perhaps Paine instead would have found only greater frustration.

Chadwick himself spoke approval of *Azara*, citing its "many beauties of thought and much interesting instrumentation,"[261] and Arthur Farwell called *Azara* Paine's "summit."[262]

In 1908 Mrs. Paine arranged for publication of the full score of

Azara, along with 33 orchestral parts, by Breitkopf & Härtel, and paid
the cost of $2,000.[263] A beautiful volume, its copies have lain unused in
libraries or perhaps even been lost through the years.

Two further compositions came from the composer's pen during the last
two years of his life. In his retirement he returned to his *Sonata in B minor*
for violin and piano (1876), and revised it extensively. It was performed
at a 22 March 1906 Boston Symphony Quartet concert by Heinrich Gebhard, piano, and Willy Hess, violin. Apparently not everyone understood
that the work was a revision, for the *Transcript* announced that the concert
would include "a new sonata for piano and violin by Professor Paine—
the first fruits of his new leisure. . . ."[264] Reviewer Herbert I. Bennett
shows the same misapprehension in his praise for the performance:

> . . . Mr. Gebhard gave his usual musicianly consideration and treatment to the new
> sonata for violin and piano in B minor, by John K. Paine, of Harvard University.
> Willy Hess scored a brilliant success with the violin part of the new work, and at the
> conclusion Professor Paine was obliged to step forward and acknowledge the plau-
> dits, together with the artists. This sonata is characterized by brilliancy and tonal
> effects of a pleasing character. Professor Paine is an American composer, by the way,
> who writes the sort of music that serves to elevate the American school. . . .[265]

But the *Transcript* did describe the work accurately in its report:

> . . . The evening was notable chiefly for the first-time performance, by Heinrich
> Gebhard and Mr. Hess, of John K. Paine's newly rewritten sonata for piano and
> violin. . . .[266]

A second and much more substantial project was a new orchestral work.
For it, Paine went back to a subject he had treated almost 40 years earlier
in his *Funeral March*—President Abraham Lincoln. An early announcement of his plans appeared in October 1904:

> It is said that Prof. John K. Paine of Harvard University is at work on a tone-poem,
> entitled "Lincoln." What will his colleague, Prof. Barrett Wendell, say to the choice
> of such a low and vulgar subject?[267]

Obviously, Paine did not share Wendell's disdain for American subjects.
He continued to work on the tone poem, and in early April 1906 an item
read:

> John K. Paine is finishing a large symphonic poem to be called "Lincoln."[268]

But the composer died on 25 April before completing it. The full score
of *Lincoln: A Tragic Tone Poem* is now in the Houghton Library at Har-

vard University, handsomely bound. A piano score is also in the Houghton collection, and a score may be found at the Library of Congress.

One may wonder in what direction Paine would have progressed as a composer, had he had another five, ten, or more years to live. Although his musical language had remained basically conservative, he had become more and more progressive since the late 1870s, and had assimilated many later 19th-century practices and innovations into his style, even keeping pace with many contemporary composers in Europe. We may reasonably assume that he would have retained his openmindedness and continued to be influenced by current developments.

9

The Remaining Years

Although the last decades of Paine's career as a composer had become increasingly frustrating and embittering—for his interest to the general musical public apparently had already begun to diminish in favor of younger, more progressive composers—his success in other areas was undiminished. With the addition of music courses into the Harvard curriculum in 1871, and Paine's later attainment of a full professorship, the security of his position in higher education was assured. Moreover, his influence and his role in the development of American music and music education was already beginning to be recognized. He had become a celebrity in the music field—his opinions were solicited on musical questions, his attendance was noted at concerts and lectures, and his private life grew interesting to the public. Many details of this period of his life have been recorded, and we may gain insights into his involvement at Harvard as well as his activities in the community and at home.

Where Paine lived during his earlier years at Harvard seems not to have been recorded except in the faculty pages of the university catalog. His residence from 1864 (when he was 25!) through 1868 was given only as "Mrs. S. Hymphrey's," with no further location indicated. For 1869, the year of his marriage, the entry was "Linden St." In 1870 the Paines moved to 8 Frisbie Place, a university-owned duplex adjoining the campus, where they remained through 1882. In 1883 they were at 20 Berkeley Street, near the Fiskes, where they lived until their house at 23 Hawthorn Street was completed early in 1885.

The Paines took the first step toward owning a home in 1881, when on 4 February they brought a lot on Hawthorn Street from the estate of Samuel Batchelder.[1] The street frontage of the lot was 95 feet, its area was 11,716 square feet, and its back boundary adjoined the property of Henry Wadsworth Longfellow. Certainly the Paines looked forward to the prospect of having Longfellow for a neighbor, but this was not to be their privilege, for the great poet died the following year.[2] Construction of the house was begun on 10 July 1884.[3] The subcontractor completed the cellar on 27 December,[4] and on 10 January 1885 the entire structure was finished.[5] A $3000 mortgage, payable in four years and three months, was granted by the Cambridge Savings Bank.[6] Architects Van Brunt & Howe had supervised the project, and described the building as "a two story house with cottage roof. . . ."[7] This was the Paines' home for the remainder of the composer's life. Sometime after his death Mrs. Paine sold the house to R. A. Daly, Professor of Theology, and moved to an apartment, also on Hawthorn Street.[8]

Details of the Paines' private life are quite spotty, as has already been discussed; many personal papers were destroyed after Mrs. Paine's death as a condition of her will, and remaining sources are few. Some informal activities involving the Paines are mentioned in the collected letters of John Fiske, and these would be typical of many other times that were not recorded. During the academic year the Paines attended many concerts, lectures, receptions, and college functions that received mention in the press. The largest gaps in our knowledge occur during the summer vacation months,[9] when concert activities and social life in Boston were at a near standstill. Fortunately, Paine's summer plans usually were considered newsworthy, and for most years there is at least a brief one-sentence description. From 1878 through 1890 the Paines spent some time in most years at the Shoals; definitely mentioned were 1878, 1880, and 1888–90. At the Shoals they renewed friendships with poet Celia Thaxter, the Fiskes, Horatio Lamb, William Mason, Julius Eichberg, and others active in society or the arts. No later mention is made of the Shoals, however, and after Mrs. Thaxter's death in 1894 perhaps the community of vacationers had changed. The Paines did return at last in July 1905. In a 23 July letter to Allan A. Brown, written in honor of the librarian's 70th birthday, Paine mentioned that they were "here at the Shoals for the summer," and "the sea air is doing me good."[10] It was probably during this stay that the following occurred, as related by Mrs. Paine's nephew, Hugh Payne Greeley:

> During his last years diabetes tried to discourage him, but he was buoyant and responsive even with waning vitality. . . . Shortly before his death he was at the Isle of Shoals, with his nephews. They were about to take a plunge in the swimming pool, an arm of the sea, enclosed by a small bay. In spite of age and infirmity, his spirit prompted him to join them. He hired a bathing suit, ran out on the diving board and plunged in with a perfect dive. Having swam out he was distressed because he could not find his glasses. He had forgotten to remove them and the pool was emptied that night and they were recovered.[11]

Nothing is known of the summers of 1891 through 1893, except that the Paines were at home in mid-August 1892, when the composer played his new *Columbus March* for John Fiske. In 1895 he came "in from the country" to attend an opera,[12] and in 1896 the couple stayed at Crawford House in New Hampshire.[13] Paine attended Portland Old Home Week in August 1900,[14] and in July 1902 wrote a letter to Mabel Daniels from Westport Inn on Lake Champlain in New York state.[15]

There were as many as four times when the Paines traveled to Europe. In 1879 they toured England and Germany, partly to generate interest in the new *Spring* symphony; Fiske's description of their visit with him in London has been quoted earlier. In June 1894 the *Advertiser* announced, in a Harvard item, that Paine "will travel on the continent. . . ,"[16] but no further word confirmed this. Similarly, the *Musical Courier*, in May 1901, disclosed that Paine, among others, "has gone or is about to go" to Europe,[17] but nothing more appeared concerning such plans. However, in 1903, the Paines definitely made a trip to Europe, for the professor represented Harvard at the October unveiling of a Wagner monument in Berlin. Paine very nearly missed this honor, according to Mrs. Paine's nephew, William Roger Greeley, for President Eliot had already announced his designation of Henry L. Higginson, Boston Symphony Orchestra founder, as the Harvard delegate. Mrs. Paine argued with Eliot, and persuaded him to issue a second announcement naming her husband as representative.[18] Greeley did not state how far in advance Eliot had made this change, but on 7 July the Berlin correspondent for the *Musical Courier* reported that the Wagner monument committee had received a cablegram from Harvard

> . . . in which the committee is informed of the fact that Prof. John Knowles Paine will attend the Wagner monument consecration as official delegate of the old renowned American high school of learning.[19]

Soon after this apparently last-minute switch, the Paines left for Europe, sailing from New York aboard the *Finland* on 18 July[20] and docking at Antwerp 10 days later.[21] After a two-month tour, they were on hand at the Tiergarten in Berlin on Thursday, 1 October, for the festive unveiling of the monument. Prince Eitel represented the royal family, and the crowd-pleasing music included the *Kaisermarsch* and choruses from *Die Meistersinger*.[22] At the banquet that evening many speeches were heard, including one by Paine. His evaluation of Wagner and his music contrasted markedly with the opinions stated in his lectures during the 1870s:

> . . . I am highly honored in being called upon to speak for my countrymen who have assembled here to render homage to the transcendent genius of Richard Wagner, the great master whose world wide influence grows more and more potent year by year since he completed his unique and wonderful life work.
>
> I have come from America as the official representative of Harvard University, our most ancient and renowned seat of learning, and I am glad to assure you of the

warm interest felt there and elsewhere in the United States in the dedication of the Wagner monument and the festivities connected therewith.

We share this enthusiasm with our English colleagues and friends. The presence here of representatives from various nations testifies to the cosmopolitan idea and object of this celebration.

We all realize that most of the forms of modern music have been developed to the highest point by the great masters of Germany—from Bach to Wagner. Through their supremacy the strict national limits of musical style have been greatly modified. It is no longer a question of purely German, Italian, French, Slavonic or Anglo-Saxon music, but cosmopolitan music. No doubt certain national characteristics will continue to exist, but I believe in the future composers will be distinguished more by their individuality of style than by nationality, or what is called local color. It is with this strong conviction that I enthusiastically propose the toast: "The Future of International Music."[23]

Although Paine had come to agree with many of his younger colleagues on the positive value of Wagner's music, he still obviously differed with them on nationalism in music; the reader will recall his earlier rejection of Dvořák's proposal for an American school based on Negro and American Indian melodies.

The festival continued on Friday with three historical concerts, devoted to the music of Gluck through Wagner, to the romantics, and to modern music—all were limited to instrumental music.[24] On Saturday, Richard Strauss conducted *Die Meistersinger* at the Royal Opera House. Then on Sunday evening was the International Concert, rather a marathon event, lasting over 3½ hours, with 17 composers represented on the program. Paine's *Oedipus* prelude was the only American work to be heard. Edgar Stillman Kelley's *Aladdin* suite also had been scheduled to be included, but Kelley withdrew it after the rehearsal time proved insufficient. With the Kelley suite and excerpts from Moritz Moszkowski's opera *Boabdil der Maurenkönig*, also omitted, the program reportedly would have lasted more than five hours. Paine's work, led by Stuttgart conductor Carl Pohlig, was well received, according to the *Musical Courier* correspondent:

> . . . Then came Prof. John K. Paine's prelude to "Oedipus Tyrannus," which fine tone poem with its grandiloquent, noble themes and classical mold, as well as perfection of form, was received with loud and prolonged applause, and our esteemed countryman was thrice called upon the platform. . . .[25]

Although the festival, as a whole, "proved more or less of a fiasco, not to say a farce," according to the *Musical Courier* correspondent, certainly it must have been a thrill for Paine to attend. In his capacity as Harvard's official delegate, however belated the appointment, he was one of very few Americans among the dignitaries present. And with his Prelude the only American composition to be heard in all of the concerts during the festival, Paine's stature as an international composer was affirmed—at least, perhaps, in his own mind. It was a fitting honor, especially to occur so near the end of his career.

There were other occasions, of course, when recognition was given to Paine's contributions to American musical life. He was initiated into the Harvard Phi Beta Kappa chapter in 1865, and elected a full member of the American Academy of Arts and Sciences in 1871.[26] He was early elected an honorary member of the Philadelphia Manuscript Society.[27] In 1890 Yale University awarded Paine an honorary Doctor of Music degree.[28] In 1896 he was one of those who founded the American Guild of Organists.[29]

On a number of occasions Paine's musical knowledge and experience brought him before the general public. One especially interesting instance centered around a United States Circuit Court hearing regarding the first Boston performance of Gounod's new oratorio, *The Redemption*, in 1883; Paine was called to testify. Theodore Thomas had obtained exclusive United States rights from Novello, the publisher, to perform the work with full orchestra; he was planning a yet unscheduled performance with the Handel and Haydn Society. But a local Boston musician, Joseph G. Lennon [Lennox?], had announced a performance of the oratorio, complete with orchestra, at the Boston Theatre on 21 January 1883. Thomas filed for an injunction with this explanation:

> . . . The work, if produced at all by defendants, must be produced with orchestration arranged from a pianoforte score, which arrangement it is alleged cannot be a fair representation of the composer's orchestration, a copy of which is in possession of plaintiff, and that such misrepresentation will be prejudicial to a fair judgment of the work, and will tend to impair the value of the copy of the original in possession of plaintiff. . . .[30]

Lennon's performance would certainly detract from the novelty of the later Handel and Haydn Society concert. A possible loss in ticket sales would be compounded by the requirement that Thomas pay Novello a rental fee of £20 per performance for the orchestral parts.[31] The response of Lennon's attorney reflects the disregard for professional ethics shown by some nineteenth-century musicians:

> . . . It was claimed that the oratorio was performed in Birmingham, England, in August, 1882; that a printed copy of the work has been presented to and is in the library of the British Museum, and that Thomas knows that the work has been fully published in its different parts, together with a conductor's score, upon which the places assigned to the several instruments are shown. A book has been published by Oliver

Illustration 6.   Photograph of Paine at the opening of the
Wagner Memorial at Berlin, 1903 (from Edwards, *Music
and Musicians of Maine*).

Ditson & Co., containing a score, with directions for the introduction of the several instruments, and that the music in the book is sufficient to enable a competent composer to construct an orchestral score therefrom. This book, together with all its contents, is the public property of the people of the United States and is open to everybody. Defendant also avers that the words "Gounod's Redemption," convey to the public the idea of the work, not as given by the original score, but as given in the published book. He denies that he employed any person to take notes, at a performance in New York, from the work as played under direction of Mr. Thomas. . . .[32]

The trial made front-page news, and attracted large crowds of spectators, including a number of prominent musicians. An upright piano was moved into the courtroom as a means of explaining points in the argument. Among those to testify for Thomas were George Chadwick, Paine, and W. F. Apthorp; Signor Vincenzo Cerillo, B. E. Woolf, and August Damm spoke for the defense. Paine provided some technical background during the 16 January session:

. . . Professor John K. Paine of Cambridge explained the process of composition and orchestration; the vocal part was composed first, and afterwards the orchestral part. He explained how it was impossible to produce anything more than an outline of an orchestral score on the pianoforte. He said that Gounod's original score and one arranged from the pianoforte score were essentially different. In his cross-examination, witness said an arrangement from a pianoforte score might take a variety of effect; it might disgust Gounod to hear another than his own orchestration. . . .[33]

This summary of his testimony, essentially the same in all papers, oversimplified Paine's explanation and perhaps weakened his argument. The composer clarified his ideas in a 17 January letter to the *Transcript*:

. . . In your report of my evidence given on Tuesday before the United States Court there was a misstatement which I beg leave to correct. I was reported as saying that in the process of musical composition "the vocal part was composed first and afterwards the orchestral part." What I did express on this point was, substantially, that able masters in composing a vocal work, similar to Gounod's "Redemption," would naturally create the vocal part and the general features of the orchestration simultaneously, details of scoring being worked out by degrees subsequently, and that the orchestration is as much a matter of inspiration as the vocal part.[34]

In enlightening the layman regarding the subtleties of orchestration, Paine also gave an insight into what must have been his own procedures of composition. Many organist-composers have seemed to conceive their works first in keyboard terms, waiting until later to "score up." But Paine's training in orchestration was intensive, and he obviously was able to think and to compose outright in orchestral terms.[35]

After several postponements, the court heard all testimony and then made its decision in favor of Thomas. But Lennon was allowed to proceed with his concert on 21 January, provided that the accompaniment be limited to organ and piano. The sanctioned Handel and Haydn Society performance was scheduled later for Good Friday, 23 March 1883.

Another circumstance that placed Paine in the public eye—although in a more accustomed role—was a series of 25 lectures on music history that he gave during the 1884–85 season. This seems to have been a time of cultural awakening on the part of the Boston music audience. The new Boston Symphony Orchestra was in its fourth season and providing expertly performed symphonic music. Other lectures were given, too, including a series on the structure of the Beethoven symphonies—in conjunction with their orchestra performances—given by B. J. Lang and George Chadwick.[36] Paine's series attracted much attention in the press. An early announcement read:

> . . . Professor John K. Paine proposes also to enter the lecture field in Boston, bringing to the desk 25 lectures chosen from his portfolio of those which he has been in the habit of delivering at Harvard College. They will be of a graver and more formal character than Mr. Lang's, historical and critical in their scope, and the audience will be advised to take notes and pursue some course of parallel reading to fill out the outlines of the discourses.[37]

The first lecture was announced for noon on 15 November 1884 at Chickering Hall, to last an hour. Topics announced were similar to those of the series in the early 1870s:

> . . . After an introduction, which will discuss ancient music, Ambrosian and Gregorian music, the first attempts in harmony, mensural music, etc., the subjects will be—the old Netherland and Italian schools and the English madrigalists; the origin of dramatic music; instruments and instrumental music from the sixteenth century to Bach; Protestant church music; the comic opera, and the opera under Gluck, Mozart, Rossini, and the other leading modern Germans and Italians; modern instrumental music, both classical and dramatic; singers, virtuosos, theorists and musical writers of the eighteenth and nineteenth centuries; Wagner and the musical drama. Mr. Paine will have the assistance of resident solo artists and a chorus, and at each lecture specimens from the works of representative masters of each epoch and school will be performed. In this manner the lectures will be rendered attractive as well as instructive, both to the musical public and to special musical students.[38]

Press coverage of the lectures was extensive, and lengthy summaries (often with quaint misspellings and naive misquotations) appeared regularly, both in the daily papers and in music periodicals. In announcing the final lecture, the *Advertiser* commented on the series:

> . . . If the [title] "historical concerts" had been given to this course it would have been more apt and conveyed a better idea of what was to be given. It seems a great pity that the much boasted musical public of Boston has let slip such an excellent

opportunity, both to get an accurate and popular account of what probably the most prominent and ablest representative American composer has to say of the merits and defects of the great composers of the world. The audiences have not been large, when they should have filled Chickering Hall to its limit. Apart from the knowledge gained at these lectures, the concert portion has alone been a delight. At each lecture from three quarters of an hour to an hour has been devoted to the rendering of some of the best and most characteristic compositions of the composers discussed in the previous half hour. The programmes have been admirably made, and the public given an opportunity to hear well given music which they rarely have a chance to hear, and well given too. Every effort seems to have been made to make the concert portion a success. The vocal soloists have had among their numbers, Mr. George Osgood; Miss Emma Eames, soprano; Miss Edmands, contralto, and others; also a quartette and sextette. The instrumental soloists have been unusually good, including Listemann, Loefler, [sic] Lichtenberg, Campanari, Perabo, Lang, Petersilea and others; also the Campanari quartette, trios and duos. . . . The audiences have taken the greatest interest, and those who went once went again. . . .[39]

Eames, who was to become an internationally famous diva, made a very favorable first impression upon the audience. She considered it a valuable experience; her recollections have been quoted earlier in this study. One criticism of the series was its great length, and the *Advertiser* reviewer recommended that a group of 12 to 15 lectures be given in future years. Paine had already shortened the course to 10 lectures, and presented them in Cambridge during March, April, and May, 1885 "with great success."[40] But he did not attempt the Chickering Hall series again.

Much of the knowledge displayed in these historical lectures, however, Paine was able to call upon in his next project. He, Theodore Thomas, and Karl Klauser began to edit a multi-volume history, *Famous Composers and their Works*, issued by J. B. Millet of Boston. The publication was a symposium, and articles were solicited from prominent American, English, French, and German writers. Louis C. Elson, writing in the *Advertiser*, gave his impression of the first eight parts to be released:

. . . While the name of Prof. John K. Paine, who is the editor, gives responsible indorsement to the whole, the views of many different writers of prominence give great variety of treatment to the topics within its covers. One can find in its pages the clearly expressed opinions of a Spitta, the fiery and pronounced ideas of a Woolf, the philosophizing of a Krehbiel, and the spicy terseness of a Hale, the wit of a Henderson, the historical care of a Fiske and the keen analysis of Prof. Paine himself, and all this in even the first eight parts of a series which is to consist of 30 parts.
. . . The addition of musical selections from the compositions of each of the men whose lines and theories are described, adds peculiar force to the lesson which is given, and the amount of pictorial art which is brought to bear on each subject makes this lesson a popular one, while it causes the whole work to assume the character of an *edition de luxe*.
The last named element is used in presenting many different pictures of each composer, specimens of his musical handwriting, birthplace, etc. The musical selec-

tions are made with especial reference to typical works, and here Messrs. Theodore
Thomas, Karl Klauser and Arthur Mees are at work. . . . The work as a whole bids
fair to be one of much importance, and has begun with extraordinary eclat.[41]

Paine's contributions to the symposium included an 11-page article, "Beethoven as Composer," and a lengthy essay, written with the assistance of
Leo R. Lewis, "Music in Germany." The latter occupied 36 pages and
dealt with all composers whom the authors considered important, except
for Wagner, who was discussed separately in a "spicy and earnest article
. . . by W. J. Henderson."[42] Authors of articles included, besides those
names in Elson's earlier review, were Americans George P. Upton, Howard Ticknor, Arthur Foote, and W. S. B. Mathews, and Frenchmen Arthur Pougin, Oscar Comettant, and Adolphe Jullien. Essays were printed
attractively and were supplied with photographs and reproductions of
composers' manuscripts. Each article closed with a facsimile of the author's signature. In 1909 the set was augmented by a "New Series" edited
by Louis C. Elson. Among the additions were Arthur Elson's "The Great
Operas," the editor's "Some Orchestral Masterpieces," and Henry C.
Lahee's "Standard Oratorios."

Many of the contributors to *Famous Composers and their Works*
were close friends and colleagues of Paine. Some had been his students
at Harvard. Certainly all were aware of his influence in the field and felt
his editorship added to the prestige of the venture.

The Paines, long established residents of Cambridge by the 1880s, continued to enjoy social contract with many prominent people in the community. As an example, after the season's opening concert of the Boston
Symphony Orchestra on 15 October 1898, a newspaper social columnist
noted that the professor was sitting with Mrs. Gericke, the conductor's
wife, and Mrs. Kneisel, whose husband led the Kneisel Quartet.[43] Another social item announced that soprano Caroline Gardner Clarke (Mrs.
James Washington Bartlett) gave an "informal studio supper" on
17 November 1899 to Professor Paine, Mr. and Mrs. Henry M. Rogers,
and Mrs. Evelyn Benedict.[44] And an undated note from Paine to Charles E.
Norton, Professor of Art at Harvard, accepts an invitation "to be present
and to hear the music . . ."[45]—probably one example of many such occasions. Similarly, a March 1887 invitation from Norton's daughter, Sara,
was answered by Mrs. Paine:

It will give us great pleasure to accept your kind invitation for Wednesday evening,
& Mr. Paine will be *delighted* (so he says) to play Bach's Sonata with you.[46]

Understandably, the Paines were desirable social companions to many cultured citizens, both because of Professor Paine's musical knowledge and ability and because of their active involvement in the Harvard community. Another Harvard acquaintance, Horatio Appleton Lamb (1850–1926; A.B. 1871), was a member of the Tavern and St. Botolph clubs. Paine on occasion would meet him at these locations, and would attend the St. Botolph concerts upon his invitation. Several of Paine's letters to Lamb have been preserved in the Harvard University Archives, and the following witticism is typical of the composer's style:

> . . . I called at your office this forenoon, but found the bird flown (if I may call a dear lamb a bird). . . .[47]

The Lambs vacationed at Shoals, as is evident in a 2 September 1889 letter from Paine, sent from that vacation retreat:

> . . . We miss you & your sister very much at the Shoals. . . . The gulls of Duck Island send you kind remembrances and wish you back again.[48]

The primary purpose in writing this 1889 letter was to thank Lamb for a loan he had advanced for John Towers, Paine's fellow student during the Berlin years, who had just accepted the post of Singing Master at the Indianapolis Conservatory of Music:[49]

> I am very much obliged to you for the check which I will send soon to Indianapolis for my friend Towers. I will enclose the receipt for him to sign. I hope he will be successful in his new sphere, and able ultimately to return the amount of the loan. It is very kind of you to do this favor for me. . . .

In arranging for this loan, the Harvard professor displayed the sympathy and commitment that he felt toward his fellow musicians; his father earlier had exhibited this trait in inviting Professor Crouch to Portland and in befriending the stranded Kotzschmar. Another musician to be encouraged was the singer Emil Tiferro, former director of the Cologne opera, who had come to the Chicago World's Fair to participate in what proved to be an unsuccessful venture in German opera. Paine urged him to try his fortune in Boston, and he attained some success as a concert artist during the mid 1890s,[50] leaving in 1896 to continue his career in Denver. In another instance, a benefit concert for Harrison W. Bennett, bass, was given on 1 October 1900 at Brattle Hall, Cambridge, "under the direct auspices of Prof. J. K. Paine;"[51] Bennett left within the week for Italy to begin several years' study. And in November 1900 Carl Armbruster delivered four lectures on "Song Writers of the World;" the *Herald* praised the "good judgment shown by Prof. John K. Paine in urging Mr. Armbruster to come to this city."[52]

Old friendships remained strong, especially with the Fiskes. Although John Fiske was often away now on lecture tours, the two men continued to enjoy each other's company, by attending concerts together,[53] occasionally with informal composition coaching, and sometimes with intellectual sparring on a friendly basis—Fiske recounted one such occurrence in a 20 April 1890 letter:[54]

> My classmate and friend James Herbert Morse of Salem wrote a poem entitled "Come, Silence, Thou Sweet Reasoner", which I have set to music for a chorus of men's voices. The words of the poem contained the following line: "The cricket tunes his slender throat." Brother Paine objected to the line as a basis of musical expression inasmuch as it was entomologically incorrect. This led to an animated discussion between us as to the limits of artistic license in poetical and musical composition. I maintained that the poet or musical composer was not entirely confined to the literal facts of nature in his composition. Finally the discussion reached the point of Shakespeare's practice in this respect, did he adhere strictly to the truth of Nature?

Fiske felt that Shakespeare's writings would illustrate his point of view, rather than the precise, literal attitude that Paine held. The two friends agreed that Fiske should consult his acquaintance, American Shakespearian scholar Horace Howard Furness (1833–1912), who gave a delightful response supporting Fiske's view:

> . . . You have asked me a devilish hard question,—nothing less than to furnish you with a citation which shall prove the divine William to have been zoologically wrong,—when my motto is, that under all circumstances Shakespeare is *always* right. However, the cause for which you ask is so good that for its sake and for your own sweet sake I have been cudgelling my brain to recall a passage to serve your turn. Let me premise by saying that I reëcho every word you say about the weakness of any objection to the tunefulness of the cricket's throat—you might just as well urge that no throat is tuneful, only the vocal cords which are in the throat. The first thing that occurred to me is that Shakespeare talks of the cricket's singing, and singing implies a throat. You remember Iachimo's first words, when he creeps out of the chest in Imogen's bed-chamber, are, "*The crickets sing* and man's o'erlabored sense repairs itself by rest," etc. If you need justification I think you have really sufficient here. Tennyson, too, will countenance you—in his "Marianna in the South" he says, "At eve a dry cicada sung," etc. But if you will force me to recall a phrase in Shakespeare where a literal, prosaic interpretation involves an error, why, then take Titania's command to her fairies,—and be darned to you. She tells them to
> "take from the bees their waxen thighs,
> And light them at the fiery glow-worm's eyes."
> Now, we all know that, as Dr. Johnson remarked, a glow-worm's light is not in its eyes, but in its tail. But I'd like to examine the bumps of a man who would change the phrase to entomological correctness.—"Her eyes the glow-worm lend thee," says Herrick to Julia, and the glow-worm ought to jump at the chance.—When Hamlet's father says, "The glow-worm 'gins to pale his ineffectual fire," Brother Paine would say, " 'T ain't *fire* at all. There's no oxygen combustion about it!"

Indeed, I think literature must be full of allusions to the song of the crickets, and if a song, then there must be a throat.—Lady Macbeth says, "I heard the owl scream and the crickets *cry*"—and Paine would substitute *fiddle*. Have I given you any help? If I have I'll praise Heaven. . . .[55]

After such an enlightening defense of artistic license by so renowned an expert, Paine must surely have silenced his objection to Morse's poem, whether he was actually persuaded by the argument or not. But he certainly must have continued to guide his friend's efforts at composition. Their families continued also to enjoy informal musicales; one held during the 1898 Christmas season was described by Fiske:

Sunday *climbed* through snow 4 feet deep to the Paine's—unfortunately Abby couldn't go. There was quite a gathering, several students, Dr. and Mrs. Mixter—Mixter Farm, Hardwick—Mrs. Miriam Thayer Richards, Miss Bôcher and others. Beautiful piano playing by Miss Jansen, and songs by Miss Ailie [sic] Haughton who has a fine voice, and is a handsome woman.[56]

One of the artists Fiske named, Alison Haughton, gained popularity during the following years in a series of voice recitals. One such program, on 30 April 1900, typically attracted "a large and distinctively smart audience at the Tuileries. . . ," according to the *Herald* society reporter.[57] Mary Elizabeth Paine was one of the 60 patronesses for the concert. Mrs. Paine gave similar support to other singers. She was one of 13 patronesses for Bertha Wesselhoeft Swift's 6 February 1900 recital at Brattle Hall, Cambridge;[58] Paine was represented on Miss Swift's program, and the composer and his wife were both there.[59] Fourteen patronesses, including Mrs. Paine, supported Emma Noyes' song recital on 16 April 1902.[60] And the composer's wife similarly promoted voice recitals by Marguerite Fiske on 13 May 1903 and 11 April 1905, both at the Cambridge home of Mrs. Francis J. Child.[61] A larger event, for which she was one of 53 patronesses, was the performance of the *Roman Festival Mass* by Sig. Augusto Rotoli (1847–1904), head of the voice department at the New England Conservatory, at Tremont Temple on 18 November 1896;[62] she was in attendance, but there was no mention of Professor Paine being there.[63] The previous year, on 24 March 1895, Paine had attended a performance of Rotoli's *Stabat Mater* given at the voice professor's home by a group of his women pupils, accompanied by piano and organ.[64] And on 28 March 1900 Rotoli's *Mass* was again produced at Tremont Temple, this time with his *Easter Offertory*, both given by a 200-voice chorus and four soloists; Elizabeth Paine was among the 101 patronesses, and she and her husband were present at the concert.[65] In 1905 Professor Paine was mentioned among the patrons of two events—George Turner Phelps' "Parsifal Lectures" on 21 February and 3 March in Brookline,[66] and Amy Murray's monologue and folk song recital on 27 November at Steinert Hall.[67] These without doubt are typical of many other concerts, recitals, and lectures for which the Paines provided endorsement.

As has been implied earlier, concerts and musical lectures were important social events in fin-de-siècle Boston, and prominent people seen at these occasions were regularly named in the newspaper society pages. Because of this, it is evident that the Paines were active concertgoers, for obviously they were considered newsworthy and their names appeared frequently in these columns. They regularly attended the Boston Symphony Orchestra concerts, both at Music Hall or Symphony Hall in Boston and at Sanders Theatre in Cambridge; twice they were listed among season subscribers. They subscribed yearly to Julia Terry's Vocal Chamber Series from 1898 to 1906. And naturally they were among the subscribers to the Harvard University chamber series, beginning in 1897, for Paine had organized these concerts. Paine also subscribed to Louis Elson's four lectures on music history, given in March 1900,[68] and to a series of art song recitals by Max Heinrich in 1903.[69] Concerts by the Kneisel Quartet or by the Theodore Thomas orchestra were sure to attract the Paines. Internationally recognized musicians regularly performed in Boston, either in solo recital or as guests with the Boston Symphony. Among the concerts that the Harvard professor attended were those given by Ignace Paderewski (December 1891), Moriz Rosenthal (16 November 1898), Ernst von Dohnányi (31 March 1900), Marcella Sembrich (14 December 1900), and Fritz Kreisler (14 March 1901). On 19 April 1904, Richard Strauss conducted the Boston Symphony Orchestra in Beethoven's Eighth Symphony, Wagner's prelude to *Tristan and Isolde*, and his own *Don Juan, Don Quixote*, and the love scene from *Feuersnot*.[70] Paine was there, and afterwards attended a 10:30 P. M. dinner reception for Strauss at the Hotel Lenox.[71]

Several opera productions numbered the Harvard composer among their audiences. For the last performance of Lewis S. Thompson's comic opera, *The Sphinx*, at the Tremont Theatre on 6 July 1895, Professor Paine was among "the many who came in from the country to hear the opera. . . ."[72] The following year the Damrosch Opera Company included Boston on its tour, and on 10 February gave the premiere of Walter Damrosch's new opera, *Scarlet Letter*, before a packed house. Paine was there, as were also the H. L. Higginsons, the B. J. Langs, Arthur Foote, and Nellie Melba.[73] Four days later Paine saw *Fidelio*, produced by the same company, and on 6 May he was in the audience when the Bostonians performed Reginald De Koven's *Robin Hood*.[74] The Paines were regular subscribers to English-language opera productions in Boston.[75]

Many student activities at Harvard and Radcliffe received the Paines' support, and Elizabeth's name appeared frequently on patroness lists. One of the most popular of these activities was the presentation of original operettas. Those given by the Pi Eta Society were most often favored by the composer's wife, beginning with *The Alcayde* in May 1896, with music by Frederick E. Barry ('97).[76] The following April *Fool's Gold*, composed by John A. Loud ('98), was given in the Pi Eta's new theater at Winthrop Square in Cambridge;[77] again Mrs. Paine helped in sponsoring the production, and in April 1898 did the same for *The Shoemaker's Holiday*.[78] Four later Pi Eta operettas receiving her patronage were John Loud's *The Viking* (April 1901),[79] *Queen Philippine* (April 1902)[80] and *Prince Punjab* (April 1903), both with music by Arthur W. Denison ('03)—although orchestration of *Punjab* was done by conductor Max Zach[81]—and *Will o' the Wisp* (April 1904), composed and directed by Archibald T. Davison ('06),[82] who later became Professor of Music at Harvard. Elizabeth Paine was also a patroness for two Hasty Pudding Club operettas, *Boscabello* (May 1898)[83] and *The Catnippers* (April 1903).[84] And she supported four Radcliffe student productions, *The Orientals* (May 1898)[85] and *Princess Perfection* (April 1899),[86] both composed by Josephine Sherwood ('99), *A Copper Complication* (May 1900), written by Mabel Wheeler Daniels ('00)[87] and *An Island Idyl* (December 1902), by Florence E. Heath and Grace Hollingsworth.[88] Daniels, musically the most prominent among these young women, had also been in the cast of *Princess Perfection*. After graduating, she composed another operetta, *The Court of Hearts*, which was given in May 1901 under the auspices of the Class of 1900; Mrs. Paine was a patroness,[89] and she and her husband were present.[90] On 30 April 1902, at the Tremont Theatre, *The Court of Hearts* was again performed, this time to aid the Peabody Home for Crippled Children; musically prominent patrons included the Paines, the George Chadwicks, the Arthur Footes, the Louis Elsons, and Julia Ward Howe.[91] In 1905, two Gilbert and Sullivan operettas, *The Mikado* (March-April) and *The Pirates of Penzance* (November-December) were performed at Jordan Hall, Boston, by Radcliffe and Harvard graduates to benefit the Radcliffe library. Andrew Carnegie had offered $75,000 to the college, provided that additional funds were raised by the school. Mrs. Paine was a patroness for both events.[92] The composer's wife did not confine her support of activities at Radcliffe to those musical in nature: in April 1900 she and 14 other women were the patronesses for a basketball game between Radcliffe sophomores and juniors.[93]

Social events involving the music department were regular pleasures. Typical occasions were an 11 January 1901 tea at Brooks House, hosted by the Paines and the Spaldings, honoring students enrolled in music courses and members of Harvard musical organizations,[94] and a student musicale at George Osgood's house in Brookline on 10 December 1903.[95]

It is clear from the events discussed above that Professor and Mrs. Paine were people of standing in the Boston-Cambridge community, that they participated in activities that were usual among people in this class, and that they were considered important enough that details of their social life attracted the interest of newspaper society reporters. This is to a large extent the result of Paine's Harvard associations. When Charles Eliot was inaugurated President in 1869, Paine was merely an employee of the university, with no academic standing at all. But with the introduction of the elective system in 1870 and the offering of the first music course for academic credit in 1871, his relation to the university changed. And upon his election to a professorship in 1875, he could take his place among such renowned scholars and educators as James B. Greenough, G. P. Baker, LeBaron Briggs, W. G. Farlow, Charles Eliot Norton, Barrett Wendell, George Palmer, and Arthur Gilman. Mrs. Paine, in her work with the many musical events discussed previously, was often associated with the wives of many of these men, as well as other prominent women such as Mrs. Henry L. Higginson, Mrs. Louis Agassiz, and Longfellow's three daughters.

Upon assuming his professorship, Paine became a full-fledged member of the college faculty and was thereby entitled to take part in setting policy and making decisions. The faculty met about six times each academic year, discussing curriculum, taking disciplinary action against erring students, recognizing superior scholarship, and discussing changes in policy to be submitted to the President and Fellows of Harvard and to the Board of Overseers, who possessed final power. Paine's attendance record at faculty meetings was irregular, but he certainly must have kept informed on current issues and developments, regardless. One issue that raised prolonged debate was the proposal to modify or eliminate mandatory chapel attendance. Sentiment among the faculty grew in favor of change, and at the 31 May 1880 meeting a motion passed concerning a revision of student regulations:

> Voted to strike out—subject to the approval of the Corporation and the Overseers—§38, which requires attendance at daily prayers, and to insert in its place a statement that daily prayers are held in Appleton Chapel at which attendance is voluntary.[96]

A number of faculty members were absent from the meeting, including Paine, and the Registrar was instructed to poll them before the next meeting and enter their votes on the record. When contacted, Paine voted in favor of the motion. This action of the faculty was to have no immediate effect, however, for the Overseers and the Corporation refused to eliminate the attendance requirement. Voluntary chapel did not come about until 1886. The topic, of course, was not forgotten, and two years later it resurfaced during a discussion of regulations for unmatriculated students. To a paragraph,

> Special Students shall be subject to all the general regulations of the Undergraduate Department . . .

it was moved to add the phrase,

> . . . except those relating to religious exercises. . . .

Paine supported this motion also, but it failed in the faculty vote, 13–18.[97]

Although chapel services remained compulsory for the meantime, their content and focus began to undergo a change. Spalding described their former nature:

> When Paine became organist and choirmaster in 1862, the music at compulsory morning prayers was led by an informal group of students, and the organ was a very inadequate instrument. Paine, though a gifted organist—a recognized virtuoso, in fact, in Bach's organ works—had little of the patience and practical experience which are necessary for a successful choirmaster. As his time and strength became fully occupied with the new Department of Music, it was decided to try the experiment of a choir of boys and men trained by a professional musician. For this duty Warren Andrew Locke (A.B. 1869), who had studied in Europe and later became organist of St. Paul's Church, Boston, was chosen.[98]

Unitarian services had been held consistently in the chapel, but this practice was ended in 1881, and a group of clergymen representing several different denominations began conducting services there.[99] Locke began his duties as organist in 1882 and organized his choir, obtaining boys from the considerable supply available in the Cambridge schools. The choir was upgraded in 1886, when chapel attendance finally became voluntary, for a higher standard of musical performance would help to attract worshipers, who were no longer required to attend.

Another issue that provoked faculty discussion was that of class attendance. On 2 February 1880 a committee was appointed to consider "certain propositions relating to the regularity and diligence of students. . . ." They proposed the following regulation, which was approved by the faculty at its 17 February meeting:

> When a student has been admitted to any course of study, he is expected to attend the appointed exercises and to perform systematically the work prescribed by the instructor.[100]

There was some disagreement over this policy of required class attendance, for at the 1 March meeting, a motion was proposed deleting the words, "to attend the appointed exercises and. . . ." It failed by a vote of 9–14. Paine was among those who favored the motion.[101]

In 1889 the Board of Overseers sent a communication to the Faculty requesting that every undergraduate be required to report in person early every morning, that class attendance be more rigidly enforced, and that daily absence reports be collected and recorded from each class.[102] Apparently the faculty action taken in 1880 had not been effective. However, the faculty felt that these Overseers regulations would be too cumbersome, and at a 5 February 1889 meeting took action

> . . . not for transmission to the Overseers:—Voted: that in the opinion of this Board it is inexpedient to require a daily morning report in person.[103]

The motion was approved 26–5; Paine was among those voting *yea*. Despite the intended lack of communication between the two bodies, members of the Board of Overseers must have learned of this faculty reaction, for another faculty meeting convened a week later, on 12 February. At this time the Overseers proposals were approved, with some modifications.[104] The vote was 36–10 in favor (Paine voted *yea*); perhaps the controversy explains the increased attendance at this second meeting.

An amusing incident, reported in the papers following the freshman elections in 1886, shows that Paine at times had to take part in routine disciplinary procedures. The newly arrived students, gathered in Boylston Hall, had seated themselves in groups according to the schools from which they had come, and rivalries were noisily apparent.

> . . . The meeting was as void of order as a football contest. The main idea seemed to be that the candidates were to be elected on the lung power of their supporters.
> . . . About the time of the latter election [Endicott, treasurer], when the howling and shouting had reached an elevated pitch, a parietal committee from the faculty, consisting of Professor J. K. Paine, Professor Greenough and Registrar C. J. White, filed into the room and had a short conference with the president. Their entrance was greeted with a terrific silence. In response to their request that the meeting be adjourned immediately, the president assured them that the meeting was only noisy; that there was no prospect of serious disorder.

The elections proceeded without further delay, the parietal committee remaining standing within the railing throughout the meeting. . . .[105]

By the latter half of the 1880s, course offerings in the music department had reached a level that was not to change in great degree before Paine's retirement in 1905. The first course to be offered—"Theory of Music.— (Harmony.—Counterpoint and Choral Figuration.—Free Composition.— Song, march, dance, and rondo forms)."[106]—attracted 11 students. Paine summarized these beginning years in an 1895 department report:

> Previous to the administration of President Eliot no regular instruction in the theory of music was offered to the students of Harvard University. The duties of the musical instructor were simply to direct the College choir and play the organ in Appleton Chapel. For the first time in the history of Harvard College the higher study of music was represented by a full course of lectures on the history of music, given by me in 1870–71. During the same year the College Faculty, at my suggestion, voted to introduce harmony and counterpoint as an elective study. For several years the instruction was contributed on my part with the confident hope that this branch of learning would secure a permanent place in the curriculum.
>
> Canon and fugue, free thematic music, history of music, and instrumentation were subsequently added, and the usefulness of these studies was demonstrated. This led to my appointment, in 1873, as Assistant Professor, and in 1875, as full Professor of Music. Meanwhile, the College Faculty established Honors in Music. . . .[107]

Apparently Paine, as an Instructor, continued to receive the same salary despite his added teaching load, and it was only after his promotion to Assistant Professor that he received an appropriate raise in pay.

During the first five years that music courses were offered for academic credit—1871–72 through 1875–76—an additional course was added each year. These were, in the order added (with earlier descriptions being revised, omitting topics covered in newer courses):

> Imitative Counterpoint.—Canon.—Fugue (in two or three voices).—Free Composition (Thematic Treatment).[108]
>
> Fugue (in three and four voices; Double Fugue, etc.)—Sonata and Symphonic Forms.—Instrumentation.—Lectures on the History of Music.[109]
>
> History of Music.—Gregorian Music.—Mediaeval and Modern Music.[110]
>
> Canon.—Free Thematic Music.[111]

These courses were open to all Sophomores, Juniors, and Seniors who could demonstrate their competency. Music courses were not officially open to Freshmen until 1888–89, but certain freshmen were enrolled in department courses almost every year from 1874–75 on. Graduate students began to be included in these courses, also, starting in the fall of 1875, and a statement appeared in the 1875–76 catalog:

> Prof. Paine will meet graduates once a week for advanced instruction in musical theory and composition.[112]

During the previous spring a vote of the President and Fellows, approved by the Board of Overseers, made it possible for a Doctor of Philosophy degree to be obtained in Music.[113] Although such a doctorate was not to be awarded for another 30 years, Harvard conferred its first A.M. in Music upon Arthur Foote at the spring 1875 commencement.

In 1876–77 the number of undergraduate music courses was reduced to four: *Fugue* and *Canon* were combined into *Canon and Fugue.—Free Thematic Music*.[114] The following year a fifth course was added, *The Instrumental Music of Haydn, Mozart, Beethoven, and their successors*,[115] and in 1878–79 *Canon and Fugue* . . . was divided into two graduate-level courses, *Canon and Fugue* and *Free Thematic Music.—Forms of Modern Instrumental Music*.[116] Course enrollment totaled 54 that year, and increased to 74 in 1879–80 for the same offerings.[117] In 1882–83 *Haydn, Mozart, Beethoven* was combined with the two-hour *Harmony* course to form a three-hour offering. It was restored the following year, but was dropped permanently after 1884–85. *Canon and Fugue* and *Free Thematic Music* ceased to be listed as graduate courses in 1882–83, and were instead grouped with the other music offerings; the following year they received permanent designations as Course 5 and Course 6. Department enrollment peaked at 111 in 1884–85, resulting primarily from the record number of 81 in History of Music.[118]

Harvard *Annual Reports* through 1889–90 included a summary of the material given in each course; in later issues the format was altered and this information was not supplied. By reading these descriptions one will discover the content of Paine's classes during their first two decades. The summaries for 1887–88 are typical:

> 1. Harmony.—Richter's Harmony, with illustrations and explanations.—Written exercises on figured basses and given melodies.—Chorals and national airs harmonized.—Exercises in Strict Counterpoint, in 2, 3, and 4 voices, were introduced during the latter part of the year.
> 2. Counterpoint.—Richter's Counterpoint.—Written exercises on given themes, in the following order: Chorals and other melodies harmonized, using passing notes; different orders of Counterpoint in 2, 3, and 4 voices; Double Counterpoint; Free Imitative Counterpoint; introduction to Canon and Fugue. Organ preludes and songs were also composed.
> 3. History of Music.—Lectures, with collateral reading.—Ritter's Student's History of Music.

*6. Free Thematic Music.—Bussler's and Pauer's text-books on Musical Form.— Symphonies and Sonatas of Beethoven, Mozart, and other masters were analyzed. Various forms of free instrumental music were composed, including a piano sonata. Two, three, and four-part Fugues and Canons were composed.[119]

Canon and Fugue was not offered that year; it and *Free Thematic Music* had begun to be offered only in alternate years, until Paine's load was lightened when Walter Spalding joined the department in 1895. The 1888–89 description of *Canon and Fugue* shows some similarity to *Free Thematic Music*:

*5. Canon and Fugue.—Jadassohn's Canon and Fugue.—Practice in musical composition.—Piano pieces and a string quartet were composed.[120]

In 1888 an additional upper-level course, *Instrumentation*, was offered for the first time:

*7. Instrumentation.—Exercises in scoring for various combinations of orchestral instruments, and for the full orchestra.—Score reading.—The scores of Beethoven's Symphonies and other works played in the class-room.—Study of the orchestral scores of classical oratorios, operas, and cantatas.

A graduate course, Music 20, *Course of Research*, enlisted one student in 1892–93.[121] Two years later it was listed as *Seminary in Music*, meeting fortnightly, and according to the catalog, "At the meeting of the Seminary advanced students will present original musical compositions for performance and discussion."[122]

Textbooks were named in some of the course descriptions. For *Harmony*, Paine had specified Richter's *Harmony* from 1879–80 through 1887–88, then changing to Jadassohn's *Harmony*. Similarly, in *Counterpoint* he had used Richter's treatise from 1874–75 through 1887–88, switching then to Jadassohn's *Counterpoint*. And in *Canon and Fugue*, Richter's *Canon and Fugue*, in use since 1880–81, was replaced in 1888–89 by Jadassohn's *Canon and Fugue*. Pauer's *Musical Form* was used in *The Instrumental Music of Haydn, Mozart, Beethoven, and their successors*, and it and Bussler's *Musical Form* were both studied in *Free Thematic Music*, as well as Jadassohn's *Canon and Fugue* when the alternate course was not given. *History of Music* students did unspecified collateral reading, but in 1881–82 they did utilize Von Dommer's *Musikgeschichte*, and in 1886–88 Ritter's *Student's History of Music*.

The instruction given in these courses seems to have been very technical and practical in orientation, with little emphasis given to the passive study more in favor in today's B.A. curriculum. This was intentional; Paine outlined department objectives in his 1895 report:

> . . . 1st, to provide a thorough training for students who intend to follow the musical profession as teachers and composers; 2d, to offer a course of technical study to those who wish to devote themselves to musical criticism and literature, and the cultivation of musical taste. . . .[123]

Average annual enrollment was about 50 students, a number Paine conceded was small when compared to other departments. But he justified the situation by an explanation of the need for strict standards:

> . . . 1st, decided talent is not common; 2d, no place is given to the study of harmony in the preparatory schools, as it is not one of the requirements for admission to College; 3d, as the piano and organ are the only solo instruments which are able to produce the complete harmony and combined voices of a musical composition throughout the compass of tone, proficiency in piano or organ playing is required of all who elect the courses in music. Many students are debarred on this account. Every year a number of applicants have been refused; though a few exceptions have been made in favor of advanced players on the violin and other orchestral instruments. . . .

Paine advocated teaching harmony in the preparatory schools, in order that entering students could skip the year of elementary training and achieve better results in advanced courses. Despite the present difficulties, however,

> . . . the number of students who have gained distinction in music is relatively large, owing perhaps, to the fact that those who pursue the study are generally assiduously devoted to it. During the last fifteen years twenty-one students have taken honors in music; of this number, ten have received highest honors. Five, since graduation, have become professional musicians, and four others are now pursuing advanced studies at home and abroad with this end in view. Six have published compositions, and several have gained some reputation as composers. Several have taken the degree of Master of Arts. Two have devoted themselves to musical criticism. . . .

To train these students more thoroughly as practicing musicians, Paine advocated the establishment of an applied music department at Harvard:

> In order to enlarge the scope of the musical department, a course of four years in practical and theoretical music ought to be established in the Lawrence Scientific School, for the thorough training of musical artists.
>
> Advanced theoretical instruction should be combined with the highest training in piano, organ, and violin playing, under eminent masters, appointed as teachers in this course. No student should be admitted without an elementary knowledge of harmony, considerable executive ability on one or more instruments, and decided musical talent. Such a four years' course, with the degree of Bachelor of Music, would set a high standard for the musical profession in this country, and would surely attract the best talent here, and add to the renown of the University. . . .

> Though Harvard still maintains its preëminence in the number and variety of its courses in theoretical music, other institutions offer practical training as well, and it is imperative that this side of the art should soon be represented by Harvard in the Scientific School. . . .

This suggestion apparently did not gain serious consideration, for the topic was not mentioned again, and applied music did not enter the curriculum. Spalding in 1929 explained department policy:

> . . . The question has often been asked why Harvard has not included in its musical curriculum the teaching of playing and singing, and at times great pressure has been applied to the Department to change its policy in this respect. This question, however, has been settled by the advantages of the locality. There have always been in Boston and Cambridge so many teachers of singing and of every instrument—the New England Conservatory being specially important—that Harvard has been able to devote itself exclusively to the creative and artistic aspects of music without being under indictment for neglecting the executive side. . . .[124]

The proposal to add applied music was one of several suggestions Paine offered in his 1895 report; others gained more positive results. Most immediate was the response to his plea for an increase in faculty:

> . . . There is pressing need of the appointment of an instructor in harmony and elementary counterpoint, in order that I may devote more work to the advanced courses in music. For nearly a quarter of a century all the courses in music have been taught by me without assistance.[125]

That fall, Walter R. Spalding, A.B., A.M., member of the class of 1887, was appointed Instructor, and began teaching Music 1, *Harmony*. Two years later, in 1897–98, he also took over Music 2, *Counterpoint*, which was renamed *Advanced Harmony and Counterpoint* after a year. Spalding added two more courses, Music 4, *Musical Form, with analysis of the works of the great composers*, a half-course, in 1900–01,[126] and Music 2a, *Vocal Counterpoint, with analysis of choral works of the great composers*, also a half-course, in 1901–02,[127] as well as assisting Paine in Music 7, *Instrumentation*; in 1902 he was appointed Assistant Professor. A third faculty member was added in 1903, Frederick S. Converse, A.B. *summa cum laude* 1893, with the rank of Instructor. Converse taught Music 5, *Canon and Fugue*, and in 1904–05 began Music 1a, *Harmony (advanced course)*. Other additions to the faculty during Paine's tenure included Henry Leroy Stone (A.B. 1901, honors 1902), appointed Assistant in 1902, Daniel Gregory Mason (A.B. *cum laude* 1895), who taught two courses in the 1902 summer term, and L. A. Coerne, who taught similarly a year later.

A third suggestion in Paine's 1895 report concerns the problem of presenting music performances to classes in a time before the development of adequate recordings and loudspeakers.

> . . . The department is also in need of a convenient lecture-room in connection with a hall for chamber concerts. A hall, with a large wooden stage and seating capacity for 400 to 500 persons, is greatly needed for the larger lecture courses as well as chamber concerts. . . . There will be need for such a hall in the near future, as it is my plan to give a full course of lectures on the history of music, with twenty or more illustrative chamber concerts, if money can be provided for this purpose.
>
> These concerts would supply a long felt want in teaching musical history. Brief selections from complex scores, read at the piano during the lecture hour, are wholly inadequate to give a true idea of the beauties of musical style and the relative characteristics of great composers. . . .

Paine proposed securing top ensembles, such as the Kneisel, Adamowski, and Molé quartets, and leading singers and performers for these concerts. Expenses could be partly met by admitting non-students for an admission charge. These concerts would also help to upgrade the *History of Music* course:

> Since 1890 the history of music has been given as a half-course on alternate years to advanced students only. Previously it had been given as a literary course to a much larger number of students. Most departments find it advantageous to offer one or more courses that appeal to students in general. I am convinced that the usefulness of the musical department would be increased if the history of music were given as a full course, open to all students able to read music well. Examinations, written descriptions of musical works, theses, and collateral reading should be required. The concerts should take place on different days from the lectures.

Two years later the plan of concerts came into being, but held in Sanders Theatre, not in a new recital hall. Paine offered a new course, Music 8, *Chamber Music of Beethoven and other masters, with analysis of their principal works*, a lecture course with 10 illustrative concerts.[128] The press provided generous publicity:

> Ten chamber concerts, supplementary to a course of lectures given to students by Prof. J. K. Paine on the chamber music of Beethoven and other modern masters, are to be given in Sanders Theatre, Cambridge, on Tuesday evenings. . . .
>
> The programmes have been selected to represent most of the forms of modern chamber music—the piano sonata, the piano and violin sonata, the piano quintet, the piano septet, and the string quartet, quintet, septet and octet. Among the larger works are Beethoven's septet, for strings and wind; Hummel's piano septet, Schubert's octet for strings and wind, and Mozart's quintet for piano and wind, and Schubert's quintet for piano and strings. Among the novelties is a quintet for piano and strings by Mr. Arthur Foote, which will be heard at the concerts for the first time. . . .[129]
>
> . . . Such well known artists as the Kneisel quartet, the Adamowski quartet, Mr.

Baermann, Mr. Joseffy will appear, and, no doubt, the many music lovers of Boston, as well as those resident in Cambridge, will be only too glad to hear such music in such surroundings. These concerts, while illustrating the same subject, are entirely distinct from the lectures by Prof. Paine.[130]

Manager of the concerts was F. R. Comee, assistant manager of the Boston Symphony Orchestra and member of the class of 1875. The concerts were successful financially, and part of the receipts were set aside against expenses of a second season.[131] The public received these programs enthusiastically, and demonstrated its appreciation at the last concert on 26 April 1898:

. . . At the close of the concert, after the artists had been recalled, there was a decided desire on the part of the audience to give Prof. Paine, the founder of these concerts, a well deserved ovation, but the gentleman modestly declined to appear.[132]

According to the *Herald*, acclaim was widespread:

. . . The critical opinion of the entire country commended Prof. Paine in the highest terms, the New York Tribune describing the series of concerts as "a most noble and commendable project. . . ."[133]

Paine announced another series of ten concerts for the 1898–99 season; eight featured the Kneisel quartet, one the Adamowski quartet, and one the Dannreuther quartet of New York. Assisting artists were to be Adele Aus der Ohe, pianist Antoinette Szumowska (wife of Joseph Adamowski), Helen Hopekirk, Carl Baermann, Alexander Siloti, Ernst Perabo, "probably" Rafael Joseffy, and "several members of the Boston Symphony Orchestra." Twenty-seven works were announced, including Paine's *Larghetto and scherzo for piano, violin and violoncello in B-flat major*. A third series of 10 concerts, "partly illustrative of a course of lectures given to students by Prof. John K. Paine, on the 'History of Music,' " extended from 24 October 1899 to 24 April 1900.[134]

Opportunity for learning in *Instrumentation* improved in 1902–03, for under the course listing in the catalog appeared the following:

. . . Orchestral musicians will be employed in the classroom to exhibit the characteristics of all the instruments of the orchestra.[135]

Improvement in facilities had resulted from a growth in interest and enrollment in the department.

. . . The Corporation has shown its appreciation of this growth by enlarging the teaching staff and by continuing the annual appropriation for the purchase of or-

chestral scores and other necessary music, and for the engagement of orchestral
players who illustrate to the students in Instrumentation the tone quality and technical
characteristics of all the instruments found in the modern orchestra. . . .[136]

Paine had first advocated a fund for orchestral players to give demonstrations in *Instrumentation* in his June 1900 department report. At the
same time he reported the acquisition of an orchestrelle from the Aeolian
Company of New York, which was used to demonstrate orchestral examples in the History of Music course.[137]

An additional degree of prestige befell the department with the introduction of entrance exams in Harmony and Counterpoint in 1903. At
its 20 January meeting, the Faculty approved Paine's motion:

I move that Music be added to the list of studies for admission to Harvard College:
Harmony as an Elementary Study, to be placed among the group of optional studies
in Science—Physics, Chemistry, Physiography, Anatomy—and counting 2 points;
Counterpoint to be placed among the optional Advanced Studies (counting as 2
points). Harmony to be held/considered *[sic]* as Elementary to Counterpoint.[138]

Paine described the requirements of the examination in Counterpoint:

The examination will be adapted to the proficiency of those who have studied Counterpoint in a systematic course of three lessons a week through one school year, and
presupposes training in pianoforte playing. As Counterpoint applies the principles of
harmony to the melodious treatment of the several voice-parts in combination, and
as the art of musical composition begins properly with this study, the work should
consist principally of written exercises on given themes. . . .[139]

Excellence on the part of composition students was encouraged in 1904
when Francis Boott (Class of 1831) left a bequest of $10,000 to provide
an annual prize of $100 for the best concerted vocal piece composed by
an undergraduate or graduate student.[140]

These developments showed recognition by the university and alumni
of the growth and success of the Music Department. However, the increase in size intensified the problem of inadequate space. During Paine's
last years the department engaged upon a campaign to raise funds for a
new Music Building, a project that did not reach fruition until after his
retirement and death. Inadequate facilities had been a problem of the
department since its inception. Already in 1875 Dwight had complained
about inappropriate recital space. Classes were held in a room in Boylston
Hall into the 1880s; a schedule for 1881–82 specifies "Boylston 5."[141] A
reporter interviewing Paine about his *Columbus March and Hymn* in 1893
disclosed that the composer's office was in the basement of the old law
building. Spalding, in a March 1903 appeal for the new building, observed

that the department had changed its location three times in the past 12 years:

> . . . Only seldom has [the Department of Music] been able to command the exclusive use of hours available for lectures, for research, and for the undisturbed consultation of music-scores. This year the Department has nearly 200 students; one of the courses is taken by 80 men, another by about 50, and yet the lecture room of the Department will contain comfortably no more than 40. For the last five years, Holden Chapel, which consists merely of this single room, has been assigned to the work of the Department, but generally lectures in several other courses have also been given there. Although a building may be hallowed by tradition, it is absolutely necessary for practical purposes that it should be well ventilated. Holden Chapel, however, is wholly lacking in any system of ventilation, is generally either too hot or too cold, and yet it is used continuously for lectures and for consultation hours, from nine o'clock in the morning to three or four o'clock in the afternoon.[142]

Paine and Spalding's joint department report in December 1904 gave further testimony to the inadequacies of Holden Chapel:

> . . . As a result of this marked interest on the part of the students, the present quarters of the Department—the single room in Holden Chapel, seating comfortably about 75 persons—become more and more inadequate. For instance, the students in Music 3, the course on the History of Music, 130 in number, are huddled together in this room, many actually being seated on the floor. And even these quarters are not secured to Music students alone, as notwithstanding primitive means of ventilation, Holden Chapel when not in use by the Department of Music is at once turned over to courses in Elocution. . . .[143]

At this stage, plans for the new building had already been drawn, and were, in fact, published with Spalding's 1903 appeal. They were drawn by architect J. M. Howells, a Harvard graduate and son of William Dean Howells, who with a fellow Harvard alumnus had established a partnership, Howells & Stokes, in New York. Paine had written to the elder Howells on 22 January 1902, telling of his hopes:

> . . . I remember your son both as a small boy and as a college student. I have a most pleasant impression of him. I have heard such high praise of his taste and ability as an architect that we are fortunate in having him to draw sketches for the proposed building for the Musical Department, and I hope his services will be engaged to build the hall, in case we succeed in our object. Will you kindly ask him if we cannot meet soon either in Cambridge or New York? It will be necessary to confer with him with regard to the rooms required and other details, before a definite plan can be made. President Eliot is interested in the matter; he & I have selected the probable site on Holmes Field. I shall be able to go to New York for a day or two after Jan. 29. I know nothing to prevent me from starting a week from tomorrow, Thursday, Jan. 30. Mr. Morris has invited me to stay with him if I go.
>
> I hope we shall raise enough money to provide the department with a good building and a handsome surplus for running expenses. . . .[144]

According to Spalding's 1903 report, the idea of a new building was first seriously discussed early in 1902 by "prominent alumni of the College in both New York and Boston." Howells & Stokes then drew the plans under Paine's supervision. Building materials were to be Harvard Brick and yellow limestone; a suggested site was the ground between the Jefferson Physical Laboratory and the new Engineering Building—"here more quiet and retirement could be secured than is possible in the present situation." On the first floor would be found three classrooms and offices for a professor and an assistant. The second floor would include a small music library and two practice rooms, as well as a concert hall:

> . . . Perhaps the greatest gain, in addition to the three separate class rooms, will be that of having on the second floor a hall with sloping seats, capable of holding about 500 persons. This may be used both for chamber concerts and for large lecture courses. At the back of the hall is a space available for the introduction of a pipe organ,—an instrument which the Department has needed for many years. . . .

Construction would not begin until $100,000 had been subscribed. This would cover the estimated cost of $80,000 for the building, $10,000 for the pipe organ, and another $10,000 as a fund for running expenses. Another appeal in December 1904[145] again announced the need for $100,000, but named $75,000 instead for the building, and $25,000 as an endowment for running expenses; there was no mention of an organ. Spalding also ventured a suggestion for some generous graduate to donate the entire amount, ". . . and thus to secure the privilege and glory of having it called by his name." Such a gift did not materialize, the fund drive proceeded slowly, and after Paine died it was decided to name the new building in his memory.

In his last years with the department, Paine relinquished more of his teaching duties, and from 1899 onward taught only the *History of Music* and two or three advanced or graduate courses a year. Additional lower level courses added to the curriculum during these years were taught by Spalding or Converse. In his last two years Paine taught just the history course, *Advanced Counterpoint and Fugue/Free Composition*, and, jointly with Spalding, *Instrumentation*. Incidentally, the History of Music course attracted large enrollments—75, 121, and 98—for Paine's last three years.

On 22 May 1905 Paine resigned his professorship, effective the following September.[146] He was honored at a dinner at the Harvard University Club, Boston, on 20 June 1905, at which occasion he received a silver tea service designed by Denman W. Ross. An inscription written by Charles Eliot Norton read:

> To John Knowles Paine, the Gift of Pupils, Admirers and Friends desirous to testify to him their sense of the value of his teachings, the beauty of his compositions, and the service he has rendered to the Art of Music.

At the same event, his last class presented him a loving cup.[147] He also was given a handsome album containing signature cards of many friends— fellow professors at Harvard, former students, and admirers in general.[148]

Clearly Paine's courses had not lost their popularity, judging from the enrollment figures and the above-mentioned presentations, even as his active career was nearing its end and he was looking forward to retirement. It will be recalled that his lecture style was quite dry, and probably he had a greater influence on his music students through informal individual contact than in the classroom. But his sense of humor remained ever active, especially in small classes. Mabel Daniels recalled one such incident in a 1903 letter to a former classmate:

> . . . Do you remember the day when Miss R— brought her dog into the class, and Professor Paine, after peering at it mildly over his glasses from his seat behind the table, made some witty remark about the increased interest in his lectures which now drew the very beasts to hear him? And later, how kindly but firmly he insisted that Miss R— leave her pet at home hereafter, inasmuch as he had already punctuated his paper on Haydn, and he did not consider the assistance of the dog, who broke in every now and then with sharp barks, at all necessary.[149]

E. B. Hill recalled that a fellow student in Paine's harmony class

> . . . spent much of the time in class gazing abstractedly through a nearby window. Underestimating Paine's quickness of perception behind the professorial spectacles he ventured to submit some long overdue harmony exercises. With a quick glance Paine commented briefly "Back numbers."[150]

There were students in the later years who received a rather negative opinion of Paine and his teaching. Percy Chase Miller took all of his courses while a student at Harvard in the late 1890s, and considered Paine to be "the poorest teacher he had ever had in any subject."[151] Charles Seeger, who did not study with Paine, "thought he was an old fogey and paid no attention to him at all."[152] Composer Daniel Gregory Mason (1873–1953) found Paine's classes so uninspiring, according to John Tasker Howard, "that he virtually dropped his music while he was in college, except for writing the music for the Hasty Pudding Club shows."[153] Mason found Paine's conservatism and academic manner stifling:

> . . . Prof. Paine struck me from the start as arbitrary, as lacking in that first and last gift of the teacher, the ability to see things from the angle of the student. Typical, to give an example, was his blue-pencilling of a dissonance with which I had begun a song. He said it was "unprepared"—as undoubtedly it was; but to me it seemed seizing and exciting, and his prohibiting it merely cold-blanketed my enthusiasm without showing me the way to a wiser one. . . .[154]

Among Paine's strongest critics was one from outside academic circles, *Musical Courier* Editor-in-chief Marc A. Blumenberg, who voiced disapproval of many aspects of the music establishment. In mentioning Paine's retirement Blumenberg observed:

> Harvard honored Professor Paine last week by presenting him with some silver dishes. But it has not yet been decided whether it was because of or in spite of the fact that Professor Paine has just retired as the musical director of the institution. . . .[155]

Naturally such a hostile assertion would elicit a storm of indignation. One such reaction published two weeks later was a letter to the editor from pianist Amy Fay, in which she attempted to answer Blumenberg's criticisms:

> The silver service presented to Professor Paine on the occasion of his resignation from the musical chair of Harvard was given by subscriptions from his pupils, irrespective of their being students of the university.
> It is only fair that the pupils of this most learned and distinguished professor should show their colors, and for my part, while I should not venture to assert my claim as one of his "eminent" pupils, I nevertheless did enjoy the privilege of taking a course in Bach's music under Professor Paine in my girlhood, and I regard it as an epoch in my musical life.
> Professor Paine was a pioneer in introducing Bach's great organ compositions, . . . and I well remember the awe with which we listened to his playing in the college chapel of them. Only the other day he told me that he had been teaching Harvard students for forty years, and he thought he was "entitled to a rest."
> If Harvard University would do something worthy of Professor Paine and of itself it would not be satisfied with offering him a silver service, but would busy itself with raising a subscription for the production of his beautiful opera, "Azara. . . ."
> This year a pupil of Professor Paine, Coerne, has graduated a "Ph.D.," and has written an opera which was accepted in Berlin. The well-known musical critic of the Evening Post, Henry T. Finck, so often quoted in your columns, was in Professor Paine's class while at Harvard, and so was S. B. Whitney, the admirable organist of the Church of the Advent in Boston, where the music is of a high order.
> Doubtless a list of Professor Paine's pupils would be interesting and would reveal many distinguished names. Harvard will not find it so easy to replace this gifted and genial instructor. . . .[156]

But Fay's argument did little to satisfy Blumenberg, for later in the summer he again criticized Paine, although indirectly:

> Harvard has not yet filled the post made vacant by the retirement of Prof. J. K. Paine. Incidentally, it is interesting to learn from a Boston paper that when the Harvard students "get up a few tunes for the annual Pi Eta or the 'Pudding' musical comedies, none of them can orchestrate their effusions, but have to get George Lowell Tracy or Max Zach to straighten things up in the mysteries of cut and dried scoring for small orchestra." What in the name of Orpheus, then, do the music students learn at our universities?[157]

The theme continued in October:

> . . . So far nothing of value musical has come from our universities, although Professor Paine had been at work at Harvard for a long period and Parker, of Yale, has been doing herculean work. It does not seem to fructify. . . . Counterpoint, harmony, orchestration studies—all these are not in demand. . . .[158]

And even in an editorial observing Paine's death, Blumenberg inserted a note of criticism:

> . . . As a man, Professor Paine was universally popular, and he had a host of friends in the musical profession and among the thousands of pupils who studied theory with him at Harvard. No great musician was ever turned out of that institution, but Professor Paine did a good and useful work there nevertheless. . . .[159]

In the same editorial are listed some of the reasons why the writer felt Paine's music had fallen out of favor:

> . . . Professor Paine was educated musically in Germany, and to this fact are attributable some of the best elements in his music, but also some of their less worthy ones. His workmanship was always solid and correct, but his scores suffered at times from decided monotony of tone coloring. He set himself rigorously against French and Italian music, when the assimilation of its influences and travel and sojourn in those lands would have supplied his own creative efforts with those very factors which prevented him from producing anything vitally original and really great, according to modern estimates and requirements. And, also, Professor Paine's constant activity as an organist militated against his acquirement of that warm and acute color sense which was so strikingly absent in his orchestral scores. . . . Professor Paine was not a genius or even a great composer, but he was an excellent theoretician, who could also write music. . . .

Many musicians did not share this criticism, however. An editorial in *The*

Nation at the time of Paine's retirement voiced a far more positive assessment of his career:

> Professor Paine is not only the Nestor of American composers, he is also the first native musician who mastered the larger musical forms and created works that won fame abroad as well as at home. His opera, "Azara," has not yet been produced. He regards it as his principal work; but even if it should fail of success, his orchestral works, notably his second symphony and his symphonic poems, "The Tempest" and "An Island Fantasy," and his music to the "Oedipus Tyrannus" of Sophocles and "The Birds" of Aristophanes, will always ensure him an honorable position in the front rank of American composers. These works will in all probability be better known to the next generation than to his contemporaries, in obedience to what seems to be a law of nature, compelling the best composers to write chiefly "music of the future." But in the other field in which Mr. Paine has done pioneer work—that of creating a department of music in American universities—the present generation is already reaping a rich harvest.
>
> Although some women's colleges may have taught practical music—piano playing and singing—before Mr. Paine began his courses at Harvard, he was the first to establish music as a branch of academic study, and he had to fight against great odds. In a few years this feeling died out, and is now a thing of the past. It is singular that so much hard and persistent effort should have been necessary to gain a foothold for music, for the academic study of music is no new thing in Europe. . . .
>
> It is quite true that, as Professor [Albert Augustus] Stanley of Ann Arbor has said, regarding Professor Paine at Harvard, "his influence as a teacher has been very great, and for many years he has been an inspiration to the men who have been under his instruction, while his example has been of incalculable benefit to American music"; it is also true that Professor Paine trained about a score of the best-known composers, teachers, and critics in this country. Yet it is likely that he would have done still more for the honor and profit of American art if he could have converted the energy expended in teaching into creating more of his splendid orchestral works. The same can be said of Mr. MacDowell. . . . Apparently, therefore, one must advise our universities to keep their hands off our composers. To be sure, the poor fellows have to live; perhaps, some day, the generous rich will take account of and make provision for them.[160]

To the end of his life, Paine remained undaunted in his desire to compose, and his main reason for retiring from Harvard, other than poor health, was to devote his entire time to composition. This period of time proved short, of course, resulting in only the revision of the Violin Sonata and the incompleted tone poem, *Lincoln*. Even with his increasingly poor health, he remained alert and professionally active. He was a subscriber to a testimonial for Boston Symphony Orchestra conductor Wilhelm Gericke, presented on 24 April 1906, just the evening before his death.[161] But death came quickly:

> [He] had not been in good health for a year or more, but he was not confined to his home and was out as late as last Sunday [22 April 1906]. On that day he contracted a cold and this developed quickly into pneumonia. . . .[162]

The official cause of death was pneumonia, although the contributory cause was Diabetes Mellitus,[163] an ailment that had troubled him for many years. Insulin was not yet available, and the disease could be controlled only to a limited extent by dieting. For several weeks before his death, Paine was mostly confined to his bed.[164]

The funeral service was held at Appleton Chapel on Friday afternoon, 27 April, at three o'clock. Rev. M. L. Kellner of the Episcopal Theological School led the service, and the Apollo Club sang. In the gallery a section was reserved for Harvard graduates and former students of Paine. Following the service the body was taken to Mount Auburn Cemetery for cremation.[165]

It is apparent that the musical world had already largely dismissed Paine as an important figure by the time of his death, for there was a complete absence of comment, save for obituaries. No memorial concerts were given, and there were no reports of pieces played in his memory on scheduled programs. One circumstance which may have contributed to this was the attention paid to the disastrous San Francisco earthquake and fire, which had occurred on 18 April. The newspapers were full of photographs, reports, eyewitness accounts, and human interest stories. Special concerts were given to raise money for disaster relief; in other circumstances, some of this attention might have been directed toward recognition for Paine's life and contribution.

But Paine was not forgotten. A substantial tribute appeared in the September 1906 *Harvard Graduates Magazine*, written by Philip H. Goepp ('84):

> . . . He lived for composing, and so he was a vital stimulus to his pupils. But, single-minded in his creative work, he was quick to kindle the spirit of his students. He had the kindly sense that sees the possibility rather than the reality. None of his pupils can forget the personal interest that seemed out of all proportion to their own desert. . . .
> . . . It seems that those who know the work of John K. Paine must stand for a certain higher estimate than is frequently heard. The very quality of his broad mastery in all the forms seemed to endanger a true appreciation of his worth. . . . There is in the highest effort an element of complete sincerity, a devotion to the least detail for the sake of its own beauty, that somehow is not felt by the instant audience, that appeals to a quieter, later judgment.[166]

Goepp's evaluation was not unique; others continued an interest in Paine's works. His compositions still appeared on Harvard concerts and even on occasional Boston Symphony Orchestra programs, and the performance of *Azara* was still ahead. His many students cherished their memories of him, and the department that he built continued to flourish and grow.

II
Works

10

The Music: Explanatory Notes

John Knowles Paine's reputation and importance may stem from his position as a founder of the modern music curriculum at Harvard and subsequently adopted by American colleges and universities. His essential contribution was to make music and its history a part of the liberal arts, rather than a subdivision of mathematics as in the medieval university or the study of performance and craft as in the European conservatory. Yet the main reason for a serious review of his career today is his worth as a composer, a value steadily appreciating and appreciated as time passes by.

A study of Paine would be incomplete without a thorough examination of his works. They are little known today, but during his lifetime the music public was acquainted with many of them from frequent performances, and sales of a number of published works justified additional reprintings. Paine's many students, through whom he was able to influence American musical tastes and standards, would have known his works well, having heard them, performed them, studied them in class work, and used them as models for composing. Perhaps most important, Paine's compositions give an effective portrait of the man, showing his rigorous training, his tastes and musical standards, his changing attitudes toward composers such as Wagner, Liszt, and Chopin, and his own colorful personality.

The following chapters comprise an analytical and descriptive survey of the extant compositions of Paine, grouped by genre, and including also other known works that are now apparently lost. Within each category, compositions are given in approximate chronological order, using as criteria manuscript dates, first performances, publication dates, and first mention in the press or in other contemporary sources. Paine's opus numbers are not particularly reliable. Many works did not receive numbers, the designations of some numbers are obscure and others conflicting, and the assignment of at least the earlier numbers seems to have been done without concern for precise chronology—for example, the earliest known work, the youthful String Quartet, is designated Opus 5, preceded in the sequence by keyboard works that Paine composed later during his student days in Berlin.

Bibliographic material for each entry includes inscription (when known), author of the text (for vocal works), location of all existing manuscripts, publication history, and instrumentation (for orchestral works). Also, as a convenience, the location of published copies in major collections is indicated by the abbreviations noted in the front of this book (see pp. ix-x).

The major portion of each entry consists of a performance history, where information is available, and an analytical discussion. Performance information in some instances may be abridged if the work has been discussed at length in the biographical chapters. Analyses are provided for all published works, as well as some representative unpublished compositions, in order to provide a comprehensive view of Paine's oeuvre. These descriptive analyses are intended to provide a clear idea of each work and an overall impression of the nature and quality of Paine's style. Omitted are extensive formal analyses of each movement or detailed comparisons between differing versions of the same works. Rather, an attempt has been made to present typical or unique thematic, rhythmic, harmonic, formal, and textural material to provide a picture of Paine's craft, to place each composition within his total oeuvre, and to evaluate his work.

Instrumental compositions are presented first, beginning with the piano works, which span most of the composer's career and display most of his musical characteristics in microcosm. Next are other instrumental genres requiring increased performing forces, followed by vocal and choral music, ending with opera and *Azara*, Paine's most ambitious work and the culmination of his career.

Musical examples are supplied in sufficient number and length to provide the reader, to whom the works are probably unfamiliar, with an adequate, true impression both of the device under discussion and of Paine's style in general. Examples are reproduced in several different ways. The chamber works with piano have been simply hand copied from the manuscripts. The string quartet and orchestral works are given in two-stave reductions by the present writer, to facilitate reading at the piano while still depicting the instrumental textures involved. For the most part, the remaining works are reproduced electrostatically from the original engraved editions. For economy of space in the choral and opera examples, vocal parts originally appearing on two staves have usually been combined onto one. Choral music examples are taken from the published vocal scores; their accompaniments are merely piano arrangements and do not adequately portray the actual instrumentation. But the examples from *Azara*, while also taken from the vocal score, have been extensively retouched by the present writer after comparison with the full score, in order to provide a more accurate portrayal of Paine's orchestration.

11

Keyboard Music

Piano Works

A study of the compositions of John Knowles Paine may begin most conveniently with the piano works, which are representative of the composer's entire career from his student days in Berlin to only two decades before his retirement. As a youthful performer, Paine was known primarily as an organist of virtuoso ability, his greatest activity taking place during the 1860s; but by the time of his appointment as full professor he seems to have abandoned the organ almost entirely. Although, as a pianist, his exposure was not as great, he continued to perform publicly throughout his lifetime and he seems to have been equally skilled, judging from his repertory. Among his earliest known performances as a piano soloist were the three fund-raising concerts in Portland in the spring of 1858, prior to his departure for Berlin; one of the last was his playing of the orchestral scene (in piano transcription) from Act II of *Azara* in May 1903.

Paine's writing for the piano is generally quite idiomatic, with textures similar to those used by major composers for the piano, including Schumann and Chopin. But certain passages contain sonorities, especially doublings, that suggest that Paine had conceived them in orchestral terms; typical examples are seen in *Romance*, Op. 25, No. 2, and *Wayside Flowers*, both discussed below. Other passages that suggest Paine orchestral devices include accented quasi-brass chords punctuating the dancelike *Gipsies*, and the treble-bass dialogue in *Romance*, Op. 39. A favorite textural tool of Paine—really a cliché—that occurs in many orchestral works as well as the piano pieces is the dotted triplet figure:

Although Paine's harmonic vocabulary is fairly consistent throughout his oeuvre, one may notice an increased use of superficial chromaticism in the later works, primarily caused by a greater use of chromatic non-harmonic tones. Altered chords appear regularly, as do typical chromatic progressions such as the "omnibus progression."[1] Paine's avoidance of what he considered a cliché—the straightforward authentic cadence—resulted in various decorations, including suspensions and non-harmonic figurations, dominant ninths and thirteenths, pedal points, and plagal progressions. Occasional passages will avoid—or delay—defining a specific tonality; examples are seen in *Romance*, Op. 12, and *Gipsies*.

Melodies are tuneful and expressive, sometimes sentimental. Suspensions and appoggiaturas often decorate the themes, and much in evidence is the "ri mi" cliché, implying an augmented dominant chord or diminished seventh chord on the raised supertonic resolving to the tonic triad. Also favored was the melodic turn. Certain of Paine's themes contain pentatonic elements, suggesting an association with folk music or even an influence of Yankee tunesmith music in Paine's background.

Predictability in Paine's melodies is minimized by a use of varied phrase lengths, a common device in much of Paine's music. A similar technique is the implication of irregular meters, as seen in the *Romance*, Op. 12. Traditional simple forms, such as ABA and Rondo, are used in the published piano works; freshness is obtained by stressing keys a third away in contrasting sections and by varying repetitions.

Sonata No. 1 in A Minor, Op. 1
>   Autograph Manuscript in Houghton Library, Harvard University.
>   Unpublished.

Sonata No. 2 in F sharp Minor, Op. 4
>   Manuscript not extant.
>   Unpublished.

These two sonatas seem to have been Paine's first compositions for piano—or at least the first of which any record has survived. *Sonata No. 1* is dated "Berlin, December 1859," according to the manuscript, and seems to be the earliest composition with an assigned opus number, aside from the *String Quartet*, Op. 5, which dates from the Portland years. One performance is known—Paine played the first Sonata on a New England Conservatory of Music chamber concert at Chickering Hall on 13 May 1868.[2] The *Sonata No. 2* is known only by its inclusion on published lists of Paine's works (such as in Champlin). The manuscript no longer exists, and no performances seem to have been mentioned in the press or in other sources.

Christmas Gift, Op. 7
>   Manuscript not extant.
>   Published by G. D. Russell & Co., Boston (1864).
>   Copies: LC.

This was the first composition of Paine's to be published (except for the *Harvard Commencement Hymn*, published in 1862 doubtless only for the college community) and available to the general public. No records survive of any performances, but the work must have been successful, for Russell later published two sets of piano pieces, *Four Characteristic Pieces*, Op. 25, and *In the Country*, Op. 26.

The opening and closing bars of the manuscript are reproduced in Edwards, *Music and Musicians of Maine*, 134–35, where it is dated "Dec. 25, 1862." According to Edwards, "A Christmas Piece"—as it was titled—was written for and dedicated to Paine's sister Helen.

Christmas Gift is a simple gigue-like dance piece. Its thematic material is derived in part from two pentatonic figures announced near the beginning (Example 11–1). The form is a simple ABA, but an extensive coda unexpectedly introduces a quickstep (Example 11–2), which persists, except for a hint of the opening theme, until the close of the piece. Paine's avoidance of a plain authentic cadence (which he considered a cliché) at the close may be observed here: a series of plagal cadences (incidentally with parallel fifths in the bass) is followed by a tonic pedal beneath another series of authentic progressions, the last of which receives a deliberately weak resolution (Example 11–3).

A Funeral March in Memory of President Lincoln, Op. 9
    Manuscript not extant.
    Published by Beer & Schirmer, New York (1865).
    Copies: LC, Port.

Following the shock of Lincoln's assassination, Paine chose this means of expressing the remorse he shared with his fellow countrymen. Doubtless there were a number of performances of the *Funeral March* during the first months after the tragedy, though there are no records of any. Two later performances are known: Paine played his *Marcia Funèbre* on the 13 May 1868 New England Conservatory chamber concert mentioned above, and pianist Annette Essipoff, pupil of Leschetizky, included it on a program of American piano music she played in New York and Boston during May 1877.[3]

With its ABA form and an arch in dynamics, the piece suggests a *patrol*—a processional approaching from the distance, building to a fortissimo, then fading again into the distance. Constant 4-bar phrases normally expected in a march are varied by extensions, such as the 5-bar phrase in the first section (Example 11–4). Again Paine avoids a conventional final cadence, this time using a dominant ninth with a suspension (Example 11–5).

The printed copy included a portrait of Lincoln on the title page, and each page of music was bordered in black.

Welcome Home to my Darling Lizzie! From John.
March 31, 1868, Cambridge.
    Autograph Manuscript in Houghton Library, Harvard University.
    Unpublished.

Here is a delightful gift to the woman who became the composer's wife during the following year (Example 11–6). Apparently because of its personal nature it was never published; also, no opus number seems to have been assigned to it (unless it was included in the *Vier Character-Stücke*, Op. 11—see below). One performance is known: Paine's 13 May 1868 recital mentioned above.

Valse Caprice
> Autograph Manuscript in Houghton Library, Harvard University.
> Unpublished.

The manuscript of this undated composition was given to Harvard by Mrs. Paine's nephew, Hugh Payne Greeley; possibly it had some family associations as did *Welcome Home*. The composition is relatively long, occupying 12 pages. No performances are known. (Example 11–7)

Vier Character-Stücke für Piano-forte, Op. 11 (1868)
> 1. *Vivace*
> 2. *Large*
> 3. *Con moto*
> 4. *Giojoso*
> [Individual titles from N.E.C.M. concert program]
> Manuscript not extant.
> Published by Rob. Forberg, Leipzig, and Koppitz, Prüfer, & Co., Boston (1872); seemingly no copies have survived.

Paine performed these four pieces on a 14 December 1868 New England Conservatory of Music chamber concert.[4] The published version was reviewed in the October 1872 issue of *Atlantic Monthly*:

> We rejoice to be able to give Mr. Paine's four "Character-pieces" almost unqualified praise. We know of very few men in this country who could have written anything so good. Although they are most free in form and full of genuine, unforced, at times almost startling originality, they show how thoroughly the composer has mastered the technical details of composition and musical form. The second piece, marked "Feierlich,"—solemn,—shows also great depth of feeling and true sentiment, and the bubbling-over animal spirits and genial joyousness of the final "Welcome" cannot fail to fascinate even those who might possibly find the other movements somewhat obscure at first. The only point at which we can take exception is that they do not lie quite so easily under the fingers as might be desired, though where there is so much genuine merit, such a consideration becomes of secondary importance.[5]

Perhaps the "Welcome" that concluded the set was *Welcome Home to my Darling Lizzie*, discussed above.

Romance, Op. 12
> Manuscript not extant.
> Published by Koppitz, Prüfer, & Co., Boston (1869).
> Copies: BPL, HMA, LC, Wellesley.

Paine's first *Romance* was inscribed: "To my friend Mr. Casimir Constable." The composer performed it on his 14 December 1868 concert mentioned earlier; on it the composition was listed as "Fantasie Stück, Op. 12"—perhaps a more suitable title, for the piece is of a far more restless nature than his two later *Romances* for piano. (Example 11–8)

The *Romance* is written in a *da capo* Song and Trio form, with E-flat major for the basic tonality and A-flat for the contrasting Trio. Paine, however, seems to have been experimenting with a wider tonality in the first section, for the feeling of key is exceedingly vague—with hints of C minor, G minor, and D minor—and only in the last four bars is the key of E-flat clearly established (Example 11–9). This indefinite tonal orientation is produced with half cadences followed by change of key or through an avoidance of cadence formulas altogether, along with irregular phrase lengths and minimized phrase articulations. Additional tonal uncertainty results from chromatic progressions, including series of diminished-seventh chords and modifications of the "omnibus progression," employing diminished sevenths in place of regular dominant sevenths (Example 11–10). Paine continues to avoid the conventional final authentic cadence, for the last clear cadences are plagal, followed by a tonic pedal (see Example 11–9).

The Trio begins with a pentatonic figure, perhaps a hint at Paine's Yankee background. Accents are displaced in the first phrase, giving the effect of irregular meters—³ ² ³ or even ⁵ ³ (Example 11–11). In the second section, a sudden modulation changes the key from A-flat to its lowered submediant, notated enharmonically as E major.

Prelude and Fugue in B Minor, Op. 15, No. 1
Prelude in F-sharp Minor, Op. 15, No. 2
Fugue in 3 Voices in A Major, Op. 15, No. 3
    Autograph Manuscripts in Houghton Library, Harvard University.
    Unpublished.

These possibly were student compositions; there are no indications that they were performed publicly. Only the first page of the *Prelude and Fugue in B Minor* has survived. Apparently the *Prelude in F-sharp Minor* was intended at first to be part of a similar work, for the beginning of a fugue is crossed out in the manuscript. The *Fugue in 3 Voices* is listed as "incomplete" in the Houghton catalogue, but the ink copy was finished in pencil.

Four Characteristic Pieces for Pianoforte, Op. 25.
    1. *Dance*
    2. *Romance*
    3. *Impromptu*
    4. *Rondo Giocoso*

Manuscript not extant.

Published by G. D. Russell & Co., Boston (1876). Reissued by Oliver Ditson & Co.;
  included in *Album of Pianoforte Pieces*.

Copies: LC, NECM, PPL (album, also Dance separately).

The *Four Characteristic Pieces* were dedicated to German-born pianist Ernst Perabo (1845–1920), who in 1866 had begun a performing and teaching career in Boston. He performed a number of Paine's piano and chamber works, especially in his series of chamber concerts held during the mid-1870s. It was at one of these concerts at Wesleyan Hall on 10 November 1876 that he first performed this set of four pieces.[6] Later Perabo performances included "Romance" and "Rondo Giocoso" at a June 1877 concert at Wellesley College, and "Dance" and "Romance" on an April 1881 recital at the Meionaon.[7] Bostonian John Orth (1850–1932) programmed the "Romance" on two April 1880 concerts,[8] and Carl Baermann, in his American debut concert with the Boston Philharmonic Society, played Beethoven's G-major concerto and three solos, including Paine's "Rondo Giocoso."[9]

In *Dance* may be seen a number of details characteristic of Paine's works, such as phrase units of irregular lengths—the first period is of 11 bars (Example 11–12), and, after a written-out repetition, is followed by a second period 15 bars in length. Suspensions and appoggiaturas—often chordal as well as melodic—dominate the thematic material, as may be seen in the above example. A raised supertonic resolving to the tonic triad occurs just before the reprise of the first theme (Example 11–13). The rhythmic pattern of a dotted eighth and sixteenth on the first beat, followed by two quarters or four eighths, pervades the piece, giving the effect of a mazurka, or perhaps a polonaise. This is most noteworthy in the middle section, where the unbroken rhythm is combined with chordal suspensions, resulting in the feminine progressions characteristic of these dance types (Example 11–14). The *Dance* concludes with another evasion of the common cadence, this time with an imperfect authentic cadence, with the dominant chord in second inversion, and the third in the final tonic triad (Example 11–15).

The *Romance* is a gentle, expressive, introspective piece, similar in mood to the longer *Romance*, Op. 39, but differing sharply from Op. 12. Its first four measures (Example 11–16) illustrate several practices to be found elsewhere in Paine's works, including a tonic pedal at the beginning, chromatic progressions (major to minor subdominant triads, and the augmented dominant seventh), and a decorated half cadence with a secondary dominant thirteenth. In bar 7 the melody is doubled at the suboctave (Example 11–17), suggesting an orchestral sonority and showing

Paine's skill and sensitivity to timbre. The last cadence is modified by a lengthy tonic pedal and final chromaticism (Example 11–18).

The vigorous, very Brahmsian *Impromptu*, in A minor, exudes energy through contrasting rhythmic values—eighths, triplet eighths, and sixteenths, plus Paine's favorite pattern, the dotted triplet (♪·♪♪), which enters at climaxes (Example 11–19). A gentler mood prevails in the F-major middle section, in $^6_8$; the expressive theme makes extensive use of decorated non-harmonic tones (Example 11–20). Typical cadential formulas may be noted as well, including a temporary dominant 13th sonority formed with an "E" appoggiatura (Example 11–21a) and a half cadence that, because of non-harmonic tones, resembles in function the famous progression in the prelude to *Tristan and Isolde* (Examples 11–21b & c). The final cadence is authentic, but the last accented chord occurs on a weak beat, as far as notation is concerned. Musically, however, he has transformed the meter to $^6_8$ for the final five pulses, which in itself is noteworthy for his freedom from the tyranny of the bar-line (Example 11–22).

The playful *Rondo Giocoso* begins with a tonic pedal, soon followed by a dominant pedal (Example 11–23). Phrase extensions result in a period of 14 bars. A contrasting section is used to create an overall ABABA form. However, the first "B" is in the major mediant key (E major) instead of the dominant—a key relationship by third also to be encountered in the *Spring Symphony*. The middle section contains examples of the raised supertonic diminished seventh chord resolving to tonic (Example 11–24), a favorite device.

In the Country: Sketches for the Piano, Op. 26
  1. *Woodnotes*
  2. *Wayside Flowers*
  3. *Under the Lindens*
  4. *Shepherd's Lament*
  5. *Village Dance*
  6. *Rainy Day*
  7. *Mill*
  8. *Gipsies*
  9. *Farewell*
  10. *Welcome Home*
      Manuscript not extant
      Published by G. D. Russell & Co., Boston (1876). Reissued by Oliver Ditson & Co.; included in *Album of Pianoforte Pieces*. *Farewell* publ. in *Musical Record* #476 (1 September 1901).
      Copies: HMA, LC, NECM, PPL (album).

Dedicated to "Madame Madeline Schiller," *In the Country* received the greatest number of documented performances among Paine's piano compositions. The first complete performance seems to have been on

8 May 1877 by Amy Fay, at Lyceum Hall in Old Cambridge; she repeated five of the set the following October at Union Hall.[10] Fay also played the first five in New York City in January 1900 and the entire set a year later in Peekskill.[11] Annette Essipoff included three (nos. 2, 3, and 5) from the set on her May 1877 American concerts mentioned earlier. William H. Sherwood included "Farewell" and "Welcome Home" on a January 1879 recital.[12]

Woodnotes is a delicate piece with an ornate melodic figuration imitative of bird song (Example 11–25). Typically, the first period is extended to the irregular length of nine bars, and the final cadence is modified by a tonic pedal and by dominant thirteenth and lowered ninth sonorities.

Accented non-harmonic tones characterize the themes of *Wayside Flowers* (Example 11–26a & b), and incidental thirteenths and ninths decorate the cadences. Paine varied the reprise of the opening theme, first with a quasi-orchestral sonority similar to that in *Romance* in the previous set (but with doubling at the tenth below), then with a modified melody and chord figuration (Example 11–27).

Under the Lindens develops a lengthy melody, with many suspensions, and a cascading broken-chord accompaniment (Example 11–28). Notable is a clash in measure 8 between the C-sharp of an implied dominant augmented triad and the C-natural of the accompanimental dominant seventh.

The Shepherd's Lament is a short, subdued, expressive piece, opening above a tonic pedal, with appoggiaturas producing momentary thirteenths (Example 11–29). An omnibus progression, modified by the use of diminished sevenths, occurs in a modulation from C-major back to the original A-minor. The opening chord in measure 13 resembles the "Tristan" chord, but differs from it in function (Example 11–30). A Neapolitan chord precedes a relatively straightforward cadential formula at the close.

Village Dance develops an opening pentatonic figure into a delightful quick dance movement (Example 11–31). Occasional third-beat accents provide rhythmic variety.

Rainy Day, in G minor, uses a staccato pattern to accompany its themes, derived entirely from an initial two-note descending motive (Example 11–32). The middle section, also derived from the motive, differs in its use of accented non-harmonic tones, which are completely avoided in the outside parts. The melancholy mood is enhanced by an emphasis on Neapolitan harmony.

A recurring left-hand 16th-note figure portrays the subject of *The Mill*; its theme is characterized by frequent articulations and accented non-harmonic tones (Example 11–33). The consequent period is varied, and the repeated periods are also modified and enlarged. Concluding cadential progressions are stated over a tonic pedal (Example 11–34).

The E-minor tonality of *Gipsies* is clouded throughout the piece by a frequent use of secondary dominant progressions (Example 11–35)—perhaps to depict the wandering nature of its subject—and is definitely affirmed only at the final cadence. In the middle section, "brass" fanfares, alternating with rapid passagework, recall similar passages in such orchestral works as *The Tempest* and the *Spring Symphony* (Example 11–36).

Farewell is a fine example of Paine's skill in creating a somber, expressive mood (Example 11–37). The theme utilizes chromatic accented non-harmonic tones, and is supported by frequent altered chords. Parallel tenths above the bass line produce a sonority comparable to that in *Wayside Flowers*, mentioned above. In the second phrase (measures 5–8) is seen an anticipation of the second theme group of the *Spring Symphony*, first movement (Example 11–38). One may note another "Tristan" sonority—also with a differing function—in measure 149 of this movement. *Farewell* ends with an excursion quite far from tonic (Example 11–39).

Welcome Home is a joyful, brilliant conclusion to the set (Example 11–40). Paine's favorite rhythm, ♪ ♪ ♪ , dominates the texture.

Romance for Piano, Op. 39
    Manuscript not extant.
    Published by Oliver Ditson & Co., Boston (1883); also included in *Album of Pianoforte Pieces*.
    Copies: HMA, LC, NECM, PPL (album).

The *Romance* is dedicated to James Bradstreet Greenough, Harvard Professor of Latin (to which rank he was elected in the year of its composition) and author of the *Harvard Commemoration Hymn* that Paine set. No performances are known.

The tranquil beginning contrasts an initial pentatonic figure with chromatic non-harmonic tones and altered chords (Example 11–41); the melodic turn in measure 4 is found in numerous other Paine works. Tension increases at the end of this passage, and a treble-bass dialogue recalls similar devices in Paine orchestral works (Example 11–42). After a diversion, the opening theme returns *fortissimo*, and after a final climax, diminishes in a chromatic progression incorporating part of the "omnibus" progression (Example 11–43a). Another progression in the following bars suggests a similar passage in the *Spring Symphony* (Example 11–43b). The final plagal progression recalls the mood of the beginning.

Three Piano Pieces, Op. 41
    1. *A Spring Idyl*
    2. *Birthday Impromptu*
    3. *Fuga Giocosa*

Manuscripts not extant.
Birthday Impromptu privately printed (1882).
Three Piano Pieces published by Arthur P. Schmidt & Co., Boston (1884).
Copies: 1. HMA, LC, NECM, Wellesley.
        2. BPL (1882 ed.), HMA, HMus (1882 ed.), LC, NECM, Summy, Wellesley.
        3. BPL, ESM, HMA, LC, NECM, PPL, Summy, Wellesley.

A Spring Idyl, dedicated to Miss Sarah D. Hoppin, imitates bird song with an extremely ornate right-hand part (Example 11–44), somewhat similar to that in *Woodnotes* mentioned above. In contrast to the earlier composition, however, the harmonic vocabulary of *A Spring Idyl* is richer, with unresolved tonic sevenths, longer held appoggiaturas, and more intense chromaticism. Two public performances are known—one, cited by Sumner Salter, was part of a 3 July 1884 program at Case Hall in Cleveland, and a second was included on a May 1885 recital by Calixa Lavallée.[13]

The brief *Birthday Impromptu*—only 38 bars—was dedicated to Harvard Professor W. G. Farlow by means of a musical pun: "A mon ami" and a low F written on the bass staff—"fa low," or "Farlow." Thematic material springs from decorated pentatonic motives in measures 1–2 and 5–6 (Example 11–45). The piece ends with an elaborate cadence, including several incidental thirteenth sonorities (Example 11–46). No public performances are known. It may be assumed, however, that the *Birthday Impromptu* appeared on a number of recitals, for its publication elicited favorable reviews.

The impact of the *Fuga Giocosa*, based on the popular ditty, "Over the fence is out, boys," has been mentioned elsewhere in this study. Although it was used as a textbook example of fugue, it is by no means a dry, academic specimen, for the wit and humor of the composer is always apparent. A three-voice exposition gives a relatively standard beginning to the fugue (Example 11–47), and numerous strettos provide contrapuntal interest (Example 11–48). Abrupt dynamic contrasts abound, and the episodes are full of harmonic and tonal variety (Example 11–49). The fugue ends with a stretto *con fuoco* on the head motive of the subject, and a final bravura flourish above one last statement (Example 11–50). One performance is known—Emil Liebling included it on a May 1886 recital in Chicago.[14]

Nocturne for Pianoforte, Op. 45
Manuscript not extant.
Published by Arthur P. Schmidt, Boston (1889).
Copies: LC, NECM, Summy, Wellesley.

According to W. S. B. Mathews, this *Nocturne* was not a new composition at the time of its publication, for Paine had played it frequently "for years" privately before even writing it down; after it was committed to manuscript, it remained unpublished for "quite a long time."[15] Internal evidence would tend to support this, for the harmonic vocabulary is more conservative than that in op. 39 and 41. Typical Paine trademarks may be seen—a melodic turn near the beginning (Example 11–51), and pedal points, such as at the climax of the middle section (Example 11–52). At the close, thirteenth-chord sonorities and chord suspensions modify the authentic cadence (Example 11–53). Paine was present at a 27 February 1891 recital at Tremont Temple when Mrs. H. H. A. Beach played the *Nocturne*.[16] Another performance of the piece was part of a January 1901 program in Evanston, Illinois.[17]

Organk Works

Prelude and Fugue in G Minor
   Autograph Manuscript in Houghton Library, Harvard University.
   Unpublished.

The *Prelude and Fugue in G Minor* is a product of Paine's student days in Berlin, and is written very much in the style of Bach. The fugue is dated "Apr. 30, 1859" in the manuscript, and the prelude, "June 21, 1859." Paine performed the work in a Berlin recital in late 1859 or early 1860. A reviewer for the London *Musical World*, in reporting the concert, declared that this piece

> proves Mr. Paine to be not only a player, but a thorough comprehender of the king of fugues. The subjects are well chosen, and treated with all the skill of an experienced contrapuntist.[1]

No other performances are known.

Prelude in C Minor
   Autograph Manuscript in Houghton Library, Harvard University.
   Unpublished.

This work is written in a later style than the preceding, and does not reflect such a strong direct influence of Bach. Its precise year of composition cannot be established, for the manuscript is undated and no performances are know. The *Prelude* apparently has been performed, however, for penciled pedal markings have been added to the inked manuscript.

Fantasia and Fugue in E Minor, Opus 2, No. 1
   Autograph Manuscript in Houghton Library, Harvard University. Another manuscript (incomplete), plus an additional beginning page (titled *Fantasia and fugue #1*, op. 3) also in Houghton collection.
   Unpublished.

The *Fantasia and Fugue* (or *Fantasia and Double Fugue*) was composed in Berlin in 1860, according to the manuscripts. Paine first performed it during the summer of that year as part of a recital he presented in "a parochial church" in Berlin.[2] At least five additional performances were heard in Boston or Cambridge between 1862 and 1867. At the 30 March 1867 inaugural concert of the New England Conservatory, Paine's performance of it was encored.[3]

Double Fugue on "God Save the Queen," Opus 2, No. 2
[*Doppel Fuge über "Heil dir im Siegeskranz"*]
> Two autograph manuscripts (one with English title, one with German) in Houghton Library, Harvard University; the former manuscript is "incomplete," according to the catalogue, and an indication on the score originally read, "Op. 2, No. 4." The latter manuscript is grouped with the E-minor *Fantasie and Fugue* and titled, *Zwei Concert Stücke für die Orgel . . .* , Op. 2. Unpublished.

The *Fugue*, based on the melody of the national anthems of England and Germany, is the first of three Paine organ works that treat patriotic airs. No performances are known, but the work may well have been included in one of Paine's student recitals that he played in Berlin, other German cities, or London. The manuscript with the German title is marked, "Berlin 1860."

Concert Variations on the Austrian Hymn, Opus 3, No. 1
> Inscribed: "To Mr. S. B. Whitney, Organist, Church of the Advent, Boston."
> Manuscript not extant.
> Published by Oliver Ditson, Boston, in 1876.
> Copies: BPL, HMA, LC, NECM.

Paine first played his *Variations* in the Summer 1860 Berlin recital mentioned above; the work was named, *Concert-Variationen über ein Thema von Haydn*. He repeated it on his final Berlin recital on 19 April 1861,[4] in Portland that summer,[5] and on his first Boston recital at Tremont Temple on 1 November.[6] Several additional performances in Boston are known between 1862 and 1872, as well as one in New York,[7] and New York organist William C. Carl included the work on recitals in 1890 and 1897.[8]

The harmonization of the theme is similar both to its use in Haydn's *Emperor* Quartet and to typical hymnal versions (Example 11–55). Variation I contains an interplay between the left hand and pedal. An octave difference between the parts, not evident in the notation, results from the registrational instructions, with the pedal part sounding an octave lower than the printed note (Example 11–56). Variation II places the theme in the tenor voice, with a reed stop dominating its timbre. Constant eighths and sixteenths form the accompaniment for a separate manual and pedals (Example 11–57). The ensuing variation embraces the parallel minor mode, *poco meno mosso*, and its four-part texture is played either on a single manual, with 8- and 16-foot stops, or divided between the manual and the pedals. The final line becomes rather chromatic, and an almost complete *omnibus* progression precedes the final half cadence (Example 11–58). Variation IV features a virtuoso pedal part (Example 11–59), and leads directly into the Fugue (Example 11–60), also virtuosic in nature, and a final energetic statement of the hymn.

Concert Variations upon Old Hundred
("Herr Gott dich loben alle wir")
>Autograph Manuscript in Houghton Library, Harvard University.
>Published by Harvard University Press, Cambridge, in 1916.
>Copies: HMA, HMus, LC, NECM, NYPL.

These variations were written during Paine's study in Berlin, and were included on his 19 April 1861 recital there. He performed the work in Boston at least five times between 1862 and 1865, at Tremont Temple, West Church, and the Music Hall, also on a February 1864 recital at St. George's Church in New York.[9] Apparently no opus number was assigned to this work.

Paine's treatment of the theme is more consistently polyphonic than in the preceding set of variations, perhaps following the model of Baroque chorale partitas. After the theme is announced in hymnal fashion, the first variation places the cantus firmus above a three-voice imitative accompaniment (Example 11–61). Variation II contains a more intricate texture, with an imitative dialogue between the Choir and Swell manuals (played by the right hand) and a rapid 16th note left-hand accompaniment on the Great, with the melody played by the pedals and registered to sound an octave higher (Example 11–62). Variation III displays a flowing accompaniment in compound meter, with the cantus firmus in the tenor on a contrasting manual (Example 11–63). The fourth variation, a minor-key setting marked "Grave," ends with a Neapolitan emphasis and a half cadence followed by the "Coda"—actually a fifth variation with a brilliant arpeggiated version of the theme (Example 11–64). This last leads directly to the fugue and a final version of the theme over a rapid virtuoso pedal figuration (similar to Variation IV of the *Austrian* variations).

Concert Variations on the Star-Spangled Banner
>Opus 3, Number 2
>Autograph Manuscript in Houghton Library, Harvard University; holograph score in Boston Public Library (dated July 1861).
>Published by Oliver Ditson, Boston, in 1865; later reissued (Library of Congress copy dates from the 1890s).
>Copies: BPL, HMA, LC, NECM.

The *Star-Spangled Banner* variations were also probably written during Paine's student days in Berlin—or just after his return—for he performed them in a July 1861 recital in Portland just a month after his arrival from Germany, and again at his farewell recital in September. He is known to have played the piece at least six more times during the next seven years, with performances at Tremont Temple, West Church, and Music Hall.[10] With publication of the score, other organists contributed to its popularity. C. H. Morse, H. M. Dunham, Harrison Wild, Mabel Wood, J. Warren Andrews, and James W. Hill performed the work at least eight times between 1879 and 1906, in Boston, Wellesley, Haverhill, Mass., Chicago, New York, and St. Louis. Doubtless the secular, patriotic character of the theme gave this work more appeal to American audiences than Paine's other works in this genre.

The theme that Paine used is a different version than that familiar to most 20th-century Americans; he presented it in a simple harmonization that could be used to accompany group singing (Example 11–65). In Variation I the opening arpeggio is filled by stepwise eighth-note motion (Example 11–66); a footnote claims that the method for indicating pedalling (specifying the use of right or left foot, heel or toe), now commonly used, was invented by Haupt, Paine's teacher in Berlin. Variation II uses a texture not found in the other variation sets—the melody, played *tenuto* as the lowest pitch of figurated triads, is combined with detached chords on a second manual and a legato moving bass in the pedals (Example 11–67). Variation III assigns the melody to the pedals, with a graceful accompaniment in compound meter (Example 11–68). The usual *minore* variation is next, full of expressive indications; the final phrase even includes a recitative (Example 11–69). A half cadence prepares for the fugue, based on a subject from the first four bars of the theme. Although possessing more than its share of passage work, this section still maintains its exuberant momentum. A pedal solo consists of five figurated diminished seventh chords in succession, necessitating a lively tempo to avoid monotony; a pedal trill proceeds to the final *pleno* statement of the theme. John Sullivan Dwight admired this piece, despite its popular origin; following a 10 September 1864 performance at Music Hall he observed,

> . . . Shy as we are of fantasias on national airs, we cannot help thinking his Variations on the "Star-spangled Banner" one of his happiest and most artistic compositions. It is all dignified, all in keeping; all organ-like and polyphonic in structure; laid out symmetrically, with good contrast and balance, as a whole, while elegantly wrought in detail. The most striking parts to us were where the deep bass murmurs the melody, while soft stops in the upper parts keep up a sort of pastoral figure; the noble minor variation: and, led into by a very ingenious cadence with trill in the pedals, the imposing reproduction of the essential subject of the air in a grand fugue with figurative counter-subject.[11]

Fantasia in F, Opus 6
    Manuscript not extant.
    Unpublished.

Paine played the *Fantasia* on a Music Hall 1 April 1865 recital, but no additional performances are known. The fact that an opus number was assigned to it would suggest that the composer valued the work, but like others of his organ works, the manuscript has been either lost or destroyed. Apparently there had been earlier performances, for Dwight seemed to have been acquainted with the work when he reviewed the 1865 concert, speaking of "his brilliant Fantasia in F major, which is one of his earlier Berlin efforts."[12]

Reverie suggested by Longfellow's "Song of the Silent Land"
    Manuscript not extant.
    Unpublished.

Paine first performed his Longfellow study, programmed as *Illustration: Longfellow's "Song of the Silent Land,"* on a 25 October 1862 West Church recital. It must have been decidedly Romantic in nature, for Dwight described it as

> . . . a sort of twilight reverie in tones, using the swell freely with a rich combination of stops, in which he illustrates with some warmth and beauty of poetic feeling, Longfellow's lines: "Into the Silent Land." This was particularly enjoyed by most.[13]

The reviewer for the *Boston Musical Times* found the *Illustration* to be "an original and highly satisfactory composition, exhibiting a genius for musical invention, and a pure and noble taste for poetical expression,"[14] and requested that the composer repeat the work on a future recital. Paine did this, including the *Reverie* on the second program dedicating the new Music Hall Organ, on 5 November 1863,[15] and on three more recitals from 1863 to 1865.[16] No further performances are known, and the manuscript seems subsequently to have been lost or destroyed.

Fantasia Sonata in D Minor, Opus 17 (?)
    1. *Grave—Allegro agitato*
    2. *Andante con variazioni*
    3. *Presto*
        Complete manuscript not extant. Autograph manuscript of *Andante con variazioni*, Opus 17, (in A) with one page of a *Presto* in D minor, both probably from this Sonata, in Houghton Library, Harvard University.
        Unpublished.

Apparently Paine gave only one complete performance of his *Fantasia Sonata*, at the seventh program on the new Music Hall organ on 22 November 1863. He played part of it on a 17 January 1864 recital on the same instrument—according to a *Transcript* announcement he was to play the opening movement, but Dwight later reported hearing the *Andante con variazioni*.[17] This movement was also included on an 18 June 1866 concert in Appleton Chapel, one of three to raise funds to pay for repairs to the organ. Dwight found the variations "musician-like, of rather a tamely respectable old cut."[18]

Caprice
> Manuscript not extant.
> Unpublished.

The *Caprice* received its first performance on Paine's 17 January 1864 recital on the Music Hall organ. He played it again at Music Hall in February 1866,[19] and on the 18 June 1866 Appleton Chapel program mentioned above; after this last performance Dwight described it,

> something like a song without words, captivating by its grace and freedom; and somewhat original. . . .[20]

Paine also played the *Caprice* on a 25 May 1870 Music Hall recital sponsored by the New England Conservatory of Music.

Deux Préludes pour l'orgue, Opus 19
> 1. *Larghetto* (D flat)
> 2. *Con moto* (B minor)
> Autograph Manuscript of No. 1 in Houghton Library, Harvard University; manuscript of No. 2 not extant.
> Published by Arthur P. Schmidt, Boston, in 1892.
> Copies: BPL, HMA, LC, NECM, Summy.

In 1864 Paine composed two pieces, both entitled "Offertoire," that seem to be those later published as *Préludes*. The first he performed on a 2 March 1864 Orchestral Union concert at Music Hall. Dwight, who disliked the *offertoires* written by typical French organists of the period, wrote approvingly of Paine's effort:

> . . . An *Offertoire*, of his own composition, a serious, calm, religious one, not a captivating *effect* piece; not catching the general ear like the French brilliants by that name, not particularly striking in its themes, but harmonizing well with serious meditation, organ-like in style and spirit, musician-like in treatment. . . .[21]

The second, in B minor, was heard for the first time at a 30 July 1864 recital, also given by Paine at Music Hall. Again Dwight was generally pleased:

> Mr. Paine's *offertoire*, a new one, has at least the merit of being in a serious, religious vein, and not after the operatic, showy, Verdi-ish French offerings by that name which have been so liberally contributed to these Organ concerts. It is moreover a pleasing, clearly connected, contrapuntal piece of writing, with only perhaps a little

too much repitition [*sic*] here and there of form and phrase without addition to the meaning.[22]

On a 9 October 1864 Music Hall recital Paine played a "Religious Offering," but which of the two was not specified; the second *Offertoire* again was played two years later.[23] Following publication of the two *Preludes* in 1892, other organists also began to play these works. Three performances of the first Prelude are known—on a 7 April 1900 recital by William C. Carl at Old First Presbyterian Church in New York City, on a 4 February 1904 program by Arthur Foote at Old First Church, Boston, and again by Foote a year later.[24] No additional performances of the second Prelude are known.

The first Prelude is a quiet song without words, in a simple part form. The beginning is characteristic of other similar Paine pieces, with the tonic pedal, melodic ornamentation (m. 3), and raised supertonic (m. 8) being common features (Example 11–70)). A continuing passage starts a gradual crescendo, and an eighth-note ostinato in the pedal contributes to greater rhythmic activity. The climax of this phrase is obtained by an increase in registration, accented doubled chords, and an active pedal part (Example 11–71). A later phrase introduces a temporary modulation to the lowered submediant key, written enharmonically (Example 11–72), a favored progression in Paine's music from this period. A change back to the original key prepares a return of the first theme in a modified version—also consistent with Paine's practice. Rather than building to another climax, the subsequent passage remains subdued, and contains an intricate chromatic progression (Example 11–73), whose longer note values unfortunately encourage a feeling of monotony in performance. A final plagal cadence (Example 11–74) is another example of Paine's avoidance of the traditional authentic progression.

Prelude No. 2 is more contrapuntal, as Dwight had observed; it also begins subdued, over a pedal point, although more sturdily than the earlier of the pair (Example 11–75). A graceful contrasting theme in the relative major is more animated, and contains several familiar Paine elements, including a pedal point, chromatic embellishing chords, and a melodic turn (Example 11–76). A German sixth chord serves as the means to modulate to E flat and C minor; a fugal section then ensues (Example 11–77). After an energetic climax the first two themes return, the second now in B major. One instance of "perhaps a little too much repetition" that Dwight possibly had referred to is the extended conclusion, a series of chromatic chords over an undulating pedal; monotony may result if the tempo is too stately. Again at the close a straightforward authentic cadence is evaded, this time by multiple suspensions.

Fantasia on the "Portuguese Hymn"
1. *Pastorale*
2. *Interlude for the Piffaro*
3. *Alla Marcia*
   Manuscript not extant.
   Unpublished.

Paine first played the *Fantasia* on a 5 March 1864 Music Hall recital, and repeated it the following September.[25] Doubtless there were other hearings besides the only other known performance, in April 1869. The three movements were based on the familiar *Adeste fideles* melody. The Interlude would have featured the Piffaro stop on the Music Hall organ, a two-rank voice on the Solo manual, presumably imitative of shepherds' pipes, that spoke at both an octave and two octaves above actual pitch. Dwight commented following the first performance:

> . . . The "Portuguese Hymn" made a good theme for Mr. Paine; the three movements of his Fantasia were well contrasted, and had pleasing matter in them. . . .[26]

Pastorale
   Manuscript not extant.
   Unpublished.

Little is known of this composition. Its only mention is in a list of original works that Paine performed between October 1864 and June 1866, published in *Dwight's Journal of Music*. According to the listing, the *Pastorale* was heard four times.[27] None of these recitals received any mention in the *Journal*, however, nor apparently in any other periodical.

Fantasie über "Ein' feste Burg," Opus 13
   Three manuscript scores in Houghton Library, Harvard University—one a rough copy, with many corrections, one a later copy, and the third apparently in a copyist's hand.
   Published by Harvard University Press, Cambridge, in 1916.
   Copies: HMA, HMus, LC, NECM.

The fantasy on *A Mighty Fortress is our God* seems to have been one of the last organ pieces that Paine composed. He performed it apparently for the first time on a Music Hall concert in April 1869, the only recital that he played that season.[28] He also included it on Music Hall recitals in May 1870 and May 1871, both sponsored by the New England Conservatory. None of the concert reports included any impressions or opinions of this piece.

Bold statements of chorale phrases, interspersed with triplet arpeggiated chords, open the Fantasy (Example 11–78). The first line of the melody is developed in this portion, including two quotations in diminution over a triplet pattern in the pedals. A change in manuals and dynamics brings a quiet section based on the central portion of the chorale (Example 11–79), in the dominant key. A half cadence leads to a fugal treatment of the opening notes of the chorale (Example 11–80). After the climax, including a statement of the subject in double pedal, Example 11–79 returns, but in the subdominant key (G major). Another fugal section follows, a step lower than in Example 11–80. At its conclusion the opening material returns, and at the close a five-measure recurring G-minor triad (over triplet figuration in the pedals) resolves to a tonic triad for a solid plagal cadence.

Example 11–1.   *Christmas Gift:* a. Measures 1–5.
                           b. Measures 13–19.

a.

b.

Example 11–2.   *Christmas Gift,* Measures 70–77.

Example 11–2.   (continued)

Example 11–3.   *Christmas Gift*, measures 116–131.

Example 11–4.   *A Funeral March . . .* , measures 9–13.

Example 11–5.   *A Funeral March . . .* , measures 64–67.

Example 11–6.   *Welcome Home to my Darling Lizzie!*, measures 1–2.

Example 11–7.   *Valse Caprice,* measures 1–3.

Example 11–8.   *Romance,* Op. 12, measures 1–8.

Example 11–9.   *Romance,* Op. 12, measures 41–47.

Example 11–10.   *Romance,* Op. 12, measures 33–36.

Example 11–11. *Romance,* Op. 12, measures 48–53.

Example 11–12. *Dance,* measures 1–11.

Example 11–13.   *Dance,* measures 61–63.

Example 11–14.   *Dance,* measures 47–50.

Example 11–15.   *Dance,* measures 79–82.

Example 11–16.   *Romance,* measures 1–4.

Example 11–16   (continued)

Example 11–17.   *Romance,* measures 7–8.

Example 11–18.   *Romance,* measures 39–43.

Example 11–19.   *Impromptu*, measures 1–10.

Example 11–20.   *Impromptu*, measures 31–34.

Example 11–21.   *Impromptu:*
> a. Measures 45–46.
> b. Measures 61–62.
> c. Wagner, Prelude to *Tristan and Isolde*, measures 1–3.

Example 11–22.   *Impromptu*, last 3 measures.

Example 11–23.   *Rondo Giocoso*, measures 1–11.

Example 11–24.   *Rondo Giocoso*, measures 59–63.

Example 11–25.   *Woodnotes*, measures 1–4.

Example 11–26.   *Wayside Flowers:*
    a. Measures 1–4.
    b. Measures 13–16.

Example 11–27.   *Wayside Flowers*, measures 28–36.

Example 11–28.   *Under the Lindens*, measures 1–8.

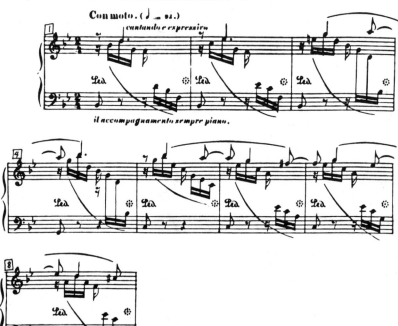

Example 11–29.   *The Shepherd's Lament,* measures 1–4.

Example 11–30.   *The Shepherd's Lament,* measures 13–17.

Example 11–31.   *Village Dance,* measures 1–10.

Example 11–32.   *Rainy Day,* measures 1–5.

Example 11–33.   *The Mill,* measures 1–8.

Example 11–34.   *The Mill,* measures 45–49.

Example 11–35.   *Gipsies,* measures 1–8.

Example 11–36.   *Gipsies,* measures 22–29.

Example 11–36   (continued)

Example 11–37.   *Farewell,* measures 1–8.

Example 11–38.   *Spring Symphony,* First movement, measures 149–152.

Example 11–39.   *Farewell*, measures 34–43.

Example 11–40.   *Welcome Home*, measures 1–6.

Example 11–41. *Romance*, Op. 39, measures 1–9.

Example 11–42. *Romance*, Op. 39, measures 19–23.

Example 11–43.   *Romance* and *Spring Symphony.*
        a. *Romance,* Op. 39, measures 57–65.
        b. *Spring Symphony,* Third movement, measures 165–172.

a.

b.

Example 11–44.   *A Spring Idyl*, measures 1–7.

Example 11–45.   *Birthday Impromptu*, measures 1–8.

Example 11–46.   *Birthday Impromptu,* measures 33–38.

Example 11–47.   *Fuga Giocosa,* measures 1–14.

Example 11–48.   *Fuga Giocosa,* measures 57–61.

Example 11–49. *Fuga Giocosa,* measures 69–76.

Example 11–50. *Fuga Giocosa,* measures 89–96.

Example 11–51. *Nocturne,* measures 1–4.

Example 11–51   (continued)

Example 11–52.   *Nocturne*, measures 37–38.

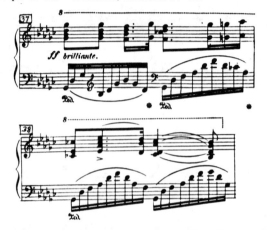

Example 11–53.   *Nocturne*, measures 72–73.

Example 11–54.   *Fantasia and Fugue in E Minor*, measures 1–2.

Example 11–55.   *Concert Variations on the Austrian Hymn*, measures 1–4.

Example 11–56.   *Concert Variations on the Austrian Hymn*, Variation I, measures 1–2.

Example 11–57.   *Concert Variations on the Austrian Hymn*, Variation II, measures 1–2.

Example 11–58.   *Concert Variations on the Austrian Hymn*, Variation III, measures 17–21.

Example 11–58   (continued)

Example 11–59.   *Concert Variations on the Austrian Hymn,* Variation IV, measures 1–2.

Example 11–60.   *Concert Variations on the Austrian Hymn,* Fugue, measures 1–4.

Example 11–61.   *Concert Variations upon Old Hundred,* Variation I, measures 1–5.

Example 11–62.   *Concert Variations upon Old Hundred,* Variation II, measures 1–2.

Example 11–63.   *Concert Variations upon Old Hundred,* Variation III, measures 1–3.

Example 11–63   (continued)

Example 11–64.   *Concert Variations upon Old Hundred,* Coda, measures 1–5.

Example 11–65.   *Concert Variations on the Star-Spangled Banner,* Theme, measures 1–8.

Example 11–66. *Concert Variations on the Star-Spangled Banner,* Variation I, measures 1–8.

Example 11–67. *Concert Variations on the Star-Spangled Banner,* Variation II, measures 1–4.

Example 11–68. *Concert Variations on the Star-Spangled Banner,* Variation III, measures 1–4.

Example 11–69.   *Concert Variations on the Star-Spangled Banner,* Variation IV, measures 25–34.

Example 11–70.   *Prelude No. 1,* measures 1–9.

Example 11–71.   *Prelude No. 1,* measures 21–39.

Example 11–72.   *Prelude No. 1,* measures 49–56.

Example 11–73.   *Prelude No. 1,* measures 108–120.

Example 11–73.   (continued)

Example 11–74.   *Prelude No. 1*, measures 129–138.

Example 11–75.   *Prelude No. 2*, measures 1–8.

Example 11–76.   *Prelude No. 2*, measures 35–41.

Example 11–77.   *Prelude No. 2*, measures 59–69.

Example 11–78.   *Fantasie über "Ein' feste Burg,"* measures 1–8.

Example 11–78.   (continued)

Example 11–79.   *Fantasie über "Ein' feste Burg," measures 33–38.*

Example 11–80.   *Fantasie über "Ein' feste Burg," measures 61–71.*

12

Chamber Music

Quartet, Op. 5 *[Violin Quartette]*
1. *Moderato*
2. *Andante*
3. *Presto molto*
4. *Andante grazioso con variazioni*; *Allegro molto (Fuga)*
    Autograph manuscript in Houghton Library, Harvard University.
    Published by The New York Public Library, New York, in 1940 (edited by Sydney
        Beck)—"reproduced cooperatively by Works Projects Administration and The
        New York Public Library."
    Scored for two violins, viola, and cello
    Copies: BPL, NYPL.

Paine's *Quartet* was a product of his early study with Kotzschmar in Portland, reportedly composed at the age of 16.[1] Very likely the piece was performed at that time, although no details survive. Two later public hearings are known, however. The third and fourth movements were included on a 28 March 1863 concert at Chickering Hall to raise funds for the "circulation in the Army of the little Song-Book (made by Prof. F. J. Child) called 'War Songs for Freemen,' a fourth edition of which has just been printed. . . .";[2] Paine had arranged the concert. The two movements, performed by Julius Eichberg and Carl Meisel, violins, Carl Eichler, viola, and Wulf Fries, cello, were "nicely played," according to Dwight, and

> made a very agreeable impression, although they would have been more justly appreciated, had the first movement also been given. For so youthful an effort it showed much artistic skill and genial conception. The variations were particularly ingenious and interesting. . . .[3]

The entire quartet was heard at a 26 February 1883 Mueller-Campanari Quartet Concert;[4] the work was not mentioned in any of the reviews.

The first movement is organized according to traditional sonata design, although it is essentially monothematic. The opening passage—the principal theme (Example 12–1)—serves as the basis for the entire movement. A bridge passage, derived from the principal theme, begins as the first of several fugal expositions that appear in the movement; the viola first announces the subject (Example 12–2). With a modulation to the dominant and a cadence, the second theme ensues, also based on the opening theme (Example 12–3). After extensive motivic development and a temporary emphasis on F major, a resolution to A and a short codetta ends the 69-bar exposition. The development, 54 measures in length, is for most of its length in A minor, and contains a double fugue derived from the opening theme (Example 12–4). A modulation to B minor leads to the 15-bar retransition, limited harmonically to alternating D-major and G-minor chords. The plagal character of this passage is intensified when a plagal half-cadence is reached, *pianissimo*, followed by rests, before the *fortissimo* opening theme begins the recapitulation. This last portion is analogous to the exposition except for the usual differences in key. In addition, all themes are varied in some way, such as rescoring, incorporating sixteenth-note triplets, or including a new countertheme. The movement ends with a coda, *più mosso*, that quotes the development's double fugue (Example 12–4), with the sixteenth-note passage modified to sextuplet sixteenths. After three statements of the subjects, the final 15 bars contain a series of plagal progressions, ending *pianissimo* with an effect similar to that of the retransition. This avoidance of the traditional authentic cadence resembles the procedure found in many later Paine compositions. Perhaps this reflected the preference of his teacher, Kotzschmar. Certainly it must have been Paine's German-trained mentor who guided his development in fugal composition; perhaps he also suggested that the young composer incorporate this texture within the sonata form. That Paine could produce a well-crafted composition with such a high degree of originality at this early age is quite remarkable.

The second movement is also in a sonata design. Its ornate opening theme is treated somewhat fugally, with each instrument stating it in turn, alternating between tonic and dominant (Example 12–5). Subsequent themes are related, and progress through G minor to the dominant, F major. A short development, in D minor and G minor, treats fugally the bridge theme from the exposition. Unfortunately, a page is missing from the manuscript, and the first half of the recapitulation is lost. However, the remaining portion of the recapitulation is analogous to that part of the exposition, and in the New York Public Library edition Sydney Beck has been able to reconstruct the missing section to enable the movement to be performed.

The *Scherzo* is based on an aggressive theme, announced at first in unison and homophony (Example 12–6). In the second reprise it is treated fugally. A constant pedal point figure dominates the Trio (Example 12–7). The *Scherzo* was later transcribed for organ, to become the last movement of the *Fantasia Sonata*, Op. 17.

A short two-part theme, harmonized with triads and a variety of seventh chords, forms the basis for the last movement (Example 12–8). The first variation is similar, but for a passing eighth-note figure (Example 12–9). In the next variation ornamentation increases, with a greater amount of sixteenth-note figuration (Example 12–10). A change in texture is encountered with the *spiccato* perpetual motion line in the viola contrasted against *pizzicato* and bowed figures in the other parts (Example 12–11). The *Minore* variation follows, in $\frac{6}{8}$ meter, and leads to the coda, the *Fuga*. This closing section, of major proportions, is in sonata design; its principal theme is that of the variations and is treated fugally (Example 12–12).

Trio in D Minor for Piano, Violin and Violoncello, Op. 22
   1. *Allegro ma non troppo*
   2. *Adagio*
   3. *Allegro giojoso*
      Inscribed: "To my friend, Mr. John Fiske."
      Autograph manuscript full score and parts in Houghton Library, Harvard University; another full score, in a copyist's hand but with numerous corrections and additions by the composer, also in Houghton collection.
      Unpublished.

Paine's *Trio* was "brought out" at the John Fiske home at one of Fiske's "Parlour Concerts" on 18 December 1874; the audience numbered 100.[5] The performers were not named in Fiske's letter from which the above information was taken, but it may be assumed that Paine was the pianist. One additional performance is known, by Carlyle Petersilea, Leandro Campanari, and Wulf Fries, at a 16 February 1882 concert at Wesleyan Hall.[6]

The opening *Allegro* exhibits a rhythmic propulsion, vigor, and dramatic flair similar to some of the earlier Brahms piano works, complete with Neapolitan harmony and hemiola (Example 12–13). The motive first announced in the cello in measure 2 dominates the movement, although a lyrical second theme (in F, the relative major) provides contrast near the close of the exposition; the tonic pedal in the piano part is a typical Paine characteristic (Example 12–14). The development section, based entirely on the principal themes (Example 12–15), begins with an immediate "Romantic third" modulation from F to D flat. Key changes are frequent, touching on D flat, B-flat minor, F sharp, B minor, A minor, B, E, B-flat minor, and A; commontone direct modulations are frequent. After a climax, a decrescendo leads to the recapitulation, in which the themes are restated as in the exposition, appropriately modified. After the second theme is heard in D major, a short coda brings a return of the principal theme, announced in a *fortissimo* tutti, and an energetic conclusion in D minor.

The *Adagio*, cast in an abbreviated sonata design, contains themes quite consistent with those in other of Paine's slow movements or slow one-movement compositions. The first theme (Example 12–16) begins with a leap of a sixth (m. 1), a pedal point (m. 2), a melodic turn (m. 5), accented non-harmonic tones (mm. 6–7), and a raised second degree over dominant harmony (m. 8). A short bridge passage contains a typical fanfare-like rhythm also seen in numerous other works (Example 12–17). The second theme (Example 12–18)—in D flat, a third away, rather than the expected dominant key—also has common Paine features, including several accented passing tones or suspensions. The unexpected trills in the second phrase create an extension, giving an asymmetrical 4 + 5 period. Following a lengthy *più mosso*, a *stringendo* passage, introduction of a new motive (Example 12–19), frequent changes of key, and a *fortissimo* climax, the original theme returns, followed by the bridge and the second theme, all in the tonic key, B flat, and rescored. Another climax, though smaller, arrived through the motive from Example 12–19. At the close a coda that the composer added later presents a relaxed version of the original theme (Example 12–20).

A dancelike spirit, almost operatic in grandeur, pervades the *Allegro giojoso*, evident immediately in the first theme of the sonata design (Example 12–21). The bridge theme continues the mood (Example 12–22). The second theme, in the dominant, apparently is the result of a later revision; its triple meter provides contrast while continuing the gaiety (Example 12–23). Following the recapitulation, an *allegro vivace* coda provides an energetic conclusion to the movement.

Sonata for Piano and Violin in B Minor, Op. 24
    Original version:
        1. *Allegro con fuoco*
        2. *Larghetto*
        3. *Allegro vivace*
    Revised version:
        1. *Allegro appassionato*
        2. *Larghetto teneramente* [formerly, *Larghetto dolce e teneramente*]
        3. *Allegro vivace*
    Autograph manuscript, with revisions by the composer, in Houghton Library, Harvard University; another manuscript (fragment—opening, end of second movement, part of third movement) and a third, in a copyist's hand, also in Houghton collection. Autograph manuscript (original version) in Music Division, Boston Public Library—dated 1875. [Manuscript fragment is identified in Houghton catalogue as "op. 29," the number assigned to *Four Songs with Pianoforte*.]
    Unpublished.

Pianist Ernst Perabo and violinist J. C. Mullaly gave the première of Paine's *Violin Sonata* as part of a George L. Osgood concert at Me-

Illustration 7.   Sonata for Piano and Violin in B Minor, Revised Version; Opening of Autograph Manuscript.

chanics Hall, Boston, on 11 May 1876, a year after its composition. The piece was welcomed eagerly by the listeners; according to Dwight,

> . . . the delight of the audience culminated in such enthusiastic and repeated plaudits that the composer had to rise in his seat and bow his acknowledgments.[7]

A reviewer for the *Boston Daily Advertiser* described the movements:

> The opening *Allegro con fuoco* is written in a strong, spirited style, and has melody abundant enough and well enough defined to save it from barrenness in ears that crave tunes; the *Larghetto* in canon form, though less absorbing than the more rapid movements, has a grave and tranquil beauty, and the concluding *Allegro vivace* is exceedingly brilliant throughout, at times excitingly so by reason chiefly of a certain fierce dramatic quality which also characterized the symphony of Mr. Paine [Symphony No. 1] which was brought out by Mr. Thomas last winter. . . .[8]

Perabo and Mullaly repeated the work on a Perabo Chamber Concert the following October. From 1881 to 1887 there were at least six more performances of the sonata in Boston, Wellesley, and New York, after which time it seems to have been neglected. Following his retirement, Paine extensively revised the work, and the newly rewritten sonata was included on a Boston Symphony Quartet concert in Brattle Hall, Cambridge, on 22 March 1906; the performers were Heinrich Gebhard, pianist, and Willy Hess, violinist. Unless otherwise noted, examples for the present study will be quoted from the revised version.

The opening *allegro*, in sonata design, begins with an aggressive, dramatic theme (Example 12–24) containing rhythmic motives that dominate the movement. A bridge theme, lyrical although retaining the rhythmic momentum, begins in the parallel major but quickly modulates to its mediant major, written enharmonically as E-flat major (Example 12–25). The second theme, a *cantabile* melody also in E flat, appears first in the piano (Example 12–26). As the section reaches a climax, a further theme is heard (Example 12–27) as a closing subject. The development is devoted mainly to the opening subject, with some working also of the second theme; chief key areas are G minor, A flat, and G major. The recapitulation is regular, except for the appearance of the second theme in the Neapolitan key, C major. An enharmonic German-chord modulation returns the tonality to B. Another hint of C and A flat is followed by an energetic coda and a B-minor cadence.

Dwight found "much beauty" in the *larghetto*, "in which we confess we should not have suspected, by mere hearing, the presence of the *Canon*." The canon technique is used throughout the movement, although the interval of imitation changes in the middle section of the 3-part design; in the outside portions the imitation is at the upper fourth, while in the central part it is a fourth lower. All melodic material seems to be derived from the opening theme (Example 12–28).

The final movement, essentially in a sonata design, begins with a theme in canonic imitation (Example 12–29), although this device is soon abandoned; the degree to which Paine revised the sonata is seen when this theme is compared with its original version (Example 12–30). The second theme is in D, the relative major (Example 12–31); its short regular phrases contrast with those of the opening. A closing subject, *fortissimo* but *cantabile* (Example 12–32), has as its accompaniment a rhythmic figure introduced in the second theme group. The development, though giving the effect of a contrasting section, is not new but actually develops both the first and second themes; key areas include B flat, C, and E. With the recapitulation all themes from the exposition are restated, mostly rescored. The second theme occurs first in D flat, then in B major. A coda based chiefly on material presented early in the development, closes the movement in the tonic major.

Romanza and Scherzo for Piano and Violoncello, Op. 30; in A major and A minor
1. *Adagio*
2. *Allegro con fuoco*

> Autograph manuscript in Houghton Library, Harvard University. Another copy of the cello part only, also in Houghton collection, appears to be a revision; it is designated, "Op. 28," and the word "Scherzo" is crossed and changed to "Humoreske," in the composer's hand.
>
> Unpublished.

Paine's *Romanza and Scherzo* received its première at an Ernst Perabo chamber concert at Wesleyan Hall, Boston, on 3 November 1876. Perabo, pianist, and Adolphe Hartdegen, cellist, performed the work, which "made quite a pleasant impression, especially the Scherzo," according to Dwight, "though hardly a work of such mark as his Sonata Duo."[9] The *Advertiser* gave a similar assessment:

> A new Romanza and Scherzo . . . was received with interest by the audience, and, though less in itself and its pretensions than its author's sonata in B-minor for piano and violin, gave more delight to the listeners, the *Allegro con fuoco* being distinguished by a sparkling and almost playful quality, quite removed above triviality by its fancifulness. . . .[10]

On the following 17 January Perabo and Hartdegen performed the two movements on a Sanders Theatre subscription concert. Dwight was more favorably impressed, and found that the work

> . . . improved upon a second hearing, and gave decided pleasure; especially the Scherzo *(Allegro con fuoco),* full of genial life and fire. The Romanza, too *(Adagio)*

> moves on in a broad, full stream of deep and tender melody, well harmonized, and,
> if less original, is far from wearisome. . . .[11]

The *Advertiser* mentioned "the melodic sweetness and elevation of its *adagio*, and the brilliant originality and gayety of its *allegro*. . . ."[12] Perabo and Hartdegen performed the work a third time at a June 1878 concert at Wellesley College.

Three different opus numbers were assigned to this composition. For the three performances mentioned above, the designation was "Op. 27"—a number later given to the *Centennial Hymn*. The "Op. 28" on the *Romanza and Humoreske* manuscript was assigned to the *Overture to "As You Like It."* "Op. 30," the eventual designation, was not without conflict, for the *Larghetto and Scherzo*, Op. 32, for piano trio, was announced as "Op. 30" for its first performance.

Larghetto and Scherzo in B Flat for Piano, Violin and Violoncello, Op. 32
> Autograph manuscript full score and two complete sets of parts in Houghton Library,
> Harvard University; another copy of the Scherzo also in Houghton collection.
> Unpublished.

Ernst Perabo's 1876–77 series of chamber concerts, on which Paine's *Violin Sonata*, *Romanza and Scherzo*, and *Four Characteristic Pieces*, Op. 25 were performed, proved to be so successful that he announced an "extra" concert for 9 February 1877. Included on the program were "two trio movements by J. K. Paine, written for this matinee. . . ."[13] Perabo, pianist, Bernhard Listemann, violinist, and Adolphe Hartdegen presented the work; Dwight found it ". . . genial, refined, and interesting, and finely played. . . ."[14] The *Advertiser* review stated that the two movements

> . . . had those characteristics of their author which we may now call well known—
> viz.: remarkable force, vividness and grace. The scherzo in particular had great
> melodic beauty and a strong rhythmic sweep.[15]

The three musicians repeated the *Larghetto and Scherzo* at an 11 December 1877 subscription concert at Sanders Theatre. Dwight was more generous in his second assessment of the work:

> . . . Mr. Paine's Larghetto and Scherzo seemed to us the finest of the several compositions he has given us in this form. The Scherzo is quite original and piquant, in striking contrast, yet well related to the rich and thoughtful slow movement that precedes it. . . .[16]

Four or five additional performances of Opus 32 are known. In August 1879 the Larghetto only was included on a faculty concert of the New England Conservatory's Normal Institute.[17] On a 20 March 1891 Carl Baermann concert at Union Hall, Boston, pianist Baermann, violinist Timothee Adamowski, and cellist John Adamowski included the work on this chamber program. Louis C. Elson, in reviewing the concert, seemed unaware that the trio had been composed at least 14 years previously:

> . . . The new work by Prof. J. K. Paine was worthy of this leading American composer, who in these later days is writing in a more romantic and earnest manner than ever before. In the "St. Peter" days, he was controlled by rules, but now he is their master, and the earnest depth of the larghetto and scherzo for piano, violin and cello and the freedom of the form, reminded of Schumann in his best period.
>
> The larghetto had a climax absolutely grand, and the scherzo was rather of the dramatic Chopin type than in the playful Mendelssohnian vein. . . .[18]

The two Adamowskis teamed with pianist Arthur Foote to perform the work on a 29 December 1898 Association Hall concert in Brooklyn, Reviewer "A.E.B." noted,

> The trio for piano, violin and 'cello, by Prof. J. K. Paine is a scholarly piece of writing in two parts, a larghetto in B flat in 2-4 time, and a scherzo in G minor in 3-4 time. The melody of the first has a most dainty accompaniment, embroidered with triplets and trills, while the second was vivacious and was handled in a manner to impress one with the particularly good balance of the instruments. . . .[19]

The *Larghetto and Scherzo* were also included on one of the ten Harvard chamber concerts in Sanders Theatre during the 1898–99 season.

One possible additional performance of the *Larghetto and Scherzo* occurred at a 4 December 1899 Kneisel Quartet concert at Association Hall, Boston. Mrs. Maas-Tapper (Mrs. Thomas Tapper?), pianist, joined members of the Quartet in performing "J. K. Paine's Trio for piano, violin, 'cello (MS., first time). . . ."[20] Unfortunately, no opus number was supplied. There is no extant trio among Paine's works that had remained unperformed until this time. The performance may have used the revised manuscript, and this version may have been performed for the "first time" in Boston. On the other hand, the revision of the Trio, Op. 22, may have been prepared for this concert, to be performed for the "first time." Or of course there may have been another work that has since been lost or destroyed. Regrettably, no reports of the concert provided any description of the composition, not even naming the movements, and no clues exist to guide the identification.

Example 12–1.   *Quartet,* First movement, measures 1–4.

Example 12–2.   *Quartet,* First movement, measures 12–14 (violins and cello *tacent*).

Example 12–3.   *Quartet,* First movement, measures 36–38.

Example 12–4.   *Quartet,* First movement, measures 77–82.

Example 12–5.   *Quartet,* Second movement, measures 1–8.

Example 12–6.   *Quartet,* Third movement, measures 1–16.

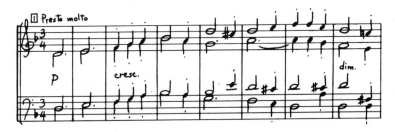

Example 12–6   (continued)

Example 12–7.   *Quartet,* Third movement, measures 316–324.

Example 12–8.   *Quartet,* Fourth movement, Theme, measures 1–8.

Example 12–9.   *Quartet,* Fourth movement, Variation 1, mm. 1–4.

Example 12–10.   *Quartet,* Fourth movement, Variation 2, mm 1–4.

Example 12–11.   *Quartet,* Fourth movement, Variation 3, mm 1–4.

Example 12–12.   *Quartet,* Fourth movement, Fugua, measures 1–12.

Example 12–12   (continued)

Example 12–13.   *Trio,* First movement, measures 1–12.

Example 12–13   (continued)

Example 12–14.   *Trio,* First movement, measures 48–53.

Example 12–14   (continued)

Example 12–15.   *Trio,* First movement.

a. Measures 67–70.

Example 12–15 (continued)

b. Measures 75–76, violin only.

c. Measures 84–87, piano only.

d. Measures 92–94.

Example 12–16.   *Trio,* Second movement, measures 1–8 (violin *tacet*).

Example 12–17.   *Trio,* Second movement, measures 18–20.

Example 12–18.   *Trio*, Second movement, measures 28–36.

Example 12–19.   *Trio,* Second movement, measures 57–58.

Example 12–20.   *Trio,* Second movement, measures 151–157.

Example 12–20   (continued)

Example 12–21.   *Trio,* Third movement, measures 1–4.

Example 12–21   (continued)

Example 12–22.   *Trio,* Third movement, measures 16–21.

Example 12–22   (continued)

Example 12–23.   *Trio,* Third movement, measures 36–39.

Example 12–24.   *Violin Sonata,* First movement, measures 1–5.

Example 12–25.   *Violin Sonata,* First movement, measures 20–23.

Example 12–26.   *Violin Sonata,* First movement, measures 31–36 (violin *tacet*).

Example 12–27.   *Violin Sonata,* First movement, measures 64–67.

Example 12–28.   *Violin Sonata,* Second movement, measures 1–5.

Example 12–29.   *Violin Sonata,* Third movement, measures 1–7.

Example 12–29   (continued)

Example 12–30.   *Violin Sonata* (original version, after manuscript in Boston Public Library), Third movement, measures 1–3.

Example 12–31.   *Violin Sonata,* Third movement, measures 36–41.

Example 12–31   (continued)

Example 12–32.   *Violin Sonata,* Third movement, measures 60–61.

13

Orchestral Works

Symphony No. 1 in C Minor, Op. 23
    I. *Allegro con brio*
    II. *Allegro vivace*
    III. *Adagio*
    IV. *Allegro vivace*
        Scored for 2 flutes, 2 oboes, 2 clarinets, 2 bassoons, 4 horns, 2 trumpets, 3 trombones, timpani, and strings.
        Autograph manuscript full score in Houghton Library, Harvard University; composer's holograph score in Music Division, Library of Congress. An 8-bar excerpt of the opening of Movement 3, reduced to 2 staves, titled "adagio cantabile e espressivo," autographed, dated "Lucerne, Aug 23, 1879"; in Treasure Room, Werner Josten Library, Smith College, Northampton, Mass.
        Score and 23 parts published by Breitkopf & Härtel, Leipzig, in 1908 (copyright by Mary E. Paine); score reprinted by DaCapo Press, New York, 1972 (ed. H. Wiley Hitchcock).
        Copies: BPL, BU, Dart, ESM, Fleisher, HMA, HMus (+ parts), LC, Mich, NYPL, Smith, Wellesley, Wis, Yale.

The C-minor *Symphony*, begun around 1872 and completed in 1875, was Paine's first major work after *St. Peter* and his first for orchestra alone. It contains a wealth of attractive themes and exhibits great skill in writing for orchestra—a result of his studies with Wieprecht and his practical experience gained while composing the *Mass*, *St. Peter*, and other shorter works for chorus and orchestra. Unfortunately, Paine was far too repetitious in his manipulation of themes. Particularly disappointing is his overreliance on certain Beethoven clichés such as motivic fragmentation, as in Example 13–1, from the development section of the first movement. By itself this excerpt is perfectly acceptable, but it follows a 30-bar repetitive treatment of another motive, and bars 197–200 of this example are twice repeated, outlining B-flat major and minor triads. The lengthy development section—144 bars out of a total of 530—lacks momentum, in part because of too great a dependence on such formulas.

    Some contemporary writers criticized this extensive use of material, as has been mentioned earlier in this study, and many remarked about its length—about 40 minutes with repeats, not including breaks between movements. But most listeners received it eagerly—Osgood enthusiastically proclaimed it "perfect in its form"[1]—for it was a novel achievement for an American. Theodore Thomas' orchestra gave the first performances—the première was in Boston on 26 January 1876, and three more followed soon thereafter, two in February in New York and again in Boston, and in July at the Centennial Exposition in Philadelphia. After a Cambridge performance by the Thomas orchestra in February 1877, the Symphony seems to have been eclipsed by later Paine orchestral works, for it received only one additional complete performance, in 1882 by the Boston Philharmonic Society.

Paine's C-minor *Symphony* is in four movements, organized in form and tempo according to the precedents set in the symphonies of Beethoven—the two outside movements are in sonata form, and the second movement is a scherzo and trio, followed by a slow third movement in song form. The first movement opens with a dramatic, aggressive gesture as its principal theme—what Fiske termed the "resistless hammer of Thor"[2] (Example 13–2). Following a climax, a transition section ensues with an attractive, restless theme (Example 13–3). A modulation to the relative major prepares the secondary theme, a pleasant dance-like melody (Example 13–4), showing the influence of operatic composers. The closing section (Example 13–5) of the Exposition is an energetic march, perhaps the most satisfactory portion of the movement. It is not repeated, but leads directly to the Development by diminishing to a soft string tremolo, over which the first of many Beethovenian motivic formulas is displayed. Dominating this section is the principal theme, which, in the process of fragmentization, inevitably results in the familiar rhythm ♪♫♩ —showing even closer resemblance to Beethoven's C-minor symphony. At the close of the Development, a lengthy dominant pedal and a crescendo lead to the Recapitulation, with the principal theme rescored for orchestra *tutti*, again in the manner of the Beethoven work. The transition theme is modified (Example 13–6), losing much of its restless character and exhibiting a lyricism found in many Weber opera melodies; assigning the theme to the solo clarinet recalls the earlier composer's frequent use of this instrument.[3] The remainder of the Recapitulation is analogous to the Exposition, except for its key area being the major tonic. Like the Exposition, it does not reach a strong cadence, but instead dissolves into a following section, in this case a 75-bar Coda that unfortunately repeats many of the developmental formulas that already were overused in the Development section.

The Scherzo is primarily based on its opening measures (Example 13–7), especially the rhythm of the first bar, which appears often in Paine compositions. Structurally this portion of the movement is ABA, although the 34-bar "A" section is dwarfed by the following 170-bar "B" section. The opening section soon modulates to E major, the major mediant key, where it remains for half of the passage before returning to a tonic half-cadence. There is a repeat, and on replaying, the half cadence leads abruptly into a modulation to D minor to begin the "B" section. This latter part is a development of material derived from Example 13–7, using techniques already encountered in the first movement. The effect is more satisfactory, however, perhaps because of the constant rhythmic momentum. At the close, section "A" returns, suitably lengthened to establish a tonic cadence. An unaccompanied horn begins a transition to the Trio, where a solo clarinet unfolds a graceful Schumannesque melody (Example 13–8) reminiscent of *Warum?* from the *Fantasiestücke* or passages from the Piano Concerto. The use of the raised fourth degree of the scale in measure 278 and the parallel tenths framework seem to be a characteristic of Paine's instrumental music. An accompanimental rhythm in the strings will recur in *As You Like It* (see Example 13–22). The design of the Trio is tripartite two-reprise; woodwind solos are featured. Again a transition is started by an unaccompanied horn—a favorite device in Paine's orchestral works. The Scherzo returns in a written-out *da capo*, and is extended with a 44-bar conclusion.

The Adagio is a lovely *romance* quite consistent with others of his compositions in this mood. It begins with an expansive melody in the cellos and first violins, harmonized smoothly over a tonic pedal (Example 13–9). A raised fourth degree (m. 3) and a melodic turn are among the significant features of Paine's melodic style to be observed, and the chromatic passages involving the lowered sixth degree (mm. 4 & 7) and the raised fourth (mm. 8–9) are clichés identified with his melodic-harmonic style. A "horn" cliché in measure 4 (the last three eighths in the melody) begins an 8-note pentatonic passage in the melody, somewhat unusual in this harmonic context. Recurrences of this theme throughout the movement are always rescored. Design of the movement is a modified rondo— ABCABA. Section "B," in the relative minor, breaks the contemplative mood with an increase in rhythmic activity (Example 13–10). A gradual crescendo leads to another increase in rhythmic momentum—the introduction of 32nd-note scale passages in Example 13–11 is a device Paine was to repeat in many later orchestral works. A decrescendo leads not to a reprise of "A" but instead to the "C" theme (Example 13–12), in the tonic minor. A long modulatory transition, ending with a dominant pedal, finally returns to the first theme, now with a more elaborate accompaniment and a hint of a countermelody. Section "B" begins as in Example 13–10 above, but subsequently is modified—Example 13–11 is transposed, and a shorter decrescendo returns to "A," now over a string tremolo and a dominant pedal, with a more clearly identified counter-melody. A short coda continues the mood, with little disruption of the slow harmonic rhythm or pedal points.

The final *Allegro vivace*, like the first movement, is in sonata form. Its primary theme (Example 13–13) dominates the entire movement, es-pecially the motive in mm. 1–2 and the rhythmic figures in mm. 7–9. The imitation between treble and bass at the beginning is a favorite technique of Paine. As in the Scherzo, the tonality of C soon modulates to E, the mediant major, and the second theme group begins in this key (Example 13–14). There is no clear theme; rather, motives derived from the first theme are developed in dialogue and sequentially. Eventually the chro-maticism reaches a greater complexity than elsewhere in this symphony (Example 13–15), with even a hint at the "omnibus" progression, although passages similar to this are found with more frequency in later works. G major, the dominant key, is not affirmed until the closing group (Ex-ample 13–16), again based on the primary theme of the movement. There is a repeat indicated for the Exposition; the second ending leads without break to the Development, which occupies a third of the movement. This section exhibits many of the problems to be found in the first movement, but the greater number of rhythmic figures available helps forestall mo-notony. Also, at about the point where the motive from Example 13–14, mm. 52–53, had been developed exhaustively, Paine used it then as an accompaniment for a new theme (Example 13–17). Similarly, the triplet figure a bit later accompanies this melody (Example 13–18). An expected dominant pedal and crescendo lead to the Recapitulation. As in the first movement, it dissolves into the Coda. Here, however, the effect is better, for there is a *poco più allegro*, the motives are treated a bit differently, and the section is not as long—only 90 bars out of the total 543. Another example of Paine's chromaticism is seen not far from the end, outlining in parallel tenths an interior tonic pedal (Example 13–19); again, such a passage is more typical of Paine's later works.

Overture to Shakespeare's "As You Like It," Op. 28.
>   Scored for piccolo, 2 flutes, 2 oboes, 2 clarinets, 2 bassoons, 4 horns, 2 trumpets, 3 trombones, timpani, and strings.
>   Autograph manuscript full score and piano 4-hand arrangement in Houghton Library, Harvard University; copyist's score at Library of Congress.
>   Score and 24 parts published by Breitkopf & Härtel, Leipzig, in 1907.
>   Copies: BPL, ESM, Fleisher, HMA, HMus, LC, NYPL, Smith.

The *Overture to "As You Like It"* is one of the most attractive and accessible of Paine's orchestral compositions, for its brevity eliminates the monotonous repetitions found in some other works, and its themes are light and tuneful. It was first performed at Sanders Theatre, Cambridge, on 21 November 1876 by the Theodore Thomas orchestra, which repeated it the following February in Boston. The Harvard Musical Association performed it in March 1877, and the Boston Philharmonic Society in May 1881. Four later performances were given between 1889 and 1901 in Chicago, New York, and Boston.

As You Like It is cast in the design found in most overtures of the period: an opening slow introduction, followed by a concluding allegro in sonata form. Paine's overture is not specifically programmatic—no themes are assigned to characters or events in the play. Rather, the music evokes the joyful mood of the Shakespeare comedy. The introduction begins with a lyrical pastoral theme in the solo clarinet that bears a rather interesting family resemblance to the *Adagio* theme of the C minor Symphony (Example 13–9) in its melodic contour, harmony, pedal point, and chromatic alterations. Parallel tenths are evident in measures 5–10 (Example 13–20). A middle section becomes more turbulent, with a crescendo treated in the Paine fashion with treble-bass alternation (Example 13–21) and increasing rhythmic activity. The third section restores the mood of the beginning and leads without break into the *Allegro vivace*, whose principal theme (Example 13–22) is a graceful melody related to the opening clarinet theme in the introduction, and with the raised fourth (m. 63) and rhythmic accompaniment similar to that found in the C minor Symphony. The transition section (Example 13–23) grows out of the rhythmic pattern begun in m. 65, and leads to the second theme (Example 13–24), scored for woodwinds with another clarinet melody. Paine's choice of A major— the mediant major key—for this theme group, rather than the dominant key usually encountered in major-key sonata movements, shows Paine's interest in key relationships a third apart. The finale of the C-minor Symphony contains a similar relationship, while in the first and last movements of the *Spring Symphony* (A major) the second theme groups are in the lowered submediant (F major) and lowered mediant (C major) keys, respectively.

Symphonic Poem: Shakespeare's "Tempest," Op. 31
> In four connected movements.
> > I. *Allegro furioso*. The Storm.
> > II. *Adagio tranquilo*. Calm and happy scene before Prospero's cell.
> > III. *Allegro moderato e maestoso*. Prospero's Tale.
> > IV. *Allegro non troppo*.
> > > The happy love of Ferdinand and Miranda.
> > > Episode with Caliban.
> > > Triumph of Prospero's "potent art."
> > Performance: about 25 minutes long.
> > Scored for piccolo, 2 flutes, 2 oboes, 2 clarinets, 2 bassoons, 4 horns, 2 trumpets, 3 trombones, tuba, timpani, harp, and strings.

Autograph manuscript full score in Houghton Library, Harvard University; another
manuscript full score in Mills Music Library, University of Wisconsin at Madison.
Madison.
Score and 26 parts published by Breitkopf & Härtel, Leipzig, in 1907.
Copies: BPL, ESM, Fleisher, HMA, HMus, LC, Mich, NYPL, Smith, Yale.

The Tempest is Paine's most detailed programmatic work, and received strong criticism from John Sullivan Dwight, a strong advocate of
classical forms, who dismissed the symphonic poems of Liszt and Saint-
Saëns. Paine's close friend and apologist, John Fiske, wrote a detailed
description[4] of the piece, explaining its thorough grounding in classical
tradition, but succeeded more in amusing Dwight than persuading him.
The first performance originally was scheduled for a March 1877 Harvard
Musical Association concert, but *As You Like It* had to be substituted.
Theodore Thomas' orchestra gave the première in New York at Steinway
Hall on 2 November of the same year, and repeated it at Sanders Theatre
in Cambridge later in the month and at Music Hall, Boston, in December.
The next performances were in March, 1883, in Boston and Cambridge,
when Paine conducted the Boston Symphony Orchestra in a revised ver-
sion of the work. Eight more hearings of the revision were given between
1884 and 1898 in Boston, Brooklyn, Chicago, New York, and Philadelphia.

It is not possible to determine the precise amount of Paine's revision,
for the original version is no longer extant. But a *Nation* review of an
1884 Brooklyn performance revealed:

Some improvements . . . have been recently made in the instrumentation; the second
movement has been enlarged, and the coda rewritten. . . .[5]

Fiske's description of the 1877 version shows us also that the "Episode
with Caliban" originally followed the first "Ariel" interlude and immediately preceded "Prospero's Tale."

As noted above, the symphonic poem opens with a depiction of the
storm. The "prelude form" of which Fiske writes is a series of three
crescendos and diminuendos (or "surges" of the storm), each growing
more intense. Tonality is not clearly affirmed until the close of the scene,
and key areas change with each new surge. The movement opens with a
timpani roll and a half cadence in D minor, incorporating a German 6th
chord in root position over a turbulent bass (Example 13–25). A restless
figure in the strings combines with an ascending woodwind motive (Example 13–26) to begin the crescendo. Near the peak of the crescendo
appears the expected Paine treble-bass counterpoint (Example 13–27),
followed by resonant wind chords combined with rushing strings, and a
diminuendo ending with a repetition of material from Example 13–25. In
the first surge the tonality shifts from D minor to G minor, and the second

reaches C minor. The third moves through C-sharp minor, and reaches a final cadence in E minor.

"Prospero's Cell," in E major, is in direct contrast to the storm scene. Pedals and long sustained chords are prevalent in the three-part movement. The opening theme (Example 13–28) contains several augmented dominant sevenths (mm. 126 & 128), parallel tenths (mm. 125–127), and raised supertonic diminished sevenths resolving to tonic (m. 125, and, borrowed from A major, mm. 124–125). A final sustained passage uses a portion of the "omnibus" progression to lead to the short "Ariel" interlude (Example 13–29), a delicate cadenza-like passage for high woodwinds over sustained string chords and harp arpeggios. The progressions prepare C major, the key of the next movement.

"Prospero's Tale" begins with a warm string melody (Example 13–30) that will recur throughout the remainder of the piece. Interestingly, it is almost entirely pentatonic. Present also are the raised fourth (mm. 196, 197), raised second (mm. 196, 198), and pedal points in both keys. A following phrase for woodwinds and harp (with a G pentatonic melody) provides a brightly contrasting timbre recalling some of the orchestral writing in *Lohengrin*. A subsequent period begins a crescendo, which includes the following material reminiscent of a processional (Example 13–31). Prospero's theme is restated several times in this movement, with modulations to A, E minor, and B minor. Near the end of the section brass fanfares (a Paine staple) introduce a majestic brass and woodwind chorale (Example 13–32); a sudden diminuendo to *pianissimo* string chords follows. In his *Advertiser* essay, Fiske praised this section, declaring it as "a passage over which I believe that Beethoven would have clapped his hands." The sustained chords allow a return of "Ariel" and a modulation to D major, the key of the last movement.

"The happy love of Ferdinand and Miranda" discloses a rich Brahmsian[6] melody as its principal theme; a hint of Prospero's theme is heard in the lower strings (Example 13–33). A melodic figure in mm. 280–281 suggests similar uses in other Paine works, particularly the second theme of the Spring Symphony's first movement (see Example 13–43, mm. 151–152 below). Other characteristic touches—the melodic turn (m. 283), the raised second to the third degree (mm. 276, 278), raised fourth to the fifth degree (mm. 276, 278), raised fifth to the sixth (mm. 277, 280), non-dominant ^{4} chords (mm. 279, 281), and parallel tenths (mm. 276–281)—cause this passage to sound very much like Paine. This final movement is in a modified sonata form—the usual development section is replaced by the "Episode with Caliban." The principal theme (Example 13–33) is followed by a transition section (Example 13–34) introducing a dotted-note figure that will recur a number of times. A modulation to

B major, the submedient major (again, a key relationship by third), ushers in the second theme group in the woodwinds (Example 13–35). Contrasting phrases introduce a variety of graceful, dancelike melodic ideas, many incorporating the rhythmic figure from Example 13–34. An energetic closing section leads to a short modulating transition section and the "Episode with Caliban." The music depicting this grotesque, comical character predictably features the bassoon (Example 13–36); repeated phrases are rescored, with prominence given to other woodwinds and the harp. To the Caliban theme is added the primary theme of the movement (Example 13–37), thus beginning the Recapitulation (in the subdominant key); again present are the parallel tenths and chromatic pitches of Example 13–33. An aggressive transition section again leads to the second theme, this time in D major, the tonic. The energetic closing group ends inconclusively on a diminshed seventh, and unaccompanied horns modulate to E flat for a quotation of Prospero's theme and a hint of Ariel. A coda, back in D major, combines Prospero's theme in the bass with a motive from the Ariel passage just heard (Example 13–38), producing a brilliant conclusion to the work—the "Triumph of Prospero's 'potent art.' "

Duo concertante for solo violin and violoncello, Op. 33
> I. *Allegro non troppo*.
> II. *Andante molto e cantabile*.
> III. *Allegro non troppo*.
> Autograph manuscript full score in Houghton Library, Harvard University. Unpublished.

This is Paine's only venture into the concerto form and seems to have been something of a stepchild among his orchestral works. It was probably completed by early 1877, for in January 1877 Paine was already working on the Spring Symphony.[7] When the latter work was not ready in time, the *Duo Concertante* was played instead by the Thomas orchestra at a 23 April 1878 Sanders Theatre concert, its only performance. Dwight found the scoring rich and brilliant, but commented that soloists Brandt and Hemmann were often covered over by the orchestral texture.[8]

Symphony No. 2 in A Major, Op. 34 (*Im Frühling*)[9]
> I. Introduction. *Adagio Sostenuto*.
>   *Allegro ma non troppo*.
> II. *Scherzo. Allegro*.
> III. *Adagio*.
> IV. *Allegro giojoso*.
> Scored for 2 flutes, 2 oboes, 2 clarinets, 2 bassoons, 4 horns, 2 trumpets, 3 trombones, timpani, and strings.
> Autograph manuscript full score in Houghton Library, Harvard University.
> Score and parts published by A. P. Schmidt, Boston, in 1880; simultaneously released by August Cranz, Hamburg, and C. A. Spina, Vienna.

Piano 4-hands arrangement by the composer, published by A. P. Schmidt, Boston, in 1880.

"Adagio," arranged for organ by H. M. Dunham, included in Dunham's *Select Arrangements for the Organ*, published by A. P. Schmidt, Boston, in 1888.

Copies (full score): BPL (+ piano 4-hands), ESM, Fleisher, HMA (+ piano 4-hands), HMus (+ parts), LC, Mich, NECM (+ piano 4-hands), PPL (+ piano 4-hands), Smith (piano 4-hands only), Summy (+ piano 4-hands, Adagio organ arr.), Wis, Yale.

The *Spring Symphony,* which Elson reported as Paine's favorite among his orchestral works,[10] is an excellent example of the mature composer's best work and deserves extended comment. No longer bound by the strictness of his training, Paine produced a Second Symphony that was more typical of mid nineteenth-century symphonists, well crafted, and sufficiently satisfying musically to deserve a place in the modern repertory. A happy result of two differing influences on Paine, this symphony seems to reflect both the traditional standards of Beethoven as the supreme symphonic composer and the exciting experiments in form, melody, and harmonic materials by much later masters as Mendelssohn, Schumann, Berlioz, possibly the young Brahms, Bruckner, and even Liszt and Wagner. The work differs greatly in this respect from the composer's earlier C-minor Symphony, whose first movement shows an obvious reliance on Beethoven's Fifth Symphony as a model. To be sure, references to Beethoven may still be seen—such as the lower strings' *quasi recitativo* in the first movement introduction (Example 13–39), suggesting the similar passage in the introduction to the Ninth Symphony finale, and a typical Beethoven *crescendo* in the Scherzo (Example 13–40). But the composer's palette has been broadened extensively, and the many new influences have been assimilated to such an extent that the resulting composition demonstrates most notably the personality of its composer.

Paine's Second Symphony received its first performances on 10 March 1880 at Sanders Theatre by the Boston Philharmonic Society, Bernhard Listemann, conducting, and the following day at Music Hall, Boston, by the Harvard Musical Association, conducted by Carl Zerrahn. Seven more performances were given between 1881 and 1892 in Boston, Chicago, Brooklyn, and New York. In addition, F. X. Arens included the work, or movements from it, in his 1892 concerts of American music in Berlin, Weimar, and Vienna.

The programmatic element in the *Spring Symphony* was not stressed at first, perhaps because of Paine's reluctance to arouse criticism from conservative musicians unconvinced of the value of program music. One may recall John Fiske's vigorous defense of Paine's 1877 *Symphonic Poem on Shakespeare's "Tempest"* as absolute music, and imagine why no titles of individual movements were included in the 1880 published score of the symphony or on programs printed for early performances. Reviewers of these concerts seem to have been unaware of these titles, also, for some provided their own descriptions of the movements. Apparently it was not until 1889 that these topics were made public as part of a discussion of the work in A. J. Goodrich's *Complete Musical Analysis*, and there seem never to have been any specific statements by Paine regarding the programmatic aspects of his symphony. The movement titles given by Goodrich are:

> I. Introduction. *Adagio sostenuto*. "Departure of Winter."
> *Allegro ma non troppo*. "Awakening of Nature."
> II. *Scherzo. Allergro*. "May-night Fantasy."
> III. *Adagio*. "A Romance of Springtime."
> IV. *Allegro giojoso*. "The Glory of Nature."[11]

With this background, one may expect the "Spring" of Paine's symphony to be only a general portrayal of moods, with little in the way of literal description, aside from some ornate flute solos that could suggest bird songs. There is no evidence, moreover, of an attempt to describe a New England spring; rather, the work follows very much in the tradition of similar compositions by Europeans. One may compare the movement titles with those at first associated with Schumann's *"Spring" Symphony*:

> I. Spring's Awakening
> II. Evening
> III. Merry Playmates
> IV. Full Spring

A much closer parallel is seen with Joachim Raff's *Symphony No. 8 "Frühlingsklänge"* (1878):[12]

> I. Nature's Awakening
> II. Walpurgis Night Revel
> III. First Blossoms of Spring
> IV. The Joys of Wandering

Rupert Hughes and Arthur Elson called Paine's symphony "program music of the most legitimate sort . . ."—that which has

> . . . no aim of imitating springtime noises, but seeks to stimulate by suggestion the hearer's creative imagination, and provoke by a musical telepathy the emotions that swayed the nympholept composer. . . .[13]

The "musical telepathy" did enable Hughes and Elson to recognize the "chill and icy" and the "rushing wind" motives, both found in the first movement introduction (see Examples 13–42a and 13–39), the "coda of vanishing bird-wings and throats," and the "moonlit revel of elves" in the Scherzo, complete with a "single hobgoblin bassoon." The third-movement Romance displayed a "love-lorn iteration of themes," and the Finale, "a halleluiah," ended with "a many-hued rainbow."[14] Such details would have delighted the most dedicated admirer of program music, but there is no indication that any of these descriptions were Paine's; more likely the "telepathy" was merely imagination on the part of the authors. The individual movements, though conveying moods appropriate to the theme, were doubtless planned primarily to be satisfactory as absolute music, and such minute details of program as suggested above would have been unlikely.

Paine's Second Symphony is long, when compared to his earlier essay in the form; an uncut performance would last about an hour, not including breaks between movements. Reportedly the 1883 Brooklyn performance lasted twice as long as that of Beethoven's Eighth Symphony which shared the concert. A medium orchestra is specified—pairs of flutes, oboes, clarinets, and bassoons, 4 horns, 2 trumpets, 3 trombones, timpani, and strings. Scoring is competent and effective—such a standard was usual in Paine's orchestral works. Sonata-form recapitulations and rondo reprises are extensively rescored.

A decided improvement over the C-minor Symphony may be seen in Paine's treatment of symphonic form. The earlier composition suffered from motivic over-development, extensive repetition of methods and formulas, awkward joinings, and occasional lack of stylistic unity, especially in themes. In composing the Spring Symphony, Paine appears to have been far more comfortable in his use of form. His transition passages are smoother, in the main, and he shows greater variety of treatment in developmental sections. He continues to observe the four-movement convention, as in the earlier symphony, and again follows the later-Beethoven model in providing a scherzo as the second movement, followed by a slow third movement in a song-form-with-variations design. The tonal plan of the four movements, however, shows a departure from Beethoven's models, and follows more the precedents set by Schumann:[15]

I— A minor (intro.); A major
II— D minor (subdominant made minor)
III— F major (submediant of tonic minor)
IV— A major

A similar relationship of keys occurs in the first movement, where the secondary theme group also appears—in the Exposition—in the key of F major, the submediant of tonic minor. And in the Exposition of the Finale, the secondary theme group is presented in C major, the mediant of tonic minor. Features such as these are hardly innovative, but they certainly contradict the common impression that Paine's music was dry, pedantic, and reactionary. The symphonies of Mendelssohn and Schumann are the chief models and points of departure for the Spring Symphony, which may be compared favorably with symphonies by European composers in the German-dominated musical world.

An evidence of Paine's continued development in compositional style is his changed concept of thematic function in the first-movement form. In the earlier Symphony in C Minor there are clearly differentiated primary and secondary theme groups, and both are extensively developed prior to the Recapitulation. But in the first movement of the Spring Symphony, only the principal theme (Example 13–41) and a "winter theme" (Example 13–42) from the slow introduction—used motivically throughout the movement—possess important functions in the form. (Motivic derivation in Example 13–42 is derived in part from Goodrich's analysis.)

The secondary theme section begins with a six-bar passage that does not recur until the analogous place in the Recapitulation; the section continues with the principal and "winter" themes combined, recast, and developed (Example 13–43). A greater thematic unity results from this avoidance of a secondary theme contrast. The main duality of themes exists, instead, between the principal theme and the "winter" motive, a difference that is minimized by their frequent combination.

Paine's use of themes simultaneously in combination is consistent with the practice of other nineteenth-century composers, who employed this technique—following the precedent established by Berlioz in his programmatic works—to heighten climaxes and to obtain dramatic interest. An early instance of thematic combination in the present symphony occurs in the second theme group of the first movement, mentioned above, where the "winter" theme—now less forbidding in its change to the major mode—is heard above the "awakening" motive of the principal theme (see Example 13–43). The extramusical associations of these two themes provide an element of dramatic conflict to an otherwise serene passage of counterpoint. Later in the exposition the closing theme is combined with the "awakening" motive, providing a feeling of culmination to the section. At the analogous place in the recapitulation the climax is intensified, for to these two themes is added the head motive of the "winter" theme in half notes, played by the trombones (see Example 13–42e). Near the close of the development another combination is discovered; in this instance the sixteenth-note accompaniment figure in the violins, associated with the "awakening" motive in the exposition, is here paired with the "winter" motive, presented in canon by the trombones.

It has been noted earlier that the "winter" motive which opened the introduction recurs throughout the first movement—usually in an altered form of the first phrase (see Examples 13–42b, 13–43) or in a shorter motive incorporating the opening second (sometimes enlarged to a third, sometimes with direction reversed) and the large upward leap (see Examples 13–42c, d, e). But similar motives may be found throughout the succeeding three movements, possibly to be interpreted programmatically as a constant contrast between the barrenness of winter and the joy, growth, playfulness, passion, etc., to be encountered during springtime. The clearest statement of the "winter" motive occurs early in the finale, where the head motive—predominantly in half notes—is combined with a quicker dance-like theme (Example 13–42m); soon thereafter another motive—in short note values and in the "giojoso" spirit of the movement—is clearly derived from the original "winter" theme (Example 13–42n). Motives in the second and third movements (Examples 13–42f–h and i–l) are more loosely related to the model, but the presence of such a number of melodic fragments—most with an initial second, all with the upward leap and conjunct descent—is more than coincidental and provides an added degree of musical and programmatic unity through this common cyclic device.

Nineteenth-century symphonists displayed an increasing interest in the effect that each musical element would produce in the overall form, and Paine was definitely a part of this trend. One means of stressing larger dimensions was to blur the outlines of smaller units—motives, periods, phrases, etc.,—to more easily integrate them into a larger context. Many Paine themes reveal his studied avoidance of small-term melodic symmetry, preferring instead units of irregular length that de-emphasize formal joinings and contribute instead to a sense of larger-scale growth. Typical examples may be found in the first movement. The principal theme begins with a 17-bar period, which may be broken, somewhat arbitrarily, into two-bar units and regrouped into a 6+6+5 bar plan (see Example 13–41). The first two phrases of the secondary theme number 6 and 8 bars, and may be broken down into 2+4 and 4+5 bar constructions (see Example 13–43). Dimensions of this latter phrase are rendered ambiguous, moreover, by the combination of the two themes—"winter" and principal—referred to above; their differing lengths and cadence implications contribute to a larger-scale feeling of growth and development. Regular phrases are seen, however, in the broad "hymn" melody, the second theme of the finale, which shows a basic pentatonic structure (Example 13–44).

Rhythmic variety, maintained throughout the four movements, is another indication of Paine's skill and craftsmanship. Diversity is obtained by such means as frequently changing rhythmic patterns (sixteenths, eighth-note triplets, dotted notes, etc.), writing melodic bass lines, often in syncopation (as well as in counterpoint) with the soprano line, and employing many different accompanimental textures and styles.

Paine's harmonic vocabulary, as seen in the *Spring Symphony*, is typical of many of his European peers—grounded in the practices of Mendelssohn and Schumann. Basic staples include primary and secondary chords from the parallel major or minor key, the Neapolitan sixth, augmented sixths—used for chromatic intensification or (often in root position) for enharmonic modulation—, dominant ninths, dominant augmented triads, and diminished sevenths—used for tension, modulation, and for tonal instability. Typically, primary thematic material is quite stable harmonically, with a strong emphasis on tonic and dominant sonorities—unless, of course, a feeling of instability or turbulence is to be implied. But an exception may be found in the main theme of the May-night Scherzo, which, after an opening flourish, refers to the tonic triad only obliquely, although remaining within the tonality, and reaches the dominant only at the end of the section (Example 13–45). A novel progression is the A minor triad in measure 9 followed by an A-flat major triad in the following bar. Complexity and tonal ambiguity occur more often as themes are developed and extended, particularly at the point of musical and dynamic climaxes. An example may be seen in a moment of great passion in the third movement, where regular progressions (secondary leading-tone chords to their tonics) are succeeded by root progressions by thirds and finally free progressions by chromatic inflection and enharmonic common tones (G half-diminished seventh, A major triad, root-position German) (Example 13–46). A typical common-tone modulation is seen a bit later in the movement, linking the temporary tonalities of E major and C major; two favorite Paine devices, rushing scale figures and brass fanfares, accompany the transition (Example 13–47). Two interludes in the finale—one part of the transition from the first theme to the broad "hymn" theme (Example 13–48a), the other near the end of the coda (Example 13–48b)—provide contrast from the straightforward diatonic nature of the themes by their greater chromaticism, tonal ambiguities, and quicker harmonic rhythm.

As in the earlier *St. Peter*, Paine often avoids what he considers a cliché—the clear-cut traditional authentic cadence. Devices he commonly substitutes include tonic pedals, dominant ninths, delayed resolutions, emphasis on the Neapolitan sixth, plagal cadences, and plagal-type progressions, such as the diminished seventh chord on the raised super-tonic resolving to tonic. At the conclusion of the third movement, a dominant seventh resolves unexpectedly to a mediant diminished seventh, followed by a submediant half-diminished seventh. Further chromatic progression leads to the final authentic cadence over a tonic-dominant double pedal (Example 13–49). A second example, from the close of the second movement trio, stresses the subdominant; appoggiaturas give a hint of Wagnerian influence (Example 13–50). Occasional examples of intense chromaticism may be seen, including a passage in the introduction moving from F minor to C major that incorporates part of the "omnibus progression," (Example 13–51) and a harmonic sequence leading to the closing theme of the first-movement Exposition (Example 13–52).

There are compositional devices that Paine made use of in numerous works that may be considered characteristic of his style. Many of these may be seen in the *Spring Symphony*. One common device—repeated-note brass fanfares—is often found at dynamic climaxes. A typical example, from the first-movement introduction, is combined with another device commonly used for intensification—shorter note values, usually thirty-second notes (Example 13–53; see also Example 13–47). Another means of increasing tension that Paine often employed is the progression from chordal texture to counterpoint, usually between soprano and bass lines. Canon often plays a part in thematic development—both the first-movement "winter" motive and the main theme of the third movement are so treated (see Examples 13–4b and 13–10). Three other clichés that almost become Paine trademarks, because of their regular use from the C-minor Symphony through *Azara*, are the triplet figure ♩.♫ , the melodic turn, and the parallel tenths skeletal framework.

In the main, the *Spring Symphony* shows evidence throughout of being well planned and well crafted. Only one short passage raises a question regarding the composer's judgment—the transition from the introduction to the exposition of the first movement. These 16 measures are required to change the mood from the stormy, desolate "winter" of the introduction to the joyous, dance-like "spring" of the principal theme. Paine chose to do this with a measured *accelerando*. Four notes—E, D, B, D—are sounded by the first violins, first as half notes, then in groups of quarters, eighths, and sixteenths, becoming then an accompaniment to the beginning of the new theme (the conclusion of this device may be seen in Example 13–41). Regrettably, it is difficult to prevent this from sounding calculated or contrived; suspense and anticipation, rather than mathematical precision, would be desirable here. Fortunately, the transition from the development to the recapitulation, although similar, avoids this rhythmic problem. Rather, the first violins make only one metric change, from eighth-note triplets to sixteenths.

Paine's Second Symphony is a work of integrity and worth, one that can be listened to and enjoyed for its musical values, regardless of its historical importance as a great American symphony. To be sure, it is a product of its time, and in many turns of phrase one may hear a suggestion of Mendelssohn, Schumann, or even Brahms—whose own symphonies were contemporaneous with the present work. But Paine's own stamp is evident throughout, and the *Spring Symphony* definitely deserves a place in the modern repertory, to be studied, performed, and enjoyed.[16]

Prelude to "Oedipus Tyrannus," Op. 35

> Scored for 2 flutes, 2 oboes, 2 clarinets, 2 bassoons, 4 horns, 2 trumpets, 3 trombones, timpani, strings.
>
> Manuscript full score of entire work in New England Conservatory of Music library; manuscript of prelude alone not extant.
>
> Score of Prelude and 23 parts published in 1903 by Arthur P. Schmidt, Boston; score reprinted by Edwin F. Kalmus, New York.
>
> Copies: BPL, Fleisher, HMus (+ parts), LC, Mich, Summy (+ parts), Wis.

Paine's music for Sophocles' play, *Oedipus Tyrannus*, was hailed as a landmark in American music almost from the day of its première at Harvard on 17 May 1881. The Prelude, moreover, achieved a popularity and an identity of its own, and was performed more frequently than any of Paine's orchestral works. Paine conducted the first performance at a Boston Symphony Orchestra concert on 11 March 1882. Five more were given by this organization between 1886 and 1923. Eight other performances in this country are known—in New York (the earliest, 1885), Boston, Cambridge, Washington, Buffalo, Cincinnati, and Cleveland (the most recent, 1953). In addition, it was performed twice in Europe—in 1889 in Frank van der Stucken's concert of American music at the Trocadéro Palace in Paris, where Julien Tiersot labelled it as of the *école allemande néo-classique*, and in 1903 during the Wagner festival in Berlin.

With this work, Paine continued his experiments with thematic unity begun in the *Spring Symphony*; as H. Wiley Hitchcock has observed, the Prelude "is quite Lisztian in its design and its thematic transformations."[17] It opens with a slow introduction, using bass recitative figures and brass fanfares (Example 13–54). A reiteration of the patterns effects a modulation from C minor to B major, preparing the Adagio, the first entrance of the theme (Example 13–55), which later recurs in the second chorus. The languid mood is shortlived, and increasing agitation accompanies a bass melody complementary to the theme (Example 13–56). A dynamic climax with quarter-note triplets soon diminishes to random string pizzicato chords and a soft timpani roll. With the *Allegro moderato* appears the most important transformation of the theme (Example 13–57), one that returns in the final chorus of the incidental music. Development of the theme is constant; among other transformations are a horn statement with a shift of accent (Example 13–58a) and an inversion (Example 13–58b).

After a pause, the original version of the theme returns, *Adagio*, this time in C major, with the passage doubled in length. The climax material from Example 13–56 recurs, followed by the timpani roll. At this point the original version utilized material from Example 13–57 to reach a quick conclusion, and the first chorus of the incidental music would follow after a pause. But for concert use Paine supplied a different ending, a 23-bar coda, which provides yet another transformation of the theme (Example 13–59). Through much of this part, a prevailing D-flat over the tonic pedal produces a strong Phrygian flavor.

An Island Fantasy, Op. 44

Scored for piccolo, 2 flutes, 2 oboes, English horn, 2 clarinets, 2 bassoons, 4 horns, 2 trumpets, 3 trombones, tuba, timpani, harp, and strings.

Two autograph manuscript full scores, plus another full score (copy) and parts in Houghton Library, Harvard University.

Score and 27 parts published by Breitkopf & Härtel, Leipzig, in 1907; score titled, *"Poseidon und Amphitrite" — Eine Meer-Phantasie. Symphonische Dichtung. — An Ocean Fantasy: Symphonic Poem.*

The following description appears in the score:

This work was suggested by the memory of summer days at the seaside amid the changing moods of ocean life, calm and sunshine, murmuring breezes and rippling waves alternately with surge and storm.

Copies: BPL, ESM, Fleisher, HMA, HMus, LC, NYPL.

An Island Fantasy was completed in the spring of 1888, and was premiered by the Boston Symphony Orchestra under Wilhelm Gericke on 19–20 April 1889. Six other performances occurred between 1890 and 1895 in Detroit, Chicago, New York, Worcester, and Boston. It was inscribed to artist J. Appleton Brown, whose two pastels depicting scenes from the Isles of Shoals inspired the composition. Louis C. Elson described the musical form, using information supplied by Paine:

. . . The principal section of the work is in one of the simpler "rondo" forms, containing two varied statements of the principal theme, two elaborate episodes and a coda. To this is prefixed an introduction in which fragments of the themes, elaborated later on, are used as the foundation of music which depicts in a masterly manner the summer sunshine and calm and the summer storm, which are the contrasted subjects of Mr. Brown's paintings.[18]

The introduction begins in G-sharp minor with a cello melody whose opening ascending fourths anticipate the main theme of the rondo (Example 13–60). In fact, the main theme soon appears, sounded by the horn in m. 5 as a countermelody. Fragments of both themes recur as the orchestration becomes increasingly elaborate and the tonality shifts to B major, E major, and A major. At this point rhythmic momentum increases, tonal stability decreases, and the summer storm ensues (Example

13–61). At the close of the final surge, a half cadence in G-sharp minor leads to the rondo, with its main theme in A flat, sounded by muted cellos under undulating muted strings (Example 13–62). In consequent phrases woodwinds are added to the melody; a repeat of the theme adds violas and horn to the theme and harp arpeggios to the string background. A sudden recurrence of the storm material, followed by cadenzas for harp and violin, provides a transition to the first episode, a delicate ornate pastoral theme (Example 13–63). A modulation to B major leads again to the storm, this time with some new thematic material (Example 13–64); it returns the listener to the main theme in A flat. The English Horn and French Horn sing the melody in unison, and the harp receives a more prominent accompanimental part. Woodwinds are added to the melody in the consequent phrases, which modulate to B major, and the repetition of the theme (in B) combines English Horn, French Horn, and cello, with added accompanimental decoration in the flutes. A last surge of the storm, more severe than the preceding ones, leads to the second episode, an intense recitative for solo clarinet (Example 13–65). An abbreviated reference to the main theme leads directly to the coda, based on the main theme and built entirely around a 36-bar tonic pedal point. Many chromatically altered chords, including German and French 6ths, are alternated with tonic chords, often with added 6ths (Example 13–66).

Lincoln: a tragic tone poem (unfinished)
> Autograph manuscript full score and piano score in Houghton Library, Harvard University; autograph manuscript full score in Music Division, Library of Congress. Unpublished.

Paine was at work on this tone poem in October 1904.[19] According to an April 1906 note he was "finishing" it at that time,[20] although what amount remained to be composed cannot be known. Paine's later orchestral compositions continued to make effective use of the orchestra, requiring a larger group of performers and achieving increased variety in timbre. Cyclic form and thematic transformation replaced classical designs as the predominant methods of formal organization. Harmonically, his vocabulary became more current, with eclipsed progressions, root movement by thirds, and non-functional chromatic harmony much more in evidence. But the rhythmic, melodic, and harmonic traits that marked Paine's individuality in his earlier works are equally visible here, and the inspiration and careful craftsmanship of these works argue strongly for their study and performance.

Example 13–1.   *Symphony No. 1,* First movement, measures 193–201; two-stave reductions by the present writer.

Example 13–2.   *Symphony No. 1,* First movement, measures 1–6.

Example 13–3.   *Symphony No. 1,* First movement, measures 31–37.

Example 13–3   (continued)

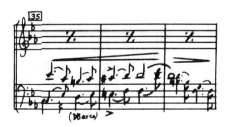

Example 13–4.   *Symphony No. 1,* First movement, measures 71–77.

Example 13–5.   *Symphony No. 1,* First movement, measures 124–127.

Example 13–6.   *Symphony No. 1,* First movement, measures 352–359 (string and horn
             parts omitted).

Example 13–7.   *Symphony No. 1,* Second movement, measures 1–11.

Example 13–8.   *Symphony No. 1,* Second movement, measures 276–291.

Example 13– 8   (continued)

Example 13–9.   *Symphony No. 1,* Third movement, measures 1–9.

Example 13–10. *Symphony No. 1,* Third movement, measures 33–36.

Example 13–11. *Symphony No. 1,* Third movement, measures 48–51.

Example 13–12.   *Symphony No. 1,* Third movement, measures 61–64 (clarinet, bassoon, and string parts omitted).

Example 13–13.   *Symphony No. 1,* Fourth movement, measures 1–9.

Example 13–14.   *Symphony No. 1,* Fourth movement, measures 47–54.

Example 13–14   (continued)

Example 13–15.   *Symphony No. 1,* Fourth movement, measures 86–95.

Example 13–16.   *Symphony No. 1,* Fourth movement, measures 110–115.

Example 13–17.   *Symphony No. 1,* Fourth movement, measures 235–242. (Clarinet 8va
                   lower; string parts omitted).

Example 13–18.   *Symphony No. 1,* Fourth movement, measures 254–256. (Flute 8va higher;
                   clarinet, bassoon, string parts omitted).

Example 13–19.   *Symphony No. 1,* Fourth movement, measures 515–523.

Example 13–19   (continued)

Example 13–20.   *As You Like It,* measures 5–12.

Example 13–21.   *As You Like It,* measures 22–23.

Example 13–22.   *As You Like It,* measures 57–67.

Example 13–23.   *As You Like It,* measures 85–87.

Example 13–24.　*As You Like It,* measures 97–102.

Example 13–25.　*Tempest,* measures 1–5 ("Storm").

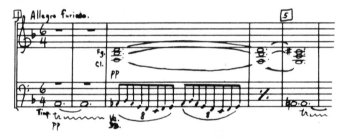

Example 13–26.　*Tempest,* measures 11–13 ("Storm").

Example 13–27.   *Tempest*, measures 21–22 ("Storm").

Example 13–28.   *Tempest*, measures 123–128 ("Prospero's Cell").

Example 13–29.   *Tempest*, measures 179–187 ("Prospero's Cell," "Ariel").

Example 13– 29   (continued)

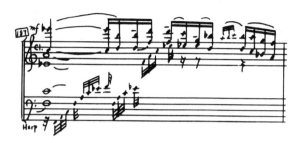

Example 13–30.   *Tempest,* measures 194–201 ("Prospero's Tale").

Example 13–31.   *Tempest,* measures 205–207 (''Prospero's Tale'').

Example 13–32.   *Tempest,* measures 244–251 (''Prospero's Tale'').

Example 13–33.   *Tempest*, measures 276–283 ("Ferdinand & Miranda").

Example 13–34.   *Tempest*, measures 302–303 ("Ferdinand & Miranda").

Example 13–35.   *Tempest*, measures 313–317 ("Ferdinand & Miranda").

Example 13–35   (continued)

Example 13–36.   *Tempest,* measures 368–369 ("Caliban").

Example 13–37.   *Tempest,* measures 404–407.

Example 13–38.   *Tempest,* measures 534–537 ("Triumph").

Example 13–39.   *Spring Symphony,* First movement, measures 11–14.

Example 13–40.   *Spring Symphony,* Second movement, measures 90–120.

Example 13–40   (continued)

Example 13–41.   *Spring Symphony,* First movement, measures 73–91 (principal theme).

Example 13–41   (continued)

Example 13–42.   *Spring Symphony,* "Winter" theme and motives.
a. First movement, measures 1–9.

Example 13–42   (continued)
b. Measures 46–49.

c. Measures 54-55.

d. Measures 276–282.

e. Measures 472–475.

f. Second movement, measures 92–94.   g. Measures 239–242.

Example 13–42   (continued)
h. Measures 280–285.

i. Third movement, measures 11–12.   j. Measures 16–18.

k. Measures 39–40.

l. Measures 87–91.

m. Fourth movement, measures 5–9.

n. Measures 19–20.

Example 13–43.   *Spring Symphony,* First movement, measures 139–152.

Example 13–44.   *Spring Symphony,* Fourth movement, measures 99–102 (1st violin part only).

Example 13–45.   *Spring Symphony,* Second movement, measures 1–23.

Example 13–46.   *Spring Symphony,* Third movement, measures 33–39.

Example 13–47.   *Spring Symphony,* Third movement, measures 72–77.

Example 13–47   (continued)

Example 13–48.   *Spring Symphony.*
a. Fourth movement, measures 60–64.

b. Fourth movement, measures 445–451.

Example 13–48b   (continued)

Example 13–49.   *Spring Symphony,* Third movement, measures 157–172.

Example 13–50.   *Spring Symphony,* Second movement, measures 311–332.

Example 13–51.   *Spring Symphony,* First movement, measures 18–24.

Example 13–52.   *Spring Symphony,* First movement, measures 179–188.

Example 13–53.   *Spring Symphony,* First movement, measures 38–42.

Example 13–53   (continued)

Example 13–54.   *Prelude, Oedipus Tyrannus,* measures 1–8.

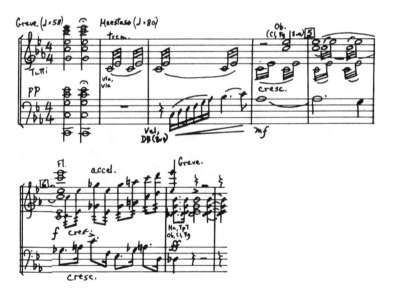

Example 13–55.   *Prelude, Oedipus Tyrannus*, measures 27–30.

Example 13–56.   *Prelude, Oedipus Tyrannus*, measures 38–44.

Example 13–57.   *Prelude, Oedipus Tyrannus,* measures 55–58.

Example 13–58.   *Prelude, Oedipus Tyrannus.*

a. Measures 79–80.

b. Measures 85–86.

Example 13–59.   *Prelude, Oedipus Tyrannus.*

a. Measures 149–154.

b. Measures 160–162.

Example 13–60.   *Island Fantasy,* measures 1–8.

Example 13–61.   *Island Fantasy,* measures 44–46.

Example 13–62.   *Island Fantasy,* measures 106–117.

Example 13–62   (continued)

Example 13–63.   *Island Fantasy,* measures 160–161.

Example 13–64.   *Island Fantasy,* measures 184–187.

Example 13–65.   *Island Fantasy,* measures 275–284.

Example 13–66.   *Island Fantasy,* measures 299–303.

14

Solo Songs

The art song seems to be a genre in which Paine was not widely involved, for only 11 songs may be numbered among his compositions. Yet, of these, eight were published, and some achieved a notable degree of popularity for their charm and are deserving of study and performance. They are well written for voice, expressive, lyrical, with interesting, effective accompaniments, and would afford a pleasant surprise to an audience of sensitive amateurs of the *Lied* or art song.

Four Songs, Op. 29.
    1. *Matin Song*
        Text: Bayard Taylor.
        Autograph manuscript in Boston Public Library.
        Printed in *Atlantic Monthly* XXXIX (January 1877), 110–11.
        Published by Oliver Ditson & Co., Boston, in 1879; reissued 1907. Included in Rupert
            Hughes (ed.), *Songs by Thirty Americans* (Ditson, 1904).
        Lower-key version (F major) issued 1889.
        Copies: BPL, HMA, HMus (low key), LC (+ 1907 ed.), PPL.
    2. *I wore your roses yesterday*
        Text: Celia Thaxter.
        Manuscript not extant.
        Published by Oliver Ditson & Co., Boston, in 1879.
        Copies: HMA, LC, PPL.
    3. *Early Springtime*
        Text: Rev. Thomas Hill.
        Autograph manuscript in Houghton Library, Harvard University.
        Published by Oliver Ditson & Co., Boston, in 1879.
        Copies: HMA, LC, PPL.
    4. *Moonlight—Mondnacht*
        Text: Joseph Eichendorff (German and English words; English translator not identified).
        Autograph manuscript in Houghton Library, Harvard University.
        Published by Oliver Ditson & Co., Boston, in 1879.
        Copies: HMA, LC.

    Matin Song was the most popular of Paine's songs, judging from contemporary records.[1] Clara Doria, accompanied by Ernst Perabo, gave the première performance at a 17 January 1877 Sanders Theatre subscription concert. The present author has learned of nine additional hearings between 1877 and 1905, including performances by Fanny Kellogg, Mrs. Otis Rockwood, Lillian Stoddard, Mrs. Anne Kennard-Martin, Paul Savage, and Harrison Bennett. When soprano Kate Percy Douglas included a Paine song on a 23 April 1897 New York recital of songs by 19 Americans,[2] most probably she chose the *Matin Song*.

The melodic line of *Matin Song* shows Paine at his best—sympathetic word setting, gracefully shaped phrases, and rhythmic variety, resulting, as William Treat Upton observed, in "great interest and spontaniety"[3] (Example 14–1). Two verses are set; the same music is used for both, with the exception of a few minor differences of text-setting, demonstrating Paine's sensitivity to the prosody of the lyric. Certain Paine characteristics or mannerisms are seen in this piece, including first-beat appoggiaturas or suspensions (see especially the freely resolved appoggiatura in measure 3, Example 14–1), the melodic turn (see m. 9), pedal point, plagal progressions, subdominant and supertonic chords borrowed from parallel minor (see mm. 3 and 5), and the raised supertonic resolving to the mediant (in the augmented dominant seventh chord in m. 10). The poem is set in regular 4-bar phrases, except for the last which is extended to five bars because of a long appoggiatura (Example 14–2). The cadence in the piano postlude is decorated with a dominant minor ninth and a dominant thirteenth, as well as raised fourths which emphasize a typical chromatic preparation for the fifth degree.

I wore your roses yesterday sets a poem by Paine's friend, Celia Thaxter. Upton pronounced it "delightfully lyric and graceful," and complimented the unobtrusive but attractive imitative effects in the piano accompaniment[4] (see Example 14–3 for the beginning measures). Two performances are known—George L. Osgood sang it on an Adamowski concert on 7 February 1881, and an unnamed singer included it on an Evanston, Illinois, Woman's Club program on 8 January 1901.

Two verses are set; the second is related musically to the first, but is extensively rewritten. Paine ends the first verse with a temporary feeling of C major, the major mediant key—an example of his fondness for key relationships by thirds. Phrase lengths are not as regular as in *Matin Song*, partially a result of text repetitions. There is not the emphasis on non-harmonic tones—pedal point, appoggiaturas, suspensions—that is found in some Paine compositions. The only prominent pedal point appears in the most evocative piano postlude (Example 14–4). Appoggiaturas are reserved for the final cadences of each verse, where they create temporary dominant thirteenth sonorities (see Example 14–7 for the end of verse 2). A melodic turn appears in measure 5 (see Example 14–3); in the same measure a raised supertonic in the melody results in an augmented dominant seventh. Other altered chords include a diminished seventh on the raised submediant, which embellishes a dominant seventh during the piano interlude between the two verses (Example 14–5). The most complex chromatic progression, in a perhaps overly dramatic setting of "defying all the storms of fate," incorporates a portion of the "omnibus" progression (Example 14–6). A far more appropriate rendering of the text is the delicate setting of "ev'ry thought of you a rose," with its emphasis on the supertonic key and its graceful vocal line (Example 14–7).

The manuscript of *Early Springtime* is dated 28 June 1866, placing its composition during the time when Rev. Thomas Hill, author of the text, was President of Harvard University. No performances are known, but contemporary authors have commented favorably on the song. Rupert Hughes called *Early Springtime* "most curiously original,"[5] and Henry T. Finck found it to have "a peaceful, almost religious character, suggesting the composer's sacred works."[6] Hill's text has a definite religious nature, for the final lines give an Easter connotation:

> "Death is but frost"
> Lo! the eternal Springtime of Heav'n shall come.

The text is prose, and is divided into two verses. Music for the two sections is similar, but the second is substantially rewritten. The tonality is unclear, shifting between C-sharp minor and E major. Both verses begin in the minor and end with a clear cadence in E major; however, the piano postlude concludes with an unresolved half cadence in C-sharp minor. The "religious" character may be observed at the beginning, where the absence of the raised leading tone in C-sharp minor gives a modal feeling (Example 14–8). Appoggiaturas or suspensions are absent, except for a single example at the end of the line, "Tender and sweet remembrance filling my heart gives me assurance" (Example 14–9). The subsequent measures, " 'Death is but frost,' " contain a startling progression including a second-inversion A-minor triad, suggesting a remote key but immediately contradicted by a dominant seventh in C-sharp minor. The somewhat exotic flavor of these three measures in heightened by the augmented second from C to D# in the vocal line.

The two verses of Eichendorff's *Mondnacht* are set to different music, save for the first line of each verse. The conception is quite different than that in Schumann's *Liederkreis*, Op. 39, except for the common key of E major. Both German and English words are given for Paine's song, although the German words fit the music far more gracefully. Some of the English version seems awkward (see the portion in Example 14–11), and the distribution is different in sections with repeated lines, with excessive repetitions of some English lines and a resulting tendency toward monotony. No performances are known, although doubtless many singers included this song and others by Paine on recitals that were not covered in the press. Finck found *Moonlight* "charming."[7]

The opening of the song is straightforward and lyric, although the submediant cadence at the end of the first phrase is surprising (Example 14–10). Phrase structure is regular in the first verse. However, the second verse soon makes use of text repetition, chromatic progressions, melodic sequence, and an avoidance of internal cadences to build to a climax and conclusion over a 16-bar span; the final portion is given in Example 14–11. Chord progressions in this passage are often the result of chromatic voice leading or enharmonic spelling, rather than traditional harmonic logic. After diatonic triads are reached in measure 39, interest is sustained by the syncopation of 2nd-beat accents. Two favored clichés, the melodic turn and a momentary dominant thirteenth, appear at the cadence.

Spring
    Text: Author unknown.
    Autograph Manuscript in Houghton Library, Harvard University.
    Unpublished.
The fountain. Song: "A Spring in the desert I found"
    Text: G. P. Lathrop.
    Autograph manuscript in Music Division, Library of Congress.
    Unpublished.
The clover blossoms kiss her feet
    Text: Oscar Laighton.
    Autograph manuscript in Houghton Library, Harvard University.
    Unpublished.

Spring, written in A flat and beginning with the words, "Gentle Spring! in sunshine clad," was dated, "Aug. 9, 1869, Constableville, N. Y." It is identified as Op. 20, No. 6 in a hand other than Paine's— apparently an error, for Op. 20 was assigned to the oratorio, *St. Peter*. Perhaps "Op. 29, no. 6" was intended, for *Spring* dates from a time similar to *Early Springtime* and *Mondnacht*, the only songs from Opus 29 whose dates of composition are known.

The Fountain was composed around 1878. *The clover blossoms kiss her feet* is dated 1 October 1882, and sets a text by Oscar Laighton, brother of Celia Thaxter and a manager of the Appledore House on the Isle of Shoals, where the Paines often vacationed.

No performances of any of these three songs are known.

Four songs, Op. 40

1. *A bird upon a rosy bough*
   Text: Celia Thaxter.
   Manuscript not extant.
   Published by Arthur P. Schmidt & Co., Boston, in 1884.
   Copies: HMA, LC, PPL.
2. *A farewell*
   Text: Charles Kingsley.
   Manuscript not extant.
   Published by Arthur P. Schmidt & Co., Boston, 1885.
   Copies: HMus, Summy.
3. *Beneath the starry arch*
   Text: Harriet Martineau.
   Manuscript not extant; measures 1–13 reproduced in Louis C. Elson, *The History of American Music*, 168.
   Published by Arthur P. Schmidt & Co., Boston, 1885.
   Copies: HMA, HMus.
4. *Music when soft voices die*
   Text: Percy Bysshe Shelley.
   Manuscript not extant.
   Published by Arthur P. Schmidt & Co., Boston, 1885(?).

A bird upon a rosy bough is a setting of a two-verse poem by Celia Thaxter; both verses use essentially the same music except for the concluding parts. Upton found interesting the "rich and sonorous piano score"[8] and Finck recalled "dainty touches."[9] Hughes found the song "old-fashioned," especially in the piano accompaniment, but "at times delicious."[10] No performances are known.

Phrase structure is regular in this song, except for the expected extensions in the last phrase of each verse. The first verse ends with a cadence in the mediant key, another example of Paine's emphasis on key relationships at the interval of a third, rather than a fifth. Typical Paine mannerisms may be observed, including appoggiaturas, suspensions, dominant thirteenths, and the melodic turn, all of which may be seen in the final seven bars (Example 14–12). This ending contrasts markedly with the playful introduction and beginning of the song (Example 14–13). Chromatic alterations at the conclusion depicted the phrase "in sobbing cadence"; a similar passage treating the line, "while sweet as love and sad as death," includes a portion of the "omnibus" progression (Example 14–14).

A farewell is quite brief—only 19 bars. The text is set strophically, and the music is repeated for the second verse. Appoggiaturas or suspensions regularly end each four-bar phrase, and the cadences at the end of the vocal part and the piano postlude both include dominant thirteenth sonorities. The opening phrase begins with a 4-note pentatonic figure

(Example 14–15), and a subsequent phrase is also basically pentatonic (Example 14–16). The only known performance was by George J. Parker on an Arthur Foote concert in Chickering Hall, Boston, on 15 March 1887.

    Beneath the starry arch is a setting of a three-verse poem; verses 1 and 2 are set strophically, while different music is provided for verse 3. Regular phrases are found except at the end of the last verse, where text repetition and chromatic progressions delay the final cadence (Example 14–17). The opening melody is pentatonic, except for an A-flat (Example 14–18). Accented non-harmonic tones are numerous, as at "resteth" and "arch" (chordal) in the above example and at the final cadence in Example 14–17. In the piano introduction (see Example 14–18) may be seen a melodic turn, as well as the lowered submediant, borrowed from the parallel minor as a color device. In measure 14 the prevailing accompaniment pattern is interrupted, and staccato chords punctuate "Hark to the foot fall"—an unexpected depiction of the text (Example 14–19).

    No copies of *Music when soft voices die* seem to exist. The major libraries with Paine collections, including the Library of Congress, do not possess it. Contemporary writers did not mention it, and no performances are known. One almost begins to question its very existence after encountering lists of Paine compositions such as that contained in John D. Chaplin (ed.), *Cyclopedia of Music and Musicians* (1890), which lists only three songs in Opus 40.

Example 14–1.   *Matin Song*, measures 1–11.

Example 14–2.   *Matin Song,* measures 34–42.

Example 14–3.   *I wore your roses yesterday,* measures 1–5.

Example 14–3 (continued)

Example 14–4. *I wore your roses yesterday,* measures 56–60.

Example 14–5. *I wore your roses yesterday,* measures 26–27.

Example 14–6.   *I wore your roses yesterday,* measures 33–37.

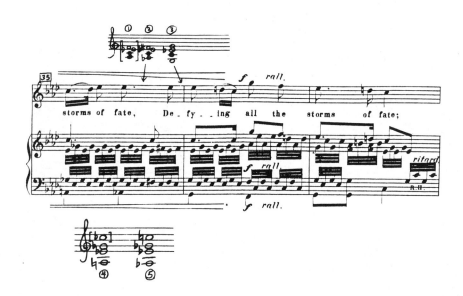

Example 14–7.   *I wore your roses yesterday,* measures 47–54.

Example 14–8.   *Early Springtime,* measures 5–7.

Example 14–9.   *Early Springtime*, measures 25–30.

Example 14–10.   *Moonlight*, measures 1–5.

Example 14–11.   *Moonlight,* measures 33–43.

Example 14–12. *A bird upon a rosy bough,* measures 38–44.

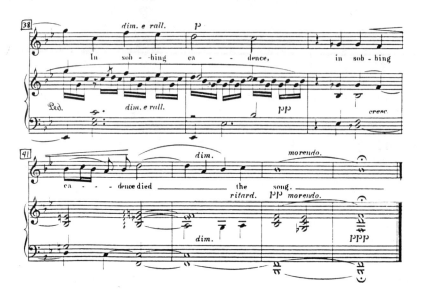

Example 14–13. *A bird upon a rosy bough,* measures 1–5.

Example 14–14.   *A bird upon a rosy bough,* measures 14–17.

Example 14–15.   *A farewell,* measures 1–4.

Example 14–16.   *A farewell*, measures 6–8 (vocal part only).

Example 14–17.   *Beneath the starry arch*, measures 34–44.

Example 14–17   (continued)

Example 14–18.   *Beneath the starry arch,* measures 1–7.

Example 14–19.   *Beneath the starry arch,* measures 14–15.

15

Choral Music

Agnus Dei (1861)
Benedictus (1861)
    Manuscripts not extant.
    Unpublished.

The *Agnus Dei* (1861) and *Benedictus* (1861) are the earliest known of Paine's compositions for vocal ensemble. Soon after he returned to America from his studies in Berlin in 1861, a report appeared mentioning his compositions,

> . . . among them an "Agnus Dei," composed in the strict church style, for the choir of the first parish in Portland, as remarkably fine.[1]

In September, before moving to Boston, Paine gave a farewell concert at the First Parish Church in Portland, and the choir performed both his "Benedictus" and the "Agnus Dei."[2] Later, in Boston on 1 November, Paine gave a concert in Tremont Temple, and among his own compositions was performed the Vocal Quartette, "Agnus Dei." According to reviewer "B—," it "showed marks of skill and severe study."[3] No further performances of either are known except for the inclusion of the "Benedictus" on a 15 January 1864 concert that Paine gave at Boston's Music Hall.[4]

There is a possibility that Paine incorporated these movements into his *Mass in D*, completed in 1865, which may explain why they were not published by themselves and why their manuscripts do not exist. But unfortunately, no descriptions survive in published reviews to serve as a basis for comparison, although both movements in the *Mass in D* require a 4-part ensemble, as do the 1861 movements.

Hymn for Commencement
    Text: James Bradstreet Greenough.
    Manuscript not extant.
    Published privately in 1862; a sextodecimo copy is in the music collection of the Library of Congress.

Published by A. P. Schmidt, Boston, in 1883; included in *Music Sung by the Alumni at the Two Hundred and Fiftieth Anniversary of the Foundation of Harvard University, November Seventh, 1638–1886*, published by Schmidt in 1886.
Copies: BPL (1885 broadside), HMA, LC, NYPL (in collection), Summy.

Paine's *Harvard Hymn* was a setting of a Latin text by James Bradstreet Greenough, later a Professor of Latin at Harvard from 1883. It became a traditional part of annual commencement ceremonies at Harvard, and was sung as a *Commemoration Hymn* during the 250th anniversary observance in 1886. The tune has appeared in several Protestant hymn books.

The tune is sturdy, consistent with other Paine hymn-type melodies. A pentatonic influence may be seen in the opening bars (Example 15–1). Notable are Paine's inclusion of non-dominant seventh chords (measures 3, 5), incomplete ninth chords (measures 9, 13), and a complete ninth chord (measure 7).

Domine salvum fac Praesidem nostrum, Op. 8

Autograph manuscript full score in Houghton Library, Harvard University. Another manuscript at Boston Public Library.
Vocal score published by Harvard University Press, Cambridge, in 1915; piano accompaniment arranged by Arthur Foote.
Copies: BPL (full), BU (vocal), HMA (full; vocal), HMus (vocal).

Domine salvum fac was composed for the inauguration of Thomas Hill as President of Harvard University on 4 March 1863 at the First Parish Church (Unitarian), Harvard Square. Paine directed the choir—comprised of the college choir and members of the Harvard Musical Association—and the Germania Orchestra in the performance. Seven years later the work was repeated at the inauguration of Charles William Eliot as Harvard's next president, on 19 October 1869. One additional performance is known, at a 28 March 1863 concert at Chickering Hall to raise funds to distribute Francis J. Child's *War Songs for Freemen* among members of the Union Army. Paine conducted the same 30-voice choir and the Germania Orchestra; the opening words were changed to "Domine, salvum fac Patriam nostram."

Paine's inauguration anthem sets the following traditional ceremonial Latin text:

Domine salvum fac Praesidem nostrum. Et exaudi nos in die, qua invocaverimus te. Gloria Patri et Filio et Spiritui Sancto, sicut erat in principio et nunc et semper et in saecula saeculorum. Amen.[5]

The work opens in the style of a Handelian French overture, introducing a long phrase in the chorus, setting the first sentence of the text (Example 15–2). A second phrase leads by way of an accelerando to an *Allegro maestoso*, the main body of the work. The first sentence of the text is again set, but with word and phrase repetitions to fit with the two- and four-bar phrase structure faithfully adhered to (Example 15–3). A middle section, treating the second sentence of the text, provides several elements of contrast. A solo quartet begins the section, *piano* and *pianissimo* markings are given, and the key changes to D minor (tonic minor) and its relative major, F major; the quartet is unaccompanied during this last change of key. With the reentry of the chorus, different methods of text setting are used, including simultaneous treatment of two phrases in different voice parts, and assigning syllables to detached notes (Example 15–4). Following a climax, the material from Example 15–3 returns for the "Gloria patri," modified to reach a conclusive cadence at the close.

Funeral Hymn for a Soldier, Op. 14, No. 1
Minstrel's Song, Op. 14, No. 3
Peace, peace to him that's gone
The summer webs
> Autograph manuscripts of *Funeral Hymn, Peace . . .* , and *The summer webs* in Houghton Library, Harvard University.
> Autograph manuscript of *Minstrel's Song* in Music Division, Library of Congress.
> Unpublished.

These are short 4-part settings for unaccompanied male chorus. Only the *Minstrel's Song* is dated—"ca. 1863," not in the composer's hand—but doubtless the others are from the same period. The identity of Op. 14, No. 2 is not known; perhaps one of the latter two songs would belong there. No performances of any of these songs is known, but it may be assumed that they were sung by the college choir and the Harvard Musical Association.

Texts are set simply and homophonically in the main. Typical is the opening of *Funeral Hymn*, a hymn-like dirge in C minor (Example 15–5). A note on the manuscript, "Transpose to D minor," supports the assumption that the work was performed.

Radway's Ready Relief
> Manuscript not extant.
> Published in 1883 by the Apollo Club, Boston, "Copyright, 1883, by Davenport Bros."—
> a copy is in the Music Division, Boston Public Library. "Composed by Dr. Dolore."
> Reprinted by Oliver Ditson & Co., Boston; a copy of this printing is in Music Library, Harvard University.

Here is a mock pretentious setting of a testimonial for a patent medicine whose advertisements saturated the newspapers of the early 1860s. The following text reproduced the commercial message in its entirety:

> Twenty years of sleepless nights William Sydney Myers, Esq., of Havana, Cuba, the correspondent of the London Times, suffered with acute and chronic rheumatism. For five and twenty years he had not enjoyed one whole night's calm rest. He applied

> Radway's Ready Relief. It immediately gave him rest and secured him the first calm
> and undisturbed sleep during the twenty years. The continued use of Radway's Ready
> Relief cured him. Always ask for Radway's Ready Relief, take no other! Price per
> bottle twenty-five cents, utterly too cheap! And for sale everywhere by all apothe-
> caries in the land, including Chelsea Beach.

This composition, an unaccompanied partsong for male chorus, is full of
musical humor, using many conventions and clichés to set totally inappropriate or incongruous texts. The opening words are set to a bland
progression, perhaps melodramatically depicting the sameness of the
twenty-year period (Example 15–6). Following three repetitions of the
opening words, a change of tempo provides an animated setting of the
client's name, especially the word, "Esquire," pronounced in Yankee
fashion (Example 15–7). Soon afterward, the word, "Cuba," provides
the nonsense syllables to accompany an extended diversion, instrumental
in character, full of sequences and ending in a half cadence (Example
15–8). When the woeful details of Myers' ailment are disclosed, the music
becomes appropriately *doloroso* (Example 15–9). The staccato bass part
provides another instrumental effect. After a picture of "one whole night's
calm rest," a *vivace e con fuoco* section reports the application of the
famed remedy; a bass solo recitative gives the result of the treatment,
reminiscent of oratorio writing in works such as Haydn's *Creation* (Example 15–10). A return of the *vivace e con fuoco* and the music used for
"William Sydney Myers, Esq." leads to perhaps the greatest bit of humor
in this composition, a quotation of the closing section of Beethoven's
Egmont Overture (Example 15–11). A following portion of this parody
involves the tenors in a patter song figuration with the repeated words,
"ev'rywhere for sale by all apothecaries." The ending includes Beethoven's piccolo part; the Apollo Club edition indicates, "To be whistled," but the Ditson printings add, "or played by Piccolo Flute."

Paine wrote, in reply to an 1884 magazine inquiry, that he composed
Radway's Ready Relief in 1864 for some friends of his in Portland.[6] The
published scores give the year of composition as 1863. Its first performance was on 25 April 1883 by the Apollo Club, who repeated it the
following year. Other performances are known by organizations in Cincinnati, Albany, and New York, and John Fiske recalled an informal rendition at the Shoals.[7]

Soldier's Oath
   Text: C. T. Brooks.
   Manuscript not extant.
   Printed in program booklet, "Harvard College, Commemoration Day, July 21, 1865." A
      copy is in the Music Division, Library of Congress; another copy is bound into
      Sibley's Private Journal, unpublished manuscript in Archives Collection, Widener
      Library, Harvard University.

Commemoration Day, 1865, was held on the Friday of Commencement week to honor the 528 Harvard sons who had fought for the Union in the Civil War and to revere the memory of the 93 who had died. It was a festive day, opening with a service in the chapel, during which Paine led a 60-voice mixed choir and a 26-piece orchestra in four works, including the "Gloria" from his *Mass in D*. Later, there was a dinner under a large tent, with speeches, poems, music from the Gilmore Band, and three part-songs from a 30-voice male chorus led by Paine. The first song was Paine's *Soldier's Oath*, setting a 5-verse poem by Rev. Brooks. Following Massachusetts Governor Andrew's speech, the chorus sang Flemming's *Integer vitae*, but with new words for the occasion. Then came poems from Julia Ward Howe and Oliver Wendell Holmes, and speeches by Ralph Waldo Emerson, President Hill, and others, after which the chorus sang Holmes' "Union and Liberty," fit to Lvov's *Russian Hymn*. John Sullivan Dwight found Paine's *Soldier's Oath* to be "a spirited part-song," although all the chorus music

suffered from the vast size of the place, the pervading and distracting noises, and the insufficient numbers of the choir.[8]

Soldier's Oath demonstrates the skill that the 26-year-old musician had developed in producing interest and variety within a very limited format. The first nonpredictable device is a half cadence in the relative minor, D minor, at the end of measure 4. This does not provide the degree of punctuation that a cadence in the expected tonic key would, and consequently the music flows without break, as does the poetry. Unison octaves in measures 5–6 are a welcome contrast in texture, and boldly emphasize the words. Rhythmic imitation and a sequence figure in measures 9–11 provide yet another contrast. The music shows a kind of prototypical glee club sonority in terms of its TTBB medium and close harmony. It certainly is of a style distinct from SATB church harmony. Perhaps one distinction lies in the equality of the vocal duets or pairing. The entire 16 bars of this composition are given below (Example 15–12); the setting is strophic, and the remaining four verses are also sung to this music.

O bless the Lord, my soul
    Text: Isaac Watts.
    Manuscript not extant.
    Published by Boston Music Co., Boston (octavo no. 2567) in 1911.
    Copies: LC; photostatic copies may be obtained from the publisher.

It may be assumed that this anthem for men's voices was composed for the Harvard chapel choir. No performances are known.

Paine's skill in writing for a male chorus is seen in this straightforward tripartite setting of a Watts hymn text (Example 15–13). Characteristic features include parallel tenths, non-dominant sevenths, and a melodic turn. The middle portion provides contrast in texture—in part by using solo voices—and key area (A minor, C, and F), and the closing section is extended, building to a final *fortissimo*.

Mass in D, Op. 10
    Inscribed: "To my teacher and friend Herr August Haupt of Berlin."
    Autograph manuscript full score in Houghton Library, Harvard University; another
        manuscript copy (not in the composer's hand) in Music Division, Library of Congress.
    Piano vocal score and chorus parts published by Beer & Schirmer, New York, in 1866.
    Copies: BPL, Dart, HMA, HMus (+ chorus parts), LC, Mich, NECM, NYPL.

The *Mass in D*, the first of Paine's large scale works, was written for a large mixed chorus, solo quartet, orchestra, and organ, and takes nearly two hours to perform. It was completed in 1865, and on Harvard Commemoration Day, 21 July 1865, Paine conducted a 60-voice mixed chorus and a 26-piece orchestra in four numbers during the chapel service, including "a rich and stirring *Gloria* from a Mass which Mr. Paine has recently composed."[9] When the work was begun would be difficult to determine. There is a possibility, mentioned above, that the 1861 *Agnus Dei* and *Benedictus* were incorporated into the *Mass in D*; however, an analysis of the corresponding movements in the later work would not support such an assumption. The "Agnus Dei" of the *Mass*, written for soprano and alto duet with chorus, could easily be performed by a quartet, as was done in the 1861 performance. However, the movement is not complete in itself. It is written in B minor, but modulates to D near the end, and without a conclusive cadence—the final choral sonority is a first-inversion supertonic seventh chord—leads directly into the final movement, "Dona nobis," thereby not forming a satisfactory excerpt by itself. After a performance on 15 January 1864, Dwight remarked that Paine's 1861 *Benedictus*, "conforming more to the Catholic style than is his wont, has beauty . . ."[10] but made no mention of the very difficult *fiorature* that permeate the solo parts—especially the tenor—of this movement of the *Mass*. The effectiveness of this movement would suffer greatly in a performance by quartet and organ only, for the intricate violin solo would suffer in transcription, and the choral crescendo and fortissimo in the "Osanna" would be sacrificed.

American performances of the *Mass* during Paine's lifetime were limited to brief excerpts, the first being the "Gloria" mentioned above.

Three other movements, "Confiteor," "Quoniam," and "Dona nobis," were included on a 20 June 1866 concert at Appleton Chapel at Harvard, performed by a 16-voice chorus with organ accompaniment. Dwight published the following remarks:

> The chorus: *Confiteor* a part of the *Credo*, impressed us as learned, ingenious in treatment, both of voice parts and accompaniment, and full of strong religious confidence in tone,—free from what is commonplace, or dry, or feebly sentimental,—churchlike and not operatic. The *Quoniam*, a tenor solo, has some rather original phrases, while the whole melody is developed and sustained with so much grace and freedom, and was so beautifully sung, that it had to be repeated. We were most struck, however, by the power and beauty of the *Dona Nobis*, which the composer has treated gravely, and not in that light, almost playful operatic style in which so many Masses, those of Haydn and Mozart included, have indulged. The individuality of style was also marked. . . .[11]

The reviewer for the *Boston Musical Times* agreed with Dwight's assessment of the works, and added that the unaccompanied Confiteor, "with its peculiar rhythm, proved highly effective."[12]

On 16 February 1867 Paine conducted a full performance of his *Mass in D*, at the *Singakademie* hall in Berlin, with a chorus of over 200, Karl Liebig's 50-piece orchestra, and four soloists. The audience that filled the hall included Crown Princess Victoria and other members of the royal family. Paine had traveled to Europe the previous summer to prepare such a performance, and had to overcome the inertia of the Berlin musical establishment. Details surrounding this performance are discussed elsewhere in this study. After Paine returned to America, a performance was projected for 12 April 1868, to feature the Handel and Haydn Society, the Harvard Musical Association orchestra, and soloists; however, the subscription drive must have failed, for the performance never materialized. At least in part, this could have been owing to a lack of enthusiasm for the idealogy of a Catholic ritual. Certainly, for Paine, a Yankee Protestant, the Mass could not but have been an acquired taste and at a relatively late age. His *Mass in D*, however, was intended for concert performance; its length prevents it from being included within a liturgical context. Specific works that may have served as models or influences include Beethoven's *Missa Solemnis* and Mozart's *Requiem*, both of which he had opportunity to hear during his study in Europe, and Cherubini's *Requiem*, portions of which he conducted in performance at Harvard.

The *Mass in D* is divided into 18 numbers. No. 1, "Kyrie," begins with a short orchestral introduction based on a one-bar motive (Example 15–14); this passage soon leads to the first entrance of the chorus, a unison passage for altos and tenors, with the motive continuing in the orchestra (Example 15–15). A fugal section soon follows, *più mosso* (Example 15–16). The third and fourth entries of the subject, in soprano and bass, form a false stretto, and after a modulation to A minor, a three-voice false stretto is heard over a dominant pedal in that key. The fugal section does not return to the original key, modulating instead to F major and leading directly to the "Christe," opening with a sustained phrase in 4-part treble chorus over the original motive in the orchestra (Example 15–17). A climax is attained in the full chorus, *più moto*, with modulations to F minor and D flat and a half cadence in the original D minor. An orchestral interlude leads to the closing "Kyrie" section, which begins as in Example 15–15 above. Soprano and alto begin the exposition of the fugal section, a means of varying that Paine used consistently in this work. The fugue is extended with additional false strettos and increases in tempo. A recurrence of the opening motive in the orchestra, combined with homophonic textures in the chorus, results in a final cadence in D minor.

The *Gloria in excelsis Deo* text of the Mass is divided into four movements, a common treatment in a work of this scope. No. 2, "Gloria," for chorus, is organized according to a rondo design. The opening line is set homophonically, with broad choral phrases over a characteristic rhythmic motive in the orchestra (Example 15–18). Choral accents on the second beat of duple measures provide syncopation, and a more complex syncopation is seen in the orchestral transition leading to the "Et in terra pax" (Example 15–19). This section, in the dominant key, A major, provides contrast in meter and dynamics. Another orchestral interlude brings a return of the opening material, but in A major, for the "Laudamus te"; imitative entries accompany "Glorificamus te." The second contrasting section of the rondo begins with "Gratias"—a rather awkward melodic figure is assigned to the solo quartet (Example 15–20), in A minor. The chorus re-enters at the "Domine Deus," with a meter change to ^{2} and a *più mosso* indication. The mood becomes increasingly majestic and martial as the keys of C major, F major, and E minor are touched upon. With the setting of "Deus Pater omnipotens" (Example 15–21), this portion reaches an extended climax; a modulation to D major prepares a return to the opening material and the words, "Domine Fili." An accelerando and new material for "Filius Patris" help produce intensification for the coda and the final plagal cadence.

"Qui tollis," No. 3 of the *Mass*, in G minor, is written for Alto solo and 8-part chorus. The chorus is used primarily to respond to the solo passages, as with the words, "misere nobis," and often is used as a 4-part male or 4-part treble chorus. Cello and violin solos are prominent, as may be seen in the opening bars (Example 15–22). The organ is used to accompany the chorus or the instrumental solos, as well as in dialogue with the orchestra. Such a passage may be seen in the second of the three implorations, which is set for chorus without soloist (Example 15–23). The "miserere" is accompanied by organ, and punctuated by orchestral chords. Some chromatic trickery is heard here: in measure 51 the listener would expect a half cadence in B flat, with a return to the chord heard on the first beat of measure 50; instead, a C-major triad appears. The pattern is repeated a fifth higher in the following three bars. A climax soon occurs and a long D pedal point prepares G minor and a return of the first material for "Suscipe deprecationem" in the Alto solo; the chorus answers with an extended "miserere."

No. 4, "Quoniam," for tenor solo, displays a formal plan common to other solo numbers in this *Mass*. The movement opens with an orchestral introduction, later repeated literally for a coda. The vocal portion is three-part, ABA, with the third section modified and extended; there is no thematic relationship between the orchestral beginning and the remainder of the movement. Writing for the voice is lyrical and broad (Example 15–24). In the central section there is an increase in dynamics, along with a *poco agitato* marking. A subsequent passage contains florid writing, *ad libitum*, over sustained chords in the orchestra. Two high A's occur, both in settings of "altissimus." Writing throughout is sympathetic and showy for the tenor soloist, and one may understand the audience's wish for an encore at the 1866 performance of this movement.

The conclusion of the *Gloria in excelsis Deo*, "Cum sancto spiritu," No. 5, opens with a solemn trumpet fanfare and a single triad in the chorus—unaccompanied except for an organ pedal—swelling from pianissimo to forte and back and intensifying with divided parts in the upper voices (Example 15–25). A slow progression of chords eventually reaches the key of D major and the "In gloria Dei Patris," set as an energetic fugue. The alto is the first to announce the subject, and proceeds to a counter-subject against the soprano answer (Example 15–26). Following the exposition and other miscellaneous entries of the subject, a lengthy episode introduces two motives, a scalar ascending whole-note figure and a one-bar eighth-note pattern on "amen," both of which are combined in Example 15–27. A second exposition—really, a "recapitulation"—follows the long episodic section and a rather static 10-bar whole-note organ transition. Voice order is changed in this second exposition—the tenor is answered by the alto—and it starts in C major, but by the third statement, in the bass, the original key of D major is regained. The ending is extended and intensified with pedal points, dramatic pauses, and homophonic writing for the chorus.

Numbers 6 through 12 are settings of portions of the *Credo*. No. 6 is in a rounded design, beginning with an energetic figure in B flat (Example 15–28); homophony is alternated with incidental imitation. With the words, "factorem coeli," the passage is repeated, although substantially modified to fit the text. A pianissimo setting of "et invisibilium" modulates to F major and a flowing imitative passage, "et in unum dominum, Jesum Christum," in ⁶ meter (Example 15–29). Sustained choral sounds for "et ex patre natum," accompanied by moving quarters in the orchestra, begin a modulation to D flat. An 11-bar orchestral interlude elaborates an A-flat dominant seventh chord, and a *crescendo* and *accelerando* prepare for a change of mood. "Deum de Deo" is given a bright, triumphant setting, with the chorus set high in close structure (Example 15–30). With no decrease in intensity, the key shifts through F minor to a half cadence in B flat, at which point the tempo and dynamics relax, and the opening material returns for "genitum non factum." The movement ends softly, and with a slow harmonic rhythm, with the words "descendit de coelis"; a single B flat is held into the next movement.

"Et incarnatus," number 7 of the *Mass*, is a soprano solo. As in the earlier "Quoniam" for tenor, this movement begins with an orchestral introduction, later repeated as a coda, and the solo portion is tripartite. The melodic line throughout is subdued and broadly flowing, with regular phrase articulations (Example 15–31). The words, "et homo factus est," do not receive unique treatment, as in many Mass settings, but are fitted to the return of material from Example 15–31. A two-bar interlude proceeds directly to the "Crucifixus," No. 8, a fugue in C minor for chorus. Its very chromatic subject is consistent with traditional settings of this text (Example 15–32)—a strong precedent for chromaticism in this section is seen in the "Crucifixus" from Bach's *Mass in B Minor*. Chromaticism is also seen in measures 3–6, "etiam" in the bass part, which functions somewhat as a countersubject. The exposition ends with a slight pause, and an intensely chromatic episode follows, temporarily evading a feeling of tonality before progressing to E flat (Example 15–33). Additional statements of the subject in E-flat minor, B-flat minor, and A-flat minor lead to a contrasting section in E-flat major, primarily homophonic, at a quicker tempo. A "recapitulation" of the exposition follows, with redistribution of the voices: alto and soprano begin the section. After the fourth entry, in the bass, a homophonic treatment of individual phrases causes a shift of accents, suggesting four bars of $\frac{3}{2}$ instead of three of $\frac{4}{2}$ (Example 15–34). The closing phrase ends in a C major tonic triad.

"Et resurrexit," No. 9, provides the expected sharp contrast with a rhythmic, animated subject in C major and triple meter (Example 15–35). The music becomes smoother and more flowing at the words, "et ascendit," and a rhythmic figure with an eighth and two sixteenths becomes more prominent. Momentum increases at the words, "sedet ad dexteram

Patris," and builds to a climax, *poco più Allegro*, at "cum gloria." With "vivos et mortuos" a decrescendo ensues—the last "mortuos" is sung pianissimo—but an orchestral fanfare builds again and leads to a recapitulation of the opening material for the words, "cujus regni non erit finis," never allowing the excitement generated in this movement to diminish until the last orchestral fanfare.

Great contrasts may be seen in the bass solo, "Et in spiritum sanctum," Number 10, between gentle legatos and angular fortissimo passages with dotted-note figures. There seems to be little of the text implied in the music. Perhaps this was one of the movements that prompted Berlin critic Alexis Hollaender to write:

> The Mass made a much more unfavorable impression in regard to its poetic conception. The individual parts of the Mass are characterized only in a most general way. The composer has taken them as subject matter for just so many pieces of music, . . . without showing any poetic individuality. . . .[13]

Vocal writing in this movement is quite difficult, especially in the disjunct passage seen in Example 15–36.

"Confiteor," No. 11, for unaccompanied chorus, was one of the three movements performed on the 1866 Appleton Chapel concert, where it was warmly received. The four voice parts are written independently, and there is close imitation throughout (Example 15–37). The polyphony does not follow the Palestrina model, but rather is merely figurated homophony, with four- and eight-bar phrases clearly articulated throughout. It is, however, "churchlike and not operatic,"[14] and on an equal standing with many other unaccompanied 19th-century motets.

Paine did not use fugue or canon in the opening "Credo" to depict musically the act of following a creed. But in the closing movement of this part, "Et vitam venturi," No. 12, he did turn to such a technique, producing a lengthy double fugue to end this third of the composition. An orchestral *intermezzo* at first provides a transition from the "Confiteor," modulating from E minor to D, and gradually increasing in tempo and dynamics. The two subjects are first announced in tenor and bass (Example 15–38) and throughout the movement are always sounded together. A stretto between the tenor-bass and soprano-alto, using abbreviated versions of the double subjects, gives added contrapuntal interest. Final statements of the double subjects alternate with homophonic passages and are given *fortissimo* by the chorus and full orchestra, growing to a resounding climax.

Four movements are allotted to the *Sanctus et Benedictus* portion of the Mass. No. 13, "Sanctus," is set quietly and slowly. A dotted-note figure predominates, and the organ is used to accompany the chorus

(Example 15–39). At the close, the key of D major suddenly gives way to a half cadence in B, and an orchestral transition leads directly to "Pleni sunt," No. 14, in B major, a chorus full of animation, especially in the accompaniment (Example 15–40). It is three-part (ABA) in design, and the closing section changes to the minor mode, simplifying a modulation to D major in an orchestral transition to the next movement. "Osanna," No. 15, is the final example of a choral fugue in Paine's *Mass*. Unlike those appearing earlier in the work, the subject used here requires a tonally modified answer, rather than an exact, "real" repetition of the subject (Example 15–41). Toward the close, the usual "recapitulation" exposition is found, with soprano and alto parts exchanged with tenor and bass. A four-part stretto precedes a sonorous conclusion.

The "Benedictus," No. 16, for quartet and chorus, contains a very intricate, ornate melodic style, first displayed in an opening passage for solo violin (Example 15–42). The first of the three sections of this movement begins with a soprano solo, showing a similarly decorated melodic line (Example 15–43); the other soloists then enter, followed by chorus, *più mosso*, with a modulation to E major. The alto soloist begins the second part in the new key, but with basically the same music as the first part. Again the remainder of the quartet enters, modulating back to G, and after a passage by the chorus, an orchestral transition leads to the third part, another repetition. This features the tenor soloist, with some exceptionally difficult coloratura passages (Example 15–44). The quartet concludes this statement of the sentence. For the "Osanna," Paine did not choose to repeat the earlier movement, but instead continued the mood of the Benedictus without any break. The chorus enters at this point, and the solo violin is featured as at the beginning. The final "in excelsis" increases to a *fortissimo* before fading to a *pianissimo* in the final bar.

"Agnus Dei," No. 17, is written for soprano-alto duet and chorus. A prominent bass line is heard throughout the movement; often, the vocal parts seem to grow out of this part (Example 15–45). The "Agnus Dei" would not seem to be particularly "churchlike"; rather, because of its strong rhythmic figures, it has the dramatic flair of an opera excerpt, or, at least, a similarity to religious works by predominantly operatic composers, such as Rossini's *Stabat Mater* or Verdi's *Requiem*. The "miserere nobis" that follows could easily have been written by one of these two composers (Example 15–46). There is not a conclusive ending to this movement; rather, a modulation to D and a supertonic sonority in the chorus lead directly to the final chorus, "Dona nobis," No. 18. To Dwight's relief, this was not written as a noisy, energetic climax to the work, as is found in many Classic and early Romantic Mass settings, such as Haydn's

Nelson Mass, *Harmoniemesse*, and *Heiligmesse*, and Mozart's *Corona-tion Mass*, but rather is a slow pastorale, with broad choral lines (Example 15–47); a similar mood is found in the "Dona nobis" of Beethoven's *Mass in C*. The predominant dynamic marking is *pianissimo*, and although there is one *fortissimo* peak, it soon diminishes, and the final measures in the orchestra soften to a *pianississimo*. The final 10 bars of the chorus (Example 15–48) show the skill and finesse of many Mendelssohn's choruses, as in the concluding portions of "Happy and blest are they," from *St. Paul*, and "He, watching over Israel," from *Elijah*.

St. Peter: An Oratorio. Opus 20.
  Text selected from the Bible, plus three Lutheran chorales.
  Autograph manuscript full score in Houghton Library, Harvard University.
  No. 5, *Choral*, "How lovely shines the Morning Star," and No. 35, *Chorus*, "This is the witness of God," included in *Music to be performed at the World's Peace Jubilee and International Musical Festival in Boston, June 1872*, published by Oliver Ditson & Company, Boston, in 1872.
  Vocal score published by Oliver Ditson & Company, Boston, in 1872.
  Copies: BPL, ESM, HMA, LC, Mich, NECM, NYPL, PPL, Smith, Tufts, Wellesley.

    St. Peter, hailed as "the first oratorio written on American soil,"[15] was the first major work of Paine's to be performed in his native country. His friend, John Fiske, wrote following the Portland première, somewhat extravagantly:

> This event is important, not only as the first appearance of an American oratorio, but also as the first direct proof we have had of the existence of creative musical genius in this country. . . . With the exception of Mr. Paine, we know of no American hitherto who has shown either the genius or the culture requisite for writing music in the grand style, although there is some of the Kapellmeister music, written by our leading organists and choristers [including Dudley Buck and Arthur Whiting], which deserves very honorable mention. . . . It must at least be said . . . that Mr. Paine's oratorio has fairly earned for itself the right to be judged by the same high standard which we apply to these noble works of Mendelssohn and Handel.[16]

William F. Apthorp, in discussing the Handel and Haydn Society performance in Boston in 1874, related his impressions of Paine's development as a composer since the *Mass in D*:

> As originality of matter and conception must sooner or later necessitate originality of form, we find that that mastery over musical form which Mr. Paine had so perfectly acquired, did not stand him in so good stead, as his original conceptions began to develop themselves, as it had while his aesthetic conceptions were more or less the reflex of other minds. Indeed, the old finished perfection of form began gradually to disappear from his compositions as the matter grew in strength and vitality. His power of completely realizing his conceptions has decreased. In fact, we may say that his ideal has slipped the leash, and that his life-work is henceforth to be a life-chase after it. And is this not one of the distinctions between the man of genius and

the man of mere talent? The man of talent always has his ideal where he can drop his pinch of salt upon it, take it in his hand and tangibly present it to the world; the man of genius follows his high ideal through life, ever drawing nearer to it, without winning it. . . .[17]

Paine began composing *St. Peter* in 1870, and had completed it by February 1872.[18] The first excerpts to be heard in public were sung by alto soloist Mrs. C. A. Barry, with piano accompaniment by Paine, at a 2 April 1872 New England Conservatory concert; included were No. 12, a recitative, "And lo! Judas came with a great multitude," and No. 18, air, "The Lord is faithful and righteous."[19] Two more excerpts, the Lutheran chorale, "How lovely shines the Morning Star" (No. 5), and a chorus, "This is the witness of God" (No. 35), were performed by the massed choir, orchestra, and organ on 17 June 1872, the opening day of Patrick Gilmore's World's Peace Jubilee; Paine conducted the excerpts before the crowd of some 50,000.[20]

The first of the two complete performances of *St. Peter* was given in Portland on 3 June 1873 by the Haydn Association. The 150-voice chorus was trained by Paine's first teacher, Hermann Kotzschmar, although Paine attended the last rehearsals and conducted the concert himself. The orchestra engaged was the Germania Orchestra, also known as the "Harvard Orchestra," for by that time it was sponsored by the Harvard Musical Association. Soloists were soprano Mrs. H. N. Weatherbee of Portland, and Bostonians Adelaide Phillipps, alto, George L. Osgood, tenor, and J. F. Rudolphsen, bass. The concert was given at the City Hall, and nearly 3,000 attended[21]—almost a tenth of the entire population of the city. The chorus was too small to render effectively the biggest climaxes, there was no organ, and the orchestral playing was quite ragged, but the concert was considered an overwhelming success.

On 9 May 1874 the Handel and Haydn Society performed *St. Peter* during its Third Triennial Festival at Music Hall, Boston. The chorus was more massive than that in Portland, the orchestra was far more skilled— having the Theodore Thomas orchestra as its nucleus—and the large Music Hall organ was used to add to the climaxes. Soloists were Mrs. Julia Houston West, soprano, Adelaide Phillips, alto, Nelson Varley, tenor, and J. F. Rudolphsen, bass; Carl Zerrahn conducted the performance. According to Dwight,[22] Rudolphsen performed the bass arias—those characterizing Peter—"for the most part with good effective style and just expression." Varley, "though suffering from fatigue apparently," sang "with fine expression." Dwight also complimented the soprano and alto soloists equally, although their arias "suffered somewhat for the want of more rehearsal with the orchestra." This last observation was repeated in his overall comment concerning the performance: "The choral part of the performance was excellent; but as a whole this work . . . needed more rehearsal with the orchestra.''

Much was written in contemporary reviews and essays about the great degree of originality displayed in *St. Peter*. To be sure, it shows far more craftsmanship than most American religious music of this era, while remaining free of many of the clichés dominating much of this literature. But Paine's oratorio shows the strong influence of its models, those of Bach and Mendelssohn. The influence of Bach seems strongest in the recitatives, especially those animated, dramatic passages that suggest similar places in the St. Matthew and St. John Passions. Mendelssohn is the dominant influence for the arias and choruses. Many textures, harmonic progressions, and melodic figures show a kinship to passages in *Elijah, St Paul*, or *Christus*. A number of arias and choruses in *St. Peter* are based on two contrasting ideas and are organized formally as ABA, ABAB, or ABAC—a plan common to many movements in Mendelssohn oratorios. Typical examples are "If with all your hearts" (ABA), "Blessed are the men who fear Him" (A, B, A+B)—both from *Elijah*—"Sagt es, die ihr erlöset seid" (ABAB) from *Lobgesang*, "He, watching over Israel" (A, B, A+B, C) from *Elijah*, and "There shall a star from Jacob shine forth" (ABAC) from *Christus*. The inclusion of traditional Lutheran chorales was a usual practice in the works of Bach, but these portions of *St. Peter* reflect the tradition more as it was adapted in the works of Mendelssohn.

The 39 numbers of *St. Peter* are divided into two parts. Part I includes "The Divine Call" (Introduction and Nos. 1–8) and "The Denial and Repentance" (Nos. 9–19); Part II continues with "The Ascension" (Nos. 20–26) and "Pentecost" (Nos. 27–39).

A 45-bar orchestral introduction begins Part I of the oratorio. Somber in mood, it contains frequent contrasts between slow, languid melodies, disjunct *fortissimo* passages, and lyric cantabiles. An opening horn statement provides a motive that recurs throughout the movement (Example 15–49). Toward the close, a series of modulations leads to the key of C, and this theme is transformed, first in the bass instruments, beginning in measure 35, then in the horns three bars later (Example 15–50). A gradual crescendo then leads—in an effect similar to that at the opening of *Elijah*—directly to the first chorus, "The time is fulfilled" (Example 15–51a), an overwhelming effect with an adequate number of performers. The majestic character of this opening is contrasted by the following passage in which the word "repent" is set to a descending diminished seventh (Example 15–51b), perhaps a gesture of humility. Both sections recur, outlining an ABAB plan, and the chorus ends quietly. A tenor recitative relating Jesus' call to Simon Peter and his brother, Andrew, is followed by No. 3, a soprano air, "The spirit of the Lord is upon me.''

The opening bars show a marked resemblance to Mendelssohn's style in its tonic pedal, appoggiaturas, and the tonic chord with lowered seventh in measure 6 (Example 15–52). The air is in two parts, with the second part of the text being set differently each time, resulting in an ABAC design.

No. 4, "We go before the face of the Lord," features a 12-voice male chorus, representing the 12 disciples. A melody first sung in unison by this chorus (Example 15–53) recurs several times during the number, in 4-part harmony by this chorus, by the full chorus, or in a combination of the two groups. The chorus is followed by No. 5, "How lovely shines the morning star." Paine's harmonization differs only in minor details from the versions found in many modern hymnals.

The scene surrounding the question, "Whom do men say that I am?" is treated in the recitative, No. 6. The first response, "Some say that thou art John the Baptist. . . ," is sung by the 12-voice male chorus. Later, Peter's "Thou art the Christ" receives special treatment (Example 15–54), as Fiske wrote, "powerfully rendered by the entrance of the trombones." Jesus' charge to Peter is set in a dramatic *recitativo accompagnato* similar in power to the Commendatore scene in Mozart's *Don Giovanni*, although related perhaps more closely to the Baal episode in *Elijah* and other similar writing in Mendelssohn's oratorios (Example 15–55). Peter's reaction to these events is set forth in the aria, "My heart is glad," No. 7, an attractive, singable melody in three-part design. Its accompaniment includes non-dominant sevenths, accented non-harmonic tones, and parallel tenths (Example 15–56). The scene closes with the chorus, "The Church is built upon the foundation of the apostles and prophets," No. 8. This opening text is set majestically, with a fanfare motif in the orchestra. A repetition of the text receives a contrasting setting, with dramatic changes in dynamics (Example 15–57). As in other choruses in this work, "The Church is built" is written along an ABAB design. The second section treats the following two-bar motive imitatively (Example 15–58). This not too promising motive is developed extensively to the degree that monotony is difficult to avoid; Dwight found it "light and frivolous, not worth the elaboration it receives."[23] Fortunately, both "B" sections end homophonically, with active orchestral accompaniments, and interest is regained.

Part I continues with "The Denial and Repentence." The scene at the Mount of Olives begins with a recitative, No. 9, that includes some quite dramatic writing for Tenor (Jesus) and Bass (Peter). A tenor arioso is interrupted at the words, "strengthen thy brethren," by an orchestral *agitato*, and Peter's words, "to prison and to death," show a graphic drop in range (Example 15–59). A tenor air, "Let not your heart be troubled" (No. 10), follows the scene. A subdued, contemplative number, it is in three parts, each of which begins with the same musical phrase (Example 15–60). This movement shows some strong features of Paine's style, including excellent accompanimental figuration (measure 10), non-dominant seventh and eleventh chords (measures 11, 12), parallel voice leading (measure 13), contrary motion between soprano and bass, and a basically pentatonic melody. Dwight called this movement "one of the sweetest and purest of all the Arias," but felt that there should have been "a little more repose in the accompaniment."[24] The air is followed by No. 11, "Sanctify us through thy truth," a graceful larghetto for quartet (Example 15–61); the full chorus appears in the middle section, and alternates with the quartet at the close.

Judas' betrayal of Jesus is related in an alto recitative, No. 12, "And lo! Judas come with a great multitude," one of the excerpts performed on the 1872 New England Conservatory concert. The use of string tremolo and chromatic chord progressions to depict turbulence is well within the traditions of operatic recitative (Example 15–62). Verses from Isaiah LIII make up the text for the following chorus, No. 13, "We hid our faces from him." The opening measures contain imitation (Example 15–63), perhaps conveying the fear and uncertainty felt by the disciples. The pentatonic subject and the short interval of imitation gives the flavor of a fuging tune. At the words, "he was despised," the texture changes abruptly to a forceful homophony (Example 15–64). A shift of accent suggests three measures of $\frac{3}{4}$ producing an effect similar to a Handelian hemiola; such a device also appeared in the "Crucifixus" of the *Mass in D* (see Example 15–34). With the words, "He was brought as a lamb to the slaughter," an *allegro* is reached, and the homophonic writing in the chorus, accompanied by constant dotted figures in the orchestra, suggest the influence of "Surely he hath borne our griefs" from *Messiah*. Both sections recur, in the expected ABAB design, and a strong Neapolitan harmony in the last portion enhances the archaic flavor (Example 15–65). The influence of Bach's crowd scenes in the Passions may be felt in the following recitative, No. 14, where Peter's denials of Jesus are answered by boisterous outbursts from the chorus (Example 15–66). Peter's deep remorse after realizing the significance of his disloyalty is portrayed in the orchestral "Lament," No. 15. An opening bass passage (Example 15–67) contains an *appoggiatura* sobbing pattern, which appears throughout the lament. A slight *accelerando* and *crescendo* lead to an emotional melodic figure (Example 15–68), which also recurs. The tonality of B-flat minor is deemphasized by an abundant use of chromatic progressions—perhaps this was "the new disease, the restlessness that leadeth nowhere, of the music of our day" that Dwight so deplored. Two separate climaxes are reached; the second, over a dominant (F) pedal, is followed by a diminuendo and half cadence, which proceeds without break into the bass air, "O God, my God, forsake me not!" (No. 16), in B-flat minor. Its expressive melodic line (Example 15–69), reminiscent of Chopin's *Waltz in A minor*, Op. 34, No. 2, caused it to be a favorite excerpt for bass singers. (One known performance was by George E. Holmes on an 8–9 April 1892 Chicago Symphony Orchestra concert that Paine attended.) The form is the usual ABAB; the first appearance of the contrasting section, in D minor (Example 15–70), demonstrates Paine's use of key relationships by thirds. This place in the oratorio recalls Elijah's aria, "It is enough," and the assuring comfort from a chorus of angels. Peter's cry of despair is answered by No. 17, Chorus of Angels, "Remember from whence thou art fallen," beginning with a passage for 4-part treble chorus, "to be sung by a small chorus of select voices." The voices are unaccompanied, and the requisite harp provides arpeggios between phrases (Example 15–71), with a modulation to the major mediant key. At a change to *allegro*, the full chorus enters with the words, "And he that overcometh shall receive a crown of life." An alto air, "The Lord is faithful," No. 18, features a solo cello obbligato. The opening alto melody is calm and flowing (Example 15–72A), contrasting with a more dramatic setting of "if we walk in the light"; the formal design is ABAC. Toward the close appears an incomplete appearance of the "omnibus" progression, a rare use of the chromatic harmonic formula at this stage of Paine's compositional career (Example 15–72B). Part I of the oratorio closes with the exciting chorus, "Awake, thou that sleepest," No. 19. Dramatic contrasts in texture and dynamics produce an arresting beginning (Example 15–73). The chorus must be strong enough here to hold its own against the orchestra, however. Fiske, in his review of the Portland première, complained that the unaccompanied choral sound in measure 5 was almost obliterated in the following bar at the entrance of the brass, rather than being reinforced and enriched, the intended effect that would have occurred with a much larger chorus. An effective fugal idea, highly acclaimed by reviewers, is used for the text, "The darkness is past," (Example 15–74) and forms the basis for the main part of the movement. With references to the opening motive and temporary modulations to B major, C major, and B-flat major, the chorus continued to build interest, giving a grand conclusion to this half of the oratorio.

Part II of *St. Peter* opens with a portrayal of "The Ascension." No. 20, a chorus, "The Son of man," begins with a somber melody for unison chorus (Example 15–75). "He was crucified" is set chromatically in 4 parts, with an accompaniment of soft brass chords. With the words, "and on the third day he rose again," the tempo changes abruptly to

allegro assai e giojoso, and a fanfare-like melody rises above fanfare figures in the trumpets. Following is the Lutheran chorale, No. 21, "Jesus,
my Redeemer, lives," whose harmonization is straightforward and traditional. Unfortunately, the one-bar introduction in divided strings and
similar interludes between phrases detract because of dated harmonic
clichés, such as overly rich successions of secondary dominant sevenths.
Next is heard the scene between Jesus and Peter, No. 22, with the three-
time question, "lovest thou me?" An arioso for tenor and bass uses sustained chords for Jesus and an agitated accompanimental pattern for Peter's responses. A soprano recitative, "And he lifted up his hands"
(No. 23), is accompanied by harp chords, with arpeggios at the words,
"and carried up to heav'n." The succeeding chorus, "If ye then be risen,"
No. 24, is in three parts, each of which is based on an ascending motive
first announced in the bass line of the orchestra. In the second part this
motive is treated in close imitation, and a brilliant orchestral accompaniment in the third part (Example 15–76) produces the climax for the movement. A soprano air, "O man of God" (No. 25), begins with a vigorous
theme (Example 15–77), doubtless requiring a powerful singer to perform
it effectively. In its middle section, which modulates to B major, the words
"eternal life" are set to extensive melismas or long held notes (Example
15–78); the quoted portion bears a resemblance to the Shaker melody,
" 'Tis the gift to be simple." The solo quartet that follows, "Feed the
flock of God" (No. 26) reveals an almost Mozartean treatment of the
voices (Example 15–79). Throughout the movement an English Horn and
a solo violin play prominent parts. They are heard first in the extensive
introduction (Example 15–80), whose syncopation Dwight found
"puzzling."

The final portion of the oratorio is entitled "Pentecost" and contains
some of its most colorful writing. Especially notable is the opening tenor
recitative, "And when the day of Pentecost was come" (No. 27). Dramatic orchestral writing dominates the passage, with abundant contrasts—in dynamics alone there are nine indicated changes from loud to
soft or vice versa within the 39 bars. The depiction of the "rushing wind"
is especially attractive (Example 15–81); the reduction from the piano
score can give only a pale idea of the full orchestral effect. Later, a
pianissimo marking for "Holy Ghost" produces a striking result (Example
15–82), while requiring great control from the soloist. This is followed by
a chorus, "The voice of the Lord," No. 28, which Dwight called "graphic
and impressive," and Fiske "mysterious." With its *allegro con fuoco*
tempo it possesses a forceful, driving character, beginning strong and
building to an early *fortissimo* climax. A second section is more subdued,
although without relaxation of tension, and with sudden changes in dy-

namics; perhaps this is one of Fiske's "mysterious" passages (Example 15–83). Other keys are reached, including the Neapolitan, F major, and the final portion of the ABAC design is in E, the parallel major. Another chorus soon follows, "Behold, are not all these who speak Galileans?" (No. 29). It is short (38 bars), primarily homophonic, and confined for the most part to its original key, B-flat major—an effective foil to the chorus just discussed.

Peter's final aria, "Ye men of Judea" (No. 30), a setting of the words of the prophet Joel, is in direct contrast with the lyricism and remorse of the two earlier arias, Nos. 7 and 16. The sternness and vehemence of the words are matched in the music, placing this aria in the same genre as "For he is like a refiner's fire" from *Messiah* and "Is not his word like a fire?" from *Elijah*. Following a *maestoso* introduction, the main portion of the aria begins *allegro moderato ma con fuoco*. Peter's quotation of Joel starts dramatically, punctuated by orchestral chords (Example 15–84). Momentum increases as the imagery appears in the text, and the orchestral writing becomes more animated as well (Example 15–85). Key changes are frequent in this passage, with the temporary tonal centers including B flat, A, F minor, D flat, E, and A. The first section then returns, in D minor, and with the words, "and every one that calleth on the name of the Lord shall be saved," the major mode predominates throughout the remainder of the movement. The contralto aria, "As for man," No. 31, is of a more contemplative nature. Its carefully shaped phrases are comfortable to sing, and the 9th-chord sonorities (see measure 5) and cadential appoggiaturas (see measure 6), though predictable, are aids to an expressive performance (Example 15–86). Word painting possibilities are not overlooked; the line of text, "for the wind passeth over it, and it is gone," is treated quite vividly (Example 15–87). Continued exhortation by Peter (recitative, No. 32) leads to a short chorus, *con moto ed energico*, "Men and brethren, what shall we do to be saved?" (No. 33). Peter's response, "Repent, and be baptised" (recitative, No. 34), uses the same descending diminished seventh for the word "repent" as was heard in the first chorus (see Example 15–51B). The disjunct line suggests similar recitatives in the works of Bach (Example 15–88). An *andante* melody is repeated and extended by the male chorus, the Twelve Disciples. This scene is concluded with the chorus, "This is the witness of God," No. 35, a cheerful work fashioned after the Mendelssohnian model in "Lord our Creator" at the conclusion of *Elijah*. The opening motive is treated imitatively (Example 15–89). A second motive appears in a contrasting section (Example 15–90) and also is used in imitation. The motives recur later in the chorus, and both are combined at the conclusion.

The remaining four numbers of the oratorio form an epilogue to the work. No. 36, Choral, "Praise to the Father," is a quotation of another Lutheran chorale, "Lobe den Herren den mächtigen König der Ehren." The translation employed is less familiar than those used in the other two chorales: it appeared in John Henry Hopkins' *Carols, Hymns and Songs* (1866).[25] Paine's harmonization is close to the usual hymnal versions; the prominence he gave to the harps in the orchestration seems inconsistent with the majestic character of the chorale. No. 37, "Now as ye were redeemed," combines the bass soloist (Peter), the male chorus (Twelve Disciples), and the full chorus in an elegant *andantino*, similar in mood to the quartet, No. 11, but richer in texture. A bright duet for soprano and tenor, "Sing unto God" (No. 38), is full of rhythmic momentum, attractive melodic motives, and imitation between the voices. Its orchestration appears to be light and colorful (Example 15–91). The horn fifths, syncopation, and pentatonic line not only sound very American, but actually appear in a waltz in Virgil Thomson's opera *The Mother of Us All*. The final chorus, "Great and marvellous" (No. 39), is appropriately majestic. It is sectional—the massive beginning (Example 15–92) alternates with imitative passages, one of which is unaccompanied. Several soft passages relieve the overwhelming dynamic level and enable the forces to build to a satisfying final cadence (a dominant ninth is used to avoid the cadential "cliché"). Paine's craftsmanship is very much apparent here, as it is throughout the oratorio. *St. Peter* is a very important milestone in American music and a successful work of art, despite some faults. It certainly is deserving of revival.

Centennial Hymn, Op. 27
> Text: John Greenleaf Whittier.
> Autograph manuscript full score at Houghton Library, Harvard University.
> Autograph manuscript score at Boston Public Library, (includes letters of Paine, W. D. Howells, and J. R. Hawley), a holograph at Sibley Library, Eastman School of Music.
> Score published by H. O. Houghton, Boston, in 1876. Republished as *Whittier's Centennial Hymn* by Oliver Ditson, Boston, in 1930. Vocal score with piano reduction (and without orchestral interpolations) published in *Atlantic Monthly* XXXVII (June 1876), 744–45, and in 10 May 1876 issue of *Philadelphia Inquirer*.
> Copies: BPL, ESM, HMA, LC (vocal; full), PPL.

Paine's *Centennial Hymn* was one of three works commissioned by Theodore Thomas for the opening ceremonies of the Centennial Exposition in Philadelphia on 10 May 1876; the other works were Dudley Buck's *The Centennial Meditation of Columbia*, a cantata setting a text by Sidney Lanier, and the *American Centennial March* by Richard Wagner, whose high fee and questionable ethics were the source of heated controversy. The ceremonies were held outdoors, with an 800-voice chorus, an orchestra of 150, and an H. L. Roosevelt pipe organ sounding from a nearby building. There were a number of additional performances during the centennial year, including ones in Boston, Groton, Portland, and Worcester. And the T. M. Carter band performed it in several popular concerts in Boston during the summers of 1876 and 1880.

The *Centennial Hymn* is a simple 24-bar strophic setting for the six verses of Whittier's poem. The harmonization is in four parts—the typical hymnal format. Its melody is much more syllabic than the earlier *Harvard Hymn*, which assigns many syllables to duplets. Melodic peaks are well controlled, with the highest occurring at the beginning of the last phrase (Example 15–93).

Oedipus Tyrannus of Sophocles. Music for Male Chorus and Orchestra, Op. 35
  Text by Sophocles, in Greek; English version also included (translator not identified).
  Autograph manuscript full score and parts in New England Conservatory of Music Library; autograph manuscript full score and 1st violin part in Houghton Library, Harvard University.
  Piano vocal score published by Arthur P. Schmidt, Boston, in 1881. Revised edition of piano vocal score published by Schmidt in 1895; reissued in 1908. Orchestral score published by Schmidt in 1908. (*Prelude* published separately by Schmidt in 1903).
  Scored for 2 flutes, 2 oboes, 2 clarinets, 2 bassoons, 2 trumpets, 2 horns, 3 trombones, timpani, and strings; tenor soloist and 4-part male chorus.
  Copies: BPL (full, 1881 vocal), Dart (full; 1881, 1895 vocal), ESM (full, 1895 vocal), HMA (full, vocal), HMus (1881, 1895 vocal), LC (full, 1881 vocal), Mich (vocal), NECM (full; 1881, 1895, 1908 vocal), NYPL (full, vocal), PPL (1908), Smith (1881 vocal), Summy (vocal, full, parts), Wellesley (1895 vocal), Yale (1881 vocal).

The "beautiful, strong, fitting, manly music"[26] that Paine wrote for the 1881 Harvard production of Sophocles' *Oedipus the King* in Greek was hailed as "the finest piece of work we have yet had"[27] from him, "the highest point which his genius as a composer has reached,"[28] and even "the most finished specimen of musical workmanship produced in this country."[29] More recent writers have agreed that the *Oedipus* music was among the most successful and satisfying of Paine's output. Certainly the Harvard Greek play was an outstanding accomplishment of the departments of Music and of Classics, and it excited interest throughout the nation.

The original production of the play, with Paine's music, was performed entirely in Greek at Sanders Theatre, Harvard University, on 17, 19, 20, and 27 May 1881. Elocution instructor George Riddle played the leading role, George Osgood sang the tenor solo, and Paine conducted the musical performance. In the following year another production was prepared to present the play "on the road." For a week in January 1882, performances were given at the Globe Theatre in Boston, the company then moving to Booth's Theatre in New York; George W. Chadwick conducted the performances at both locations. Consistency of language was not an aim here—Riddle gave his lines in Greek, but the other characters all spoke in English translation. There were no further performances of the play, but a number of concert performances of Paine's music took place in the following years. Two complete performances are known—in November 1895 the Apollo Club gave the work in Boston and in Cambridge, and in 1921 it was given at Harvard as part of the 50th anniversary observance of the play. At least 13 performances of separate choruses were given between 1882 and 1903 in Boston, New York City, Brooklyn, Milwaukee, Chicago, and San Francisco. (For a detailed discussion and documentation of these performances, see Chapter 7 of the present study.) The *Prelude* gained a popularity of its own; its performance history is discussed elsewhere in this study.

Sophocles' choruses in *Oedipus Tyrannus* are divided into strophes and antistrophes, and were performed by a chorus of 15. Paine, however, assigned only the strophes to the on-stage chorus of 15, while writing the antistrophes for a 60-voice supplementary chorus—mostly from the Apollo and Boylston clubs—seated in a semicircle with the orchestra, in front of the stage; he had decided, "in composing the music, . . . that it would be best to sacrifice the letter of the custom for the sake of the grand effects to be produced by a larger number of voices."[30] The orchestra, headed by Listemann, numbered 35, including 19 string players. For a full discussion of the production, see Chapter 7 of the present study. A detailed description of the play, music, sets and costumes (with photographs), and press coverage is given in Henry Norman, *An Account of the Harvard Greek Play* (Boston, 1882).

The first chorus is begun in procession, the singers representing the old men—citizens—who have been called by Oedipus to hear his plans to solve the murder of Laius. After an 18-bar introduction, the onstage chorus begins a unison melody (Example 15–94)—Strophe I—that contains the rhythmic patterns used throughout the movement. The supplementary chorus answers with Antistrophe I, which is set to the same music with the addition of some 4-part harmonization. In this chorus, as well as in numbers 2, 3, and 5, Paine generally assigned the same music to Strophe and Antistrophe pairs, minor differences occurring only in harmonizations, cadential extensions, and text underlay. (At times he seems to have composed with the English text in mind, which fits the musical phrases more comfortably than does the Greek.) The music of Strophe I (and Antistrophe I) often modulates quickly to the mediant—E minor; following a return to C, the passage ends in A minor, the submediant. Strophe II introduces the first 4-part harmonization for the onstage choir, sung unaccompanied to heighten its effect (Example 15–95). D minor is the main key of emphasis here, but a modulation returns to an A-minor cadence. Strophe III and Antistrophe III differ more from each other, but much of their music is shared. The closing measures contain one of the ''grand effects'' that the use of the larger chorus would ensure (Example 15–96).

Following is the scene in which Teiresias, the old blind prophet, reveals that Oedipus himself had murdered Laius, who was his father (unknown to him), and had subsequently committed incest by marrying Laius' widow Jocasta, thereby bringing the curse of plague and barrenness upon the nation. Oedipus refused to believe this statement and accused Teiresias of treason. The chorus understandably was very confused, for Oedipus was a very popular king, but Teiresias also was highly respected. But their mood is depicted in the second chorus, which, unlike the first chorus, is full of contrasts. The first strophe begins with a broad, tragic melody, with many marks of expression (Example 15–97). A subsequent section, *allegro con fuoco*, expresses the urgency to flee the condemnation of fate. Paine's setting conveys this restlessness with rapid note values and by unstable nonfunctional chromatic harmony (Example 15–98). This section is repeated, with minor differences (such as a cadence in B flat, rather than D minor, at the end of the first passage), for Antistrophe I. The restless mood continues with the beginning of Strophe II. A four-note melodic pattern fits the short English phrases perfectly, but conflicts decidedly with the Greek syllabification (Example 15–99). With an expression of confidence in Oedipus, a warm peaceful melody, richly harmonized, changes the mood substantially (Example 15–100)—this is the theme that formed the basis of the *Prelude* (see Example 13–55). A later phrase (Example 15–101) also appears briefly in the *Prelude*, although somewhat modified (see Example 13–56, measures 43ff). This passage reaches a quiet conclusion, and the entire material of Strophe II returns for Antistrophe II.

    No. 3 is an interchange between Oedipus, Jocasta, Creon (Jocasta's brother), and the Chorus, and is written partly as melodrama, lines for the three characters being spoken, while the Chorus parts are sung. It follows a heated argument between Oedipus and Creon, whom the king accuses of plotting treason with Teiresias. Jocasta, on entering, urges reason and trust. The chorus begins the Strophe with a solemn melody, in conversation with Oedipus (Example 15–102); spoken lines are delivered during orchestral pauses. The final portion of the Strophe begins with a dramatic crescendo, which leads to a lyrical melody (Example 15–103) that touches on D minor before finally modulating to B minor. An orchestral interlude, with spoken dialog between Oedipus and Creon, leads to the Antistrophe, which repeats the music of the Strophe; the main speaking character is Jocasta. The scene continues as Jocasta and Oedipus agree to summon an old shepherd, who as a servant was the only survivor of the murder of Laius and his companions and who would be able to state whether or not Oedipus was there. After they leave, the Chorus comments on justice and fidelity to the gods in No. 4. Strophe I is a sturdy hymn of loyalty, primarily pentatonic at the beginning (Example 15–104). Antistrophe I, describing tyrants who disregard justice, introduces an agitated theme (Example 15–105). Pictorial phrases are graphically set, as in Example 15–106.[31] The theme immediately switches to loyalty to the nation and to the gods, with an appropriately sweeping melody (Example 15–107). Strophe II resumes the mood of the first part of Antistrophe I, but with new material. Momentum increases, and the *alla breve* changes to $\frac{6}{8}$ meter, *l'istesso tempo*. Antistrophe II returns to the music of Strophe I, somewhat abridged, with an expanded ending. The mood of the text is different, however—instead of loyalty, the message is a protest against the lack of respect accorded the gods and their oracles, and an imploration to Zeus to notice and correct this.

The next movement, No. 5, provides relief from the growing tension and the increasing premonition of tragedy. Jocasta, having realized that her husband Oedipus is really the cursed son that she and Laius had banished, had rushed off stage griefstricken, to be discovered later a suicide. Oedipus awaited the arrival of the old shepherd, who besides being with Laius at his murder had also been the one who had failed to destroy Laius and Jocasta's infant son. While waiting, he imagines himself the child of Fortune, and the chorus joins in the diversion. Most of the movement features the tenor soloist, whose broad melody, with frequent appoggiatura figures, is similar to other Paine songs and arias (Example 15–108). An interlude (Example 15–109), leading to the first appearance of the chorus, contains a motive also used in the *Prelude* (see Example 13–56, measures 38–39). With the combining of the chorus and soloist, a sonorous effect is the result, including some colorful harmonic progressions (Example 15–110). The Antistrophe is an exact repeat of the music of the Strophe, except for an added bar and one reharmonization.

Before the sixth chorus, the old shepherd appears, and, though reluctant, is forced to reveal Oedipus' true identity. Oedipus and the other characters leave the stage in a state of horror, with the chorus remaining to comment upon the situation. The musical design of No. 6 is basically a rondo, ABACABA, with a Coda based on material from "B." The opening melodic figure (Strophe I) is found in the *Prelude* (see Example 13–58b); its accompaniment figure occurs throughout the *Allegro mod-*

erato of that movement (Example 15–111). A modulation to G minor brings a new theme (Example 15–112). The climax to this passage contains several dissonant clashes, adding to the emotional heightening (Example 15–113); a similar passage is found in the *Prelude* at measures 93–96. Antistrophe I follows with a return of the opening melody. A fanfare-like theme modulates to A-flat minor, B, and C (Example 15–114). The triumphant sound of this theme is shortlived; with a diminuendo, Strophe II soon brings a return to the original material, in F minor. Example 15–113 is heard again, in C minor, and Antistrophe II returns to the final statement of the first theme, modified to fit the text. The closing coda includes a reference to Example 15–113, expanded to include a strong Neapolitan flavor.

No additional music is provided for the rest of the play. Remaining action includes the Messenger's long monologue relating in grisly detail Oedipus' desperate search for Jocasta, his discovery of her body hanging by her bed, and his blinding himself by gouging his eyes with her gold brooches. Oedipus then relinquishes the throne and the custody of his two daughters to Creon, and prepares to enter exile. A final statement for the Chorus ends the tragedy. According to Norman, there was music here:

> The music sounds again in pathetic tones, and the Coryphaeus [a chorus member] expresses for his fellows the lesson of life. . . .
> With bowed heads the old men of Thebes retire to the city, and the play is over.[32]

Also, reports of concerts including excerpts from the *Oedipus Tyrannus* music mention an "Orchestral Postlude." Further information seems to be lacking.

The Realm of Fancy, Op. 36
    Text: John Keats.
    Autograph manuscript full score, copyist's full score, and instrumental parts in Houghton Library, Harvard University. Autograph piano vocal score in Music Division, Boston Public Library.
    Piano vocal score published by Arthur P. Schmidt, Boston, in 1882.
    Scored for mixed chorus, solo quartet, and orchestra.
    Copies: BPL, LC, NECM, Summy.

The Realm of Fancy was performed by the Boylston Club, with orchestra, at Music Hall in Boston on 2 March 1882; George Osgood conducted the concert. It is a short cantata, lasting about 10 minutes, that contains four connected movements. An opening horn figure sets the pastoral scene (Example 15–115). Soon the tempo increases, and the orchestra explodes with the first choral entrance (Example 15–116). This 4-part harmony is soon alternated with numerous imitative passages, and the key changes first to D, then moving through E minor, A minor, and D minor to arrive at F minor, with a unison chorus over simple chords (Example 15–117). A mysterious passage moves from C minor to B major by hinting at the "omnibus" progression (Example 15–118). Another modulation causes the chorus to end in E flat, and a 16-bar interlude, after flirting with B major again, returns to E flat for the soprano solo (Example 15–119). Its light tuneful melody is characteristic of Paine's products of this type, with clear phrases, accented non-harmonic tones, and little corroboration of material except for sequence. A quartet follows, with the bass soloist first to be heard; his warm melody is combined with a counter-melody in the orchestra (Example 15–120). Alto and tenor then join in, and the quartet produce a graceful Mendelssohnian effect (Example 15–121). The chorus then enters, alternating with the quartet. At the end of this section an interlude similar to the opening introduction leads to a reprise of the first chorus, but with different text. It is extended also, allowing the quartet to enter in, and a change of key scheme permits the work to end in G. Several sonorous fortissimo chords for eight-part chorus near the close lead to a fugato, *più allegro*, and a brilliant conclusion.

The Realm of Fancy received another performance on 25 March 1897 by the Newton Centre "Singers," conducted by George A. Burdett.

Phoebus, Arise! Op. 37

> Text: William Drummond, of Hawthornden (1585–1649).
>
> Autograph manuscript full score, copyist's full score, and instrumental parts (no vocal parts) in Houghton Library, Harvard University. Copyist's manuscript piano vocal score in Music Division, Library of Congress.
>
> Piano vocal score published by Arthur P. Schmidt, Boston, in 1882.
>
> Scored for tenor solo, male chorus, and orchestra.
>
> Copies: BPL, HMA, HMus, LC, NECM (+ original Apollo Club edition), NYPL, Summy.

Summons to Love, as *Phoebus, Arise*! was originally called, received its first performance at Boston's Music Hall on 26 April 1882 by the Apollo Club—for which it was written—and orchestra, conducted by B. J. Lang. Reviewers praised the colorful setting of the picturesque text, and found the strengths of the *Oedipus* music equally present here. *Phoebus, Arise*! was performed by the Orpheus Club of Cincinnati and again by Boston's Apollo Club, both in 1902. And on 3 June 1925 the Harvard Alumni Chorus included it on a concert at the Harvard Club of Boston.[33] The short cantata, which would take about 11 minutes to perform, is continuous, with four connected movements or sections.

A 29-bar orchestral introduction paints a picture of the sunrise. The pre-dawn solitude is found in the opening bars (Example 15–122a). Instruments are added gradually, and volume and tempo gradually increase;

along with Paine's typical fanfare-like figurations are heard a chord progression a major third away—D flat (= C Sharp) to A major—a device first actively embraced by him in the early 1880s (Example 15–122b). The opening chorus is grand, with resonant homophonic scoring for the voices (Example 15–123). Variety is sustained through changes in texture, including antiphonal and polyphonic exchanges between sections of the choir, and changes in key, reaching G, A, and F-sharp minor before arriving at a final cadence in A. An orchestral interlude quickly modulates to A flat and leads to the tenor solo, a graceful melody with somewhat irregular phrasing (Example 15–124). Certain characteristic melodic or harmonic clichés are evident here, including the raised supertonic resolving to the third of the tonic triad (m. 100), and the German sixth resolving to the tonic triad, second inversion, in a type of plagal progression (measures 103–104). The solo modulates to E, and an interlude returns to A flat for a repeat of the tenor melody, now by the chorus, with an extended line in the solo. A following section for chorus breaks the placid mood entirely, with a depiction of the winds (Example 15–125). A lull then follows—the stillness before sunrise—and then the movement resumes. Intricate choral writing (Example 15–126), with a busy orchestral accompaniment, provides a climax to the section and leads to a reprise of the first chorus. As with *The Realm of Fancy*, this is modified, with some revoicing, opportunities for the soloist to be heard, and a revision of the key scheme to provide an ending in C major. Toward the end, chorus parts are placed high for brilliance, and the Tenor I part contains As and B-flats, as well as one B natural. The voices have the last word: when the orchestra concludes, the chorus holds its tonic traid for two additional bars (Example 15–127).

The Nativity, Op. 38

> [in the revised edition of the published score, listed as Op. 39, the number assigned to the *Romance for Piano*, published in 1883.]
>
> Text: John Milton, *On the Morning of Christ's Nativity* (1629), 11 of 27 stanzas.
>
> Autograph manuscript full score, copyist's full score, and parts in Houghton Library, Harvard University.
>
> Piano vocal score published by A. P. Schmidt, Boston, in 1883; revised edition of piano vocal score published by Arthur P. Schmidt, Boston, in 1903.
>
> Scored for mixed chorus, solo quartet, and orchestra.
>
> Copies: BPL (orig.), BU (orig.), ESM (rev.), HMA, HMus (orig., rev.), LC (orig., rev.), Mich (orig.), NECM (orig., rev.), NYPL (orig.), Summy (orig.), Wis, Yale (rev.).

Paine's *The Nativity* was composed for the sixth triennial festival of the Handel and Haydn Society in 1883, and was performed at the second concert of the festival on 2 May. Soloists were Emma Thursby, soprano, Mathilde Phillipps, alto, George W. Want, tenor, and Myron W. Whitney, bass; Paine conducted. The Society repeated the work in a January 1888 concert at Music Hall. Frank van der Stucken conducted the middle movement in a Chickering Hall Symphonic Concert in New York in 1886. Pittsburgh's Handel and Haydn Society performed the entire cantata during their 1887–88 season, as did the People's Choral Union and the Boston Festival Orchestra, conducted by Samuel W. Cole, in March 1903.

The Nativity is a cantata with three separate movements. Of greater proportions than the two works discussed above, its first movement alone is of a comparable length and variety. An orchestral introduction sets a pastoral mood; the opening unaccompanied line has a pentatonic basis (Example 15–128). Following a *crescendo* and *stringendo*, the tempo relaxes. After some harp arpeggios, the chorus enters, with the theme first given in the sopranos (Example 15–129). The tenor voices answer, followed by the unison chorus; eventually, polyphonic writing predominates in this portion. A second section in A major, for soprano solo and chorus, continues the peaceful mood, although the tempo is quickened slightly (Example 15–130). A reference to war, "spear and shield," and "hooked chariot" brings an agitated setting (Example 15–131), although these features of conflict are named as being absent. But this turmoil contrasts dramatically with "and kings sat still," which follows immediately, with chromatic chords under a choral unison chant; the chromatic movement produces, beneath the tonic pedal, a V_2^4 of iv, a diminished seventh, a supertonic half-diminished $\frac{4}{3}$, a V_3^4 of iv, and another diminished seventh— vii°7 of V (Example 15–132). Soon the martial references are past, and the opening material returns, in C major. Elaborate orchestral effects accompany "the winds, with wonder whist, smoothly the waters kissed." Additional descriptive filigree—probably bowed and fingered string tremolo with sustained horns—occurs with "birds of calm," (Example 15–133), along with rather special chord progressions by thirds (A flat, F, E-flat minor, C flat); the splendid sonority of these bars perhaps goes back to Weber's metaphor for "birds" in *Der Freischütz* and to Beethoven's Symphony No. 6. Key changes are frequent, until a half cadence on the dominant is reached. The soprano soloist then begins the last section, again based on the opening theme. More harmonic coloring is included (Example 15–134), and Neapolitan harmonies are heard in A (measure 288) and soon afterward in C (measure 293). The chorus soon enters, and the combined forces build to a grand conclusion, with an optional high C for the soloist.

The second movement, for quartet and chorus, has its rustic, playful mood stated colorfully in the orchestral introduction, which shows a certain amount of pentatonic flavor (Example 15–135). The basic theme is first given by the tenor soloist (Example 15–136), answered by bass and alto. Most of the writing is polyphonic, with numerous 16th-note melismas and running passages. A modulation to B major and harp arpeggios announce a new theme for the soprano soloist (Example 15–137). The quartet later joins in this section, then returns to the opening section (in A flat), now harmonized in four parts. In a coda the full chorus joins the quartet, first in A major, then abruptly in A flat. Paine's expanded harmonic vocabulary is evident in a series of progressions relating the tonic triad to the subdominant, lowered submediant, and lowered mediant keys (Example 15–138).

The final chorus is majestic and joyful, an effective movement for a massed choir. Fanfares and massive choral sounds provide an arresting beginning (Example 15–139). Imitation follows, to offer a change in texture (Example 15–140). Soon are heard the graphic settings of "the base of heaven's deep organ" and "ninefold harmony," (Example 15–141), the grand effect discussed in Chapter 8 of the present study. A middle section, in G major, relaxes the mood (Example 15–142). Modulations suggest G minor and C minor before leading to a reprise of the beginning portion and a magnificent climax. Paine must have found the effect at the end of *Phoebus, Arise!* to be successful, for here again he wrote for the last chord in the voices to be held for a measure after the last written notes of the orchestra. Several critics noted their pleasure at this device.

Hymn, Divine Love
    Text: Charles Wesley ("Love Divine, all loves excelling").
    Manuscript not extant.
    No record of any publication.

Paine's hymn, setting the "Love Divine" text by Charles Wesley, was included on an afternoon worship service at Portland City Hall, Sunday, 4 July 1886, as a part of the Portland Centennial celebration. The music was performed by the choirs of the State Street and First Parish churches.[34] Paine was invited to attend—which apparently he did not—and to provide the music for the hymn. The setting seems not to have survived or to have been mentioned elsewhere. Perhaps a setting was not written fresh, but rather the text simply paired with an existing tune. For example, the Wesley words would go well with the *Harvard Hymn*.

Song of Promise, Op. 43
    Text: George E. Woodberry, from *My Country*.
    Autograph manuscript full score, copyist's full score, and instrumental parts in Houghton Library, Harvard University. Full score (probably a copy) in Music Division, Library of Congress.
    Piano vocal score published by the John Church Co., Cincinnati, in 1888.
    Scored for mixed chorus, soprano solo, orchestra, and organ.
    Copies: HMA, HMus, LC, NECM, NYPL, PPL, Wis.

The *Song of Promise* was commissioned for the Cincinnati "Centennial" May Festival of 1888, and was performed on 22 May. Paine had selected the words from Woodberry's ode, *My Country*, which had been published in the July 1887 issue of *Atlantic Monthly*. Theodore Thomas, music director for the festival, conducted the 600-voice chorus and his 108-piece orchestra from New York. Soprano soloist was Lilli Lehmann, and Arthur Mees was organist; Paine was present for the concert. The cantata received no further performances, except for a January 1892 Boston Philharmonic concert that included only the soprano aria, with Alice Wentworth, soloist.

Song of Promise is in three connected movements and would last about 30 minutes in performance. Woodberry's highly patriotic ode is full of phrases descriptive of America's beauty and high purpose. Paine treats the multitude of expressed ideas with an equal variety of musical themes and textures. Traditional formal schemes are unworkable, as a result, and the first and last movements are basically continuous in design. However, in both choruses the opening portion returns later in the movement, creating a rounded effect and a sense of recapitulation. Moreover, the concluding section of the first chorus, with minor modifications, returns as the conclusion of the last chorus, adding to the overall unity of the cantata.

The first movement begins with a 31-bar orchestral introduction. Harp arpeggios precede the entrance of the soprano soloist—this association is used consistently. The melody begins with a pentatonic figure (Example 15–143). After an animated, poetic description of the sun's voyage west over the continent, a 26-bar interlude produces a change of key and tempo for the first entrance of the chorus, a bright, hymn-like, almost pentatonic theme (Example 15–144). Choral textures vary between 4-part harmony, quasi polyphony, and unison or octave doubling. An example of the last technique is found later in this section, depicting the stillness before the dawn (Example 15–145). Independent voice leading, with some imitation, soon follows in a warm, expressive passage (Example 15–146). The dawn accomplished, the many physical features of the countryside are announced, with primary emphasis on mountains; "Look forth, O Land" (Example 15–147), begins this section, and modulates from the original key of A to B flat and A minor. One of the many spectacular choral effects pictures the burst of sunlight upon the mountains, changing from a unison to a brightly voiced *fortissimo* chord (Example 15–148). Key centers move to D major, B major ("the Appalachian gold"), E flat ("thousand, thousand rivers"), and A flat ("the sea-horizoned lakes"); new themes are given for all these subjects. Musical fireworks erupt for the storm (Example 15–149), abruptly contrasted by a placid suggestion of Renaissance polyphony, portraying the timelessness of Mount Shasta in California (Example 15–150). When all subjects have been illustrated, another series of harp arpeggios returns to the key of C for the soprano soloist. Her melody is different from the opening passage, but the opening pentatonic figure is the same and the general formal effect is that of a beginning recapitulation. This is confirmed after a modulation to A major, when the chorus enters with, "O Land of Promise, joy!" to the material of the opening choral section (Examples 15–144 and 15–145). A concluding section is based on a short ascending phrase first announced by the chorus men, "While the chorus never-ending" (Example 15–151). With the words, "Triumph of the peoples," Paine indulged in a two-fold "omnibus" chromatic progression, with nearly complete series based on the dominant sevenths on G and E (Example 15–152).

After an overwhelming conclusion, a short interlude leads directly to the second movement, where a 30-bar introduction, complete with harp arpeggios, moves through A flat to the key of F and sets a quiescent mood. The soprano aria is in an AABA design, and begins with a gentle line over a tonic pedal point (Example 15–153). Following a second section, slightly modifying the material ("Of holy hymns and famous deeds"), the harp appears and modulates to D flat for the contrasting section. The initial pentatonic figure is the same as in the first movement (Example 15–154). An interlude is related to material from the introduction, although not a repetition; with arrival at F major, the first section returns ("Thy wondrous spring") over an accompaniment of undulating sixteenths. The theme is extensively modified, and the soloist has free opportunity to display her high range. Arpeggios fade away to end the movement.

The last movement begins with a series of chords in dialogue (Example 15–155), producing a sober, grave effect. The 17-bar introduction leads to a somber unison theme (Example 15–156), modulating from G-sharp minor to B major, and then to A flat and E flat. The fanfare from the introduction announces another theme, in E, "Again, O mighty hymn, begin," which results in the first *fortissimo* of the movement. An abrupt modulation from E to C, with another fanfare, prepares a tempo change to *Allegro*; this section develops the idea of America as a haven of peace. Over an accompaniment of triplets, a basically pentatonic melody is sung in the higher voices (Example 15–157). A cry against imperialism causes an increase in tempo and a spirited exchange between sections (Example 15–158). The key remains B minor through an extended development of this idea, but with the text, "So hard, surpassing War, doth Peace assail," a more tranquil melody appears, and this portion closes in D. Following is a recapitulation of the opening, now in G minor and B flat. The instrumental chords are augmented by an added choral part, "O Harbor of the sea-tossed fates," and the melody of Example 15–156 now expresses, "Mother, whose heart divinely holds Earth's poor within her breast." A brief modulation to G and an animated choral interlude in A brings in the finale, a 121-bar reprise of material from the first movement, including that in Examples 15–146, 15–151, and 15–152. The first portion uses a different text, and the order of material is altered. However, with "While the chorus never-ending," both text and music correspond to that in the first movement, including the placement of Examples 15–151 and 15–152. Occasional phrase extensions heighten the resounding climax, with very effective, sonorous composition for massed voices.

Columbus March and Hymn

    Text by the composer.

    Autograph manuscript full score and copyist's full score in Houghton Library, Harvard University.

    Chorus edition of the Hymn, Columbus March and Hymn (without march) published with piano accompaniment by Oliver Ditson Company, Boston, in 1892. Piano arrangement of March and Hymn (two hands) by Arthur Foote also published by Ditson in 1892.

    Scored for piccolo, 2 flutes, 2 oboes, English Horn, 3 clarinets, timpani, bass and snare drums, triangle, cymbals, strings, organ, and mixed chorus.

    Copies: BPL (chorus, piano), HMA, HMus (chorus), LC (chorus, piano), NECM (piano), NYPL.

The *Columbus March and Hymn* was commissioned for the opening ceremonies of the World's Columbian Exposition at Chicago, where it received its premiere performance on 21 October 1892, when the Exposition buildings were dedicated. Theodore Thomas, Musical Director of the Exposition, conducted the *Hymn*, along with works by Chadwick, Mendelssohn, Haydn, Handel, and Beethoven; singers numbered in the thousands, and there were about 300 musicians. On 1 May 1893 the Exposition was formally opened to the public, and a performance of Paine's *March and Hymn* was again included in the ceremonies. The work was heard at least three more times in concerts at the Exposition. In addition, two orchestras included the work on concerts during their 1893 season—the Chicago Orchestra, under Thomas, in January, and the Boston Symphony Orchestra, conducted by Arthur Nikisch, in February.

Paine's *March* was written as a concert piece, flowing continuously, and not divided into the sections to be found in military marches. The composer provided an extensive analytical description of the piece, printed in *Musical Record* and later reprinted in the program booklet for the Chicago Orchestra performance; the reader is referred to Chapter 8 of the present study, where this essay is quoted in full. The work lasted about 15 minutes in performance, and the accompaniment for the Hymn was so scored that the chorus parts could be omitted. Orchestral scoring is brilliant and colorful, while the choral writing is simple and straight-forward—unisons, straight homophony, and moving quarters. The melody begins within a pentatonic framework, and stays limited almost entirely to a D major diatonic scale, with a range of a tenth (Example 15–159). For the second half, the melody is reharmonized, modified, and extended, and the orchestral accompaniment becomes more elaborate. A short codetta ends the piece, with a long sonorous chord for the choir; meanwhile, the orchestra produces a hemiola that recalls earlier uses of this device in the *Mass* and *St. Peter* (Example 15–160).

"Freedom, Our Queen": National Song for the School Children of Chicago
  Text: Oliver Wendell Holmes.
  Manuscript vocal score in Harvard Musical Association collection.
  Published by Novello & Co., London, in 1893. Vocal score of arrangement for 4-part chorus or quartet published by Novello, Ewer & Co., New York, in 1902.
  Scored for orchestra and chorus.
  Copies: ESM, HMus, LC, PPL.

Paine's second commissioned work for the World's Columbian Exposition was written for the Exposition Children's Chorus, directed by William L. Tomlins. The first performance was given at their first concert about the beginning of June 1893; it was sung by the group of 1,200 voices, and Theodore Thomas conducted the chorus and orchestra. Two more performances were given during the Exposition. In July 1904 the song was performed by a children's chorus concert during the Saengerfest des Norwesterns in Milwaukee, with the choir and orchestra conducted again by Thomas.

Two verses are set. The same melody is used for both, although the second is extended by an additional phrase, allowing a more conclusive ending. Harmonizations are identical, except for the close. An 11-bar introduction precedes the choral entrance, and the two verses are separated by a short interlude. At the end, this orchestral material returns, extended, and the chorus enters for a final plagal cadence. The orchestral introduction typically does not use melodic material from the choral portion, and includes a crescendo with increased note values (triplets). The melody is primarily diatonic, with a range of an eleventh (Example 15–161).

Scenes from "The Birds" of Aristophanes
  Text: Aristophanes; English version by Austin Hall Evans.
  Manuscript full score and instrumental parts, another full score, two manuscript piano vocal scores (one "evidently a latter version"), and mimeographed vocal parts (dated 1939) in Houghton Library, Harvard University. Manuscript full score (copy) in Music Division, Library of Congress. *Prelude* only: two manuscript full scores, 3 sets of parts in Houghton Library, Harvard University.
  Piano vocal score, with English text only, published by G. Schirmer, Jr. (The Boston Music Company), Boston, in 1902; manuscript orchestral material and the Greek text

were available from the publisher. *Prelude to the Scenes from The Birds of Aristo-
phanes*, for piano, 4-hands, published by G. Schirmer, Jr., Boston, in 1905.
Scored for male chorus, tenor soloist, and orchestra.
Copies (vocal score): BPL, ESM, HMA (+ prelude for piano), HMus, NYPL, PPL,
Wis, Yale.

Paine's music for *The Birds*, completed before the end of December
1900, was written for a performance of the Aristophanes play by Harvard's Classical Club, given at the Fogg Art Museum on 10 May 1901; a
public dress rehearsal had been held on 6 May, with a private performance
two days later. The performance was in Greek. As in the *Oedipus* production, a small choir performed on stage, with a supplementary chorus
in the orchestra. Appleton Chapel organist-choirmaster Locke directed
the small 20-voice chorus, with members mostly from the Harvard Glee
Club; the supplementary chorus was made up of Harvard graduates, for
the most part. No orchestra was available—Paine played the accompaniment on the piano. On 7 March 1902 the Apollo Club, conducted by
Emil Mollenhauer, performed the *Scenes* on a Chickering Hall concert;
again, Paine played the accompaniment. The *Prelude* alone received four
orchestral performances: by the Chicago Orchestra, with Theodore
Thomas, on 27–28 February 1903; at a 9 March 1904 Chickering Hall
concert in Boston, with Paine conducting; by the Boston Symphony
Orchestra on 17–18 November 1905 with Wilhelm Gericke; and a
28 December 1905 Cambridge concert, also by the Boston Symphony
Orchestra.

The *Prelude*, which received several hearings on its own and which
was the only portion of the work to be performed by an orchestra, draws
its thematic material from the choruses that follow. Unlike the *Prelude* to
Oedipus Tyrannus, there is not a tightly knit unity of themes here; rather,
the movement is more of a potpourri, containing a greater variety of
themes. A beginning fanfare leads to the triumphant melody from the
wedding scene at the close of the play, quite operatic in effect (Example
15–162). A hint at Zeus' thunder, from Chorus III, proceeds to a quotation
from the tenor solo, Movement V, Paethetaerus' "Come follow us, ye
birds who may!" (Example 15–163). The continuation of this theme is
delicately rescored; a *più mosso* and a change of mood include a quotation from an interlude in Chorus I. Zeus' thunder leads to a fugato
based on a theme from the first chorus (Example 15–164). The entire
theme soon appears in B major, and dissolves into a related melody of
wide range, quoted from the end of Movement II where it accompanies
the Chorus Leader's speech (Example 15–165). The abrupt modulations
to keys a major third away had become a common device by this point
in Paine's career; the undulating major seventh, ninth, and added sixth
sonorities give a greater flavor of Liszt and Wagner. Another transition

returns to a fanfare and a repeat of the wedding theme, given in Example 15–162. As a Coda, Paine quotes the "Singing Hymen! Hymenaio!" refrain that closes Choruses IV and VI (Example 15–166); the quick modulation to C flat, the lowered submediant, is another progression by major third. In the agitation leading to the final cadence, Paine includes a series of authentic progressions, starting on C and continuing downward by major second (with chromatic bass) the distance of a major tenth (Example 15–167). Additional emphasis on the lowered submediant precedes the final plagal cadence.

Aristophanes' comedy is centered around Euelpides and Peithetaerus, two elderly Athenians escaping taxation and the penalties for being in arrears, who enter the area of the Birds and organize its citizens to establish a kingdom—called Cloudcuckooland—and to erect a wall between Heaven and Earth. Animal sacrifices were thus prevented from being sent from Earth to Heaven, and earthmen were encouraged to direct their offerings to the Birds, instead; gods were not allowed to pass through the gates of the wall without permission, with imprisonment or death (to the immortals!) as a penalty. Earthmen welcomed these new rulers, and flocked to visit the Kingdom and learn the new fashions; the gods, in contrast, resented their loss of power and, no longer receiving the sacrifices, were growing quite hungry. A delegation from the gods approached Peithetaerus, the spokesman for the nation, to discuss a truce, and reluctantly agreed to his terms—recognition of the Birds' sovereignty and the promise of Zeus' daughter Basileia's hand in marriage. The play ends in the wedding celebration, with hymns to the happy couple and expressions of praise and gratitude to Zeus.

The first chorus of Paine's music appears quite late in the play—line 1366 in the 1657-line work; the earlier passages for Chorus, much of them in verse, some quite lengthy, would have been spoken in the Harvard production. The first chorus, in four strophes, spans the most dramatic action of the six numbers. Strophes 1 and 2, sung in succession, are rather nonsensical verses sung while Peithetaerus and his helpers are off stage delivering wings to the tens of thousands of men who have arrived in Cloudcuckooland and wish to dress as birds. The jovial chorus is very much in the spirit of an excerpt from a Gilbert and Sullivan operetta (Example 15–168). The second strophe enters after a short interlude, much of whose material was heard in the Prelude. This second section contains a varied orchestration, although the vocal parts are the same. Following a short orchestral tag, there is a break for more dramatic action. Prometheus, a Titan outcast from Heaven for disclosing to man the gods' secret of fire, approaches Peithetaerus to suggest a strategy against the gods, including the details of sovereignty and marriage. As they leave, the chorus sings Strophe 3, an equally jovial but decidedly macabre verse, with music related to the earlier portion (Example 15–169). Imitation and chromatic progressions occur as the coward Peisander observes the bat Chairephon approach his sacrificial camel-lamb (Example 15–170). Another break for action occurs—the scene of the confrontation between Peithetaerus and the gods, and his eventual success. As Peithetaerus leaves to prepare for the wedding, the Chorus resumes, amid harp flourishes and woodwind coloring. Two short passages, set to nonsense syllables, "pum, pum, pum" lead to a reprise of the first chorus, to a verse condemning the mutilation of Greek by foreigners; the music is extensively modified, incorporating changes from Strophe 3.

Chorus II begins the wedding scene, opening with harp arpeggios as Peithetaerus and his bride descend from Heaven in a flying car. The chorus sings a fanfare, "Room for the company!" and then a grand hymn to the bride's beauty and to the couple (Example 15–171). The orchestra continues as the Chorus Leader speaks, an example of melodrama technique. The interlude proceeds without break into Chorus III, the hymn to the couple, with an angular, rhythmic theme (Example 15–172). A second verse repeats the same music. Further speech is accompanied by the orchestra, including a display of Zeus' power (Example 15–173). Following without interruption is Chorus IV, a turbulent movement, marked "Stormy and Wild," expressing awe of Zeus and his storms. The triumphant theme heard in the Prelude (Example 15–162) first appears in quite another guise (Example 15–174). But praise is then expressed and the triumphant E-flat melody surfaces (Example 15–175), with the chorus in unison. A spirited refrain ends the section, "Singing Hymen!" (Example 15–176). Closing chords, dominated by harp, lead to No. 5, the tenor solo, quoted in Example 15–163 above. Brightly scored processional music is followed by Chorus VI, a rousing fanfare and a broad operatic melody (Example 15–177). The final bars are the same as those that end the Prelude, but with the addition of the chorus.

Hymn of the West
    Text: Edmund Clarence Stedman.
    Manuscript full score and piano vocal score in Houghton Library, Harvard University.
    Piano vocal octavo published by Thiebes-Stierlin Music Company, St. Louis, in 1904.
      Music and words printed in *New York Daily Tribune*, 1 May 1904.
    Copies: HMA, LC, NECM, PPL.

Paine's *Hymn of the West* was commissioned for the Louisiana Purchase Exposition, held in St. Louis in 1904—the St. Louis world's fair. It was performed at the opening ceremonies on 30 April 1904 by a chorus of 450 led by Alfred Ernst. Two further performances were heard during the following year—in a 19 February 1905 Handel and Haydn Society concert at Symphony Hall, Boston, and opening a 25 April 1905 concert for the Syracuse Music Festival; conducting both concerts was Emil Mollenhauer.

The five verses of Stedman's hymn are set strophically, preceded by a 41-bar orchestral introduction. The melody is more varied rhythmically and more conjunct than the *Centennial Hymn* or the *Columbus Hymn*, and does not show a pentatonic influence (Example 15–178). Verses one and two are sung without break, to the same music; the orchestra largely doubles the voices. An interlude, with material abridged from the introduction, follows the second verse. The last verses are sung to basically the same harmonization, but the orchestration is enlarged; a note in the score directs that the interlude be repeated before the last stanza if all five are sung. The introduction opens with a drum roll and trumpet fanfare. Full orchestra enters in D with a version of the opening phrase of the Hymn, the descending line treated canonically between treble and bass (Example 15–179). Soon there is a modulation a major third upward to F sharp, and then to G. A sudden increase in tempo near the close produces a favorite Paine device, a repeated-note fanfare for brass, with the interval of a third (Example 15–180). At the close of the Introduction, D major is reestablished, and an upward scale passage ends in two detached dominant chords that lead directly to the first verse of the Hymn.

Example 15–1.   *Hymn for Commencement,* measures 1–16; stanzas 2–4 omitted.

Example 15–2.   *Domine salvum fac,* measures 1–12 (from piano vocal score).

Example 15–2   (continued)

Example 15–3.   *Domine salvum fac*, measures 19–26 (accompaniment omitted; tenor parts sound an octave lower than written).

Example 15–4.   *Domine salvum fac,* measures 61–81 (piano vocal score).

Example 15–4   (continued)

Example 15–5.   *Funeral Hymn,* measures 1–4.

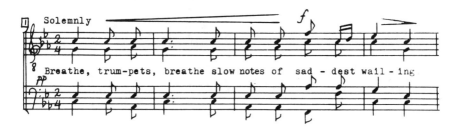

Example 15–6.   *Radway's Ready Relief,* measures 1–3.

Example 15–7.   *Radway's Ready Relief,* measures 10–14.

Example 15–8. *Radway's Ready Relief,* measures 20–29.

Example 15–9. *Radway's Ready Relief,* measures 43–46.

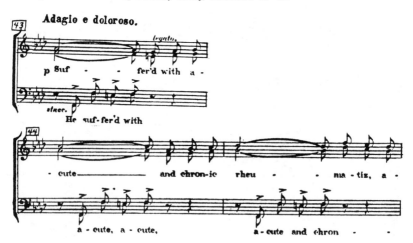

Example 15–9   (continued)

Example 15–10.   *Radway's Ready Relief,* measures 70–78.

Example 15–11.   *Radway's Ready Relief,* measures 102–109.

Example 15–12.   *Soldier's Oath.*

Example 15–13.   *O bless the Lord, my soul,* measures 1–9.

Example 15–14.   *Mass in D,* measures "Kyrie," measures 1–4 (all examples based on
                  piano vocal score).

Example 15–15.   *Mass in D,* "Kyrie," measures 14–17.

Example 15–16.   *Mass in D,* "Kyrie," measures 26–34.

Example 15–16   (continued)

Example 15–17.   *Mass in D,* "Kyrie," measures 74–77.

Example 15–18.   *Mass in D,* "Gloria," measures 1–7.

Example 15–18   (continued)

Example 15–19.   *Mass in D,* "Gloria," measures 41–51.

Example 15–20.   *Mass in D,* "Gloria," measures 125–134.

Example 15–21.   *Mass in D,* "Gloria," measures 187–190.

Example 15–22. *Mass in D,* "Qui tollis," measures 1–9.

Example 15–23. *Mass in D,* "Qui tollis," measures 49–54.

Example 15–23   (continued)

Example 15–24.   *Mass in D,* "Quoniam," measures 9–14.

Example 15–25. *Mass in D,* "Cum sancto spiritu," measures 1–7.

Example 15–26. *Mass in D,* "Cum sancto spiritu," measures 38–49 (accompaniment doubles voices).

Example 15–27. *Mass in D*, "Cum sancto spiritu," measures 97–103 (accompaniment doubles voices).

Example 15–28. *Mass in D*, "Credo," measures 1–8.

Example 15–29. *Mass in D*, "Credo," measures 104–111.

Example 15–30.   *Mass in D,* "Credo," measures 163–170.

Example 15–31.   *Mass in D,* "Et incarnatus," measures 17–24.

Example 15–32.   *Mass in D,* "Crucifixus," measures 1–8 (accompaniment omitted).

Example 15–33.	*Mass in D,* "Crucifixus," measures 24–28 (accompaniment doubles voices).

Example 15–34.	*Mass in D,* "Crucifixus," measures 78–82 (accompaniment doubles voices).

Example 15–35.   *Mass in D*, "Et resurrexit," measures 1–5.

Example 15–36.   *Mass in D*, "Et in spiritum sanctum," measures 13–16.

Example 15–37.   *Mass in D*, "Confiteor," measures 9–12.

Example 15–38. *Mass in D,* "Et vitam venturi," measures 34–48 (accompaniment doubles voice parts).

Example 15–39. *Mass in D,* "Sanctus," measures 1–2 (accompaniment doubles voice parts).

Example 15–40.   *Mass in D*, "Pleni sunt," measures 1–4.

Example 15–41.   *Mass in D*, "Osanna," measures 1–7 (accompaniment doubles voice parts).

Example 15–42.   *Mass in D*, "Benedictus," measure 1.

Example 15–43.   *Mass in D,* "Benedictus," measures 8–9.

Example 15–44.   *Mass in D,* "Benedictus," measure 15 (accompaniment omitted).

Example 15–45.   *Mass in D,* "Agnus Dei," measures 1–7.

Example 15–46.   *Mass in D,* "Agnus Dei," measures 65–77.

Example 15–47.   *Mass in D,* "Dona nobis," measures 1–5.

Example 15–48.   *Mass in D*, "Dona nobis," measures 39–48.

Example 15–49.   *St. Peter,* "Introduction," measures 1–5 (all examples after piano vocal score).

Example 15–50.   *St. Peter,* "Introduction," measures 34–41.

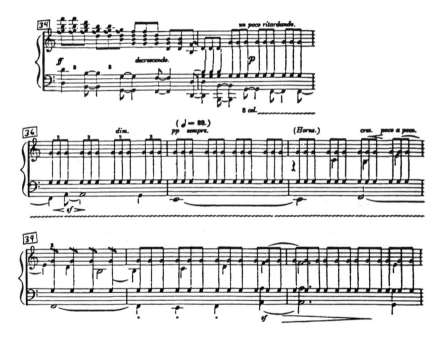

Example 15–51.   *St. Peter.*

a. "Introduction," measures 44–45.

Example 15–51   (continued)

b. "The time is fulfilled," measures 1–4.

Example 15–52.   *St. Peter,* "The spirit of the Lord," measures 1–8.

Example 15–53.   *St. Peter,* "We go before the face of the Lord," measures 1–10.

Example 15–54. *St. Peter,* "And he asked his disciples," measures 16–24.

Example 15–55. *St. Peter,* "And he asked his disciples," measures 37–49.

Example 15–55   (continued)

Example 15–56.   *St. Peter,* "My heart is glad," measures 7–11.

Example 15–57.   *St. Peter,* "The Church is built," measures 19–24.

Example 15–58.   *St. Peter,* "The Church is built," measures 26–27, Soprano part only.

Example 15–59.   *St. Peter,* "And when Jesus and his disciples," measures 14–22.

Example 15–60.   *St. Peter,* "Let not your heart be troubled," measures 10–13.

Example 15–61.   *St. Peter,* "Sanctify us through thy truth," measures 10–13.

Example 15–62.   *St. Peter,* "And lo! Judas came with a great multitude," measures 11–18.

Example 15–62   (continued)

Example 15–63.   *St. Peter,* "We hid our faces from him," measures 1–7.

Example 15–64.   *St. Peter*, "We hid our faces from him," measures 7–10.

Example 15–65.   *St. Peter*, "We hid our faces from him," measures 44–52.

Example 15–65 (continued)

Example 15–66. *St. Peter*, "But Peter followed him," measures 12–23.

Example 15–66   (continued)

Example 15–67.   *St. Peter,* "Lament," measures 1–6.

Example 15–68.   *St. Peter,* "Lament," measures 15–18.

Example 15–69. *St. Peter,* "O God, my God, forsake me not!" measures 1–6.

Example 15–70. *St. Peter,* "O God, my God, forsake me not!" measures 28–33.

Example 15–71.   *St. Peter,* "Remember from whence thou art fallen," measures 1–8.

Example 15–72.   *St. Peter,* "The Lord is faithful."
           a. Measures 9-13.

b. Measures 41-51.

Example 15–72b   (continued)

Example 15–73. *St. Peter,* "Awake, thou that sleepest," measures 1–11.

Example 15–74. *St. Peter,* "Awake, thou that sleepest," measures 30–36, vocal parts only.

Example 15–75.   *St. Peter,* "The Son of man," measures 9–13.

Example 15–76.   *St. Peter,* "If ye then be risen," measures 37–48.

Example 15–77. *St. Peter*, "O man of God," measures 1–11.

Example 15–78. *St. Peter*, "O man of God," measures 59–69.

Example 15–79.   *St. Peter,* "Feed the flock of God," measures 14–21.

Example 15–80.   *St. Peter,* "Feed the flock of God," measures 1–6.

Example 15–81.   *St. Peter,* "And when the day of Pentecost was come," measures
12–20.

Example 15–82.   *St. Peter,* "And when the day of Pentecost was come," measures
                    29–33.

Example 15–83.   *St. Peter,* "The voice of the Lord," measures 36–49.

Example 15–83 (continued)

Example 15–84. *St. Peter,* "Ye men of Judea," measures 14–22.

Example 15–85.   *St. Peter,* "Ye men of Judea," measures 37–47.

Example 15–86.   *St. Peter,* "As for man," measures 1–6.

Example 15–87.   *St. Peter,* "As for man," measures 24–31.

Example 15–88.   *St. Peter,* "Repent, and be baptised," measures 1–3.

Example 15–89.   *St. Peter,* "This is the witness of God," measures 3–10.

Example 15–90.   *St. Peter,* "This is the witness of God," measures 19–21, soprano part only.

Example 15–91.   *St. Peter,* "Sing unto God," measures 1–21.

Example 15–92.   *St. Peter,* "Great and marvellous," measures 1–8.

Example 15–93.   *Centennial Hymn* (after piano reduction).

Example 15–94.   *Oedipus Tyrannus*, No. 1, measures 19–29; all examples after piano vocal
score, Greek text omitted.

Example 15–95.   *Oedipus Tyrannus*, No. 1, measures 150–161.

Example 15–95   (continued)

Example 15–96.   *Oedipus Tyrannus*, No. 1, measures 424–448.

Example 15–96   (continued)

Example 15–97.   *Oedipus Tyrannus*, No. 2, measures 7–14.

Example 15–97   (continued)

Example 15–98.   *Oedipus Tyrannus*, No. 2, measures 51–68.

Example 15–98   (continued)

Example 15–99.   *Oedipus Tyrannus*, No. 2, measures 157–164 (Greek text transliterated).

Example 15–100.   *Oedipus Tyrannus*, No. 2, measures 185–189.

Example 15–101.   *Oedipus Tyrannus*, No. 2, measures 201–205.

Example 15–102.   *Oedipus Tyrannus*, No. 3, measures 1–10.

Example 15–103.   *Oedipus Tyrannus*, No. 3, measures 32–45.

Example 15–103   (continued)

Example 15–104.   *Oedipus Tyrannus,* No. 4, measures 1–6.

Example 15–104   (continued)

Example 15–105.   *Oedipus Tyrannus*, No. 4, measures 56–60.

Example 15–106.   *Oedipus Tyrannus*, No. 4, measures 84–90.

Example 15–107.   *Oedipus Tyrannus*, No. 4, measures 91–94.

Example 15–108.   *Oedipus Tyrannus*, No. 5, measures 1–5.

Example 15–109.   *Oedipus Tyrannus*, No. 5, measures 25–32.

Example 15–109 (continued)

Example 15–110. *Oedipus Tyrannus*, No. 5, measures 40–47.

Example 15–110   (continued)

Example 15–111.   *Oedipus Tyrannus,* No. 6, measures 1–6.

Example 15–112.   *Oedipus Tyrannus,* No. 6, measures 21–23, accompaniment omitted.

Example 15–113.   *Oedipus Tyrannus,* No. 6, measures 25–29.

Example 15–114.   *Oedipus Tyrannus,* No. 6, measures 48–51, accompaniment doubles
vocal parts.

Example 15–114 (continued)

Example 15–115.   *The Realm of Fancy*, measures 1–4.

Example 15–116.   *The Realm of Fancy*, measures 17–24.

Example 15–116   (continued)

Example 15–117.   *The Realm of Fancy,* measures 72–75.

Example 15–118.   *The Realm of Fancy,* measures 92–100.

Example 15–119.   *The Realm of Fancy,* measures 146–159.

Example 15–120.   *The Realm of Fancy,* measures 209–216.

Example 15–120   (continued)

Example 15–121.   *The Realm of Fancy,* measures 225–228.

Example 15–122.   *Phoebus, Arise!* (all examples from the piano vocal score).

a. Measures 1-8.

Example 15– 122   (continued)

b. Measures 17-21.

Example 15–123.   *Phoebus, Arise!,* measures 30–35.

Example 15–124.   *Phoebus, Arise!*, measures 100–107.

Example 15–125.   *Phoebus, Arise!*, measures 179–187.

Example 15–125   (continued)

Example 15–126.   *Phoebus, Arise!,* measures 226–238, vocal parts only.

Example 15–127.   *Phoebus, Arise!*, measures 304–310.

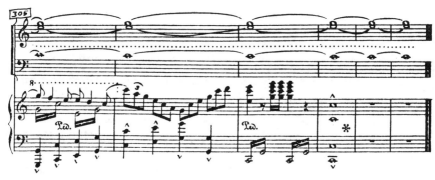

Example 15–128.   *The Nativity,* No. 1, measures 1–6 (examples after piano vocal score, revised edition, with corrections in composer's hand).

Example 15–129.   *The Nativity,* No. 1, measures 33–42, soprano part only.

Example 15–130.   *The Nativity,* No. 1, measures 83–88.

Example 15–131.   *The Nativity,* No. 1, measures 131–134.

Example 15–131   (continued)

Example 15–132.   *The Nativity,* No. 1, measures 163–169.

Example 15–133.   *The Nativity,* No. 1, measures 231–235.

Example 15–133   (continued)

Example 15–134.   *The Nativity,* No. 1, measures 284–295.

Example 15–134   (continued)

Example 15–135.   *The Nativity*, No. 2, measures 1–14.

Example 15–136.   *The Nativity*, measures 22–30; accompaniment omitted.

Example 15–137.   *The Nativity,* measures 138–145.

Example 15–138.   *The Nativity,* No. 2, measures 331–339; chorus parts double quartet in
measures 336 ff.

Example 15–138   (continued)

Example 15–138   (continued)

Example 15–139.   *The Nativity,* No. 3, measures 1–9.

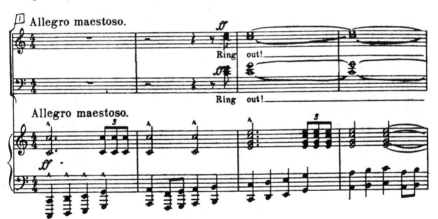

Example 15-139   (continued)

Example 15-140.   *The Nativity,* No. 3, measures 21–25, accompaniment omitted.

Example 15-141.   *The Nativity,* No. 3, measures 29–41.

Example 15–141   (continued)

Example 15–142.   *The Nativity,* No. 3, measures 58–62.

Example 15–143.   *Song of Promise,* No. 1, measures 32–36; all examples after piano vocal score.

Example 15–143   (continued)

Example 15–144.   *Song of Promise,* No. 1, measures 92–96.

Example 15–145.   *Song of Promise,* No. 1, measures 126–132.

Example 15–146.   *Song of Promise,* No. 1, measures 143–150, accompaniment omitted.

Example 15–146 (continued)

Example 15–147. *Song of Promise,* No. 1, measures 174–179.

Example 15–148.   *Song of Promise*, No. 1, measures 198–206.

Example 15–149.   *Song of Promise*, No. 1, measures 275–278.

Example 15–149   (continued)

Example 15–150.   *Song of Promise*, No. 1, measures 285–290.

Example 15–151.   *Song of Promise,* No. 1, measures 400–404.

Example 15–152.   *Song of Promise,* No. 1, measures 413–421.

Example 15–152 (continued)

Example 15–153. *Song of Promise*, No. 2, measures 31–34.

Example 15–154. *Song of Promise,* No. 2, measures 89–93.

Example 15–155. *Song of Promise,* No. 3, measures 1–15.

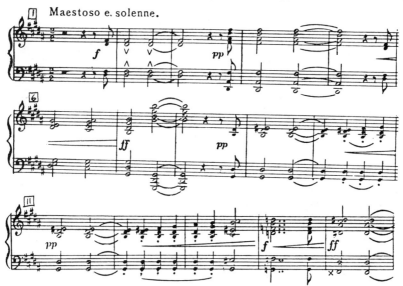

Example 15–156. *Song of Promise,* No. 3, measures 18–26.

Example 15–157.   *Song of Promise,* No. 3, measures 88–95.

Example 15–158. *Song of Promise,* No. 3, measures 162–169.

Example 15–159.   *Columbus March and Hymn*, conclusion of March and measures 1–8
of Hymn, after chorus edition.

Example 15–160.   *Columbus March and Hymn*, measures 50–56 of Hymn, choral parts
omitted.

Example 15–161.   *Freedom, Our Queen*, measures 1–19, after score of 4-part arrangement.

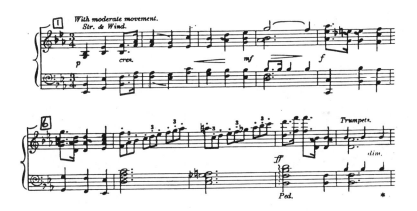

Example 15–161   (continued)

Example 15–162.   *Scenes from The Birds, Prelude,* measures 1–12; all examples after
piano vocal score.

Example 15–162   (continued)

Example 15–163.   *Scenes from The Birds, Prelude,* measures 30–34.

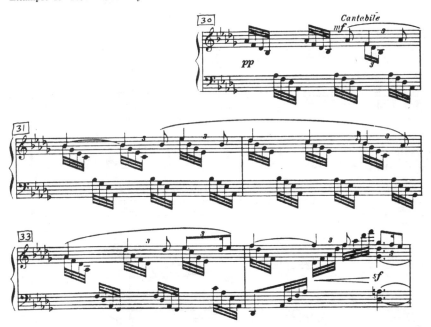

Example 15–164.   *Scenes from The Birds, Prelude*, measures 73–78.

Example 15–165.   *Scenes from The Birds, Prelude*, measures 96–103.

Example 15–166.   *Scenes from The Birds, Prelude,* measures 164–170.

Example 15–167.   *Scenes from The Birds, Prelude,* measures 176–182.

Example 15–168. *Scenes from The Birds*, No. 1, measures 14–20.

Example 15–169. *Scenes from The Birds*, No. 1, measures 108–113.

Example 15–170.   *Scenes from The Birds,* No. 1, measures 129–137, accompaniment
                    omitted.

Example 15–171.   *Scenes from The Birds,* No. 2, measures 27–34.

Example 15–172.   *Scenes from The Birds,* No. 3, measures 1–5.

Example 15–173.   *Scenes from The Birds,* No. 3, measures 44–50.

Example 15–174.   *Scenes from The Birds,* No. 4, measures 13–16, tenor part only.

Example 15–175.   *Scenes from The Birds,* No. 4, measures 36–44.

Example 15–176.   *Scenes from The Birds,* No. 4, measures 52–56.

Example 15–177.   *Scenes from The Birds,* No. 6, measures 1–8.

Example 15–177   (continued)

Example 15–178.   *Hymn of the West*, Hymn, measures 1–9.

Example 15–178   (continued)

gird The earth with splen - dor round,
show The mar - vels God hath wrought

Example 15–179.   *Hymn of the West,* Introduction, measures 6–13.

Example 15–180. *Hymn of the West,* Introduction, measures 28–36.

16

Opera

Il Pesceballo ("The One Fishball")
Mirabel in 4 acts, unfinished
Falstaf, unfinished

   The One Fishball was prepared for a series of Civil War benefits in Boston and Cambridge in 1862. It was based on a ballad by Professor George Martin Lane; Professor Francis J. Child wrote the Italian libretto, and James Russell Lowell provided an English translation. The music was assembled from airs by Mozart, Rossini, Bellini, and Donizetti; Paine arranged the score and provided recitatives, interludes, and other connecting passages. No score of the music has survived, except for a short incipit in the published libretto.[1] *Mirabel* and *Falstaf* are items in published biographical discussions on Paine; whether they ever actually existed is uncertain and a bit doubtful. The first, listed as a "romantic opera in 4 acts (MS., not yet finished)," was included in an 1890 article in Champlin's *Cyclopedia of Music and Musicians*.[2] W. S. B. Mathews wrote in 1900, "For a long time [Paine] was at work upon a 'Falstaf' which has never been performed. . . ."[3] Whether either of these was eventually transformed into *Azara*, or for that matter ever existed at all in the composer's mind, is subject only to conjecture.

Azara

   Libretto by the composer; German singing translation by Karl Pflueger.

   Autograph manuscript full score (in 3 volumes) and piano vocal score in Houghton Library, Harvard University. Another autograph manuscript piano vocal score in Boston Public Library, another (copy) in Music Division, Library of Congress.

   Excerpts also in Houghton Library: Introduction and part of Scene I from Act III, manuscript score for voices and piano; Introduction and Orchestral Scene from Act II, for concert use, manuscript full score and parts; Moorish Dances, manuscript full score.

   Piano-vocal score published by Breitkopf & Härtel, Leipzig, in 1901. Full score (*f. d. Privatgebrauch*) and 33 parts published by Breitkopf & Härtel, Leipzig, in 1908. Ballet Music (3 Moorish Dances), arranged for piano solo, also published by Breitkopf & Härtel.

Copies:

    Vocal score—BPL, BU, ESM, HMA, LC, Mich, NECM, NYPL, Phila, PPL, Smith, Tufts, Wellesley, Wis.

    Full score—BPL, ESM, Fleisher (Orchestral Scene, Three Moorish Dances only), HMus (+ parts), LC, NECM.

    Piano selections—HMA, PPL (2nd Moorish Dance only), Wellesley.

    Librettos—BPL, HMus.

Scored for 3 flutes, piccolo, 2 oboes, English horn, 2 clarinets, bass clarinet, 3 bassoons, 4 horns, additional horns on stage, 3 trumpets, additional trumpets on stage (12 or 6), 2 trombones, bass trombone, tuba, tambourine, timpani, bass drum, cymbals, triangle, harp, and strings.

Characters: Rainulf, King of Provence (bass); Gontran, his son (tenor); Azara, ward of Aymar (soprano); Aymar, Count and vassal of Rainulf (baritone); Odo, Count and royal page (mezzo-soprano); Malek, a Saracen chief (baritone); Garsie, a shepherdess (mezzo-soprano); Colas, a shepherd (alto); a Huntsman (tenor); Moorish Minstrels and Dancing-girls; Trumpeters; Chorus (Knights, Men at Arms, Lords, Ladies, Pages, Guards, Burghers, Maidens, Saracens, Attendants, etc.).

Azara required 15 years to reach completion; Paine started his opera in the spring of 1883,[4] and it was finished and in process of translation into German by July 1898.[5] Its performance history, of course, was quite disappointing. The work was never staged; it received only three concert performances, none of which was complete. The first, directed by Ephraim Cutter, Jr., was held at Chickering Hall on 7 May 1903; Cutter accompanied at the piano. Included were the first half of Act I, Scenes 1, 2, 4, and 5 from Act II, and the last half of Act III.[6] In addition, Paine played the piano arrangement of the introduction to Act II.[7] Cutter conducted a similar performance at his home on 14 March 1905.[8] The only performance with orchestra was at a 9 April 1907 Cecilia Society concert at Symphony Hall, conducted by B. J. Lang. Essentially the entire opera was sung, but cuts were still made, including all orchestral music—the preludes to each act, the Orchestral Scene from Act II, and the ballet music in Act III. The concert lasted 2½ hours; restoring the cuts would have added about 30 or 45 minutes to the performance.[9] Other programs included excerpts from *Azara*; soprano Alice Bates Rice and baritone Stephen Townsend both performed arias during 1902 and 1903. A popular orchestral excerpt was the ballet music, the *Three Moorish Dances*. The Boston Symphony Orchestra, under Gericke, was the first to perform them. They were included in March and April 1900 concerts in Boston, Cambridge, Philadelphia, Brooklyn, and Providence; in December 1903 they were heard again in Boston, and during the following month in Cambridge, Philadelphia, Brooklyn, New York, and Hartford.[10] The Chicago Orchestra under Theodore Thomas performed the Moorish Dances in October 1900,[11] and the Sousa Band played arrangements of them in 1902 and 1908.[12] Additional information regarding performances and their reception in the press may be found in Chapter 8 of the present study.

Paine based his libretto upon *Aucassin and Nicolette*, an early 13th-century French *chante-fable* in alternating prose and verse. This medieval love romance deals with Aucassin, son of a Provençal count, and his love, Nicolette, a captured Saracen. Details of the plot—their separation by the count, their escape and capture by the Saracens, Aucassin's becoming Count upon the death of his father, Nicolette's identification as the Saracen king's daughter, her return to Provence in minstrel disguise, and the lovers' happy reunion[13]—all are paralleled in Paine's version. Following is a synopsis of the plot of *Azara*, with parts selected from two contemporary sources:

> Rainulf, King of Provence, is at war with the Saracens under Malek; and, being infirm, awaits in his castle news from the near-by battle in which his son Gontran commands and in which the enemy are beaten. Gontran claims his promised reward, which was to be of his own choice, and specifies Azara, a beautiful Moorish girl, who is the ward of Rainulf's vassal, Count Aymar.
>
> The King is struck by her charms and decides on taking possession of her himself, ordering his son to make a political match with a Spanish princess and sending [Azara] away with her guardian. Gontran is duly exasperated, but pleads for his due until he loses patience with his father, sets free his captive, the chieftain Malek, renounces his allegiance after threatening his father with his sword and charging him with various iniquities. This brings to a vehement close a tumultuous and stormy act in which the rays of fight and conquest and the animosities of races and peoples have been contrasted. In the hurly-burly Malek has escaped. It hardly needs to be said that Azara and Gontran are deeply in love with one another, and the purpose of the opera is to unite them happily.
>
> The second act shows Azara as a more active figure in the circumstances of her own fate. Aymar has fled with her from the royal castle, and they are resting in the wood till daybreak. Shepherds tell him that Gontran was not killed in the quarrel with his father, as they supposed, and the old man goes in search of him. As Azara waits alone with her fancies, . . .[14] Malek appears, and discovers that Azara is the lost daughter of the caliph, of whom he has been sent in search. He urges her to return with him, and pleads his love. She refuses, reminds him in vain of Gontran's generosity to him, and is rescued from enforced submission only by Gontran's appearance. Rainulf arrives, and claims the care of Azara. But Gontran shows a papal edict, excommunicating Rainulf for former crimes.[15] The previous quarrel is renewed, and in the midst of it an ambushing party of Saracens fall upon them; in the struggle the king is killed, living just long enough to entreat his son's forgiveness, while Malek bears Azara in triumph to his galley and sails away with his prize, while his men yell their war cry and the Provençals shout for vengeance as the act ends.
>
> A year is supposed to elapse. Gontran, now king, still mourns his lost Azara, and finds small comfort in Aymar's assurance that Malek has had to render her up to her father, at whose [Moorish] court she lives. It is a day of festivity, with joyous songs and brilliant dances.
>
> Malek appears in the disguise of a minstrel and lets it be known that he is again in pursuit of Azara, who has escaped from her home and probably is trying to make her way to Provence. A young troubadour enters, whom Malek recognizes as Azara, and who sings to the assembly a veiled story of her love and her vicissitudes. She

throws off her mantle and reveals her identity to Gontran, when Malek, unable to restrain longer his jealous passion and determination to possess or kill her, springs upon her, but is disarmed and repelled. Then, in a burst of remorse and despair, he throws himself at her feet and begs for pardon. Then he suddenly draws another dagger, which he had concealed, as William Tell his second arrow, and kills himself. A little thing like that does not disturb "the general joy of the whole table" at a brisk mediaeval festival. His body is carried forth, and the lovers break out into an enraptured amorous song, with which are blended the acclamations and jubilations of the multitude.

Except for the *Scenes from "The Birds"* and the *Hymn of the West*, both relatively minor, *Azara* was the last composition that Paine completed. A period of 15 years elapsed between inception and completion, a major portion of his life, and the opera may be seen as a summation of his compositional career. The fact that he also wrote the libretto—entirely in rhymed verse and in a somewhat archaic form of the language, reflecting the medieval period of the story—underscores his total commitment to the work. His choice of a plot based on historical fable, with its elements of family and religious strife, betrayal, kidnapping, masquerade, and final triumph of love are common to the nineteenth-century European tradition, particularly German. The flow of the music is continuous within each act, but individual arias, ensembles, and choruses are clearly recognizable. The individual roles are eminently vocal, and, moreover, ample opportunity is provided for traditional virtuoso display. The orchestra plays an exceedingly important part in the work, although never overwhelming the voices. Changes in mood, characterization, and plot are effectively depicted, and independent orchestral movements—introductions to Acts II and III, the Orchestral Scene from Act II, and the ballet music—are especial examples of Paine's orchestral skill, color, and variety.

There are some weaknesses in the plot of *Azara*. Rainulf's attraction to Azara seems too hasty to justify his jealous disinheritance of his son Gontran. In Act II it is surprising to learn later that all during Azara and Gontran's love duet he had harbored the knowledge, learned only that morning, that Rainulf had murdered his mother and now was excommunicated from the Church. Most disconcerting because of its historical improbability is the Saracen chief, Malek, who carries a portrait of the caliph's dead wife and uses it to identify Azara as her daughter; a devout Moslem such as he would certainly follow the injunction of his religion forbidding pictorial representations of persons. But these are no more serious problems than are encountered in many operas whose popularity seems not to be affected by such details. Musical value and theatrical effectiveness prove to be much more important qualities.

Azara was hailed by contemporary writers for its strong Wagnerian characteristics, especially for a composer who had so vehemently criticized Wagner earlier in his career. True, much of Paine's later music was influenced by Wagner, as was most music composed at the end of the nineteenth century. But Wagner's innovations—in opera form, harmony, and orchestration—were absorbed into the common musical vocabulary, and such features in Paine's compositions do not necessarily imply a heavy direct reliance upon the earlier composer. In communications to Henry T. Finck, Paine himself acknowledged a debt to Wagner but denied wholesale imitation:

> . . . You will find that I have entered upon a new path in all respects—in form, thematic treatment, instrumentation, etc. All dramatic composers must learn from Wagner, yet I have not consciously imitated him in style, etc. . . .

> . . . I have followed throughout the connected orchestral rhythmic flow, and truth of dramatic expression characteristic of Wagner. . . .[16]

A technical feature of *Azara* that may be called Wagnerian is the use of recurring themes. But in the main these are complete melodies that return in a sense of recapitulation or reprise, not *Leitmotive* that are transformed or modified to permeate the texture as in Wagner's *Ring* operas. Two themes, however, are treated in such a manner throughout the work. The first, associated with the Moors and with Malek, is heard at the very beginning, first in the orchestra and then by a chorus of Saracens, "Allah illa Allah!" (Example 16–1) sung behind the curtain before the first scene begins. Subsequent recurrences are mainly in the orchestra: to introduce Malek's aria following his release by Gontran in Act I (Example 16–2A); to announce his entrance in the scene with Azara in Act II (Example 16–2B); later in the act as Rainulf's knights are attacked by the Saracens, who kidnap Azara (Example 16–2C); in the last act, with Malek and Azara both in minstrel disguise, as he declares his intention to kill Gontran (Example 16–2D); and in the final measures, accompanying the triumphant notes of the chorus and soloists (see Example 16–43, measures 435–437). The other *Leitmotiv*, which appears only in the orchestra, is associated with Azara herself. It is first heard, delicately scored, as Gontran leads Azara before Rainulf, to announce their plans to marry. The melody elaborates a sustained tonic triad, using the added sixth and major seventh; a subsequent German sixth returns again to the tonic chord (Example 16–3). This theme recurs over a moving bass line in the orchestral introduction to Act II (Example 16–4A), and soon afterward, in Scene 1, is heard in a manner similar to the original, as Aymar sings,

Ah me! how shall I keep mine eyes awake
And watch the weary hours for her dear sake?

There are two appearances in the Orchestral Scene that follows: the first, in the "Dawn and Daybreak" portion, varies the beginning of the theme and treats it canonically, while the bird calls that are heard throughout this section continue above (Example 16–4B); soon afterward, the Azara theme begins the climactic "Broad Daylight" portion that concludes the scene (Example 16–4C). A quotation appears at the close of Azara and Gontran's duet in Act II (Example 16–4D), with added emphasis on the German 6th; a similar quotation is included in the final chorus of the last act. The theme is also heard softly in the last act as Azara enters, disguised as a Spanish troubadour, and again after she sings, "God strengthen me to prove the faithfulness of Love." Azara herself sings the theme in the last act, where it forms the basis for her troubadour song ballad, sung in disguise (Example 16–4E).

Other instrumental motives are found in the second act, three appearing in the introduction. The first, in the opening bars, appears later to suggest Gontran's supposed death (Example 16–5); a second (Example 16–6) is associated with Azara's pensive mood over the loss of Gontran; and the third depicts Rainulf, the tyrant (Example 16–7). This last motive first appears in the opening scene after Aymar sings,

> God guard her slumbers till the waking morn
> Bring hope to guide us to the distant bourne
> Beyond the sea, far from the tyrant's hand.

In a later scene it is preceded by the first motive, as Aymar refuses to believe the news from Garsie, Colas, and the Huntsman that Gontran is alive (Example 16–8). The "tyrant" theme is sounded once more in Scene 6 as Rainulf and his attendants appear following Azara and Gontran's duet. Azara's pensive theme appears at the beginning of the "Dawn and Daybreak" portion of the Orchestral Scene, and again as she comes on stage after Malek's Act II aria, before she is aware of his presence.

Recurring themes assigned to singers in the main are confined to the first act, where they function as recapitulative devices to produce an element of design in the unbroken hour-long section. A study of these themes and others reveals a familial relationship to other Paine melodies, especially in the choral works and art songs. Beginning upward leaps of a sixth or a fourth are common, and the latter interval is frequently found in interior positions, often a product of pentatonic construction. Accented appoggiaturas and suspensions are still found regularly, and chromatic pitches, both nonharmonic and as part of altered chords, are more numerous than in earlier works. Pedal points still dilute harmonic activity at the beginnings of many melodies, but authentic cadences are less often evaded; altered dominants are common, however, especially the augmented triad, usually with a minor seventh. Deceptive resolutions of the dominant seventh may often be found at phrase endings, modulating either to the lowered submediant or to the key a half step below tonic (with the dominant seventh resolving enharmonically as a German sixth). Chromatically altered pitches include the raised second and fourth degrees of the major scale, resolving to the third and fifth, respectively, of the tonic triad.

The first theme to be emphasized through repetition is heard as Rainulf reacts in surprise to the news that his son is a hero. Leaps of sixth and fourths, a tonic pedal, and emphasis on the raised second and fourth scale degrees are typical of Paine's style (Example 16–9). Rainulf repeats the melody, with the opening bars slightly changed, after meeting Azara—"A newborn passion sways my longing heart." Later the first part of the melody is heard after Gontran enters, as Rainulf sings, "My son, bend not the knee as one who pleads." A second melody Rainulf sings in the opening portion of the scene as he gazes upon Azara for the first time (Example 16–10). Throughout, a tonic pedal point is maintained, ensuring a sense of tonal stability; most harmonies serve to embellish the tonic triad, including a respelled German sixth (measure 116) and a lowered submediant triad (measure 118), both of which resolve to tonic by means of elliptical progressions—those that avoid the traditional syntax (see analysis staff in Example 16–10). The initial leap of a fourth, the accented appoggiatura on "divine," and the chromatic altered pitches are consistent with the composer's melodic style; the delicate scoring— a favored sonority in Meyerbeer's operas, especially measure 117—is similar to some appearances of the "Azara" theme discussed above. After Azara's royalty is disclosed by Aymar, and she pleads with Rainulf to allow her to marry Gontran, he again begs her hand, "Whate'er thy sovran craves, deny him not," with a repeat of the theme and its orchestration.

Gontran's love song (Example 16–11), directed to Azara before Rainulf and the crowd, contains the same features—an initial ascending fourth, accented appoggiaturas on "warms" and "spring," and a raised fourth scale degree in measure 294. Chromatically altered chords, for coloristic purposes, include a minor subdominant triad (measure 292), a German sixth, resolved with irregular voice leading (measure 293), and a lowered sub-mediant triad (measure 295)—basically the same chord as the German sixth, used as a pivot to modulate to E-flat. Typical Paine features include the triplet figure in measures 292–293, seen in nearly all major works since the *Mass in D*, and the melodic turn in measure 295. The opening phrase is quoted in Act II as Gontran enters. Another theme, shared by Gontran and the chorus, shows similar features, such as the opening ascending fourth, although differing greatly in mood—it is first heard as Gontran prepares to release Malek after his plea for Azara's hand is rejected by Rainulf (Example 16–12). Following Malek's extended aria, after Gontran prevents the guards from obeying Rainulf's order to seize the Saracen chieftain again, the chorus repeats this theme with "O prince! thy headlong rashness we deplore," and following Rainulf's banishment of Gontran, sings, "Alas! ill-fated son! ah bitter woe!" This final passage leads directly to a related melody sung by Gontran (Example 16–13), which serves as the basis for the ensemble and chorus that concludes the act. Here again are melodic fourths, emphasized appoggiaturas and suspensions, and a melodic turn. The C-major key eventually is shown to be the Neapolitan of the prevailing B minor. The closing measures of the act display resonant choral writing and an energetic orchestral part, incorporating the favorite dotted-note triplet rhythm (Example 16–14). As the curtain falls, two triads, G minor and E flat, have only a remote relationship to the final tonic chord, forming a series of tonic to lowered-submediant progressions that recall the elliptical progressions of Example 16–10. Quite possibly Paine thought of this as the ultimate in harmonic daring. Similar to the theme in Example 16–13 is the melody sung by Gontran in Act III, while hoping that Azara is safe in her father's castle (Example 16–15); again, the emphasis on sixths, fourths, accented non-harmonic tones, and the melodic turn may be noted, along with a polonaise rhythm in the accompaniment that gives a quite non-Wagnerian effect to the passage.

An opening ascending sixth may be seen in two of Rainulf's themes, the first sung as he commends his soldiers on the victory in battle (Example 16–16). The opening pitches, identical to those in Example 16–9, are mostly pentatonic; Paine's dotted-note triplet serves as an accompaniment. This theme recurs as Rainulf disapproves of Gontran's promise to Azara and announces plans for Gontran to marry the princess from Aragon: "With honor crowned, O serve the ends of state!" Later in the act another theme with the same opening interval—only in minor—is sung by Rainulf; rhythmically it is far more aggressive, and again uses two of Paine's favorite patterns—the dotted note triplets and alternating treble and bass—in the accompaniment (Example 16–17).

Azara's melodies exhibit similar characteristics—ascending large leaps, skips of a fourth, emphasized appoggiaturas, and regular use of the raised second or fourth scale degree in major. Harmonically, added sixth, major ninth, and chromatically altered chords are regular sonorities. Her first main aria begins desperately (Example 16–18), after Rainulf has ordered that she become his queen; irregular phrase lengths, dissonant chords (such as the 13th chord on "heart" in measure 571), and chromatic progressions seemingly without clear direction (measures 573–574) add to the sense of turbulence. A subsequent section modulates to the relative major, with thoughts directed toward Gontran; an expressive climax and release of tension are achieved with several very effective ninth and thirteenth sonorities, especially in measures 596–597 (Example 16–19).

Azara's solo is followed by a lovely ensemble and chorus that provides a climax for this part of the scene. At the beginning is a duet between Gontran and Azara, with irregular phrase lengths, metric and rhythmic changes, and disjunct melodic motion giving interest to a rather ordinary harmonic scheme (Example 16–20). After an abrupt modulation to A flat, the singers are joined by Rainulf and Odo, the page (a mezzosoprano). The voices enter imitatively, with Rainulf and Odo repeating the melody the king had sung when seeing Azara (Example 16–10). Azara, on the other hand, sings the melody of Gontran's love song (Example 16–11), and Gontran's entrance is also based on this theme; the two melodies begin similarly, and the effect of imitation is preserved (Example 16–21). An arpeggiated theme follows, its first gesture entirely pentatonic (Example 16–22). In the first phrase the harmony embellishes tonic, in the main, and a tonic pedal point is repeated throughout. A return of the duet melody from Example 16–20 shows some effective close harmony for the quartet, especially the parallel V$^6_5$ chords in measures 717–18 (Example 16–23). This passage, followed by a crescendo, stringendo, and entrance of the chorus, shows the great skill in writing for chorus that Paine achieved through his many choral works.

In Act II Azara participates even more extensively, with several short arias plus her *scena*. First is her reaction to the news that Gontran is alive. A spirited melody (Example 16–24), incorporating the Paine triplet, includes appoggiaturas ("throbbing," "undaunted"), added sixth ("fly"), and French sixth ("knight"). The leaps for "On Hope's" and "O fly" are effective portrayals of the text, as well as being attractive vocally. Azara is then joined by the two Shepherds, the Huntsman, and Aymar. Garsie and Colas introduce themselves in a charming duet, very much in the character of a folk song of a clearly identifiable Paine flavor on account of its pedal with chromatics. The accompaniment is scored for woodwinds (primarily double reeds), lower strings *divisi*, and a horn drone, adding greatly to the pastoral image (Example 16–25). Soon the Huntsman takes part, and the number concludes as a quintet. As the others leave, Azara begins her *scena* over an undulating accompaniment (Example 16–26), a rather unique rhythm, possibly a pseudo-Arabic or Moorish dance rhythm, for a similar pattern occurs in the third Moorish Dance in Act III (see Example 16–59). The resulting effect is quite different from anything found in operas by Wagner or Verdi. Upward skips of a fourth in the opening phrase give a pentatonic effect; feminine cadences on "trembling leaves" and "caress" sustain the gentle mood. With a modulation to A flat, the "Azara" theme is heard in the orchestra; Azara herself embellishes it (Example 16–27). A nightingale is heard, and Azara entreats it to carry her message to Gontran. The reminder of danger brings the "tyrant" theme in the orchestra, followed in the brass by what is almost Wagner's "Fate" motive from his *Ring* cycle (Example 16–28), but the nightingale's song is again reassuring. As Azara retreats, Malek enters, who observes her and then realizes that she is the lost Moorish princess. When she returns to find him, she is apprehensive and hostile, but receives the tale of her parents with emotion. As she looks at her mother's portrait, she sings a quiet expressive melody, with ascending fourths, and accompanied by a harmonic sequence, tonic-dominant progressions a major third apart, in E flat, C flat, G, and again E flat (Example 16–29), again involving the lowered submediant triad in a series of deceptive resolutions. This passage is similar, especially in its scoring, to a passage in the Coronation Scene of Meyerbeer's *Le Prophète*. After Malek leaves, Gontran appears. A short melody, accompanied by the "Azara" theme, is followed by a lengthy (182 measures), dramatic duet, based mainly on themes from the first act duet and chorus (see Examples 16–20 and 16–22). The conclusion is quite brilliant, with demanding lines for the singers (see Example 16–4D above). Typical Paine features are the triplet accompanimetnal figure, the Neapolitan harmony (measure 234), and quotation of the "Azara" theme in measure 239ff. This passage in the main is a repetition of the conclusion of Gontran's aria in Act I, where he proclaims, "Azara shall be my bride!"

The role of Malek contains some of the most original writing in *Azara*. Such an exotic character would have been quite in fashion in the late nineteenth century, and according to Henry Taylor Parker in his *Transcript* review of the 1907 concert performance, Paine spent much time researching Arabian music in order to achieve the proper effect. The two most common devices he incorporates are rapid melismas and the melodic augmented second. Following a "Tristan" chord (in function, not sonority), a melisma is heard in Malek's first utterance, upon being freed by Gontran and receiving his sword (Example 16–30); an augmented second follows soon after (Example 16–31). In the main, harmonic progressions are simpler and less chromatic in Malek's music; as a result, the melodies are more straightforward rhythmically and usually have a more sharply defined profile. Modal inflections add to the exotic flavor; occasional C naturals give momentary Lydian color to the main melody of this aria (Example 16–32). In the second act Malek's part at first is similar to that of the other roles, including singing over the orchestral "Azara" theme as he compares her face with that on the portrait he carries. But when he addresses her, occasional syllables sung to short triplets suggest characteristic melismas (Example 16–33). His aria entreating her to accompany him is attractive rhythmically and melodically; an augmented second retains the oriental flavor (Example 16–34). Malek expresses his love for Azara more vehemently as she repeatedly spurns him; an apparently authentic Arabic melodic figure clashes effectively with the E-minor harmony at the words, "to call thee mine" (Example 16–35). The scene ends with a duet. Following the kidnapping and battle, Malek is seen holding the unconscious Azara aboard the Saracen ship as it sails past. His melody is derived from the "Allah illa Allah" theme, and contains extensive melismas at the ends of periods (Example 16–36).

In Act III Malek enters in minstrel disguise, tired and disheartened, and his initial music is turbulent but not characteristically oriental. Upon recognizing Azara, disguised as a troubadour, he sings an ardent melody, typical much more of the operatic mainstream than the Middle Eastern music used in the earlier acts. However, a later passage suggests the "Allah illa Allah" theme, and the word "fly" brings a substantial melisma (Example 16–37). A thought of Gontran brings hatred and a recurrence of the "Allah illa Allah"-based melody (see Example 16–2D) first heard at the conclusion of Act II (see Example 16–36). While listening to Azara's tale to Gontran, he grows insanely jealous, and as she removes her disguise, he attempts to kill her. Unsuccessful, and immediately remorseful at his act of violence toward her, he sings above a very chromatic background (Example 16–38), and after a final melisma, he stabs himself and dies.

Paine's music for the chorus shows a decided skill and craftsmanship, as was noted earlier, which stems from more than 30 years' experience in writing for massed voices. The chorus is first heard as Gontran and his knights return victorious from battle. Following trumpet fanfares from off stage (scored for 12 or 6 trumpets in B flat), the chorus enters, hailing the victors, with a brilliant orchestral accompaniment (Example 16–39). A vigorous march melody follows, in a predictable operatic style but nevertheless bearing melodic traces of pentatonic flavor at key points; men of the chorus (Knights) begin it in unison, and later the setting is increased to the 4-part mixed chorus. Following Rainulf's praise to his soldiers (Example 16–16), the chorus returns, with more elaborate choral writing including a short canon; directions in the score allow this section to be cut. At this point the SATB chorus again sings "Hail" as Gontran, Aymar, and the remaining knights enter and salute the king (see Example 16–51), then sing a broad hymn to Gontran and

Provence (Example 16–40). Complete with pentatonic elements (measure 134), this resembles patriotic melodies Paine had previously composed, including the *Centennial Hymn* and *Columbus Hymn*, and the first phrase has a marked similarity to the opening of the *Hymn of the West*; curiously, all are in the key of D major.

As the act unfolds, the chorus has an important role in reacting to the drama, especially between Rainulf and Gontran. At the conclusion, the chorus joins Gontran in his last aria, leading to a grand ending (see Example 16–14). In Act II, the male chorus participates in the battle, both Knights and Saracens. After the fighting, the Ladies somehow appear on stage to complete the ensemble. The interplay between the Saracens and the members of the Provençal court is quite effective (Example 16–41).

Choruses in Act III are joyful. As part of the Maytime festivities, the Lords and Ladies sing another paean to Gontran, who is now their king (Example 16–42). This chorus, in triple meter with a polonaise rhythm, is much more joyous, less stately, than the hymn presented in the first act. Ever typical of Paine's style are appoggiaturas (measures 30, 35), other accented nonharmonic tones (measures 40, 41), and the melodic turn (measure 34). The 4-part harmonization is skillful, and a hint of imitation is implied at measure 32. At the end of the opera, the chorus joins Gontran and Azara in a continuation of their last duet. These final measures (Example 16–43) are an indication of Paine's choral skill and his understanding of the value of a chorus in producing an overwhelming climax. The choral and vocal writing is high and full; some details were added after the piano vocal score was published. Rhythmically the accompaniment is propelled by Paine's triplet figure. An expanded harmonic vocabulary is seen, especially with an "omnibus" progression in measures 430–31 and other non-functional harmony in measures 431–34. The Neapolitan chord is stressed in measures 418–19 and 436. Prominent thematic quotations include the "Azara" theme in measures 424–27, and "Allah illa Allah" at measure 435.

The harmonic vocabulary of *Azara* is consistent with that of other recent works, especially the *Island Fantasy*. Added sixths are common in a conclusive sonority (see Example 16–4D, measures 246–50), and major ninths are often sustained and figurated without a strong feeling for immediate resolution (see Example 16–9). Tonic pedal points, emphasized melodic nonharmonic tones, and decorated cadences, with ninth and thirteenth sonorities, remain common devices. Progressions of chords or chord sequences a major third away may often be found, as in the final bar of Act I (see Example 16–14) and in Azara's solo as she views her mother's portrait (see Example 16–28). Modulations at this distance are also frequent. For example, the Act I quartet that begins with Example 16–21 thereafter arrives at a cadence in B-flat major. The triad is followed by a direct shift to F-sharp major (to prepare Example 16–22), and the common B flat/A sharp is the only link between the keys. Less abrupt modulations, but still surprising, occur in Azara's reply to the Shepherds' good news in Act II (Example 16–44). The key of E flat (with a hint of C minor) changes to C flat (a major third away) at measure 216, and then returns to E flat at measure 219; in both instances the supertonic chord resolves to the tonic triad, second inversion, in the new key. A quick glimpse at several keys is seen in a short excerpt from the third Moorish dance (Example 16–45). Within eight bars deceptive resolutions and chromatic progressions lead from A flat to C flat, E minor, G major, B major, E-flat major, and back to A flat.

A chromatically altered chord encountered regularly in *Azara* is the German sixth, used both as an embellishment for the tonic triad and as a means for enharmonic modulation. A typical example of the embellishing usage is seen in Example 16–4D. The first occurrence (measure 241) has the chord in second inversion, with a tonic pedal remaining throughout—this is the "Azara" theme, and most of its appearances utilize this harmonization. A return to the German sixth in measures 243–45 has the usual inversion. The chord is then respelled as a dominant seventh, but still resolves as a German sixth. Another similar use of the German sixth to embellish tonic, with pedal point, occurs at the beginning of Aymar's aria in Act I telling of Azara's background (Example 16–46); unfortunately (or perhaps deliberately), this passage bears a strong resemblance to the *Liebesruhe* theme from Wagner's *Tristan und Isolde*[17] (Example 16–47). In the Act I quartet a German sixth (respelled) is used as a climactic harmony, but is replaced by another supertonic sonority which progresses regularly (see Example 16–23, measure 721). An example of a German sixth used for modulation occurs early in the opera when, in the processional scene, a dominant seventh in E flat suddenly resolves as a German sixth in D (see Example 16–39, measures 22–23). A similar use occurs in Azara's Act II *scena*, where, at the Wagner "Fate" motive noted earlier (see Example 16–28, measures 92–93), a German sixth in B minor is resolved as if it were a dominant seventh in C major. This resulting C chord remains in effect until measure 96, when the singer's A sharp converts it into another German sixth, to return to B major.

Nonfunctional chromatic progressions are common during dramatic scenes. A short series of augmented triads accompanies Rainulf's command following Malek's release (Example 16–48). In the Orchestral Scene a harmonic sequence contains four units of a major triad followed by a major-minor seventh chord a tritone away (measures 130–37); neither chord resolves traditionally (Example 16–49), and triads proceed chromatically in the next three measures. Another sequence of alternating triads and major-minor sevenths is found earlier in the Orchestral Scene, colorfully scored (Example 16–50); a later repetition displays varied instrumentation. A chromatic progression of major triads (measures 126–28) accompanies Gontran's salute to the king in the triumphant processional scene of Act I; this is preceded by an almost complete "omnibus" progression (Example 16–51). Another progression similar to the "omnibus" is heard (measures 41–42) as Gontran cries out following Azara's kidnapping and Rainulf's mortal wounding in Act II (Example 16–52). A complete "omnibus" is heard near the end of the opera (see Example 16–43, measures 430–31); the passage continues with a nonfunctional progression of triads and seventh chords, with most root movement by third, tritone, or major second. In the last measures an augmented triad resolves to the final tonic sonority; this same progression ends the Act II finale (see Example 16–41, measures 103–5) and occurs near the end of the third Moorish Dance.

The orchestration of *Azara* is the result of a lifetime of writing and refining, beginning with studies under Wieprecht in Berlin and continuing with experience gained from the *Mass in D*, *St. Peter*, the symphonies, the other symphonic works, and the many compositions for chorus and orchestra. Paine called for a larger orchestra than he required in any of the orchestral works, writing parts for tripled woodwinds, greatly increased brass, a larger percussion section, and more extensive *divisi* passages in the strings. Scoring is full and sonorous, yet transparent and varied; typical—and varied—examples of climactic passages may be seen in Examples 16–1, 16–4C, 16–14, 16–39, and 16–41. Example 16–3 is a short passage containing several different colors, including muted strings with harp, woodwind chords, and a conclusion for brass. Atmospheric string writing such as this, already seen in the *Island Fantasy*, is also found in the beginning of Azara's *scena*, "Softly and balmy zephyr sighs" (see Example 16–26).

In the two major symphonic movements—the Orchestral Scene from Act II and the "Ballet: Three Moorish Dances" from Act III—may be seen the widest demonstration of Paine's mature orchestral manner. No concert performances of the Orchestral Scene in excerpt are known, but the fact that separate manuscript score and parts were prepared (and also that performance materials for this excerpt are now in the Fleisher Collection in Philadelphia) would suggest that such performances were anticipated. The opening measures depict the lapping of the waves

(Example 16–53), as well as other "mysterious forest sounds." Additional quotations may be examined in Examples 16–4B and C, 16–49, and 16–50. The Three Moorish Dances, which take place in the third act after the opening chorus praising King Gontran, and just before Malek and Azara make their appearance. These pieces are appropriate vehicles for exotic, colorful writing, and Paine's success in this medium is indicated by the many performances the dances have received.[18] Solo lines are often given to woodwinds, especially double reeds, and instrumental combinations are numerous, changing often. Paine's orchestral works do not call for percussion at all, except for timpani; in contrast, the Moorish Dances have prominent parts for tambourine and triangle, as well as bass drum and cymbals. The first dance begins with a timpani roll and a fanfare motive outlining the tritone and already setting an exotic mood. The bassoon continues with a quick-moving passage stressing the melodic augmented second, also producing an oriental flavor (Example 16–54). This grows in the first theme, a lilting melody also centering around the augmented second, played by the first violins and colored by an oboe (Example 16–55). Rapid sixteenth-note chords show great contrasts in range and color (measures 35–37). Following a repeat of the section, a new melody, in the relative major, is heard in the tenor range with violas and cellos (Example 16–56); different doublings are heard at each recurrence. The dance plunges forward relentlessly, rhythmically to an exuberant conclusion. Dance II begins leisurely with a gentle English Horn melody over a swaying accompaniment in the strings (Example 16–57). Again, orchestration is varied upon repetition, along with added countermelodies. This dance is relatively brief—only 54 bars—and is followed by a written out repeat of the first dance, with its introduction abridged and the repeats omitted. The third dance begins with an extensive introduction. A dramatic unison statement (Example 16–58) outlines the tritone and evinces a modal feeling. Colorful passages for harp alternate with the opening sixteenth-note motive, and lead to the graceful first theme, in violins, flutes, and clarinets (Example 16–59); in measure 32 there is a hint of the *Liebesruhe*, or Aymar, theme from Examples 16–46 and 16–47. A contrasting section, in A flat, has a heavier scoring, with cellos, violas, trumpet, horn, and clarinet on the alto-range melody, and the bass notes emphasized with the timpani and bass drum (Example 16–60). A later phrase (see Example 16–45) abandons the percussion, and builds from strings with woodwind melody to a fuller ensemble amplified by brass and tremolo strings. The dance serves as a climax to the ballet; it is longer—198 bars—than either of the other two, and contains two *fortississimo* peaks.

Azara is a work that definitely deserves further study and performance.
It is well written and should prove of value and enjoyment to a public that
has come to reevaluate and appreciate the contributions of nineteenth-
century composers. Paine's music is always dramatically appropriate, and
his writing is skillful and effective both for voices and for orchestra. A
large orchestra is required, but the demands are reasonable. Only two
scene changes are called for, and these are between acts. The fact that
the vocal score, orchestral score, and parts were carefully engraved and
published would greatly reduce the problems of preparing a performing
edition.[19] One may repeat the plea for performance first expressed over
75 years ago by a reviewer for the *Boston Herald*:

> "Azara" ought not to be very difficult of production, and one wishes that there
> were an ambitious and able American company to present it. Its scenery should be
> handsome, but easy for a good landscapist, and the costumes are not exacting. The
> principal singers should be good, but they need not be great. They must show strong
> feeling and behave as if they meant business; yet they might be acceptable even if
> rather conventional in action. A chorus of average excellence would do, and nothing
> unusual is required for the orchestra, which should be liberal in its wooden wind,
> the usual percussion, a harp and a few extra trumpets and horns for the stage.[20]

Example 16–1. *Azara,* Act I, Introduction, measures 23–30 (after full score; German text omitted from all examples).

Example 16–2.   *Azara*

a. Act I, Scene 3, measures 40–44; addition to Malek's part
   included from 1908 full score.

b. Act II, Scene 3, measures 129–132, and Scene 4, measures
   1–5.

Example 16–2 (continued)

c. Act II, Scene 7, measures 1–8.

d. Act III, Scene 4, measures 133–137.

Example 16–3.   *Azara,* Act I, Scene 2, measures 208–214.

Example 16–4.   *Azara.*

a. Act II, Introduction, measures 51–56.

Example 16–4 (continued)

a.

b. Act II, Scene 1b, measures 103–110.

c. Act II, Scene 1b, measures 122–129.

Example 16–4   (continued)

c.

d. Act II, Scene 5, measures 231–250.

Example 16–4 (continued)

d.

e. Act III, Scene 4, measures 224–230.

Example 16–5.   *Azara,* Act II, Introduction, measures 1–6.

Example 16–6.   *Azara*, Act II, Introduction, measures 25–31.

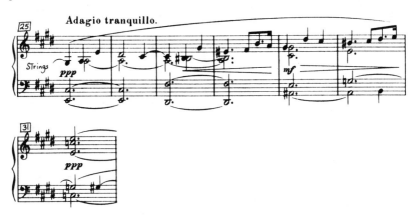

Example 16–7.   *Azara*, Act II, Introduction, measures 60–66.

Example 16–8.   *Azara*, Act II, Scene 2, measures 150–165.

Example 16–8   (continued)

Example 16–9.   *Azara*, Act I, Scene 1, measures 80–89.

Example 16–10.   *Azara,* Act I, Scene 1, measures 113–119.

Example 16–11.   *Azara,* Act I, Scene 2, measures 288–296.

Example 16–11   (continued)

Example 16–12.   *Azara,* Act I, Scene 3, measures 4–11.

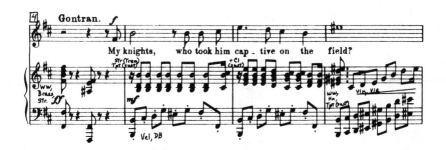

Example 16–12   (continued)

Example 16–13.   *Azara,* Act I, Scene 3, measures 386–393.

Example 16–14.   *Azara*, Act I, Scene 3, measures 425–438.

Example 16–14   (continued)

Example 16–15.   *Azara,* Act III, Scene 1, measures 104–111.

Example 16– 15 (continued)

Example 16– 16. *Azara*, Act I, Scene 2, measures 77–81.

Example 16–17.   *Azara,* Act I, Scene 3, measures 285–294.

Example 16–18.   *Azara,* Act I, Scene 2, measures 570–576.

Example 16–18   (continued)

Example 16–19.   *Azara*, Act I, Scene 2, measures 591–597.

Example 16–19   (continued)

Example 16–20.   *Azara*, Act I, Scene 2, measures 660–667.

Example 16–20   (continued)

Example 16–21.   *Azara,* Act I, Scene 2, measures 677–685.

Example 16–21　(continued)

Example 16–21   (continued)

Example 16–22.   *Azara*, Act I, Scene 2, measures 695–705.

Example 16–22   (continued)

Example 16–22   (continued)

Example 16–23.   *Azara,* Act I, Scene 2, measures 716–730.

Example 16–23   (continued)

Example 16–23   (continued)

Example 16–24.   *Azara,* Act II, Scene 2, measures 205–213.

Example 16–24   (continued)

Example 16–25.   *Azara,* Act II, Scene 2, measures 47–61.

Example 16–25   (continued)

Example 16–26.   *Azara*, Act II, Scene 3, measures 5–12.

Example 16–26   (continued)

Example 16–27.   *Azara*, Act II, Scene 3, measures 28–41.

Example 16–27   (continued)

Example 16–28.   *Azara,* Act II, Scene 3, measures 88–97.

Example 16–28   (continued)

Example 16–29.   *Azara*, Act II, Scene 4, measures 97–102.

Example 16–30.   *Azara,* Act I, Scene 3, measures 37–39.

Example 16–31.   *Azara,* Act I, Scene 3, measures 46–51.

Example 16–32.   *Azara,* Act I, Scene 3, measures 68–74.

Example 16– 32 (continued)

Example 16–33.   *Azara,* Act II, Scene 4, measures 64–69.

Example 16–34.   *Azara,* Act II, Scene 4, measures 130–137.

Example 16–34   (continued)

Example 16–35.   *Azara,* Act II, Scene 4, measures 230–240.

Example 16–35   (continued)

Example 16–36.   *Azara,* Act II, Scene 8, measures 54–64.

Example 16–36   (continued)

Example 16–37.   *Azara,* Act III, Scene 4, measures 61–73.

Example 16–37   (continued)

Example 16–38.   *Azara,* Act III, Scene 4, measures 368–376.

Example 16–38   (continued)

Example 16–39.   *Azara,* Act I, Scene 2, measures 19–40.

Example 16–39   (continued)

Example 16–39   (continued)

Example 16–40.   *Azara,* Act I, Scene 2, measures 132–141.

Example 16–40   (continued)

Example 16–41.   *Azara*, Act II, Scene 8, measures 81–105.

Example 16–41   (continued)

Example 16–41   (continued)

Example 16–41   (continued)

Example 16–42.   *Azara,* Act III, Scene 2, measures 25–43.

Example 16–42   (continued)

Example 16–43.   *Azara,* Act III, Scene 4, measures 418–442; additions and revisions in the vocal parts from the 1908 full score are included.

Example 16–43   (continued)

Example 16–43   (continued)

Example 16–43　(continued)

Curtain falls.

Example 16–44.　*Azara*, Act II, Scene 2, measures 213–220.

Example 16–44   (continued)

Example 16–45.   *Azara,* Act III, Scene 3, III, measures 86–94.

Example 16–46.   *Azara,* Act I, Scene 2, measures 432–441.

Example 16–47.   Wagner, *Tristan and Isolde,* Act II, Scene 2.

Example 16–48.   *Azara,* Act I, Scene 3, measures 164–166.

Example 16–49.   *Azara,* Act II, Scene 1b, measures 130–145.

Example 16–49   (continued)

Example 16–50.   *Azara,* Act II, Scene 1b, measures 36–42.

Example 16–51.   *Azara,* Act I, Scene 2, measures 124–130.

Example 16–51. (continued)

salutes the King. The Knights and Men-at-arms strike their shields and wave their banners.)

Example 16–52. *Azara*, Act II, Scene 7, measures 37–48.

Example 16–53.   *Azara*, Act II, Scene 1b, measures 6–15.

Example 16–54.   *Azara*, Act III, Scene 3, I, measures 1–11.

Example 16–54   (continued)

Example 16–55.   *Azara*, Act III, Scene 3, I, measures 27–38.

Example 16–56.   *Azara,* Act III, Scene 3, I, measures 61–68.

Example 16–57.   *Azara,* Act III, Scene 3, II, measures 5–12.

Example 16–58.   *Azara,* Act III, Scene 3, III, measures 1–3.

Example 16–59.   *Azara,* Act III, Scene 3, III, measures 29–37.

Example 16–60.   *Azara,* Act III, Scene 3, III, measures 70–73.

17

An Evaluation

John Knowles Paine in his own time was hailed as the "dean" of American composers, and today is considered one of the most important in the history of American music. Yet his compositions have been left virtually unperformed for over three quarters of a century. The uninformed musician may doubtless assume from this situation that the works were inferior, ephemeral pieces deserving of oblivion. However, after even a cursory study or audition of Paine's music, it becomes apparent that the neglect is undeserved, resulting from the unique circumstances of American music.

Traditionally American musicians and audiences have turned to European composers as the standard of taste and excellence. Native composers have been either ignored or patronized because they were American, in neither case allowing a fair assessment against their European peers. Paine's music was performed frequently during his lifetime, but primarily by local performing organizations and by friends or acquaintances. For example, his orchestral music was played somewhat regularly by Boston-area ensembles, and also by the Brooklyn and Chicago orchestras during the years when they were conducted by Theodore Thomas, a close friend. But the New York and Philadelphia orchestras almost completely ignored Paine's music, while regularly performing works by such Europeans as d'Albert, Goldmark, Raff, Rheinberger, Rubinstein, and Sinding. Paine, of course, was not a major composer, but his music in the main is at least equal in quality and attractiveness to the popular works of such composers. History was not in his favor, either—his works were conservative, and did not attract the controversy and interest of leading composers such as Liszt, Wagner, Mahler, and Strauss. When he died, the twentieth-century reaction against Romanticism was already underway, and his music was dismissed as hopelessly old-fashioned and quickly forgotten.

Fortunately the prospects have brightened in recent years. We have come increasingly to recognize the quality and value of much earlier American music, especially from the tunesmith era, and have published and performed it. With the revival of interest in Romantic music, nineteenth-century American composers began to receive a share of scholarly and public notice. The observance of the Bicentennial also has fostered a great increase in attention. However, as far as publication is concerned Paine was largely neglected; only a welcome volume of organ music and one chorus from *St. Peter* have surfaced, to the author's knowledge, and neither the organ music nor the earlier reissued *Symphony No. 1* score show the composer at his best. It is hoped that the present study will provide the impetus for a fair reassessment of Paine's music and its reestablishment in the repertory.

Among the most attractive of Paine's compositions are those for orchestra, for he was a master at instrumentation. His scoring is always effective and often brilliant. The best of these—and one of the finest in Paine's entire oeuvre—is the lovely "Spring" Symphony. Its four movements are equally successful formally, and entirely complementary. The graceful themes of the first movement, the witty scherzo and its lyrical trio, the intensely expressive *Adagio*, and the exuberant Finale are all highly inspired, showing Paine at his best and most characteristic. This symphony should be heard.[1] Also, the score—the first American orchestral work to be published—should be reissued. Paine's *Symphony No. 1* is flawed by excessive repetition and over-development of material, especially in the first two movements and to a lesser degree in the Finale, but the themes are fresh and attractive. The *Adagio* is a gem, a fine example of the expressive slow movements that Paine composed so successfully.[2]

Paine's symphonic poems will repay further study. Characters and events in *The Tempest* are effectively portrayed, and the contrasting themes are knit together into a convincing whole.[3] Although some themes in *An Island Fantasy* may seem to be a bit trite, they are attractively scored and effectively integrated, and the work is a worthy representative of Paine's later style. Three shorter orchestral works should become popular with audiences.[4] The *Overture to As You Like It* is pleasant, direct, handling the sonata form efficiently. Paine's *Oedipus Tyrannus* prelude is a minor masterpiece, logical, tightly knit, dramatic, and effectively scored. Despite its lack of publication, the *Overture to The Birds* is an agreeable work, with effective contrasts but well unified.

Perhaps the work that should benefit the most from a reappraisal of Paine is *Azara*. It suffered the most from the anti-native prejudice that prevailed in the musical world at the turn of the century, most evident at the Metropolitan Opera. However, the situation is far more promising now, due to the existence of many regional and university companies. *Azara* would easily qualify for such production. Dramatic, tuneful, well written and scored, with a libretto in English, it would be an attractive choice. There is much beauty in the work, including Gontran's aria from Act I ("My love is ardent as the day"), the quartet from that act, Azara's Act II scene ("Softly the balmy zephyr sighs"), and the lovers' lengthy duet later in Act II. Malek's arias in Acts II and III are especially distinctive, and the quaint song of Garsie, Colas, and the Huntsman in Act II is delightful. Choruses are especially effective, and some remarkable passages include the triumphant entry in Act I, the battle and kidnapping in Act II, and the finale to Act III. Two orchestral passages demonstrating Paine's craftsmanship—and deserving to be excerpted—are the Orchestral Scene (Act II, Scene 1b) and the Three Moorish Dances.[5]

Paine's choral music, a substantial portion of his output, also deserves performance. The two most extensive works—the *Mass in D* and *St. Peter*—are important historically, both being pioneering American examples of their respective genres. The events centering around the Singacademie première of the Mass and its enthusiastic reception remain fascinating. Finally, after 112 years, it has received a domestic performance and an excellent recording,[6] revealing a somewhat fragmented but nonetheless strong, convincing work. *St. Peter*, while paying respect to Mendelssohn, is a skillfully crafted, lyrical, dramatically effective work, definitely deserving revival. Another historically important choral work, the music to *Oedipus Tyrannus*, has enjoyed several performances in the decades since Paine's death, the latest quite recently. It still possesses much of the beauty and pathos that moved the audiences of 1881. Other of Paine's cantatas would prove of value and interest to college and community choruses, including *The Realm of Fancy*, *The Nativity*, and *Song of Promise*—also, for male voices, *Phoebus, Arise*, and *Scenes from "The Birds."*

Songs, chamber works, and keyboard music are of course pieces on a smaller scale. Nevertheless, they have a special significance, for Paine was involved with them not only as composer but also as performer. Of the songs, the *Matin Song* achieved a great popularity during Paine's lifetime; its simple charm would make it a favorite today as well. *Mondnacht*, or *Moonlight*, the equal of many popular *Lieder*, is well worth examining. Of the chamber music, both the *Violin Sonata* and the *Trio* are strong works, musically satisfying, and deserving publication and performance. The organ works all are youthful compositions and are more derivative than many works in other genres. However, they are well written, effective, idiomatic pieces, and often require virtuosity. At least they are easily obtainable in reprint, and excellent recorded performances of several are available.[7] A number of successful compositions may be found among the 22 published piano pieces still extant. The *Romance*, Op. 12, one of the larger works, evokes the dark-hued drama of some Schumann compositions or perhaps some of the Brahms rhapsodies.[8] The later *Romance*, Op. 39, is less successful because of the presence of some dated *salon* elements, but it is still an effective large-scale piece, more in the nature of a nocturne. The slow expressive melody, so admired in the symphonies and chamber music, may be found in several works, including a *Romance*, from Op. 25, and three "songs without words" from *In the Country—Wayside Flowers*, *Shepherd's Lament*, and *Farewell*. Charming miniatures, incorporating effective textures and an opportunity for technical display, include *Christmas Gift*, Op. 7, *Dance* and *Rondo Giocoso* from Op. 25, and *Village Dance*, *Rainy Day*, and *The Mill* from *In the Country*. The aggressive *Impromptu* from Op. 25, the light, exotic *Gipsies* from *In the Country*, and the rhythmic, exuberant *Welcome Home* that closes the latter set are other enjoyable recital encores. Finally, the witty scherzo, *Fuga Giocosa*, is an example of Paine's sense of humor combined with superb craftsmanship, with delightful results.

Notes

Preface

1. John Tasker Howard, *Our American Music*, 4th ed. (New York, 1965), 298.

2. Two unpublished monographs have appeared in recent years. A thesis by Kenneth C. Roberts, Jr., *John Knowles Paine* (University of Michigan, 1962), offers thorough bibliographical information on the works and provides some valuable biographical insights, but performance information is scanty and the scope of the study did not permit a thorough biographical study. J. C. Huxford's *John Knowles Paine: His Life and Works* (Ph.D. dissertation, Florida State University, 1968), placed too great an emphasis on secondary sources, chiefly Edwards' *Music and Musicians of Maine* and Spalding's *Music at Harvard*; he often was forced to conjecture to bridge gaps in his information, and many resulting statements are inaccurate.

3. Leon Edel, "The Autobiography: The Figure Under the Carpet," *The New Republic* CLXXX/6 (10 February 1979), 26.

Chapter 1

1. G. T. Edwards, *Music and Musicians of Maine* (Portland, Me., 1928; reprinted in 1970 by AMS Press, Inc.).

2. Richard Aldrich, "John Knowles Paine," *Dictionary of American Biography* (New York, 1928) XIV, 151–53; Aldrich was a New York music critic.

3. M. A. DeWolfe Howe, "John Knowles Paine," *The Musical Quarterly* XXV (1939), 257–67. Howe was a prominent biographer and historian.

4. Walter R. Spalding, "Music, 1862–1929," *The Development of Harvard University since the Inauguration of President Eliot, 1869–1929*, ed. S. E. Morison (Cambridge, 1930); and *Music at Harvard* (New York, 1935).

5. Kenneth C. Roberts, Jr., *John Knowles Paine*, unpublished M. A. thesis, University of Michigan (1962). Another study, John Calvitt Huxford's *John Knowles Paine: His Life and Works* (unpublished Ph.D. dissertation, Florida State University, 1968), contributes little to the current scholarship on Paine because of his almost complete reliance on secondary sources.

6. Ethel F. Fisk [sic] (ed.), *The Letters of John Fiske* (New York, 1940).

7. Spalding, *Music at Harvard*, 148.

8. R. T. Paine, "Notes . . . ," *Paine Ancestry: The Family of Robert Treat Paine, Signer of the Declaration of Independence*, comp. Sarah Cushing Paine (Boston, 1912), 6.

9. Josiah Paine, "Thomas Paine, of Eastham," *Paine Ancestry* . . . , 7–8.

10. Mrs. M. L. T. Alden, "The Snow Genealogy," *The New-England Historical and Genealogical Register* XLVII (1893), 82.

11. Mary W. Ferris, comp., *Dawes-Gates Ancestral Lines* (1931) II, 763–68.

12. Alden, "Snow . . . ," 187.

13. G. B. Merrick, *Genealogy of the Merrick-Mirick-Myrick Family of Massachusetts 1636–1902* (Madison, Wis., 1902), 13–18.

14. A. K. R. Meserve, comp., *Notes on Standish Families*, unpublished collection at Maine Historical Society, Portland.

15. Alden, "Snow . . . ," 187.

16. C. T. Libby, "The Knowles Family of Eastham, Mass.," *The New England Historical and Genealogical Register* LXXIX (1925), 286–97, 379–92.

17. L. E. B. Morris, *Lineages and Genealogical Notes* (Dallas, 1967), 1.

18. Samuel P. May, *The Descendants of Richard Sares (Sears) of Yarmouth, Mass., 1638–1888* (Albany, 1890).

19. Morris, 3; also, John Doane, *Deacon John Doane and the Doane Family* (Yarmouthport, Mass., 1914), 1-2.

20. Evelyn Rich, "Richard Rich of Eastham on Cape Cod and some of his descendants," *The New England Historical and Genealogical Register* LXXXIII (1929), 261–78, 394.

21. Details of Jane Small's genealogy are obtained from L. A. W. Underhill, *Descendants of Edward Small of New England*, rev. ed. (Boston, 1934).

22. A. K. P. Meserve, *History of the early settlement and settlers of Standish*, unpublished manuscript, Maine Historical Society collection.

23. The second name—"Knowles"—is given in the *Records of the Church of Christ in Standish* (Me. Historical Society collection): on 29 July 1787 "John Knowls [sic] son of Joseph Pain [sic] was baptised" (p. 218). What the "H." initial stood for is obscure. If, as with "Knowles," it was a family name in the Paine ancestry, it most likely was "Hicks," after immigrant Robert Hicks (an ancestor of both of John K. H. Paine's maternal grandparents), "Hopkins," after *Mayflower* immigrant Stephen Hopkins,

whose lineage may be traced to both Joseph and Phebe Paine, or "Howes," the family name of Joseph Paine's maternal grandmother. John Knowles may also have been the namesake of his uncle, John Knowles Rich, who died in 1787 [Rich, "Richard Rich . . ."].

24. William R. Cutter, *Genealogical and Personal Memoirs Relating to the Families of Boston and Eastern Massachusetts* (New York, 1908) III, 1299.

25. Edwards, 46.

26. Ibid., 35.

27. *Cumberland County Records* (Portland, Me.) LXXXIII, 419.

28. *Cumberland County Records* LXXXV, 459.

29. Meserve, *Notes*.

30. *Standish, Maine, Vital Records 1759–1900*, 126; in Maine Historical Society collection.

31. W. G. Davis, "Intentions of Marriage in Limington, Me., 1792–1810," *The New England Historical and Genealogical Register* LXXXVII (1933), 126.

32. Edwards, 68.

33. Howe, "John Knowles Paine," 257.

34. Edwards, 122.

35. Ibid., 323.

36. *Tri-weekly Argus* (Portland, Me.), 2 October 1833, 4.

37. Edwards, 330. "Saccarrappa" was the early name for Westbrook, an industrial town adjoining Portland to the northwest [*Maine: a Guide "Down East"* (Boston, 1937), 382]; the "Sacarappa Falls" on the Presumscot River are nearby [William Willis, *History of Portland* (Portland, 1865), map]. Possibly this use of the term "Saccarap" alludes to the primitive backwoods nature of the organization.

38. *The Portland Directory; containing the names of the inhabitants . . . and the city register . . .* (Portland, 1834), 94.

39. *Tri-weekly Eastern Argus*, 14 October 1833, 1.

40. S. B. Beckett, *The Portland Reference Book and City Directory for 1847–48* (Portland, 1847), 97, 136.

41. *Portland Transcript*, 14 June 1851, 71.

42. *Tri-weekly Eastern Argus*, 8 November 1833, 2.

43. *Portland Directory* . . . (1834), 94.

44. "Value of Real Estate owned . . . none." *Schedule I—Free Inhabitants in Ward No. 5, City of Portland . . . enumerated . . . on the 19th day of August 1850. . . .*

45. Edwards gives his place of birth as "a two and one-half story house on Oxford Street in Portland . . ." and provides a photograph of the dwelling. Possibly this was the current Jacob Paine residence, or else the home of John's grandmother, Mrs. Jane Paine. Her address in the 1847 directory is listed as "9 Portland Street," but the lot, purchased by her husband in 1833, bordered on both Portland and Oxford streets. Edwards obtained his information from Julia Norton Deland, who was a neighbor of the Paines during John's childhood.

46. L. D. Rich, *The Coast of Maine; An Informal History* (New York, 1956), 134.

47. Population figures supplied by Edith H. McCaulcy, Assistant Reference Librarian, Portland Public Library, in an 18 January 1977 letter to the present writer.

48. Edwards, 117.

49. Jacob Paine distributed his umbrellas in the surrounding region, as may be seen from the advertisement quoted earlier.

50. *Maine: A Guide "Down East" Written by Workers of the Federal Writers' Project of the Works Progress Administration for the State of Maine* (Boston, 1937), 72.

51. From advertisement in *Eastern Argus*, 16 April 1830, 4.

52. From advertisements in *Eastern Argus*, 8 July 1850, 1.

53. From advertisements in *Eastern Argus*, 9 July 1860, 1.

54. *Maine: A Guide "Down East,"* 71.

55. Advertisement, *Eastern Argus*, 8 July 1850, 1; the Atlantic and St. Lawrence information that follows is also from this issue.

56. *Maine: A Guide "Down East,"* 71.

57. From advertisements in the 1850 and 1860 issues of *Eastern Argus* cited above.

58. From letter of Edith H. McCauley, 18 January 1977.

59. Edwards, 79.

60. Quoted in Edwards, 112. It was published in Portland by Hyde, Colman & Chisholm; a copy is in the Boston Public Library. Two compositions of David Paine—*Te Deum, in C* (New York: Beer & Schirmer, 1866) and *Christmas Anthem: Let Us Now Go* (Boston: Davenport, 1868)—and two more of his compilations—*The Social Minstrel*

(Boston: Crocker & Brewster, 1845) and *The Jenny Lind Glee Book* (Boston: Ditson, 1851)—are also to be found in the Boston Public Library.

61. *Portland Transcript*, 12 October 1850, 206.

62. Quoted in Edwards, 84.

63. Quoted in Edwards, 81, from which the details of this episode were obtained.

64. Controversy seems to have been a family characteristic. Crouch's daughter, Cora Pearl, was a famous Parisian courtesan of the Second Empire [*Baker's Biographical Dictionary of Musicians*, 5th ed., ed. Nicholas Slonimsky (New York, 1958), 335].

65. Edwards, 122.

66. *Portland Transcript*, 21 September 1850, 183.

67. The roster also included singers Julia and Alonzo P. Wheelock, pianist Hermann Kotzschmar, and cellist and flutist Henri Jungnickel (from an advertisement, *Portland Transcript*, 1 May 1852, 22).

68. *Records, Portland Sacred Music Society*; in Maine Historical Society collection.

69. "Adjourned annual meeting," 10 June 1851, *Records.* . . .

70. *Records* . . .; punctuation appears as in original. John L. Shaw, who made the motion, was a First Vocal Conductor in 1848, served as a Councillor, and appeared frequently as a soloist [Edwards, 77–78].

71. *Records.* . . .

72. *Portland Transcript*, 4 March 1854, 374.

73. Edwards, 122.

74. H. Earle Johnson, *Musical Interludes in Boston, 1795–1830* (New York, 1943), 151.

75. Ibid., 132.

76. Ibid., 126.

77. Edwards, 58.

78. Johnson, 289.

79. Ibid., 153.

80. Edwards, 111.

81. John Tasker Howard, *Our American Music*, 4th ed. (New York, 1965), 170.

82. "Pillars of Portland.—XXII. Hermann Kotzschmar.—Our Pillar of Music," *Portland Transcript* clipping, ca. 1883, preserved in *Kotzschmar Scrapbook*, Portland Public Library.

83. *Hermann Kotzschmar* (Portland, 1909), 9, 33.

84. Unidentified clipping, ca. 1890, preserved in *Kotzschmar Scrapbook*, Portland Public Library.

85. They were the third group to reach America that year; the Germania and Gungl orchestras had come over earlier.

86. Apparently no connection with William Henry Fry, who was in Europe at the time; possibly his brother, Joseph R. Fry, headed the company.

87. "Pillars. . . ."

88. Unidentified clipping, ca. 1896, preserved in *Kotzschmar Scrapbook*, Portland Public Library.

89. Unidentified clipping, ca. 1890. . . .

90. *Portland Daily Press*, 1 July 1899, 2; clipping preserved in *Kotzschmar, Scrapbook of miscellaneous material*, Portland Public Library. The sentence that follows is also based upon this article. Any relationship between Reinecke and the pianist-composer, Carl Reinecke, has not been established.

91. "Pillars. . . ."

92. *Hermann Kotzschmar*, 35.

93. Edwards, 167.

94. Ibid., 80.

95. Ibid., 167–68.

96. Ibid., 117.

97. Unidentified clipping, ca. 1890. . . .

98. *Hermann Kotzschmar*, 36.

99. *Portland Transcript*, 1 April 1854, 406.

100. *Portland Transcript*, 6 July 1850, 94; the title page lists Paine, but names E. H. Wade, Boston, as the publisher.

101. *Portland Transcript*, 3 August 1850, 126.

102. *Portland Transcript*, 26 October 1850, 222.

103. *Portland Transcript*, 7 December 1850, 270.

104. *Portland Transcript*, 10 April 1852, 413.

105. *Portland Transcript*, 29 May 1852, 54.

106. *Portland Transcript*, 17 March 1855, 390.

107. Copies of all the above-named compositions are on file in the Portland Public Library.

108. Edwards, 332.

109. Ibid., 167.

110. Ibid., 382.

111. Quoted in Edwards, 267.

112. Edwards, 123. Two movements from this quartet were performed at a 28 March 1863 concert at Chickering Hall, Boston; John Sullivan Dwight commented: "For so youthful an effort it showed much artistic skill and genial conception" [*Dwight's Journal of Music* XXIII/1 (4 April 1862), 7].

113. *Portland Boys' high school. Lists of master: E. N. Pomeroy & others*; in Maine Historical Society collection.

114. *Semi-Annual Report of the Portland High School for Boys for the Term ending August 2ᵈ, 1851*; in Maine Historical Society collection.

115. *Semi-Annual Report . . . Term ending July 30, 1852*.

116. *. . . Term ending March 4, 1852; . . . Term ending August 5, 1853*.

117. S. B. Beckett, *The Portland Directory and Reference Book for 1852–53* (Portland, 1852), 286.

118. *Portland Transcript*, 14 October 1854, 211.

119. From *Portland Transcript* announcements.

120. *Portland Transcript and Eclectic*, 28 June 1856, 94.

121. *Portland Transcript and Eclectic*, 19 July 1856, 118.

122. *Portland Transcript and Eclectic*, 9 August 1856, 140.

123. *The Eastern Argus* (Portland, Me.), 11 August 1856, 3.

124. *The Eastern Argus*, 27 September 1856, 2.

125. *Portland Transcript and Eclectic*, 4 October 1856, 206; this report was in itself a special tribute, for the *Transcript* rarely printed obituaries.

126. *Eastern Argus*, 8 October 1856, 2.

127. Edwards, 331.

128. Ibid., 87, 261–62.

129. Ibid., 87, 119.

130. Ibid., 170.

131. *Eastern Argus*, 1 January 1857, 3.

132. *Eastern Argus*, 28 March 1857, 3.

133. *Eastern Argus*, 27 January 1857, 2.

134. *Eastern Argus*, 25 July 1857, 2; the Downing and Kotzschmar publications that follow were also included in this announcement.

135. Advertisement in *Eastern Argus*, 30 May 1857, 3.

136. *Eastern Argus*, 1 June 1857, 2.

137. Edwards, 123.

138. *Records, Haydn Association* (Portland, Me.), 44; in Portland Public Library.

139. Edwards, 117.

140. *Eastern Argus*, 27 April 1857, 3.

141. *Eastern Argus*, 8 August 1857, 2.

142. *Portland Transcript and Eclectic*, 28 March 1857, 406.

143. *Portland Transcript and Eclectic*, 13 June 1857, 79, and 27 June 1857, 97.

144. *Eastern Argus*, 23 December 1857, 3.

145. *Records, Haydn Association*, 55.

146. *Eastern Argus*, 28 December 1857, 2.

147. *Eastern Argus*, 4 January 1858, 2.

148. *Portland Transcript and Eclectic*, 9 January 1858, 318.

149. *Eastern Argus*, 21 December 1857, 3.

150. *Records, Haydn Association*, 57.

151. 4 January 1858 meeting, *Records, Haydn Association*, 58.

152. 27 January 1858 meeting, *Records, Haydn Association*, 61.

153. *Eastern Argus*, 22 January 1858, 3.

154. *Eastern Argus*, 30 January 1858, 2.

155. *Eastern Argus*, 6 March 1858, 3.

156. *Eastern Argus*, 11 March 1858, 2.

157. Advertisement for 31 March concert, *Eastern Argus*, 27 March 1858, 3. Twitchell had established a good reputation in Boston as a contralto soloist, hence this billing. In the 1870s mention of her performances—now "Mrs. Jennie Twitchell Kempton"— occurs frequently in concert reviews. She boasted ". . . the great advantage of the tuition of the best masters abroad" (*Boston Daily Globe*, 16 September 1874), and for a while was associated with Carlyle Petersilea's music school (*Globe*, 14 January 1874). Sometime later she moved to Los Angeles. An announcement of a 1901 recital by her pupils affirmed:

> Mrs. Kempton numbers among her pupils not a few of the most prominent singers of Los Angeles, and her recitals partake of the character of artistic concert work rather than that of the usually amateurish efforts to be heard in recitals of the sort [*Musical Courier* XLIII/20 (13 November 1901), 10].

158. *Eastern Argus*, 12 March 1858, 2.

159. *Eastern Argus*, 25 February 1858, 2.

160. *Portland Transcript and Eclectic*, 6 March 1858, 382.

161. *Eastern Argus*, 15 March 1858, 2; this review is the source of the two quotations that follow.

162. *Portland Transcript and Eclectic*, 20 March 1858, 398; the latter was a popular work by Hans Christian Lumbye (1810–78).

163. Ibid.

164. *Eastern Argus*, 15 March 1858, 2.

165. Advertisement in *Eastern Argus*, 27 March 1858, 3.

166. *Eastern Argus*, 2 April 1858, 2.

167. *Portland Transcript and Eclectic*, 10 April 1858, 6.

168. *Dwight's Journal of Music* XIII/2 (10 April 1858), 15; hereafter, *DJM*.

169. Spalding, *Music at Harvard*, 150. On 4 March 1854 Helen married William Allen, Jr. (1832–1900), who was engaged in the wholesale fruit business and later headed a successful fire insurance agency. They had three children, two of whom survived Helen (d. 1891)—Mrs. John T. Brown and Miss Alice Maude Allen (who later married Dr. John W. Bowers); only Alice Maude was living at William's death. [Information from *Portland Obituary Scrapbooks* I, 41 and *Post scrapbook* VI, 6; in Maine Historical Society collection.]

170. Advertisement in *Eastern Argus*, 15 March 1858, 3.

171. Advertisement in *Eastern Argus*, 19 April 1858, 3.

172. Advertisement in *Eastern Argus*, 29 April 1858, 3.

173. *Eastern Argus*, 7 May 1858, 2.

174. Advertisement in *Eastern Argus*, 21 May 1858, 3.

175. *Records, Haydn Association*, 77.

176. Ibid., 81.

Chapter 2

1. *Portland Transcript and Eclectic*, 10 April 1858, 6.

2. *New-York Daily Tribune*, 20 July 1897, 7. Mason had greatly increased his collection in 1852 by purchasing the large library of the Darmstadt organist Johann Christian Heinrich Rinck (1770–1846); all was donated to Yale University at Mason's death [W.S.B. Mathews, *A Hundred Years of Music in America* (Chicago, 1889), 44]. It was quite probably this addition on which Thayer labored.

3. *New-York Daily Tribune*, 20 July 1897, 7.

4. John Tasker Howard, "Alexander Wheelock Thayer," *Dictionary of American Biography*, XVIII (New York, 1943), 401–2.

5. *New-York Daily Tribune*, 20 July 1897, 7.

6. *New-York Daily Tribune*, 8 July 1858, 5.

7. Identified as Paine by Dwight in the 26 March 1859 issue.

8. *Records, Haydn Association*, 77.

9. Quite possibly this was an outgrowth of the Grand Musical Congress of 1854 held in the immense Crystal Palace, supposedly with the sponsorship of P. T. Barnum; Fry strongly supported the venture in his *Tribune* editorials [W. T. Upton, *William Henry Fry, American Journalist and Composer-Critic* (New York, 1954), 147–48].

10. Musical information from *New-York Daily Tribune*, 14–29 June 1858.

11. Mary L. Booth, *History of the City of New York* (New York, 1867), 780–81.

12. John William Leonard, *History of the City of New York 1609–1909* (New York, 1910), 362–64.

13. *New-York Daily Tribune*, 24 June 1858, 7.

14. *New-York Daily Tribune*, 3 July 1858, 7; Converse was visting New York.

15. *New-York Daily Tribune*, 8 July 1858, 8.

16. A. W. T[hayer], "The Diarist Abroad—Berlin, September 1, 1858," *Dwight's Journal of Music* XIII/27 (2 October 1858), 209. The September 1858 date of a farewell concert in Portland, cited in Edwards, *Music and Musicians of Maine*, 123, is in obvious error.

17. Ibid.

18. *DJM* XIV/2 (9 October 1858), 218; the quotation that follows is also from this source.

19. "Diary Abroad—Monday, Aug. 23d, noon," *DJM* XIV/4 (23 October 1858), 238–39.

20. Gerhard Masur, *Imperial Berlin* (New York, 1970), 46–50.

21. "A.W.T.," "Musical Correspondence—Berlin, Sept. 17," *DJM* XIV/5 (30 October 1858), 244; above titles conform to Thayer's original.

22. "A.W.T.," "Mozart's 'Magic Flute'—Berlin, Sept. 30, 1858," *DJM* XIV/7 (13 November 1858), 257.

23. "A.W.T.," *DJM* (30 October 1858), 245.

24. "A.W.T.," "Musical Correspondence—Berlin, Jan. 9," *DJM* XIV/20 (12 February 1859), 368.

25. "A.W.T.," "Musical Correspondence—Berlin, Dec. 13, 1858," *DJM* XIV/15 (8 January 1859), 325.

26. "A.W.T.," *DJM* (30 October 1858), 245. Similar evaluations are found in Carl Freiherr von Ledebur's *Tonkünstler-Lexicon Berlin's* (1861)—"Haupt . . . is gegenwärtig jedenfalls einer der ausgezeichnetsten Orgel-Virtuosen"—and Hermann Mendel (ed.) *Musikalisches Conversations-Lexikon* V (1875)—"einer der ausgezeichnetsten Orgelvirtuosen der Gegenwart."

27. Frederick F. Bullard, "Music in Boston: Zerrahn, Paine, Lang and Chadwick," *Musical Courier* XXXVII/1 (4 July 1898), unpaged.

28. Ledebur, 227.

29. "Orgelstil," *Musikalisches Conversations-Lexikon*, ed. H. Mendel & August Reissmann, VII (1877), 415–20.

30. Hans Klotz, "Orgelspiel," *Die Musik in Geschichte und Gegenwart*, ed. Friedrich Blume, X (1962), col. 387.

31. *Boston Morning Journal*, 28 October 1862, 4.

32. Henry T. Finck, *My Adventures in the Golden Age of Music* (New York, 1926), 78.

33. *Boston Journal*, 6 November 1863, 2.

34. *Boston Herald*, 13 November 1904, Women's Section, 6.

35. From an explanatory note in the score.

36. *Neue Zeitschrift für Musik* LIV/21 (17 Mai 1861), 184.

37. *Haupt's Theory of Counterpoint, Fugue, and Double Counterpoint, prepared expressly for the Royal Institute for Church Music, at Berlin, Prussia*, trans. H. Clarence Eddy (New York, 1876).

38. "A.W.T.," *DJM* (12 February 1859), 368.

39. "A.W.T.," *DJM* (8 January 1859), 325.

40. Quoted in *DJM* XVII/21 (18 August 1860), 168.

41. *Musical Record* #467 (1 December 1900), 521.

42. F. H. Jenks, "John Knowles Paine," *A Dictionary of Music and Musicians*, 1st ed., ed. George Grove (London, 1880), II, 632. W.S.B. Mathews, *A Hundred Years . . .*, 675, states that he studied piano and composition with Wieprecht and Teschner. *Cyclopedia of Music and Musicians*, ed. John D. Champlin (New York, 1890), III, 66, lists Fischer, not Teschner, as Paine's singing teacher; *Baker's Biographical Dictionary of Musicians*, 5th ed., rev. Nicolas Slonimsky (New York, 1958), 1199, repeats this statement.

43. *Boston Musical Times* II/15 (30 November 1861), 229.

44. John Knowles Paine letter to John Sullivan Dwight, Berlin, 5 November 1866, *Dwight— Correspondence Musical Boston, 1861–1892* II, Boston Public Library.

45. *Boston Musical Times* IV/3 (2 May 1863), 46.

46. *Neue Berliner Musikzeitung* XII/13 (24 März 1858), 101.

47. Writers mentioning the *Hochschule* include Krehbiel (*Grove's*, 2nd ed.) and Edwards; Upton, *Art-Song in America*, mentions the Kullak Academy.

48. "A.W.T.," *DJM* (30 October 1858), 245.

49. Ibid., 246.

50. "A.W.T.," *DJM* (8 January 1859), 325.

51. Writers who do not mention a school include Jenks, Krehbiel ("Music in America," *Famous Composers and Their Works*, IV), Bullard, Mathews (*A Hundred Years; The Great in Music*), Howe, and Goepp (*Harvard Graduates Magazine*).

52. *DJM* XIV/26 (26 March 1859), 416.

53. *DJM* XIV/24 (12 March 1859), 398; the quotation that follows is also from this source.

54. John Towers, "Personal Recollections of Notable Musicians," *American Art Journal* LIX/18 (13 August 1892), 427; at the time of this article, Towers had recently founded Towers' School of Vocal Music in New York City. He had formerly directed the English Select Choir of London, and had been a student of Pinsuti of London and Kullak and Marx of Berlin. In 1904 Towers moved to St. Louis and became head of vocal instruction at the Kroeger School of Music.

55. *Portland Transcript*, 27 October 1860, 239.

56. Krehbiel, *Grove's*, 2nd ed., III, 597; Mathews, *A Hundred Years*; and others.

57. *Dictionary of American Biography* (New York, 1928) XIV, 151.

58. Reprinted in *DJM* XVI/21 (18 February 1860), 375–76.

59. Reprinted in *DJM* XVII/21 (18 August 1860), 168; the quotations that follow are also from this source. A sign of the friendship between Paine and Grimm may be seen in the inscription in a copy of Emerson's *The Conduct of Life* (now in the Houghton Library at Harvard University)—"Hermann Grimm/ Weihnachten 1860/ Mr. Payne [*sic*] zum abschied/ am 21 April 1861/ Berlin."

60. *DJM* XVI/24 (10 March 1860), 399.

61. *The Musical Review and Musical World* (New York) XII/23 (9 November 1861), 270.

62. *DJM* XVI/21 (18 February 1860), 375–76.

63. Thomas-M. Langner, "Orgelmusik: 19. und 20. Jahrhundert," *Die Musik in Geschichte und Gegenwart*, ed. Friedrich Blume, X (1962), col. 367.

64. *DJM* (18 August 1860), 168.

65. *Voss'sche-Zeitung* (Berlin, 21 April 1861); English trans. in *Musical World* (London) XXXIX/17 (27 April 1861), 266; *Boston Musical Times* II/7 (18 May 1861), 107; and *DJM* XIX/8 (25 May 1861), 60.

66. *Neue Zeitschrift für Musik* LIV/21 (17 Mai 1861), 184.

67. *Voss'sche-Zeitung* (21 April 1861).

68. *Musical World* (27 April 1861), 266.

69. *Boston Musical Times* II/14 (2 November 1861), 214.

70. *Eastern Argus* (Portland), 18 June 1861, 2.

71. Advertisement, *Portland Transcript and Eclectic* XXII/37 (18 December 1858), 295.

72. *Boston Musical Times* II/11 (10 August 1861), 166.

73. *Portland Transcript* report printed in *DJM* XIX/19 (10 August 1861), 149.

74. "A few weeks ago" as of the 10 August *Boston Musical Times*; the quotation is from this issue.

75. *Boston Musical Times* II/13 (5 October 1861), 198.

76. *The Musical Review and Musical World* (New York) XII/23 (9 November 1861), 270.

77. *DJM* XX/6 (9 November 1861), 254; the quotation that follows is from this source.

78. *Records of the Committee of the West Boston Society Corporation* I (1806–1864), 253 (in the collection of the Boston Public Library).

79. Ibid., 250 (entry of 8 April 1861); the price was $4,000, less $300 for the old organ.

80. *Boston Herald*, 18 December 1900, 4.

81. *Boston Musical Times* II/15 (30 November 1861), 229.

82. *Treasurer's Accounts—West Boston Society (1847–1893)* (in the collection of the Boston Public Library).

83. *Boston Musical Times,* 30 November 1861, 229.

84. "Old Boston Landmarks: The West Church," *Roxbury Gazette* (undated clipping in archives of the Unitarian-Universalist Association, Boston).

85. Mrs. Lucy G. Wadsworth, *West Church, Boston*, n. d. (typescript in archives of the Unitarian-Universalist Association, Boston).

86. *Records of the Committee* I, 257 (entry of 12 December 1862).

87. Letter to Hon. Nathaniel Silsbee from A. P. Peabody, Cambridge, 25 April 1862, *Letters of Acting President Andrew P. Peabody*, 31-32 (Harvard University archives).

88. Letter to Hon. John A. Lowell from A. P. Peabody, Cambridge, 25 March 1862, ibid., 22.

89. Paine was last paid on that date, according to *Treasurer's Accounts*.

90. *DJM* XXIV/2 (16 April 1864), 223.

91. *Records of the Committee*, 261 (entry of 5 December 1863).

Chapter 3

1. Spalding, "Music, 1862–1929," 107.

2. *DJM*, 21 July 1855.

3. Quoted in Spalding, "Music, 1862–1929," 107.

4. *A Catalogue of the Officers and Students of Harvard University for the Academical Year 1861–62, First Term* (Cambridge, 1861), 35.

5. *Boston Daily Advertiser*, 11 March 1862, 1; hereafter, *BDA*.

6. Letter from A. P. Peabody to Hon. John A. Lowell, 18 March 1862, *Letters of Acting President Andrew P. Peabody*, 16; in Harvard University archives.

7. Ibid.

8. *Harvard College Papers*, Second Series, XXIX (1862), 38–39; in Harvard University Archives. Crowninshield's son, Benjamin (A.B. 1858, A.M. 1861), had become acquainted with Paine while in Berlin in 1858–60.

9. Peabody (1811–93), Plummer Professor of Christian Morals and University Chaplain, had served as Acting President since the death of President Cornelius Conway Felton on 26 February 1862.

10. Letter from Peabody to J. K. Paine, 18 March 1862, *Letters . . .*, 15.

11. Letter from Peabody to Lowell, 25 March 1862, *Letters . . .*, 22.

12. Letter from Peabody to Nathaniel Silsbee, 23 October 1862, *Harvard College Papers*, Second Series, XXIX, 331.

13. *BDA*, 31 March 1862, 2.

14. *Life of Henry Wadsworth Longfellow, With Extracts from his Journals and Correspondence*, ed. Samuel Longfellow (Boston, 1886) III, 15.

15. Letter from Peabody to Henry G. Spaulding, 20 March 1862, *Letters* . . ., 18–19.

16. *A Catalogue . . . for the Academical Year 1862–63*, 35.

17. *Harvard College Papers*, Second Series, XXIX, 328.

18. Letter from W. G. Stearns to President Thomas Hill, 9 January 1863, *Harvard College Papers*, Second Series, XXX, 10.

19. Letter from Peabody to Nathaniel Silsbee, 14 April 1862, *Letters* . . ., 34.

20. Letter from Peabody to Silsbee, 25 April 1862, *Letters* . . ., 47.

21. *BDA*, 31 March 1862, 2.

22. Letter from Peabody to Silsbee, 25 April 1862, *Letters* . . ., 47; the quotation that follows is also from this source.

23. *BDA*, 31 October 1862, 1.

24. *DJM* XXII/5 (1 November 1862), 247; XXII/6 (8 November 1862), 255.

25. *BDA*, 19 February 1863, 1.

26. *DJM* XXII/17 (24 January 1863), 343.

27. The Germania Orchestra, comprised of German musicians with a love of freedom and a missionary zeal, held great prestige during its American tours from 1848 to 1855, including performing at President Taylor's inauguration in 1849, traveling with Jenny Lind, and giving long seasons in New York, Philadelphia, Boston, Baltimore, and Newport. Because of waning public support, the organization was dissolved in 1855, and its conductor, Carl Zerrahn, came to Boston where he led his "Philharmonic Orchestra" until 1863. After the Civil War, Zerrahn's orchestra was sponsored by the Harvard Musical Association ["A Debt to Musical Germany," *New England Conservatory Magazine-Review* VI/2 (December 1915–January 1916), 43–45].

28. *BDA*, 5 March 1863, 2; the information that follows is also from this source.

29. *BDA*, 17 March 1863, 1.

30. *BDA*, 1 June 1863, 1.

31. *BDA*, 23 September 1863, 2.

32. Spalding, "Music, 1862–1929," 112.

33. *DJM* XXII/26 (28 March 1863), 411. Child (1825–96), Boylston professor of rhetoric and oratory at Harvard, produced two definitive works on the ballad, *English and Scottish Ballads* (1857–58) and *English and Scottish Popular Ballads* (1883–98).

34. *DJM* XXIII/1 (4 April 1863), 6–7; the next sentence is also based on this material.

35. *BDA*, 3 November 1863, 1.

36. Ibid.

37. Mathews, *A Hundred Years*, 675.

38. *Boston Musical Times* II/11 (10 August 1861), 166.

39. *BDA*, 9 March 1863, 1.

40. *BDA*, 30 March 1863, 1.

41. Annie Fields, *Authors and Friends* (Boston, 1893), 37.

42. *DJM* XXIII/17 (14 November 1863), 133–34; the report of the occasion that follows is derived from this source.

43. *BDA*, 26 October 1863, 1.

44. *DJM* XXIII/17 (14 November 1863), 134; punctuation and spelling according to source. W. Eugene Thayer (1838–89), student of Paine, reportedly decided at about this time to study music seriously; after work with Haupt and Wieprecht in Berlin (1865–66), he held several important organist posts in Boston and in 1875 opened one of the first private organ studios in the country. George Washbourne Morgan (1822–92), a native of England, had left an organ and conducting career in Gloucester to come to New York in 1853; currently he was organist of Grace Church, New York. Benjamin Johnson Lang (1837–1909), a student of Liszt and an early champion of Wagner, was a local concert pianist as well as organist for the Handel and Haydn Society and Old South Church; he later became conductor of the Apollo Club (from 1871), the Cecilia Society (from 1874), and the Handel and Haydn Society (1895–97). Samuel Parkman Tuckerman (1819–90), longtime organist for St. Paul's Church in Boston, had just returned from eight years of study in England to become organist of Trinity Church in New York City. John Henry Willcox (1827–75) became Tuckerman's successor at St. Paul's Episcopal Church in 1850; later he became organist at the Church of the Immaculate Conception, where the Hooks had installed a large instrument.

45. *Harper's New Monthly Magazine* XXVII (January 1864), 275.

46. *BDA*, 16 October 1863, 1.

47. *Harper's New Monthly Magazine* XXVII (January 1864), 275; the quotation that follows is also from this source.

48. *DJM* XXIII/17 (14 November 1863), 134.

49. *BDA*, 3 November 1863, 1.

50. *Boston Journal*, 3 November 1863, 2.

51. "George Washbourne Morgan," *American Art Journal* LIX/14 (16 July 1892), 347–48.

52. *Boston Journal*, 3 November 1863, 2.

53. *DJM* XXIII/17 (14 November 1863), 134.

54. *BDA*, 3 November 1863, 1; the sentence that follows is also based on this source.

55. Quoted in *DJM* XXIII/21 (9 January 1864), 163. If the weight given for Paine was accurate, it would tend to confirm the physical description of him as "portly" by A. W. Thayer.

56. *Boston Journal*, 6 November 1863, 2.

57. *BDA*, 6 November 1863, 1.

58. *DJM* XXIII/24 (20 February 1864), 192.

59. *Musical Review and Musical World* XV/4 (13 February 1864), 54.

60. John K. Paine reports dated 18 May 1863 and 16 October 1863, *Visitation of the University, 1863 (Overseers-Supplement)*, 34, 88; in Harvard University Archives; the information that follows about the 1862–63 academic year is also from this source. Total enrollment figures for the fall and spring semesters, 1862–63, were 64 and 57. Class totals were: Freshmen, 16 and 14; Sophomores, 22 and 20; Chapel Choir (Juniors and Seniors) 26 and 23.

61. John K. Paine reports dated 1 May 1864 and 18 October 1864, *Academic Series I: Reports to the Overseers II*, 58 and *I*, 430; in Harvard University Archives.

62. *Records of the College Faculty 1860–65*, 437; in Harvard University Archives. Perhaps this was a victory for Paine.

63. John K. Paine reports dated 1 May 1865 and 17 October 1865, *Academic Series I: Reports to the Overseers II*, 183, 150. Sunday Choir numbered 13 members in the fall and 10 in the spring; Morning Choir retained 12 for both semesters.

64. *DJM* XXIV/2 (16 April 1864), 223.

65. "Mrs. Mary E. Paine," *Lewiston* [Me.] *Evening Journal*, 15 September 1920; clipping preserved in *Portland obituary scrapbook* III, 134; in Maine Historical Society, Portland. The William E. Greeley family was originally from Portland, where the three children—William Henry, Josephine Ficklen, and Mary Elizabeth—were born. Greeley's business activities brought the family to Salem and then to Boston. According to William Henry Greeley's son, Dr. Hugh Payne Greeley, the brother had looked forward to becoming a college professor; however, when William E. Greeley died, he assumed responsibility for his two sisters' welfare, and began a career in merchandising to support them [from a telephone interview between Hugh Payne Greeley and the present writer, 8 June 1974].

66. *A Catalogue of the Officers and Students of Harvard University for the Academical Year 1862–63* (Cambridge, 1862), 7.

67. *City of Portland Record of Deaths* V (1849–1866), 229.

68. *Cumberland County Records* (Portland, Maine), CCCXVIII, 431.

69. John Spencer Clark, *The Life and Letters of John Fiske* (Boston, 1917) I, 299.

70. Fisk (ed.), *The Letters of John Fiske*, 132.

71. *DJM* XXV/10 (5 August 1865), 79. The quotations and information that follow are also from this source.

72. Howe, 264.

73. *DJM* XXVI/8 (7 July 1866), 270–71. The three quotations that follow are also from this article, as is mention of the Boston soloists' names.

74. *Boston Musical Times* VII/7 (7 July 1866), 4.

75. *Boston Evening Transcript*, 7 June 1866, 3.

76. *Boston Evening Transcript*, 16 June 1866, 1.

77. *DJM* XXVI/8 (7 July 1866), 270–71.

78. *DJM* XXVI/9 (21 July 1866), 279.

79. *Boston Evening Transcript*, 26 April 1866, 2.

Chapter 4

1. *Boston Evening Transcript*, 18 July 1866, 2.

2. *DJM* XXVI/8 (7 July 1866), 270.

3. "George Laurie Osgood," *The National Cyclopaedia of American Biography* (New York, 1892, 1897) VII, 436.

4. *College Records* X (1857–1866), 15; in Harvard University Archives.

5. *Boston Musical Times* VII/8 (4 August 1866), 5.

6. *Boston Evening Transcript*, 6 August 1866, 4.

7. John K. Paine letter to John Sullivan Dwight, Berlin, 5 November 1866, *Dwight— Correspondence Musical Boston, 1861–1892* II, 122; in Boston Public Library.

8. *Boston Evening Transcript*, 28 July 1866, 2.

9. *DJM* XXVI/9 (21 July 1866), 279.

10. Paine letter to Dwight, 5 November 1866.

11. *DJM* XXVI/14 (29 September 1866), 319.

12. Paine letter to Dwight, 5 November 1866.

13. Translation from *DJM* XXVI/26 (16 March 1867), 413.

14. G[eorge] L. O[sgood] letter to the editor, Berlin, 27 February 1867, *Boston Daily Evening Transcript*, 16 March 1867, 2; further statements of Osgood are from this source.

15. LXIII/15 (5 April 1867), 131.

16. Translation from *DJM* XXVI/18 (24 November 1866), 352.

17. Paine letter to Dwight, 5 November 1866. The four quotations that follow are also from this source.

18. *Boston Musical Times* VIII/3 (2 March 1867), 23.

19. *DJM* XXVI/26 (16 March 1867), 413. The statements of Geyer that follow also are taken from this source.

20. II/11 (13 März 1867), 91; trans. J.C.S.

21. Translation from *Boston Daily Advertiser* quoted in *Boston Musical Times* VIII/4 (6 April 1867), 27.

22. *Boston Daily Evening Transcript*, 14 March 1867, 2; hereafter, *BDET*.

23. *Boston Musical Times* VIII/3 (2 March 1867), 23.

24. *DJM* XXVI/9 (21 July 1866), 279.

25. *Corporation Papers 1867*, Harvard University Archives. Francis Augustus Carpenter (A.B. 1866) was organist for Rev. Mr. Alger's church and a law student. Because of poor health, he resigned both activities in the fall of 1867, and died of tuberculosis in December.

26. *BDET*, 19 February 1867, 2–3.

27. *BDET*, 28 March 1867, 3.

28. *DJM* XXVII/2 (13 April 1867), 15.

29. *Annual Catalogue and Circular of the New England Conservatory of Music, Music Hall, Boston, Mass. February, 1868* (Boston, 1868), 2.

30. *BDET*, 20 May 1867, 3, and later issues.

31. *DJM* XXVII/16 (26 October 1867), 127.

32. *DJM* XXVII/19 (7 December 1867), 150.

33. *BDET*, 14 November 1867, 2, and 26 November 1867, 2.

34. First appearance in *BDET*, 10 September 1867.

35. Clark I, 332.

36. *BDET*, 31 October 1867, 2.

37. *BDET*, 16 January 1868, 2.

38. *DJM* XXVII/23 (1 February 1868), 183.

39. *Boston Musical Times* IX/2 (1 February 1868), 14.

40. *DJM* XXVII/25 (29 February 1868), 199.

41. Most notably Howe, 261, and Huxford, 46.

42. *DJM* XXVIII/16 (24 October 1868), 335. Perhaps another reason for the cancellation of the Easter concert was the Society's first Triennial Festival, which began on 5 May, less than a month later. Preparations for the festival may have left the singers with inadequate rehearsal time for the *Mass*.

43. The *Mass in D* received its American première on a 12 May 1972 concert of the New England Conservatory Orchestra and Chorus, conducted by Gunther Schuller.

44. *BDET*, 7 April 1868, 2.

45. *BDET*, 14 April 1868, 2.

46. *Boston Musical Times* IX/8 (1 August 1868), 61.

47. *Boston Musical Times* IX/6 (6 June 1868), 47.

48. *Annual Catalogue . . . of the New England Conservatory of Music . . .* (Boston, 1869), 38.

49. Spalding, "Music, 1862–1929," 112.

50. *Reports to the Overseers—President and Fellows Series I* II (1865–1870), 200; in Harvard University Archives.

51. *Marriages Registered in the City of Cambridge for the Year Eighteen Hundred and Sixty-nine* CCXVIII, 128.

52. "Mrs. Mary E. Paine," *Lewiston [Me.] Evening Journal*, 15 September 1920; in *Portland obituary scrapbook* III, 134, Maine Historical Society collection, Portland.

53. Edwards, 138.

54. From a letter quoted in Kenneth C. Roberts, *John Knowles Paine*, 71.

55. Spalding, *Music at Harvard*, 193–94.

56. Quoted in Howe, 266.

57. ". . . All letters and diaries found in my effects [are to] be burned without examination, . . ." Mary E. Paine, Cambridge, Will #178648. The Rev. Dana McLean Greeley, son of William Roger Greeley, wrote the present author on 26 June 1970: ". . . I am sorry to say that when my father's aunt died, he burned all of her papers and personal diaries, at her request. . . ."

58. "Mrs. Mary E. Paine," *Lewiston Evening Journal*, 15 September 1920; the obituary quotation that follows is also from this source.

Chapter 5

1. Text printed in *The Musical Times* [=*Boston Musical Times*] X/10 (October 1869), 58–59, from which the excerpts that follow are taken.

2. Quoted in *Folio* II/1 (January 1870), 6. Perhaps "Dr. Peck (or Peek)" was one of the large musical Peak family, who were known especially as bell-ringers, although some of their number were also singers or violinists. See F. O. Jones, *A Handbook of American Music and Musicians* (Canaseraga, N. Y., 1886), 130.

3. *College Records* X, 218.

4. *Folio* III/5 (November 1870), 106.

5. *Folio* III/3 (September 1870), 58.

6. *Folio* III/1 (July 1870), 7.

7. *DJM* XXXI/8 (15 July 1871), 64.

8. *Folio* III/4 (October 1870), 84.

9. *DJM* XXX/21 (31 December 1870), 371.

10. *DJM* XXX/22 (14 January 1871), 377.

11. *DJM* XXX/23 (28 January 1871), 387.

12. *DJM* XXX/27 (25 March 1871), 420.

13. *DJM* XXXI/1 (8 April 1871), 8; the Beethoven lecture that follows was also printed in this issue.

14. *DJM* XXXI/2 (22 April 1871), 11–12; Paine's Wagner lecture was also included in this issue.

15. *DJM* XXX/21 (31 December 1870), 371.

16. *DJM* XXX/23 (28 January 1871), 387.

17. *Nation* XIII (17 August 1871), 111.

18. A printed copy is contained in the music collection of the Boston Public Library.

19. *Historical Register of Boston University—Fifth Decennial Issue 1869–1911* (Boston, 1911), 28.

20. *North American Review* CXVI (April 1873), 217–45.

21. Finck, *My Adventures in the Golden Age of Music*, 78; the quotation that follows is also from this source.

22. *Nation* XXXIV (2 February 1882), 101–2.

23. Finck, 79; the two quotations that follow are also found in this source.

24. Edwards, 136.

25. *Arthur Foote, 1853–1937, An Autobiography* (Norwood, Mass., 1946), 33.

26. Henry M. Dunham, *The Life of a Musician woven into a Strand of History of the New England Conservatory of Music* (New York, 1929), 69; the quotation that follows is also from this source.

27. Edwards, 139.

28. Ellis Gray, "The Mission of Music," *Harper's New Monthly Magazine* LI (October 1875), 744.

29. Finck, 76–77; the quotation that follows is also from this source.

30. *A Catalogue of the Officers and Students of Harvard University for the Academical Year 1871–72* (Cambridge, 1871), 46.

31. *Forty-seventh Annual Report of the President of Harvard College, 1871–72* (Cambridge, 1873), 46.

32. *DJM* XXXIV/9 (8 August 1874), 278.

33. Quoted in *DJM* XXXIV/8 (25 July 1874), 270; the excerpts that follow, describing Paine's courses, are also from this report.

34. *Forty-eighth Annual Report . . . , 1872–73* (Cambridge, 1874), 45.

35. *Reports to the Overseers—President and Fellows Series I* III (1871–1874), 320.

36. *Records of the Overseers . . .* XI (1871–1882), 92–93.

37. Course titles and enrollment figures from *Forty-ninth Annual Report . . . , 1873–74* (Cambridge, 1875), 44, 47; other facts and quotations from *DJM* XXXIV/9 (8 August 1874), 278.

38. *DJM* XXXV/12 (18 September 1875), 94; the course descriptions that follow are derived from this passage.

39. The course descriptions that follow were published in *Fiftieth Annual Report . . . , 1874–75* (Cambridge, 1876), 50: *Music 1*, Harmony.—Chorals in four-part Harmony [10 enrolled]; *Music 2*, Counterpoint (Richter's Treatise) [5 enrolled]; *Music 3*, Imitative Counterpoint.—Canon.—Fugue in Two and Three Voices; *Music 4*, History of Music. Ancient Greek Music.—Gregorian Music.—Medieval and Modern Music [6 enrolled].

40. *DJM* XXXIV/9 (8 August 1874), 278; the quotation in the sentence that follows is also from this source.

41. *DJM* XXXV/12 (18 September 1875), 94.

42. Reprinted in *DJM* XXXV/13 (2 October 1875), 103–4.

43. *DJM* XXXV/12 (18 September 1875), 94; the quotation and information about the concerts that follow are also from this source.

44. *Records of the Overseers . . .* XI (1871–1882), 200.

45. *Reports to the Overseers—President and Fellows Series II* I (1874–1878), 107.

46. Gray, "The Mission of Music," 744.

47. *Records of the Overseers . . .* XI, 202, 205.

48. *DJM* XXXV/10 (21 August 1875), 78.

Chapter 6

1. *Folio* III/3 (September 1870), 58.

2. *Folio* VI/2 (February 1872), 42.

3. From collected programs, New England Conservatory of Music library.

4. Unidentified review quoted in Eleanor Miller, *The History and Development of The New England Conservatory of Music*, unpublished B.Mus. thesis, New England Conservatory of Music, 1933.

5. English translation from *Jubilee Days* #11 (28 June 1872), 48.

6. *Music to be performed at the World's Peace Jubilee and International Musical Festival in Boston, June 1872* (Boston, 1872), 113–14.

7. *DJM* XXXII/9 (27 July 1872), 179–80; the Dwight quotations that follow are also from this source.

8. Newspaper clipping from *William T. Campbell scrapbook*, 40; in collection of the Boston Public Library. The *Post* item that follows is also contained in this source.

9. John Knowles Paine, *St. Peter: An Oratorio* (Boston, 1872), iii.

10. Such as the "quite remarkably difficult" solo writing noted in the *Leipziger Allgemeine Musikalische Zeitung* review.

11. Louis C. Elson, *The History of American Music* (New York, 1904), 166. One of O'Neill's most famous pupils was Lillian Nordica, who studied with him for three years "and can attest to his superiority and skill in training the voice. . . ." [*American Art Journal* LXI/18 (12 August 1893), 409].

12. Letter of 5 June 1873; Fisk, 223. Paine, who had been guiding Fiske's meager talent, said of Fiske's Mass that "the melody and harmony are good, some of the themes grand . . ." and that it contained much that "a great composer need n't *[sic]* be ashamed of" [Clark I, 414].

13. *DJM* XXXII/23 (8 February 1873), 392.

14. Quoted in *DJM* XXXIII/3 (17 May 1873), 20–21.

15. The article was unsigned; Mathews was identified as its author in Frederic Field Bullard, "Music in Boston: Zerrahn, Paine, Lang and Chadwick," *Musical Courier* XXXVII/1 (4 July 1898), unpaged.

16. *Nation* XVI (13 February 1873), 116–17; the Mathews quotations that follow are also from this review.

17. *Atlantic Monthly* XXXI (April 1873), 506–7; the Apthorp quotations that follow are also from this passage.

18. *Records, Haydn Association*, 245; the quotation that follows also appears at this source.

19. Ibid., 256.

20. Ibid., 257.

21. John Knowles Paine letter to Hermann Kotzschmar, Cambridge, 7 June 1873, included in *Kotzschmar. Scrapbook of miscellaneous material*, Portland Public Library.

22. *Records*, 259; the "Harvard Orchestra of Boston," rather than the Germania, appeared on the handbill, showing the orchestra's actual identity.

23. Ibid., 259–61.

24. Fisk, 223. Portland had a population of 31,413 at the time of the 1870 census.

25. *Atlantic Monthly* XXXII (August 1873), 248–51; the four quotations that follow are from this review.

26. *Folio* IX/1 (July 1873), 10.

27. Paine letter to Kotzschmar, Cambridge, 7 June 1873.

28. Charles C. Perkins and John S. Dwight, *History of the Handel and Haydn Society, of Boston, Massachusetts* (Boston, 1893), 333.

29. *Boston Daily Globe*, 6 October 1873, 8.

30. *DJM* XXXIV/5 (13 June 1874), 246–47; further Dwight comments are from this review.

31. *Boston Daily Globe*, 11 May 1874, 4.

32. *History of the Handel and Haydn Society*, 348–49.

33. Reported in *Boston Daily Globe*, 11 May 1874, 4.

34. *Atlantic Monthly* XXXIV (August 1874), 250–52.

35. *Atlantic Monthly* XXX (October 1872), 505; no copy of op. 11 appears extant.

36. Clark I, 418–19.

37. Fisk, 334–35.

38. Programs for the earlier two concerts are in the New England Conservatory library. Paine included his *Caprice* on the 1870 program, and closed both with an improvisation and his *Ein' feste Burg*.

39. *DJM* XXII/18 (14 December 1872), 351.

40. *Folio* X/4 (April 1874), 110.

41. *Boston Daily Globe*, 20 March 1874, 5.

42. *DJM* XXXI/26 (23 March 1872), 207.

43. The spelling, *theatre*, was used almost exclusively during the period of this study.

44. *Boston Daily Globe*, 8 June 1874, 4.

45. *Boston Daily Globe*, 22 June 1874, 8.

46. *New York World*, 6 February 1876; quoted in *DJM* XXX/23 (19 February 1876), 181–82.

47. *DJM* XXXV/22 (5 February 1876), 175.

48. *Atlantic Monthly* XXXVII (May 1876), 633.

49. Fisk, 339.

50. *Atlantic Monthly* XXXVII (June 1876); Fiske's authorship is revealed in his 12 July 1876 letter quoted in Fisk, 351.

51. *Boston Daily Advertiser*, 27 January 1876, 1.

52. *New-York Tribune*, 7 February 1876; quoted in *DJM* XXX/23 (19 February 1876), 181. The quotations that follow are taken from reviews in the *New York World* (6 February 1876), the *New York Times* (6 February 1876), and the *Saturday Evening Gazette* (29 January 1876), all reprinted in this issue of *DJM*.

53. Reprinted in *DJM* XXXV/22 (5 February 1876), 173.

54. *Nation* XXII (30 March 1876), 216–17.

55. A difficult problem exists in establishing the authorship of 19th-century music criticism in newspapers and periodicals. Most articles were unsigned, although some closed with a pseudonym (such as "Der Freyschutz"—W.S.B. Mathews in *DJM*), initials, or the author's full name. Initials are helpful only when they are distinctive; unfortunately, "C.H." is not. Probable authorship of an unsigned article may be ascertained if one knows the music critic on the staff of the publication for that particular time; however, such attribution can seldom be made without some remaining doubt.

56. *DJM* XXXVI/9 (5 August 1876), 280.

57. *DJM* XXXVI/8 (22 July 1876), 271–72.

58. *DJM* XXXVI/4 (27 May 1876), 238–39.

59. Rose Fay Thomas, *Memoirs of Theodore Thomas* (New York, 1911), 117–18.

60. Quoted in *DJM* XXXVI/4 (27 May 1876), 238.

61. *Atlantic Monthly* XXXVIII (July 1876), 124.

62. *Atlantic Monthly* XXXVII (June 1876), 744–45.

63. *DJM* XXXVI/6 (24 June 1876), 254.

64. *BDA*, 6 July 1876, 1.

65. *Records, Haydn Association*, 318.

66. *DJM* XXXVI/15 (28 October 1876), 328.

67. *DJM* XXXVI/17 (25 November 1876), 342.

68. *BDA*, 26 August 1876, 4.

69. *DJM* XXXVI/4 (27 May 1876), 239.

70. *BDA*, 13 May 1876, 4.

71. *DJM* XXXVI/16 (11 November 1876), 335.

72. *BDA*, 6 November 1876, 2.

73. *BDA*, 13 November 1876, 4.

74. *BDA*, 22 November 1876, 1.

75. *DJM* XXXVI/18 (9 December 1876), 350.

76. *BDA*, 19 February 1877, 4.

77. *DJM* XXXVI/22 (3 February 1877), 382.

78. *BDA*, 18 January 1877, 1; the details of the concert that follow are also from this source.

79. *DJM* XXXVIII/10 (17 August 1878), 288.

80. *DJM* XXXV/25 (18 March 1876), 198.

81. *BDA*, 2 March 1876, 1.

82. *BDA*, 13 April 1876, 4.

83. *BDA*, 13 March 1876, 4.

84. *BDA*, 21 March 1876, 4.

85. *BDA*, 28 April 1876, 4.

86. Fisk, 351–52.

87. Huxley (1825–95) was the principal exponent of Darwinism in England; Fiske had met him in an 1873 visit to England. Although also an evolutionist, Fiske did not share Huxley's agnosticism, and attempted to reconcile evolution and Christianity in his *Outlines of Cosmic Philosophy* (1874).

88. Fisk, 353; Petersham was the home of the Brooks, Mrs. Fiske's family.

89. Clark II, 90.

90. *Dwight—Correspondence*, 125.

91. Fisk, 368.

92. *BDA*, 9 October 1876, 4.

93. John Knowles Paine letter to William Dean Howells, Cambridge, 4 [?] April 1877, in Houghton collection, Harvard University.

94. *BDA*, 2 March 1877, 4.

95. *BDA*, 29 March 1877, 4.

96. *DJM* XXXVII/1 (14 April 1877), 6.

97. Henry C. Lahee, *Annals of Music in America* (Boston, 1922), 73.

98. Quoted in *DJM* XXXVII/16 (10 November 1877), 128.

99. Clipping preserved with collected programs, Boston Public Library.

100. *BDA*, 14 November 1877, 4.

101. *DJM* XXXVII/17 (24 November 1877), 134–35.

102. Published in *BDA*, 6 December 1877, 2.

103. *DJM* XXXVII/19 (22 December 1877), 150, a review of the 8 December concert, upon which the report that follows is based.

104. *BDA*, 22 January 1877, 4; 10 February 1877, 2.

105. A. A. Brown (compiler), *Programmes of Concerts in Sanders Theatre*, in collection of Boston Public Library.

106. *DJM* XXXVII/19 (22 December 1877), 151.

107. *BDA*, 7 May 1877, 1.

108. *BDA*, 8 May 1877, 1.

109. *BDA*, 6 April 1876, 2.

110. *DJM* XXXVII/16 (10 November 1877), 127.

111. *DJM* XXXVII/7 (7 July 1877), 55.

112. Quoted in *Music, a Monthly Magazine* XIX/4 (February 1901), 432.

113. *New-York Daily Tribune*, 5 May 1877, 11.

114. *DJM* XXXVII/4 (26 May 1877), 32.

115. Derived from advertisements in the *New-York Tribune*, 5 May 1877, and *BDA*, 11 May 1877. The name "Brandeis" appears as "Mandeis" in the advertisements, apparently an error of the typesetter.

116. *BDA*, 14 May 1877, 2.

117. *DJM* XXXVIII/29 (11 May 1878), 229.

118. *DJM* XXXVIII/23 (16 February 1878), 183.

119. *BDA*, 20 August 1877, 1.

120. *Fifty-second Annual Report of the President of Harvard College. 1876–77* (Cambridge, 1878), 52.

121. Report quoted in *DJM* XXXVIII/5 (8 June 1878), 247.

122. *BDA*, 25 April 1877, 1.

123. *BDA*, 15 October 1877, 2.

124. *BDA*, 1 January 1877, 4.

125. *BDA*, 9 October 1877, 1.

126. *BDA*, 19 February 1877, 2.

127. *DJM* XXXVIII/29 (11 May 1878), 229–30.

128. *BDA*, 8 July 1878, 1.

129. Fisk, 372–73.

130. From a 10 September 1878 letter quoted in *Letters of Celia Thaxter* (Boston, 1895), 93. Mrs. Thaxter's mother, whom she had cared for for 11 years, had died in 1877. Paine would often repeat Thaxter's favorite Beethoven sonatas, op. 109 and 110 [ibid., 139].

131. George F. Whicker, "Celia Laighton Thaxter," *Dictionary of American Biography* XVIII (1936), 397–98.

132. *BDA*, 11 July 1878, 2.

133. William Mason, *Memories of a Musical Life* (New York, 1901), 252; the quotation that follows is also from this source.

Chapter 7

1. *BDA*, 17 May 1879, 1.

2. *BDA*, 23 June 1879, 1.

3. *DJM* XXXIX (5 July 1879), 110.

4. The score was released in Europe by August Cranz of Hamburg and its associated firm, C. A. Spina of Vienna. Schmidt also published a piano-four hands arrangement at the same time.

5. Clark II, 73.

6. Fisk, 408; the quotation that follows is also from this source.

7. Ibid., 409. Host of the party was publisher Frederick Macmillan (1851–1936), who had become partner in the Macmillan firm three years earlier; guests named were biographer and historian James Sime (1843–95), George Grove (1820–1900), who was preparing his *Dictionary of Music and Musicians*, librarian and Russian scholar W. R. S. Ralston (1828–89), American publisher Henry Holt (1840–1926), novelist Hardy (1840–1928), and Elise C. Otté (1818–1903), Scandinavian scholar and historian. Fiske's other acquaintance named in the passage above was London publisher and scholar Nikolaus Trübner (1817–84), "the prince of social entertainers" (Clark II, 150).

8. Ibid., 409–10.

9. Clark II, 150–51; the quotation that follows is also from this source. Guests not previously identified were: Scottish journalist William Fraser Rae (1835–1905); Harvard professor and historian Henry Brooks Adams (1838–1918); clergyman Moncure Daniel Conway (1832–1907), who held a pastorate in London during 1864–84; publisher George Haven Putnam (1844–1930), president of G. P. Putnam & Sons; and Willard Brown (1853–1910), a Harvard law student who later became a prominent lawyer in New York City. Among those not attending were: Viscount James Bryce (1838–1922), jurist, historian, diplomat, Oxford law professor, and mountain climber; John Williams White (1849–1917), the American Hellenist who in 1880–81 would co-produce Sophocles' *Oedipus Tyrannus* at Harvard, with Paine composing the incidental music; and philosopher and evolutionist Herbert Spencer (1820–1903), whose books were widely circulated in America.

10. Fiske's comment—"*he's* all right"—about Paine's drinking freely suggests that the composer seldom indulged himself to such an extent.

11. *Musical World* LVII/29 (19 July 1879), 452. Davison's tastes were quite conservative, and he condemned Wagner and especially Verdi regularly.

12. *Musical World* LVII/32 (9 August 1879), 501.

13. *BDA*, 26 September 1879, 2.

14. *Harvard College Class of 1875—Fiftieth Anniversary Report, 1875–1925* (Norwood, Mass., 1925), 36.

15. Ibid.

16. *DJM* XXXIX (8 November 1879), 184.

17. *BDA*, 14 October 1878, 2; 21 October 1878, 1.

18. *Musical Record* II (27 December 1879), 197.

19. "1. Harmony; 2. Counterpoint; 3. History of Music; 4. The Instrumental Music of Haydn, Mozart, Beethoven, and their Successors"—all undergraduate courses—and two graduate courses: "24. Canon and Fugue; 25. Free Thematic Music" (*The Harvard University Catalogue*. 1879–80).

20. *DJM* XL (28 February 1880), 40.

21. *DJM* XXXIX (5 July 1879), 110.

22. *DJM* XXXIX (20 December 1879), 208.

23. *DJM* XXXIX (6 December 1879), 199. This increase is interesting, for 40 players is still a small orchestra for a symphony.

24. *DJM* XL (27 March 1880), 54; the program that follows is also found at this source. The Harvard orchestra was larger; probably most players performed in both organizations.

25. *DJM* XL (27 March 1880), 53.

26. Ibid., 54.

27. Contained in Allen Augustus Brown (comp.), *Programmes of Concerts in Sanders Theatre*, Boston Public Library; reviews of both concerts from the *Gazette*, *Courier* (for which Brown doubtless was the reviewer), and *Transcript* are found in this collection.

28. *Musical Record* II (20 March 1880), 389.

29. *BDA*, 12 March 1880, 1.

30. *BDA*, 11 March 1880, 1.

31. "John Knowles Paine," XIV, 151–53.

32. Unidentified newspaper clipping contained in the Brown scrapbook cited earlier.

33. *DJM* XL (4 December 1880), 198.

34. *DJM* XLI (29 January 1881), 21.

35. *BDA*, 4 February 1881, 1.

36. *DJM* XLI (26 February 1881), 36.

37. *Musical Record* III (12 February 1881), 309; hereafter *MR*.

38. *BDA*, 3 January 1881, 1.

39. Information supplied in a letter to the present writer from Richard G. Appel, Cambridge, Mass., 7 May 1970.

40. *American Art Journal* LIX/8 (4 June 1892), 211.

41. Arthur William Foote (comp.), *Three Scrap-books of Clippings, Programs, etc., relating to music* II (Boston, 1881–1907), in the collection of the Boston Public Library.

42. *Signale für die Musikalische Welt* L/11 (1892), 168; trans. J.C.S.

43. *DJM* XXXIX (21 June 1879), 96.

44. *BDA*, 28 May 1879, 1.

45. From collected programs, New England Conservatory library.

46. *MR* III (18 June 1881), 595.

47. *DJM* XLI (26 March 1881), 53. This song was the second in a set of four published by Ditson in 1879 as Op. 29; the other three were *Matin Song*, *Early Springtime*, and *Moonlight*.

48. *DJM* XXXIX (15 February 1879), 30.

49. *BDA*, 31 March 1880, 1.

50. *MR* II (17 April 1880), 453.

51. *BDA*, 12 April 1881, 1; 14 April 1881, 1.

52. *MR* I (23 August 1879), 325.

53. *DJM* XLI (4 June 1881), 94.

54. Programs contained in Foote, *Three Scrap-books* I.

55. *DJM* XXXIX (29 March 1879), 55.

56. *BDA*, 13 February 1879, 1.

57. Foote, *Three Scrap-books* I.

58. *BDA*, 3 March 1879, 2.

59. *BDA*, 16 February 1881, 4.

60. *DJM* XL (23 October 1880), 176.

61. *DJM* XL (20 November 1880), 192.

62. Quoted in Fields, *Authors and Friends*, 247.

63. Sara Norton and M. A. DeWolfe Howe, *Letters of Charles Eliot Norton, with Bio-graphical Comment* (Boston, 1913) II, 114–15.

64. *BDA*, 17 March 1881, 1; the publication information that follows is also from this advertisement. A post-publication notice in *DJM* XLI (9 April 1881), 61, quotes one dollar as the price for the vocal score.

65. *BDA*, 19 March 1881, 1; the quotations that follow are also from this source.

66. *BDA*, 5 April 1881, 1.

67. *BDA*, 5 May 1881, 1.

68. *DJM* XLI (21 May 1881), 82–83.

69. Identified in Henry Norman, *An Account of the Harvard Greek Play* (Boston, 1882), 127.

70. *BDA*, 30 June 1881, 1. Burdett left for Europe the following year to pursue a Ph.D., but had to abandon his plans because of poor health. Returning to Boston, he entered the business world, joining H. S. Ballow & Co. in 1885 and Chamberlain, Burdett, & Co., bankers and brokers, in 1889. But in 1895 he retired from a financial career and devoted his time to teaching, conducting, lecturing, and composing [*Harvard College Class of 1881—Fiftieth Anniversary* (Cambridge, 1931), 58–59].

71. *BDA*, 16 May 1881, 1; the quotations that follow are also from this source.

72. *BDA*, 18 May 1881, 1.

73. *DJM* XLI (21 May 1881), 84; Dwight's statement is also from this source.

74. Norton and Howe, II, 120–21.

75. Quoted in *DJM* XLI/12 (4 June 1881), 90–91.

76. *BDA*, 24 May 1881, 1.

77. *BDA*, 26 May 1881, 4.

78. *BDA*, 28 May 1881, 1; the quotation that follows is also from this source.

79. Quoted in *BDA*, 23 August 1881, 4.

80. Quoted in *BDA*, 4 October 1881, 4.

81. *BDA*, 6 February 1882, 5.

82. *BDA*, 23 January 1882, 8.

83. *BDA*, 24 January 1882, 8; the material and quotations that follow are from this source.

84. Reviews quoted in *BDA*, 1 February 1882, 8.

85. *New York Times*, 31 January 1882, 5.

86. *Nation* XXXIV (2 February 1882), 101–2.

87. Ibid.

88. Collected programs of the Brooklyn Philharmonic are found in the Lincoln Center music collection of the New York Public Library.

89. *Brooklyn Daily Eagle*, 19 March 1882, 5.

90. *New York Times*, 18 March 1882.

91. *Nation* XXXIV (23 March 1882), 254.

92. *MR* III (22 October 1881), 53.

93. *New York Tribune*, 19 March 1882, 7.

94. *BDA*, 16 February 1882, 8; the following quotations and other material are also from this source.

95. Wilson, *Boston Musical Year Book* I (1884).

96. Program in Foote, *Three Scrap-books* I.

97. *BDA*, 30 November 1887, 8.

98. *BDA*, 10 January 1883, 8.

99. *BDA*, 27 May 1884, 4; 29 May 1884, 4.

100. Wilson, *Boston Musical Year Book* V (1888).

101. *BDA*, 11 June 1885, 4.

102. Wilson, *Boston Musical Year Book* VII (1890).

103. Program in Foote, *Three Scrap-books* II.

104. *Boston Herald*, 19 April 1903, 39.

105. *MR* #370 (November 1892), 8.

106. *Boston Herald*, 24 November 1895, 16; 1 December 1895, 27.

107. Howe, 263.

108. *MR* IV (18 March 1882), 389.

109. *Boston Herald*, 12 March 1882; this and the reviews that follow of this concert are preserved as clippings inserted in the collected Boston Symphony Orchestra programs in the Boston Public Library collection.

110. *MR* #299 (December 1886), 8.

111. Information from the files of the Boston Symphony Orchestra.

112. *MR* #295 (August 1886), 5.

113. From the collected programs of the Boston Philharmonic Orchestra.

114. Foote, *Three Scrap-books* III.

115. *Boston Evening Transcript*, 23 May 1908, III, 4.

116. *MR* #279 (April 1885), 5.

117. Wilson, *Boston Musical Year Book* VII (1890).

118. *American Art Journal* LXIII/12 (30 June 1894), 214.

119. *Musical Courier* XXXVIII/24 (21 June 1899), 12.

120. G. H. L. Smith, *The Cleveland Orchestra: Thirty-sixth Season (1953–54)*, 203–5.

121. *Etude* VII (August 1889). French musicologist Julien Tiersot's account of the concert was rather discouraging to the Americans:

La jeune école américaine a présenté à son tour quelques-unes de ses productions orchestrales dans un concert donné aujourd'hui au Trocadéro. Cette jeune école, bien digne de ce nom, puisque ces principaux réprésentants n'ont guère dépassé la trentaine, ne se fait pas encore remarque par des tendances ni un tempérament très caracterisés. Elle prend ses inspirations de préférence dans l'école allemande néo-classique: Mendelssohn, Brahms, Raff, paraissent être ses modèles préférés; on peut relever aussi une certaine influence wagnérienne, mais superficielle dans certains agencements harmonique, certaines combinaisons de timbres. Parfois aussi, elle fait penser à la musique de nos maîtres français les plus connus, Massenet, Gounod, même Ambroise Thomas. Mais à défaut d'originalité, la facture est sérieuse, correcte, solide, et toujours pratique. Et surtout les jeunes compositeurs américains paraissent donnés d'une grande activité, car leu école à peine formée compte déjà un grand nombre de représentants et un important répertoire. Sans m'arrêter sur les oeuvres, je me borne à citer les noms des compositeurs exécutés au Trocadéro, car nous en retrouverons certainement plus d'un dans l'avenir. . . . [Julien Tiersot, *Musiques Pittoresques*. *Promenades Musicales à l'Exposition de 1889* (Paris, 1889), 55].

122. *Musical Courier* XLVII/17 (21 October 1903), 7.

123. Philip H. Goepp, "John Knowles Paine," *Harvard Graduates Magazine* XV (September 1906), 21–27.

124. *Boston Evening Transcript*, 23 May 1908, III, 4.

Chapter 8

1. L. C. Elson, "Musical Boston," *Music and Drama*, 3 June 1882, 5.

2. "John Knowles Paine," *Appleton's Cyclopaedia of American Biography*, rev. ed., ed. James Grant and John Fiske (New York, 1888, 1898), IV, 629.

3. *MR* #329 (June 1889), 6.

4. *BDA*, 23 April 1894, 4.

5. H. T. Finck, *Songs and Song Writers* (New York, 1900), 232.

6. H. E. Krehbiel, "Music in America," in Albert Lavignac, *Music and Musicians*, 4th ed., trans. William Marchant (New York, 1903), 492–93; the quotation that follows is also from this source.

7. *BDA*, 26 December 1887, 5.

8. Quoted in *MR* #352 (May 1891), 7. Reference to the one young composer may have been MacDowell or Chadwick; Horatio Parker had yet to write *Hora Novissima*.

9. *BDA*, 3 March 1882, 8; the quotation that follows is also from this source.

10. The vocal score, published in 1882, gave the opening line, *Phoebus, Arise!*, as the title. Later performances continued this substitution.

11. *MR* #188 (6 May 1882), 531.

12. *BDA*, 27 April 1882, 4; the three quotations that follow are also from this source.

13. *Boston Herald*, 28 March 1897, 13; hereafter, *BH*.

14. *Musical Courier* XLIV/16 (16 April 1902), 28.

15. *BH*, 14 November 1902, 9.

16. *BH*, 16 November 1902, 30.

17. The revised edition of the piano-vocal score, published in 1903, identifies the work as op. 39, the number assigned to his *Romance for Piano* (Ditson, 1883).

18. Dwight's article, originally published in advance of the concert, was quoted in his *History of the Handel and Haydn Society, of Boston, Massachusetts* (Boston, 1893), 437–39, and reprinted in the *American Art Journal* LXII/11 (30 December 1893), 234.

19. *BDA*, 3 May 1883, 5.

20. *BDA*, 2 February 1883, 5.

21. *BDA*, 3 May 1883, 5; other quotations from the *Advertiser* pertaining to this concert are from this source.

22. *Boston Evening Transcript*, 3 May 1883, 1; all remaining quotations are from the *Advertiser* article cited earlier.

23. Dwight, *History of the Handel and Haydn Society*, 489.

24. *BDA*, 30 January 1888, 4; the quotations dealing with this concert that follow are also from this source.

25. Wilson, *Musical Year-Book, Season 1886–87*, 12.

26. *MR* #310 (November 1887), 3.

27. *BH*, 8 March 1903, 39.

28. *BH*, 12 October 1902, 44.

29. *Musical Courier* XLVI/12 (25 March 1903), 18.

30. *BH*, 23 March 1903, 4; the *Herald* quotation that follows is from this source.

31. *Boston Evening Transcript*, 23 March 1903, 7; hereafter, *BET*.

32. Greenough (1833–1901) had joined the Harvard faculty in 1865 as tutor in Latin; in 1873 he became assistant professor, and was elected Professor of Latin in 1883. An influential publication was his *Analysis of the Latin Subjunctive* (1870), and he spent much time in producing textbooks, including editions of Caesar, Cicero, Virgil, Horace, Livy, Ovid, and Sallust, all benefiting from his own research [C. B. Gulick, "James Bradstreet Greenough," *Dictionary of American Biography* VII (New York, 1931), 588].

33. Spalding, *Music at Harvard*, 89.

34. *MR* #299 (December 1886), 8.

35. *Music Sung by the Alumni at the Two Hundred and Fiftieth Anniversary of the Foundation of Harvard University, November Seventh, 1638–1886* (Boston, 1886), 27.

36. Program contained in Foote, *Three Scrap-books*, I; a program of the following Mueller-Campanari Quartet concert is also found in this source.

37. Wilson, *Musical Year-book*, Season of 1884–85, 29.

38. Wilson, *Musical Year-book,* Season of 1887–88, 23.

39. Programs of this and the following concert contained in Foote, *Three Scrap-books*, I.

40. *BDA*, 21 March 1891, 4.

41. *Musical Courier* XXXVIII/1 (4 January 1899), 21; hereafter, *MC*.

42. *MC* XXXVII/16 (19 October 1898), 31.

43. *BH*, 3 December 1899, 11, and 10 December 1899, 30.

44. *MR* #267 (April 1884), 2.

45. *BDA,* 26 April 1883, 5; the *Advertiser* quotation that follows is from this source.

46. *BET*, 26 April 1883, 1; the quotation that follows is also from this source.

47. Wilson, *Boston Musical Year-book*, Season of 1883–84, 51.

48. Wilson, *Musical Year-book*, Season of 1887–88, 43.

49. Wilson, *Musical Year-book*, Season of 1890–91, 5.

50. From an unidentified, undated clipping glued into a copy of the score; in the collection of Boston Public Library.

51. 25 August 1890 letter in Fisk, 581. Clara Kathleen Rogers (1844–1931)—"Clara Doria"—an English-born soprano, came to America in 1871 with the Parepa-Rosa Company, and later established a teaching career in Boston.

52. Program in Foote, *Three Scrap-books* I; a clipping of the following *Post* review is also found in this source.

53. *BDA*, 16 March 1887, 4. Doubtless more of these songs were heard in concert, but since voice recitals usually did not receive detailed reviews, and since incidental songs in programs of larger works were seldom named in notices, such performances are difficult to document.

54. Both in Foote I.

55. Foote II.

56. *BH*, 3 March 1895, 16.

57. *MC* XLII/2 (9 January 1901), 33.

58. *MC* XLVII/23 (2 December 1903), 6.

59. *MC* L/21 (24 May 1905), 6.

60. *MC* LI/21 (22 November 1905), 34B.

61. Although it was copyrighted in 1883, the Library of Congress copy was received on 4 February 1884.

62. *BDA*, 25 February 1884, 4.

63. *BDA*, 4 April 1884, 4; the publication notice quoted for the following set, op. 41, is also from this issue, although Ditson was listed as the publisher.

64. Unidentified, undated clipping contained in Foote, *Three Scrap-books* I.

65. *Music and Musicians of Maine*, 133.

66. However, in our time, H. Wiley Hitchcock uncharitably has found the fugue "unbelievably dry" [*Music in the United States: A Historical Introduction* (Englewood Cliffs, N. J., 1969), 132]. The *Fuga giocosa* does not display the broad humor of many later Ives works, of course. But the unlikely juxtaposition of this jaunty informal ditty and the strict framework of the fugue calls to mind Paine's ready wit and healthy sense of humor. The piece, when performed at a lively tempo, is far from "dry."

67. W. S. B. Mathews (ed.), *The Great in Music: A Systematic Course of Study in the Music of Classical and Modern Composers* (Chicago, 1900) I, 177; the information that follows also is from this reference.

68. Sumner Salter, "Early Encouragements to American Composers," *Musical Quarterly* XVIII (January 1932), 78.

69. Wilson, *Boston Musical Year Book* (1884–85), 29.

70. *MR* #281 (June 1885), 1.

71. *MR* #293 (June 1886), 8.

72. *American Art Journal* LVI/21 (7 March 1891), 322.

73. *MC* XXXVII/15 (12 October 1898), 11.

74. *MC* XL/2 (10 January 1900), 29.

75. *MC* XLII/5 (30 January 1901), 41.

76. *DJM* (9 July 1864), 271.

77. *DJM* (6 August 1864), 287.

78. *DJM* (23 June 1866), 262.

79. Among American organists who studied with French teachers were Issac V. Flagler (1844–1909) [Edoard Batiste], Raymond Huntington Woodman (1861–1943) [Franck], James Hotchkiss Rogers (1847–1940), Homer A. Norris (1860–1920), William C. Carl (1865–1936), George Waring Stebbins (1869–1930), Clarence Dickinson (1873–1969), and Seth Bingham (1882–1972) [all with Guilmant]. Fewer Americans now studied in Germany. The most popular German teachers were Haupt, in Berlin—Paine, Eugene Thayer (1838–1889), Samuel P. Warren (1841–1915), Nathan H. Allen (1848–1925), Clarence Eddy (1851–1937), James H. Rogers, and Gerrit Smith (1859–1912)—and Rheinberger, in Munich—G. W. Chadwick and Horatio Parker.

80. *MC* XL/15 (11 April 1900), 25.

81. Foote, *Three Scrap-books* III.

82. *American Art Journal* LIV/33 (24 February 1890), 545; hereafter, *AAJ*.

83. *MC* XXXIV/15 (14 April 1897), 21, and XXXIV/16 (21 April 1897), 16.

84. *AAJ* LXVI/6 (16 November 1895), 84.

85. *AAJ* LXV/6 (18 May 1895), 84.

86. Program contained in Foote, *Three Scrap-books* I.

87. Wilson, *Musical Year-book*, Season 1892–93, 203.

88. *AAJ* LVIII/24 (26 March 1892), 522.

89. *MC* XLVIII/18 (4 May 1904), 19.

90. *MC* XLIX/26 (28 December 1904), 32.

91. *New Music and Church Music Review* V (March 1906), 791.

92. *New York Times*, 31 March 1883, 4.

93. *Brooklyn Daily Eagle*, 1 April 1883, 5.

94. *New York Daily Tribune*, 1 April 1883, 7.

95. *Nation* XXXVI (5 April 1883), 298.

96. *BDA*, 3 March 1884, 4.

97. *BDA*, 18 June 1885, 4.

98. Foote, *Three Scrap-books* I.

99. *BDA*, 11 April 1892, 5; the quotation that follows is also from this article. In 1904, writing in his *History of American Music*, Elson still spoke highly of the symphony, declaring that Paine "now . . . became master of the rules [of music], and his poetry began to assert itself," and finding the finale almost comparable with the last movement of Schumann's *Spring* symphony [Louis C. Elson, *The History of American Music*, rev. ed. (New York, 1915), 166].

100. Philo Adams Otis, *The Chicago Symphony Orchestra; Its Organization, Growth and Development, 1891–1924* (Chicago, 1924), 34.

101. From a J. K. Paine letter to Anna Lyman (Mason) Gray, Cambridge, 6 April 1892; in Houghton Library, Harvard University.

102. *MC* XXXVIII/14 (5 April 1899), 17.

103. *BDA*, 21 March 1883, 2.

104. *BDA*, 12 March 1883, 2; further *Advertiser* quotations pertinent to this concert are from this issue.

105. *MR* #233 (17 March 1883), 464.

106. *BET*, 12 March 1883, 1.

107. *Nation* XXXIX (4 December 1884), 483.

108. *Brooklyn Daily Eagle*, 30 November 1884, 7.

109. *New York Tribune*, 30 November 1884, 7.

110. *New York Times*, 29 November 1884, 4; the quotations that follow are also from this article.

111. *BDA*, 9 November 1885, 4.

112. Information from collected programs, *Theodore Thomas and His Unrivaled Orchestra: Summer Garden Concerts—In the Exposition Building*; copy contained in Brooklyn Public Library.

113. Wilson, *Musical Year-book*, Season 1887–88, 54.

114. *New York Times*, 18 February 1888, 4.

115. Wilson, *Musical Year-book*, Season 1887–88, 76.

116. Information from the collected Chicago Orchestra programs, season 1899–1900; in New York Public Library.

117. Wilson, *Musical Year-book*, Season 1889–90, 34.

118. *MC* XXXIII/23 (2 December 1896), 12.

119. *BH*, 26 November 1899, 20.

120. *MC* XXXIX/23 (6 December 1899), 19.

121. *BH*, 27 January 1901, 17.

122. *AAJ* LVII/1 (18 April 1891), 4.

123. "John Knowles Paine," *Cyclopedia of Music and Musicians*, ed. John D. Champlin, Jr. (New York, 1888–90) III, 66–68. A confusing abundance of titles has been given to this work, including *Seebuilder, An Ocean Fantasy*, *Eine Meer-Phantasie*, and *Poseidon und Amphitrite*—the latter three appearing on the published score (Breitkopf & Härtel, 1907).

124. *BDA*, 19 April 1889, 4.

125. Mary E. Paine, Will No. 178648, Middlesex County, Massachusetts.

126. *AAJ* LV/12 (5 July 1890), 210.

127. *AAJ* LXI/14 (15 July 1893), 315.

128. *BDA*, 22 April 1889, 4.

129. H. E. Krehbiel, *The Philharmonic Society of New York: A Memorial* (New York, 1892), 160; J. G. Huneker, *The Philharmonic Society of New York and its Seventy-fifth Anniversary: A Retrospect* (New York, 1917) lists no further performances.

130. *New York Daily Tribune*, 13 January 1890, 6; *Tribune* quotations that follow are also from this article.

131. *New York Times*, 11 January 1890, 4.

132. *AAJ* LV/19 (23 August 1890), 319.

133. Ibid., 320.

134. *AAJ* LXI/14 (15 July 1893), 315.

135. *AAJ* LXII/3 (4 November 1893), 53.

136. *BH*, 3 March 1895, 7.

137. The following letter from Paine to Woodberry is in the Houghton Library of Harvard University:

> Harvard University
> June 22, 1887
>
> Mr. George E. Woodberry.
> My Dear Sir,
>   It is my present intention to compose and publish a Cantata for Chorus & Orchestra for a musical festival to be given next year, and I should esteem it a great favor if you will give me permission to select the words for this purpose from your noble Ode—"My Country," which I have read again & again with great delight. If you grant my request I should like to meet you at your convenience to consult with you. The best musical treatment would render it necessary to omit a considerable part of the poem. In composing Milton's Hymn to the Nativity I took this indispensable liberty. If you will kindly appoint a time & place of meeting I shall be much obliged.
>
> Yours truly, John K. Paine
>
> P.S.   I have written to Messrs. Houghton, Mifflin & Co. to ask their consent also. I should like to keep this matter a secret for the present.

138. *MR* #317 (June 1888), 7.

139. *MR* #318 (July 1888), 3.

140. Rose Fay Thomas, *Memoirs of Theodore Thomas*, 311–12.

141. Unidentified newspaper clipping bound with collected programs of the Boston Philharmonic Orchestra, in the Boston Public Library; the quotations that follow are also from clippings contained in this source.

142. "Music in Chicago," (27 December 1891), *AAJ* LVIII/13 (9 January 1892), 289.

143. *AAJ* (9 January 1892), 295; George W. Chadwick, not MacDowell, eventually composed the ode.

144. "Our Boston Budget," *AAJ* LIX/2 (23 April 1892), 67.

145. Fisk, 612.

146. *BDA*, 22 August 1892, 2.

147. *MR* #369 (October 1892), 8.

148. *AAJ* LX/2 (22 October 1892), 28.

149. *MR* #371 (December 1892), 14; this description, with minor changes, also appeared in the program booklet for the 20–21 January 1893 matinée and concert of the Chicago Orchestra at the Chicago Auditorium, Theodore Thomas, conductor.

150. G. P. Upton, "Reminiscence and Appreciation," *Theodore Thomas: A Musical Autobiography* (Chicago, 1905) I, 196.

151. Rose Fay Thomas, *Memoirs . . .*, 381–83.

152. *BDA*, 22 October 1892, 1.

153. *AAJ* LXI/14 (15 July 1893), 317.

154. *AAJ* LXI/2 (22 April 1893), 29.

155. *AAJ* LX/22 (11 March 1893), 491.

156. Quoted in *AAJ* LXI/7 (27 May 1893), 149. Probably this was sent in response to W.S.B. Mathew's request for support. A 12 May 1893 telegram from Mathews to Arthur Foote asked Foote to wire "all good names" in Thomas' behalf; telegram contained in Foote *Scrap-book*, Boston Public Library.

157. Quoted in Upton, "Reminiscence . . ." I, 199.

158. *AAJ* LXI/14 (15 July 1893), 316.

159. *AAJ* LXI/18 (12 August 1893), 414.

160. *AAJ* LXII/3 (4 November 1893), 53.

161. *AAJ* LXI/18 (12 August 1893), 414.

162. Wilson, *Musical Year-book*, Season 1892–93, 239.

163. *AAJ* LXI/9 (10 June 1893), 197.

164. *AAJ* LXI/12 (1 July 1893), 271.

165. From the collected programs, in Music Division, New York Public Library.

166. *BDA*, 6 February 1893, 5.

167. *MC* XLIX/1 (6 July 1904), 12.

168. *MC* XLVIII/12 (23 March 1904), 27.

169. *MC* XLVIII/19 (11 May 1904), 23; the correspondent for the *Boston Herald* (1 May 1904) reported a chorus of 500.

170. An octavo edition of the *Hymn*, with the orchestral introduction and accompaniment arranged for piano, was published prior to the first performance by the official music publisher for the exposition, Thiebes-Stierlin Music Co., St. Louis.

171. *BH*, 20 February 1905, 12.

172. Ibid, 4.

173. *MC* L/18 (3 May 1905), 14.

174. Fisk, 693.

175. *BH*, 6 May 1901, 12.

176. *BH*, 7 May 1901, 9; the quotation that follows is also from this source.

177. *BH*, 9 May 1901, 3.

178. *BH*, 2 March 1902, 31.

179. *BH*, 8 March 1902, 9.

180. *MC* XLVI/9 (4 March 1903), 30.

181. Quoted in *BH*, 15 March 1903, 39.

182. *BH*, 13 March 1904, Women's Section, 3.

183. *BH*, 10 March 1904, 8.

184. *MC* LI/21 (22 November 1905), 34A.

185. *BET*, 18 November 1905, II, 4.

186. *MC* LII/1 (3 January 1906), 47.

187. *MC* LI/15 (11 October 1905), 31.

188. *MR* #245 (9 June 1883), 107.

189. *MR* #287 (December 1885), 8.

190. Spalding, *Music at Harvard*, 156. No record of such offers seems to exist. But Howells' attitude toward opera seems to have been inconsistent. In his early days he termed it a "stumblingblock and a foolishness." And in 1906 he wrote that

opera is terrible to me. . . . It is perhaps because of the light gossamer which now alone protects my scalp that music seems to get in its merciless work, and make an evening at the Metropolitan like a sojourn in a boiler factory.

However, he enjoyed Italian opera, and praised Caruso in *L'Elisir d'Amore*. He termed the Gilbert and Sullivan operettas "the most charming things in the world," and reflected their influence in *A Sea Change*, on which he collaborated with composer Georg Henschel [Information and quotations from Edward Wagenknecht, *William Dean Howells: The Friendly Eye* (New York, 1969), 142].

191. Quoted in Edwards, 138.

192. Finck, 79.

193. From the program for a concert performance of *Azara* by the Cecilia Society, Boston, 9 April 1907; copy in Music Library archives, Harvard University.

194. *The Forum* XIII (June 1892), 507–18.

195. *BDA*, 9 October 1886, 8.

196. *MR* #298 (November 1886), 4.

197. *Cyclopedia of Music and Musicians*, ed. Champlin, III, 67.

198. *The Great in Music* I, 173.

199. From the European edition of the *New York Herald*; quoted in *AAJ* LVII/26 (10 October 1891), 418.

200. *MC* XXXV/22 (1 December 1897), 26.

201. *MR* #379 (August 1893), 4.

202. Quoted in *BH*, 26 April 1896, 31.

203. Three copies of the libretto may be found in the Music Library of Harvard University, the first dated "c. 1896–98," the second published in 1898 by Riverside Press, Cambridge, the third dated 1903.

204. *Harvard Graduates Magazine* V (1896–97), 462.

205. Frederick F. Bullard, "Music in Boston: Zerrahn, Paine, Lang and Chadwick," *MC* XXXVII/1 (4 July 1898), unpaged.

206. *MC* XXXVII/16 (19 October 1898), 28.

207. Quoted in Howe, 266.

208. Ibid., 265; the quotation that follows is also from this source.

209. Finck, 79; the quotation that follows is also from this source.

210. L. C. Elson, *The History of American Music* (New York, 1904), 169.

211. *The Great in Music* . . . I, 175–76.

212. *MC* XL/11 (14 March 1900), 31; the quotation that follows is also from this source.

213. *BH*, 11 March 1900, 3; the quotations that follow are also from this source.

214. From records of the Boston Symphony Orchestra.

215. *MC* XLI/18 (31 October 1900), 17.

216. *BET*, 21 December 1903, 9.

217. *BH*, 20 December 1903, 7.

218. *BH*, 6 January 1904, 10.

219. *MC* XLVIII/2 (13 January 1904), 29.

220. *MC* XLIV/20 (14 May 1902), 32.

221. Foote, *Three Scrap-books* III.

222. Unidentified clipping, ibid.

223. A copy of the subscription notice is contained in Foote, *Three Scrap-books* III.

224. "Seldom has there been such an exodus of musicians from [Boston] as has been going on for the past month and will continue far into June, all bound for that Mecca—Europe. . . . John K. Paine, of Harvard College, has gone or is about to go. . . ." ["Boston Music Notes, May 25, 1901," *MC* XLII/22 (29 May 1901), 28].

225. J. K. Paine letter to Mabel Daniels, Westport-on-Lake-Champlain, New York, 28 July 1901; in Harvard University Archives.

226. *BH*, 20 October 1901, 30.

227. *BH*, 10 November 1901, 44.

228. Ibid.

229. Translation from *BH*, 19 January 1902, 34.

230. *Music* XXI/2 (January 1902), 178.

231. *BH*, 3 November 1901, 30.

232. "Boston Music Notes, November 23, 1901," *MC* XLIII/22 (27 November 1901), 18.

233. *BH*, 9 February 1902, 30.

234. *BH*, 5 February 1902, 8.

235. *MC* XLIV/7 (12 February 1902), 28.

236. *BH*, 8 January 1905, Women's Section, 6.

237. *BDA*, 9 May 1885, 2.

238. Emma Eames, *Some Memories and Reflections* (New York, 1927), 33–34.

239. Louis C. Elson, "At the Exposition, Paris, Aug. 24," *BDA*, 10 September 1889, 5.

240. Louis C. Elson, *European Reminiscences, Musical and Otherwise* (Philadelphia, 1896), 222.

241. *MC* XLIV/11 (12 March 1902), 17.

242. *BH*, 16 April 1902, 9; the quotation that follows is also from this source.

243. *BET*, 19 March 1903, 3.

244. *BH*, 3 May 1903, 39; the list of performers that follows was obtained from this source.

245. *BH*, 8 May 1903, 10; the quotation that follows is also from this source.

246. *MC* XLVI/19 (13 May 1903), 25.

247. *BH*, 8 May 1903, 10.

248. *BET*, 8 May 1903, 3; the quotation that follows is also from this source.

249. E. E. Hipsher, *American Opera and Its Composers*, 2nd ed. (Philadelphia, 1934), 352–53.

250. *BH*, 7 April 1903, 9; Damrosch's opera finally was produced in 1913.

251. *BH*, 24 May 1903, 39.

252. *BH*, 20 December 1903, 7. Impresario Henry Wilson Savage (1859–1927) began producing opera in English in 1897 with his Castle Square Opera Company in Boston; the company undertook several tours, including a season in Chicago in 1899. In 1900 Savage formed his English Grand Opera Company. Special troupes toured nationally with *Parsifal* in English in 1904–05 and *Madama Butterfly* in 1906–07.

253. *MC* L/7 (15 February 1905), 24.

254. *New Music Review and Church Music Review* IV (October 1905), 472.

255. Finck, 79–80.

256. Hipsher, 353.

257. Ibid.

258. *Musical America* V/22 (13 April 1907), 5.

259. *BET*, 10 April 1907, 21.

260. Victor Yellin, *The Life and Operatic Works of George Whitefield Chadwick*, unpublished Ph.D. thesis, Harvard University (1957), 248–50.

261. G. W. Chadwick, "American Composers," *History of American Music*, ed. W. L. Hubbard (Toledo, 1908), 3.

262. Arthur Farwell and W. Dermot Darby, *Music in America* (New York, 1915), 336.

263. Finck, *My Adventures in the Golden Age of Music*, 80.

264. *BET*, 17 March 1906, II, 4.

265. *MC* LII/13 (28 March 1906), 25.

266. *BET*, 23 March 1906, 9.

267. *BH*, 16 October 1904, Women's Section, 6.

268. *MC* LII/14 (4 April 1906), 25.

Chapter 9

1. *County of Middlesex Land Registration Records* MDLX, 65.

2. Paine played for his funeral at Appleton Chapel on 26 March 1882 [*BDA*, 27 March 1882, 1]. Later in the year he "expressed an intention of setting some of his poems to music" [W. Sloane Kennedy, *Henry W. Longfellow: Biography, Anecdote, Letters, Criticism* (Cambridge, 1882), 187], a plan that did not reach fruition.

3. *County of Middlesex Land Registration Records* MDCXCIII, 373.

4. Ibid. MDCXCII, 109–10.

5. Ibid. MDCXCIII, 373.

6. Ibid. MDCXCIII, 555–58.

7. Ibid. MDCXCII, 110.

8. From a 2 July 1970 telephone interview with Hugh Payne Greeley.

9. Summer vacations at Harvard gradually increased in length during Paine's years there. In 1864–65, classes lasted from 1 September to 19 July, leaving only six weeks for vacation. In subsequent years, fall classes began about a week later, but the mid-July commencement was retained. In 1869, commencement was moved to the end of June, and the 1870 beginning date was changed to the end of September, lengthening the summer vacation to two months. This schedule continued throughout the remainder of Paine's tenure.

10. John K. Paine letter to Allan A. Brown, Appledore House, Shoals, off Portsmouth, N. H., 23 July 1905, *Allan A. Brown Scrapbook* I, Boston Public Library.

11. From a 1927 letter to George Thornton Edwards, quoted in *Music and Musicians of Maine*, 138–39. Greeley confirmed the probable year 1905 in an 8 June 1974 telephone conversation with the present writer.

12. *BH*, 7 July 1895, p. 2.

13. *BH*, 12 July 1896, p. 27, 9 August 1896, p. 27.

14. *MC* XLI/8 (22 August 1900), 22.

15. Letter contained in Harvard University Archives collection.

16. *BDA*, 2 June 1894, p. 4.

17. *MC* XLII/22 (29 May 1901), 28.

18. From a 31 October 1961 letter from Greeley to Kenneth C. Roberts, quoted in Roberts' unpublished thesis, *John Knowles Paine*, 71.

19. *MC* XLVII/4 (22 July 1903), 11.

20. *BH*, 19 July 1903, 31.

21. *BH*, 29 July 1903, 12.

22. *Monthly Music Record* XXXIII/395 (1 November 1903), 215.

23. Quoted in *MC* XLVII/17 (21 October 1903), 5–6.

24. *Monthly Musical Record* (1 November 1903), 215.

25. *MC* (21 October 1903), 7; the quotation that follows is also from this source, p. 5.

26. Information from Roberts, 105.

27. *MC* XXXIX/25 (20–27 December 1899), unpaged.

28. H. E. Krehbiel, "John Knowles Paine," *Grove's Dictionary of Music and Musicians*, 2nd ed., ed. J. A. Fuller-Maitland (New York, 1907) III, 597. Paine's "Mus.D." was included with his faculty listing in subsequent Harvard catalogs.

29. *MC* XXXII/22 (27 May 1896), 21.

30. *BDA*, 17 January 1883, 8.

31. *BET*, 23 January 1883, 4; Novello had only two sets of parts available for America, one for Thomas and the other for a Canadian, Torrington.

32. *BET*, 16 January 1883, 1.

33. *BDA*, 17 January 1883, 8.

34. *BET*, 17 January 1883, 4.

35. During an interview for *Music* magazine in March, 1896, John Lathrop Mathews (son of editor W. S. B. Mathews) asked Paine, after hearing him play the Moorish dance from *Azara*, how he went about composing such a piece. " 'Why,' said he, 'I have an idea—and jot down a sketch of it. Then bit by bit it grows and gets plainer and I increase my sketch, until at last I have the thing complete. Then when I feel in the mood I sit down and write the full score.' " [*Music* IX (1896), 645–46]

36. M. A. DeWolfe Howe, *The Boston Symphony Orchestra, 1881–1931* (Boston, 1931), 68–69.

37. *BDA*, 24 October 1884, 4.

38. *BDA*, 30 October 1884, 2.

39. *BDA*, 9 May 1885, 2.

40. Ibid.

41. *BDA*, 23 February 1893, 5.

42. From a review by Louis C. Elson, *BDA*, 9 October 1893, 5.

43. *BH*, 23 October 1898, 31.

44. *BH*, 19 November 1899, 31.

45. Letter from John K. Paine to (Charles E.) Norton, Houghton Library, Harvard University.

46. Letter from Mary Elizabeth (Greeley) Paine to Sara Norton, Houghton Library, Harvard University.

47. Undated John K. Paine letter to H. A. Lamb, Harvard University Archives.

48. J. K. Paine letter to H. A. Lamb, Shoals, 2 September 1889, Harvard University Archives; the quotation that follows is also from this letter.

49. *AAJ* LIV/7 (31 August 1889), 103. Later, in 1903, Towers opened a studio in St. Louis, and then joined the Kroeger School of Music there as head of vocal instruction [*MC* XLVIII/2 (13 January 1904), 31]. He compiled a *Dictionary-Catalogue of Operas and Operettas Which Have Been Performed on the Public Stage* (Morgantown, W. Va., 1910).

50. *AAJ* LXIV/12 (29 December 1894), 218.

51. *BH*, 30 September 1900, 30.

52. *BH*, 21 October 1900, 13.

53. Such as a Boston Symphony Orchestra program at Sanders Theatre on 27 December 1900 featuring composer Helen Hopekirk [*BH*, 30 December 1900, p. 30].

54. Fisk, 575.

55. Quoted in Fisk, 575–76.

56. Fisk, 673.

57. *BH*, 6 May 1900, 31.

58. *BH*, 28 January 1900, 31; the 13 ladies represented "the best in the university set," according to the Social Life editor.

59. *BH*, 11 February 1900, 31.

60. *BH*, 13 April 1902, 30.

61. *BH*, 3 May 1903, 31, and 9 April 1905, Women's Section, 3.

62. *BH*, 8 November 1896, 27. Rotoli had taught at the Academy of St. Cecilia in Rome from 1868, where, reportedly, Adelina Patti had studied with him. In 1885, at the invitation of Eben Tourjée, he came to Boston to join the New England Conservatory faculty [*BH*, 27 November 1904, 15].

63. *BH*, 22 November 1896, 27.

64. *BH*, 31 March 1895, 27.

65. *BH*, 11 March 1900, 31, and 1 April 1900, 31.

66. *BH*, 19 February 1905, Women's Section, 3.

67. *BH*, 19 November 1905, Society Section, 3.

68. *BH*, 18 March 1900, 31.

69. *BH*, 22 March 1903, 31.

70. *BH*, 14 April 1904, 11.

71. *MC* XLVIII/17 (27 April 1904), 29.

72. *BH*, 7 July 1895, 27. Thompson earned his A.B. *summa cum laude* in 1892 from Harvard, and had been a student of Paine.

73. *BH*, 16 February 1896, 27.

74. *BH*, 10 May 1896, 27.

75. *Music* IX (1896), 644.

76. *BH*, 10 May 1896, 27.

77. *BH*, 3 April 1897, 7.

78. *BH*, 1 May 1898, 26.

79. *BH*, 7 April 1901, 30.

80. *BH*, 6 April 1902, 31.

81. *BH*, 12 April 1903, 31.

82. *BH*, 24 April 1904, Editorial and Women's Section, 3.

83. *BH*, 17 April 1898, 27.

84. *BH*, 29 March 1903, 31.

85. *BH*, 29 May 1898, 31.

86. *BH*, 16 April 1899, 31.

87. *BH*, 15 April 1900, 30. Daniels received her A.B. *magna cum laude* in 1900, after working with Paine; she studied further with Chadwick and H. Carleton Slack, and then continued her education abroad. A book resulted: *An American Girl in Munich— Impressions of a Music Student*. She achieved recognition as a composer. Her father, George Frank Daniels of Brookline, was a president of the Handel and Haydn Society.

88. *BH*, 7 December 1902, 31.

89. *BH*, 19 May 1901, 31.

90. *BH*, 2 June 1901, 30.

91. *BH*, 27 April 1902, 31.

92. *BH*, 5 March 1905, Women's Section, 3, and 10 November 1905, 5.

93. *BH*, 15 April 1900, 31.

94. *BH*, 13 January 1901, 30.

95. *BH*, 13 December 1903, 31.

96. *Faculty Records, New Series* II (1877), Harvard College, 365.

97. *Faculty Records, New Series* III (1880), Harvard College, 137 (16 January 1882).

98. Spalding, "Music, 1862–1929," 108.

99. *Reports of the President and the Treasurer of Harvard College*, 1903–04 (Cambridge, 1905), 47–48.

100. *Faculty Records, New Series* II (1877), Harvard College, 323.

101. Ibid., 327.

102. *Faculty Records, New Series* V (1887), Harvard College, 175–76.

103. Ibid., 177.

104. Ibid., 180–81.

105. *BDA*, 8 October 1886, 8.

106. *A Catalogue of the Officers and Students of Harvard University for the Academical Year 1871–72* (Cambridge, 1871), 46.

107. "Music at Harvard," *The Harvard Graduates Magazine* III (1894–95), 311–12. Paine apparently was unaware of the music theses that had been written by Harvard students during the seventeenth and early eighteenth centuries; these were filed in the college library and were destroyed in a fire. This information was available in George Hood, *A History of Music in New England* (Boston, 1846), 50–51.

108. *The Harvard University Catalogue 1872–73* (Cambridge, 1873), 73.

109. *The Harvard University Catalogue 1873–74* (1874), 84.

110. *The Harvard University Catalogue 1874–75* (1874), 62; apparently beginning with this issue the catalogues were published in advance.

111. *The Harvard University Catalogue 1875–76* (1875), 64.

112. Ibid., 150.

113. Meeting of 24 March 1875, *Overseers Records* XI (1871–1882), 173–4.

114. *The Harvard University Catalogue 1876–77* (1876), 60.

115. *The Harvard University Catalogue 1877–78* (1877), 82.

116. *The Harvard University Catalogue 1878–79* (1878), 176.

117. Information gathered from *Annual Report* volumes; totals do not allow for possible student duplications between courses. See Appendix 2 for enrollment tabulation.

118. Paine's *Lecture Notes* for the History of Music course were published that year by W. H. Wheeler, Cambridge, perhaps as a result of this large enrollment. A copy is contained in the Harvard University Archives collection. Paine was preparing a music history textbook at the time of his death. The manuscript, complete only through the Classical period, was edited by Albert A. Howard and published as *The History of Music to the Death of Schubert* (Boston: Ginn and Co., 1907; reprinted AMS Press, Inc., New York).

119. *Annual Reports . . . 1887–88* (Cambridge, 1889), 66; the asterisk indicates the requirement of prior approval from the instructor before registering for a course.

120. *Annual Reports . . . 1888–89* (1890), 77, the following quotation is also from this source.

121. *Annual Reports . . . 1892–93* (1894), 68.

122. *The Harvard University Catalogue 1894–95* (1894).

123. "Music at Harvard," *Harvard Graduates Magazine* III, 312–13; the three quotations that follow are also from this source.

124. "Music, 1862–1929," *Development . . .* , 110.

125. "Music at Harvard," *Harvard Graduates Magazine* III, 314; the two quotations that follow are from pp. 313 and 314 of this report.

126. *Annual Reports . . . 1900–01* (1902), 68.

127. *Annual Reports . . . 1901–02* (1903), 81.

128. *Annual Reports . . . 1897–98* (1899), 81.

129. *BH*, 19 September 1897, 29.

130. *BH*, 3 October 1897, 26.

131. *MC* XXXVI/18 (4 May 1898), 33.

132. *BH*, 1 May 1898, 27.

133. *BH*, 9 October 1898, 13; the information that follows, on the 1898–99 season, is also from this source.

134. *MC* XXXIX/16 (18 October 1899), 24.

135. *The Harvard University Catalogue 1902–03* (1902), 392.

136. J. K. Paine, "Music," *The Harvard Graduates Magazine* XI (March, 1903), 416–17.

137. *The Harvard Graduates Magazine* VIII (June 1900), 538.

138. *Faculty of Arts and Sciences, Reports and Papers* V (1900), 345.

139. Ibid., V, 365.

140. *The Harvard Graduates Magazine* XII (June 1904), 622.

141. "Tabular View of Elective Studies for Undergraduates, 1881–82," *Faculty Records, New Series* III (1880), 122–23.

142. *The Harvard Graduates Magazine* XI (March 1903), 377–78.

143. *The Harvard Graduates Magazine* XIII (December 1904), 284–85.

144. John Knowles Paine letter to William Dean Howells, Cambridge, 22 January 1902, in Houghton Library, Harvard University.

145. *The Harvard Graduates Magazine* XIII (December 1904), 285.

146. *Reports of the President and the Treasurer of Harvard College, 1904–05* (Cambridge, 1906), 324.

147. *The Harvard Graduates Magazine* XIV (September 1905), 198. Later Mrs. Paine gave the tea service to the Harvard Faculty, and it was "ordinarily" used at the weekly meetings [John Hays Gardiner, *Harvard* (New York, 1914), 94].

148. *The Harvard Graduates Magazine* XIV (December 1905), 285–86; the album is now in the Harvard University Archives collection.

149. Quoted in Mabel W. Daniels, *An American Girl in Munich—Impressions of a Music Student* (Boston, 1912), 177.

150. E. B. Hill, "Musical Boston in the Gay Nineties; Halcyon Days at Harvard," *Etude* LXVII (January 1949), 9.

151. From a letter from Edward Ballantine to Kenneth C. Roberts, Jr., quoted in Roberts' *John Knowles Paine*, 96.

152. From a letter to Roberts, ibid., 97.

153. Howard, *Our Contemporary Composers* (New York, 1941), 40.

154. D. G. Mason, *Music in My Time, and Other Reminiscences* (New York, 1938), 39.

155. *MC* LI/1 (5 July 1905), 18.

156. *MC* LI/3 (19 July 1905), 21.

157. *MC* LI/7 (16 August 1905), 18.

158. *MC* LI/16 (18 October 1905), 20.

159. *MC* LII/18 (2 May 1906), 20; the quotation that follows is also from this source.

160. *Nation* LIII (8 June 1905), 452.

161. *MC* LII/17 (25 April 1906), 28.

162. *Portland Post*, 25 April 1906; clipping preserved in *Post Scrapbook* V, 145, Maine Historical Society.

163. *Commonwealth of Massachusetts Death Records* XXV, 415.

164. From a 2 July 1970 telephone interview with Hugh Payne Greeley.

165. *BET*, 26 April 1906, p. 1.

166. Goepp, 26–27.

Chapter 11

Keyboard Music

1. According to Victor Fell Yellin, in a paper read before the American Musicological Society in 1972, the "omnibus progression" is "a chain of five chords beginning with (1) a dominant-seventh in the first inversion, root in the soprano, and ending with (5) the chord in root position. While the inner voices remain stable as pedals, the two outer voices expand by contrary motion in three chromatic steps. . . ."

An early discussion of the progression is found in S. Jadassohn, *Lehrbuch der Harmonie* (1883). The paper, "The Omnibus Idea," is summarized in *Abstracts of Papers Read at the Thirty–Eighth Annual Meeting of the American Musicological Society, Dallas, Texas, November 2–5, 1972*, 20–21. In 1888 Paine adopted Jadassohn's book as a text for his Harmony course at Harvard.

2. *BMT* IX/6 (6 June 1868), 47.

3. *New-York Daily Tribune*, 5 May 1877, 11; *DJM* XXXVII/4 (26 May 1877), 32.

4. *Annual Catalogue . . . of the New England Conservatory of Music* (Boston, 1869), 38.

5. *The Atlantic Monthly* XXX (October 1872), 505.

6. *BDA*, 13 November 1876, 4.

7. *DJM* XXXVII/7 (7 July 1877), 55; *BDA*, 14 April 1881, 1.

8. *BDA*, 31 March 1880, 1; *Musical Record* II (17 April 1880), 453.

9. *Musical Record* #481 (1 February 1902), 40; F. O. Jones, *A Handbook of American Music and Musicians* (Canaseraga, N. Y., 1886), 10.

10. *BDA*, 8 May 1877, 1; *DJM* XXXVII/16 (10 November 1877), 127.

11. *MC* XL/2 (10 January 1900), 19, and XLII/5 (30 January 1901), 41.

12. *DJM* XXXIX/987 (15 February 1879), 30.

13. Sumner Salter, "Early Encouragements to American Composers," *Musical Quarterly* XVIII (January 1932), 78; *Musical Record* #281 (June 1885), 1.

14. *MR* #293 (June 1886), 8.

15. Mathews, *The Great in Music* I, 177.

16. *AAJ* LVI/21 (7 March 1891), 322.

17. *MC* XLII/2 (9 January 1901), 33.

Organ Works

1. Quoted in *DJM* XVI/21 (18 February 1860), 375.

2. *DJM* XVII/21 (18 August 1860), 168; the recital took place in Haupt's church, the *Parochialkirche*.

3. *DJM* XXVII/2 (13 April 1867), 15. Other performances were 1 November 1862 at West Church [*DJM* XXII/6 (8 November 1862), 255], 11 July 1863 at West Church [*BMT* IV/6 (1 August 1863), 86], an Orchestral Union Concert on 4 May 1864 at Music Hall [*DJM* XXIV/5 (28 May 1864), 247], and 18 June 1866 at Harvard's Appleton Chapel [*DJM* XXVI/8 (7 July 1866), 270].

4. *DJM* XIX/8 (25 May 1861), 60.

5. *BMT* II/13 (5 October 1861), 198.

6. *DJM* XX/6 (9 November 1861), 254.

7. Boston performances: 27 January 1862 at Tremont Temple [*DJM* XX/18 (1 February 1862), 350–51]; 1 November 1862 [cited in footnote 3]; 9 October 1864 at Music Hall [*DJM* XXIV/16 (29 October 1864), 335]; and 9 March 1872 at Music Hall [*DJM* XXXI/26

(23 March 1872), 207]. New York performance: 9 February 1864 at St. George's Church [*Musical Review and Musical World* XV/4 (13 February 1864), 57].

8. Performances at Church of the Incarnation, New York, in February 1890 [*AAJ* LIV/33 (24 February 1890), 545], and Mendelssohn Glee Club Hall, New York, on 23 April 1897 [*MC* XXXIV/16 (21 April 1897), 16].

9. Boston performances included 8 February 1862 at Tremont Temple [*DJM* XX/20 (15 February 1862), 367], 25 October 1862 at West Church [*DJM* XXII/5 (1 November 1862), 247], 22 November 1863 at Music Hall [*DJM* XXIII/18 (28 November 1863), 143], 17 January 1864 at Music Hall [*DJM* XXIII/23 (6 February 1864), 182], and 1 April 1865 at Music Hall [*DJM* XXV/2 (15 April 1865), 14]. For New York performance see footnote 7.

10. Boston performances include 27 January and 8 February 1862 at Tremont Temple, 25 October 1862 at West Church [*DJM* XXII/4 (25 October 1862), 239], and 24 December 1863 [*DJM* XXIII/21 (9 January 1864), 166], 10 September 1864 [*DJM* XXV (17 September 1864), 311], and 8 April 1868 [*BDET*, 7 April 1868, 2], all at Music Hall.

11. *DJM* XXIV/13 (17 September 1864), 311.

12. *DJM* XXV/2 (15 April 1865), 14.

13. *DJM* XXII/5 (1 November 1862), 247.

14. *BMT* III/9 (1 November 1862), 135.

15. *DJM* XXIII/17 (14 November 1863) 135; see discussion of the dedication of the Music Hall organ in Chapter 3 of the present study.

16. 22 November 1863 [cited in footnote 9], 9 October 1864 [see footnote 7], and 1 April 1865 [see footnote 9], all at Music Hall.

17. *BET*, 15 January 1864, 3; *DJM* XXIII/23 (6 February 1864), 182. Paine also played the *Andante* on his February 1864 New York recital.

18. *DJM* XXVI/8 (7 July 1866), 270.

19. *DJM* XXV/25 (3 March 1866), 199.

20. *DJM* XXVI/8 (7 July 1866), 270.

21. *DJM* XXIII/25 (5 March 1864), 199.

22. *DJM* XXIV/10 (6 August 1864), 287.

23. For 1864 recital citation, see footnote 7; for later citation, see footnote 19.

24. Carl recital reported in *MC* XL/15 (11 April 1900), 25; programs of both Foote concerts contained in his *Three Scrap-books* III.

25. 10 September 1864 citation given in footnote 10; April 1869 recital cited in footnote 28.

26. *DJM* XXIII/26 (19 March 1864), 207.

27. *DJM* XXVI/7 (23 June 1866), 262.

28. *DJM* XXIX/2 (10 April 1869), 14, and XXIX/9 (17 July 1869), 70.

Chapter 12

1. H. E. Krehbiel, "Music in America," *Famous Composers and Their Works*, ed. John K. Paine *et al.* (Boston, 1891) IV, 947.

2. *DJM* XXII/26 (28 March 1863), 411.

3. *DJM* XXIII/1 (4 April 1863), 7.

4. Foote, *Three Scrap-books*, I.

5. Fisk, 334–35.

6. Program contained in Foote, *Three Scrap-books*, I.

7. *DJM* XXXVI/4 (27 May 1876), 239; the quotation that follows, concerning the *larghetto* movement, is also from this source.

8. *BDA*, 13 May 1876, 4.

9. *DJM* XXXVI/16 (11 November 1876), 335.

10. *BDA*, 6 November 1876, 2.

11. *DJM* XXXVI/22 (3 February 1877), 382.

12. *BDA*, 18 January 1877, 1.

13. *DJM* XXXVI/22 (3 February 1877), 383.

14. *DJM* XXXVI/23 (17 February 1877), 391. In this report the work is listed as "op. 30"; the *DJM* review of the second performance the following December gives "op. 32."

15. *BDA*, 10 February 1877, 2.

16. *DJM* XXXVII/19 (22 December 1877), 151.

17. *MR* #47 (23 August 1879), 325.

18. *BDA*, 21 March 1891, 4.

19. *MC* XXXVIII/1 (4 January 1899), 21.

20. *MR* #456 (1 January 1900), 42.

Chapter 13

1. *DJM* XXXV/22 (5 February 1876), 173. The writer most critical of the work and its excessive repetition was the reviewer for the *New York Times*, who presented his views following the first New York performance with Thomas.

2. *Atlantic Monthly* XXXVII (June 1876), 763.

3. For example, the solo passages in the overtures to *Oberon* and *Der Freischütz*, and the lyrical themes in the clarinet concertos.

4. Published in *BDA*, 6 December 1877, 2. Dwight's initial criticism appeared in *DJM* XXXVII/17 (24 November 1877), 134–35; his response to Fiske's description included in a review of the December 1877 Music Hall performance, published in *DJM* XXXVII/19 (22 December 1877), 150.

5. *The Nation* XXXIX (4 December 1884), 483.

6. There is no knowledge, apparently, that Paine ever knew Brahms, although the possibility exists that they may have met during one of Paine's European visits. Certainly he must have been acquainted with many of Brahms's compositions when composing these works; whether there was direct influence asserted would be difficult to determine. Both Paine and Brahms were students of the same masters, and it is reasonable to assume that somewhere they should use similar musical locutions.

7. *BDA*, 1 January 1877, 4.

8. *DJM* XXXVIII/29 (11 May 1878), 229–30.

9. Originally announced in 1879 as Op. 32; subsequent listings give Op. 34, as does the published score.

10. Louis C. Elson, *The History of American Music*, rev. ed. (New York, 1915), 166.

11. A. J. Goodrich, *Complete Musical Analysis* (Cincinnati, 1889), 285–89.

12. Cited in Rupert Hughes and Arthur Elson, *American Composers* (Boston, 1900), 146–47.

13. Ibid., 147–48.

14. All terms ibid., 148–50.

15. For example, in Schumann's First Symphony in B-flat Major, the second movement is in E-flat (subdominant), the third in D minor (mediant). In the Third Symphony ("Rhenish") in E-flat Major, the second movement is in C major (submediant made major), the third is in A-flat Major (subdominant).

16. The *Spring Symphony* has been recorded for the Society for the Preservation of the American Musical Heritage by the Royal Philharmonic Orchestra, Karl Krueger, Conductor. Lamentably, huge cuts were made, including the entire recapitulation sections of the first and last movements and a similar amount from the third; only the Maynight Scherzo survived with minimal trimming.

17. *Music in the United States: A Historical Introduction*, 131.

18. *BDA*, 19 April 1889, 4.

19. *Boston Herald*, 16 October 1904, Women's Section, 6.

20. *MC* LII/14 (4 April 1906), 25.

Chapter 14

1. Many performances of songs went unrecorded, for voice recitals often did not receive detailed coverage in the press. Performance details of *Matin Song* were gained from newspaper reviews in the *Boston Daily Advertiser*, concert reports in *Dwight's Journal of Music* and *Musical Courier*, and program leaflets and clippings contained in Arthur Foote's *Three Scrap-books*.

2. *MC* XXXIV/15 (14 April 1897), 21.

3. W. T. Upton, *Art-Song in America* (Boston, 1930), 78.

4. Ibid., 78.

5. Hughes & Elson, *American Composers*, rev. ed., 163.

6. H. T. Finck, *Songs and Song Writers* (New York, 1900), 232.

7. Ibid.

8. Upton, 78.

9. Finck, *Songs*, 232.

10. Hughes and Elson, 163.

Chapter 15

1. From *Boston Musical Times*; published in *DJM* XIX/21 (24 August 1861), 166.

2. *Boston Musical Times* II/13 (5 October 1861), 198.

3. *The Musical Review and Musical World* XII/23 (9 November 1861), 270.

4. Advertisement, *BET*, 15 January 1864, 3.

5. One may wonder at the appropriateness of the "Gloria patri" as a part of a ceremony in a Unitarian church on behalf of an institution with traditional Unitarian ties.

6. *MR* #267 (April 1884), 2.

7. 25 August 1890 letter in Fisk, 581.

8. *DJM* XXV/10 (5 August 1865), 79; all details of Commemoration Day mentioned earlier are obtained from this source.

9. *DJM* XXV/10 (5 August 1865), 79.

10. *DJM* XXIII/23 (6 February 1864), 182.

11. *DJM* XXVI/8 (7 July 1866), 270.

12. *Boston Musical Times* VII/7 (7 July 1866), 5.

13. *Neue Zeitschrift für Musik* LXIII/15 (5 April 1867), 131; trans. J.C.S.

14. *DJM* XXVI/8 (7 July 1866), 270.

15. Louis C. Elson, *The History of American Music* (New York, 1904), 166.

16. *The Atlantic Monthly* XXXII (August 1873), 248.

17. *The Atlantic Monthly* XXXIV (August 1874), 251.

18. *Folio* VI/2 (February 1872), 42.

19. From collected programs, New England Conservatory of Music library.

20. *DJM* XXXII/9 (27 July 1872), 179–80. Several later writers have stated mistakenly that Paine's excerpts were performed at the earlier 1869 Peace Jubilee; among them were G. W. Chadwick, "American Composers," *History of American Music*, ed. W. L. Hubbard (Toledo, 1908), 2; and W. A. Fisher, *Notes on Music in Old Boston* (Boston, 1918), 46.

21. 5 June 1873 letter of John Fiske to his mother, quoted in Fisk, 223.

22. *DJM* XXXIV/5 (13 June 1874), 247; the quotations that follow are from this source.

23. *DJM* XXXIV/5 (13 June 1874), 247.

24. *DJM* XXXIV/5 (13 June 1874), 247.

25. John Julian, *Dictionary of Hymnology*, 2nd rev. ed. (1907; repr. 1957), 683.

26. *DJM* XLI/1 (21 May 1881), 84.

27. *Boston Saturday Evening Gazette* review quoted in *DJM* XLI/2 (4 June 1881), 90–91.

28. *BDA*, 18 May 1881, 1.

29. *Nation* XXXIV (2 February 1882), 101–2.

30. *BDA*, 19 March 1881, 1.

31. However, the Greek text for these measures, *enth' ou podi chresimo chretai*, is not the equivalent, but rather a following line that seems to be unaccounted for in the English version Paine used—"and there its feet are no service" [translation by David Grene, in Sophocles, *I. Three Tragedies*, ed. D. Grene and R. Lattimore (Chicago, 1954), 48].

32. Henry Norman, *An Account of the Harvard Greek Play* (Boston, 1882), 103.

33. A program of this last concert was included with a 7 May 1970 letter from the late Richard G. Appel to the present writer.

34. John T. Hull (ed.), *Centennial Celebration: An Account of the Municipal Celebration of the One Hundredth Anniversary of the Incorporation of the Town of Portland, July 4th, 5th and 6th, 1886* (Portland, 1886), 149.

Chapter 16

1. Roberts, *John Knowles Paine*, 4–5.

2. *Cyclopedia of Music and Musicians*, ed. J. D. Champlin, Jr. (New York, 1890), III, 67.

3. *The Great in Music: A Systematic Course of Study of the Music of Classical and Modern Composers*, ed. Mathews, I, 173.

4. *MR* #245 (9 June 1883), 107.

5. Frederick F. Bullard, "Music in Boston: Zerrahn, Paine, Lang and Chadwick," *MC* XXXVII/1 (4 July 1898), unpaged.

6. *Boston Herald*, 3 May 1903, 39.

7. *MC* XLVI/19 (13 May 1903), 25.

8. E. E. Hipsher, *American Opera and Its Composers*, 352–53.

9. *BET*, 10 April 1907, 21.

10. From records of the Boston Symphony Orchestra.

11. *MC* XLI/18 (31 October 1900), 17.

12. *MC* XLIV/20 (14 May 1902), 32, and Foote, *Three Scrap-books* III.

13. "Aucassin and Nicolette," in *The Reader's Encyclopedia*, 2nd ed., ed. William Rose Benét (New York, 1965), I, 62–63.

14. *Boston Herald*, 10 November 1901, 44.

15. Arthur Elson, "The Great Operas," *Famous Composers and their Works*, New Series, ed. Louis C. Elson (Boston, 1909), II, 159; the remainder of the synopsis is from the *Herald* article.

16. Letters of 25 March 1900 and 27 May 1900, quoted in Finck, *Adventures*, 79.

17. Yellin, *The Life and Operatic Works of George Whitefield Chadwick*, 289.

18. The reader may judge for himself. The second dance has been recorded by the Royal Philharmonic Orchestra, conducted by Karl Krueger, for the Society for the Preservation of the American Musical Heritage in 1966. This seems to be the only portion of *Azara* ever to have been recorded.

19. Mrs. Paine paid $2,000 to have the full score and parts published. Incidentally, Paine did some revisions following the publication of the vocal score in 1901, mainly in the form of additions to the vocal lines. These may be found in the full score, and the composer wrote them into a copy of the vocal score now in the Harvard music library. Such changes would need to be made in any future reprinting of the vocal score.

20. *Boston Herald*, 10 November 1901, 44.

Chapter 17

1. Four of the orchestral works were recorded in the 1960s by conductor Karl Krueger in the Music in America series of the Society for the Preservation of the American Musical Heritage. Historically these recordings are extremely important, for they enable us to hear and evaluate each work aesthetically. Most regrettable, however, was the decision to present most of these compositions in abridged versions, for the results cannot be considered definitive. For example, the recording of the *Spring Symphony* with Krueger and the Royal Philharmonic Orchestra (MIA-120) would be adequate, were it not so drastically cut. A new and authentic recording is needed.

2. The recording (MIA-103), also by Krueger, although somewhat unpolished in ensemble, will suggest the effect of an expert performance.

3. The Krueger recording (MIA-130), although heavily cut, is well done.

4. Two of these have been recorded. Krueger's recording of *As You Like It* (MIA-141) is uncut and well performed; the work was earlier recorded by conductor Richard Korn (Allegro 3149). Also, in the 78 r.p.m. era, Howard Hanson and the Eastman-Rochester Orchestra recorded the *Prelude to Oedipus Tyrannus*; this performance should be released again.

5. The second Moorish Dance may be heard in a recording by Krueger and the Royal Philharmonic Orchestra (MIA-132).

6. Performed by Carmen Balthrop, Joy Blackett, Vinson Cole, and John Cheek, soloists, the St. Louis Symphony Orchestra and Chorus, with Gunther Schuller, conductor; released by New World Records (NW 262-263).

7. The *Fantasie über ein feste Burg* is performed by Richard Morris on a New World recording (NW 280). Organist Janice Beck included the *Concert Variations on the Austrian Hymn* and *Prelude No. 2 in B minor* in a recording for the Musical Heritage Society (MHS OR A-263). Organist Richard Ellsasser also recorded the *Austrian variations* (Nonesuch, 71200) but unfortunately used an abridged, simplified arrangement and omitted the fugue.

8. *The Romance*, Op. 12, and *Fuga Giocosa* are included on a New World recording (NW 206) of American piano music by Malcolm Frager.

Appendix 1:
Opus Numbers

1. Sonata No. 1 in A minor, for piano (1859)

2. Zwei Concert Stücke für die Orgel (1860)
    1. Fantasie und Fuge in E moll
    2. Doppel Fuge über "Heil dir im Siegeskranz" or "God save the queen"

3. Two compositions for organ
    1. Concert Variations on the Austrian Hymn (1860)
    2. Concert Variations on the Star-Spangled Banner (1861)

4. Sonata No. 2 in F-sharp minor, for piano

5. String Quartet (1855)

6. Fantasia in F, for organ (1865)

7. Christmas Gift, for piano (1864)

8. Domine, salvum fac Praesidem nostrum (1863)

9. Funeral March in memory of President Abraham Lincoln (1865)

10. Mass in D (1865)

11. Vier Character-Stücke für Piano-forte (1868)
    1. Vivace
    2. Largo ["Feierlich"]
    3. Con moto
    4. Giocoso ["Welcome"]

12. Romance in C minor, for piano (1868)

13. Fantasie über "Ein' feste Burg" (1869)

14. Partsongs and motets
    1. Funeral Hymn (TTBB) "Breathe, trumpets, breathe"
    2. (unknown)
    3. Minstrel's Song (SATB) (ca 1863)

15. Preludes and fugues for piano
    1. Prelude and Fugue in B minor
    2. Prelude in F-sharp minor
    3. Fugue in 3 voices in A

16. Partsongs and motets (unknown)

17. Fantasia Sonata in D minor, for organ (1863)
    1. Grave—Allegro agitato
    2. Andante con variazioni
    3. Presto

18. Partsongs and motets (unknown)

19. Deux Préludes pour l'orgue (1864)
    1. Prelude No. 1 in D flat (Larghetto)
    2. Prelude No. 2 in B minor (Con moto)

20. Oratorio, "St. Peter" (1872)

21. (Unknown)

22. Piano Trio in D minor (1874)

23. Symphony No. 1 in C minor (1875)

24. Sonata in B minor for Piano and Violin (1876; rev. 1906)

25. Four Characteristic Pieces, for piano (1876)
    1. Dance
    2. Romance
    3. Impromptu
    4. Rondo Giocoso

26. In the Country: Sketches for the piano (1876)
    1. Woodnotes
    2. Wayside Flowers
    3. Under the Lindens
    4. Shepherd's Lament
    5. Village Dance
    6. Rainy Day
    7. Mill
    8. Gipsies
    9. Farewell
    10. Welcome Home

27. Centennial Hymn in D (1876)

28. Overture to "As You Like It" (1876)

29. Four Songs
    1. Matin Song (publ. 1877)
    2. I wore your roses yesterday (publ. 1879)
    3. Early springtime (1866)
    4. Mondnacht (1867)

30. Romanza and Scherzo for cello and piano (1876)

31. Symphonic Poem, "The Tempest" (1877)

32. Larghetto and Scherzo in B flat for Piano Trio (1877)

33. Duo Concertante in A for Violin, Violoncello, and Orchestra (1877)

34. Symphony No. 2 in A, "Im Frühling" (1879)

35. Music for "Oedipus Tyrannus" of Sophocles (1881)

36. The Realm of Fancy, cantata (SATB) (1882)

37. Phoebus, Arise, cantata (TTBB) (1882)

38. The Nativity, cantata (SATB) (1883)

39. Romance in D flat, for piano (1833)

40. Four Songs
    1. A bird upon a rosy bough (1884)
    2. A farewell (1885)
    3. Beneath the starry arch (1885)
    4. Music when soft voices die

41. Three pieces for piano
    1. A Spring Idyl (1884)
    2. Birthday Impromptu (1882)
    3. Fuga Giocosa (1884)

42. (Unknown)

43. A Song of Promise, cantata (SATB) (1888)

44. Symphonic Poem, "An Island Fantasy" (1888)

45. Nocturne in D flat, for piano (publ. 1889)

Works Without Opus Numbers

Piano Works

Valse Caprice in E
Welcome Home (1868)

Organ Works

Prelude and Fugue in G minor (1859)
Prelude in C minor
Concert Variations upon Old Hundred (1861)
Reverie suggested by Longfellow's "Song of the Silent Land" (1862)
Caprice (1864)
Fantasia on the "Portuguese Hymn" (1864)
Pastorale (1865)

Orchestral

Lincoln: a tragic poem

Songs

Spring [possibly Op. 29, No. 6] (1869)
The Fountain. Song: "A Spring in the desert I found" (ca 1878)
The clover blossoms kiss her feet (1882)

Choral Music and Partsongs

Agnus Dei (1861)
Benedictus (1861)
Hymn for Commencement (1862)
Peace, peace to him that's gone (TTBB)
The summer webs (TTBB)
Radway's Ready Relief (TTBB) (1864)
Soldier's Oath (TTBB) (1865)
O bless the Lord, my soul (TTBB)
Hymn, Divine Love
Columbus March and Hymn (1892)
Freedom, Our Queen (1893)
Scenes from "The Birds" of Aristophanes (TTBB) (1901)
Hymn of the West (1904)

Opera

Il Pesceballo (1862)
Azara

Appendix 2: Music Course Enrollment at Harvard, 1871–1905

	1871– 1872	1872– 1873	1873– 1874
Music 1. Theory	11	6	5
Music 2. Imit. Cpt.		3	3
Music 3. Fugue, Instr.			2

	1874– 1875		1875– 1876
1. Harmony	10	1. Harmony	9
2. Cpt.	5	2. Cpt.	4
3. Imit. Cpt. Canon, Fugue	1	3. Canon Free Th. Mus.	2
4. Hist. Mus.	6	4. Fugue	2
		5. Hist. Mus.	13

	1876– 1877	1877– 1878
1. Harmony	12	7

2.
Cpt.   6   6

3.
Can. & Fg.
    Free Th. Mus.   1   2

4.
Hist. Mus.   9   6

5.
Inst. Mus.
    Haydn, Mozart,
    Beethoven, etc.   3

	1878– 1879	1879– 1880	1880– 1881	1881– 1882
1. Harmony	14	24	12	14
2. Cpt.	8	5	9	3
3. Hist. Mus.	17	36	22	14

4. Instr. Mus.
    Haydn, Mozart
    Beethoven
	15	9	3	8

Graduate:
    Can. & Fugue,
    Composition
			6	6

Graduate: Instr. Mus.				7

	1882– 1883

1. Harmony
Instr. Mus.
    Haydn, Mozart
    Beethoven
	18

2. Cpt.	7

3.

Hist. Mus. 15

4.

Can. & Fugue 1

5.

Free Them. Mus. 1

	1883–1884	1884–1885	1885–1886	1886–1887	1887–1888
1. Harmony	14	16	10	15	10
2. Cpt.	6	4	6	2	4
3. Hist. Mus.	28	81	50	55	37
4. Inst. Mus. Haydn, Mozart, Beethoven	9	4			
5. Canon & Fugue, Composition	3	3	2	4	
6. Free Th. Mus., Composition	3	3	2	1	4

	1888–1889	1889–1890	1890–1891	1891–1892	1892–1893	1893–1894	1894–1895
1. Harmony	19	22	18	18	18	27	16
2. Cpt.	9	10	11	10	7	8	15
3. Hist. Mus.		17		11		8	
5. Canon & Fugue	3		5		9		5
6. Free Th. Mus.		5		7		7	

Life and Works of John Knowles Paine

7.
Instrumentation	4		7	9		5

20.
Research				1		

	1895–1896
1. Harmony	[Sp]31
2. Cpt.	9
3. Hist. Mus. (half)	16
5. Can. & Fugue	9
6. Adv. C & F / Free Th. Mus.	4

	1896–1897	1897–1898
1. Harmony	[Sp]27	[Sp]27
2. Cpt.	10	[Sp] 9
3. Hist. Mus. (half)		8
5. Can. & Fugue, Free Th. Mus.	3	3
6. Adv. C & F, Free Comp.	3	4
8. Chamber Mus.		24

	1898–1899	1899–1900
1. Harmony	[Sp]21	[Sp]26
2. Adv. Harm. & Cpt.	[Sp] 9	[Sp] 9
3. Hist Mus.		10
5. Can. & Fugue, Free Th. Mus.	5	3
6. Adv. C & F Free Comp.	2	2

7.

    Instr. (half)   10

	1900–1901	1901–1902	1902–1903	1903–1904	1904–1905
1. Harmony [Sp]	31	33	41	38	38
1a. Advanced [C]					2
2. Adv. H & C [Sp]	14	16	14	25	19
2a. Vocal Cpt. (half) [Sp]		7	7	9	10
3. Hist. Mus.	24	28	75	121	98
4. Musical Form (half) [Sp]	13	10	11	19	24
5. Free Th. Mus. Can. & Fugue	2	2	6	[C] 4	[C] 7
6. Adv. C & F, Free Compos.	3	2		3	2
7. Instr. [P & Sp]	5	5	4	8	9

	Summer:	1902	1903	1904
I. Grammar & Principles		[M]2	[LC]9	[St]4
II. General Course		[M]3	[LC]3	

All courses were taught by Paine, unless indicated:

[C] Frederick S. Converse	[P&Sp] Paine and Walter R. Spalding
[LC] Louis A. Coerne	[Sp] Spalding
[M] Daniel Gregory Mason	[St] Henry Leroy Stone

Appendix 3: A Selective List of Individuals Who Studied with Paine

Names and information gleaned from standard reference works, studies on Paine, Harvard catalogs, records, and reports, class anniversary volumes, and periodical and newspaper articles.

Abbott, Ernest Hamlin [A.B. magna cum laude, 1893] Associated with the theological weekly, *The Outlook*.

Aldrich, Richard (1863–1937) [A.B. 1885] Music critic (*Providence Journal*, 1885–89; *Evening Star*, 1889–91; *N.Y. Tribune* asst., 1891–1901; *N.Y. Times*, 1902–23).

Allen, Paul Hastings (1883–1952) [A.B. 1903] Boston composer.

Apthorp, William F. (1848–1913) [A.B. 1869] Music critic *(Atlantic Monthly, Boston Eve. Transcript);* annotator of Boston Symphony programs; taught at New England Conservatory, Boston University.

Ashton, J. N. [grad. stu. 1891–95] Prof. of Music, Brown University.

Atherton, Percy Lee (1871–1944) [A.B. magna cum laude 1893] Boston composer; studied with Rheinberger, Sgambati, Widor.

Atkinson, Robert Whitman (1868–1934) [A.B. summa cum laude 1891] Led Freshman and Varsity Glee Clubs, wrote songs in University collections, composed the first all original Hasty Pudding operetta (1892); studied with Rheinberger; active in Tavern Club, Boston.

Ayer, Clarence Walter [A.B. cum laude 1885]

Beatley, James A. [A.B. 1873] Boston public school music director.

Blanchard, Arthur F. [A.B. 1904]

Botume, J. F. [A.B. 1876] Composer.

Brackett, Frank [Honorable mention in music, 1880]

Brown, Allen A. Head of Music Division, Boston Public Library.

Burdett, George Albert (1856–1943) [A.B. summa cum laude 1881] Abandoned Ph.D. studies because of poor health; began financial career (1885) with H.S. Ballow & Co., then (1889) with Chamberlain, Burdett & Co. (bankers & brokers); retired from financial career in 1895 to compose, lecture, conduct, and teach; organized New England chapter, American Guild of Organists; organist at Central Church, Boston (20 years), Harvard Church, Brookline, and First Unitarian Society, Newton.

Burlingame, Edward L. Editor, Scribners.

Burton, Frederick Russell (1861–1909) [A.B. summa cum laude 1882] Editorial work for Boston and New York newspapers; researched music of the Ojibway Indians north of Lake Superior, published as *American Primitive Music*; composed cantata, *Hiawatha* (perf. New York, 1898), other works.

Carpenter, John Alden (1876–1951) [A.B. summa cum laude 1897] Prominent composer; also in shipping supply business.

Clapp, Philip Greeley (1888–1954) [A.B. 1908] Composer and teacher (Harvard, Dartmouth, Univ. of Iowa, Juilliard).

Clark, John T. (1875–?) [A.B. 1898, honors in music] Faculty (Romantic Philology), University of California, Berkeley.

Class, Franklin Morris [A.B. 1903]

Coerne, Louis Adolphe (1870–1922) [Ph.D. 1905] Composer; taught at Smith College, Olivet College, Univ. of Wisconsin, Connecticut College for Women.

Colburn, Samuel C. [Special Student; Honors, Francis Boott Award, 1905]

Comins, Danforth [A.B. 1893] Attorney.

Converse, Frederick S. (1871–1940) [A.B. summa cum laude, 1893] Prominent composer; studied with Baermann, Chadwick, Rheinberger; taught at New England Conservatory, Harvard.

Cumming, Robert [A.B. 1882; Honorable mention in music]

Daniels, Mabel Wheeler (1878–1971) [A.B. 1900, Radcliffe] Studied with Chadwick, Thuille; taught at Radcliff, Simmons College; composer.

Davis, Wendell Phillips [A.B. 1882; Honorable mention in music]

Davison, Archibald T. (1883–1961) [A.B. 1906] Studied with Widor; taught at Harvard (1910–54); many editions and arrangements of music; books.

Densmore, John H. (1880–1943) [A.B. 1904] Wrote Hasty Pudding Club operettas while at Harvard; composer—mostly choral works.

Dodge, Edward S. [A.B. 1873] Musician (organist).

Dodge, Frank Faden [Honorable mention in music, 1880]

Dole, Nathan Haskell [A.B. 1874] Writer of musical biographies.

Dunham, Henry M. (1853–1929) Studied with Paine at Boston University College of Music; organist at several churches; taught at New England Conservatory (1876–1929); composer.

Elson, Arthur (1873–1940) [A.B. 1895] Writer on music.

Endicott, Samuel [A.B. 1903]

Fairchild, Blair (1877–1933) [A.B. 1899] Studied with Buonamici, Widor; composer; spent several years in U. S. diplomatic service in Turkey and Persia.

Fay, Amy (1844–1928) Pianist; took Bach course under Paine; studied with Tausig, Kullak, Liszt; wrote *Music-Study in Germany* (1881).

Fenollosa, William Silsbee (1854–?) [A.B. 1875, A.M. 1876] Pianist, teacher in Boston, Salem; taught Paine's Harvard classes Sept. 1879; conducted Salem Oratorio Society (1898–).

Finck, Henry T. (1854–1926) [A.B. 1876] Music critic (*The Nation*, 1881–1924; *N.Y. Evening Post*, 1888 on); editor and journalist; early admirer of Wagner.

Fleisher, Edwin A. (1877–1959) [A.B. 1899] Music patron; founded a Symphony Club in Philadelphia (1909); amassed large collection of orchestral scores and parts, later presented to the Free Library of Philadelphia.

Foote, Arthur (1853–1937) [A.B. 1874, A.M. 1875] Prominent composer, organist, and teacher in Boston.

Gardner, R. R.

Goepp, Philip H. (1864–1936) [A.B. 1884, honors in music] Philadelphia organist, teacher, and writer; program annotator for the Philadelphia Orchestra (1900–21).

Gulick, F. C. (1876–1902) [A.B. 1900, honors in music]

Hamlin, Charles Eugene [A.B. 1884, honors in music]

Heard, Richard [A.B. summa cum laude, 1879] A member of Fridtjof Nansen's expedition to the North Pole (1893–96).

Hebard, A. P. [A.B. 1889, honors in music]

Heilman, William Clifford (1877–1946) [A.B. summa cum laude 1900] Composer; studied with Rheinberger, Widor; Harvard music faculty 1905–30.

Henry, Bertram C. (1864–1945) [A.B. summa cum laude 1886] Taught at Georgetown College School of Music (Ky.); then in California and Idaho.

Hiler, Ernest Osgood (1871–1931) [A.B. 1893, honors in music] Boston lawyer, retired in 1924 because of poor health.

Hill, Edward Burlingame (1872–1960) [A.B. summa cum laude 1894] Prominent composer, mostly instrumental music; studied with Bullard, Chadwick, Whiting, Widor; taught at Harvard (1908–40).

Hobbs, Charles Austin [Honorable mention in music, 1880]

Hood, Frederick Clark [Honorable mention in music, 1886]

Hood, Helen (1863–1949) Song composer; Boston. Studied with B. J. Lang, Chadwick, Moszkowski.

Howe, Mark Antony DeWolfe (1864–1960) [A.B. 1887] Writer and editor; associated with *Atlantic Monthly*; wrote biographies of Phillips Brooks, Charles Eliot Norton, Barrett Wendell, John Jay Chapman, and others.

Hyde, A. P.

Johns, Clayton (1857–1932) [Special student at Harvard] Boston pianist and composer; studied with Paine for 2 years (1879–81), also with Sherwood, and in Berlin with Kiel, Raif, Rummel.

Johnson, William Lyman. Studied with Paine and F. F. Bullard; wrote a "Wagnerian" *Communion Hymn* (text by Mary Baker Eddy).

Leichtentritt, Hugo (1874–1951) [A.B. 1894] Prominent musicologist.

Lewis, Leo Rich (1865–1945) [A.M. summa cum laude 1889] Studied with Rheinberger; head of music, Tufts College (1895–1945); writer on music.

Locke, Arthur W. [A.B. 1905, honors in music]

Longworth, Nicholas [A.B. 1891] Studied violin with S. E. Jacobsohn, Chicago Musical College.

Lynes, Frank (1858–1913) Studied with Paine at New England Conservatory and privately; Boston composer and organist; other study with B. J. Lang, Reinecke, Jadassohn.

Markham, George D. [A.B. 1881] Senior member, W. H. Markham & Co., insurance; Chief of Bureau of Music, St. Louis World's Fair.

Marston, George W. (1840–1901) Portland organist, choral conductor, and composer; according to Edwards *(Music and Musicians of Maine)*, he studied with Paine in Portland about 1858.

Mason, Daniel Gregory (1873–1953) [A.B. cum laude 1895] Prominent composer, educator, and writer; grandson of Lowell Mason, son of Henry Mason (Mason & Hamlin); studied with Whiting, Goetschius, Chadwick, d'Indy; music faculty, Columbia Univ. (1910–42).

Mason, Edward Palmer [Honorable mention in music, 1881]

McKenzie, Kenneth (1870–?) [A.B. 1891, honors in music] Professor of Italian, Princeton University.

Morrill, Sam Henry [A.B. 1882, honors in music]

Morse, Charles H. (1853–1927) Studied with Paine (organ, harmony, composition) at Boston University College of Music; organist; taught at Wellesley, other schools in Boston, Minneapolis, Brooklyn.

Morse, Robert G. [A.B. 1896]

Munro, John Cummings [A.B. 1881, honorable mention in music]

Osgood, George L. (1844–1922) [A.B. 1866] Singer, vocal teacher; studied organ with Paine, led Glee Club; studied with Haupt and Robert Franz; settled in Boston; conducted Boylston Club (1875–93).

Palmer, Franklin Sawyer [Honorable mention in music, 1886]

Parker, Henry Taylor (1867–1934) [A.B. 1889] Music critic, writer; drama & music critic of *N.Y. Globe* (1903–05), *Boston Transcript* (1905–34).

Royce, Edward (1886–1963) [A.B. 1907] Composer; studied at Stern Conservatory, Berlin; taught at Middlebury College, Ithaca Cons., Eastman School of Music (Prof. of Theory, 1923–47).

Ruggles, Carl (1876–1971) [Special student, 1903] Eminent composer.

Ryder, Arthur Hilton (1875–1944) Organist and composer, Boston and neighboring towns.

Salter, Sumner (1856–1944) Studied with Paine at New England Conservatory; organist, composer, arranger; other study with J.C.D. Parker, E. Thayer, Osgood; director of music, Williams College (1905–23).

Sanborn, John Pitts (1879–1941) [A.B. 1900, A.M. 1902] Music critic (*N.Y. Globe*, 1905–23; *N.Y. Evening Mail*, 1924–31; *N.Y. World Telegram*, 1931 on).

Sleeper, Henry Dike (1865–1948) Studied in Hartford, Chicago, Philadelphia, London; taught at Beloit College, Georgetown College (Ky.), Univ. of Wisconsin, and Smith College (1898–1924; head of music 1904–24); organist, composer; edited two hymnals.

Spalding, Arthur C. (1877–?) [A.B. 1899, honors in music] Organist, lawyer, banker; Lowell, Mass.

Spalding, Walter Raymond (1865–1962) [A.B. 1887, A.M. 1888, honors in music] Studied with Guilmant, Widor, Rheinberger; Harvard music faculty from 1895; texts.

Stone, Henry Leroy [A.B. 1901, honors in music 1902] Appointed "Assistant" to Harvard music faculty in 1902; taught summer course in 1904.

Surette, Thomas Whitney (1861–1941) [A.B. 1891] Music educator; taught at Oxford Univ. extension div., Bryn Mawr, Rocky Mountain Coll. (N.C.); helped shape New England public school curriculum; founded Concord Summer School of Music (1914); with A. T. Davison edited "The Concord Series" of educational music; composed operetta, *Priscilla*, other works.

Szemelényi, Ernest (1852–1919) [A.B. 1875] Tenor, Glee Club; translator, researcher for U. S. Patent Office.

Taylor, M. A. [A.B. 1889, honors in music]

Thayer, W. Eugene (1838–89) Boston organist; studied with Haupt, Wieprecht; opened a private studio in 1875.

Thompson, Lewis Sabin [A.B. summa cum laude 1892] Boston organist; composed operettas.

Turner, Alfred D. (1854–88) Studied with Paine at Boston University College of Music; pianist; taught at New England Conservatory and Boston University.

Whitney, Samuel Brenton (1842–?) Studied with Paine from 1870, was his assistant at Appleton Chapel; organist, Church of the Advent, 1871 on; faculty, New England Conservatory, Boston University.

Whittemore, Frank B. (1875–?) [A.B. summa cum laude 1896] Led Glee Club; cond. '96 Hasty Pudding show "Branglebrink," composed some of its music; New York businessman (bonds), also organist-choirmaster.

Wister, Owen (1860–1938) [A.B. summa cum laude 1882] Trained as a composer; also studied in Leipzig. Novelist, short-story writer, and biographer; his novel *The Virginian* was a model for later cowboy fiction; he was one of the actors in the Greek play, *Oedipus Tyrannus*, in 1881. Descendant of actress Fanny Kemble Butler (1809–93), daughter of Charles Kemble of Convent Garden, and wife (until divorced in 1848) of Pierce Butler of Philadelphia and Georgia.

Witherle, William Russell (1869–1897) [A.B. 1891, honors in music] Treasurer, Beacon Trust Co., Boston; organist, music critic.

Bibliography

Academic Series I: Reports to the Overseers I–II (1859–74). Harvard College. In Harvard Archives collection.

Alden, Mrs. M. L. T. "The Snow Genealogy," in *New-England Historical and Genealogical Register* XLVII (1893).

Aldrich, Richard, "John Knowles Paine," in *Dictionary of American Biography*. Edited by Dumas Malone. New York: Charles Scribner's Sons, 1934. XIV.

American Art Journal LIV–LXXIX (1889–1902). Edited by William M. Thoms. New York.

Annual Reports of the President and the Treasurer of Harvard College, 1878–79. Cambridge: University Press, 1880. Successive issues through 1904–05.

Atlantic Monthly XXX–XLVIII (1872–1881). Boston.

"Aucassin and Nicolette," in *The Reader's Encyclopedia*. Second Edition. Edited by William Rose Benét. New York: Thomas Y. Crowell, 1965. I, 62–63.

Beckett, S. B. *The Portland Directory and Reference Book for 1852–53*. Portland: Brown and Thurston, 1852.

—————. *The Portland Reference Book and City Directory for 1847–8*. Portland: Thurston, 1847.

Booth, Mary L. *History of the City of New York*. New York: W. R. C. Clark, 1867.

Boston Daily Advertiser, 1862–63, 1876–94. Boston.

Boston Daily Globe, 1873–74. Boston.

Boston Evening Transcript, 1864–1907. Boston.

Boston Herald, 1894–1905. Boston.

Boston Morning Journal, 1862–63. Boston.

Boston Musical Times II–X (1861–69). Edited by Henry Tolman, later George W. Stratton. Boston.

Brooklyn Daily Eagle, 1882–84. Brooklyn, N. Y.

Brown, Allan A., comp. *Programmes of Concerts in Sanders Theatre*. Unpublished Collection. Boston Public Library, Boston.

Brown, Allan A., Scrapbook I. Boston Public Library, Boston.

Bullard, Frederick F. "Music in Boston: Zerrahn, Paine, Lang and Chadwick," in *Musical Courier* XXXVII (4 July 1898), unpaged.

Campbell, William T., Scrapbook. Boston Public Library, Boston.

Catalogue of the Officers and Students of Harvard University for the Academical Year 1861–62. Cambridge, 1861. Successive issues through 1904–05 (later title: *Harvard University Catalogue*).

Chadwick, George W. "American Composers," in *History of American Music*. Edited by W. L. Hubbard. Toledo, Ohio: Irving Squire, 1908.

Champlin, John D., Jr., ed. *Cyclopedia of Music and Musicians*. New York: Charles Scribner's Sons, 1888–90.

Chase, Gilbert. *America's Music from the Pilgrims to the Present*. Revised second edition. New York: McGraw-Hill, 1965.

Clark, John Spencer. *The Life and Letters of John Fiske*. Boston: Houghton Mifflin, 1917.

Class of 1882, Harvard College—Seventh Report of the Secretary, 1882–1932. Boston, 1933.

College Records X–XI (1857–73). Harvard College. In Harvard Archives Collection.

Corporation Papers (1867). Harvard College. In Harvard Archives Collection.

County of Middlesex Land Registration Records. Cambridge, Mass.

Cumberland County Records. Cumberland County Court House, Portland, Maine.

Cutter, William R. *Genealogical and Personal Memoirs Relating to the Families of Boston and Eastern Massachusetts*. New York: Lewis Historical Publishing Co., 1908.

Daily Eastern Argus, 1853, 1856–58, 1861. Portland, Maine.

Daniels, Mabel W. *An American Girl in Munich—Impressions of a Music Student*. Boston: Little, Brown, and Co., 1912.

Davis, W. G. "Intentions of Marriage in Limington, Me., 1792–1810," in *New England Historical and Genealogical Register* LXXXVII (1933).

"A Debt to Musical Germany," in *New England Conservatory Magazine-Review* VI (December 1915–January 1916), 43–45.

Doane, John. *Deacon John Doane and the Doane Family*. Yarmouthport, Mass.: C. W. Swift, 1914.

Dunham, Henry M. *The Life of a Musician Woven into a Strand of History of the New England Conservatory of Music*. New York: Richmond Borough Publishing and Printing Co., 1929.

Dwight, [John Sullivan]—Correspondence, Musical, Boston, 1861–1892. Unpublished Manuscript Collection. Boston Public Library, Boston.

Dwight's Journal of Music XI–XLI (1857–81). Edited by John Sullivan Dwight. Boston.

Eames, Emma. *Some Memories and Reflections*. New York: Appleton, 1927.

Edwards, George T. *Music and Musicians of Maine*. Portland: Southworth Press, 1928.

Eleventh Report of the Class of 1871 of Harvard College, June 1921, Fiftieth Anniversary. Cambridge, 1921.

Elson, Arthur. "The Great Operas," in *Famous Composers and Their Works*, New Series. Edited by Louis C. Elson. Boston: J. B. Millet Co., 1909. II, 147–72.

Elson, Louis C. *European Reminiscences, Musical and Otherwise, Being the Recollections of the Vacation Tours of a Musician in Various Countries*. Philadelphia: Theodore Presser, 1896.

————. *The History of American Music*. New York: Macmillan, 1904; revised edition, 1915.

————. "Musical Boston," in *Music and Drama*, 3 June 1882.

Faculty of Arts and Sciences, Reports and Papers I–VI (1873–1903). Harvard College. In Harvard Archives collection.

Faculty Records, Harvard College, New Series, II–V (1877–87). In Harvard Archives collection.

Farwell, Arthur, and W. Dermot Darby. *Music in America*. New York: National Society of Music, 1915.

Ferris, Mary Walton, comp. *Dawes–Gates Ancestral Lines*. 1931.

Fields, Annie. *Authors and Friends*. Boston: Houghton, Mifflin & Co., 1893.

A. F. [Fields, Annie] and R. L. [Rose Lamb], eds. *Letters of Celia Thaxter*. Boston: Houghton, Mifflin and Co., 1895.

Finck, Henry T. *My Adventures in the Golden Age of Music*. New York: Funk & Wagnalls, 1926.

————. *Songs and Song Writers*. New York: Charles Scribner's Sons, 1900.

————. *Success in Music and How it is Won*. New York: Charles Scribner's Sons, 1913.

Fisher, William Arms. *Notes on Music in Old Boston*. Boston: Oliver Ditson Co., 1918.

Fisk, Ethel F., ed. *The Letters of John Fiske*. New York: Macmillan, 1940.

Folio II–XI (1870–75). Edited by Dexter Smith, George Lowell Austin, T. D. Tooker and C. A. White. Boston.

Foote, Arthur. *Arthur Foote, 1853–1937, An Autobiography*. Norwood, Mass.: Plimpton Press, 1946.

————. comp. *Three Scrap-books of Clippings, Programs, etc., relating to music*. Unpublished Collections. Boston Public Library, Boston.

Forty-first Annual Report of the President of Harvard College to the Overseers . . . for the Academical Year 1866–67. Cambridge: Welch, Bigelow, and Company, 1867. Successive issues to 1877–78.

Gardiner, John Hays. *Harvard*. New York: Oxford University Press, 1914.

Goepp, Philip H. "John Knowles Paine," in *Harvard Graduates Magazine* XV (September 1906), 21–27.

Goodrich, A. J. *Complete Musical Analysis*. Cincinnati: The John Church Co., 1889.

Gray, Ellis. "The Mission of Music," in *Harper's New Monthly Magazine* LI (October 1875).

Gulick, C. B. "James Bradstreet Greenough," in *Dictionary of American Biography*. Edited by Allen Johnson and Dumas Malone. New York: Charles Scribner's Sons, 1931. VII.

Harper's New Monthly Magazine XXVII, LI, LXVI (1864, 1875, 1883). New York.

Harvard Class of 1906: Twenty-fifth Anniversary Report, June, 1931. Cambridge, 1931.

Harvard College. Class of 1866. Class Report, July, 1866, to June, 1869. Boston, 1869.

Harvard College Class of 1875—Fiftieth Anniversary Report, 1875–1925. Norwood, Mass., 1925.

Harvard College Class of 1881—Fiftieth Anniversary. Cambridge, 1931.

Harvard College Class of 1891: Secretary's Eleventh Report. Cambridge, 1941.

Harvard College Class of 1896: Fiftieth Anniversary Report. Cambridge, 1946. Similar volumes for Classes of 1893, 1898, and 1899.

Harvard College Papers, Second Series XXIX–XXX (1862–63). Harvard College. In Harvard Archives collection.

Harvard Graduates Magazine I–XV (1892–1906).

Hill, E. B. "Musical Boston in the Gay Nineties; Halcyon Days at Harvard," in *Etude* LXVII (January 1949).

Hipsher, E. E. *American Opera and Its Composers*. Second Edition. Philadelphia: Theodore Presser, 1934.

Hitchcock, H. Wiley. *Music in the United States: A Historical Introduction*. Englewood Cliffs, N. J.: Prentice-Hall, 1969.

Historical Register of Boston University—Fifth Decennial Issue 1869–1911. Boston: University Offices, 1911.

Howard, John Tasker. "Alexander Wheelock Thayer," in *Dictionary of American Biography*. Edited by Dumas Malone. New York: Charles Scribner's Sons, 1936. XVIII.

————. *Our American Music*. Fourth Edition. New York: Thomas Y. Crowell, 1965.

————. *Our Contemporary Composers. American Music in the Twentieth Century*. New York: Thomas Y. Crowell, 1941.

Howe, M. A. DeWolfe. *The Boston Symphony Orchestra, 1881–1931*. Boston: Houghton Mifflin Co., 1931.

———————. "John Knowles Paine," *Musical Quarterly* XXV (July 1939), 257–67.

Hughes, Rupert, and Arthur Elson. *American Composers.* Revised Edition. Boston: The Page Co., 1914.

Hull, John T., ed. *Centennial Celebration: An Account of the Municipal Celebration of the One Hundredth Anniversary of the Incorporation of the Town of Portland, July 4th, 5th and 6th, 1886.* Portland: Owen, Strout & Co., 1886.

Huneker, James Gibbons. *The Philharmonic Society of New York and its Seventy-fifth Anniversary: A Retrospect.* New York: The Society, 1917.

Huxford, John Calvitt. *John Knowles Paine: His Life and Works.* Unpublished Ph.D. dissertation. Florida State University, 1968.

Jenks, F. H. "John Knowles Paine," in *Dictionary of Music and Musicians.* First Edition. Edited by George Grove. London: Macmillan, 1880. II, 632–33.

Johnson, H. Earle. *Musical Interludes in Boston, 1795–1830.* New York: Columbia University Press, 1943.

Jones, F. O., ed. *A Handbook of American Music and Musicians Containing Biographies of American Musicians and Histories of the Principal Musical Institutions, Firms and Societies.* Canaseraga, N. Y.: F. O. Jones, 1886.

Jubilee Days, 1872. Boston.

Julian, John. *Dictionary of Hymnology.* Second revised edition. London: Murray, 1907; reprinted 1957.

Kennedy, W. Sloane. *Henry W. Longfellow: Biography, Anecdote, Letters, Criticism.* Cambridge: Moses King, 1882.

Klotz, Hans. "Orgelspiel," in *Die Musik in Geschichte und Gegenwart.* Edited by Friedrich Blume. Kassel: Bärenreiter, 1962. X, col. 385–96.

Kotzschmar, Hermann. Portland, 1909.

Kotzschmar Scrapbook. In Portland Public Library, Portland.

Kotzschmar. Scrapbook of miscellaneous material. In Portland Public Library, Portland.

Krehbiel, H. E. "John Knowles Paine," in *Grove's Dictionary of Music and Musicians.* Second Edition. Edited by J. A. Fuller-Maitland. New York: Macmillan, 1900. III, 197–98.

———————. "Music in America," in *Famous Composers and their Works.* Edited by John K. Paine, Theodore Thomas, and Karl Klauser. Boston: J. B. Millet, 1891. IV, 933–60.

———————. "Music in America," in Albert Lavignac, *Music and Musicians.* Fourth Edition. Translated by William Marchant. New York: Henry Holt and Co., 1903.

———————. *The Philharmonic Society of New York: A Memorial.* New York: Novello, Ewer, and Co., 1892.

Lahee, Henry C. *Annals of Music in America.* Boston: Marshall Jones, 1922.

Langner, Thomas-M. "Orgelmusik: 19. und 20. Jahrhundert," in *Die Musik in Geschichte und Gegenwart.* Edited by Friedrich Blume. Kassel: Bärenreiter, 1962. X, col. 364–81.

Ledebur, Carl Freiherr von. *Tonkünstler-Lexicon Berlin's von den ältesten Zeiten bis auf die Gegenwart.* Berlin: Ludwig Rauh, 1861.

Leipziger Allgemeine Musikalische Zeitung II (1867). Leipzig.

Leonard, John William. *History of the City of New York, 1609–1909.* New York: Journal of Commerce and Commercial Bulletin, 1910.

Letters of Acting President Andrew P. Peabody. Unpublished Collection. In Harvard University Archives collection.

Libby, C. T. "The Knowles Family of Eastham, Mass.," in *New-England Historical and Genealogical Register* LXXIX (1925).

Longfellow, Samuel, ed. *Life of Henry Wadsworth Longfellow, With Extracts from his Journals and Correspondence.* Boston: Houghton Mifflin & Co., 1886.

Maine: a Guide "Down East." Written by Workers of the Federal Writers' Project of the Works Progress Administration for the State of Maine. Boston: Houghton Mifflin, 1937.

Mason, Daniel Gregory. *Music in My Time, and Other Reminiscences.* New York: Macmillan, 1938.

Mason, William. *Memories of a Musical Life.* New York: Century, 1901.

Masur, Gerhard. *Imperial Berlin.* New York: Basic Books, 1970.

Mathews, W. S. B., ed. *The Great in Music: A Systematic Course of Study in the Music of Classical and Modern Composers.* Chicago: Music Magazine Publishing Co., 1900.

————. *A Hundred Years of Music in America.* Chicago: G. L. Howe, 1889.

May, Samuel P. *The Descendants of Richard Sares (Sears) of Yarmouth, Mass., 1638–1888.* Albany: Joel Munsell's Sons, 1890.

Mendel, Hermann, ed. *Musikalisches Conversations–Lexikon.* Berlin: Robert Oppenheim, 1875.

Merrick, George B. *Genealogy of the Merrick-Mirick-Myrick Family of Massachusetts, 1636–1902.* Madison, Wis.: Tracy, Gibbs, & Co., 1902.

Meserve, A. K. R. *History of the early settlement and settlers of Standish.* Unpublished manuscript. Maine Historical Society collection, Portland.

————. *Notes on Standish Families.* Unpublished collection. Maine Historical Society, Portland.

Miller, Eleanor. *The History and Development of The New England Conservatory of Music.* Unpublished B.Mus. thesis. New England Conservatory of Music, 1933.

Mills, William. *History of Portland.* Portland: Bailey and Noyes, 1865.

Monthly Musical Record XXII (1892), XXXIII (1903). London.

"Morgan, George Washbourne," in *American Art Journal* LIX (16 July 1892), 347–48.

Morris, Louise E. B. *Lineages and Genealogical Notes.* Dallas: B. & W. Printing, 1967.

Music; A Monthly Magazine IX–XXII (1896–1902). Edited by W. S. B. Mathews. Chicago.

Music Review II (1892–93). Edited by Calvin B. Cady. Chicago.

Musical America V (1907). Edited by John C. Freund. New York.

Musical Courier XXXII–LII (1896–1906). Edited by Marc A. Blumenberg. New York.

Musical Record, Nos. 38–481 (1879–1902). Edited by Dexter Smith, Lorin Deland, Philip Hale, and others. Boston.

Musical Review and Musical World XII–XV (1861–64). Edited by Theodore Hagen. New York.

Musical World XXXIX (1861), LVII (1879). Edited by J. W. Davison. London.

The Nation XIII–LIII (1871–1905). New York.

Neue Zeitschrift für Musik LIV (1861), LXIII (1867). Leipzig.

New England Conservatory Magazine-Review V–VIII (1915–17). Boston.

New Music Review and Church Music Review IV–V (1905–06). New York: Novello, Ewer & Co.

New-York Daily Tribune, 1858, 1877, 1882–84, 1890, 1897. New York.

New York Times, 1877, 1882–84, 1888–90, 1906. New York.

Norman, Henry. *An Account of the Harvard Greek Play.* Boston, 1882.

Norton, Sara, and M. A. DeWolfe Howe. *Letters of Charles Eliot Norton, with Biographical Comment.* Boston: Houghton Mifflin, 1913.

"Osgood, George Laurie," in *The National Cyclopaedia of American Biography.* New York: James T. White, 1892. VII, 436.

Otis, Philo Adams. *The Chicago Symphony Orchestra: Its Organization, Growth and Development, 1891–1924.* Chicago: Clayton F. Summy Co., 1924.

"Paine, John Knowles," in *Appleton's Cyclopaedia of Biography*. Revised edition. Edited by James Grant and John Fiske. New York: Appleton, 1898. IV, 629.

Paine, John Knowles. "Beethoven as Composer," in *Famous Composers and their Works*. Edited by John K. Paine, Theodore Thomas, and Karl Klauser. Boston: J. B. Millet, 1891. II, 337–48.

————. *History of Music. Lecture Notes*. Cambridge: W. H. Wheeler, 1885.

————. *The History of Music to the Death of Schubert*. Edited by Albert A. Howard. Boston: Ginn and Co., 1907.

————. "The New German School of Music," in *North American Review* CXVI (April, 1873), 217–45.

————. "Shall we have Endowed Opera?" in *Forum* XIII (1892), 507–18.

———— and Leo R. Lewis. "Music in Germany," in *Famous Composers and their Works*. Edited by John K. Paine, Theodore Thomas, and Karl Klauser. Boston: J. B. Millet, 1891. III, 569–608.

Paine, Josiah. "Thomas Paine, of Eastham," in *Paine Ancestry: The Family of Robert Treat Paine, Signer of the Declaration of Independence*. Compiled by Sarah C. Paine. Edited by C. H. Pope. Boston, 1912.

Paine, Robert Treat. "Notes upon the foregoing extracts," in *Paine Ancestry: The Family of Robert Treat Paine. . . .* Compiled by Sarah C. Paine. Edited by C. H. Pope. Boston, 1912.

Perkins, Charles C., and John S. Dwight. *History of the Handel and Haydn Society, of Boston, Massachusetts*. Boston: Alfred Mudge & Son, 1893.

Portland Directory; containing the names of the inhabitants . . . and the city register. . . . Portland: Arthur Shirley, 1834.

Portland Boys' high school. Lists of master: E. N. Pomeroy and others. In Maine Historical Society collection, Portland.

Portland Obituary Scrapbooks. In Maine Historical Society collection, Portland.

Portland Transcript and Eclectic, 1850–1863. Portland, Me.

Post Scrapbook. In Maine Historical Society, Portland.

Pratt, Harry Rogers. "Music Study at Harvard," in *Musical World* III/7 (July, 1903), 109–11.

Records, Haydn Association. In Portland Public Library, Portland.

Records of the Board of Overseers of Harvard College X–XII (1862–91). In Harvard Archives collection.

Records of the Church of Christ in Standish. In Maine Historical Society, Portland.

Records of the College Faculty (1860–65). Harvard College. In Harvard Archives collection.

Records of the Committee of the West Boston Society Corporation. Unpublished volumes. In Boston Public Library, Boston.

Records, Portland Sacred Music Society. In Maine Historical Society collection, Portland.

Report of the Class of 1858 of Harvard College. Boston, 1888.

Reports to the Overseers—President and Fellows Series I, (1865–70); *Series* II, I-VI (1874–1900). Harvard College. In Harvard Archives collection.

Rich, Evelyn. "Richard Rich of Eastham on Cape Cod and some of his descendants," in *New England Historical and Genealogical Register* LXXXIII (1929).

Rich, Louise D. *The Coast of Maine; An Informal History*. New York: Thomas Y. Crowell, 1956.

Roberts, Kenneth C., Jr. *John Knowles Paine*. Unpublished M.A. thesis. University of Michigan, 1962.

Salter, Sumner. "Early Encouragements to American Composers," in *Musical Quarterly* XVIII (January 1932), 76–105.

Semi-Annual Report of the Portland High School for Boys for the Term ending August 2d, 1851. Successive issues dated July 30, 1852, March 4, 1852, and August 5, 1853. In Maine Historical Society collection, Portland.

Sibley, John Langdon, comp. *Sibley's Private Journal*. Unpublished volume. In Harvard Archives collection.

Signale für die Musikalische Welt, No. 11 (1892). Leipzig.

Slonimsky, Nicholas, ed. *Baker's Biographical Dictionary of Musicians*. Fifth Edition. New York: G. Schirmer, 1958.

Smith, G. H. L. *The Cleveland Orchestra: Thirty-sixth Season (1953–54)*. Program notes.

Sophocles. "Oedipus the King," in *Three Tragedies*. Trans. David Grene. Chicago: University of Chicago Press, 1954.

Spalding, Walter R. *Music at Harvard*. New York: Coward-McCann, Inc., 1935.

————. "Music, 1862–1929," in *The Development of Harvard University since the inauguration of President Eliot, 1869–1929*. Edited by S. E. Morison. Cambridge: Harvard University Press, 1930.

Standish, Maine, Vital Records 1759–1900. In Maine Historical Society collection, Portland.

Thaxter, Celia. *Among the Isles of Shoals*. Nineteenth Edition. Boston: Houghton, Mifflin & Co., 1895.

Thomas, Rose Fay. *Memoirs of Theodore Thomas*. New York: Moffat, Yard & Co., 1911.

Thomas, Theodore: A Musical Autobiography. Edited by George P. Upton. Chicago: A. C. McClurg & Co., 1905.

Tiersot, Julien. *Musiques Pittoresques. Promenades Musicales à l'Exposition de 1889*. Paris: Librairie Fischbacher, 1889.

Treasurer's Accounts—West Boston Society (1847–1893). Unpublished volume. In Boston Public Library, Boston.

Tri-weekly Eastern Argus, 1833. Portland, Me.

Underhill, L. A. W. *Descendants of Edward Small of New England*. Revised Edition. Boston: Houghton Mifflin, 1934.

Upton, G. P. "Reminiscence and Appreciation," in *Theodore Thomas: A Musical Autobiography*. Chicago: A. C. McClurg & Co., 1905.

Upton, W. T. *Art-Song in America*. Boston: Oliver Ditson, 1930.

————. *William Henry Fry, American Journalist and Composer-Critic*. New York: Thomas Y. Crowell, 1954.

Visitation of the University, 1863 (Overseers-Supplement). Harvard College. In Harvard Archives collection.

Wadsworth, Lucy G. *West Church, Boston*. Unpublished typescript. In Unitarian-Universalist Association archives, Boston.

Wagenknecht, Edward. *William Dean Howells: The Friendly Eye*. New York: 1969.

Whicker, George F. "Celia Laighton Thaxter," in *Dictionary of American Biography*. Edited by Dumas Malone. New York: Charles Scribner's Sons, 1936. XVIII, 397–98.

Wilson, G. H. *The Boston Musical Year Book. Vol. I, Season of 1883–84*. Boston: Geo. I. Ellis, 1884. Volume II similarly titled.

————. *The Boston Musical Year Book and Musical Year Book in the United States. Vol. III, Season of 1885–86*. Boston: Ellis, 1886.

_____ . *The Musical Year-book of the United States.* Vol. IV, Season of 1886–87. Boston: Alfred Mudge and Son, 1887. Volumes V through X similarly titled. (Vols. VIII and IX publ. Chas. Hamilton, Worcester; Vol. X publ. Clayton F. Summy, Chicago, 1893.)

Yellin, Victor, *The Life and Operatic Works of George Whitefield Chadwick.* Unpublished Ph.D. thesis. Harvard University, 1957.

_____ . "The Omnibus Idea," in *Abstracts of Papers Read at the Thirty-Eighth Meeting of the American Musicological Society, Dallas, Texas, November 2–5, 1972.*

Index

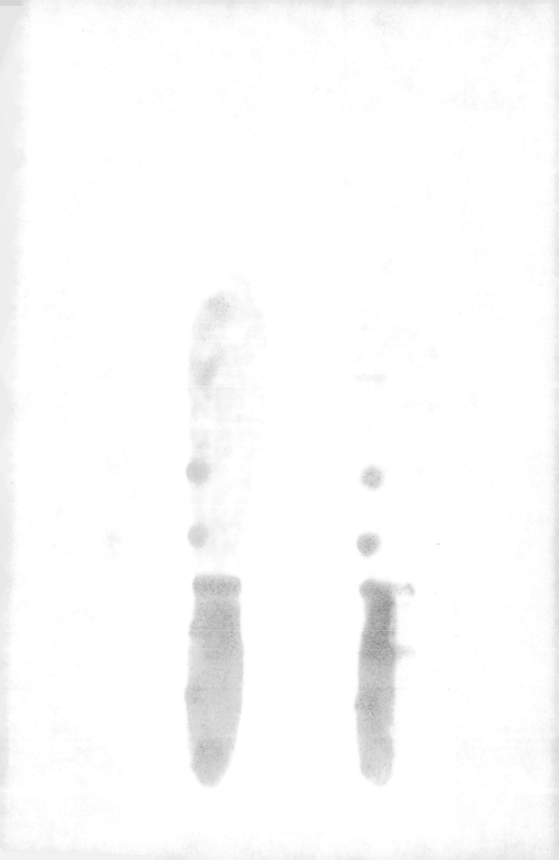

DATE DUE	
MAY 1 4 2002	
JUN 06 2016	

GAYLORD   PRINTED IN U.S.A.